Village Japan

RICHARD K. BEARDSLEY · JOHN W. HALL · ROBERT E. WARD

Village Japan

THE UNIVERSITY OF CHICAGO PRESS

CHICAGO AND LONDON

THE UNIVERSITY OF CHICAGO PRESS, CHICAGO 60637
The University of Chicago Press, Ltd., London

Library of Congress Catalog Card Number: 58–13802

Contents

Illustrations

Tables

Foreword

This is the study of a small, rice-growing community in Japan named Niiike.[1] It is located in the prefecture of Okayama, which lies in the southwestern portion of the island of Honshu, midway along the northern shore of the Inland Sea. Within limits which will be explained, we regard Niiike as reasonably representative of rice-growing communities in most areas of Japan's three southern islands.

This is not to say that the study purports to be a key which will unlock the secrets of Japanese "national character." In fact, after seven consecutive years of fieldwork and study in Japan by various members of the group, none of us believes that total "national character" has been scientifically defined with any success. Perhaps it cannot ever be defined. The more one learns of a people and a culture, the more one becomes conscious of the basic limitations and inaccuracies of any holistic generalization. For all its seeming homogeneity, Japanese culture is rich and diversified. Major variations occur on regional, class, age, educational, and environmental bases. The present study is based upon a keen awareness of such variations. It attempts to isolate and portray the ways of life of a particular segment of the Japanese people—farmers living and working in rice-growing villages. Even when limited in this way, we are uncomfortably aware of the range of cultural variation to be encountered in Japanese farm villages. Patterns of social organization are quite different, for example, in the villages of Tōhoku (northeastern Honshu), while the technical problems of farming vary somewhat in any of the areas of reclaimed land. The full extent and social significance of such variations is yet to be determined; as a matter of fact we hope that the present study can serve as a sort of trial bench mark in just such an undertaking.

Despite such qualifications, however, our investigations lead us to believe that Niiike provides extensive and useful insights into the lives, problems, and attitudes of a major segment of Japan's population. The signifi-

[1] The name means "new pond." It is pronounced Nee'-ee-ee'-keh.

cance of this claim may not be immediately apparent. It rests upon three considerations. First, even today almost half the Japanese population is rural, dwelling and working for the most part in small, rice-growing communities like Niiike. Second, even this statistic vastly understates the cultural influence of such farm communities upon the people of Japan. A very large proportion of present city dwellers were brought up in just such rural communities and subsequently migrated to the city. Their most formative years were spent in the countryside. Third, the villages may, to a limited but significant degree, be held to represent the traditional cultural foundations of all of modern Japan. The whole country was, until quite recent times, predominantly agricultural and premodern in its economic and social organization. The entire culture has changed quite markedly since those days, but the rate of change has been uneven. It has been more rapid and more extensive in the cities; the Japanese countryside, while changing, tends to do so in slower and less comprehensive fashion. In this sense, the villages may be regarded as somewhat more representative of the nation's cultural traditions and foundations than are the cities. It is for reasons such as these that we consider a study of village Japan—and of Niiike as a partial but significant exemplar thereof—to be an important point of entry or approach to an understanding of Japanese culture as a whole. It does not necessarily define or represent Japanese culture in all or even the majority of cases; we hope, however, that it does illuminate it in many.

It may well be asked why and how we decided to study Niiike rather than some other of the fifty thousand or more similar basic communities to be found in Japan. The reasons were complex. The initial decision was to select a community in the Inland Sea region of Japan. This was chosen because it is an old and continuously settled area which has been centrally associated with all major developments in Japanese history and culture. Okayama was then selected from the eleven prefectures of this region on a variety of grounds. While primarily an agricultural and rice-growing prefecture, it also had a sizable industrial and commercial sector in its economy and might thus in an over-all environmental sense be considered as more representative of modern Japan than could such contrasting extremes as metropolitan Osaka or rural Ehime. Also its communications with other areas in the Inland Sea region were distinctly superior, a point of practical importance since the comparative checking of data throughout the entire region was held to be a matter of major importance. The absence of any sizable or important contingent of the foreign Occupation forces was an added recommendation. Finally, it developed upon investigation that the prefectural political and academic authorities were most favorably disposed toward our undertaking. The pinpointing of Niiike itself was then a product of a lengthy and extensive search based on documentary and map work, on consultations with officials and others familiar with the agricultural parts of the prefecture, and, finally, on visits to promising localities and interviews with their inhabitants.

Firm judgments as to the typicality of a community cannot be based on necessarily superficial examinations of this sort. One can only take all possible precautions and hope for the best. Niiike was chosen because it was a primarily rice-growing community with a population of manageable size which was not averse to being studied in this manner. It was also more conveniently situated than were several other communities of potentially equal promise. Other than that, it was the absence of any unusual or distinctive features which commended it to us. As our knowledge of the community developed and we became able to compare it in more meaningful terms with other settlements in the vicinity and throughout the Inland Sea region, it emerged that our choice had been a fortunate one—just how fortunate we had no way of knowing at the time.

The research underlying this study of Niiike has been carried out along co-operative and interdisciplinary lines under the auspices of the University of Michigan's Center for Japanese Studies. It is based for the most part on interviews, questionnaires, and firsthand observations. These results of our field research have been brought together in the central file of field notes located in Ann Arbor. Niiike was under more or less continual observation from April, 1950, to July, 1954. It was revisited on several more recent occasions—up to the spring of 1957—to check data and bring particular items up to date. The field data on which the book is based represent contributions from many scholars and disciplines. The bulk of the material was gathered by the three authors, who are respectively an anthropologist, a historian, and a political scientist, and by J. D. Eyre, geographer. Important contributions were also made by other geographers, economists, sociologists, psychologists, medical doctors, and specialists in Japanese literature and linguistics, as well as by other representatives of the authors' disciplines. A number of Japanese scholars have co-operated in the undertaking. The normal working procedure was to have the community under study by specialists in several disciplines at the same time. During the first year, for example—which was the period of most intensive study—Niiike was under almost daily observation by an anthropologist, a geographer, and a political scientist. It was not possible actually to live in the community, but the individuals concerned—who themselves lived and normally worked together—averaged a six-hour day, four or five days a week there or in neighboring villages, homes, or offices. Nighttime visits and occasional stays for periods up to one week were also included. During later stages of the project, this procedure underwent considerable variation, especially as comparative studies in other villages became a more important part of the work. The result has been, however, that Niiike has been studied with an intensity, over a period of time, and from a number and variety of professional viewpoints unusual in the history of community studies. Every effort has been made to give a balanced and rounded portrayal.

While our study is based primarily on observations and interviews, it should be noted that pertinent documentary sources and written materials were utilized when necessary or where available. Historical and statistical materials found in limited quantities were of disappointing utility. Of more value were various studies which could be used for comparative purposes. A substantial literature in the field of community studies exists in Japanese. The authors have consulted this extensively, primarily for background and comparative purposes, and wish to acknowledge their indebtedness to it. This literature has not been cited specifically in our work because it does not deal directly with Niiike or our major problems. In a volume so greatly dependent on field observation, we have made an effort to keep footnotes to a minimum.

A study of this sort depends primarily on relations between observer and observed, on the attitude and status each acquires or attributes to the other. We asked the people of Niiike to accept our intrusion into their lives on a study of scholarly and international significance. They responded magnificently, bearing up courteously for a long four years under the more or less continual presence of outsiders, sometimes regrettably inarticulate in Japanese, who were professionally obliged to be persistently and minutely curious about all aspects of individual and community life. Their time was pre-empted, no matter how much we minimized our demands, for matters ranging from brief queries to extensive physical examinations and batteries of psychological projective tests. Yet they not only gave time ungrudgingly; they also took up the intellectual challenge of learning how to inform us, conscientiously and accurately, about things in their lives to which they never before had given any conscious thought. This willingness, of course, did not make everything easy. Some of our inquiries dealt with matters that were sensitive for one reason or another; our having the status of foreigners, guests, and scholars in the eyes of Niiike's people sometimes facilitated these inquiries but occasionally complicated them. On certain subjects, such as money or taxes or various family relations, we naïve foreigners could raise questions that no Japanese could well ask without seeming ridiculous or causing alarm. On the other hand, informal though we might be, we were considered guests and scholars, a status which made it difficult for persons of any age or sex to pass us the choicest gossip, to chat unrestrainedly about social discrimination, sex, or quarrels, or to abandon completely the attitudes or treatment which our status demanded. Our own research arrangements required us usually to live as a group in the city rather than in Niiike itself, in order to keep our cross-disciplinary exchange at its best level; and Niiike was too small to accommodate any of us overnight except for brief periods; hence, none of us was able fully to overcome the disadvantages of "guest" status in Niiike. It by no means inhibited friendships, however, and those of us who were most frequently among the men, women, and children of Niiike cherish the warm affections that developed.

We were occasionally able to be of some assistance to the community and, over a period of time, our relations with many of Niiike's families became very friendly. We are happy to say that it continues so today, though we sometimes wonder, if it were to be done over again, whether they would willingly repeat the experience. Fortunately, the question is purely academic. We would like to make quite clear, however, the fact that this study was made possible only by the patient co-operation and kindness of the people of Niiike, in whose debt we will permanently remain.

The question inevitably arises in connection with a project of this kind: To what extent did our presence in the community distort its normal patterns of conduct? In the early stages of research we worried a good deal about this, as well as about the accuracy and completeness of the answers to our questions. An outsider can never be certain on these scores, but as our knowledge of Niiike and its people deepened, we grew steadily less concerned. It is conceivable that a close-knit group of 130 persons might effectively dissemble their normal ways on particular occasions or for relatively short periods of time. That they should do so on such a variety of occasions, day in and day out for four years, and with such skill as to mislead a large number of well-informed and critical observers seems to us highly improbable. We do not for a moment believe that we achieved that chimerical status often referred to as "becoming members of the community." We doubt that any foreigner has ever been so accepted in Japan. It is just that over a period of time Niiike grew used to us and our activities and, in some cases, acquired a quite positive interest in what we were doing. Where the honesty and completeness—the latter is the more serious issue—of the information we received is concerned, it varied with situations and individuals. We were quite well aware of the fact that on some particularly sensitive matters, such as personal debts, illegal acts, etc., even our best friends occasionally lied, evaded, or sought to mislead us. Similarly, we discovered through experience and cross-checking that some members of the community were much more reliable and satisfactory informants than others. This is only to be expected, and it is foolish to sacrifice its advantages to a passion for random sampling. All possible precautions were regularly taken against either deliberate or unintentional deceptions on the part of our informants. These took the form of a variety of cross-checks over long periods of time, our general familiarity with the normal institutions and ways of life in a Japanese village, and extensive comparisons of what we were told about Niiike with our investigations in other villages. On the basis of this experience, we concluded that we were normally told the truth. We also learned, however, that it is likely to take several interviews to secure a reasonable semblance of the whole truth. Time and patience are of the essence in a study of this kind.

The assignment of appropriate credit for a work of this sort is difficult. Our debts are very numerous. We have no doubt, however, about where our primary obligation lies. It is to Professor Robert B. Hall, the first director of the University of Michigan's Center for Japanese Studies. Professor Hall was responsible for both the establishment of the Center and of its Field Station in Okayama. He had more to do with the original formulation of the present study and its subsequent support and encouragement than did any other person. He took part in the early stages of the fieldwork and in the selection of Niiike, and he returned frequently to the village in later years. He contributed extensively to many phases of the field notes and on several occasions served as director of the project in Okayama. The authors are heavily indebted to him on a variety of scores and want to take this occasion to express their deep appreciation.

Preparation of the study for publication has been the result of a long and intricate process. After the first round of field research had been completed in 1953, a general plan for a published report was drawn up by the members of the Center for Japanese Studies. From the outset, primary responsibility rested with Richard Beardsley. The lengthy sections on the political aspects of village life became the prime concern of Robert Ward, while John Hall handled the historical dimension of the study. Various specialized contributions were made by fieldworkers in Niiike. In 1954–55, Richard Beardsley returned to Okayama and conducted a second year of observation, this time with the report in mind. Robert Ward, in the course of a year of field research in Japan during 1956–57, also had the opportunity to return to Niiike to check and revise his previous observations.

Writing began in 1954. During the year 1956–57 a draft manuscript was submitted for review to a number of participants in the Niiike field study, both in this country and in Japan. Simultaneously in Ann Arbor the manuscript was discussed at a weekly staff seminar of the Center for Japanese Studies and was given editorial revision. The manuscript as revised was again carefully reworked by the three primary authors functioning as a team. Every effort was made to assure integration of material. Thus, the published book bears the imprint of many hands. It is possible, however, to indicate the division of primary responsibility for most of the chapters, and the authors wish to make this clear. Chapter 3 was written by John W. Hall, who also contributed to chapters 1 and 6; chapters 2 and 6 are derived from manuscripts initially contributed by J. D. Eyre but extensively reworked by the authors; chapter 8 rests on a systematic study of Niiike's economy made by Charles F. Remer; chapters 12 and 13 are the work of Robert E. Ward. The remaining chapters were written by Richard K. Beardsley. In addition to the preparation of the manuscript, the work of preparing illustrations, maps, and charts, and integrating the manuscript as a whole has been shared by the three primary authors. Thus, our work is in every respect a joint effort.

The number of Japanese scholars, officials, and just plain people who assisted us through advice, encouragement, and support is so great as to preclude separate mention. We must acknowledge with deep gratitude, however, the unfailing courtesy and invaluable aid we received from the officials of Okayama Prefecture, Okayama City, and the village of Kamo. Among these, special recognition must be accorded to governors Nishioka and Miki and to mayors Yokoyama, Tanaka, Migaki, and Namba. Through the participation of many Japanese scholars, in particular the members of the *Seto Naikai Sōgō Kenkyūkai*, the project became to an unusual extent a deeply satisfying and mutually enriching experiment in intercultural and international academic co-operation.

Other American participants in the project have also been numerous. To varying extents almost everyone who has been regularly stationed at our Okayama Center has contributed to the field notes on which the present study is based. This includes faculty members and graduate students from at least three universities besides the University of Michigan. We would like to express our gratitude and obligation to all these individuals. They are: Grace Beardsley, Cecil C. Brett, Ardath W. Burks, Jane Burks, John B. Cornell, George A. DeVos, Paul S. Dull, Olga Eyre, Gladys Ishida, James A. Kokoris, David H. Kornhauser, Douglas H. Mendel, Jr., Edwin L. Neville, Edward Norbeck, Forrest R. Pitts, Gaston J. Sigur, Robert J. Smith, Joseph L. Sutton, Mischa Titiev, David A. Wheatley, and Joseph K. Yamagiwa.

Finally, acknowledgment must be made to the Carnegie Corporation, the University of Michigan and its Horace H. Rackham School of Graduate Studies for the financial and academic support which sustained the Center for Japanese Studies, this project, and its authors during the long years of research and writing. Various members of the group would also like to express their gratitude for individual assistance received from the Ford Foundation, the Fulbright Commission, and the Social Science Research Council in addition to the previously mentioned sources. None of these institutions, however, is responsible for any opinions expressed in this book.

R. K. B.

J. W. H.

R. E. W.

1. Introduction

Niiike is a small rice-growing settlement in the western half of Honshu, Japan's principal island. One hundred thirty people live in its twenty-four houses clustered at the base of a pine-covered hill. Their physical surroundings, daily activities, organized relations, and the beliefs and values that give meaning to their lives are reported here, as a starting point toward understanding the people of rural Japan.

We are interested in these one hundred thirty persons not as so many individual Japanese but as members of a community. Niiike is a clearly defined, natural sociocultural unit, large enough to be the setting for most situations and events that are the basic stuff of a way of life, yet small enough to let us see this way of life at close quarters. As members of communities ourselves, we will recognize familiar conditions and problems among those that confront the people of Niiike. Certain other situations are peculiar to Japan or to this particular locality. But the solutions, even of those problems with which we are familiar, are often not what we would expect. Niiike's style of dealing with life's situations is what makes it distinctively Japanese rather than some other nationality, rural rather than urban, Niiike rather than some other settlement. Yet much of Niiike's way of life is also customary and normal in a great many other Japanese communities. By observing the conditions of this way of life, and by comparison with the ways of various other communities, we hope to achieve a better understanding of rural Japan, especially in terms of the intimate aspects of its people, their life, their problems, and their aspirations.

The people of Japan are divided almost equally between country and city. The rural population includes only about 3 or 4 per cent non-cultivators, such as fishermen, miners, and forestry workers. Farmers comprise the remainder. The urban population inhabits communities ranging in size from small cities up to giant metropolitan centers such as Tokyo and Osaka. More than fifteen million Japanese, almost 17 per cent of the entire population, live in the six largest cities of Japan. Japan is highly urbanized

1

among Asian countries yet at the same time clearly more oriented to rural ways of life than the United States. What is the relationship of the farmers whose ways are the concern of our study to the town and city folk? To what extent is city life based upon or different from country life in Japan? To these questions there have been diametrically opposed answers. Some maintain that the modern mores of the city form no more than a thin veneer over ingrained traditions of people but recently removed from the country. It must be granted that country-born persons constitute a high proportion of the population in the mushrooming urban centers. But others answer that the past century of industrialization and modernization has split Japanese society in two, that urban people in Japan may well feel more akin to city dwellers of Western countries than to their own country folk.

Inescapably our reaction to urban Japan is tempered by the direction from which we approach it, whether from a foreign urban environment or from rural Japan. If a Western traveler comes to Japan from abroad, landing probably at a large seaport or airfield, the Japanese scene will press upon him with many unfamiliar and exotic qualities. And yet the unfamiliar will be largely submerged beneath the familiar attributes of a Western urban environment. Under the familiar factory smoke hanging in the sky are modern concrete and steel buildings. Plate glass shop-windows reflect crowds of pedestrians in Western dress. By night, snatches of jazz band music and the clangor of fast-flowing auto traffic mingle on neon-bright streets. Modern stores, offices, and theaters are filled with city-bred people who are not only familiar with Western ways of life but in tune with them. These features of the city linger in our minds when we visit the countryside. Small wonder, then, that barefoot villagers going about their bucolic tasks or gathering a few paces away to gaze unblinkingly at the foreigners seem a world apart. It is a far cry from the city to the oxen plowing across tiny fields, the straw thatch roofs, and the open wells of the countryside. Perhaps urban Japanese really are further removed from all this than from the West.

But let us return to the city, fresh from the country, and explore again. Now we will remember whole farmland communities—houses, lands, and all—crowded on acreages not broad enough to fill a single ordinary American farm; and we will recall the ubiquitous, ever working men and women. Back in the city we will rediscover this compression of population. People are packed four or five times more densely into Japanese cities than into even the most crammed of American cities. Another feature of the country shared by the city is revealed as we move out of the cosmopolitan districts into the smaller side streets. Here the unexpectedly cheap purchase and the bargain price of a haircut or shoe repair remind us of the low value set on human time, whether expressed in city goods and services or in long hours of hand labor in the fields. Similar conditions of economy, as of demography, link city and country.

But there is more than this in common. The urban Buddhist temple, half-hidden behind a row of shop-front houses, and the Shinto shrine, reached from the city street by a path leading under a torii gate, are fully interchangeable with those of the country. In the city the religious ceremonies and pageants follow a sequence of dates parallel to that in the country. They are celebrated by residents of a city district who form a collectivity for mutual help and public works in much the same way as in a country village.

The farmer in Japan need not feel out of his element in the city. On the contrary, he will be able to find there almost any familiar feature of his own life, even down to the croaking of frogs in sun-warmed patches of paddy, for rice fields intrude well into the limits of even the large Japanese city. However, what exists as a whole way of life in the rural community is only one layer of city life. Here for the last century the effects of industry, commerce, modern education, and new modes of communication have produced an overlay of many new patterns of behavior. A flood of customs and ideas from abroad have created still another layer. These layers are distinct only in theory. Actually they are juxtaposed and intermingled in a confused and changing tangle.

By contrast, life in the countryside is much less distorted by the strains of accommodation. The rural culture is a full, traditional, stable way of life. It is founded on the requirements of intensive agricultural technology and agrarian economy, which were dominant through centuries of Japanese history. The continuing importance of intensive agriculture gives this cultural tradition great durability today and makes it a living reservoir of traditional norms that are distinctively Japanese.

To distinguish this stable, conservative tradition from the more recently emergent, foreign-influenced ways of the city is not to say that the rural tradition is fixed and unchanging. New ways are entering the rural community, some from the city or from abroad via the city, some spontaneously from changing circumstances in the countryside itself. A good share of the attention of our study is given to the forces of change and to the intertwining of change and continuity. By absorbing change without losing balance, the rural tradition is proving its vitality and contributing equilibrium to the whole of Japanese society.

Our study concentrates on the life of people in a rural community called a "buraku." In non-technical terms, the buraku is a small rural settlement, a social entity consisting of households grouped into a community.

We retain untranslated throughout this study the Japanese word "buraku," because it has no appropriate counterpart in our experience and in order to avoid confusion with two other Japanese terms, "ōaza" and "mura," which refer to successively larger divisions of the rural countryside. From a purely geographical point of view these terms are generally so related that several buraku lie within each ōaza and several ōaza lie within each mura. But these terms connote more than a difference in geographic size. Outside the cities and towns, all of Japan is divided into mura: units of territory fitting border to border to furnish a blanket of government over the entire country, including hills and open fields as well as settlements. The mura has a full apparatus of government; it is the smallest legal administrative unit of Japan and may be considered the administrative village. The ōaza beneath it is also a territorial unit with a vestige of administration inherited from the period of Japanese history prior to 1872. Neither the mura nor the ōaza, however, is a community all of whose inhabitants have constant and face-to-face social interaction. The buraku is just such an entity; its government is largely unofficial, and the borders of its land are only hazily defined; but it is a clearly defined social community. Its inhabitants have a strong sense of group identity. For this reason, it is a useful and convenient unit of study.

To call this community by its Japanese title, Niiike buraku, unfortunately does not relieve us of all terminological difficulties. The same sort of community in some other parts of Japan is called an *aza*, while "ōaza" may be used to refer to only the principal community among a group of *aza*, all of them together composing a mura, or administrative village. Moreover, almost all over Japan, there is popular use of the term buraku in speaking of segregated settlements of the onetime classless people, the outcast *Eta*. Even in the vicinity of Niiike, this pejorative connotation may color the word in conversational use. But the usual meaning of "buraku" is the perfectly honorable one of "small rural settlement."

But we still must ask how appropriate Niiike is as an example of a buraku. It lies on the coastal plain of Okayama Prefecture in one of Japan's more prosperous farming areas. Among Japanese country folk, the farmers of this plain are regarded as generally up to date and forward looking. Niiike is run of the mill within the area. It is neither particularly old-fashioned nor progressive, rich nor poor, specialized nor diversified. It is a representative community of the Okayama coastal plain. But no one community can be fully representative of more than a limited area; its historical background, its present degree of prosperity, its size, its topographic and climatic setting, and its products, to name only a few features, differ slightly or grossly from those of other communities. Therefore, we have on occasion drawn comparisons, to show the variety of alternatives and necessities from which the people of Niiike and the Okayama coastal plain have shaped their living. These comparisons also make us aware of the diversity of rural Japan and of the importance of a region's history to the character of its communities.

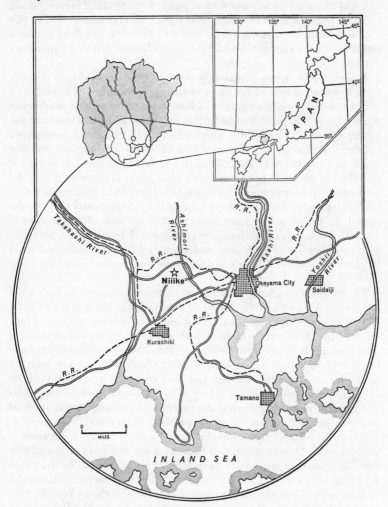

FIG. 1.—The location of Niiike in Okayama Prefecture, Japan

In taking up the study of Niiike, we are concerned with a community and through the community with a way of life, a culture, common to much of rural Japan. Every student of culture is aware that his analysis inevitably distorts the whole, because it begins at one point and proceeds linearly to related points. A community is an organic whole; its culture is a union of many intimately interlocked parts. The culture of Niiike, strung point by point through the pages of this book, is thus distorted. For this reason we wish to start our study with a brief sketch of salient points, a sort of bird's-eye view of the whole culture, before moving in to explore the details.

The visitor to Niiike inescapably observes that survival here depends upon squeezing a living from an exceedingly small portion of land. Niiike and the twenty-nine other buraku of Kamo (the mura), with a total population of over thirty-five hundred persons, occupy an area of less than one square mile. This area is filled with houses, roads, bridges, shrines, public buildings, and uncultivated ridges in addition to the irrigated and dry fields. In comparison to many localities in Japan, productive acreage is abundant in Kamo. For the nation as a whole, only 15 per cent of the total land area can be cultivated, to supply food and industrial crops for 90 million Japanese. One-sixth of the total national food supply must be imported. In Kamo, arable land makes up 69.4 per cent of the total area. The rich coastal plain farm land is so crowded with farmers that, in Niiike, a household of five to six persons controls only 2.7 acres of fields and wood lot. Less than half of its crops feed the household; the rest goes to the city markets.

The fabulously high production from such small acreage (Japan's average irrigated acre yields three tons of rice; China's, one and a half tons; Indonesia's, one ton) requires the most intensive farming practices. Copious fertilizer, multiple use of fields, and, above all, prodigious amounts of skilled effort coax the crops of rice, dry grains, vegetables, and fruit from the soil. The sensitive human hand wielding simple tools has long been the most effective instrument for this task, but ingenuity is increasingly finding a place for small-scale machinery in the actual tasks of cultivating as well as in the processing of crops after harvest. To this day, the heavy food requirements of the dense population and the heavy man-labor requirements of the food production methods have made a nearly closed circle of production and consumption and thus set a low ceiling on material welfare. The Japanese farmer seldom gets fat at his own table. To be sure, in Niiike there is a flow of income from the outside—from city salaries and market sales—that checks the circle's tendency to close. Yet the near closure of the production-consumption circle narrows the farm child's opportunity to cast aside his limited patrimony and seek other means of living.

Each person remains intimately bound to his household. The household and the family have an enormously potent claim on the loyalty and affections of every member. Self-sacrifice in behalf of one's kindred is commonly expected. The high and constant praise of self-sacrifice expresses its importance to the social system. Individuality is suppressed for the sake of household solidarity, for the individual is dependent on the household's limited land and resources. In its turn, the Niiike household is dependent on the community; for its fields are scattered among those of its neighbors, and all of them are appended to a system of drainage and irrigation works, flood controls, access paths, and other vital adjuncts to food production that must be maintained and operated jointly and co-operatively over a wide area beyond the buraku.

Apart from his other social involvements, when even the very crops he must plant and the schedule of tending and reaping them are determined through group action, it is small wonder that the Niiike cultivator rarely shows pronounced individualism. Conflicts between what the Japanese call *giri* ("obligation") and *ninjō* ("human feelings or personal interest") do occur. This tension provides the raw material of Japan's greatest dramatic plots. But when the play is finished, on the stage or in real life, obligation has won out over personal interests. The Japanese onlooker is satisfied, not so much because he knows the individual is lesser and weaker than the group, but because he conceives of individual well-being as a function of group well-being when it comes to most of life's major decisions.

Willing submission to higher authority, however, has certain limits; it is not absolute and unqualified. The Niiike householder recognizes two distinct systems of authority outside his family circle. In one, at the local level, he is participant and beneficiary in concrete, understandable fashion. He joins his fellow householders in monthly prayers and helps them in crisis as they also assist him if disaster strikes. He assembles with his more distant neighbors for shrine ceremonies and for common problems of irrigation and field management, and he co-operates with communities still farther removed along the course of the large canal that irrigates his fields. These persons and communities share with him a traditional system of understandings and controls. This is *his* government, often unofficial but real. The other government is external to this world of interlocked communities. It intrudes with controls, regulations, and demands which the farmer had no hand in formulating and which often conflict with his own or his community's interests as he sees them. This outside government levies taxes, takes them out of sight, and spends them in distant places for ill-comprehended purposes. To a population that equates civic duty with doing right by one's neighbors and love of country with close attachments to the Okayama Plain and Inland Sea, the abstract "national welfare" used to justify new tax assessments and crop requisitions still seems to mean the welfare of outsiders. The co-operative system of local authority, as an extension beyond family and the face-to-face community, is accepted as just and proper even when painful. But submission to the separate, outside system of legal authority is reluctant and evasive. Compromise, concession, and concealment are the tactics that continue to be used on both sides, pending the time when there may emerge the concept of responsible government based on the popular will.

One agency which may foster the emergence of such a new concept is Japan's educational system, prized by outside authority and villager alike. Roughly speaking, of Niiike's three generations, the younger two have gone through four to nine years of public schools. This schooling is bringing not only literacy but the development of new views of the world and man. These views are not easily assessed, for they may gently transmute the stuff of village affairs without affecting the outer contours.

Religious matters well exemplify the preservation of outer contours. Traditionally religion has been permissive, not requiring any special declarations of faith or moral resolve or even unanimous participation in the recurrent ceremonies. How many of the villagers today, doing obeisance before the Buddhist tablets commemorating their ancestors, make a personal prayer to these spirits, and how many simply offer this overt gesture of respect to the memory of bygone generations? Among the visitors to the Shinto shrine, are there many who attend without belief, but go to reaffirm their participation in the social group assembled for the ceremony? With either a supernatural or a natural outlook, the villager can participate sincerely and without pretense. In either case, one of the ends of religion is served: making manifest and visible the order and meaning of the relations of man to the rest of the world. The outer contours of religious observance have been preserved while allowing considerable latitude of inner conviction.

What we are about to narrate of Niiike's work, society, and conceptions has been learned by watching and talking with the people who make up the buraku. The villagers of Niiike are all surnamed either Hiramatsu or Iwasa, whereas other hamlets of similar size often have half a dozen surnames. But a common surname does not guarantee relationship. The lineages or groups of kindred in Niiike are five, three Hiramatsu and two

Iwasa, each lineage comprised of from three to seven households. Though general etiquette in Japan makes it difficult even for rather close acquaintances to drop the surname, villagers customarily use the given name, its contraction, a sometimes humorous nickname, or, most often, the appropriate household kinship term for address within their own small hamlet. This custom has an especially practical advantage in Niiike, limited as it is to only two surnames. The same consideration leads the people of Niiike to make a point of having no two living inhabitants carry the same given name. In this book we abide by village custom; given names are used except when the surname is important.

But the name is not the person. Who are the people of Niiike? Is there a typical person to represent the community? As we cast about the village, Hiramatsu Mitsusaburō, aged seventy-two, comes readily to mind. He is casually called "Sensei" (teacher, leader) in deference both to his past career as a schoolteacher and principal and to his present widespread reputation for wisdom, patience, and sound advice. These qualities have given him unusual standing outside the community as well as within. His health is failing now. He lost good rice land in the agricultural land reform, and he has neither son nor grandson of his own, only a daughter and granddaughters. Yet he works lovingly on the land where he has spent his life and lives in modest comfort by local standards. But already we have said enough about him to indicate an unusual rather than typical man. Iwasa Sōichi, aged sixty, may be more typical. In contrast to the Sensei's courtly diction, Sōichi's blunt speech buzzes with the accents of local dialect. His strong, spare hands get their full contentment not from books but from working in the rich earth and dandling his infant grandson. Sōichi seems completely of the village, taking a respected but not obtrusive place among the elders, the grandfathers, the competent cultivators. But Sōichi grew up in a hill village miles away, coming to Niiike as an adult by adoption and marriage into a household where the mental deficiency of the natural son prevented the normal succession of househeadship. So Sōichi is not a native son and scarcely typical.

Can we find the typical villager among the younger men? Iwasa Minoru, who is twenty-nine years old, was born and reared in Niiike. His landholdings, his crops, his household consisting of mother, wife, and infant son, are ordinary. His father, Kakuji, like Sōichi an adoptive husband from the hills, brought with him skills no man of Niiike could match, first in carpentry and second in lusty singing and drinking. If Minoru is more sedate, more deliberate in speech and action, perhaps he reflects the burden of separation from his first wife for sterility and the death of his first son born of his second wife. We must concede that these are not entirely typical family problems. Let us try another man, say, Hiramatsu Jun, aged thirty-three. In his case, the usual seven years of schooling, followed by military training, work in the family fields as eldest son and heir, marriage and two children make up a standard background. A leaning toward puckish humor is perhaps his salient, though still slight, quirk of character. Yet of Jun people ask why his parents broke custom by moving into the new home built for his younger brother instead of remaining in the old family home with Jun. Was it really for greater comfort, or to watch over flighty young Yukuji, or maybe to ease tension with Jun's wife?

It is no easier to find the typical woman. Compare three older women: Iwasa Koyoshi, Hiramatsu Kuma, and Hiramatsu Hisa, aged seventy-three, fifty-eight, and seventy-one, respectively. Koyoshi is five times a grandmother. In bearing three sons, she fulfilled any mother's ordinary ambition. But only the second-born, not the eldest, stayed at home. The other two went to America, and only one returned. Kuma is also a grandmother but under rather different circumstances. She was born near the city and might not have come so far into the country for marriage except that her husband was the first son of the first family in Niiike. Her early fears of lonely country life and her later grief at the successive deaths of two infants have faded. Her surviving daughter has provided her with grandchildren. Kuma's kindly warmth is a good foil to her husband's consciousness of his role as head of Niiike's leading house and makes her one of the best liked women in the village. Hisa, a cheery little chirping bird of a woman, is well loved, too. But she is childless, aunty to everyone but mother to none. This makes her a tragicomic figure in the community, where children are a necessary part of every ordinary woman's life. None of these women could be described as truly ordinary or typical.

Even when we find women closely alike with respect to children, other sharp distinctions appear. Hiramatsu Chizue, forty-two years old, has five daughters and one son. Iwasa Matsuko, aged forty-eight, has four daughters and one son. Now, a proper wedding for any girl is a costly affair; weddings for four or five are a heavy burden to have on one's mind. But intelligent Chizue, wife of Niiike's leading farm-school graduate, looks cheerfully to the future as she throws her effort and encouragement behind his ventures in cash-crop farming. Matsuko and her husband are wartime evacuees from the bombed city who have only a poor relative's portion of land. They scrape and extemporize to make life possible from day to day and look despairingly at the weddings that loom ahead. Possibly no two women are more different in Niiike than these. Is one typical, the other not?

As in any community, then, our search is fruitless. There is in Niiike no typical man, woman, or child. Each is unusual, distinct, unique. As closer acquaintance reveals individuality in each villager, we come to realize the range of experience within the grasp of a country farmer, even though his chief companionship throughout his life is drawn from but a hundred or so fellow villagers. But as we discover ever new facets of individuality, we also come to recognize common patterns of experience and behavior that hold true for the total membership of the community. Into the unique and rich variety of personal experience there is everywhere interwoven the common experience which forms the fabric of Niiike life. Hence, every man, woman, and child is the typical villager for whom we search, for each individual both bears and enriches the patterns of life that typify Niiike. These common patterns can be recognized as we set each person against the background of the entire community. From the whole assembly of persons we learn the contours of rural living. In the same way, Niiike is a unique village which, together with other distinctive villages, reveals the patterns of the total fabric of life of village Japan.

2. *Geographical* SETTING

Niiike lies at the western border of Kamo village in the southern or coastal-plain sector of Okayama Prefecture, about eight miles from Okayama City, the prefectural capital. In appearance it is almost indistinguishable from nearby communities. A simple cluster of houses and outbuildings nestles at the foot of a long, steep-sided but low hill covered with pine and bamboo grass. Before it paddy fields spread across the narrow valley floor. Halfway out into the valley Niiike's fields merge with those of a neighboring buraku. Similar settlements, slightly larger or smaller, are ranged every few hundred yards along the foot of the hills, and to the east some are set out in the middle of the valley floor where it broadens toward the Ashimori River. Some thirty such buraku, on both sides of the Ashimori River, make up Kamo mura (see Fig. 2). Beyond the low hills to the north, west, and south, and beyond the Ashimori River to the east, the coastal alluvial plain is dotted with hundreds of buraku looking very much like Niiike except in minor details of house arrangement and topographic setting.

Taking a wider view of the Okayama plain, in which Niiike occupies a roughly north central position, we find that it is bordered on the north by narrow stream valleys that cut through the foothills from the mountains beyond and on the south by newly created fields wrested from the shallows of the Inland Sea. If we travel from Niiike in either direction we see a gradual change in the form of buraku; the houses become more scattered, their clusters harder to define. Toward the hills, irregularities of landscape encourage a straggle of houses and outbuildings. Along the coast, in the newest reclaimed tracts with a clean slate to start on, parallel rows of houses are regularly spaced, each equidistant from its neighbors, along the preplanned checkerboard network of drainage and irrigation canals. Niiike's compaction is characteristic of the older settlement areas of the Okayama Plain. As a settlement ages and new households branch from old ones, the new houses are built very close to the old, both to main-

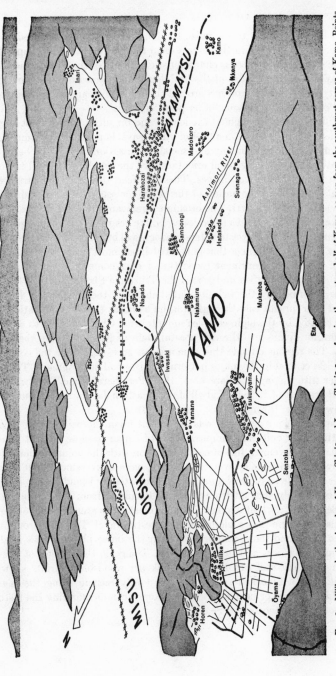

Kamo Village Boundary

FIG. 2.—Niiike and other buraku of Upper Shinjō and Lower Shinjō ōaza, forming the western half of Kamo, as seen from the southwest corner of Kamo. Points of interest include the Ashimori River, crossing Kamo as it flows to the right across the center of view; Harakozai of Takamatsu, the closest shopping town, hugging the railroad on the far side of the river; Inari, with its famed shrine and inns, at the head of the valley beyond Harakozai; and the tomb-mound, Tsukuriyama (at left lower center) rising over the fields south and east of Niiike.

tain family ties and to minimize the land area taken out of production. Often in an old buraku the houses seem to sit in one another's laps. This close settlement pattern is characteristic not only of the older areas of the Okayama Plain but also of the half-dozen other coastal plains ranged at thirty- to fifty-mile intervals around the Inland Sea and of upland basins and coastal plains in some other parts of Japan.

Villages differ throughout the length and breadth of Japan, not only in settlement pattern, but in a host of other ways: in material equipment and techniques, in the economy and social organization, and in the behavior, emotional tone, and general orientation of the inhabitants. And the contrast is not limited to villages. These, in fact, derive their character in great degree from the nature of the larger socioeconomic regional setting of which they are a part. The broadest significant grouping we are able to make divides Japan into three zones. Niiike lies within a broad region embracing nearly all of western Japan which will be referred to as the "Core Zone." The Core Zone is that portion of Japan most intimately associated with the Asiatic continent by virtue of easy communication along the axis of the Inland Sea and across the Tsushima Strait. The heart of the zone is formed by the well-populated shores of the Inland Sea. But the total area spreads east through Honshu as far as the communication barrier created by the high, complex mountains of Chūbu and north over the mountain divide into the rich coastal plain of Nagano facing the Japan Sea. The regions outside this zone are less accessible from the continent and less central to the major patterns of historical development. They fall either into an intermediate area, the "Peripheral Zone," or, with the southern part of Kyushu and all of northeastern Japan, into an outer ring known as the "Frontier Zone" (see Fig. 3).

Japan for long centuries was dependent upon the neighboring Asiatic continent for cultural stimulus. Areas of Japan in close contact or in a relatively convenient line of communication with the point of stimulation enjoyed an advantage over those which were more remote. The Inland Sea's 280-mile passage of quiet water, protected by island masses and yet not completely shut off from the open Pacific or from the Korea Strait, made it an important avenue of communication to areas outside of Japan and at the same time a highroad of domestic travel. The water route was often surer and more comfortable than the horse paths in this land of mountain barriers and turbulent rivers. Today, in the villages of this region one may still run across the folk art wood-block prints showing flotillas with blazoned sails bearing a lordly retinue along the island-studded waters, or hear folk songs or stories commemorating the historic importance of the Inland Sea.

Ease of communication favored development of the Inland Sea region, both in early days when it brought crafts and organizational skills from the sophisticated civilization of the continent and in later centuries when it nurtured internal development. Moreover, the waters and shores of the Inland Sea provided a favorable environment. Rich fisheries and high

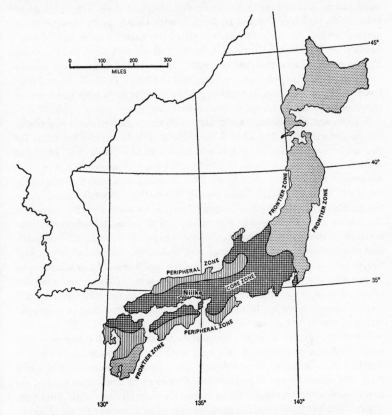

FIG. 3.—Japan, showing the Core, Peripheral, and Frontier zones of development

agricultural productivity permitted the rise of a dense population, which in turn provided the labor force as well as the stimulus for further increases in production. Intensive agriculture was favored further by the mild winter climate and relative freedom from the disasters of typhoon and earthquake that plague Japan elsewhere. Until nature and man combined successfully to create fertile land from long stretches of swampy or submerged coastline, however, the broadest agricultural acreage was at the eastern end of the Inland Sea and in the connected valleys beyond (see Fig. 4). There, in the upland basins of Yamato and Nara, the seats of government flourished for the first thousand years of the islands' history. It was only within the last few centuries that political power shifted eastward to the Kanto Plain, the region now dominated by Tokyo. But the Inland Sea region continued to flourish with Osaka as its greatest commercial center. Although in modern times the nation's main axis of communication has shifted overseas, bringing fortune to Tokyo and the other Pacific ports, Osaka and the secondary cities of the Inland Sea remain major centers of population, finance, and industry. Thus the Inland Sea, heart of the Core Zone, has either set the pace or kept step in each new phase of national economic development.

Niiike's location midway along the north shore of the Inland Sea places her in the center of the Core Zone. Today this heartland stretches far enough beyond the Inland Sea to encompass all of Japan's cities of over a million population, the bulk of the nation's industrial strength, the best-developed network of rail and road communications, and the most productively managed agricultural land of the nation. Most farm communities in this area, the mountain buraku only somewhat less than those on the plains, have been deeply influenced by the industrial-urban environment enveloping them. The cities provide expanding markets for specialized cash crops, their commercial and industrial enterprises are a key source of employment and cash income for members of farm households. Earning power, thus supplemented, allows a scale of living and the purchase of equipment and material goods formerly beyond the farmer's grasp. Though these are latter-day phenomena, often still in an emergent stage, the area has a record of relative advantages stretching over two millenniums or more. It is this fact and its social and cultural consequences which distinguish villages of this area from the rural communities of the Frontier Zone in northeastern Japan. Such frontier communities are still relatively self-sufficient in production, cling more to traditional modes, are poorer and often organized along hierarchical social lines outmoded elsewhere. The physical conditions of the Frontier Zone are harsh. Neither today nor in the past have the physical and social contexts of the Frontier Zone buraku been as advantageous as those of the Core Zone. However, within this Core Zone, not all rural communities have benefited equally. Those situated among mountains or in isolated plains have been partially excluded from the main course of development. Topographic and climatic conditions thus explain certain variations among the communities of the area.

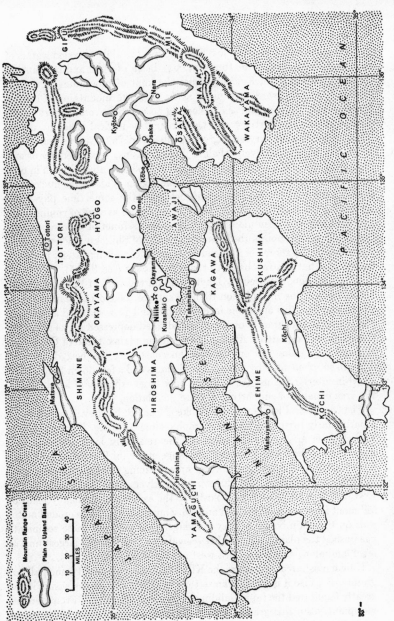

Fig. 4.—Prefectures around the Inland Sea. Note that cities are in the restricted coastal plains and upland basins where irrigated crop yields are highest

INLAND SEA TOPOGRAPHY

The Inland Sea, one of the loveliest and most heavily traveled waters of the world, is the central feature of a large basin of plain and sea rimmed by mountain arcs which emerge from the knot of mountains in central Japan, curve westward, and unite again with the mountains of central Kyushu (see Fig. 4). The sea, according to one of several theories, was created in recent (Tertiary and Quaternary) geological times by down-faulting. Because of varying degrees of subsidence in its several parts, it is composed of six relatively shallow major basins, separated by island groups. Water still covers a large portion of the basin area, though in past ages it spread over all the lowlands of the region. This water nucleus integrates the region's land-based life while at the same time physically separating the encircling land masses. Its use as an avenue of communication probably has been more important than its function as a separating factor, for at two points the arcs of the coast of Shikoku reach to within ten miles of the shores of Honshu. Plateaus descend like steps from the mountains that rim this basin to the water's edge (see Fig. 5). Up to two millenniums ago, the present Okayama Plain was part of this shallow sea with islands rising in profusion from its surface. Like other plains around the Inland Sea, this one came into existence and grew seaward as streams ate away the soft granite of the hills and filled depressed segments along the edges of the plateau. Among the resulting plains, those of Okayama, Hyogo, and Osaka—all on the Honshu coast—are the best developed. Though supplemented by lesser alluvial plains and a few down-faulted and silted-in interior basins, they are the only large expanses of level land in the area capable of supporting a dense population.

The Okayama Plain, on which Niiike is located, has developed through a particularly favorable set of geographic circumstances. First, the rivers and streams arising to the north in the relatively large, bowl-shaped watershed of the Chūgoku mountain range and Kibi Plateau converge on a relatively small isle-studded water area. Gaining size and erosive power as they rush seaward, the three primary rivers—the Takahashi in the west, Asahi in the center, and Yoshii to the east—pick up heavy loads of sediment from the Kibi plateau and subsequently drop these eroded materials on the plain below as they converge. Deposition of these sediments has pushed the plain front steadily seaward and created the largest unit of level land along the Inland Sea west of the Osaka Plain.

Unlike most areas of Japan, the Kibi Plateau is composed principally of granite. Because it is a soft granite that weathers and erodes easily, it has greatly facilitated the rapid building of the Okayama Plain. From another viewpoint, also, this granite base is an asset to the region, for it marks geological stability greater than that of the majority of areas where the same forces that extrude volcanic rock also produce frequent and severe earthquakes. But such soft parent material makes for soil conditions that are naturally inhospitable to the growth of trees. Scarcity of soil in rain-eroded areas has hindered natural seeding and replacement. At the same time, relatively light rain during much of the year, coupled with poor

Fig. 5.—Topography of Okayama Prefecture. The Kibi Plateau, forming an upland intermediate between the Chūgoku Range and the Okayama Plain, perpetuates in its name the ancient title of the province. Okayama's three primary rivers converge on the plain.

retention of available moisture, tends to kill the young trees which do take root. Man has contributed to this problem. Under primeval conditions, broad-leaf trees, such as oaks, made up the natural forest cover of western Japan. That these trees survive almost nowhere testifies to man's expending of what forest cover there was. From prehistoric times, cutting for household fires has been a continuous drain. In the seventeenth and eighteenth centuries additional heavy demands for fuel arose from the establishment of many small furnaces for the smelting of iron from river sand, the development of many small commercial pottery kilns, and the needs of salt driers of the coastal area. Subsequent reforestation programs in the nineteenth and twentieth centuries covered the hills once more with quick-growing black and red pine, but meanwhile the soil had been contributing at ever faster rates to the gradual silting-in of the plain below.

Thus, several physical conditions, operating over a large area, favored the development of the Okayama Plain. In the later extension of this plain, man has been fully as active as nature in pushing back the sea. In fact, from a structural viewpoint, there are three successive fronts of the Okayama Plain which correspond with the historical development of farming and reclamation there. The inner or northern part pushes seaward from the lower reaches of the Kibi Plateau and was the first area to be silted in. As early as the first century B.C., this delta region was being farmed by the ancient Japanese (see chap. 3). The central zone corresponds to the area reclaimed for manors in the Middle Ages, principally during the thirteenth century (see Fig. 6). The outer or southern zone is the area of latest silting-in, and reclamation there has been underway from the late sixteenth century. Thus the work of reclamation along the edge of the bay, extending over four centuries, has sped the natural process of sedimentation and land creation and has added appreciably to the cultivated area of Okayama Plain.

INLAND SEA CLIMATE

The agricultural success of this area, a success that long antedates the modern period, is attributable to the mild climate for which the Inland Sea borderlands are famed. Relatively slight rainfall coupled with the many sunny days makes the plain one of the pleasantest places in Japan in which to live. Summer temperatures are high, but winters are mild and especially attractive with chilly, crisp air and brilliant sunshine interrupted only occasionally by overcast skies and slight snowfalls. The late onset of cold days—January is the coldest month—permits winter wheat and naked barley to get a good start in the late fall, and sunny winter days permit the soil to absorb enough warmth to keep the mean temperature of the earth's surface as high as 37.2° F. in January.

The average annual rainfall in the area around Niiike is only 42 inches. This places it nearly at the bottom of the rainfall range of 40 to 120 inches for Japan as a whole. This moderate rainfall is accompanied by comparatively low humidity, and the area actually loses more moisture by evaporation throughout the year than it gains through precipitation, even though few weeks go by without an overcast sky and at least a light rain. The rain is concentrated in two seasonal downpours with relatively dry periods between. Late spring, especially June, is marked by the "plum rains," a fine continuous drizzle accounting for 15 per cent of the year's total precipitation. The other rainy season occurs in September, the month of typhoons, although these storms, which strike other parts of southwestern Japan with such destructive force, seldom penetrate the Inland Sea Basin with sufficient power to do serious damage.

These characteristics—sunshine, relatively little rainfall, and a long growing season—together with gentle winds, are in large part the effect of the surrounding mountain ridges that protect the region from weather extremes. The mountain areas surrounding the basin are almost twice as wet as the lowlands around Niiike and are enough colder to have an appreciably shorter growing season. In summer Niiike's prevailing winds come from the south. They bring tropical monsoon air which has lost much of its moisture crossing the Shikoku ranges. In descending and crossing the Inland Sea, the air is warmed and tends to hold its remaining moisture until it rises to cross the Chūgoku Range to the north. During the winter the prevailing winds blow from the opposite quarter, toward Japan from Siberia. As they travel in a southeasterly direction across the Japan Sea they gather a good deal of moisture, subsequently deposited as heavy snowfalls covering the Japan Sea side of the mountains, with somewhat lighter fall on their Inland Sea side. But as the winds descend into the Inland Sea Basin, they warm a bit, the sky clears, and the resultant mild weather permits winter crops to be grown in the paddy fields of the southern third of Okayama Prefecture.

The precipitation pattern, with its long periods of limited rainfall, has been both a help and a hindrance to successful agriculture. In winter, the farmer benefits from the prevailing dryness which permits the paddy fields to be drained, aerated, and planted to cool-season crops, chiefly mat rush and winter wheat and some naked barley. But rainfall is also light during the hot summer when rice, the main staple of the region, and other crops demand the greatest water supply. Faced with summer water shortages that reach drought proportions more frequently than in any other region of Japan, Inland Sea farmers have pushed irrigation facilities to a high point of development. Most of the rivers that drain the coastal plains have been diked and tapped to help supply paddy fields with irrigation water and, at the same time, to protect the surrounding countryside from the periodic floods that sweep seaward on the elevated river beds. Further effort, over the course of centuries, has dotted the surface of many lowlands in the eastern Inland Sea region with a remarkable concentration of water storage ponds. Other ponds built into slopes along the plain's edges likewise help to ease the seasonal water shortage and enable irrigated fields to climb slopes that were formerly available only for the less productive dry-field cultivation. With the combination of rainless, sunny summer weather and large-scale water storage, Okayama fruit orchards prosper in the sunshine as almost nowhere else in Japan, even while the rice is stem-deep in the vital water.

There are other formidable problems the farmers have to face. Except in the dry summer, rivers, whose stream beds are elevated above the adjacent farmland, pose a threat of flood which even ambitious diking does not completely remove. Flood waters occasionally break through and rampage destructively through the most heavily settled parts of the plain. Drainage still is not adequate in many low-lying spots to permit double cropping of paddy fields, and in newly reclaimed areas the saline soil is of limited productivity despite repeated washings to remove the salt. Other soils tend to become overly acid because of too much moisture, resulting in crop losses in early fall when the heads of rice are heavy with grain. Niiike shares some of these physical handicaps with the rest of the region, and later chapters will show how its farmers have evolved ways of overcoming them.

PHYSICAL DESCRIPTION OF OKAYAMA PREFECTURE

As we scan the geographical profile of Okayama Prefecture, we see features that are repeated in most of Japan's forty-six major political units, certainly in the eight prefectures that cluster around the Inland Sea: Osaka, Hyōgo, Okayama, Hiroshima, and Yamaguchi in Honshu; Kagawa and Ehime in Shikoku; and Oita in Kyushu. The modern prefectures of Japan are of relatively late origin. Although the earlier provinces were abolished in 1871, it was only after some two decades of experimental rearranging that the present-day prefectures were established. Most prefectures are amalgams of several former provinces, and it is apparent that the central government in combining these units attempted, as far as topography permitted and without too greatly violating either historical precedent or natural boundaries, to create each new préfecture as a compound of relatively prosperous coastal plain and relatively unproductive interior mountains. This linking of plain and mountain into single administrative units permits the government to draw upon assets of the tax-rich industrial and agricultural plains areas to offset the deficits of the mountain areas. However, no amount of ingenuity has sufficed to make the various prefectures equally self-sustaining. Thus we find that the annual proceeds of national taxes in Okayama exceed the amount that the prefecture receives in national subsidies. The reverse is true of neighboring Tottori and a number of other prefectures. Like most other prefectures, Okayama Prefecture began its official life with one major urban and commercial center, the primary castle town that dominated the coastal plain in feudal times. After 1871 this city continued its dominant position as the prefectural capital, Okayama City.

Okayama Prefecture occupies a roughly rectangular segment of western Honshu, an area referred to as the Chūgoku region. Spread out over the southern or "sunny" flank of this region, the prefecture is about as deep inland as it is broad along the seacoast and comprises about four-fifths of the total breadth of Honshu at this point. It includes the Okayama Plain, the Tsuyama Basin, and several smaller fault depressions of the interior, the rounded hills and mountains of the intervening Kibi Plateau, and the southern flank of the Chūgoku Range, backbone of the island. From elevations of over 3,500 feet, this range sweeps swiftly down to the sea on the northern or "shady" side, providing only a narrow strip of mountain flank and plain for Shimane and Tottori prefectures, which face the Japan Sea; but it descends more gradually into Okayama. Okayama Prefecture is primarily arranged around its key lowland, the Okayama Plain, on which Niiike is located. Very irregular in shape, this plain measures some fifteen miles deep and has a maximum east-west extent of thirty-five miles. The northern margins of the plain terminate abruptly at the southern edge of the Kibi Plateau, which emerges as poorly forested, rounded hills less than 800 feet high. On the south, except near the mouth of the Takahashi River, the plain is shut away from the sea by coastal hills and the boot-shaped Kojima Peninsula. These are fault ridges running east and west, which are echoed farther inland by parallel low ridges that break the present-day plain surface. Like Kojima Peninsula, these hills were islands in earlier historical times when the Inland Sea covered the plain. Niiike itself lies at the foot of just such a hill in the western part of the plain. Shallow Kojima Bay is a remnant of the earlier waters, and what is now Kojima Peninsula is a former island which was joined at one end to the silted-in plain only within the last eight centuries (see Fig. 5).

Okayama City, astride the Asahi River just eight miles from Niiike, is the prefectural capital and the industrial and communications center of the prefecture. With a population of 235,754 in 1955, it is the leading city between Hiroshima to the west and Himeji to the east. It began as a castle town during the early sixteenth century and grew rapidly after it became the headquarters of the main feudal baron of the locality (see chap. 3). By channeling east-west traffic on the famous old Sanyō road through his new headquarters town and by developing the Asahi River as a link between the interior and the sea routes beyond Kojima Bay, the daimyo laid the foundations for the development of Okayama as the major city of the plain. During the early years of the modern period, however, Okayama was slow to convert its assets into ones suited to the new industrialization so radically altering much of urban Japan. Osaka and Yawata, the major industrial nodes at either end of the Inland Sea, drained business and capital away from Okayama and the other cities of the region. One special handicap of Okayama was that, as a river port, it could not dock large ships as could Hiroshima, a coast port. After the Russo-Japanese War, regional leadership was permanently lost to Hiroshima.

When that war broke out, the railhead of the main line from the national capital had just passed Hiroshima; the terminus, Kure, became the point of embarkation for troops and military supplies bound for the continent and, thereafter, the leading naval base in the Inland Sea region. Nearby Hiroshima thrived as a supply center and also added regional governmental offices and industries along with divisional headquarters. Hiroshima is now half again the size of Okayama and the acknowledged leading city of the central Inland Sea area. However, although Okayama City still has almost no heavy industry, industrialization has gained momentum during the past several decades. Though it is still primarily a marketing and processing center, its light industries manufacture a variety of consumer goods. A brood of smaller cities scattered along the rail line at the seaward edge of the plain have shared increasingly in this industrial development. An advanced synthetic fiber industry has grown in Kurashiki. In Tamano and Tamashima, along the Inland Sea coast, shipyards and other heavy industries are booming. Amid this competition, Okayama City's primacy as governmental capital and regional communications center is still a factor in its dominance. Transverse rail lines across Honshu to the Sea of Japan coast and via ferry to Shikoku intersect the main rail artery here. A new downriver harbor on the Asahi, built since 1953, will at last permit ocean-going freighters to dock and bring sea trade. Thus Okayama City has opportunity to grow through connections with the outer world, while it serves as the main urban service and supply center for its rural hinterland.

AGRICULTURE OF THE OKAYAMA PLAIN

Despite the urban growth along its seaward fringe, Okayama Plain still retains the pre-eminently agricultural character with which it first moved into the light of history. Urbanization, both local and national, has only intensified its importance as a major crop-producing area. Its surpluses of rice, dry grains, and vegetables move toward nearby and distant markets; truck gardening zones have emerged near its cities; its fruit is prized in the markets of Tokyo and Osaka. These are crops that bring a cash income to the farmer. Significantly, farmers are stressing the money income potential of industrial crops, chief and oldest of which is the mat rush (*Juncus effusus*) used in the manufacture of mats and the coverings for *tatami*.

Except for the hillocks and plain borders where dry fields are the rule, the surface of the Okayama Plain is covered with an almost unbroken expanse of flooded fields. In summer these paddy fields are filled with rice, which in winter is replaced by wheat, mat rush, rapeseed, and many kinds of vegetables. This endless succession of crops gives the Okayama Plain as well as the Inland Sea region as a whole the highest average land-use intensity of any agricultural region in Japan. Most farmers plant two crops a year on from 60 to 80 per cent of the total area they cultivate. This double cropping falls below 60 per cent in only a few places. Nor does the quantity of production fall markedly as a result of such intensive planting. It was only in the years following World War II that fertilizing techniques on the single-crop fields of northern Japan raised production averages above the Okayama Plain level of more than fifty bushels of rice per acre. The western plain, including the reclaimed land near Kojima Bay, is the foremost commercial mat rush growing area in Japan and accounts for one-fourth of the national production. Matting fabricated from Okayama rush brings premium prices, and its relatively steady market contributes considerably toward keeping farmers free from debt. In the eastern part of the plain, where hills and mountains are more numerous, commercial orchards planted on the warm, south-facing slopes provide the farmer with his chief source of cash income. Unblemished peaches, magnificent table grapes, and smaller amounts of Japanese pears and mandarin oranges find their way from these slopes to the markets of all Japan. In the western plain, where Niiike lies, commercial fruit-growing is confined to a few small areas because of the present preoccupation with rush and a lack of appropriate orchard sites. Only on Kojima Peninsula and in the extreme western hills are there orchard zones of any importance.

The intensive agricultural economy of the Okayama Plain, stressing both subsistence and commercial crops, is stimulated in part by the very dense rural population that the area must support. At the same time the dense population grows out of the success of the agricultural economy. Increasing population presses on the capacity of the land and, in fact, surpasses it. Although the Inland Sea region's standard of living is high for Japan as a whole, intensive agriculture by itself does not provide the income and security for an average rural family that production-per-acre figures would imply. The land held by ordinary farm households is the smallest average farm acreage in the nation. Families of six to eight members cultivate from one to two acres as a rule. This means, of course, that there are many families who are forced to maintain themselves on properties much smaller than this. In short, whereas productivity per unit is extremely high, production per person remains low.

Glancing again at national statistics, one finds the Inland Sea region has the greatest percentage of farm households dependent on non-farm employment for cash income. This dependence is most marked in areas such as Okayama Plain, which are near large industrial and commercial centers where opportunities for other jobs are abundant. Such supplemental income results in a relatively high total-family-income and provides the surplus necessary for a comfortable standard of living. As one indication of this prosperity and its use for productive investment, Inland Sea farmers use more commercial fertilizer and insecticides and employ more animal and mechanical power than farmers elsewhere in Japan. Eighty per cent of the farm households use draft animals (usually oxen) or gasoline motors in one or more farm operations. In the Sanuki Plain in Kagawa Prefecture on the southern coast of the Inland Sea, the figure is 98 per cent, highest in the nation. Another indication of this prosperity is the general evidence that Inland Sea farmers rarely put themselves in debt for such essentials of living as food and taxes, as is often the case with the farmers of northern Japan. Rather, they owe money for improvements on their houses or holdings, for fertilizer and machinery, and occasionally for other modern conveniences which have substantially increased their standard of living.

Contrasts in farm size, mechanization, and settlement pattern exist between the older interior plain, where Niiike lies, and the newly reclaimed lands of Kojima Bay. In the older areas, holdings are small—often totaling less than an acre—and are broken into tiny, scattered fields. The houses are clustered together in tightly grouped little hamlets like Niiike. On the other hand, two-thirds of the farm households in the reclaimed area have at least two and one-half acres laid out in a single block on which house and outbuildings are also situated. This rather exceptional settlement pattern has resulted from the special development through which the area has passed. The unending quest for land has encouraged the continuous reclamation of shallow coastal waters into new paddy fields. Full-scale reclamation of the Kojima Bay marshes, begun in the sixteenth century and renewed with vigor after 1899 by a private development company and finally taken over by the national government following the land reform of 1947, is now almost completed. This reclaimed area was operated from 1912 to 1947 as the largest contiguous piece of farmland owned by a single interest in Japan. Operated along scientific lines, this project became an exciting center of innovation in methods of cultivation and farm living whose influence carried over into the older adjacent areas. Settlers have come to the reclaimed area from all over western Japan, creating a social milieu of mixed origins quite unlike the older hamlets in which the same families have lived together in close physical and social relationships for generations.

Within this geographical framework of the Inland Sea region and the Okayama Plain, Niiike emerges as a moderately prosperous little agricultural community. As in generations past, her farmers work their fields with the intensity that a dense population demands and a favorable climate permits and with the skill that generations of experience have taught them. But Niiike is also part of modern Japan, neighbor to industrial urban communities that have provided markets for her surplus food and raw or processed materials and employment for her extra manpower and have taught her much about city ways. Niiike is aware of and uses modern agricultural methods, her people travel to Okayama City to shop or work, and her youth seek out its variety of entertainment. It is within the geographical framework outlined above and the historical perspective that follows that the social, political, and economic life of Niiike today must be viewed.

The area of present-day Okayama Prefecture, together with a portion of the territory of Hiroshima Prefecture to the west, is historically known as the Kibi region. Kibi, along with a number of other centers of culture in Core Japan, is an area in which the Japanese people have maintained a continuous existence for well over five thousand years. Niiike, whose origin as a community dates back only some three hundred years, is a relative newcomer to this region. Yet it clearly shares the cultural, social, and economic heritage of this long-settled portion of Japan. The complexity of land use and the intricate technology, the economic balance of its way of agriculture, and the delicate perfection of its irrigation system are all inheritances which took many hundreds of years to develop. It would be an exaggeration, of course, to claim that the pattern of Niiike life today is entirely a matter of cumulated past experience or that an understanding of Niiike must be based on knowledge of the whole history of the Kibi region. Much of Kibi's past is now forgotten and need not be recollected. Yet the depth of cultural continuity is an ever present part of the community's environment. The past is felt not only in Niiike's current way of life but in the historical monuments of the region, the ancient burial mounds and temple remains, and the local names which so often trace back to some dimly remembered age. All these are part of the cultural setting of the community we have undertaken to study.

THE EARLIEST INHABITANTS AND THEIR CULTURE

To relate the panorama of history to this community we need only climb to the top of Ōyama, the hill in front of Niiike (see Fig. 6). From this vantage point we can see across the plains which form the heart of old Kibi and imagine the sweep of over five millenniums of human history. At the time human life began in this region, the Inland Sea waters washed the edges of the slope on which we stand, and the small pine-clad hills which pierce the waves of more distant rice fields were islands. The earliest known inhabitants, coming perhaps in early postglacial times, discarded stone tools on hilltops that then were islands. No more is known of them than that they chipped stone points and blades; no skeletal remains have been found.

Somewhat later, prehistoric people formed hunting and fishing communities on the edges of the now landlocked islands. The pottery remains of this culture, named Jōmon by modern archeologists, distinguish a primitive stage of life which flourished in the Japanese islands from at least 3000 B.C. to 350 B.C. (see Fig. 6). Various Jōmon sites, marked by deposits of refuse such as pottery fragments, tools, animal bones, and vast quantities of shells tossed aside after meals of shellfish, have been found not far from Niiike. One find at Kasaoka, only thirty miles to the southwest, has revealed over a hundred skeletal remains. It is one of the outstanding Jōmon deposits in Japan.

From Ōyama, our hill overlooking Niiike, we need refocus our imagination but slightly to see the next stage of cultural development in Kibi. To archeologists, this is the Yayoi culture which extended from approximately 350 B.C. to A.D. 250. From the continent, new peoples came to Japan bringing a more advanced culture based on agriculture. There were new styles of settlement, tool-making, pottery, housing, and social systems. But above all, the addition of the technique of wet-rice cultivation was the outstanding Yayoi contribution to the advance of human civilization in Japan. Not only did rice give Japan a new and more productive economy able to support a more advanced and numerous population, but the requirements of wet-rice cultivation had a profound effect upon the subsequent patterns of life and society in Japan. In particular, the cultivation of rice put new emphasis on the combined use of land and water. There is clear evidence that the delta regions of the three rivers of the modern Okayama Plain, the Takahashi, Asahi, and Yoshii, prospered greatly during the Yayoi period. Provided with a number of sizable, well-watered lowlands, easily accessible by sea and located on the route between the major centers of northern Kyushu and the Yamato Plain, the Kibi region was a locale of rich prehistoric cultural development.

By the Yayoi period the plain of the Ashimori River, in which Niiike is located, had become considerably extended. The land had risen and the sea receded below the first range of hills to the south of Ōyama, on which we stand, thereby exposing rich lands suitable for rice production. A pattern of settlement and land use began which has been maintained in its essentials down to recent times. The settlements dotting these plains, although long since overlaid by later village communities, left behind numerous remains of pottery and other artifacts. It is commonplace for

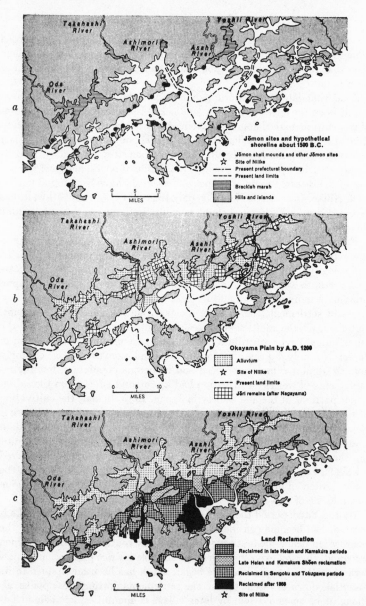

FIG. 6.—Development of arable land of the Okayama Plain, shown in three stages: *a*, The coastline about 1500 B.C., prior to the emergence of flatland and prior to the coming of plant cultivation. Jōmon sites on the hill slopes are near the water edge of this period; Yayoi sites occupy the flatland emerging at a later time. *b*, Early plains areas, identified by fields divided according to the *jōri* system about A.D. 1200. *c*, Successive major phases of land reclamation to the present day.

Yayoi relics to be dug up accidentally in the fields around Niiike, and many amateur archeologists of the region have collections. Although showing certain local characteristics, the Yayoi culture which flourished in the Kibi region was part of a general culture complex which extended from Kyushu as far north as the Kanto region. In the village of Shō, about two miles south of Niiike, some hundreds of pottery finds from an obviously permanent Yayoi settlement suggest density of settlement and show that the sea had receded beyond this line.

THE GREAT TOMB-BUILDERS

Yayoi culture was replaced by the Tomb culture, dated by archeologists as about A.D. 350 to A.D. 650. This was the high point of Japan's prehistoric civilization. The tombs for which this period was named were those of local chieftains of considerable power who were buried in artificial mounds set high on hill crests. The cultural advances of the great tomb-building period were stimulated in large part by overseas contacts, but, in some part, new ideas for organizing production and social relations developed from the Yayoi culture. By the late part of the Tomb period, mounted warriors using swords were beginning to establish an aristocracy, with a clan form of organization and a stress on purity of family line. The weapons, equipment, and social organization of this aristocracy bore remarkable resemblances to those of the people of Korea and Manchuria. It is surmised that at least some families may have been immigrants from these areas. While most people continued many of their Yayoi ways of life and buried their dead near their homes amid the rice fields, the aristocracy, almost as if they were a separate people, maintained a higher cultural tradition characterized by great tombs.

Tomb culture extended over roughly the same area as Yayoi. The most famous tombs are those identified as imperial mausoleums in the old province of Yamato, near present-day Nara and Osaka. Others, gigantic or modest, are scattered from these localities westward in some abundance along the coastal plains and basins of the Inland Sea, and thence southward. Northward they extend from the Osaka-Nara region toward the Kanto area, although in greatly diminished numbers. Jewelry of semi-precious stones and gold and silver, as well as bronze and iron grave objects, suggest the growing wealth controlled by the tomb builders; and the giant stones brought from the hills to build the later tomb chambers, as well as the masses of earth piled up to form mounds on the valley floor, testify to the immense labor force at their command. For the largest of their tombs, the Japanese chieftains developed a mound style with a square front and round back called a "keyhole" mound, which may reach twelve hundred feet in length.

Second only to the central Yamato Plain in rich Tomb culture finds, the Kibi area contains seventy-nine large burial mounds of various types. From our perch atop Ōyama, two of the six great keyhole tombs in old Kibi are visible. One, known as Misu Tsukuriyama, is about one and a half miles to the west, built on a spur of hills rising out of the plain; the other, Tsukuriyama ("Man-made Hill"), lies in the middle of the valley before Niiike no more than four hundred yards away. It is half again as long as the greatest Egyptian pyramid, a mass of earth over 90 feet high and 360 yards long. Though utilizing a natural knoll, the entire mound was modeled into the characteristic keyhole shape. Other smaller tombs are plentiful nearby. A group of six circular tombs is arranged in pairs near the straight end of Tsukuriyama. On the crest of the hill immediately behind Niiike, two small keyhole tombs rise amid the pines, one partly within the woodlot of a Niiike household. Vegetables grow on the remnant of a large circular mound at the edge of the valley east of Niiike. Probably the latest tomb to be constructed in the vicinity was a passage grave, now empty, which leads into the hillside immediately behind Iwasa Yasuta's house in Niiike. This stone-lined passage leads thirteen feet inward to a chamber, eighteen by seven feet, terminated by a single great stone slab measuring eight feet high by seven wide and vaulted by several huge slabs with exposed surfaces over four feet wide and seven feet long. Although no scientific excavations have been made in the largest tombs described here, the contents of a small stone-lined cist, just large enough for a single burial, on the hillside above Niiike suggest what the burial offerings of grander tombs may have been. This tomb, when excavated by members of our research team in 1950, revealed thirteen complete pottery vessels for food offerings and many fragments of others; iron arrow-tips and larger points, a sword and scabbard, and an iron hammer head, as well as several comma-shaped beads (*magatama*) of agate or crystal, all of which are characteristic of the Tomb culture.

To the villagers of Niiike these evidences of prehistoric grandeur have become commonplaces exciting little emotion. The shrine atop Tsukuriyama, visited periodically for buraku festivals, has no connection with the chieftain who lies buried in the mound. Children play casually in the burial chamber behind the buraku. To them this place is more awesome as a former haunt of robbers than as a tomb of a prehistoric chieftain. During the Pacific war the chamber functioned as an antiaircraft shelter for the people of Niiike and at one time as temporary housing for a wartime evacuee and his family.

Despite the remoteness of Tomb culture from more recent chapters in Japanese social development, this period is important as the starting point for many of Japan's characteristic social patterns. At this stage in Japanese agrarian society, the archeological and mythological evidence leads us to distinguish the operation of two separate but complementary forces for social cohesion. One led to the extension of genealogically centered, extended families; the other to the formation of pseudo-family groups on the basis of geographical proximity and functional homogeneity. In Tomb culture these tendencies are revealed by the appearance of two distinct social units, *uji* and *be*.

The exact nature of ancient Japan's social structure is not fully known. The evidence available tends to confirm a view that this society was divided into two parts, one consisting of *uji*, kinship-dominated extended family groups, the other of *be*, occupation-centered pseudo-family groups. Apparently *uji* groups were composed predominantly of socially or politically prominent families, while *be* groups were composed of families of subordinate status. Here is a picture of early Japanese society in which the upper social levels tended to emphasize genealogy and the lower levels were brought together on an occupational basis. Only later did the occupational groups add kinship concepts. In Japan the use of a family name was long a mark of social prestige.

We may suppose then that in the valley of the Ashimori River by the time of the tomb-builders the populace was being differentiated into clearly defined communities. Most of these were *be* which tilled the soil or performed other economic or service functions. *Uji* communities were fewer in number and tended to supervise land use and manage the *be*. There are numerous reminders of this stage of social development in names surviving in the Ashimori Valley even today. Southward across the fields from Niiike, the community of Yabe still bears the name of the *be* of arrowmakers. Hattori, across the hills behind Niiike to the east, was a community of weavers. *Uji* names are less easily distinguished. But, as we soon shall see, many of the major locale names of this region were associated with prominent *uji* of the Tomb period.

There is considerably more information regarding the internal structure of the *uji* communities than of the *be*. The *uji* community was more than a family or even an extended family. It was a group of families clustered around a central and socially prominent family, the head of which was known as the *uji* chief, *uji-no-kami*. The clustered families held various kinship and service relationships to the central family and generally all lived together forming a social and economic community. The *uji* chief held a recognized position of leadership within the group and was acknowledged as the lineal descendant of the progenitor of the *uji*. The progenitor, moreover, was looked upon with religious veneration as the protective deity of the group, the *uji-gami*. Thus the *uji* was a social unit fused together under common leadership and a common focus of religious worship. The *uji* chief combined in his person the authority of social prestige, economic power, and religious sanction.

The *be* communities, although taking shape somewhat differently from the *uji*, seemed to resemble them in structure except that they were held together less by kinship ties than by the necessities of agricultural or craft co-operation. Despite lack of genealogical relationships, the sense of kinship and mutual reliance on a central deity developed and became strong in such communities. *Be* members also looked to a leading figure, generally of *uji* status, to whom they were personally subservient. The close connection between leading *uji* and subservient *be* is to be seen in the way in which many *be* took the names of the *uji* they served, and many *uji* bore the name of the functions performed by the *be* they managed, such as weaver or swordsmith. It is also important to note that the religious symbols worshipped by the *be* communities were often closely associated with the *uji*. Today the village shrines of Japan are referred to collectively as *uji-gami*, although the term for local deity (*ubusuna-gami*) is more properly applied to many such shrines.

These details are recounted, not because of any demonstrable direct connection between the social structure of this remote age and present-day Niiike, but because modern sociologists have observed in the society of that time the origins of certain social patterns which are still observable in rural Japan. The tendency of socially prominent families to form genealogically oriented main-and-branch families (*honke-bunke*) is traced back to the *uji;* while the *be*, as functionally oriented pseudo-family groups (*dōzoku*), are seen as the prototype of certain communal organizations. As we shall see in chapters 9 and 10, an understanding of Niiike's present-day social organizations involves these concepts and terms.

THE ORIGINS OF THE HISTORIC KIBI REGION

The age of the tomb-builders brings us to the threshold of recorded history in the area around Niiike. From Chinese records, for instance, we are told that Japan of the third and fourth centuries was a land of over "one hundred countries." These "countries," no doubt, referred to the kinship or tribal units which figured as the basis of Japan's first political divisions, known as *kuni*. During the fourth century these *kuni* were brought under the hegemony of a powerful group based in Yamato, a region including the present Osaka and Nara.

Although some of the greatest tombs near Nara and Osaka are traditionally identified as the burial places of early "emperors," no such history
or tradition is attached to the imposing mounds on the Okayama Plain.
Local legend and early historical records such as the eighth-century *Kojiki*
and *Nihon-shoki* which chronicle the lives of the ancient Yamato rulers,
tell us of the origin of the name, Kibi. According to these records the
Yamato emperor Sūjin, probably in the late fourth century, sent armies
out in four directions. The army that entered the Inland Sea area to conquer the "sunny side" (Sanyō) of the island of Honshu was led by the
general, Prince Kibitsu-hiko. The story of his major battle incorporates a
widespread Old World folktale motif, the magicians' transformation contest, and explains a number of place names in the neighborhood of Niiike.
According to local legend, Kibitsu's main opponent, Ura, was wounded by
a dexterously aimed arrow from Kibitsu's bow. He tried to escape by
turning into a pheasant; Kibi became a hawk and chased him through the
woods. Just as the hawk dove to make his kill, the pheasant leaped into a
creek and became a carp. But before the carp could disappear, Kibitsu
took the shape of a cormorant, dived, and delivered the final blow. Blood
gushing from the dying carp colored the stream and gave it the name,
Chisui-gawa ("Blood-drinking Creek"). This stream flows into the Ashimori River just north of Niiike. Kibitsu's stronghold for the fight was the
site of the most ancient and famous shrine of the area, Kibitsu Jinja, located only five miles east of Niiike and still the major shrine of southern
Okayama. The chronicle goes on to state that the area pacified by Prince
Kibitsu was named Kibi-no-kuni and, after subdivision into several *kuni*,
was parceled out among the prince's descendants. In this way, we are told,
there came into existence the Kibi family line with its main branches.

This story and other local legends, together with other bits of evidence
gleaned from a study of local place names, provide further clues for the
reconstruction of the history of Kibi in the age of the tomb-building chieftains. We are able to confirm the fact that the area was under the control
of a powerful local family holding the surname of Kibi. Whether or not the
Kibi family was a branch of the "imperial" family of Yamato is not clear,
but later history shows that they maintained close relations with the
Yamato group and came to champion the Yamato cause. Branches spread
throughout the Kibi area, as evidenced by the fact that the names of most
of the *kuni* in what is now the southern portion of Okayama Prefecture are
identical with the names of the early branches of the Kibi family. These
names were perpetuated as the names of the administrative districts, or
gun, in use from the seventh century until today. Each branch of the
Kibi family had its special shrine, the most important being the one

erected to the mythological founder of the family, Prince Kibitsu-hiko. This, the Kibitsu Jinja, is located in the district formerly known as Kayō and was long tended by the Kayō family, an offshoot of the Kibi line. Chieftains of these local families must have built a great number of the graves and tombs seen today as impressive reminders of the remote past.

THE NARA PERIOD

During the fifth and sixth centuries, society underwent a number of cultural changes and moved slowly in the direction of formal governmental organization. The cultural advance in the area of Kibi domination was steady and impressive. While we know few specific details, there is evidence that there was continuous growth in population and in the extent of area under cultivation. Foreign colonists settled in the Inland Sea region and brought with them many new cultural imports from the continent. The plains of the Takahashi, Asahi, and Yoshii rivers became major centers of colonization, as many place names in the area still attest. The locally eminent Achi family, of Chinese derivation, established a community at the mouth of the Takahashi River. Apparently ancient Kibi had access to the sea through a port located on the Ashimori River in the southern portion of what is now Kamo village and almost within sight of Niiike. This leads to several interesting observations. It was then necessary for navigation to avoid the main course of the Takahashi River, a swift and treacherous stream, in favor of the more manageable waters of the Ashimori. It is possible, however, as one historian proposes, that water from the Takahashi merged with the Ashimori to give the latter more volume. Also, it is well established that the Ashimori port area was dominated by the Tsu family (a word which means harbor) probably a branch of the Kibi. Whether in reference to the port (*tsu*) or to the Tsu family, the general area around present Kamo village became organized as the Tsu district (first Tsu-no-kōri, later Tsuu *gun*). This designation was used until 1900 when Tsuu *gun* was combined with Kuboya *gun* to form Tsukubo *gun*, a term still in use.

A massive attempt at centralization and systematization of government, based on Chinese patterns of administrative organization, was attempted by the Yamato rulers during the seventh and eighth centuries. These centuries in Japan are generally referred to as the Nara period, taking the name of the city of Nara which was established as the capital city in 710. By the time of the Taika political reform of 645, which committed Japan to a Chinese-style political centralization, Kibi had already gone a long way in this direction. Kibi itself was recognized as an area existing under the jurisdiction of a single authority, the *kuni* chief, *kuni-no-*

miyatsuko, a title recognized by the Yamato court and held by the heads of either the Kibi Shimotsumichi or Kibi Kamitsumichi families. The areas of authority exercised by the major branches of the Kibi family had become delimited as districts (*agata* or *kōri*), with the branch family chieftains recognized as district chiefs (*agata nushi*).

In 670 the old region of Kibi had been divided into three provinces: Bizen, which contained the valleys of the Yoshii and Asahi Rivers, Bitchū, on either side of the Takahashi River, and Bingo, farther to the west (see Fig. 7). In 714 the northern half of Bizen was made into the province of Mimasaka. Each province had its administrative headquarters (*kokufu*), which was the seat of a provincial bureaucracy, the higher echelons of which were officials appointed by, and often sent out from, the national capital. The headquarters of Bitchū was clearly the most important among those of the provinces of old Kibi. It was located where the village of Hattori now stands, just visible to the west over the crest of the hill behind Niiike (see Fig. 7). Here, in the midst of a fertile plain during the eighth century there were erected imposing public buildings, an administrative center, a college, a garrison, and branches of the great Tōdaiji temple of Nara. Buddhism was now officially patronized and its influence extended to the provinces. Sōja City of today derives its name from the *sōja*, or central administrative shrine, of Bitchū located where the city now stands. Kokubunji, the official monastery of Bitchū, was located at the foot of the hill which separates Niiike and Kokufu. Now only stone foundations remain, the tile-roofed structures having been destroyed in the wars and fires of the feudal age. Not far from Kokubunji and closer up the hill toward Niiike was Kokubun-niji, the nunnery of Bitchū. Of the temples, perhaps the largest was Tsudera, the guardian temple of the port of Bitchū, located across the east dike of the Ashimori River in the community of Yabe (see Fig. 8). Only a single foundation stone eight by five feet and exposed three feet above the earth remains to suggest what must have been the imposing size of this structure. Altogether the remains of some fifteen temples of the Nara period can be identified in Bitchū. With the ten in Bizen, they make up what must have been one of the largest agglomerations of pre-ninth-century Buddhist architecture outside of the capital area.

Another important reminder of the vitality and symmetry of imperial institutions during the Nara period is the system of land management established by order of the imperial government. This still leaves its imprint on the land about Niiike. The program of administrative centralization under the Taika Reform asserted public ownership of all cultivated land and redistributed it in equal portions to the cultivators. The former *be* were abolished, and their members made free cultivators under the central government. To accomplish this scheme the *jōri* system of land division was put into operation. Cultivated land was divided into half-mile squares and then subdivided into thirty-six equal squares. These squares in turn were cut into ten strips of 0.245 acre each. These became basic units of land allotment among the cultivators. For a long time modern historians considered the *jōri* system a paper reform in the provinces, but recent field

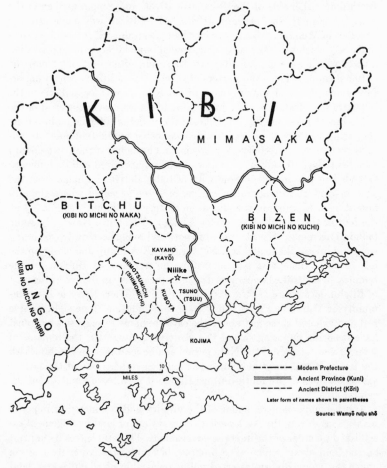

Fig. 7.—Ancient Kibi, subdivided into Bizen, Bitchū, and Mimasaka (in Okayama Prefecture), and Bingo (in Hiroshima Prefecture).

studies have revealed an unexpectedly wide distribution of *jōri* remains stetching from the Kanto Plain to northern Kyushu. Bitchū and Bizen provide some of the best examples of the survival of the *jōri* system. Largely through the indefatigable work of the local historian, Nagayama Usaburō, remains of *jōri* squares have been identified in the valley of the Oda River, in the plain between the Takahashi and Ashimori rivers, and in the plains on either side of the Asahi and Yoshii rivers. In many of these areas it is possible to find paddy fields which are still called by the original numbers assigned to them under the *jōri* system in the seventh century. These remains in the Kibi area provide us with a concrete measure of central

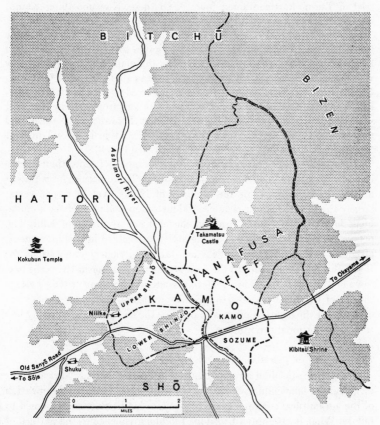

Fig. 8.—Niiike and Kamo within the Hanafusa fief (1600–1869). The several ōaza of Kamo, shown here, were legally separate mura throughout this period.

government control at this early date. They also reveal the locations of the best paddy lands of the region during the Nara period. Furthermore, a study of the southern limit of the *jōri* system gives us a fairly accurate picture of the location of the coastline at this time (see Fig. 6).

Intimately linked with the *jōri* system was the plan of local administrative divisions, fully developed during the Nara period and basically still in use today. We have already mentioned the division of old Kibi into provinces (*kuni*). These were further divided into districts (*kōri*, later *gun*), and still further into villages (*gō*, today "mura") and hamlets (*ri*). We know that there were eleven districts in Bitchū (see Fig. 7). The district of Tsu-no-kōri contained four *gō*. Of these, Kawamo (later Kamo) and Natsukawa have continued as mura names down to the present.

One final landmark of the Nara period lies directly before Niiike at the foot of Ōyama, where we have placed ourselves to view the panorama of local history. This is the road which bears the main traffic of the narrow valley and on which the Hiramatsu and Iwasa catch the bus to Okayama City. Called the Sanyōdō in Nara days, it served as a thriving thoroughfare along the Inland Sea carrying officials to and from the capital. Post stations on the road were established at Itakura, Kawabe, and Yakage, and a subsidiary post station may have been located just beyond present Niiike in what is now the buraku of Shuku (see Fig. 8).

These reminders of the glories of imperial Japan of more than twelve hundred years ago, like the monuments of the Tomb period, have passed into the commonplace for the villagers of Niiike. Yet in recent years, largely through the enthusiasm of local historians and politicians, a movement has started to instil pride in the past achievements of Kibi. The people of Niiike have yet to become actively involved in this movement, although perhaps the name Kibi has taken on richer connotations for them But a brief distance to the west across the Takahashi River the new own of Mabi was created in 1950 to perpetuate the name of Kibi's greatest son of the Nara period. He was Kibi-no-Mabi, a famous scholar and diplomat of the eighth century and perhaps the last of the Kibi family line to achieve national prominence.

THE DECLINE OF CENTRAL AUTHORITY

The Chinese-inspired systematization attempted by the Nara government did not long endure. Particularly the attempted basic reorganization of the agricultural community and system of land tenure was doomed to failure. What it attempted had done too much violence to the pattern of Japanese society. Land eventually reverted to private ownership and the land cultivators to a state of personal dependence upon families of local prominence. The decline of imperial institutions left little trace in local records, so can only be inferred from events recorded at the center of the political stage. In a general way, though, we can visualize changes in political, social, and cultural institutions as they took place around Niiike. During the ninth and tenth centuries much of the public land reverted to private estates known as *shōen*. In the province of Bitchū, while much of the land continued to be called public, in reality it became the private possession of hereditary officials. Kamo-no-*gō* was converted to a private estate, and its small settlement of Madokoro still carries, in slightly modified form, the name of the manorial office (*mandokoro*). Though we have no information about who became the owner of Kamo estate, it was customary for local landholders to put themselves under the protection of some central aristocratic family or a powerful temple. In many of the land transactions of this time Kibitsu shrine played a prominent part.

Reclaimed land provided material for many of the largest estates of the time. The urge to extend private holdings stimulated a period of active land reclamation during which the second belt of the Okayama Plain was recovered from the sea. About 1024 the large plain now dominated by Kurashiki City was brought under cultivation and made the estate of Masu (see Fig. 8). Today this area contains some of the richest paddy land of the Okayama Plain. The present village of Senō, south of Niiike, takes its name from a twelfth-century local hero who distinguished himself in reclamation and waterworks projects. He is credited with expanding the paddy system in Bitchū and with repairing the irrigation system which brought the waters of the Takahashi River through the Sōja Plain and down the valley of the Ashimori River. This is said to have been the origin of the Twelve Village (Jūnikagō) Canal system which forms the basis of irrigation for Kamo village today. Elsewhere in old Kibi, land was reclaimed on either side of the Asahi and Yoshii rivers. By the twelfth century, the entire belt of former sea marsh below the plains which had contained the administrative headquarters of Bitchū and Bizen had been converted to paddy. It was probably about this time that the owner of Kamo estate reclaimed part of the marsh between the Ashimori River and the hill against which Niiike rests. To this area was given the name Shinjō ("New Estate"), a name which the area carries to this day (see Fig. 8).

THE FEUDAL AGE

The appearance of the privately owned estates or manors and the decline of central authority ushered in further changes which served to transform the over-all pattern of Japanese social organization. The ensuing society, called feudal because of similarities to Western feudalism, lasted from the twelfth through the nineteenth centuries and left a very deep imprint on Japanese culture. So long was Japan's feudal age and so recently did it pass away that it is still common for the Japanese to label anything old-fashioned as "feudal."

Feudalism in Japan, as in Europe, was marked by decentralization and militarization of government. The bearing of arms became the prerogative of a knightly class, the *bushi* or samurai. This class, as manorial lords, estate managers, local agents of powerful court families or religious institutions, dominated the provincial scene. On the estates, ordinary people lost their relationship to the uniform law of the central government and became attached to leading families in a capacity similar to serfdom. The tendency toward the formation of pseudo-kinship groups of village-wide scope was reinforced. Among the knightly class, the manipulation of family lines and genealogies became a favorite occupation.

Again as in Europe, the feudal age in Japan was markedly religious. Buddhism, long firmly established on the monastic level, became deeply enmeshed in the fabric of rural life. Religious institutions were not only centers of arts and letters but also powerful military-economic holdings and local centers of influence. Among the many important temples of southern Bitchū the most outstanding was Hōfukuji, located in the foothills to the north of present Sōja (see Fig. 8). This monastery, which at its height boasted an estate drawing upon the resources of eleven *gō*, a group of over thirty buildings, and the special title of *gokoku* ("protector of the land"), was one of the greatest Zen monasteries of west central Japan. In the eighteenth century, even after many of its buildings had been destroyed by fire, the monastery had 159 community parishes scattered over southern Kibi. Sesshū, great artist of the fifteenth century, was a member of the order. Several objects of religious art at Hōfukuji, including some of his works, have been designated "national treasures" (*kokuhō*) by the Japanese government, a matter of considerable pride to the residents of Okayama.

Feudal militarization permeated central and provincial governments alike. The foremost figure in Bitchū now was the military protector (*shugo*) appointed by the central government located in Kamakura. The location from which the military protector exercised control over Bitchū shifted from the Kojima Bay area on the Inland Sea, headquarters of the Sasaki family in the twelfth century, to Matsuyama castle in the mountains of central Bitchū during the thirteenth and fourteenth centuries. After 1393, control was exercised by the Hosokawa family, keeper of

Kamogata castle in western Bitchū. Thus the old center of political influence of the Nara period in central Bitchū passed into eclipse.

While Bizen, during the feudal period, eventually became a major military and economic center, Bitchū remained weak and disunited. Economically, the extension of reclaimed land along the Ashimori deprived Bitchū of its port and hence of ready access to the rest of Japan. Militarily, large concentrations of feudal military power never developed in the older settled portion of Bitchū. Consequently the core of Bitchū was subjected to the constant, fragmenting pulls of outside forces during the ensuing years. The three core-districts of Tsuu, Kayō, and Kuboya became a feudal shatter zone between strong rival powers (see Fig. 7).

The history of Bitchū in this period is largely the story of struggles among small local families with occasional strong interference by forces pushing in from the east or west. To the present locality the legacy of this period is one of battle scars and castle remains. When central authority began to break down in the twelfth century, the need for self-protection induced locally influential families to fortify their residences. In the vicinity of Niiike we find evidence of some eleven such fortifications. Across the Ashimori River, branches of the Kayō family, keepers of Kibitsu shrine, fortified their residences at Niwase and Ashimori. Two more fortifications were located in the vicinity of Sōja. Such improvised defenses were not sufficient, however, when Japan moved into an age of professional warriors. Soon it was necessary to build strong castles, carefully placed to afford real military protection and strategic advantage. Mountain fortresses dotted the hilltops in the area around Niiike by the fourteenth century. Today there are remains of fifty-odd castles in the region of southern Bitchū. Not all were occupied at any one time, but they give us some idea of the intensity of former feudal competition around Niiike. From Ōyama, the sites of three castles that guarded the hill above Kibitsu shrine are visible across the Ashimori River, as well as those of four castles above the valley around Takamatsu, three above Oishi village, four above Aso, five above Sōja, and five surrounding Ashimori.

BITCHŪ AND THE WARS OF CONSOLIDATION

Between 1560 and 1600 Japan was shaken by momentous wars of political consolidation, fought out at two levels. At the top, Japan's "Three Unifiers" fought their way to hegemony over Japan. At the lower level, no less important for the national outcome, a process of local consolidation was taking place. Everywhere wars eliminated the small and weak in favor of the large and powerful. In central Japan, on either side of Bitchū, huge military powers began to take shape (see Fig. 9). To the west, with headquarters at Hiroshima, the Mōri family became a paramount contender for national hegemony. Its troops had gained control of the castles of western Bitchū by 1575. To the east the Ukida family achieved control of all Bizen and parts of Mimasaka and Bitchū. In 1568 the first of the "Unifiers," Oda Nobunaga, began his bid for national supremacy. For a while the Mōri and Ukida forces fought together against those of the Oda. But in 1578 the Ukida lord turned against the Mōri and joined with Oda Nobunaga. For the next four years lower Bitchū was an armed dividing line between the Mōri forces in the west and the Oda-Ukida forces in the

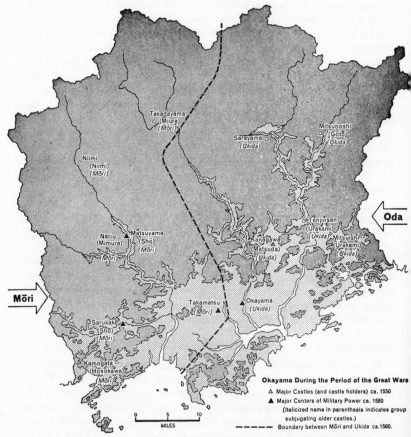

Fig. 9.—Okayama in the sixteenth century, showing how military strongholds shifted toward the plain and its communication routes.

east. The Mōri army threw up a fort in Kamo mura guarded by some one thousand men. Another was built at Hibata and a third in Yamate, all near neighbors of Niiike. These, together with the existing forts of Niwase and Takamatsu were staffed with the Mōri's front-line divisions.

Meanwhile the Ukida strengthened the hill castles above the Ashimori River valley. By 1582, Nobunaga, having pacified the capital area of Japan, was ready to move against his rivals in the west. Led by his ablest general, Hashiba (later Toyotomi) Hideyoshi, the Oda forces met those of the Mōri at Takamatsu castle in the valley of the Ashimori not two miles east of Niiike. This famous battle involved thirty to forty thousand fighters on either side and some remarkable engineering feats. Hideyoshi's troops, combined with those of the Ukida, broke through into the Ashimori Valley at the opening of the spring rainy season and surrounded Takamatsu castle. In a surprise stroke the Mōri forces broke the dikes of the Ashimori River and inundated Hideyoshi's troops. Hideyoshi, in turn, built a canal and poured water around the castle, thus isolating its defenders. Eventually the forces of east and west fought to a negotiated victory for Hideyoshi, the commander of Takamatsu castle taking his own life to save those of his men. The Mōri acknowledged Hideyoshi's suzerainty and accepted a division of territory with the Ukida at the Takahashi River. Bitchū remained divided between two forces and a frontier for both.

Perhaps, of all past events the battle of Takamatsu castle is most vividly engraved on the minds of the villagers of the Ashimori Valley today. Niiike residents recall that this historic battle took place within sight of the buraku just across the Ashimori River. Niiike children puzzle over the stone monument on the ridge just south of Ōyama where we now stand. This stone, left by Kobayakawa Tatsukage, tells of the historic meeting of the armies of Mōri and Oda. Finally the battle is remembered by many of the prominent local families as the occasion which brought their ancestors to the valley. For, as a result of the defeat at Takamatsu castle, many aristocratic members of the Mōri armies gave up their knightly privileges and settled down to become farmers.

During the last two decades of the sixteenth century, the scale of military operations continued to increase in Japan. The great feudal lords had the opportunity to consolidate their positions still further, building fortresses on wide plains to house an ever increasing number of troops and retainers. The greatest of these lords, called "daimyo," controlled territories which produced ten thousand or more *koku* of rice. (A *koku* is 5.2 bushels, theoretically a one-year supply for one man.) Some, such as Hideyoshi, held land producing over two million *koku*. In Bizen during these years, the Ukida extended their power, trimmed the independence of the outlying castle-holders, and called their forces into a great fortress built at Okayama City on the broad lower plain of the Asahi River. From here the Ukida extended their control over territory producing more than five hundred thousand *koku* of rice. But in Bitchū, many small fortified strong points continued to be staffed as the frontier outposts of the contending forces of the Mōri and Ukida.

THE TOKUGAWA ERA

Although the area around Niiike remained a military and political shatter zone, it was profoundly affected by the balance of power between the great daimyo to its east and west. Hideyoshi's short-lived hegemony over all Japan was wrested from his followers after his death by the Tokugawa family and their adherents. At the battle of Sekigahara in 1600, Tokugawa Ieyasu won undisputed leadership over Japan. In 1603 Ieyasu became shogun, and his headquarters at Edo, the present Tokyo, became the paramount center of political authority for the entire country. This system is familiar to Western literature as the "shogunate." Since both the Ukida and Mōri had opposed the Tokugawa, their fortunes declined rapidly after 1600. In 1601 Bizen was taken from the Ukida and shortly thereafter became the domain of the Ikeda family. The Mōri were replaced at Hiroshima by the Asano. Since neither the Ikeda nor the Asano were close vassals of the Tokugawa, the small domains of Bitchū, which lay between them, were used by the Tokugawa as strategic buffers and, where possible, put in the hands of Tokugawa retainers. This policy continued through the long period of Tokugawa hegemony (1600–1868) and became the immediate background of the area's development in modern times.

To the people of Niiike the Tokugawa period is noteworthy first as the time of origin of the buraku and second as a time in which many basic patterns of social and economic organization were set. The techniques of political regimentation utilized by the Tokugawa shogun and applied by his feudal vassals were thorough and far-reaching. Thus, after 1600, the whole countryside underwent a rigid pacification and a systematic political reorganization. The wars of the sixteenth century had left Japan in a state of political and social confusion. Recruitment for large armies had drawn farmers off the land into the troops of the daimyo. The fortunes of war had uprooted families and scattered them in many directions. The outcome of battles had dispossessed many high-ranking feudal families and cast their vassals and troops adrift as masterless wanderers. Completion of the Tokugawa hegemony brought both a cessation of war and a consolidation of the political and social structure at the local level.

In southern Bitchū, which had been fortified, fought over, and devastated, the problems of physical reconstruction and social reorganization were immense. But consolidation was accomplished despite the multiplicity of administrative units (see Fig. 10). In the territory encompassed by our view from Ōyama there were four small daimyo domains, each producing from ten thousand to twenty-nine thousand *koku* of rice, and some nine units of lesser holdings. These represented another category of Tokugawa holdings consisting of fiefs of less than ten thousand *koku* assigned to lesser vassals of the shogun known as *hatamoto*. Such fiefs, or *chigyōsho*, took up a large portion of the territory of southern Bitchū during this period.

Though southern Bitchū remained one of the most minutely fragmented regions in Tokugawa Japan, the area was unified by the strong authority of the shogunate. This authority extended to the various feudal lords as vassals of the shogun. But it was visibly represented in Bitchū by the placement of a deputy (*daikan*) at the town of Kurashiki. The consequent rise of Kurashiki as the political and economic center of southern Bitchū brought about the final shift of the provincial center of gravity from the Sōja Plain to the belt of land reclaimed from the sea after the Nara period.

The deputy at Kurashiki held direct jurisdiction over Tokugawa territories (*tenryō*) stretching over Bitchū and two other provinces. In Bitchū these amounted to some fifty thousand *koku* and were scattered in patchwork fashion over the province. The area of Lower Shinjō in the Ashimori Valley adjacent to Niiike is the most readily visible of these territories from where we stand. The presence of the Tokugawa deputy at Kurashiki did a great deal to stabilize the political structure of southern Bitchū and also helped to insure a remarkable degree of unity in social and economic legislation and in administrative procedures.

The impact of Tokugawa policy on the agrarian community was most extensive. The feudal aristocracy was stabilized by a nationwide registration of individuals according to social status. This registration reduced most of the masterless warriors and part-time fighters to the status of farmer or merchant. To regularize taxation, a new land survey and registry was conducted. This laid the foundation for the administrative control of the agrarian community through a system of mura units. It was in the context of this system that Niiike was founded and subsequently developed.

Niiike came into existence as part of the fief of the Hanafusa family, a holding of eight thousand *koku* in the portion of the Ashimori Valley centering on Takamatsu. The Hanafusa were *hatamoto* or direct vassals of the Tokugawa. As such, they maintained a retinue of between fifty and seventy households. But the military and bureaucratic services which they

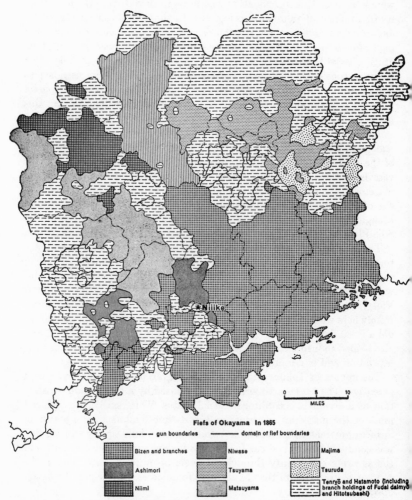

Fiefs of Okayama in 1865
- - - - - gun boundaries   ———— domain of fief boundaries

Bizen and branches

Ashimori

Niimi

Niwase

Tsuyama

Matsuyama

Majima

Tsuruda

Tenryō and Hatamoto (including branch holdings of Fudai daimyō and Hitotsubashi)

FIG. 10.—Okayama in the seventeenth to nineteenth centuries, showing the buffer belt of small fiefs and shogunal domain encircling the large Ikeda domain of Bizen.

were obliged to perform for the shogun kept the family and the major portion of its retinue in residence at Edo. To administer the Takamatsu fief and the local interests of the Hanafusa, an administrative residence, or *jinya*, was built at Harakozai. Here seven members of the Hanafusa retinue oversaw the fief's affairs, collected the tax rice, saw to its shipment to Osaka and Edo, and administered the villages, temples, and shrines of the area.

For taxation and administrative purposes the Hanafusa fief in early Tokugawa times was divided into the eight mura of Kamo, Shinjō, Nakajima, Waimoto, Harakozai, Minoshima, Oshikabe, and Tsudera. These mura constituted the taxable subdivisions of the fief, and each was given a set tax-base, assessed in *koku* of rice. Adjustments were made from time to time as the agrarian population increased. The growth of new communities was provided for by the recognition of branch villages (*eda-mura*) and if need be by the establishment of new mura. Shinjō was divided into Upper Shinjō and Lower Shinjō sometime during the eighteenth century; Kamo was divided into eastern and western parts. These four *mura* were to give rise to the modern village of Kamo. By the end of the Tokugawa period the resulting area contained the branch villages of Sempukuji, Kurozumi, Nakamura, Iwasaki, Yamane, Ōyama, Senzoku, Eta, Tsukuriyama, Mukaiba, Suenaga, Hatakeda, and, of special interest to us, Niiike, which was in Upper Shinjō (see Fig. 8).

Administration of the mura in the Hanafusa fief was carried out in orderly and comprehensive fashion from the headquarters at Harakozai. Four intendants (*daikan*), vassals of the Hanafusa, were in residence there. These officials, though of low feudal rank, were the chief link between the distant Lord Hanafusa and the villagers who supported him. The total population of the fief may have numbered ten thousand by the middle of the nineteenth century. Below the intendants, some fifty salaried villagers held positions of village-group heads (*ōjōya*) and village headmen (*Shōya*). These village officials performed the real work of administration, regulation, and tax collection. Many of the families of this class were former warriors who had been reduced to farmer status by the vicissitudes of the wars of unification. For example, Niiike fell within the jurisdiction of the Mano family, which, after the battle of Takamatsu castle, had taken up residence in what was to become the branch village of Iwasaki and functioned hereditarily as headmen in Upper Shinjō *mura*.

Tokugawa rural life was characterized by a high degree of regimentation and bureaucratic control of political, economic, and even religious matters. The mura of Tokugawa times, at first a somewhat arbitrary political ordering of rural society, became thoroughly intrenched over a period of two and a half centuries. By the end of the Tokugawa period, the mura constituted a closely integrated community, despite the fact that it usually contained several smaller settlements (dignified in the Niiike area by the term "branch village"). The legal relationship of the mura to the feudal government encouraged group solidarity. Tax payments were a joint responsibility within the mura and so, also, were tax delinquency and crime. Distribution of irrigation water, access to communal forest land, worship at shrines, and many other activities were worked out on the mura basis. Village headmen kept records of census, landholding, tax assessment, religious preference, and in innumerable ways regulated the lives of the villagers. Farm families themselves were organized into mutually responsible groups of five to twenty households (*gonin gumi*).

The people of Niiike today are little aware of the tremendous influence that the laws and attitudes of the Tokugawa period continue to exert upon them. Certainly the many years of paternalistic government produced in the farmers of Japan both a submissiveness toward authority and a suspicion of government still visible in the present generation. And many of the conservative social mores of the farming community of today stem from the injunctions of the Tokugawa period which exhorted the farmer to hard work, frugality, and modest deportment. For example, those few lingering aspects of traditional blue-cotton clothing which one sees in Niiike are a product of Tokugawa sumptuary legislation. Now worn as a picturesque mark of pride in an honored profession, these bits of clothing were once prescribed as a mark of distinct social status.

Another aspect of rural life affected by Tokugawa law was the religious. Although Buddhism and Shinto declined as spiritual influences in Japan after 1600, the Tokugawa government made important use of religious institutions as agents of social control. Beginning in 1614, and periodically thereafter—especially after the "Christian rebellion" of Shimabara in 1638—the Tokugawa Shogunate required all Japanese to deny the Christian faith by registry at a Buddhist temple or Shinto shrine. The resulting registers, eventually collected on an annual basis, were passed to the feudal authorities for their inspection. The Register of Religious Preference (*Shūmon aratame chō*) became a sort of census in which each member of each village was listed by family under the signature of the family head. Each family also maintained at its temple of registry (*dannadera*) a burial plot. These practices are further evidence of the way in which the villagers of the Tokugawa period were tied to their localities. Changes of residence required the complicated process of change of temple registry, and the whole weight of official sanctions and religious custom caused the farmer to remain close to the land of his ancestors.

It is through such records that we gain insight into the early history of Niiike. Death registers, going back to 1683, are the prime source for the dating of the origin of the buraku. The ancestors of the present Niiike inhabitants had two temples of registry. The Hiramatsu were registered at Sōrenji, the Iwasa at Renkyūji. This contrasts with most of the other neighboring buraku, whose inhabitants are registered at nearby Honryūji. The fact that Niiike families use two temples, each of which is some distance from the settlement, indicates that the Hiramatsu and Iwasa undoubtedly migrated to the present site from two different locations some time before 1683, perhaps about 1670. Family tradition has it that the Hiramatsu came from the village of Shō and the Iwasa from Madokoro (see Fig. 8).

The Hiramatsu and Iwasa temples of registry both belong to the Nichiren sect of Buddhism and here, also, lies a story which goes back to the Tokugawa period. Adherents of Nichiren, one of the more fanatical of the Buddhist sects, are not very numerous in central Japan. During the seventeenth century, however, the lord of the Hanafusa fief became converted to Nichiren and ordered all temples in his fief to follow suit. Other communities not located in the Hanafusa fief retained their former persuasions as Jōdo or Tendai followers. Even today these villagers claim to be able to distinguish a degree of religious fervor among the residents of Kamo and refer to the village as a *Hokke* mura (a Nichiren village).

For two and a half centuries, then, the ancestors of the present people of Niiike lived under a system of social controls which permeated every aspect of their lives. Small wonder that even today, almost a hundred years after the passing of the Tokugawa regime, the social boundaries of the old mura of Upper Shinjō—now an ōaza contained within the larger boundaries of modern Kamo village—continue to be visible in the behavior of the people of Niiike.

The Tokugawa period was, as we have noted, a time of stability and rigid social control. But it was also a time of considerable improvement in the techniques of government and in the standard of living. Government during the Tokugawa period, while restrictive, became more and more a matter of public record and uniform law. Although the threat of arbitrary action by feudal overlords or their subordinates was never entirely eliminated, rural administration by the nineteenth century had gone far in the direction of impersonal, bureaucratic procedure. In some of the more advanced communities of southern Kibi, landowning farmers participated in the election of village headmen, pointing to new political consciousness on the part of upper-class farmers.

Another noteworthy achievement of the Tokugawa period was widespread improvement in agricultural technology and in the methods of land use and water control. Public works of reclamation and river control sponsored by the shogunate and the various daimyo were not only more extensive but also technically more advanced than anything Japan had yet seen. Sea walls, water gates, and canal ways were improved in many ways, not the least of which was the common substitution of stone for wood as building material. Southern Kibi was especially favored by such public works. The resources of the powerful Ikeda domain, of the Tokugawa deputy at Kurashiki, and of certain prosperous Osaka merchants were utilized to push the waters of the Inland Sea yet farther southward and to improve further the system of river control and irrigation works which made the new land suitable for rice cultivation (see Fig. 6). Between 1590 and 1690 over sixty-three hundred acres of rice land were reclaimed in the deltas of the Asahi and Yoshii rivers. The Asahi River was tamed so that the new lands south of Okayama City were free from fear of flood. Westward in Kojima Bay, a large reclamation project raised fourteen hundred acres from the delta of the Ashimori River. This was the famous Kōjo village project. With its completion the island of Kojima was finally joined to the coastline, and the old sea route between it and the mainland closed. In Bitchū, under the leadership of the Tokugawa deputy at Kurashiki, the many salt marshes in the delta of the Takahashi River were reclaimed, as well as large blocks of land along the mouth of the river at Fukuda and Tamashima.

Because of the terrain, the nature of her rivers, and the constant addition of new land to the south, Bitchū developed an increasingly complex irrigation problem. The Bitchū Plain descended to the sea in three steps. Each step had its own irrigation and drainage requirements. Furthermore, because of the uncertain flow of the smaller rivers, such as the Ashimori, all three steps were best watered by the Takahashi, which lay on the extreme west of the plain. This required a lengthy and intricate series of canals and water regulation systems.

The Twelve Village (Jūnikagō) Canal system has already been mentioned. During the Tokugawa period the co-operative efforts of eleven feudal territories were harnessed to expand this system and improve the water allotment schedule. By 1850 this network of canals watered paddy land producing 46,000 *koku* of rice. Farther downstream from the Twelve Village Canal, the Eight Village (Hakkagō) system was extended to care for land producing 14,600 *koku* in Kurashiki Plain. Beyond this point, these two systems crisscrossed to take care of the newly reclaimed areas in Kojima Bay. Still farther down the Takahashi River, a third canal system, the East-West (Tōzai), carried water to new fields south of Kurashiki on either side of the Takahashi River (see Fig. 11).

In the valley which included Niiike, the most significant hydraulic development was the final taming of the Ashimori River, which had brought frequent floods to adjacent villages by sudden rises in rainy weather. During the early Tokugawa period, the Ashimori appears to have shifted its course from the east to the west side of the valley, where it now flows between sturdy protective embankments built by Tokugawa river en-

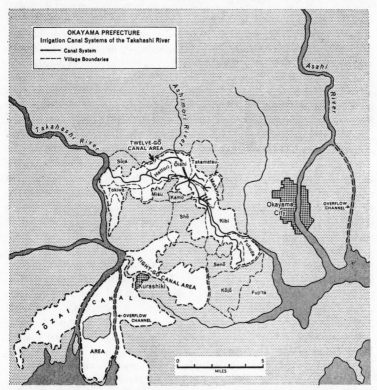

FIG. 11.—Areas served by the three large irrigation canal systems fed from the Takahashi River. Main ditches of the Twelve-Gō system are shown.

gineers. Such high containing embankments, constructed by the co-operative effort of many thousands of workers, were a favorite solution to the problem of chronic floods. The security they gave to the adjacent lands, previously subject to flash floods, made available some of the best paddy land in the Okayama Plain. Today the same embankments continue to serve the purpose of flood control, while major roads often run along their crests.

Less dramatic than the taming of the major rivers, but nonetheless important, were the many small-scale works of land improvement carried out by the Tokugawa villagers and authorities. In the Ashimori Valley, for instance, the Hanafusa fief increased its land by over two thousand *koku* through reclamation. But these works have left no record. It is through this same reclamation, however, that Niiike must have come into existence, for we know its appearance to have been intimately linked with the reclamation of land once too marshy for cultivation.

Very little concrete evidence is available to illuminate the problem of the origin of Niiike. As has already been stated, death records of 1683 show that the Hiramatsu family had moved to the present location by that time. An official map of the 1630's gives no evidence of the existence of Niiike. But a map dated 1694 shows the community of Ōbara occupying the area of present-day Niiike. It will be remembered from chapter 2 that the principal pond of Niiike is still called Ōbara. These clues support the inference drawn from temple records that the buraku was established sometime around 1670. The occasion for the migration of the first settlers was undoubtedly the completion of certain reclamation projects along the valley of the Ashimori River, perhaps the building of a new irrigation pond as reflected in the name Niiike ("New Pond"), or the reverse, the elimination of such a pond and the conversion of its bottom to paddy fields. At any rate Niiike owes its existence to the work of Tokugawa agrarian engineers.

If the Tokugawa era aided in the improvement of agricultural conditions, it also began the economic trend toward urbanization, greater agricultural diversity, and production for the commercial market. New ports which developed in Bizen and Bitchū engaged in a thriving trade through the Inland Sea. Centers of feudal power such as Okayama and Kurashiki attracted extensive urban populations, with a consumer class composed of feudal aristocracy, merchants, and various service groups. Even the small centers closer to Niiike such as Ashimori and Takamatsu became differentiated economically from the agricultural countryside.

In the villages, too, changes were taking place. Rice was now being raised not only for local consumption and for tax payment but also as a commercial crop. Bitchū became an important rice surplus area. Many villages were converted to more specialized functions by the development of trade both by land and through the Inland Sea. Those along the Sanyō road engaged in serving the many travelers on the highway. Double cropping, primarily of rice and winter wheat, gradually became more prevalent throughout Bitchū. The development of upland fields for cotton production added to the economic potential of the farmers of southern

Bitchū. That Niiike joined in raising cotton is evident from the still clearly marked but now abandoned terraces from which the pines now grow behind the village. These cotton terraces gradually fell into disuse as Niiike farmers made their rice lands more secure and began the double-crop process which put wheat, barley, or mat rush into the rice paddy fields during the winter.

For Niiike as a beginning community, the Tokugawa period provided an environment of well-organized local administration and relative economic progressiveness which was to become its legacy for the modern age. In the vocabulary of the Japanese historical geographers, Niiike is a *shinden* ("new field") village of fairly late origin; most of its neighboring communities originated at least as far back as the *shōen* period. Growing up in an area where the competition for land was severe and the possibilities of reclamation limited, it remained a small community. Perhaps for these reasons and because Niiike was settled originally by land-poor farmers, no large landlords or politically powerful villagers arose. The problems of land and water had been sufficiently solved by the Tokugawa reclamation engineers to permit settlement by the Hiramatsu and Iwasa.

NIIIKE IN THE NEW JAPAN

The 1850's were a period of great instability for Japan as the effects of Western pressures were felt throughout the country. In 1868 the political opponents of the Tokugawa government won the day. The shogunate was overthrown, and Japan entered her modern period. Many subsequent changes affected the rural areas, but few were revolutionary. Certainly the major changes in the area of Niiike were ones primarily of degree rather than of kind. Many had already been foreshadowed during the Tokugawa period.

Politically, between 1868 and 1890 Bitchū was placed under a new central government and a more systematically organized local administration. In 1888, the feudal territories were amalgamated into forty-six prefectures. The old districts (*gun*) were retained, and below these several Tokugawa mura were combined into new villages (mura or *son*). More densely populated units became towns (machi or *chō*). Thus, the old mura —Tsudera, Kamo, Sozume, and Upper and Lower Shinjō—were united to form the new village of Kamo, of which Niiike is part today. All told, more than seventy thousand Tokugawa mura were reduced to some fourteen thousand modern villages and towns by 1890. But in most instances the older units retained identity as legally recognized subdivisions (ōaza). Amalgamation, however, pushed the smaller settlements, such as Niiike, below the level of political recognition. The term "buraku" probably came into general usage about this time to designate the settlement units smaller than the ōaza.

Changes in the distribution pattern of political influence and wealth followed the passing of the Tokugawa hegemony. Opportunity was given to more adventurous individuals to take advantage of new conditions of economic and social freedom. In the rural society around Niiike, some families rose to new economic or political status, but on the whole such changes came slowly. In rural politics, for a generation and even longer the same families, prominent as headmen under the Tokugawa, continued to monopolize public office, holding such posts as village mayors, representatives to the county (gun) office or in prefectural assemblies. In Upper Shinjō, the head of the Mano family served briefly as an official at the village level before graduating from rural politics to the national stage. But many others of the former headman class continued on in their old villages and remain today the most influential and respected families of the area. Nor did the new land and tax laws of 1873 do much to disturb the pattern of landownership which had existed for centuries. The samurai, already removed from the land, did not reassert themselves as a landed class. Thus the political and social stratification of the villages changed little after 1868.

New improvements in agriculture and communications affected the whole rural populace, landholders and tenants equally. The changes in agricultural technology were not revolutionary but rather were further improvements in the system of intensive cultivation. It was a major accomplishment that Japan, in the years after 1868, in the wake of a startling increase in population, was able to make a long-term over-all improvement in the economy and the living conditions of the various segments of her population, including the farmers. This was accomplished slowly, persistently, and largely undramatically by gradual improvements in hygiene, communication, and agricultural technology and by small-scale farm mechanization. In Niiike there were also successive changes in the irrigation system which brought an increase in agricultural production. In the 1920's, a new pond on the western slope of Ōyama was completed, and the lowlands in front of Niiike were made available for paddy use. A new, concrete water gate on the Ashimori just above Niiike gave further assurance against flood. In 1904, a spur line was constructed from Sōja through Takamatsu to the main rail line at Okayama City, thus linking rural Kibi with the great cities and the world beyond. On the Sanyō highway immediately across the fields from Niiike, the ricksha, the bicycle, the bus, and the three-wheel motor truck began to pass. All have affected the orientation of village economy and attitudes.

These tangible improvements have been matched by invisible changes equally important in the life of the Niiike farmer. He has new horizons through education, assurance of occupational freedom, and a heightened sense of participation in the national destiny. He is accepting the new and looking to the future while living with equanimity amid much that is old. Our view into the horizons of the past from the top of Ōyama has suggested something of the cultural depth of the way of life of the people of Niiike. Today Niiike is both the inheritor of the past and the product of new forces. In the midst of old traditions, substitutions are being made, and life is taking on new dimensions. The uniformity that once characterized the village is gradually fading as innovations increase. But the transformation is a quiet one.

4. Niiike's People: PHYSIQUE AND TEMPERATURE

The forebears of Niiike's people, in the main, are likely to have been native to the Okayama Plain twenty or even thirty generations ago. For the last two millenniums, life in farm villages has been highly stable. History, as chronicled in the preceding chapter, shows some violent tides of military and political struggle swirling across the plain throughout this time. These events worked great changes for a few families, sweeping them up to greatness or down to extinction. Yet they did little to change the composition of the basic population.

The population stability, referred to here, is not to be confused with population uniformity. People moving through the Inland Sea as a major communication route surely left genetic traces along the way, though perhaps more among the coastal fishing populations than among farmers farther inland. Other additions to the genetic pool must have come from Korean craftsmen and others who were imported and settled in small groups from time to time in the past, eventually to mingle with the local farming population. And this local population from the earliest time when agriculture was known, according to archeology, seems to have been somewhat diverse. Hence, with the later increments, its heterogeneity is not inconsiderable. Evidence of diversity is not confined to the Inland Sea. As an entire nation the Japanese are a relatively varied people, though unmistakably of one major race. Hence, the diversity that appears in Okayama—and in Niiike—is normal. It promotes individual variation within a stock which has experienced no great transformations. Farm village populations on the Okayama Plain are made up of lineal descendants, tracing descent usually in the male line, and mates drawn from villages no more than five miles away, a distance scarcely less restricted in recent times than in ancient. This marriage habit has contributed much stability to the population of the coastal plain. Such biological continuity would scarcely be affected, moreover, by families moving a few miles from an ancestral village to found a new community such as Niiike. Hence, it seems probable that in physical makeup the people of Niiike carry the heritage of a great many generations native to the Okayama Plain.

HEALTH AND PHYSICAL APPEARANCE

In their physical appearance the people of Niiike are typical of the population of the region. Adults are short in stature. Several men are nearly as diminutive as Iwasa Genshirō, about 4 feet 10 inches tall, whereas Hiramatsu Tokujirō, at 5 feet 9 inches, seems strikingly tall. The average male height is about 5 feet 4 inches; women average about two inches shorter. As is true of many of the world's short peoples, both men and women are proportioned with trunks of moderate length but short legs, so that their appearance is one of long-waistedness. Body build is more spare than is immediately apparent to the casual eye. Faces are often quite broad across the cheekbones and suggest a well-filled body below. Loose-cut clothing also contributes to the impression of a sturdy figure. But most people are lean or even thin by American standards. Few hardworking farm men or women get fat, even though their normal diet is abundantly starchy. About four persons among all the adults are moderately plump; none is obese; a few children are pudgy, apparently as a phase of growth rather than as a permanent characteristic. Bones and musculature are typically light, sometimes quite delicate. Musculature is not at all weak, however. Japanese farmwork develops muscles of remarkable endurance even if of no great bulk.

Despite habits of working bent far over from the hips, the standing posture is more or less erect, though shoulders carried well back are seldom seen among mature and older adults. Men somewhat more than women carry the head thrust forward, their shoulders bowing slightly forward in sympathy. Certain elderly men and women, apparently afflicted with osteoarthritis, lose all ability to raise themselves erect and are bent forward from the lower back so that walking is almost impossible without a cane or other support. This particular posture of the aged, seen commonly enough in other communities as well, afflicts four persons in Niiike to a moderate or extreme degree.

Coloring of hair, eyes, and skin is dark, but with variations. The hair of some is brown-black, of others blue-black, and of others plain black. It is usually straight, sometimes gently wavy. Curly or deeply waved hair would be unknown were it not for the advent of the permanent-wave shop (*pāmu*). Hair often begins to turn gray after forty and is usually allowed to show its grayness in Niiike, whereas women who live in the city are more careful to dye it black. Baldness is uncommon, though partial loss of hair does occur. Neither men nor women have much perceptible body hair. Most men appear clean shaven who use the razor only once in several days or a week, although there is no little variation in the amount and the rate of growth of the beard. The color of eyes is brown, usually quite dark. Skin color is a very light tan, sometimes sallow, sometimes ruddy. Men often appear somewhat darker than women because of their more constant exposure, but a light skin color is admired, and both men and women go to some lengths to cover their skin from the sun in order to preserve its fairness. The precautions taken against tanning by Niiike people and the farm population in general set them apart in skin color from various laboring groups, fishing people, and others. Niiike people, incidentally, belong with a still larger majority of Japanese in wearing no tattoo on the skin. Japanese tattooing has acquired a measure of fame in the outside world for its skill and luxuriance of design, but within Japan it is confined to persons of certain occupations and classes, mostly fishermen and several lower fringe groups in cities.

Neither girls nor women blacken their teeth (*haguro* or *kanetsuke*), a custom practiced at least on ritual occasions fifty years or more ago. Yet sound white teeth in either men or women are rare enough to be memorable. Parted lips or an opened mouth usually reveal a conspicuous array of gold, silver, or other metal fillings. Such glinting metal is so common that one is almost taken by surprise by the clean white teeth of people in their twenties or younger, whose teeth are not necessarily more sound but whose fillings are of porcelain. That incidence of tooth decay is high in much of Japan, especially in rural areas, is indicated in a report by the Ministry of Welfare on a survey of its employees which shows dental caries affecting up to 90 per cent of the persons in groups examined in cities and up to 95 per cent of groups examined in the country. The people in Niiike appear to have their full share of dental problems.

As for general health, it is difficult to make positive and meaningful observations about Niiike villagers without technical comparisons and data which go beyond the scope of this book and the competence of its authors. However, a few observations may be drawn from a medical survey made in October, 1951, by members of the staff of the Okayama University Hospital and the Inland Sea Joint Research Society. Records were obtained on 118 persons in Niiike. Their medical histories and various aspects of current health were covered, and observations were made on their body build and physical tone.

The kinds and frequency of diseases recalled from childhood for this survey are much the same as in Western nations; measles has been most frequent, followed by whooping cough, tonsillitis, scarlet fever, and mumps. In the past there had been one or two instances each of typhoid, enteritis, beriberi, and malaria, the last two being incurred during service in the army. The survey showed one or more persons with active cases of tuberculosis, while X-ray plates showed healed scars in others. But this incidence is in no wise remarkable in Japan, for it is only in recent years that the introduction of BCG inoculation has brought the high national rate of tuberculosis plummeting down.

Doctors and others concerned with public health in the region remark that Niiike has relatively good standards of sanitation. Though its houses have no screens against flies and mosquitoes, no sewage system, no refrigeration, and often no full protection against contamination of food and water, its people use DDT and flypaper to control flies and are careful not to leave open buckets of ordure sitting long in the yard before taking them to fertilize the fields. One bit of evidence from the medical survey about the benefits of good hygienic practice, however, seems too good to be credited. According to stool examinations, only 10 per cent of all persons examined were afflicted with intestinal parasites of any sort, and at that even the most common (eight cases) and easily transmitted parasite, *Ascaris* or pinworm, was discovered in no more than one person of any household. Fallibility of the examination procedures must be taken into account with this finding. Other small communities examined in similar fashion by the Okayama University Hospital staff in the plains and mountains of the prefecture showed parasitic infestation among 60 per cent or more of all persons examined. The incidence rises to 90 per cent in some rural communities. Nor are intestinal parasites confined to the countryside; a rigorous medical examination, in connection with studies of atomic radiation effects, conducted on a sample of five thousand inhabitants of Hiroshima City in 1950 and 1951 showed that from 84 to 92 per cent of each age group above age three was afflicted with *Ascaris*, hookworm, *Tricocephalus*, or *Endamoeba histolytica* or their combination. As a total group, 90 per cent of the five thousand persons examined had some evidence of parasites. It seems unlikely, thus, that Niiike people are as free from parasites as the medical record suggests, despite their care and precautions in hygiene and despite their use of patent vermifuge drugs sold in every drugstore.

The people of Niiike today depend on modern science and technology for almost all their problems of health. Virtually no home remedies are used, at least not exclusively. Children receive various inoculations at school. To treat minor illnesses and accidents, people use adhesive tape, gauze, Mercurochrome, aspirin, and patent medicines from their home medicine bags. Some buy these materials at drugstores in the nearby shopping centers in the town of Takamatsu; others use items from bags of drugs and supplies left in their homes by door-to-door agents of drug companies who periodically renew the supplies and collect money for the items used. For major ills there are seventeen medical doctors among the four adjoining villages and towns of Kamo, Oishi, Takamatsu, and Makane. The ratio of doctors to the total population of these four low-land communities (*ca.* 12,000) is considerably more favorable than the ratio of 1:10,000 for the prefecture as a whole.

The distribution by age and sex of the 128 inhabitants of Niiike in 1950 is shown in Figure 12. Note that the female segment is considerably larger than the male, the more so because of the number of girls born just within the previous three years. Throughout the prefecture of Okaya-

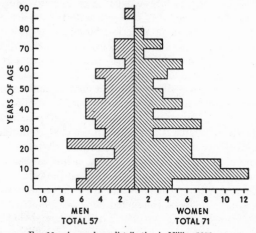

FIG. 12.—Age and sex distribution in Niiike, 1951

ma as well as in neighboring prefectures, all of which are predominantly agricultural and densely populated, women number slightly more than men because so many young men leave for work in the cities of more urbanized and industrial prefectures. In the population of the latter pre-fectures, consequently, men outnumber women. Since the rural pattern of outmigration of males is characteristic of Niiike as well as of the region, some slight predominance of resident females is consistently to be expected.

Niiike's population not only maintains itself but is increasing some-what, according to birth data gathered from Niiike mothers. The crude fertility rate is 3.15, which is to say that a total of 111 children have been born to the 35 wives who are in the years of theoretical fecundity. When only the 90 children are counted who have lived to the age of 18, the hypothetical age of reproduction used by population statisticians, the index is reduced to a net reproductive rate of 2.57. Since a net rate of only 2.00 keeps a population constant, the higher net figure for Niiike shows that the community is adding to its population. In this respect it fits the fertile rural pattern of Japan. Though in 80 years the number of persons living in Japanese villages has risen only slightly, it is their excess children, products of a consistently high birthrate, who have filled the burgeoning cities of the nation. Future reproductive patterns in Niiike and other Japanese communities, it must be noted, seem likely to differ greatly from those shown hitherto, for the new modes of family limitation described in chapter 11 are beginning to have striking effect.

The net survival rate of Niiike children has risen in recent years. This conclusion is drawn from two computations. In the first, the childbirth history of 17 younger wives (age 30–54) compared to that of 13 older wives (age 55 and above) is 3.47 births per younger wife to 3.75 births per older wife. Since this calculation omits six wives below age 30 who may not have completed their child-bearing, it seems reasonably certain that younger wives, as a rule, have been having somewhat fewer children each, though the difference is not startling. But they have been better able to keep their children alive. One-fourth of all the younger wives who have borne children lost one child by the age of six; by contrast, one-half of the older wives lost from one to three of their children, the deaths actually occurring before age four. This comparison, considering the rough similarity in reproductive rates, suggests considerably higher actual infant mortality in the past than within the last two decades.

A measurement of life expectancy for the total population of Niiike is less feasible; it may be presumed to be roughly equal to the rates for Japan as a whole. These rates recovered rapidly from a slump reflecting World War II and the subsequent period of scarcity. In 1956, Japanese women had a life expectancy of 68 years, Japanese men of 64 years, a longevity far beyond that of any other Asian nation and comparing closely with life-expectancy rates in west European countries. Except for the wartime slump, life-expectancy rates in Japan have shown a steady and rapid rise since more than a generation ago. The number of persons past age 80 (see Fig. 12) can be expected to continue or increase.

Increased longevity does not guarantee a youthful appearance in elderly persons. Rather, men and women begin to look elderly very soon past age fifty, though vigorous and hearty a few years earlier, with a spring in their walk. The rapidity of aging, it may be suspected, is not solely a matter of physiological change but reflects a social situation encouraging the mature person to reach out gladly and thankfully to old age rather than to fear it. Up through the years of full maturity one works hard to make a living and rarely if ever experiences the exhilaration of accomplishment; middle age is a hard period, and the escape to the relative leisure and prestige of old age is a release from its strains. To enter old age early is to enjoy its advantages longer. Accordingly, without conscious awareness, people take up the mannerisms of old age rather than carry on those of the middle years past age fifty.

In other ways too manifold and subtle to enumerate here with any completeness, culturally acquired mannerisms and gestures overlie and modify the physical appearance of people in Niiike. Many of their habits of body posture and movement are ones common to Japanese in general and are the ones sketched here. Noticeable is the frequent and typical bow that accompanies greeting and parting from another person, a precisely patterned movement in which one arcs both head and body simultaneously forward, resting the hands near the knees with the palms laid slightly inside the front of the thighs. The niceties of this bow are taught from earliest childhood. Other characteristic gestures are less consciously inculcated. Without particular instruction, the child learns to make his conversational gestures mainly with his forearms and hands and to use the hand as a unit, fingers together and slightly curved while gesturing or hiding an embarrassed or hearty laugh. Everyone, whether by conscious instruction or by mere observation, learns the Japanese fashion of counting on the fingers of one hand, which is to tuck thumb into the palm for "one," then wrap the forefinger and other fingers over it in succession for "two" to "five" and to reverse this order in unfolding the fingers for "six" to "ten."

As for sex differences in posture and motion, those that characterize women are perhaps more fully and explicitly set out in verbalized rules than are men's gestures. Some are almost transparently functional: the slightly bent-kneed, toed-in walk with mincing steps, with which women adapt themselves to straw sandals or wooden clogs and to the hobbling effect of the tight-wrapped kimono, or the unconscious reaching across the body to hold the kimono sleeve with one hand while reaching or serving food, to prevent dragging the sleeve across the table. Other bodily positions and motions have less superficially obvious reasons. For example, girls are instructed to sleep on their side or back, always with their legs together. Sitting up, girls and women may not sit cross-legged with knees straddled, as boys and men may, but must kneel down and rise always keeping the knees together. Finally, when standing, women in any position of rest or arrested motion characteristically should have their legs and feet placed precisely together. If one seeks a symbol of control and sexual reserve, this legs-together image of femininity, whether for reclining, kneeling, or standing, suggests itself as such a symbol in contrast with the frequent free posture of men—especially young men—feet planted conspicuously apart, arms akimbo with the hands at the joint of hip and thigh, hips thrust forward.

Much of the cultural patterning of gesture and movement alluded to is instilled without either learner or teacher being aware of the process. The teaching, in any case, is done in great part by example and physical guidance rather than in words, so that people may fail to recognize that quite precise goals of approved behavior are being reached. Hence the young mother can honestly disclaim that she would attempt to drill any manners into children younger than eight or ten, when just a moment earlier her hands were guiding her own three-year-old through the conventional low bow before her visitor.

TEMPERAMENT AND CHARACTERISTIC ATTITUDES

Characteristic habits of mind are shared in some degree among the people of Niiike, distinguishing them at least from persons of other nations, and in a few respects from other Japanese as well. To sketch these involves both some comment on their disposition, by which is meant the frame of mind in which the people do things, and some analysis of their sense of values, by which is meant their preferences or attitudes concerning how things should be done. Habits of mind are easily subject to misinterpretation; however, the comments presented here are bolstered by findings derived from projective tests of personality conducted in Niiike and subsequently analyzed by Dr. George A. DeVos.[1] In particular, the findings of these tests have helped to define and give proper weight to values held in different degree by men and women of various ages within the community and will be cited in illustration of these differences, though without the technical analysis which is needed to substantiate the findings.

An atmosphere of easy tranquillity normal to Niiike bespeaks the comfort and satisfaction with which the majority of people regard their life as farmers in a rich and beautiful countryside. Most of Niiike's residents are deeply attached to their community and to the land, though they find this attachment difficult to articulate in words. An uncalculated grace en-

---

[1] Dr. DeVos, at the time a participant in the Human Relations Joint Research Group of Nagoya University, supervised the administration particularly of Rorschach, Thematic Apperception, Problem Situation, and Authoritarian Personality projective tests in Niiike in 1954. One or more of this battery of projective devices was administered to each of 60 persons in Niiike by members of the Nagoya University Joint Research Group or of the staff of Okayama University Hospital working under Dr. DeVos' supervision.

hances many ordinary tasks; some portion of the Japanese aesthetic tradition perhaps is alloyed with pride in one's work so that even when a fence is erected temporarily or mat rush is spread out to dry in the field it is done with beautiful craftsmanship. If asked simply what gives him pleasure in ordinary life, many a man answers that his main joy is in helping things to grow, or working with the soil, or he names a specific farm task. Not all farmers in the world are as satisfied with the fitness of farming as are most of the people of Niiike.

Underlying this easy and cheerful attitude toward farm life, however, are attitudes perhaps more distinctly Japanese. For the sake of simplicity they may be summarized under two themes, control and effort.

Control is an attitude—and simultaneously a positive value—expressed in a variety of conventionally approved ways, including restraint, self-discipline, endurance, and self-sacrifice. The sense of quiet tranquillity in Niiike comes in good part from the restraint put on all expression of emotion. Exuberance is repressed; so is every form of violence. The people smile readily and often; they laugh not infrequently, but gently, never in boisterous guffaws. Noisy argument or quarreling is as rare as riotous laughter, and physical violence among adults is shocking even to think about. Japanese as individuals or groups, though outwardly as restrained as the people of Niiike, seem often to mask a genuinely volatile and mercurial temperament under the curb of self-discipline. Niiike's people appear exceptional, not in exercising restraint over the emotions, but in having relatively little strong emotion to require control. Rorschach test records, in confirmation, suggest an exceptionally flat emotional life among the respondents from Niiike. Moreover, it is men who have spent their entire lives in Niiike whose responses tend most to be empty of feeling; many of the women, raised in other communities before coming to Niiike in marriage, had a stronger surge of feeling and gave freer expression of it in response to projective tests. Niiike's neighbors pass similar judgment, viewing these people as "grinds" whose serious mien makes them good neighbors but poor drinking companions. Niiike men, on the whole, are light drinkers of sake, as if less in need of this conventional avenue for releasing exuberance and relaxing self-discipline. Release o another sort, in tears of sympathy for others, is accepted as much in Niiike as elsewhere, however. An example is the interest taken in radio broadcasts and live local performances of *naniwabushi*, which are melodramatic recitals of tales of feudal loyalty, strife, and tragedy. Tears flow, though quietly, in contemplation of these melancholy themes.

Self-discipline keeps the emotional pitch low even in the most critical moments of life. Throughout her wedding day, though it be her greatest occasion, the bride is expected to look neither joyous nor sad but, instead, aloof and unmoved. When she becomes a mother, she should not cry out in childbirth. To wail or act distraught at a funeral is most unbecoming behavior. Women are more continuously and unrelievedly under conventional restraints of this nature than are men, but the same basic conventions apply in large measure to both sexes. Where others might be restive and fretful if restrained so, Niiike's people appear to gain satisfaction from demonstrating the ability to perform a stereotyped role perfectly. Conscious and artful performance of roles offers compensatory satisfaction for the prohibition on too individual and improvised interpretation of the role. Thus, when one is guest or host, one may take pleasure in adroitly choosing from among the many stereotyped phrases appropriate to visiting instead of attempting to inject something unique and distinctive into each visit.

The very nature of farm life tends to foster patience and acquiescence in the slow, sure processes of nature. One cannot expect to harvest a crop before it is ripe or to plant before the season is ready. Niiike's people exhibit powers of endurance difficult to account for as simply the consequence of farm life; they derive more naturally from acceptance of the principle of control. In this respect, they are no more than a match for Japanese whose lives are far removed from farming but who also have been taught to practice self-discipline. Social gatherings that move at a snail's pace with long periods of inaction, though not necessarily preferred, are taken without complaint. Plotless movies, novels of similar formlessness which run as serials through a thousand issues of the daily paper, and music which repeats a simple theme over and over throughout a celebration are a part of Japanese life fully accepted in Niiike. As in other contexts, one suspects that the real savor is in texture rather than form and that the texture is to be enjoyed as long as the time permits.

Self-control carries implicitly the assumption that one gains power over the external world by disciplining one's self. This assumption can be carried into action through self-sacrifice, which thus can be seen as an opportunity rather than a duty. Such a conception is revealed in various stories made up by Niiike people in response to pictures of the Thematic Apperception Test. In these stories, a father or mother, by dying, inspires a wayward son to reform himself; whereas to people of another culture such a death would be coincidental, it is difficult to deny its purposefulness in Japanese culture, where *hara-kiri* and other traditional modes of self-sacrifice are accepted methods of bending other persons to one's will. Three such stories are given here as examples of imagined self-sacrifice.

(Respondent: male, age 40.) In a middle-class family their only child does not like to study. The mother gets worried and comes to see whether the child is working. The child gets addicted to philopon [a stimulant drug] and becomes an outlaw. The mother gets very worried, gets sick, and dies. The child reforms himself and becomes successful in the future.

(Repondent: female, age 17.) A father scolded his son for being stupid. The son walks out. The father dies, which inspires the son to work hard. He becomes successful.

(Respondent: female, age 13.) A father died and the son walked out of his home because his mother repeatedly told him to become like his father. The mother lived lonely, and when she finds her son she dies. The son becomes a hardworking man.

Note how the motif of hard work is introduced in the stories cited above as a countermotif to self-sacrifice. In the ethics of Niiike, effort expended in work has positive value, for its own sake as well as to compensate for evils and misfortunes. People are more inclined to view work as a positive opportunity to achieve success than to regard it as a burden thrust on them by circumstances or by someone in higher authority. Many of the stories made up in response to projective test pictures carry a tone of confident ambition even in the face of great obstacles. One such picture shows a boy contemplating a violin; to many respondents outside of Japan, the violin seems to symbolize the tyranny of parents who prevent the boy from joining his gang by requiring that he practice instead. The following response to the same picture is more typical of Niiike:

(Respondent: male, 16.) I like music and used to go to a teacher to take violin lessons. One day he told me I should give up the violin because I was not doing well. But I swore in my mind that I would become a good player. I practiced day and night as hard as possible, and finally my teacher had to admit I was playing well.

The comparison of leisure with work offers an interesting insight into the dynamics of value judgments. As the foregoing story suggests, Niiike's people respect work and have an affirmative attitude toward effort. Leisure by definition is opposed to work. Yet it is not necessarily condemned by those who value work. The negative view of leisure associates relaxation with laziness and condemns it; but leisure may also be viewed, more positively, as the deserved reward for hard work. Both attitudes are evident in brief stories, among those made up in Niiike in response to projective test pictures, which happen to deal with leisure. When analyzed according to the age of the respondents, the stories show that persons of one age group tend to evince a similar attitude toward leisure; and a comparison of age groups brings out a pattern of changing attitudes from youth to old age. Brief presentation of the details, following the analysis made by Dr. George DeVos and his colleagues, will make this pattern clear.

Among the total of 800 responses to projective test pictures, 102 carry some implication about leisure or relaxation. The tone of these responses is more often negative (64 responses, or 8 per cent of the total) than either neutral or positive (41 responses, or 5 per cent of the total). When responses of men and women from different age groups are examined separately, a distinct shift in attitudes appears. Young persons of both sexes (the 12–17 age group) more often view leisure indulgently than with condemnation. So, also, do their grandparents (age 65 and above), who offer only one negatively toned response out of a total of eleven responses. There is a decided swing toward responses of negative tone, however, for both men and women in all four intermediate age groups (ages 18–24, 25–34, 35–49, 50–54), culminating in the negativism of the persons between 25 and 34, whose reaction to leisure is condemnatory in thirteen out of fourteen instances. Viewed as a section across the life span of the typical person in Niiike, this pattern of response shows a clear-cut arc; the youthful attitude of indulgence toward leisure is canceled or transmuted into a condemnation of relaxation in the middle years but re-emerges as an indulgent attitude in old age. Social expectations are neatly reflected in this pattern; young people and grandparents are expected to fill roles that impose relatively few responsibilities, whereas duties lie heavy on men and women in their twenties and thirties, who are the most active providers in the household and community. The pattern is distinctively Japanese, it may be added. When the same analysis is made of Americans of different ages, their responses show a straight-line progression from condemnatory attitudes among the young toward indulgent attitudes among their elders, rather than the arc just described.

Although Niiike's people have confidence that effort will bring achievement and conceive that everyone has not only the right but the obligation to work, they also recognize that various circumstances condition this obligation. Except for some of the younger persons—especially younger women—most concede that family responsibility must prevail when, for example, a young person working away from home at the time of his father's death finds it impossible to take over family responsibility and at the same time further his ambition for himself. More limiting even than family ties is the handicap to self-advancement that besets women because of their sex.

A woman is denied most means of direct action open to men in achieving their goals, because to be feminine she must preserve an appearance of passivity, submission, and forgetfulness of self. Yet the evidence of tests and observation unquestionably shows women to be equally convinced with men that life requires effort and equally aware that the achievement of a goal may entail opposition and aggression against others. Having been declared weak, then, women use the weapons of the weak: indirection and vicarious achievement. Behind a veil of outwardly cheerful acquiescence and submission, a woman may simply fail to cooperate; she may be unresponsive to advances; she may unaccountably forget or delay things that go against her aims. Little girls playing agreeably together practice these techniques on unwanted playmates; they do not draw blame by excluding anyone from their group, but, while singing happily through a counting game, they consistently fail to choose the child who is not wanted. Being unable to retaliate openly against the teasing of a brother, a girl may "accidentally" break some prized possession or hide his school cap—and sympathetically help him search for it later. These are the methods of indirection by which strong men may be brought to heel. Alternatively, a woman who becomes a mother achieves vicariously through her children, using the same techniques within the context of love and protection, where necessary, to stimulate their ambition and sweep away obstacles to their progress.

Children come to view their parents in dissimilar ways, as is shown by their conception of the mother's role and the father's role in assisting their own efforts to achieve success. A son's relation to his mother, for reasons detailed later (chaps. 9 and 11), is apt to be very warm and intimate; it may so thoroughly condition his attitudes toward all women that his eventual relation even to his wife, as well as to other women in his family, may bear many elements of his dependent tie to his mother. This relationship, in which the mother has the position of initiative in offering protection, indulgence, and stimulation, makes comprehensible the active part attributed to the mother above in instigating and aiding her son's achievement. Her role contrasts with the role of the father toward his sons, as stories made up in response to projective tests show. A father serves as a model, an aloof source of inspiration; his influence, in fact, can be as great after his death as during his life. Two stories, each responding to a picture of an elderly man standing next to a seated younger man, illustrate the tone of this conception of the father:

(Respondent: male, age 17.) I think that this young man has not been very successful in business so far. But, since his father was a great man, I think he will remember his father and will make strong efforts to be as successful as his father.

(Respondent: male, age 23.) He is thinking of his dead father. This is the image of his father. This . . . he is recalling his father and is making up his mind to strive toward success. I don't know what his profession is. . . . Anyway, he has an ambition now.

Finally, it must be made clear that, in giving their full approval to the effort to achieve success, most people of Niiike conceive of themselves as seeking improvement and success within the bosom of the family. As in the standard American tale of the stalwart youth who sets out to make his fortune in the city, the stories which Niiike people make up very often tacitly assume that success must be sought away from home. Yet, the majority of these simple tales do not concede that leaving the home, of itself, breaks the family tie. At the very least, the hero or heroine of their tales who is physically separated from his family is making his effort for the family's sake, and the happy ending often brings him home in fact. It proves possible even to rationalize a person's refusal to return home when called as being a proper assertion of his ambition for the sake of his family.

As the individual person is considered to be responsible for his family, so the family is responsible for its members. It not only gives them support; it supervises their conduct. No one in Niiike suggests the view that might be phrased, "He's not a very good boy, but, right or wrong, he's *my* boy." A person's support from his household is conditioned upon his good behavior, for the household takes upon itself the guilt of the sinner. This means that, if a person goes wrong or falls below the standards of his house, his own kin are likely to be the first to turn upon him and, in addition, feel the necessity of expiating his wrong with their own actions. Women's responses indicate an especially marked inclination to find fault in themselves for the overt misdeeds of others, but all members of the household share jointly the responsibility of keeping the family name clean and untarnished.

In Niiike, to summarize, people tend to appreciate and value self-control, balancing this attitude with an affirmative attitude toward energetic work. It is interesting to note the interplay between these attitudes and the external conditions of life in Niiike. As later chapters will show, persons in Niiike are necessarily quite dependent on the social groups into which they are born, married, or adopted for the basic and ever present problem of making a living. There is little room for the rugged individualist, the person who acts solely for his own interest and advantage. Self-restraint, therefore, fits harmoniously with prevailing conditions that require each person to subordinate personal wants to the needs of the group. Over the years, however, changes in these external conditions have been taking place. On balance, they have increased economic security, and some have begun to open new avenues for personal choice, as later chapters will make clear. These changes have not come to Niiike unbidden, forcing themselves onto a well-adjusted but inert community. The people of Niiike themselves, by their active exertions, have helped to create their new conditions. Here is evidenced the relation of their attitude of approval of work and effort to the external world. This attitude has made them able to grasp opportunity and mold circumstances, within limits set by the welfare of the group. The concrete steps by which these changes have been made and the economic, social, and political situation that now prevails form the subject matter of the remaining chapters.

5. Community Life: MATERIAL GOODS AND EQUIPMENT

There are several approaches to Niiike. The most used route is by way of the roads and paths from Takamatsu, a small shopping town across the Ashimori River one and three-quarters miles to the east. One travels a secondary road branching from the main bus route at Takamatsu and almost at once crosses the border into Kamo. From here the course runs westward through a network of roads, crossing the Ashimori River on one of its stone-pillared bridges, and then following the edge of the northern hills to the head of the valley. Niiike lies here. The roads are too narrow for a truck to manage the sharp turns easily, but one meets a continuous trickle of bicycles and freight motorcycles as well as foot traffic. The trickle swells to a stream in the morning and late afternoon, when office workers commuting to Okayama City walk or cycle along this road to the train station at Takamatsu and students from the grammar school near the Kamo village office and the middle school at Takamatsu are on the road. Footpaths laced geometrically across the flat valley floor as divisions between paddy fields serve as short cuts and provide diversions for children in pursuit of amusement. Here the passersby must walk in single file or in pairs to avoid slipping off into the rich mud of the rice fields that lie two or three feet below the paths and roads.

Literally at the back door of the shops lined along the main street of Takamatsu, neat fields of vegetables and irrigated rice plots begin, filling the flat plain all the way to Niiike. One walks to Niiike through a landscape which long ago surrendered to human control. Above the fields, the hard, sandy surface of the side roads is banked with solid stone walls. The grassy edge of each road, like the grass along the paths, ditches, and high dikes beside the river, is cropped to a stubble the whole year. Weeds that escape the tethered plow-oxen and goats are cut off with short sickles and added to the compost heap in each farmyard. Farmers use the narrow ditch banks to plant a patch of vetch or a row or two of soybeans.

From the road skirting the north edge of the valley, one looks over a checkerboard of fields stretching fenceless to the southern hills, each field set apart by a neatly banked ditch or raised border. No stream gouges the valley floor. Run-off water has been channeled through these man-made ditches, and the one-time stream bed has long since been erased and converted into fields. An extraordinarily neat and precise orderliness, of a sort which requires long hours of daily attention with sickle and hoe, pervades these fields. Such careful techniques of cultivation and individual attention to each plant cannot be found on most farms of the Western world, except in the kitchen garden. This is why the Kamo landscape seems to Western eyes to be a continuous, extensive food garden.

Flanking the other side of the road are less productive hillsides, carrying unirrigated plots of vegetables or fruit trees on their lower slopes. The highest slopes are mantled with the deep green of the pine trees which supply each village with winter firewood as well as brush and pine needles for compost. Framed the year around by the unchanging hues of these pine-clad hills, the brilliant greens and yellows of newly planted or ripening crops on the valley floor below present a bright contrast with every advancing season.

At work in the rice fields, the dry fields, or the wood lots of the valley and hillsides are the people of Niiike and a dozen similar communities. Like their forefathers who first molded this landscape into its disciplined, productive form, the people today call themselves "pure farmers" and take pride in the traditional place of honor given their occupation.

THE FORM OF THE COMMUNITY

In the valley where Niiike lies, people are crowded 5,360 to the square mile of cultivated land. Though some parts of rural Japan are still more densely inhabited, this figure is high indeed. If this is compared with the population density of 50 to the cultivated square mile in an American agricultural state such as Iowa, it is obvious that these farmers must live very close together if they are to leave the fields clear for cultivation. The desire not to intrude on cultivable land, however, is countered by the need for each household to be within reasonable range of its fields. Hence the clusters of houses which are the buraku are small and bunched compactly so that fields will be close at hand. The road we take from Takamatsu to Niiike, for example, passes through the buraku of Nagada, Nakayama, and Yamane before it gets to Niiike and turns south across the valley to end at Ōyama. These five communities average less than 650 yards apart.

Houses are gathered into tight clusters for more reasons than the practical one of leaving the fields open. These are primary, face-to-face communities, and daily business concerning every household is more readily accomplished when the houses are close together. A household living apart is apt to miss information from government offices and elsewhere, since this is circulated by word of mouth or by passing around the *kairamban*, a board on which village notices are pasted for circulation. Moreover, the satisfactions drawn from living as an intimate part of a larger group are great. In the community of Niiike, by way of example, the young farmer Iwasa Takeshi, after marrying, moved to a location no more than fifty yards from the nearest neighbor and within two hundred yards of his father's house. Yet he later moved closer at considerable expense, partly because he felt lonesome and left out. In another instance, saving time and manpower had sufficient value to Iwasa Eikichi to induce him in 1954 to move from high on the hill to a spot nearer his fields though somewhat outside the village proper. Still, the trend is toward concentration. Today, except for Eikichi's, all the houses of the buraku, their outbuildings, drying yards, and a few vegetable plots are concentrated in a small triangular zone about half again the size of a football field. This is the total living area of the village.

For a panoramic view of all the houses of Niiike, one should approach the village along the dike path bordering a drainage canal that angles across the fields. What seems a motley cluster of grass and tile roofs can be sorted out by the practiced eye into a double row of dwellings set one above the other on the hillside, with the beginnings of a third tier higher up. Each house faces almost directly south, the direction of warmth and light from the sun. Narrow footpaths give the upper houses access to the road which passes in front of the lowermost row of houses. One of these paths, marked by an inscribed stone pillar, leads on over the hill to the neighboring buraku on the north. Another path leads to wood lots and dry fields on the hillside, and two converge on the community graveyard fifty yards to the west. The rest merely give outlet to the various houses and barns within the community.

At the western edge of the buraku are the three community-owned structures: a fire tower, a shed for storage of fuel and fire equipment, and the meeting hall, a simple, one-room building. Both the shed and the meeting hall are of frame construction with tile roofs, moderately well built but suffering from lack of upkeep. Architecturally, they are set apart from the homes. Their hip roofs and horizontally planked walls are the hallmark of public buildings in Japan. Their disrepair also contrasts with the careful upkeep of other buildings in the community, all of which belong to individual households. Just to the north of the entrance to the meeting hall stand three inscribed stones, one Shinto and two Buddhist.

Fig. 13.—Houses and outbuildings of Niiike buraku

The community graveyard is on the lower slope of the hill and apart from the houses. Here the sense of compaction is even greater than in the village of the living. Cremation permits very close placement of the tombstones. The stones are erected in family groups and face outward across the fields.

Niiike dwellings have been erected for service, not display, and have little pure ornamentation. Except in abnormal times, as during the inflation of postwar years with its extra cash, farmers have more serious uses for their money than the decoration of their houses. But the upkeep of these buildings is so scrupulous that the ones built sixty or eighty years ago, despite the perishable nature of their materials, are hardly distinguishable from newer houses. All buildings are unpainted but please the eye through the harmony of natural colors and textures of wood, clay, straw, dark tile, and white paper. One exception to the rule exists in the area. In some nearby localities tall storehouses (*kura*), following a tradition once reserved by decree for samurai, have been made eye-catching with coats of whitewash or still more striking diamond or fleuret patterns of white plaster on a black ground. Although Niiike has several storehouses, they are not treated with even this modest flamboyance but are of plain tan clay. A semidecorative treatment found in Niiike, as well as elsewhere, is the covering of the lower half of a wall with charred boards. But even this is functional, for the blackened boards protect the clay wall from the rain, and charring the boards is much less expensive than painting and more durable. To show respect for one's house—an important symbol of a stable and enduring family—one is expected to keep it neat and in perfect repair but is in no wise required to ornament it. Thus, subdued hues and a minimum of decoration give an air of restraint to the buildings of the community.

THE HOUSEYARD

The houses in Niiike have outbuildings, utility yards, and assorted farmyard structures, all of which are closely associated with the dwelling itself in very compact, approximately square or rectangular houseyards, roughly sixty feet on a side. Sometimes the whole is inclosed by a mud wall, tile topped against the rain, with an arched gate entrance (see Fig. 14), but more often the sense of inclosure arises from juxtaposition of the structures or sometimes from stone retaining walls where an attempt has been made to level off the hillside slope. There is considerable uniformity in arrangement among the houseyards of Niiike. The house is at the back of the lot. The clear space of bare ground in front of the house serves as a general utility yard and drying area for various farm products, or there are chicken houses and cow tethering posts in these days when crops can be dried in the better-drained fields.

As one follows the paths from one yard to the next, one sees almost identical houses and outbuilding groups. The principal outbuildings are erected on the east side of the yard at a close right angle to the house and face west. Together the buildings form an L (see Fig. 14). Occasional variations in this plan are dictated by the convenience of the builder or the pitch of the hillside. The west and south edges of the utility yard are often given to plots of seasonal vegetables, the southwest corner to orna-

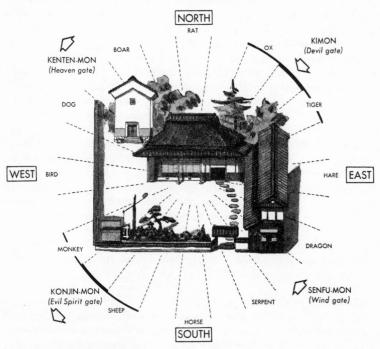

Fig. 14.—The zodiacal wheel visualized on a typical house lot. Maleficent forces enter from the northeast, beneficent forces from the southeast.

mental shrubs. Sometimes a chicken coop or a well may be ranged along the west side. Wells are also commonly placed to the north in back of the house. These are stone-lined and variously left open, covered, or roofed over, and are equipped with a wooden or tin bucket on the end of a rope which is drawn up by hand, pulley, sweep, or crank. Three houses have pumps. If there is a strong room (*kura*), it is in back of the house. Such a room is a tall, one-room storehouse built with thick clay walls and tiny barred windows and is used by a well-to-do farmer to store his rice and other valuable household possessions. Once prohibited to those below samurai rank, there are today several in Niiike. However, most villagers store their valuables, including fancy dishes and special clothing, in the attics of their houses.

Of the outbuildings along the eastern edge of the houseyard, the principal one is the workshed (*naya* or *nagaya*), a building somewhat smaller than the dwelling and built of wood or clay with a straw thatched roof. It houses the family ox and provides storage for tools, fertilizer, and crops, and work space for secondary occupations. Sometimes there is a separate structure next to it which may serve any of a variety of purposes: it may contain the family bathroom, hold the large loom for weaving floor-mat covers, or shelter the ox or, latterly, a dairy cow. One auxiliary building considered desirable is separate sleeping quarters for either the newly married couple or the retiring elderly couple. When lack of space or money prohibits a separate building, a mat-floored room is improvised in the workshed. Though auxiliary structures vary somewhat in number and kind, the minimum essentials in every houseyard in Niiike are the house and workshed, as basic as the house and barn on an American farm.

The similarity among houseyards is the result of the system of directional rules (*hōgaku*). *Hōgaku* governs the relationship of buildings and facilities in a houseyard and the arrangement of rooms within a house. It applies to each houseyard individually without immediate regard to any surrounding topographic features, unlike the Chinese fêng-shui system of relating buildings and points of human activity to the environment; nor do public buildings, shrines, or cemeteries acquire the magical orientation, but only dwellings or other spots where some person spends most of his time. This directional system has an astrological basis. In practice, a zodiacal circle is laid horizontally so that the mid-point of the house falls in the center of the circle. The features of the yard then fall variously into zodiacal zones which are used to relate the household and the activities of its members to the world at large (see Fig. 14). The good and bad luck significance of the various zones shifts according to the position of the planets on different dates and their relation to the birthdays of the individuals concerned. But certain directions have consistent qualities. For example northeast and southwest are consistently inauspicious, whereas southeast is always a fortunate direction. One should never set the clay storehouse or the well directly on the south, the sunny side from which fires arise, lest the strong room burn and the well dry up. Because income "flows" from southeast to northwest, the strong room should be in the northwest corner to gather income. Conversely, bad fortune flows from northeast to southwest, so a space should be left open in each of these directions to permit evil influence to depart once it has entered the dwelling area. Niiike makes relatively little of "circling *konjin*," a baleful force that moves regularly around the zodiac, though *konjin* is the dominant concern of directional rules in many other villages. Nevertheless, the system deeply affects those who choose to observe it. One looks for a bride who lives in an auspicious direction with relation to his house. One postpones a trip if the day is inauspicious for travel in that direction or else goes first in a different direction, then turns toward his destination. Daily life can be guided in endless detail by reference to proper direction.

Nowadays no one in Niiike has such unquestioning belief in the fateful significance of directions as to manage all his daily life by this system, although in remote parts of the country oldsters still take a serious view of the art. But in Niiike, belief has not been replaced by disbelief. Before altering a homestead or building anew, people still consult an expert in astrological lore and are very cautious in departing from the *hōgaku* rules. Regardless of his personal beliefs or convenience, a man risks the censure of his believing neighbors and of posterity if any misfortune visits his house after he has consciously violated the traditional "rules of direction." Disaster can strike even those who have carefully considered the fateful directions, but, if a person has imprudently ignored this precaution, some people will be reluctant to help him. It is better to conform and retain the sympathy and co-operation of others.

Whatever the motivation for observing these rules, the measure of their hold is what the villagers are willing to pay for them in money, time, and inconvenience. Sometimes people pay a surprisingly high price. When Iwasa Takeshi was to be married and set up a branch house in 1949, the question of where to build the house arose. His family owned a good site in the midst of the community, but it lay in an inauspicious direction from his father's house. So Takeshi set up a branch house in the low paddy fields in front of the village. Though in a fortunate direction from his original home, the site had to be raised with a gravel fill to keep the house from being perpetually damp. Even then it was not above danger from flood, and the well water was unusable. He and his wife felt lonely and estranged living even fifty yards away from the community. After he had lived in the new house for a time, and after a nearly tragic incident (see chap. 10), the direction of the preferable site his family owned could be calculated from the new house, and it was found permissible for him to move to the better place. So in 1954 his parents' household helped him tear down his house and set it up on the more desirable lot. Not counting family labor, the estimated amount spent for hired labor and materials

Kumagai Motoichi

Rice is good food

Hiramatsu Mitsusaburō, the Sensei, wears his formal *montsuki*.

Hiramatsu Fumio, eldest son of Asae, favors the young men's style of work clothes.

Dressing after a splash in the irrigation ditch. This boys' sport can be shared by girls, too, if young enough.

Hoshino Akira

Hiramatsu Chizue is the mother of six children, one of them a son.

Iwasa Koyoshi has two of her four sons and nine of her grandchildren in Niiike.

Preparation for Fall Festival guests makes Hiramatsu Isamu's kitchen a busy place

Hoshino Akira

The black castle built in Okayama for the Ikeda clan (*above*) stood on a stone platform inside the bend of the Asahi River (*below*), overlooking the park of Kōrakuen. Okayama City now spreads out on each side of the river.

Across the valley, northwest of the mound tomb and buraku of Tsukuriyama, are Niiike buraku and Ōbara Pond. Kōjin shrine is in the bare area on the crest of the tomb.

Much of Niiike's irrigation water comes from the Twelve-Gō Canal; Takahashi River water entering here at Tatai meanders east across the plain to the Ashimori River, beyond the low hills at top center.

Niiike, under the late August sun, looks over its rice fields

Ritual bamboos protect a new house near Niiike. To finish off, the builders will tile the roof and plaster clay over the bamboo-lattice wall cores.

Iwasa Minoru's house, of typical size for Niiike, gets a new thatched
roof.

The house and outbuildings of a onetime village head (*shōya*) of the
Tokugawa period on the Okayama plain conform to the rules that
govern the much smaller house lots of Niiike. Trees within the
wall make up a formal garden.

These stores, selling canned goods and fish or other foods, like other stores and shops are open in front to serve customers, while the owner lives in rooms to the rear.

Kumagai Motoichi

Harvested rice, stacked and hung for drying, fills the Okayama Plain in November

Irrigated fields being prepared near Niiike for transplanting rice in late spring depend on the natural runoff down this valley (*above*). To insure still more dependable water supply, dams are being built such as the one on the Osakabe River (*below*).

Okayama Prefectural Government

Two farmers turn the windlass that raises a water gate built during the Tokugawa period and still an important part of the irrigation system of the Okayama Plain.

The Iwasaki water gate at high water. Niiike's water comes from the Shinjō First Gate (*at left*) leaving the main current to move toward the Ashimori River (*out of sight on the right*).

Field appearance is transformed as the varied crops of spring (*top*) are succeeded by uniform rice cultivation in the summer (*below*). Dry fields cover the hill slope in the foreground.

Ox and plow are needed to prepare the fields for rice. Note the characteristic draft saddle used instead of a yoke.

Iwasa Ishita and his son bundle rice seedlings to transport them from seedbeds to the irrigated fields.

Hiramatsu Sakae smilingly shows how many rice seedlings are planted together.

Hiramatsu Mitsusaburō's wife and daughter, Masano and Sadako, work with him to dry rice harvested from their largest field.

Hiramatsu Chiyoko and her eldest daughter screen the plump grains of rice from the empty husks.

Transplanting mat rush in the frosty sunlight of January is a painfully cold task

Shaking the heavy bundles of cut mat rush clears out the short strands

Hiramatsu Isamu will try to sell his bundled mat rush when the market is right

Hand looms for weaving mat rush provide a useful task for spare time

Hoshino Akira

Niiike women fit baby-tending, housework, and fieldwork into their busy day. Iwasa Ikuno carries her grandson while turning the household mill (*left*); Hiramatsu Chieko goes with Jun, her husband, to set out tomato vines on a spring morning (*right*).

The motor-driven pump, braced with a pole to keep the belt taut.

A tractor-cultivator, heavier than the latest models, near Kojima Bay.

A communally owned insecticide spray in use on rice seedbeds.

Kumagai Motoichi

His mother's kitchen as seen by a Kamo first-grader. Above the bath stoke-hole at right are matches and a sign, "Care with Fire."

Persimmons and rice are equally important in a second-grader's view of the fall harvest.

Kumagai Motoichi

Shōji reflect the afternoon sun behind girls playing with bean bags on the veranda.

Before being repapered, *shōji* are washed carefully.

Niiike women hope for an ideal tiled kitchen like this one in the Kojima Bay area.

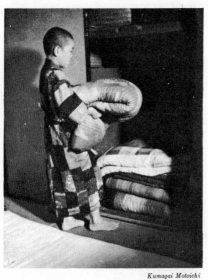

Bedding is stacked in the closet each morning

A built-in firebox heats this bath water to the scalding point.

The hand must be quicker than the maul in mixing red beans with *mochi* rice for New Year feasting.

The gilded *butsudan* of the household, with fruit offerings set before the Bodhisattva images and ancestral name-tablets.

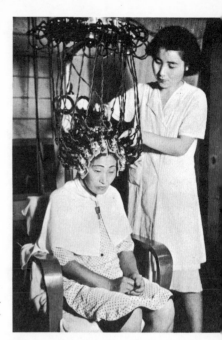

Kumagai Motoichi

The farm wife stoically submits to the old-style permanent-wave machine still used in some rural beauty shops.

Yukata-clad girls seem all the more graceful by contrast with the comic masqueraders who mingle in the Summer Festival dancing at Kibitsu, near Niiike.

To please his ancestors, during the *Bon* festival, Hiramatsu Mitsusaburō offers food and says prayers before their name-tablets in the
tokonoma (*above*), while Hiramatsu Kuma offers water and rice and
burns pine roots and incense at their graves (*below*).

Kumagai Motoichi

Dolls are arrayed on shelves for Girls' Day

Paper carp fly over the house before Boys' Day

Children's handwriting adorns colored paper slips on the bamboo frond set up for Tanabata.

Kumagai Motoichi

His neighbors watch Hiramatsu Tadashi cast his ballot in a winter meeting in the assembly hall

Government inspection of the 1950 wheat harvest, done at the time of requisition, was rigorous.

Hoshino Akira

Niiike's assembly hall. The stones beyo[...]
(*at the left*) constitute one of two gro[...]
used for community worship.

Officers of a mura of the Okayama Plain pose while inspecting an irrigation system with
Ueda Chikao, a prefectural official (*right*).

Every mura office is full of files and employees

Coeducation in many postwar grammar schools puts one boy and one girl at each double desk.

Kumagai Motoichi

Mother tends to infant needs as best she can when field work is heavy.

Kumagai Motoichi

The first day of school is a proud and exciting occasion for mother and son.

Boys play *patchi* while Hiramatsu Kazu watches from his work at the compound wall.

For small school children, especially, there are exceptions to the rule that boys and girls walk separately to school.

Hoshino Akira

Girls gather at the bridge or in someone's yard after school is out.

A branch house: Iwasa Takeshi and Toshiko, his young wife, at the entrance to their new house.

Go-betweens assist in the eating ceremony at the wedding of Iwasa Yukuji and Kimoto, his bride, in their new house. Behind the bride is the chest of drawers brought as part of her trousseau.

The priest assists at ancestral memorial services held in the cemetery at Sōrenji, temple of the Hiramatsu lineages.

Fire several times has destroyed the pagoda at the ancient temple, Kokubunji, first established in the Nara period.

The Shinto shrine has distinctive ridge ornaments. The smaller structure in the rear is the *honden*, repository of the sacred symbols.

Kumagai Motoichi

Elderly people are most assiduous in offering incense and prayers the ancestors.

was ¥70,000 (about $200). An additional ¥70,000 was spent to replace the cement tiles of the former roof by ceramic tiles. Of the total expenditure, half provided Takeshi with a calculable benefit—a sound roof for fifty years. But the remainder, about two-thirds of a full year's declared income, was an investment in the imponderable, in *hōgaku*, the art of calculating lucky and unlucky directions.

But there are increasing pressures to abandon many rules of *hōgaku* because they create inconvenience from a modern point of view. For example, traditional rules place the well on the west or southwest, clear across the yard from the kitchen and bath where most of the water is used. The latrine, in its traditional position in front of the house, collects night soil and waste bath water in a single container, so placed as to facilitate the ladling out of night soil for hauling to the fields. But, so placed, it is unsightly. Furthermore, night soil is less in need now that more and more chemical fertilizer is being used. Also, drainage from the traditional fixed spot of the latrine may run downslope to the well. Modern ideas of sanitation forbid placing a well on a downslope from a latrine no matter what *hōgaku* says. Again, women are traditionally inferior, and guests supreme. Consequently, guests are entertained in the sunny, south, main room, thus relegating all the main work areas of women—cooking, dining, and sleeping quarters—to the dim north side. But these relations are changing as women's social position improves. Hence, pressure rises to alter the traditional position of the kitchen. Finally, the traditional system permits little adjustment for comfortable living under different landscape conditions. Houses on north and south slopes are under the same restrictions. But modern values favor having the main room open on a downhill view rather than into the wall of a cutbank.

A few old rules are violated with each house that is built in Niiike. New ideas of health, sanitation, and efficiency are gradually and steadily breaking down the old rules and replacing them. Actually, from the *hōgaku* point of view, there is a noteworthy amount of unhealthy variation in the houseyards of Niiike. No two are exactly alike, and not one is perfectly in the old tradition. But from a non-traditional point of view, there is considerable uniformity, and, even with the many modern innovations, today's house and houseyard arrangements in Niiike cannot be described adequately without reference to the *hōgaku* rules.

THE HOUSE

The average dwelling is about thirty-six feet long and eighteen feet deep and is one story high with an attic above. If of different measurements, it is of the same general proportion but varies by units of three feet, the standard width of the floor mats, which must be fitted in whole units to the length and breadth of the floor. There are only three two-storied houses in Niiike, all new. Both second stories and attics are reached by a swinging ladder. Typically the floor area is divided into six rooms of roughly equal size (see Fig. 15). The two at the eastern or right-hand end are at ground level. They usually have an earthen floor, less often one of concrete. The remaining four rooms are elevated about two feet above the ground and floored with planks (shown in one room of Fig. 15). The

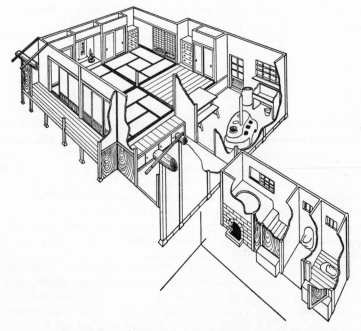

Fig. 15.—Room plan of a Niiike house, in cutaway perspective

planks, however, are rarely seen for they are solidly covered edge to edge with the thickly padded rectangular mats characteristic of the traditional Japanese house. It is the elevated floor that is considered the living area even though numerous household activities take place in the earth-floored rooms. Outdoor footgear is invariably removed upon entering the elevated rooms.

The floor mats of the elevated rooms deserve special mention. These mats (*tatami*) are a standard size, six feet by three feet; their dimensions fix the unit of construction in house-building, for floors must be a multiple of mat length or width. Room sizes are commonly given as "a four and one-half mat room" (far room of Fig. 15), "a six mat room" (two front rooms of Fig. 15), and so forth in daily conversation and in official documents. The mats have a two-inch-thick core layer of straw, the top side covered by a smooth grass-like matting made of rush, which wraps over the short edges and is bound along the long edges by fabric, usually black cotton. Every house in Niiike has *tatami* matting on its "living" floors, except occasionally in temporary quarters such as an improvised room in the workshed; even then the floor usually is spread with the same smooth grass-like cover of the *tatami* mat but without the thick straw underpad. However, poorer houses or houses in more isolated parts of rural Japan may have fewer or no *tatami*. A thousand years ago, bare boards were the floor, and straw mats, one yard square, were used as cushions for distinguished persons only. The use of *tatami* gradually increased until in Tokugawa times the samurai had most of their floors completely covered with mats, though sumptuary laws restricted the size of the largest room according to official status. The luxury of all-*tatami* elevated floors has been within reach of Niiike farmers only within the last few generations.

The outside walls of the house are nearly solid, of wattle and clay daub, on three sides, east, north, and west. The south side has numerous openings and in summer is often more open than shut. Figure 15 shows the east wall cut away to expose the interior. This wall is typically without an opening, though in recent years a window is sometimes cut through into the kitchen. This room also has a glass window on the north side over the sink and a sliding wooden door, with glass panes in the upper portion, which leads outside. The other opening on the north side of the house is a broad double door in the northwest room, a sleeping room. This opening is filled by two wooden frames which slide to either side guided by grooves in the beams above and below. The lower quarter of the frame is of lightweight natural-color wood; the large upper portion is a wooden lattice with small rectilinear openings pasted over with plain white rice paper. This type of panel door (*shōji*) is used extensively in Japanese houses. The southern wall space of the two front elevated rooms is filled almost entirely by *shōji*. The paper cuts off the view but pleasantly diffuses light. It also admits the cold of winter. When the front *shōji* are thrust aside, the rooms open on a narrow veranda (*engawa*) floored with broad boards carefully polished. On formal occasions this is the entryway for guests and in daily living a comfortable place to lounge or a place to catch whatever breeze is moving on a summer evening. But when the family goes to bed, summer or winter, heavy wooden weather doors (*amado*) are slid shut across the front of the veranda and across the *shōji* of the sleeping room. These weather doors slide in grooves following the same principle as the *shōji*. So does the solid wooden door which covers the main, every-day entrance to the house in the front earth-floored room. When the Niiike villagers go to bed at night, all exterior openings are carefully made fast. This practice causes them to toss in stifling heat in summer, but summer or winter they like to sleep feeling secure against the outside world.

The inside walls of the house create six rooms from the space the exterior walls inclose. An unpainted clay wall pierced by an open doorway separates the two earth-floored rooms—the entry (*doma*, literally "earth room") and the kitchen (*suijiba*, "cooking place"). Within the remainder of the house, rooms are demarcated by removable sliding panel doors (fusuma). These are similar to the papered, lattice exterior doors except that the wooden frame is covered front and back by a single, large, opaque sheet of thick paper, sometimes patterned or ornamented. Partition walls above the fusuma, like those over the *shōji*, or like outside walls in general, are of clay laid over a bamboo-strip core. These extend downward some two feet from the polished board ceilings. They are permanent, but the fusuma, *shōji*, and weather doors may all be easily lifted from their grooves and stacked away, leaving the house open to various degrees as desired. This adjustable arrangement gives great versatility to the living space. The whole living area may be thrown open to accommodate large numbers of people for a wedding, funeral feast, or other occasion. Since the elevated rooms contain little furniture other than storage units ranged along the solid outside wall, they are versatile in another aspect, for they are readily turned to several uses.

When the interior panels are all in place the largest inclosure is the main room (*honza* or, less usual in Niiike, *zashiki*), used principally for receiving guests and for certain family ceremonial occasions. In addition to greater size, the main room is distinguished by a rectangular alcove (*tokonoma* or *toko*) in its solid wall flanked by one or more decorative posts. (See right-hand wall section of the left front room of Fig. 15.) When properly prepared for receiving guests the *tokonoma* is always decorated by a tasteful arrangement of flowers, and a scroll appropriate to the season is hung against the wall. The scroll may be a painting in traditional style or an inscription of Chinese characters done in artistic hand. The *tokonoma* is not only a visual center of interest; it is the social focus of the whole house. Irrespective of its physical height, the *tokonoma* is spoken of literally as the high point of the house. In family affairs or the entertainment of guests, the place of honor is nearest the *tokonoma*. In descending order of importance, guests are arranged along the theoretical slope which extends from *tokonoma* to the earth-floored area at the opposite end of the house. Every room and every part of every room has indelible superior-inferior relationships with other parts of the house. Of secondary visual interest in the main room is a long, horizontal, framed scroll or plaque (*gaku*) bearing a philosophic inscription in four Chinese characters, usually hung over one of the entrances. Actually less than half Niiike's houses display *gaku*. An equally small number substitute, as an innovation, a small, framed landscape, usually European, printed in garish colors which clash in their small way with the quiet natural tones of clay, paper, wood, and matting of the rest of the room.

Between the main room and the entry is the *nakanoma* (literally "middle room") which is a kind of anteroom. The ordinary visitor who shoves back the outside door, steps into the entry, and calls out, "Excuse me!" ("*Gomen nasai!*") to announce his presence is received by the housewife kneeling in the anteroom. If the call proves to be a social one, the guest is conducted through the anteroom and into the main room. Children returning from school and the husband from the fields call, "I'm back!" ("*Kaerimashita!*"), and usually enter the living area through the anteroom. This room is the women's favorite sewing area, the school children study here, and the men stretch out for an occasional nap or to listen to the radio.

The entry is more than an entrance. It is used to store rain gear, bicycles, and the miscellaneous accumulations of household life. Doffed footgear may remain on the floor below the raised anteroom entrance or be jammed into cluttered sliding door cupboards underneath the narrow platform (Fig. 15). Some housewives keep the entry as clear and bare as possible. But more often it is a catchall with a miscellaneous assortment stacked deep along the side wall and suspended from the rafters.

The kitchen is even more dimly lit than the entry. There are various arrangements of its furnishings, all inconvenient. In Figure 15 there is a wooden, metal-lined, shallow sink under the rear windows. Next to it stands the water jar. Women draw well-water by bucket, and most have to go outdoors for water, some around the house and to the far corner of the yard if the well is where the astrological rules prescribe. Only three people in Niiike have a pump for their households: Hiramatsu Mitsusaburō, the Sensei, a retired schoolteacher; Hiramatsu Ai, a city woman transplanted to the country; and Iwasa Ishita, who spent a number of years working in the United States. Waste water runs through a hole in the bottom of the sink and is caught in a pail underneath. The large kidney-shaped object is the cookstove. Usually it is of polished black clay or, in newer houses, of red brick. Two or three open fire holes in its top support the flanged aluminum pots in which the food is cooked. For fuel, rice straw and kindling wood are fed in from the side. Though provided with a narrow metal flue, an improvement within the last forty years, these stoves contribute generously to the layers of soot on walls, beams, and other unused surfaces of the kitchen. Boiled or steamed staples, such as rice or barley, are always cooked on the main stove, but most other cooking is done on small, low, portable charcoal braziers (konrō) set on the ground. Since food preparation as well as cooking is done at ground level or on a very low table, Niiike women spend much of their time stooping or squatting in the kitchen. Supplies and containers are piled on the table and eventually overflow to be stacked on the floor along the wall or hung from nails driven into the wall posts. A few open shelves or a corner cupboard acknowledge but do not solve storage problems. When not in use, much of the kitchen equipment, and food as well, lies on the floor or rests in the sink, from which it must be moved when dish-washing starts. Needless to say, the hours Niiike women spend in the kitchen are long and arduous.

Until recently, little attention has been paid to comfort and convenience in women's affairs. Certainly improvements in cooking facilities have been very slowly adopted. Before the flue was added to the stove, most households did their cooking under a shed roof behind the house to keep from smoking up the interior. Some still do it there. But work space, light, convenience, and sanitation are as inadequate behind the house as under the main roof. Even today's talk of remodeling kitchens stems less from concern for women's needs than from a growing consciousness of the basic principles of sanitation, as taught in schools and preached in newspapers and magazines. Major changes such as tiled kitchens, glassed-in cupboards, and adequate window space are appearing here and there in the surrounding countryside. But none had appeared in Niiike until 1955, when the Asia Foundation supported a comprehensive improvement plan.

The central rear room in Figure 15, shown with exposed floor boards, is the back or inner room (okunoma), used during waking hours for after-meal lounging, listening to the radio, and reading. At night it is the sleeping room for the junior members of the household. From its kitchen side projects a broad platform (daidokoro) on which the family assembles for meals (scarcely shown in Fig. 15). As this is the favorite play space for small children and because soup or crumbs from rice bowls are spilled on it, the daidokoro surface is usually only bare boards. Traditionally and most commonly, the family eats seated on the daidokoro around a low table. But family customs vary. Also traditional but now infrequent are individual low table-boxes set one before each person, such as Hiramatsu Tokujiro uses in his household. The box top serves as a small table during meals and the interior contains the owner's personal dishes and chopsticks between meals. A more recent form is the table used by Hiramatsu Isamu's family and shown in Figure 15. It allows one to come in from the fields with muddy feet, sit on the bench to eat, and then depart without changing footgear. The other diners sit opposite on the *daidokoro*.

The principal sleeping room is the *nando* (literally "closet"), to the rear left in Figure 15. It is used customarily by the main couple of the household and their younger children. Along the west wall of the sleeping room is a cupboard where bedding is kept by day and to its right a chest of drawers for storing clothing. The sleeping room seems small and dim and is little used except for sleep itself. Children are born there, and in it the aged die. To most Niiike people this room seems somehow the least pleasant area of the house.

There is very little furniture on either the mat-covered or earthen floors. One sits or lounges directly on the mat floor, softened if he wishes by flat pillows about a foot and a half square. One or two low tables serve adequately for almost every need. Even these are frequently dispensed with. Eating, writing, or various kinds of work are often done at floor level even when a table is handy. At night very thick, comforter-like bedding, cotton covered and cotton filled, is taken from the storage cupboards in the sleeping room and back room and spread on the floor. A small, firm, brick-shaped pillow filled with rice hulls supports the head. In the morning bedding is folded and returned to the cupboards. The same cupboards, supplemented by one or two large chests of drawers, store clothing and equipment. There is often a storage bureau in the anteroom. Infrequently used items may be stored in the attic.

Though the farmhouse interior may seem underfurnished, even bare, at first to the unaccustomed eye, one soon comes to enjoy the restful quality inherent in its straightforward simplicity. Even when spread with the disorder of everyday chores and pleasures—and such is the usual aspect of most rooms, except when prepared for visitors—the intrinsically plain uncluttered surfaces are aesthetically satisfying.

The usual bathroom facilities consist of a urinal, a toilet, and a bathtub, each in a separate compartment. Usually the toilet is under the same roof with the bath, less often inside the main house than as part of the workshed or entrance gate. In Figure 15 the three items are shown in a separate inclosure adjacent to the house. The urinal, in the central position, is made of porcelain and placed in a doorless cubicle for manly use with minimum ado. The toilet, in the righthand cubicle, is an oval hole in the floor, of true outhouse character. Accommodated to squatting posture, the aperture may be rimmed by a porcelain fixture with a splash hood at one end. The opening into the receptacle below is large enough so that Niiike mothers are reluctant to let their young children go to the toilet alone. A flat wooden cover may be set over the opening. Although most people use lime in summer, an odor persists and spreads like a living thing through the house when night soil is drawn off for use in the fields. This task is generally left to the men and is felt by younger people to be most disagreeable. This repugnance to fecal odors, being learned more in the schools than at home, may not only bring changes in toilet facilities but may also encourage the impending agronomic change-over to the exclusive use of animal manure and chemical fertilizers in the fields in place of human ordure.

The bath cubicle, to the left in Figure 15, is often set near the kitchen so both stove and bath may be fired from the same straw pile, but in some homes it is set near the entrance to the yard. The tub is a circular iron pot permanently set in bricks and large enough to sit in with knees drawn up. It is filled with water and heated by a fire built underneath and fed from outside, usually a child's chore. The fuel shortage leads people in summer to draw well-water in the morning so it may warm to air temperature during the day and thereby require less fuel to heat at night. Also some households fire the bath only every two or three days as an economy. Even so, Niiike people bathe more frequently than many farmers, and the bath is a prized part of household life. At all levels of Japanese society, body cleanliness is an old and honored tradition. Near sunset, a haze of smoke hangs over every village as school children or those first in from the fields fire the water for the family bath and the stove for cooking supper. Relaxation and conviviality are firmly associated with the idea of bathing. Father and mother take the small children in to bathe with them, granny scrubs the men's backs, and relatives or neighbors who have no bath (three houses in Niiike) come to chat while waiting their turn at the end of the day. The senior male of the household finishes his bath first and the family follow in regular order of sex and age precedence. The first bather gets the hottest water. A circular board rack pushed to the bottom with the feet enables the bather to avoid scorching himself on the hot metal tub even though he risks almost scalding himself in the water. After soaking a bit in the steaming water, he stands (or sits on a low wooden stool) outside the tub on the drainboards while scrubbing himself with soap and a light towel. Then he dips a small pan into the tub and rinses off before climbing back in for the final soak. In this way soap does not cloud the bath water, but sweat and soaked off dirt are another matter. However, by consecutively using the same hot water, the whole family gets clean at a minimum cost of precious fuel.

The bath is especially attractive in winter for it offers a brief respite from the cold. The farmhouse has only the flimsiest insulation against wintry wind or low temperatures and no effective interior heating system. The sliding panels, which lend such charm in summer by opening the house to the visual pleasures of sunlit yard and fields beyond, may be closed in winter but do more to shut out the view than the cold. The only heating inside the house is a handful of glowing charcoal set on a bed of ashes inside a large, heavy ceramic jar (*hibachi*). This jar is placed on the floor beside the person whose position or age gives him most privilege. Several *hibachi* in a room can warm the finger tips and even take the edge off the chill on a not too cold night, but they do not provide enough heat to justify shedding any of the thick clothing and heavy underwear which is the farmer's mainstay against cold. People around Niiike do not use the *kotatsu* (essentially a *hibachi* sunk in the floor under a low table, covered with a thick comforter, around which people sit toasting their feet), despite their knowledge of its being in common use in many other parts of Japan. Rather they rely on *hibachi*, heavy clothing, hot tea, good hot baths, and thick bedding to see them through the winter months.

Houses are lighted by electricity, available almost everywhere in the prefecture and brought to Niiike in a low-voltage line. Most houses take advantage of minimum rates by using only two 25-watt bulbs, each on an extension cord which can be shifted from one room to another as needed. The bare bulb is suspended by the cord from a hook in the ceiling, providing a weak and graceless illumination. Three houses have had electric meters installed in order to run a small electric motor or for other purposes. But the power lines are too weak to accommodate machinery used in communities closer to the city for weaving mats, pumping water, or other purposes.

As to general security, even when house and outbuildings are inclosed by a wall, as some are in Niiike, the gate into the compound cannot be securely locked. The heavy wooden weather doors outside the house and workshed, though locked shut with slotted bars of wood, give no more security than do the compound walls against breaking and entering. A thief has only to pry the door out of its base groove in order to gain access to the house. The fear of thieves and the even greater fear of fire from the glowing charcoal of an overturned *hibachi* make it seem unwise to leave the house unattended. It is the invariable custom to leave a *rusuban*, one member of the household who stays home when the family leaves for a party or festival.

No house is complete without facilities for spiritual protection and religious worship. Each religious symbol has its special place in the dwelling. There is a Shinto "spirit shelf" (*kamidana*) above the doorway in a corner of the anteroom or overhead in the entry, to assist in protecting the household against the intrusion of harmful influences or disaster. The shelf holds a tiny vase with a sprig of the *sakaki* bush, an incense bowl, and a small bowl for the rice offering. In theory, the shelf serves Shinto guardian spirits which have no material form and are quite unrelated to the saints or divinities of Buddhism. But in practice no one objects to enshrining a small statue of Daruma (Bodhidharma, a Buddhist saint) on this shelf. In the kitchen near the stove, there is another small shelf with a rice bowl for offerings to the Shinto spirit protecting the kitchen and its food, which again is confusingly identified by a Buddhist name as Fugen (Samantabhadra, a Buddhist deity). Small slips of bamboo or paper (*o-fuda*) obtained from pilgrimages to a shrine are added, year by year, to a bundle under the eaves at the front entrance and to another bundle near the well, where a separate spirit gets an occasional offering of rice. All these spiritual outlets are Shinto rather than Buddhist. In comparison with many other communities in Japan, fewer spirits are invoked to guard the premises of Niiike and other local villages because of the region's strong Buddhist emphasis.

The Buddhist place of household worship is a large cupboard (*butsudan*) which rises from floor level against the outside wall of the back room. The brass-fitted double doors of the upper portion open to reveal two or more black tablets (*ihai*) set in gilded mounts and inscribed in gold with the death-names of deceased ancestors. Branch houses have fewer of these tablets than do main houses. Beside the tablets are small bowls for water, rice, and other food offerings, a vase for flowers or the leafy *shikimi*, and all the ceremonial implements: candles, metal and wooden bells, rosary, incense, and prayer books. Usually the cupboard also holds a few books, magazines, table condiments, or other small objects set there to be out of the way during house-cleaning. Respect for ancestors and spirits is considered compatible with treating them as members of the family. Their turn as guests comes on the midyear festival (*Bon*) and on individual memorial days, when the tablets are set in the *tokonoma* of the main room.

Much of the material used in the Niiike farmhouse and outbuildings is locally available. Pine from the hillside wood lots is used for rafters, posts, and wooden underfloor (see Fig. 16). The solid walls are made of bamboo strips from the nearby groves, woven together and plastered over inside and out with a paste of ordinary mud mixed with chopped rice straw. The roof is thatched with wheat straw, saved from the spring harvests, because it is strong and less brittle than rice straw. These materials cost something in the long run, for they would be salable if not used at home, and, furthermore, a man usually must buy extra to eke out what he already owns. But ready availability makes house materials relatively cheap.

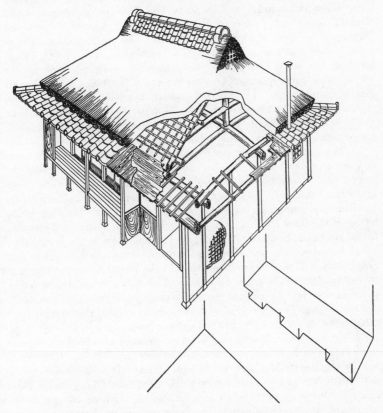

Fig. 16.—Structural elements and exterior of a Niiike house, in cutaway perspective

However, some materials and services can be supplied only from outside the village and contribute considerably to building costs. Certainly the paper for the *shōji* panels and for the interior fusuma panels must be bought outright. For the *tatami*, even if a household grows and weaves its own mat coverings, the job of packing straw bundles onto wooden frames as padding and sewing the cloth binding around the perimeter requires the skill of a professional. Special woods must be bought for certain posts, veranda flooring, and ceiling boards. Decorative posts in the main room are often made of *keyaki*, an elm-like tree; *hinoki*, related to cedar, is highly regarded for fine boards; and in the 1920's and 1930's, imported California redwood was used extensively in Niiike homes for both ceiling panels and decorative posts. The more modern houses require etched glass instead of paper for the lattice panels, bricks for the bath and stove, and tile instead of straw for the roof. One must call on a stonemason for foundations, a carpenter for setting in beams and posts, a plasterer for the walls, and a roofer for either tile or thatch roof, not to mention the "house-planner" for drawing a plan in which the astrological directions are safeguarded. The last-named expert is paid a single honorarium, whereas the artisans get ¥300-¥400 per day plus three meals. In the 1950's, Niiike people estimate, ¥400,000-¥600,000 ($1,117-$1,668) are required, apart from family labor, to build a house.

For the money and labor spent, the house which is built embodies certain features that have swept the field of Western architectural design in recent years: low, horizontal lines, emphasizing natural textures and uncluttered surfaces; "open" construction which provides shelter without severing the connection with the outdoors; "modular" building units, based on the three by six foot *tatami*, which provide a standard measure for all structural materials; flexible size for each room in the house, provided by removable partitions; and multiple functions for each room. Some of these ideas still are innovations in the West but are nothing new to the traditional Japanese farmhouse. The Niiike conventional house just described is of the pattern most commonly found throughout western, or Core, Japan. There are local variations, as in a few of the larger houses near Niiike, in which a room or rooms have been added in a third tier at the back. Very large houses may have an elevated area of three tiers of three rooms each. Of course, there are smaller quarters too. Hiramatsu Asae, was, after the war, an evacuee from the city. He lived for eight years with his wife and two children in a converted barn. They had a floor space of twelve by twenty-four feet for their living area, as well as for storage of both their household and farm equipment. Fortunately they were subsequently able to build a fine, new, two-story house, with certain urban features, right next to their old home, which then returned to being a barn. Though not in Niiike or its immediate environs, one does encounter in Core Japan houses of but one room, a dirt floor at one end and a raised wooden floor at the other. In such cases, the elevated floor is covered with some sort of thin matting, generally of rice straw.

The house plan of Niiike is not common to the whole nation. Depending on which features are regarded as diagnostic, it is possible to distinguish perhaps four principal house types, all of which have long traditions. The two most widespread are the one just elaborated for Niiike, which is dominant throughout most of western, or Core, Japan, and a second quite different plan which is prevalent in northern Honshu. The latter house is gathered about a large central room which is the center of family life. In the middle of the room is an open fire pit which has a roofed-over smoke hole in the rafters above and is surrounded by a board-floored *daidokoro*. The raised-floor rooms with special functions are grouped about the central room, as are also the workshed and cow stalls, the whole being under one main roof. Other house types present various combinations of features which are characteristic of other and smaller areas of Japan. But the kind found in Niiike is the form most consistently built throughout Core Japan.

However consistent or long in tradition the style of the Niiike farmhouse, there have been some gradual changes; the more recently built houses show an increasing number of embellishments of and changes in traditional construction. Most of the new ideas are borrowed from up-to-date city houses. Innovations over the past forty or fifty years which by now are commonplace in Niiike include such things as stove flues in the kitchen, electric lighting, a row of frosted glass panes in the *shōji*, and fire-resistant tiles in place of straw thatch, or at least tile eaves. These were not changes in the basic traditional pattern but embellishments adopted when ready cash permitted the luxury. During the inflation of 1951 to 1954, four new houses were built in Niiike: Iwasa Eikichi moved from the hill down closer to his fields, Hiramatsu Asae moved from the converted barn to a new house, Iwasa Takeshi left his ill-fated first home (chap. 10) for a fresh start on the hill, and Hiramatsu Kinjirō built a new house for his son Yukuji, when the latter took a bride. Each of these houses differed significantly from the traditional design. All had two stories rather than one, an entrance room under a separate roof at right angles to the main roof, individually distinctive room arrangements, and various high-cost features such as all glass panes in the *shōji*. These houses would fit in as well in the city as in the country. In adopting the ideas of the city, some of which are conveniences and some merely fashions, the people of Niiike reflect the extent to which they feel themselves increasingly participants in the larger metropolitan community. The sentimentalist voices regret that the industrial age is intruding upon the "natural simplicity" of the Japanese countryside. Indeed, in nearly every Niiike home the electric light protrudes as a bare bulb hanging from a heavy wire, the radio rests

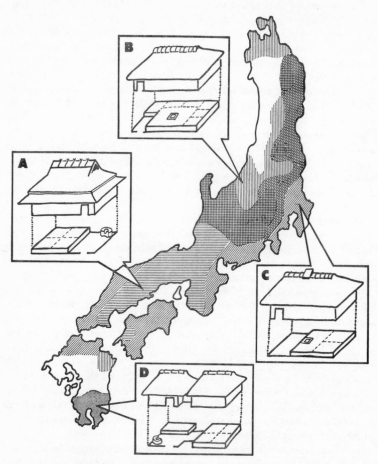

Fig. 17.—Four common house types and their distribution in rural Japan. All types have an elevated floor as part of the interior; in all the ridge beam is supported on king posts or queen posts rising from transverse beams on a four-post foundation. *A*, half-gable main roof, pent roof at each end; interior raised-floor area partitioned into four or more similar rooms. *B*, hip roof; interior partitioned into a main central room with small rooms around it. *C*, hip roof; interior partitioned into similar rooms except at one end of raised floor, which is left open for general household use. *D*, double roof; cooking area under one roof, often joined by a passage to the living area under a separate roof.

on the floor amid a tangle of wires, and gaudy, printed, Western-style calendar art decorates the walls. But the new developments in housing, whether decried or applauded, indicate the widening horizons of the Niiike villagers. There is a trend toward identification with modern, urban ways. Its continuance depends on many conditions. Certainly if the inflated postwar income currently available for property improvement decreases, as seems likely, the more costly innovations will be dropped. But the expanded participation of Niiike residents in the growing urban and industrial community and the rapidly changing national life can hardly be turned back.

HOUSEHOLD EQUIPMENT AND TOOLS

The greatest contrast between the equipment in Niiike today and that of fifty years ago is in the amount and complexity of machinery in both house and field. In earlier days, machinery was of the simplest sort: a wheelbarrow, a flail, a mortar with a pivot-beam pestle operated by foot, a rotary stone mill, a hand-turned spinning wheel, and sometimes a loom for weaving the home-grown cotton. Local specialists could easily provide any of these items, and most were not beyond the ability of the ordinary householder to make for himself. Today's machinery, though by no means elaborate, is factory-made. The machines used in the fields or in processing the crops—listed in chapter 7, pp. 169–70—need not be described here. Some, however, serve in the house and, except for repairs, are more the charge of women than of men. The sewing machine is ubiquitous; a foot treadle model is in almost every house. Each house or barn, moreover, has one or more of the special looms for weaving *tatami* covers from the mat rush grown in the fields; the loom rises about five feet from the floor and has foot treadles to change the shed. Electric looms are well known but cannot be installed in Niiike until power lines of higher capacity are laid into the buraku.

Among the very numerous items of simpler household equipment, there has been a striking change in recent years through the introduction of new materials. Up to a couple of generations ago, most household tools and utensils were made of home-grown materials: bamboo, wood, and rice straw. Metal was scarce, limited perhaps to a standard pair of kitchen knives and a few pots. Food was prepared and stored in baskets, wooden boxes, and crockery jars; it was eaten from dishes of lacquer or crockery. The few pieces of furniture were made without screws or other metal. Much of this non-metal equipment is still made at home or by local craftsmen, but today metal is common, and molded plastics have now made their appearance.

Fig. 18.—Simple tools of Niiike. All hoes and forks on the left side are classed as *kuwa*, except for the D-handle pitchfork and spade, which are Western tools recently added. Main use of these *kuwa* is in cultivating wheat and dry-field crops. The plow (*top right*) has an adjustable beam and removable share. Rice-cultivating implements (*below*) include the harrow, the transplanting guide-string with spaced beads, the wheeled grass-weeder (*jōsōki*) (*bottom center*), sickles, a one-*tō* rice measure with roller to level off the rice at the brim, and a mallet for pounding straw preparatory to making rope or other straw products.

The housewife buys iron frying pans and aluminum rice pots, meanwhile complaining because her rice burns in aluminum, and serves her meals in cheap porcelain or sometimes in plastic dishes. Yet the old ways have not disappeared. Bamboo is still a most common material, whether for a clothes rack in the drying yard, for baskets in the workshed, for a table or stand in the *tatami* rooms, or for the knife-holder and dippers in the kitchen. Though basket-making is one of the few household crafts surviving in Niiike today, bamboo basketry requires equipment as well as skill. Consequently, most baskets are bought from the co-operative. Wood is used everywhere, not only for furniture, but also for kitchen utensils: measuring boxes, storage containers, steamers, lids, and paddles. The cooper who makes and repairs wooden buckets is one of the busiest artisans of surrounding communities. Rice straw has some very common uses. Several of the older men, especially Iwasa Genshiro, now in his eighty-second year, plait rice straw into carrying baskets of several types, mostly for field use such as carrying manure or fertilizer. Almost every household has someone who makes rice-straw sandals (*waraji*) for family use, and the technique of plaiting rice-straw bags for rice shipment is an everyday skill among the men.

However, for most of their work tools and for their household goods Niiike people have long depended on the world outside. In the days of predominantly wood and bamboo implements, artisans of the surrounding region supplied many of their needs. But now, in contrast to the local house builders who are as numerous as ever, only a few tool-making artisans remain. Their work has been generally supplanted by factory production. To win the countryside to the use of their products, manufacturers are beginning to put up billboards along the railroad, scatter handbills from helicopters, sponsor exhibitions and fairs, and use other promotion methods. Thus there are in Niiike an increasing number of items that are easier and cheaper to buy than to make.

CLOTHING

The clothing styles worn in Niiike are of two origins, the traditional Japanese costume and the Western or European garb associated with industrialization. Almost every villager is able to outfit himself in either style.

Elderly people, particularly women, spend most of their time in Japanese dress, and younger adults and children usually wear Western dress, but it should be emphasized that each person's wardrobe contains some of both. Moreover, the two styles are seldom mixed. Except for knit undergarments, and perhaps Western trimmings such as bags, umbrellas, and men's hats, the Niiike villager who dons Japanese clothing will be consistently Japanese throughout. Or, if Western dress is worn, then the whole costume is Western, except for an occasional wearing of Japanese wooden clogs. In short, Western clothing has been accepted as an alternative to the native tradition, not an admixture. Merging of these two traditions occurs somewhat oftener in the city, but in Niiike the villagers rather distinctly conceive of their clothing as two separate traditions. Nor are there many adults who have completely substituted Western garb for Japanese costume. Both styles are very much in evidence.

Whereas Western costume is cut and shaped to fit human contours so closely that a few inches difference in bodily measurement necessitates a different size of garment, traditional Japanese clothing is largely unfitted. Garments are sewn from several narrow panels of cloth. Aside from infants' clothing, there are only three sizes of garments, small for young children, medium for older children, and large for adults. Individual adjustments are made by tucks of appropriate size across the shoulders and around the waist or somewhat below the sash-like belt.

A Japanese wardrobe usually includes a great variety of garments for special occasions, situations, and seasons. Broadly speaking, however, all are derived from two basic ideas; the one, a combination of trousers with a straight-cut upper garment, usually belted but sometimes tied across the front; and the other, an ankle-length, surplice-front wrapper gown, with long hanging panel sleeves, tied around the middle with a sash. One variety of the latter has come to the West as the kimono, though the word in Japanese refers to any sort of clothing. Technically speaking, whether of cotton or silk, the garments are hand sewn from cloth woven a standard fourteen inches wide. The straight cut allows each garment to be readily folded flat without wrinkles for storage. In a sense the seams are temporary, for the garments are often taken completely apart for washing, starching, and mending. No wonder the sewing machine is reserved primarily for Western sewing. There are no buttons and buttonholes or their equivalents such as the Chinese frogs or north Asian toggles. Garments are closed with either ties or a waist sash. The sash is a major element in women's formal costume, when it is known as the "obi" and is woven of stiff fabric in the fourteen-inch width traditional for Japanese material since the days of the belt loom. Warmth is regulated by number and kind of garments worn. For warm weather, light clothes of single thickness are in order. As it grows colder one puts on more clothing, changing first to lined garments, then to cold weather, cotton-padded clothing.

In general, Niiike men's work clothes are predominantly factory-made Western-style garments in summer and homemade, traditional Japanese style in winter. In warm weather, men of all ages work in a Western-style open-necked shirt and trousers worn over a single layer of underwear. The shirt and trousers are of plain cotton fabric, often white or khaki or of a sober dark hue. On their heads they may wear a broad-brimmed, factory-woven, barley-straw hat much like any American farmer's, or a white cotton headcloth, actually a small towel, either draped over the head or rolled and tied around as a sweat band. The lower legs are left bare. In the black ooze of paddy fields men go barefoot. At other times they slip their feet into homemade, flat, straw sandals (waraji, or a better quality, zōri) or purchased wooden clogs (geta) raised a couple of inches above the ground level by two parallel wooden crossbars. These footgear are kept on by a straw (for zōri) or cloth (for geta) cord gripped between the first and second toes and divided to pass around the arch of the foot and attach at either side of the sole in the rear. Even in the full heat of summer, men as well as women often wear dark cloth armlets reaching to the fingers to preserve the traditionally admired light skin. The same end is served by much of the head wrapping and by wearing the full complement of clothes right through the hottest days. Perhaps this vanity coupled with the pressure for modesty accounts for the fact that no man in Niiike ever works in his fields stripped to the waist, though such lack of cover is not unusual among city laborers or fishermen. However, on sultry days he may relax at home in only a loin cloth, though he is apt to retain, also, a flannel or ribbed-knit wool band wound around his abdomen "to keep the bowels warm." After all, summertime is dysentery time, and everyone feels strongly the need to keep his abdomen warmly wrapped to avoid sickness. If visitors arrive or if he goes outside the house, our relaxing farmer will again dress "properly."

As cold weather approaches, Japanese-style blouses and trousers begin to be worn. Their fuller cut makes for warmth and easier combinations of garments one under the other. Early in the fall most men don long, knit underwear, an early borrowing from the West. They continue to wear these heavy "longies" until the first oppressive heat of the next summer. As the weather gets more nippy, the men wrap themselves up all over. More varied headgear appears, including a plentiful supply of old army caps. They wear kerchiefs over their heads and knot them under the chin. Wool sweaters are worn underneath their shirts and padded vests under loose jackets. Cloth leggings are tied on; and on their feet are black cloth ankle-length socks with rubber soles (jikatabi), divided between great toe and second toe. Cold weather work clothing looks altogether Japanese, for the only Western garments are worn as underclothing.

Navy-blue cotton cloth dyed with indigo remains the favorite choice for work clothes for both men and women. The dark background may be enlivened by narrow longitudinal stripes of lighter hue or by small white or light-blue motifs in a traditional weave called *kasuri*. *Kasuri* is of the so-called ikat group of Southeast Asian dyeing-weaving techniques in which the pattern is formed by tie-dyeing the warp and weft threads before they are woven. The deep blue of a *kasuri* garment accented with a white head cloth and bright sash makes an eye-catching as well as serviceable costume.

The Niiike man working at a salaried job in the city sets out for work in Western costume the year around: a dark wool suit, most often navy blue, white shirt, dark four-in-hand tie, low leather shoes, and often a felt hat. In winter he will add an overcoat, but summer heat must approach the unbearable before he will discard his suit coat and wear just a white cotton shirt. Western-style wool suits are worn by almost any young or middle-aged man going to town for business or pleasure. As with so many Western features incorporated into Japanese culture, the prevailing style is that of an earlier generation in the West, particularly that of the United States in the case of clothing. To be sure, all except the oldest men feel at home in a Western suit and change to one readily from work clothing, but the approved cut and colors suggest the stiff formality of American male dress in the 1920's.

The older man ordinarily does not wear a Western suit to town or for visiting. Rather he favors a Japanese dark silk kimono, over which he wears a dark, striped silk, ankle-length overskirt divided somewhat like culottes (*hakama*). His feet are shod in dark cotton cloth socks with separated great toe (*tabi*) and thrust into wooden clogs. The whole is topped off by a Western-style dark felt fedora. As he sets off with great aplomb, as often as not on his bicycle, he will add a dark silk, thigh-length, Japanese coat (haori) if the day is chilly or carry a furled black silk umbrella if it is overcast.

Women's dress for housework in summer is usually chosen on the basis of age. Younger women most often wear a simple white cotton blouse and dark straight skirt or a light-colored, one-piece, cotton dress, plain or printed and buttoning down to the waist. Older women usually wear a Japanese, sash-tied, cotton kimono of somber hue. Before starting housework, for either style of dress, an apron is donned which is a white cotton cover-all reaching almost to the knees, fastened in back, and having long full sleeves gathered at the wrist. This last feature is effective in protecting the voluminous kimono sleeves from dragging while doing housework. Perhaps an older style of apron is that worn by the oldest women, a single fourteen-inch panel of cotton cloth reaching down the front from waist to hem and serving for little more than a convenient hand wiper. Women may go barefoot in the house or wear *tabi* if it is cold.

For field work, women wear a surplice-cut blouse of dark cotton work cloth tucked into roomy, gathered-ankle field trousers (*mompei*) of similar material. These field trousers are worn big enough so that a full kimono can be tucked in if worn in place of the long blouse. Their use became widespread during World War II at the urging of the Japanese government to replace the less convenient knee-length field gown worn in the past. On their feet women wear straw sandals or wooden clogs similar to men's except that women's clogs are not only smaller but narrower in proportion and gayer in color of cloth cord. Women protect the head with a white head-cloth, its ends tucked up variously by women of different age groups. They may also wear the same sort of broad-brimmed straw hat they buy for their husbands and are more dexterous and meticulous than their spouses in flipping off both hat and cloth with an unoccupied hand as etiquette requires when greeting an outsider. Conservative Niiike has only begun to adopt a white cotton bonnet with wide ruffles around the face. This headgear, which suggests the old-fashioned American sunbonnet, may have been introduced by a returning emigrant; it has been worn in most parts of the Okayama Plain since before World War II.

In cooler weather, the wash dresses become fewer. The kimono worn by older women and the field work clothes show little surface change but, underneath, multiple layers of underclothing are worn. Knee-length drawers, which usually go with Western costume, sometimes are worn with Japanese clothing as an alternative to the inmost, knee-length, wraparound loin skirt. Long, knit underwear forms part of the cold-weather underclothing, and various gown-length wrappers and perhaps a sweater are also added. The sweaters of men, women, and children as well as various other articles are knit by the women of the household from yarn that is reused many times. Whatever the underclothing, its extra bulk is of little consequence with Japanese-style clothes because the ties and sashes readily adjust to changing measurements; but in the case of women's Western-style clothes, for the few who wear them in winter, the size must be several inches larger than for summer clothes.

When Niiike women dress for town or visiting they are as delightfully colorful as gorgeous tropical birds in their gay, figured silk kimonos with the broad, contrasting sash (obi); these garments are as colorful and bright as the men's visiting clothes are dark in hue. On a cold day they may add a silk coat (haori). The sunlight, passing through colored parasols of silk or cotton which women carry in the place of hats, diffuses a warm tint over face and costume. Black cloth umbrellas, also constructed in Western style, are saved for rainy weather; or they carry the Japanese-style parasol, with bamboo ribs supporting a flat, lacquered paper top. On their feet women wear white cloth *tabi* and elegant sandals (*zōri*) covered with fine straw, bright cloth, or flexible plastic. The footgear and the closely wrapped skirts of the kimono and under kimonos are managed with a graceful, mincing, swaying walk which goes far toward convincing the observer that the most appealing feminine curves are, after all, those of movement.

But the lively and even riotous colors of Niiike women's social dress does not represent simply unrestrained exuberance. The total effect is the result of many careful choices. There are a multitude of conventions governing what may be worn, by whom, and when. The size of the design and the brilliance of the color must be subdued with advancing age and varied with social position, and the bird and plant designs which compose most patterns must be appropriate to the season. Indeed, for everyone there are subtle and detailed rules governing color and design according to sex, age, social position, and the season in which the garment is to be worn. Men and boys avoid all warm hues, especially red, and wear greens, blues, browns, and grays in plain fabrics, stripes, or over-all patterns of small motif. Even such small things as the ties on coats and the cords on sandals and clogs have male and female, young and old, color and pattern conventions. These ideas of what is appropriate are so pervasive that they often carry over to selection of Western-style clothing as well. No one can be insensitive to the rules of dress and expect to avoid ridicule.

For the most formal and solemn occasions, both sexes wear black silk gowns (*montsuki*), whose only ornamentation is a small, white, circular family crest printed at five scattered but particular spots. This costume, once the exclusive prerogative of the upper classes, became universal about the time of the feudal breakdown in the late nineteenth century. Today only the very poor do without at least one such gown and its accessories. The bride's wedding gown is black, also, but the lower portion from mid-thigh to hem boasts costly and elaborate multicolored embroideries. It is worn only once, to be stored away thereafter as an unused family treasure.

Some specialized garments which in cut are variations of the silk kimono may be worn by men, women, and children on appropriate occasions. The most common variant in Niiike is a cotton kimono (*yukata*) for summer use. One puts on the *yukata* after his evening bath and wears it through supper and the evening, both indoors and out. The padded equivalent for cold weather is a *tanzen*. Either garment with slightly shorter hem may be worn to bed as a sleeping costume (*nemaki*, "sleeping wrap"). City dwellers change as a matter of course from Western dress to one of these Japanese costumes at home because of their convenience and to avoid the wear and tear which kneeling and cross-legged squatting bring to trousers. But farmers are more likely to resume their daytime costume after bathing or wear a worn kimono, single or padded, for household wear or sleeping attire. Certainly few farmers' wardrobes hold each of these specialized costumes.

In rainy weather, figures seen in the distance among the fields may look for all the world like eighteenth-century "Old Japan," with their broad, conical rainhats and capes. Closer inspection may show the hat to be made of scrap aluminum and the cape hanging down the back to be thin plastic stretched over a mat rather than overlapping palm fiber tufts, but the effect is much the traditional one. Knee-length rubber boots are coming into wide use, especially for transplanting mat rush, for this task requires wading in the icy water of midwinter. Western-style raincoats and rubbers or galoshes are worn to school or on visits to town but are unhandy in the fields, where traditional rain gear that covers only the bent-over back continues to be popular among farmers.

Children's clothing is partly in the Japanese tradition and partly in the Western, as is their parents'. Shortly after birth an infant is given Japanese-style garments by the mother's family. These may be worn for some years; the broad tucks in the shoulders and around the waist are let out as the child grows. In winter, small children wear padded kimonos and seem to stay warm even with bare feet, although sweaters and narrow-ankled pants are becoming more common each year. Girls begin to wear Western-style dresses or dark pleated skirts with sweaters or blouses, especially a navy or white middy blouse, in the pre-school years, and this remains standard school and daily costume through the teens. Boys of similar age wear a white shirt with perhaps a sweater and dark shorts or long pants, or, more often, a school uniform consisting of a black brass-buttoned jacket with standing collar and long black pants. On their heads boys wear a shiny visored, black school cap. Children's feet are most frequently shod in wooden clogs or black canvas sneakers with an elastic insert in place of laces. Although school uniforms have not been compulsory in Japan since World War II, most children's school clothing continues to reflect the former requirements. The wearing of Japanese-style garments by school children is a treat reserved largely for festivals and special occasions—and then they are worn more by girls than by boys.

Since the housewife buys cloth to make some garments and chooses other items ready-made, she must be capable of a multitude of nice discriminations in her choices if her family is to be properly, attractively, and economically clothed. Tradition, practicality, advertising, and neighborhood opinion all contribute toward forming her decisions. Because they depend on the products of factories with nationwide output, Niiike people and their neighbors no longer have the colorful and distinctive local peculiarities of dress which prevailed up to four decades ago when they wove their cloth at home from home-grown cotton. And no longer do they weave or wear the hemp and ramie garments which still comprise part of the daily or special wear in some of the more remote areas of Japan. In theory, the modern department store offers a wide range of materials and designs which might add wardrobe variety and dash. But, where once they took pride in local traditions of cut and weave, today the men and women of Niiike think of themselves not as the people of a locality but as the members of an occupational class. They are farmers first, and they choose clothing which fits their social status and occupation, clothing of conservative cut and sober design. Bright, splashy patterns and highly contrasting colors are for the shopgirls of the city or, perhaps, the happy-go-lucky fishermen of the coast, whom they regard as a different class. For themselves Niiike people favor a plain, subdued costume which expresses the serious-minded, steady temperament expected of farmers.

Even more than in neighboring communities, sobriety has been a guiding principle in Niiike. The young woman who puts on lipstick or gets a permanent wave to be like her companions in outside social activities is made to feel embarrassed when she returns home and is heckled by the men in her house. But frowning on vanity does not prevent change from creeping in. A few recent brides who have come into the community continue to wear lipstick and wave their hair without being openly censured for it. Every house has one or more of the several style magazines, which tend to draw communities such as Niiike farther away from the old tradition of local variation in costume and into the realm of sweeping national fluctuations of style. The inclusion in these magazines of large sections of American styles introduces the still larger dimension of international fashion, for the new modes are carefully studied by the housewife and her daughters, even if they resist the temptation to try them out. A strong motivation acting against variety and change in fashion is that of economy. In Japanese-style clothing this force acts chiefly by keeping the number of garments at a minimum. In Western clothing it favors dark colors which are slow to soil, neutral colors and plain fabrics which go with everything, or white which does not fade. Economy also favors conservative cut which requires little cloth to make and which will not go out of style. But perhaps the biggest strain on economy is the practice of maintaining both Japanese and Western-style wardrobes.

Actually, having two kinds of clothing has advantages as well as disadvantages. Niiike people have a wide and relatively flexible choice in costume. Perhaps the teen-age girls display the most felicitous adjustment to the dual tradition, for they wear skirt, blouse, and saddle shoes becomingly and with comfort during the day, and carry themselves with equal ease, though differently, in the long, graceful white cotton *yukata* splashed with color and bound with a bright sash that they don after their evening bath. Women choose Western dresses for practicality, since they are easily washed and have no dragging sleeves or long hems to interfere with their work but switch to Japanese kimono when appearance is important, since they feel dresses are poorly adapted to the long waists and short legs which are their physical heritage.

The other side of the coin, however, is the high expense of maintaining a dual wardrobe such as is thought desirable for every season and occasion. The average man must be equipped with Japanese costumes for work in all weather, for ceremonial, semiformal, and highly formal occasions; and he must also have an adequate supply of Western work shirts and trousers, white shirts, socks, and underwear, shoes, a couple of wool suits, an overcoat, and accessories. His wife and at least the other adults in the household require a similar dual outfit. In addition, just as their wives have their bridal gowns laid by, many men keep in moth balls a full suit of morning clothes, with tail coat, striped trousers, and accessories, to be worn on very special occasions. We do not know how long farmers will be willing to pay the cost of a dual wardrobe, but one would expect this high expense to exert a continual pressure toward change in clothing habits. The trend probably will be toward increasing use of the mass-produced clothes of Western style and the integration of Japanese costume remnants with the Western apparel to form a single, consistent tradition.

FOOD AND DRINK

In the paddy fields, the dry fields, and the houseyards of Niiike, one sees a variety of produce which would make almost every household self-sufficient in food should they choose to rely entirely on their own resources: rice, barley, and wheat, eggs and meat from their chickens, various beans including soybeans, oil pressed from rapeseed, and a variety of vegetables and fruits. When we look into the cooking pots in the kitchen, at least four-fifths of what we see does come from the village's own fields. But the taste for other foods and the economic advantage in selling not only the surplus produce but also some things in short supply, such as eggs, rape oil, and fruit, prevent complete self-sufficiency.

Of the purchased foods, one-fifth of the total supply, the largest single item is fish. The peddler who brings trays of fresh fish through the settlement on the back of his bicycle weighs out for each customer minute cuts of the cheaper kinds—sardine and mackerel rather than halibut. Each sale is tiny, but he is the biggest single purveyor of foods to Niiike housewives. No meal would taste right without the flavor of fresh or salted fish. But only for a special feast does each person get more than a couple of bites, and only two or three times a year is there served the famous red snapper (*tai*) of the Inland Sea. From other peddlers, or from the man who runs a little store in Senzoku across the way, housewives buy both necessities, such as salt and sugar, and minor luxuries, such as better quality tea than they can grow themselves, rice wine (sake), cookies, and cakes. They also have begun to purchase noodles and other prepared foods and sauces, which they could make at home.

If there is any single food prized above all others, it is rice. The villagers know that nothing matches clean, steamed rice for taste and filling qualities. In its every aspect, rice is the embodiment of conscious and unconscious values—when it is first transplanted and covered with water, when the green-golden ears droop in the still air of the paddy fields covering the valley floor, and when the polished grain rests in a steaming mound in one's bowl. Story, song, art, and ceremony have constant reference to rice in one or another of its stages of growth. And rice is the one indispensable food for a satisfying meal. Yet in Niiike, as in most farm villages, rice is a luxury food which the housewife in cooking must eke out by mixing with rolled barley or some other inferior grain. The portion of barley is held down to a sixth in the New Year just after the rice harvest; and rice is even served unadulterated when peaks of work in the crop cycle demand long hours in the fields. But late in the year, when the store of rice dwindles and finally vanishes under the onslaught of the farmers' heavy appetites, meals may lack the comfort of rice altogether. Then the housewife must make shift with barley, sweet potatoes, taro, or other starchy substitutes.

In front of each house is a covered, straw-lined pit where the starchy root crops are kept: sweet potatoes, taro, and a few white potatoes. These supplement the cereals and are generally cut up and served in soups or as cooked vegetables. Wheat is used very little except when prepared as noodles. Noodles are also often made of buckwheat and are served in a soup.

In Niiike's diet there are few of the protein foods common in Western meals; the fish, meat, and an occasional egg are used more for flavor than for their food values. But soybeans and lesser quantities of red beans, broad beans, and chick-peas are served often. These beans provide some protein, and an additional amount creeps into the diet thanks to the tradition of using soy sauce, *miso*, and *tōfu*. Soy sauce is always on hand as a salty flavoring to be added during cooking or eating; *miso* (a salty paste of fermented soybean added to a wheat, rice, and bean soup) is a main ingredient of the standard breakfast soup; and *tōfu* (a custard-like curd of fermented soybeans served in chunks) is a common extender of soups and stews. Were it not for these, the protein intake from fish and from eggs and chicken meat would be low indeed, for fish seems expensive, and villagers feel themselves extravagant if they eat their own eggs and cruel if they eat their own chickens.

Meat was unknown on the table two generations ago. There are old persons still who have never violated the Buddhist taboo against eating "the flesh of four-footed creatures." Nowadays high prices of meat relative to other foods, rather than the old taboo, keep consumption low—a thin slice or two of beef perhaps once a week. Relatively few persons have developed a taste for pork, which on account of its high fat content is at odds with the pattern of "clean" greaseless cooking so firmly intrenched in Japan. But almost everyone enjoys beef or veal, although the villagers tend to associate it with "Western"—hence costly—cuisine.

A couple of generations back nobody drank milk. Until World War II, it was used mainly as an occasional last resort to encourage lactation in nursing mothers. But since the end of the war, children have learned to enjoy the bowl of milk served at school as part of a public health supplemental food program and have taken home their newly acquired taste. Even some of the adults in Niiike are now drinking milk. The new taste for milk (it comes in three- and six-ounce bottles in the city) is being spread among children throughout Japan and so affects the economy of the village, as discussed below (p. 201).

Fruit and green vegetables provide variety and seasonal change to Niiike menus. Niiike people sell little fruit, but for themselves the small orchards and scattered trees bearing loquats, figs, and persimmons provide fresh fruit in season from spring until late fall. Persimmons, sun-dried and sugary, are a special treat in the winter. Watermelons are plentiful and delicious in the summer. Apart from starchy tubers, about twenty kinds of vegetables are regularly cultivated, a few more are gathered wild, and two or three sorts which grow best at a higher altitude are bought in season. This wide range of leaf, stem, and root vegetables is what gives interest to the otherwise monotonous meals. The choice is narrowed in winter, but there remains a choice.

It is true that food shortage is not unknown in Niiike, but on the whole the diet seems adequate and well balanced, whether for children, pregnant women, and mothers, or for men doing hard physical labor. However, the food proportions in Niiike's dietary pattern are different from those of the West. It is difficult for the villagers to understand the American three-part division of a meal into meat, vegetables, and starchy food. They imagine the heart of the American meal to be a mass of bread, as theirs is a heaping bowl of rice with barley, surrounded with small but tasty side-dishes of fish, vegetables, and pickles. Whereas the Western meal contains more protein and contributes fat and sugar as well as starch directly to the body, the average Niiike meal contributes in large quantity only starch. Though soybeans are much used, their protein is not quite equivalent to that of meat. If there is a deficiency in protein intake, the body can do little to cover the shortage, but the body can and, if necessary, does manufacture sugars and fats from starches. This seems to be the usual physiological process in Niiike. The fat content of their diet is low. Few of the fish they eat are fat; rape oil, which is the standard cooking fat, is used very sparingly except to fry slices of compressed glutinous rice cakes (*mochi*) during the fall and winter holidays or to deep-fry foods in batter (*tempura*) on festive occasions. Children and adults are ravenous for sugary candy, but most often must content themselves with a saccharine or sugar-sweetened, fermented soybean paste which is neither very sweet nor served as everyday food. To compensate for these shortages in fat and sugar the appetite is keen for starch (rice-barley or its substitutes: sweet potatoes, white potatoes, noodles, taro, beans) in quantities so large as to dwarf the remainder of the meal and so invariable as to become vastly monotonous to the Western palate.

Culinary art would seem uncomplicated at first glance. Niiike lacks an oven or any method of baking. The cook, choosing between boiling, frying, and broiling, needs merely to cut each item in bits, cook it lightly, and serve it separately. Tradition lays no stress on serving foods hot. Though hot food may be relished, a meal often stands until it is lukewarm or even cold before being served. Tepid and cold meals are quite usual. Boiled rice with barley is the backbone of meal after meal, and certainly its preparation is not complicated. The new bride, it is true, is judged severely on the exact quality of her boiled rice, for, though there is no universal agreement on what constitutes good rice, the final product must combine a certain sheen, firmness of grain, and sufficient glutinousness to permit ready handling with chopsticks. Each person has his own standard and is very particular about it. Men disclaim any knowledge of cooking and, in their rare attempts, usually burn rice or boil it soggy. Even so, the consistency of rice is what is being judged, not its flavor. Nor is there much stress on manipulation of flavor in cooking other foods. It is to other aspects of cuisine that we must look for refinements.

To the foreigner it often seems that the real art in Japanese cooking lies in enhancing the appearance of food. This is an art that requires knowledge and skill, and demands a great deal of time. The creative effort of cutting ingredients into attractive shapes and arranging them tastefully on individual dishes is a highly developed tradition in Japan, well known to the countrywomen, who call it into play when guests are entertained. But for everyday most housewives have so many tasks apart from cooking that, as they quickly admit, their ordinary meals are hastily prepared and coarsely served. Given the time—and the overriding need to show every attention to a guest justifies her taking this time—the competent housewife is expected to set forth a feast for the eye and to know the properly gracious ritual for serving it. Visual appeal in the arrangement of food and the etiquette of serving it must meet high and critical standards of performance.

Normally there are three meals a day except during busy seasons. When the working hours are long and hard an extra meal or two is eaten in the field or at home before retiring. Sometimes the children bring a pot of hot tea into the fields for a mid-morning or mid-afternoon snack break. On a normal work day the housewife, up before anyone else, has breakfast ready for the others when they rise about five-thirty or six o'clock. The noon meal is eaten at twelve, pretty much by the clock. The evening meal, which is somewhat more elaborate, is served whenever convenient after the family has bathed and before they retire. Here is a representative summer menu, with an estimate of the normal adult portion.

Breakfast	Lunch
Miso soup, with noodles (1 cup)	Peas fried in rape oil ($\frac{1}{4}$ cup)
Red beans, vinegared ($\frac{1}{4}$ cup)	Cucumber slices in soy sauce (2 slices)
Pickled radish (3 slices)	Fried sweet potato (2 or 3 slices, $3'' \times 3'' \times \frac{1}{8}''$)
Rice-barley, 2:1 ($2\frac{1}{2}$ cups)	
Tea	Bean curd, deep-fried ($\frac{1}{4}$ cup)
	Rice-barley, 2:1 (2 cups)
	Water

Dinner	
Fried squid ($1\frac{1}{2}'' \times 3'' \times \frac{1}{8}''$ slice)	Pickled radish (3–4 slices)
Clear fish-soup ($\frac{3}{4}$ cup)	Rice-barley, 2:1 ($2\frac{1}{2}$ cups)
Cucumber slices in soy sauce (2 slices)	Tea
Sliced tomato (2 slices)	Fruit in season

Holiday and special meals are served perhaps twelve to twenty times a year. Both procedure and food differ from everyday practice. If guests attend, they are served in the main room rather than the *daidokoro*, and there is great rigidity of protocol in seating. The guests are placed in order of rank from the "upper" end of the room to the "lower" where the host sits at the very bottom. Each person politely protests being moved upward but is well aware of how high he should sit. Usually the women of the household are excluded except for serving the meal.

At banquets, several varieties of fish are served, including at least one whole broiled or boiled fish per person. Raw fish served in slices (*sashimi*) is a sweet and tender delicacy and so is the batter-dipped fish or shrimp fried in deep fat (*tempura*). Either of these may be served at ordinary meals, also, though raw fish is more common. Banquets are considerably richer in protein, fat, and sugar than everyday meals but are differentiated also by the serving of sake—a mild beverage of about 14 per cent alcoholic content—or the cheaper liquor *shōchū*. Both liquors by custom are preferably served with food, and the sake, at least, should be served hot. One never fills his own tiny cup with wine but keeps watch over his neighbors and urges them to drink more. The host, in particular, should refill everyone's cup as soon as a sip has been taken and see that the conversation remains brisk. Various games and rituals, such as a mutual exchange of wine cups, are brought into play to step up the drinking, which in most areas leads to speedy and hilarious inebriation. Niiike is markedly puritanical in this respect. Insobriety is frowned on in Niiike, and consumption is never high. The first man whose reddened face signals the influence of liquor (and for many Japanese a very small portion of sake brings on a flush) becomes the target of much teasing. In Niiike this teasing seems to have a hidden barb that controls the amount of drinking even while the host persists in his hospitality. A party continues as long as food is served. When finally the tub filled with boiled rice appears, the banquet is nearing its end. Each person takes a bowl or two of rice to finish his meal. Very shortly afterward the guests make their profuse stereotyped "thank-you-for-the-feast," hear the host's equally stereotyped "thank-you-for-your-effort [in coming]," and depart, each carrying home any leftover food from his portion for the women and children of his household who have not attended.

Calendric festivals are intimately linked with the cycle of food production, a fact which helps to explain their association with special foods. For most of these occasions no feast is prepared, but one or two unusual dishes may be added to the meal or served separately. The two main occasions for feasting are the Fall Festival and the New Year. At the Fall Festival cold rice flavored with vinegar and rolled into balls with centers of vegetable and fish (*sushi*) is the special food. In Niiike the Fall Festival is one of the few occasions when those who enjoy sake feel free to drink it in quantity and when the emphasis is on good food of every sort. New Year is a more extended period of feasting. By the time the rice harvest has been threshed, hulled, polished, and stored in the great aluminum vat in the workshed, winter is upon the village and there are no urgent tasks. So the New Year begins with a busy three days of visiting and feasting, then tapers off for the next four days. Festivities are revived at mid-month and again at the first of the next month. Two foods associated with the New Year are *mochi* (highly glutinous rice, steamed and pounded before being shaped into rolls and sliced) and "red rice" which is ordinary rice steamed together with red beans. Either or both of these foods may also appear at any ceremonial or happy occasion throughout the rest of the year. They are the generalized symbols of festive events while other special dishes are limited to a specific occasion.

Dining, even on ordinary occasions, has its mute rituals revealing some fundamentals of the social order, though Niiike does not regularly observe all of these. Traditionally the seating order at family meals is as rigidly prescribed as the protocol at government banquets. The household head, in the place of honor (*yokoza*) on the "upper" side opposite the kitchen area, usually is flanked by his male heirs in order of birth, while females of the household are ranged opposite, along the "lower" side. "Only priests and fools sit in the master's place." The center of reference is the master's seat. A secondary center is the wooden tub which keeps the rice warm. This is placed on the kitchen side of the eating circle under the care of the house-mistress, whose symbol of household authority is, in fact, the rice paddle she uses to fill the individual bowls from the tub. Traditionally, women and girls eat with the men and boys, but they are served last, are skimped when food is short, and do not take the initiative in mealtime conversations. Frequently, the house-mistress and her main helper are too busy cooking and serving others to eat until later. Grandparents, who once occupied the seats of command, often cook and eat separately as a sign of their retirement from the responsibility for the household. The seating and serving pattern of traditional family meals exemplifies the hierarchical organization of traditional social relations. Its repetition three or more times daily is doubtless effective in reinforcing children's awareness of the lessons in hierarchy they are given elsewhere.

Since these rigid seating patterns are still observed in many traditional Japanese communities, it is significant to note the laxity with which these rules are observed in Niiike. Most adults recognize the principle governing seating arrangements, and some households, those headed by more elderly or conservative men, follow the principle fairly strictly. But in this community of relatively weak hierarchy, not even within the household does hierarchy override other considerations. Seating arrangements tend to be flexible: the household head sometimes eats at the "lower" side where he can dangle his muddy feet over the dirt floor if he chooses to eat without scrubbing himself first; the toddling child, regardless of sex, may be seated next to the father or a grandparent who can watch over the bowl and chopsticks in tiny fingers while the mother is busy at the stove; grandparents do not eat separately, and those households which have adopted a family table with benches set on the dirt floor admit to no fixed seating order except the informal one of habit. Only at banquets does Niiike invariably use the standard patterns of hierarchical protocol and pay close heed to the conventions of seating and serving.

All considered, Niiike's habits in connection with food and its consumption are relatively conservative. As just noted, etiquette associated with eating has relaxed; also, people have added a few minor vegetables and prefer polished rice over the husked but unpolished rice that was customary several generations ago. Such changes are relatively slight, however, by comparison with changes described in connection with housing, tools, or clothing. In their conservatism with regard to food, it may be noted, they are not unlike the Japanese people in general, who are justly famed for their adaptation and experimentalism in other areas but have been "old fashioned" about their eating. Even city dwellers have gone very slowly until the last decade or so in altering their food preferences or their modes of preparing and serving food. Hence it is not strange, perhaps, that rural people such as those of Niiike use none of the available canned foods except for a few condiments and are both quite unfamiliar and totally unconcerned with exotic cuisines. Their own fields supply most of their own food. To shift diet greatly without abandoning a large measure of self-sufficiency would require changing their patterns of cultivation. No push in this direction is likely, for the simple reason that other factors in agriculture far outweigh the question of what people like to eat. Agricultural change is more likely to be the cause than the result of changing food habits, as the succeeding chapters dealing with land use and agricultural practices will make clear.

6. Land and Water

The serried paddy fields lying beneath the pine-garbed hills of the Okayama Plain give an impression of changeless antiquity. Even the unhurried, deliberate movements of the farmers as they work among their crops or in their drying yards contribute to the aura of timelessness which lies over the landscape. There are evidences of the past all about. Yet the scene itself has been constantly changing. This landscape contains few of the natural features as they were a thousand years ago. They have been modified over the centuries and are still being reshaped by man. Over the centuries men have effaced the sluggish, estuarine streams that once drained these valleys. They have diked the Ashimori River to curtail its floods and have dug ditches to drain the swamps. Men have made ponds to hold irrigation water and later have erased them to set fields in their place. Men have cut down the ancient forests, terraced the hillsides for crops, and then once more covered the hills with trees. At a pace measured in generations, from the time of first settlement through the medieval projects of drainage, clearing, and canal-building to the modern period when revision of the ditch system transformed and rationalized the entire pattern of rice fields, the farmers of this valley have transformed the landscape. These many generations of planning and reconstruction were unified by the consistent effort to feed an increasing population. Flood control, new varieties of crops, alteration of soil conditions, and the adoption of new agricultural techniques all contributed to this effort. The wasteful prehistoric chieftains, it is true, placed their great tombs in the middle of the fields, but every other move affecting the appearance of the valley floor and hills, or even the distribution of houses, can be interpreted in terms of more efficient planting and management of fields.

Rice cultivation has been the central theme in the development of Okayama agriculture. From the dawn of agriculture in Japan, irrigated rice has been the overwhelmingly important crop. Dry fields have been used largely for supplemental purposes; even the dwindling forests and meadows have been used to support rice growing, providing green cuttings to fertilize the paddy fields. Today 56 per cent of all Japan's cultivated land is in paddy. In Niiike this figure is 85 per cent. Wet rice cultivation has been a potent force shaping communities such as Niiike. Its implications must be understood before we can adequately comprehend the problems of land and water faced by the people.

Even at a simple level of technology, rice grown with ample water provides a maximum yield per unit of cultivation. Water acts as a retardant to weeds and certain insects and in other ways aids the cultivator. In particular, nitrogenous bacteria that flourish in the still water covering the fields constantly replenish the soil and make possible its repeated use. Thus, apart from the high yield, wet growing conditions minimize the need for crop rotation. These natural qualities provide a secure and constant base for an agricultural population, contrasting in important respects with the technique of dry farming familiar in Europe. Europe's traditional agricultural technology centers around grains that grow well under dry soil conditions: wheat, barley, rye, and oats. It puts a premium on diversity of land use and rotation of crops. It has fostered close integration between animal husbandry and agriculture, since the constant need for fertilizer has made the Western farmer depend on manure from his animals.

Thus, starting with cereal crops that grow well under different conditions, two distinct agricultural technologies have grown up on opposite sides of the Eurasian continent. Farmers of the Orient increasingly have emphasized intensive cultivation of land, perfecting irrigation systems and organizing their communities to manage them. They have become able to grow two or more crops annually in the same field. As units of cultivation have grown small, maximum production per unit has been achieved by lavish expenditure of human energy. In contrast, most occidental farming has more land available, so its techniques are prodigal of land, e.g., fallowing and the grazing of large animals. As acreage expands, these techniques permit less manpower per acre and lower unit costs; so the system encourages extending the acreage of each farm. Substitution of machines for man and animal power fits the logic of this *extensive* farming, which is probably most highly developed today in the American Middle West. Instead of more crops per man hour, however, *intensive* farming develops the logic of more crops per acre; it reaches a peak in Japan's small, double-cropped farms. In their version of the equation, MANPOWER UNITS + LAND UNITS = CROP UNITS. Land units are necessarily tiny, so they boost manpower in order to produce peak crops.

Intensive cultivation of rice tends to impose certain conditions on the society it supports. Its high yield stimulates dense population; its heavy requirements of manpower in turn depend on dense population. Paddy technology is complex and demanding. Preparation of paddy fields and the planting and transplanting of rice are laborious operations little amenable to types of mechanization devised to date. Rural Japan thus has long used its heavy concentration of population as a work force. Problems arise from the fact that this population is usefully employed only through a limited season; but the workers live the year around on the farm, so they often face long periods of underemployment or, as it is called in Japan today, "concealed unemployment." This lack of year-round work, however, does not contradict the reciprocal relation between rice and population; as population rises to take care of cultivation, the methods of cultivation must be intensified to produce food for the increased number of mouths.

Paddy culture is self-perpetuating in yet another way. The amount of labor and capital put into the creation of paddy land provides a continuing incentive to maintain the system. The construction of paddy fields is laborious and costly, hard for those familiar only with "natural" agriculture to comprehend. The fields must be constructed to hold water an exact inch or two deep over the entire surface. In preparing them the farmer must frequently start several feet below the surface and build up with carefully graded soils. Moreover, each paddy plot must be linked to an irrigation system, which in itself is often a major undertaking. The same irrigation system must also provide proper drainage of rain and ground water during the seasons when the fields are dried. This complex system of terraced fields and interlacing irrigation and drainage ditches is not easily assembled, nor is it easily modified. It becomes the cherished heritage of an entire community generation after generation.

In the final analysis this type of technology leaves a strong imprint on the community which engages in it. Each household, as a unit of production as well as ownership, needs internal cohesion and co-operation to keep and make the most of its landholdings. The household, in turn, must look to the local community, both as a source of co-operative labor at crucial times and as the management unit for irrigation. Close associations among households exist in most areas of Japan today, even though the forms of association vary sharply according to local conditions (see chap. 10).

Beyond the level of the family the social implications of paddy culture merge with many other molding forces, yet the effects of this technology are clearly visible. Intensive cultivation under these conditions tends to limit returns to a subsistence level. The great supply of labor tends to limit the mechanization of agriculture. In so far as the workers must be fed from their limited land, food crops cannot readily be supplanted by ones that have high market value or shifted to meet variable market demands. Farmers with low income on scarce and high-priced land tend to lose their independence and, in any case, lack income for improvement. Agricultural improvement frequently depends upon government or the wealthy and powerful. Land reclamation and water management tend to lie beyond control by the individual farmer and rest with the community, the landlord, or the feudal lord. In Japan, as in other Asian countries with similar economic features, political power has been closely related to the control of land and water.

Important though land is to contemporary Niiike, it is no longer the sole reliance for every household or for the community as a whole. Recent measures have pushed back the threat of landlordism, and the circle that leads from rising population to more intensive cultivation and back to newly increasing population has been broken by outside economic factors as well as ones internal to the community. Discussion of these factors, however, is deferred to the succeeding chapter.

LAND TYPES AND THEIR USE

Every square rod of land in the Okayama Plain is precious. The average Niiike household owns somewhat less than three acres of productive land, which must provide not only food for the household but the produce sold to the city as well. Because the premium is high on land that can be made to produce heavily and constantly and because rice outproduces every other crop, irrigable rice fields are most prized, particularly if they will produce a second crop. In ordinary conversation people take irrigated land as the measure of a family's holdings. Yet other types of land are listed on the tax records. In the productive category, two other kinds are important: dry field and wood lot. Uncultivated land, of some importance elsewhere for pasture and other purposes, is inconsequential in the vicinity of Niiike. Other private holdings include lots for farmhouses and outbuildings and privately owned ponds or canals.

Communally owned land, although minimal, also exists in Niiike. It comprises the cemetery, the lots upon which the village assembly hall and fire-equipment shed are built, and one patch of wood lot. The last is owned in common by all buraku of upper Shinjō ōaza, which use it only as a source of wood for funeral cremations. Roads, paths, canals, and streams are public property and not taxed, although responsibility for upkeep belongs to the buraku or larger entities, depending upon their location and importance. The space given to these is restricted. Cultivation is the primary goal.

The importance of paddy land can be illustrated in two ways. In 1956 in the Okayama Plain, paddy land was selling at prices ranging between $1,100 and $2,300 per acre. (The figures here approximate the real price rather than the nominal price fixed by government regulation.) At this price, most Niiike farmers have holdings worth $4,000 or more, equal in value to ten or twenty acres of farmland in the American Middle West. This comparison is inadequate, not only because the prices of other things such as housing differ, but also because there are aspects of landholding that defy calculation in monetary terms. Cultivated land is so hard to get that those who possess it often are unwilling to sell at any price, to the vexation of public officials who must then confiscate land required for public or industrial developments. The fact that cultivation can compete in cash profits with other land uses helps to explain why plots of rice may be seen growing well inside the fringes of a city. In non-economic terms, the value of paddy land can also be illustrated by a distinctive system of place names. Peaks and promontories, streams and valleys very often have no standard names. A river or stream may change its name every few hundred yards along its course, and the same mountaintop will be known by different names to the persons who live north and to the persons who live south of it. By contrast, almost every little parcel of paddy land has its distinctive name, which it has carried through generations, sometimes from as far back as the Taika Reform of A.D. 645. Dry fields and wood lots rarely have acquired names in this fashion.

Yet every household, for healthy economic balance, needs to own wood lot and dry field as well as paddy land, The wood lot, at the minimum, supplies kindling for winter warmth. Dry fields provide much of the household's food. Once minimal needs have been met, few households strive to increase their dry-field holdings. These remain nearly constant while either paddy land or forest holdings are built up. New or impoverished households, who must worry first about subsistence rather than cash production, are apt to have a high proportion of dry fields. Some conception of the balance of landholdings in Niiike is given in Table 1.

Dry-field acreage varies much less from the average than does the area of paddy land or of wood lot, as the acreage figures show. The smallest owner, Iwasa Tamaichi, one of the evacuees who took up life in Niiike on whatever land he could get during the war, is short in all three categories. He has to make up his deficiency even in dry-field produce by money earned from his side trade as a barber. Note, however, that even the largest landowner has not a great deal more dry field, for such land has little value either for current income or as investment. Dry fields are gauged to meet subsistence needs within the household but are not increased beyond this point if paddy land or wood lot can be purchased. Land reform did not touch dry-field holdings, so it has not altered this situation.

The distribution of land types shown in Table 1, while valid for the average household today, differs markedly from the balance prevailing in Niiike until a generation ago. The farmers of Niiike have shifted in recent years to an increasing emphasis upon paddy farming for a number of reasons, among them the increased importance of cash-crop farming, the collapse of the market for locally grown cotton, and the improvement of hitherto marshy paddy land. To make clear the reasons for this shift, we must briefly review the recent history of land development in the

TABLE 1

Type of Land	Average Holding		Largest Holding		Smallest Holding	
	Percentage	Acres	Percentage	Acres	Percentage	Acres
Paddy field	58.0	1.57	33.1	2.88	28.5	.18
Dry field.	10.4	.28	3.9	.34	30.8	.20
Wood lot.	31.6	.86	63.0	5.49	40.7	.26
Total.	100.0	2.71	100.0	8.71	100.0	.64

vicinity of Niiike. Although this is the history of a local change, it typifies changes which have brought about an increase of paddy land throughout Japan.

Niiike is a young settlement compared to its neighboring buraku, most of whose beginnings go much further back than the several centuries Niiike can claim. Niiike's first settlers struggled with drainage problems, for much of their land was backmarsh. To judge from the shapes of fields and their names, drainage problems first were solved nearest the river, probably because river silts deposited there raised the land level. Historical records show that cultivation near the river antedates the Taika Reform which reworked some of these fields into the regular *jōri* pattern. During the following centuries, fields closer to the head of the subsidiary valleys were brought under cultivation, and the land at the head of the side valleys was reclaimed last. Niiike, pocketed at the very head of its little valley, was the last area to be drained and cultivated. Piecemeal attacks on the ever present drainage problem up to 1925 had resulted in meandering ditches that crosscut the fields into tiny, irregular shapes. A large gash was cut across the valley floor by a diked ditch that led run-off water from the hills on the north across the valley to the prehistoric moat at the base of Tsukuriyama and thence drained into the Ashimori River. Although this ditch was built to protect the acres lying between it and the Ashimori River, floods recurred, and one tract—the Shinjō Depression— although cultivable, remained so swampy that wry jokes were made about outsiders who, blundering through its footpaths, fell in and were never seen again. The dike of the large ditch, moreover, prevented the river water from reaching the land in front of Niiike in dry periods. Irrigation water had to be supplied by a good-sized pond immediately west of the present village. The presence of this pond, according to one local conjecture, accounts for the name Nii-ike, or "new pond." Thus the Niiike settlement grew to much its present size by combining intensive use of the dry fields on the hill behind the settlement with the greatest possible use of the unsatisfactory paddy fields in front.

The worst features of this situation were corrected through a large-scale program of land improvement begun in 1925. At that time the central government, seeking a monumental enterprise to commemorate the reign of the Taishō emperor, made special funds available for irrigation and land improvement loans. All over the nation a wave of projects ensued which resulted in "Taishō ponds," "Taishō canals," and "Taishō dams." The project centering on this valley affected not only Niiike and other buraku of Kamo village but the buraku of neighboring villages as well. It never was fully completed because its cost outran the ¥240,000 fund raised to finance the project. Instead of seventy-two additional acres of fields, only twenty-four acres were created, and some land still lies too low to produce two crops each year.

Niiike, however, profited immensely from the improvements. Leveling of the entire valley floor between 1925 and 1930 made possible parallel ditches for drainage and irrigation between large, rectangular fields over most of the area; the earlier, irregular pattern, preserved where ancient tombs were not completely leveled, makes a striking contrast (see Fig. 20). A uniform grade of feeder-drainage ditches was established to enlarge and straighten the fields; a better drainage ditch carried run-off water from the hills on the north to the Ashimori without impeding irrigation from the river; in place of the large local pond, which shrank to a fraction of its former size, water became available from Taishō Pond in the hills of Yamate village. Also, a new road built from the highway across the valley past the settlement was wide enough to admit motor vehicles, thus vastly improving the village's communications.

Before this improvement of paddy land, most households in Niiike acquired their cash income from cotton grown on the hillside fields behind the buraku. Cotton was then a major product of the Okayama Plain, where some of Japan's largest spinning mills had been built after the Meiji Restoration. The mills later turned to the cheaper and more plentiful cotton imported from the United States and southern Asia. The market for domestic cotton thus declined sharply after 1910. The Niiike

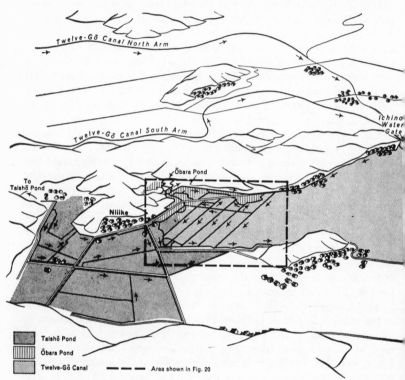

Fig. 19.—Main irrigation and drainage ditches of Niiike, 1950, showing the flow of water and the fields served by each water source.

farmer turned to raising mat rush, the basic material for the covering of floor mats. A swamp plant, this rush could be grown as a second crop even in hard-to-drain paddy fields. Intensive use of chemical fertilizer began about the same time. Household labor was needed now in the paddy fields or could be profitably employed in weaving the mat rush into *tatami* covers. Gradually cultivation of the hillside dry fields was abandoned, and pine trees were planted. Today the major part of Niiike's cash income is derived from the cultivation of rice and mat rush. Niiike became a paddy farming village.

All parts of the valley floor low enough to lead water to are utilized for paddy. As has been said, such land is not merely cleared, it is constructed, beginning with the subsoil. Where decomposed granite from the hillsides forms the subsoil near Niiike, drainage is adequate; but where the base is muck derived from the original stream or swamp, proper drainage can be insured only by adding loads of gravel to lighten the soil. Over this

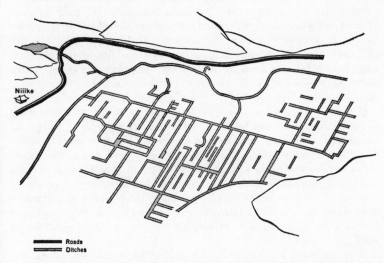

Roads
Ditches

Fig. 20.—A portion of Niiike's fields in 1892, before the revision of the ditches. Compare the crop area with the fields in the area demarcated by broken lines in Fig. 19.

base soil is the surface mud, made black by tons of organic material added through the centuries. This is carefully leveled and surrounded by a low dike. Even after such careful construction, fields are not identical in their characteristics. Some are overwatered when rains are heavy. Others go dry during a drought. The wetter fields can grow only one crop a year or three crops in two years; most desirable are the fields which bear two crops each year. The most swampy fields of all, in the Nishinuma sector, are rarely planted to anything other than vetch in winter, for they can never be drained, as is required one year in every three for growing mat rush as a winter crop. But even here the unending pressure for more crop land has led to such experiments as planting wheat in wide-spaced furrows, each furrow piled extra high to raise the roots above the standing water in the troughs.

Dry fields lie above the practical limit of irrigation. In much of the Okayama Plain, particularly the eastern half, dry fields are valuable for their orchards. The relatively dry summer climate of Okayama is beneficial for fruit. But in Niiike only two households in recent times have grown fruit for outside, city markets. Niiike's hillside fields are more important for their crops of dry grains, white and sweet potatoes, beans, and root and leaf vegetables that serve primarily for family consumption. Most of the dry fields are terraced or sloped on the hillside behind the housing area and along a strip that extends around the upper slopes of Ōbara Pond. Chemical fertilizer and compost are used chiefly in the paddy fields, but night soil is used in the dry fields. This permits their intensive use, both through cultivation of successive crops throughout the year and through intercropping or "multi-story" cropping, the system under which one sees in a single field rows of vegetables planted between rows of grain, the whole overtopped by a grape arbor or fruit trees.

One major contrast in the economic function of dry and wet fields appears in the division of household labor. Adult men, women, and young people past school age all work in the fields. The men are invariably found in the paddy fields, not merely because of plowing and other heavy work, but because these fields produce the primary cash crops. Women and young people also work in the paddy fields, particularly at periods of peak labor, but the cultivation of dry fields on the hillside is almost exclusively their concern. The household head wields a hoe or other small hand tool in a dry field only if he raises fruit, melons, or some vegetables for sale.

There is wood lot on the hillside behind the settlement which was planted when cotton-growing was discontinued forty years ago. This wood lot meets the regular needs of each household. But most families also keep some plots of trees on the mountain slope across the valley for lumber and for winter firewood. Fast-growing species, particularly red pine, predominate; these are the trees that are massed in dark green profusion on top of nearly every hill rising out of Okayama Plain. The original, native vegetation of hardwoods such as oak and maple was cut centuries ago in most localities, to provide fuel and building lumber for the dense population of the coastal plain. Even the fast-growing species must be husbanded carefully to prevent denudation and consequent erosion, a danger of which the farmers in this area of torrential rains are keenly aware. The potential commercial value of trees has led a few households to acquire additional wood lot as an investment. During the war, higher prices and government exhortation led some households to sell patches of pine which were cut, sent away, and used in an ill-starred attempt to produce aviation fuel from resin. Such patches of land have been replanted to peach trees and edible bamboo.

Most of the smoke haze that hovers over the valley from the evening bath and cooking fires comes from rice straw, the primary cooking fuel. Charcoal, produced in the mountains and bought through stores, is used in small handfuls to provide most of the winter heat. Unlike many areas of Japan, compost made from pine needles, grass, and brush swept from

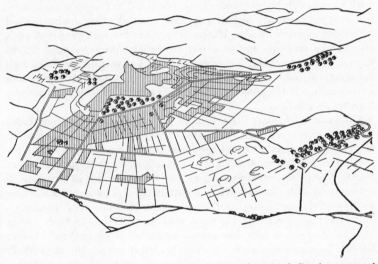

FIG. 21.—Land owned or cultivated by residents of Niiike, shown by shading, is concentrated near their houses. Wood lots, not set off here, cover the hill behind the houses and part of the hill on which we stand.

beneath the trees is only of minor importance in Niiike. Nonetheless, the wild grasses which luxuriate through the summer are cut in the fall and the ground beneath the trees raked clean to make compost piles.

As in villages throughout Japan and the Orient, the land owned and worked by any one household of Niiike buraku is fragmented into many small, scattered parcels. This fragmentation and dispersal of landholdings has been a matter of concern to agricultural economists on account of the limitations such a system imposes on farm management. The factors leading to fragmentation and scattering are real and enduring.

Roughly speaking, the buraku and its lands form a unit centered upon the housing area (see Fig. 21). Most of the fields of Niiike lie together, distinct from fields belonging to people of other buraku. Until the land reform of 1946–47, anyone was able to buy and cultivate land wherever he could obtain it. Various land reform regulations now make it difficult for a person to obtain land unless he is an inhabitant of a nearby community. However, it is the convenience of having fields near one's house, rather than any legal necessity, that tends to concentrate a buraku's landholding. The unity, however, is far from being perfect. Various households in Niiike own plots of one or another type of land relatively distant from their own community. Conversely, the farmers of nearby buraku own and work a certain number of fields close to Niiike. The fringes of each buraku's holdings are made decidedly ragged by the way they are interlocked with fields of other buraku. Habits of co-operation with people of one's own buraku make it, on the whole, somewhat more convenient not to have an outsider working a neighboring field, but there is no strong feeling against outside ownership. Thus, it is only personal convenience and a general sense of the fitness of things that brings most land of the buraku together as a unit.

The pattern of distribution of land owned by any single household, however, is quite different. The acreage held by each house is made up of patches and plots scattered here and there, the number of such plots ranging from a minimum of eight to a maximum of thirty in the case of Niiike. Except for wood lots across the valley, Niiike is fortunate in having most of its fields close to the settlement. Yet for any given household, two fields seldom lie together or even on the same path. This maximizes the time spent carrying tools, seed, and fertilizer to fields and in bringing the harvest back. The same time and effort are required whether the field be a quarter-acre in size or only a few dozen square yards. Well-established households with more fields have greater carrying distances than newer dependent households with fewer plots. But the "portal to portal" distances range from 145 to 945 feet. Actually house-to-field distance in Niiike is trifling compared with that of farmers in the foothills and mountains, who measure their house-to-field distances in terms of hundreds of yards rather than feet. But in either case a great deal of effort is consumed non-productively as a consequence of the scattering of fields. Because of the miniature scale of transport vehicles required to negotiate the narrow paths between paddy fields, several trips to a single field are often necessary for completing one operation, such as the scattering of fertilizer. This wastage of manpower is only one consideration that makes field scattering disadvantageous for farm management. Fragmentation poses great difficulties for mechanization or a possible trend toward market production of one main crop. Each field must be cultivated as a sep-

arate and distinct operation, raising tractor fuel consumption per cultivated acre to an almost prohibitive figure and canceling most of the advantages gained from working a single crop. It requires little imagination
to see how fragmentation developed. Family holdings are seldom split
among heirs but are passed on as a unit to a single heir. However, small
plots are acquired, exchanged, and sold piecemeal as family fortunes fluctuate, new fields are developed, or the balance of cultivation is shifted.
Older households, especially head households, tend to show more cluster-
ing of fields than younger or branch households, especially in areas of

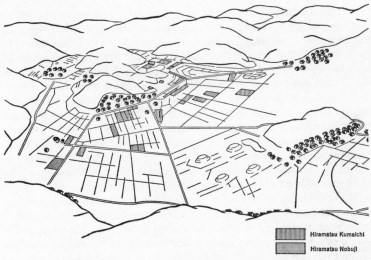

Hiramatsu Kumaichi
Hiramatsu Nobuji

Fig. 22.—Dispersal of landholdings; the fields belonging to Hiramatsu Kumaichi and those
belonging to Hiramatsu Nobuji (separately shaded) include patches in every sector of Niiike.

double-crop paddy. This is evidence of their recognition of the advantages
of having fields close together. Nonetheless, the continuance of fragmentation testifies to the centrifugal tendencies built into the traditional land
tenure system.

Yet, it should be noted that there are certain advantages in the scattering of fields. To the extent that each household is self-sufficient but
makes its living from a very small total acreage, this acreage must be
scattered in order to incorporate the different sorts of land required for
different crops. Scattered holdings also provide some local security against
natural disasters. If the crops are ruined in certain fields by flood, drought,
or blight, others may escape. Finally, the appraising eye of the tax collec-

tor, who is traditionally regarded in the same category with natural disasters, may miss one or more fields when he visits the village to compare actual holdings with the tax records. Consequently, scattered holdings do provide security, both in terms of satisfying the diverse needs of the household and in terms of offsetting natural calamities. The farmers themselves, more concerned with the lessons of past experience than with promises of future development, have not until recently shown any serious discontent with the situation as it is.

WATER CONTROL: IRRIGATION AND DRAINAGE

Let the farmer labor ever so hard and manage ever so craftily to acquire land for his family's security, this security is valueless unless he has access to water. It is meaningless to own rice land without water. In recognition of this vital connection, legal water rights automatically go with the ownership of irrigated land. Despite such interdependence, the use of land and the use of water differ in one vital respect. Land is operated by each household as a unit. However, single households do not control irrigation water, except for very small ponds. Water is managed by communities. The households of Niiike participate in water-use communities of varying sizes, all of which are larger than the buraku itself. Community management of this vital resource has extremely serious implications for social and economic organization. Land management unites the household; water management unites the community.

Water-control problems are not limited to irrigation. Drainage and protection against flood are also of constant concern. Every measure taken to prevent drought must work also against inundation. These contradictory needs, together with the conflicting demands of the various members of the irrigation community, make delicate and complicated the arrangement of water courses, water gates, ditches, dikes, and ponds. One cannot but marvel at the resourcefulness which, over the centuries, has provided for these conflicting needs. By the same token, one comes to understand that the inadequacies that remain cannot be settled by easy means.

The water needs of crops are so well controlled through irrigation that the day-to-day fluctuations of direct precipitation concern the farmer only when they pose a drainage problem. Ultimately, rainfall over the river drainage basins in the hills is more important than rain falling directly on the fields. Local rainfall is only a small part of the larger problem of controlling run-off to prevent or reduce floods, and this in turn is but one aspect of the problem of water control. Water control means holding back the water in times of overabundance, saving it for use when it is critically needed, and distributing it equitably to all who have a call on it.

The days when water problems were met by the buraku or its component households are lost in antiquity. Today these problems transcend buraku limits. They are handled at the lowest level by the various ōaza and, beyond that, by organizations of larger scope. Irrigation, in fact, involves the prefectural and the central governments; national measures for river control, dam-building, and land reclamation have direct impact upon the buraku. But, in contrast to many phases of life which the central government absorbs completely once it touches them, irrigation problems are too complex and variant to permit higher government to take over and mold the situation at will. Water control is vital to the national economy —the rice harvest as a whole may fluctuate 20 per cent or more between wet and dry years. Higher levels of government are therefore deeply concerned with irrigation and drainage. But they must rest content with sharing this responsibility with local units of government.

Among Okayama coastal plain communities Niiike has a somewhat below average proportion of irrigated land. Moreover, because of poor drainage, even this land is below average in its ability to support two crops a year. Whereas 85 per cent of Niiike's cultivated land is in paddy, Kamo village as a whole has 95 per cent in paddy. For all of Okayama Prefecture, which embraces mountain land up to the Chūgoku Divide as well as coastal plain, irrigated land amounts to 57 per cent of all cultivated and pasture land. A large sector of rugged mountains bordering Hiroshima on the west, where all villages have less than 50 per cent and sometimes as little as 20 per cent paddy land, is responsible for the low prefectural average. Everywhere else, the proportion of paddy land is above 50 per cent and rises almost to 100 per cent in some villages of the coastal plain.

The figures for irrigation facilities suggest the complexity of irrigation development in the prefecture as a whole: there are 10,000 irrigation ponds and somewhat more than 5,700 inlets from streams. Despite this, drought and flood are perpetual threats. The people of Okayama remember the severe droughts of 1925, 1945, and 1946, when pond-watered land lost up to 60 per cent of its crop. They also recall 1953 when typhoons brought floods from one end of Japan to the other. Nonetheless, Okayama Prefecture is relatively well favored. Floods are seldom as severe as elsewhere, and the folk tradition of *amagoi*, a communal gathering around a great fire built on the hillside to call for rain in time of severe drought, is less frequently encountered than in other parts of Japan. Okayama's advantage over other prefectures is partly due to its natural setting, its screen of mountains south and north that protect it from typhoons and winter storms but provide a good rain shed. Beyond this, Okayama Prefecture escapes severe damage because its water-control facilities are far advanced.

Niiike has access to almost every important type of irrigation and drainage resource. The resources for irrigation include small ponds owned and managed by individuals, ponds managed by communities, canals owned and managed by irrigation co-operatives, and rivers in the public domain. Individually owned and managed ponds are of minimal importance in Niiike, although in areas where other water facilities are limited they may be instruments of economic coercion for the benefit of their owners. Counting even the tiny ponds used primarily for raising fish or planting lotus for its edible roots, there are sixteen. These are scattered about Niiike's fields, mostly around the uphill fringes of the main pond, Ōbara. Most are the property of individual Niiike households, but two are owned jointly by a man from Niiike and a man from the buraku of Horen. One pond, remnant of the original main water resource of the buraku Einoike, serves for little save a water reserve for fire-fighting. Title to the two larger ponds providing irrigation water for Niiike is held by the central government, so that no one pays taxes on them. This arrangement at the same time precludes their being manipulated for power purposes by an individual owner. The smaller one, Ōbara, is managed by farmers of Niiike buraku alone, on a volunteer basis, a system which exemplifies the ancient tradition of water management. The second and larger pond, Taishō, supplies five buraku of Kamo and various buraku of two other villages, Misu and Yamate.

Ōbara Pond, over two acres in area, lies in an elevated hollow around a shoulder of the hill from the housing area of Niiike. Water from this pond reaches fields totaling somewhat over 10 acres (4.11 *chō*), almost all of which are owned by Niiike residents. It is operated jointly by the sixteen households whose fields receive its water. In groups of four, the heads of participating households take turns as water guards, rotating variously over a cycle of sixteen years. Those who benefit least, through having the smallest acreage involved, work the least. But the duty is not onerous. It comes principally during the one hundred days of rice growing in the summer when one to two inches of water are constantly needed on the fields. The period of transplanting mat rush during January and February again brings a brief tour of duty. This system of management exemplifies the older tradition: service is rendered by the persons who benefit, on a pattern of co-operative, rotating responsibility carried on without written rules and without a formal director. The farmers on water-guard duty receive pay for their services but at a token rate. The money comes from an assessment per acreage and is paid to the guards in two ways: a direct payment from the landowners concerned, and a payment from water taxes transmitted through the ōaza.

Formally, the ōaza is the unit in charge of Ōbara Pond and other ponds within its domain. Although it may leave the operation of the pond to the discretion of the buraku that benefits chiefly or entirely, the ōaza in effect is responsible for the system of water guards and is in charge of maintenance and repair. Each pond may be thought of as having three parts: the pond basin and dam, the lead-off ditches to the fields, and the feeder-ditches from the hills. Maintenance of small lead-off ditches is invariably the responsibility of the buraku, whatever the source of water. But the ōaza, using a portion of all irrigation assessments paid to it, employs "engineers" (who often are part-time farmers) to inspect and do minor maintenance of the ōaza irrigation system and to submit to the village office estimates of costs for major repairs.

Maintenance and repairs take place for the most part quite inconspicuously. However, each three or four years every pond must be drained in order to clean out weeds and water grasses and to inspect the ladderlike rows of outlet plugs. This becomes a festive occasion for the entire neighborhood, since the draining ordinarily takes place in the slack season while the rice fields are dry for ripening. The water guards set a convenient date and spread the word around the neighborhood. Old and young gather from all directions. Men and boys make great sport of wading through the shallows of the larger ponds to net fish and stab the slippery eels, and the spectators delightedly watch them getting splashed and muddy. The fish harvest is a respectable one, and it would be unneighborly of Niiike to take it all for itself. Anyone is welcome to join the festivities and share the catch, whether he uses the water of Ōbara Pond or not.

Taishō Pond lies to the west of Niiike in Yamate village. Pocketed in a group of higher hills, it is larger and deeper than Ōbara Pond and has twelve levels of drains as against three for Ōbara. Its water irrigates about 120 acres, divided among adjoining parts of three villages: Kamo, Misu, and Yamate. Built thirty years ago during the ditch-revision program of the 1920's, its management follows a new tradition of professionalism. Money collected on an acreage basis from all farmers who receive irrigation water goes from the respective buraku to their various ōaza and from there via the village offices to the office of Yamate. Yamate uses some of this money for maintenance and with the remainder hires a guard at a token annual salary of ¥987, less than $2.75. The present system of a single guard is a change introduced in 1947. Prior to that there had been five. One may well wonder why five guards should have been needed to do the work that obviously makes only a part-time job for one man. The original five guards were chosen from the three villages in approximate ratio to the land irrigated in each village. We may suppose the reduction was made after a generation of use had given some assurance that no disputes were likely to arise over the distribution of water and that there was no need for each village to protect its rights by having official representation.

As compared with canals, ponds occupy relatively large areas of otherwise productive farmland. But pond water has the advantage of being easily conducted directly into gravity-flow ditches, whereas canal water must always be pumped to the ditches or fields. As many as thirty outlets may pierce the pond embankment at regular vertical intervals between high and low water levels, each outlet having its own sluice to lead the water to the regular ditch system below. Yet a field directly below a pond is not necessarily free of pumping costs. In Niiike, for example, the allocation of water from Ōbara Pond changes as the pond level drops. It is reserved during low-water periods for higher fields, not for lower ones, on the ground that to force the owners of high fields to pump water all the way up from canal level while the owners of lower fields enjoy the pond water without cost would be an unfair expense to the former. Under this low-water allotment, everyone pumps; water is lifted to the high fields from the pond, to the low fields from the canal.

Water-lifting devices, accordingly, are an essential part of everyone's farm equipment. Round about Niiike, some of this work of raising water is done by various picturesque well sweeps and water wheels. These devices now do very little of the great amount of day-to-day water-lifting, yet they are worth noting as examples of methods of older times. The sweeps, which in certain places stand tilted against the sky in clusters like a flock of alarmed wading birds, function to raise and lower buckets in wells. Except where the only water to be had comes from such wells, more efficient methods are current today. Self-acting water wheels are sometimes used at the edge of a stream or canal where a steady current flows. They cannot raise water over a high dike, but they are an ancient device, and their construction is ingenious. Around the outer rim of a large double frame of wood or bamboo, sections of bamboo that form natural tubes are lashed at just the proper angle to catch up water from the stream on the start of the upswing and empty it, on the downswing, into a trough leading to a field. The fields so served are usually ones developed temporarily (and illegally) on the government-owned bottom lands inside the dikes of a stream. Water wheel, crops, and all risk being swept away when a hard rain fills the bottom with rushing floodwater.

Throughout the irrigating season every household puts to frequent use a small, foot-powered water wheel. It can easily be dismantled into several sections, each one light enough to be carried from one field to another. When in use, the wheel, composed of paddles radiating out from the hub, is seated into a wood frame sheathing one quadrant. The frame is lodged solidly against the ditch edge, its short trough projecting over the border of the field. Two poles rise from sockets in the frame sides to support an armrest on which the operator steadies himself as he steps from blade to blade, rotating the wheel so that each blade in turn catches water and lifts it up within the sheathing to the trough. When the field is adequately watered, he dismantles his contrivance and carries the wheel, sheathing frame, armrest, and supporting poles to the next small field.

Fɪɢ. 23.—Water-lifting devices of Niiike. A foot-propelled, portable water wheel is shown assembled and in use; part of a motor-driven cylindrical metal pump is cut away to show the Archimedes'-screw moving part in the interior. The large, automatic water wheel used on the river and main ditches is not shown here.

Motorized irrigation is preferred for larger fields, provided that a path is nearby. A metal cylinder, which is open at the bottom and incloses an Archimedes'-screw core, is set into the water at the edge of a ditch so that a trough from the top of the cylinder projects over the low dike into the field. From a wheel at the top, a belt is stretched to the flywheel of the household's 4.5 horsepower kerosene motor, set nearby on its carrying sledge, and the motor spins the screw to send water gushing into the field. Powering these irrigation devices is one of the principal uses for the all-purpose motor. Weighing well over one hundred pounds at the lightest, it cannot readily be used in fields that have no nearby path or firm ground. Hence the wooden foot-turned wheel continues to be used for small or distant fields even though the motor-driven screw pump has become standard equipment on the Niiike farm.

Among water-lifting devices, there should finally be noted several large, stationary electric pumps, owned by the ōaza rather than by individual households, which help in drainage rather than in irrigation. Those that concern Niiike are installed at the dike of the Ashimori River, where they work constantly throughout the irrigating season, discharging over the dike all the water that has been pumped or led onto the fields in the valley from its ponds or canals.

Canal water supplies Niiike with about half its irrigation water. Niiike's access to this water is through its membership in a large irrigation canal organization known as the Twelve-Gō Irrigation Association (Jūnikagō Yōsui Kumiai). Its canal runs eastward from the Takahashi River. Niiike and other buraku have no independent status in this organization but participate only through their respective ōaza and villages. The organization, despite its name, includes thirteen villages and towns and contains various suborganizations at different levels. More exactly, perhaps, we should describe the whole system as being made up of two co-ordinate organizations, the Twelve-Gō (Jūnikagō) and the Six-Gō (Rokkagō) irrigation associations, with subordinate units in each. Niiike is a very small part of this organization indeed, but to understand the significance of the organization to the life of people in Niiike we must step back for a large-scale view of the whole.

Eight of the thirteen villages and towns of the Twelve-Gō Canal System, including Kamo, lie in the drainage basin of the Ashimori River four to five miles east of the Takahashi River. Their access to the Takahashi River water relieves them from dependence on the capricious Ashimori, which has a dangerously torrential flow after a heavy rain but carries little water during most of the year. The Takahashi River has provided summer water to these distant villages for more centuries than to villages close by; not until recent times was a second canal system, the Eight-Gō (Hakkagō), created for the benefit of villages and towns close to the Takahashi River. The Twelve-Gō Canal, older and larger than the Eight-Gō Canal, branches from the river at Tatai, where the river first breaks out of the hills, and moves eastward across the plain, following what may once have been the bed of the Takahashi River. It soon splits into two arms. The northerly arm follows the hills on the upper edge of the plain until it spills into the bed of the Ashimori River; take-off ditches serve nearby fields en route. The southerly arm bends down to the edge of the hills along the south and, serving as a transit canal, retains all its water until just before it reaches the Ashimori River. There, at the Iwasaki water gate, it splits into three arms. One drains into the bed of the Ashimori River, mingles with the excess water of the northern arm, and flows south to be used by villages farther downstream. Of the remaining two arms, one bends around the hills on the west side of the Ashimori and eventually reaches Niiike after having been split once more into an Upper and a Lower Shinjō Canal. The remaining arm dives under the bed of the Ashimori River to re-emerge via a siphon on the east side, where it waters the lands of eastern Kamo and its neighbors. As Figure 24 shows, Niiike gets its share of Takahashi River water only after it has been diverted by two water gates (the Tatai water gate at the Takahashi River and the Iwasaki water gate near the Ashimori River) and channeled through several

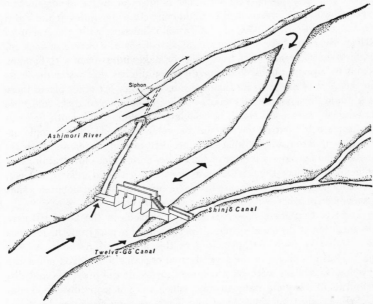

Fig. 24.—The Twelve-Gō Canal at the Iwasaki water gate. Canal water flowing from the left divides here, part crossing under the river to the far side, part going through the First Gate of Shinjō (Ichinohi) (*lower right*) and part falling into the Ashimori River bed for use downstream. In flood, the river water backs into the canal and may inundate fields between canal and river or beside the canal upstream.

branch and subbranch ditches. Niiike's lands are only a fraction of the 13,600 acres watered by the canal.

The Twelve-Gō Canal, an exceptionally important factor in the agricultural development of coastal land, is reputed to have been constructed along its present general course about A.D. 1220, serving twelve of the village-like units of the time known as "*gō*" (see p. 40). Local tradition has it that the course was laid out by Kageyasu Senotarō, who set out from the Takahashi River on horseback and had the canal dug along the twisting route he followed across the plain. Centuries afterward, as new land was created from the tide flats of Kojima Bay, the villages established there hooked onto the canal and became incorporated as downstream members of the Twelve-Gō system, which today is among the five largest irrigation systems of Okayama Prefecture.

As one follows the route of the canal and its branches today, one comes across a few control and diversion structures of recent date and modern aspect standing side by side with very humble, primitive arrangements. Prefectural loans have helped to build concrete water gates at the Tatai entrance and, since 1950, at the Iwasaki juncture with the Ashimori River. En route between the two gates, sections of concrete or rock retaining walls alternate with heavy piles or stakes interwoven with bamboo strips to support the banks. Some diversion ditches that water the fields in the vicinity are no more than holes in the bank. At other places there are crude diversion devices made of piles of submerged rocks and pine trunks laid across the canal, of calculated thickness and depth beneath the surface to control the amount of water diverted. These simple arrangements are readily displaced by accident or high water, and their reinstallation becomes a matter of sometimes acrimonious arbitration; it is difficult to replace them with more precisely measured modern devices, not only because of the expense involved, but because of jealous fears that one side or another will come out on the short end.

Tight conservatism preserves many archaisms in the administrative organization of the canal system. It derives in large part from the tensions and jealousies over the husbandry of this important resource. All the participating villages in the several canal organizations linked under the Twelve-Gō system work on a common problem: the provision and distribution of adequate water in ways which will not jeopardize flood control. But there is no single ideal solution, since some fields are disadvantaged by conditions that are ideal for others. Each unit of a canal organization is in a sense a separate sovereignty treating with others for a satisfactory working compromise. This uneasy confederation is more apt to follow historical precedent than laboratory theories of hydraulic engineering. Although co-operation is mandatory, it is not achieved without a certain amount of hard feeling or even open conflict. Serious tensions prevail at every level of the rather complex organization.

In order to use canal water from the Twelve-Gō Canal, Niiike is a member of three organizations of successively larger size, each involving it with portions of the canal farther upstream. It belongs to the smallest through its ōaza, Upper Shinjō, which joins with Lower Shinjō to clear and repair the feeder-ditch as far as the water gate at Iwasaki. The two ōaza form an organization, the Shinjō Ichinohi (Shinjō "First-Gate"). Similar minimum-level organizations composed of one to three ōaza exist all along the system. The Ichinohi ditch, it will be remembered, is only one of three ditches that branch at the Iwasaki water gate. Hence the Iwasaki gate affects not only the Shinjō Ichinohi fields but also those of the ōaza of Kamo east of the river and of the six remaining villages and towns downstream. All these, accordingly, form a co-operative, in which the several ōaza of Kamo, including the two that use Shinjō Ichinohi ditch, speak through Kamo village as their administrative unit. This is the Six-Gō organization, responsible for the Iwasaki water gate and downstream ditch maintenance. Finally, the villages of the Six-Gō co-operative, because of their interest in the head water gate at the Takahashi River and in the transit ditch from there to Iwasaki, are confederated with upstream villages as members of the Twelve-Gō organization.

Formal charters cover the structure and operation of the Twelve-Gō and the Six-Gō organizations. Several of the lower echelon organizations also have charters, but most do not. All but a few of these date from 1889, the year when present village organization was formalized, but some revisions took place about 1925, when grand plans for ditch revision focused attention on irrigation matters. Chartered associations do not differ basically from the others, for the charters did not establish them or, in essence, change them except to recognize modern village units in place of ancient ones. Each charter merely codifies tradition that has long been accepted. For example, each ōaza, as a basic participating unit of the Twelve-Gō Irrigation Association, is charged a share of the costs and allotted a percentage of water fixed to the fourth decimal point (Upper Shinjō gets 1.6071 per cent). The ratios are fixed on the basis of acreage served at some time in the distant past and have not taken into account later changes in the extent of fields. Even though charters, in a sense, merely crystallize tradition, they are nevertheless convenient and even necessary for the larger groups. Because costs vary from year to year, their apportionment in an annual budget is much facilitated by the formal organization of the irrigation group under a written charter.

The mayor of Kamo is fairly prominent in the councils of the twenty-four-man administrative board of the Twelve-Gō organization, because, by tradition, he is chief administrator of the Iwasaki water gate, located near the Kamo village office. The fact that Kamo is farthest upstream and the oldest participant in the Six-Gō system also gives him seniority.

Irrigation taxes rise as the years go by because cash expenses have gradually increased. Villagers themselves once took care of most maintenance and repair, contributing their free labor; unpaid labor is still contributed but extends only to maintenance and repair of the smallest ditches within each buraku. Cash is now needed to hire guards for each water gate, to hire workers for repair of the main canal, to pay for major improvements, and for incidental organizational expenses. These costs are met by an earmarked irrigation tax in each village budget (see p. 386).

(see p. 386)

WATER CONTROL: TENSIONS AND DISPUTES

The theoretical rights to a certain percentage of water are clearly established by charter or by tradition for each participating unit. The problem is to implement these rights in practice. The condition of the canal itself makes this difficult. At certain points, facilities are precisely and firmly fixed; for example, the dimensions of the outlet from the main canal to the Shinjō Ichinohi branch, 1.1 feet high by 3 feet broad, were fixed by arbitration and made permanent by being cast in concrete. As the people say, every man knows these figures as well as he knows his own house number. But no one has measured the precise volume and rate of flow of water either in the canal or in the river from which it comes, nor does anyone know what happens to the water as it passes over and around crumbling rock dams and rotting diversion logs before reaching the Ichinohi outlet.

Equally important as a source of friction is the tradition of unequal water rights. In time of drought the villages on the reclaimed land in Kojima Bay get shortchanged, according to their view. Their claim to this water goes back only a century, at most, and they are at the tail end of the canal. Hence, the older villages upstream claim prior right to the water. In any case they have first access to it, and it is their own people who decide, as water guards, how much to let through. Frictions, thus, are inevitable. At a still higher level, the Eight-Gō organization has gone to court against the Twelve-Gō organization in a dispute over division of the Takahashi River water. The dispute concerned the question of how high the Twelve-Gō organization ought to be allowed to build its diversionary dam. Because there is no codified law concerning water rights, the case stagnated until both parties, appalled at the mounting expense of lawyers and litigation, compromised out of court. Such friction occurs at every organizational level down to the ōaza and, in some cases, among individual farmers within the ōaza. The details of the following dispute show how difficult it is to reconcile conflicting interests.

Rice fields near the Six-Gō water gate at Iwasaki but upstream from the gate are not entitled to water from the transit canal bordering them but instead draw their water from the canal arm running along the edge of the hills to the north. The tangle of river and canal channels near the

Iwasaki gate is arranged to prevent flooding at that point but, at the same time, to water fields on the downstream side of the gate. Ordinarily, the trickle of water in the bed of the Ashimori seems much too small to justify the high dikes that border the river; the river bed serves merely as a convenient channel to carry canal water. After a hard rain, however, the river rises twelve or fourteen feet. The canal level fluctuates only slightly, owing to the fixed size of the opening from the Takahashi River. Thus, the flooded Ashimori may back up along the canal and, since no high dikes border the canal, may flood the low fields there unless the water gates are closed in time. Although the canal may serve as a safety valve for the river in flood and prevent its bursting its dikes elsewhere, farmers owning fields at this point suffer if the water gates are opened. Shortly after a heavy rain, we saw the gates standing open, the rice in low fields nearby completely under water, and a crowd of angry farmers clustered on and around the water gate. The mayor of Kamo, summoned posthaste, splashed up through the mud to learn that unknown persons, presumably those with fields at a higher level nearby, had used a bootleg crank to raise the gates and water their fields. The cultivators of the low fields, upon seeing the water rise over the top of their rice, had stormed up to the water gate and were now demanding that the gate be closed and they be compensated for damage. The mayor's decision, finally, to close the gates did not relieve him of having to hear a half-hour tirade launched against the suspected culprits, the system, and his own management, delivered with violent gestures by the disputants on both sides.

Although there is no visible end to disputes of this sort, progress can be made toward solving one of the basic irritants, periodic shortages of water. Small ponds and ditches already exploit localized ground water so thoroughly that additional water needs cannot be met except by major projects in the upstream drainage basins of large rivers. This requires action quite beyond the domain of single villages or canal co-operatives. Prefectural and national dam-building is required. Such action has been started in the postwar period. The prefecture has pushed plans for construction of major, multipurpose dams on two important rivers, the Takahashi and the Asahi. The irrigation community to which Niiike belongs is to benefit directly from the smallest of these, the Osakabe Dam. This, besides supplying 3,000 kilowatts of electricity and impounding water to diminish the flood threat along the Takahashi River, will provide irrigation water during the low-water season. A still larger dam downstream, not yet in the blueprint stage, will provide even more water than the Osakabe Dam and will further alleviate the perennial water shortage of villages on the downstream end of the Twelve-Gō Canal. The central government, which advances the entire cost to begin with, is eventually repaid 40 per cent of this amount, 15 per cent by the prefecture and 25 per cent by the participating irrigation co-operatives. This postwar dam-building, involving both local communities and the highest levels of government, is something new in water control in the Okayama Plain. It is occurring in the normal course of events rather than as a specific outcome of war or occupation. As such, it seems a token of a future in which communities such as Niiike will be linked ever more intimately into an economic and financial framework of prefectural and national scale.

WARTIME AND LAND REFORM

Niiike, like other villages, was affected by wartime and postwar developments. Men were taken away for military service, evacuees arrived, and fields changed hands under the land reform program of 1946. But none of these events struck with extraordinary force. The land reform, in fact, though almost cataclysmic in some parts of rural Japan, touched Niiike only lightly. Yet the case of Niiike illustrates very well the pattern of the problems brought by war and its aftermath.

At the end of the war Niiike was fortunate in getting most of its servicemen back safe. Hiramatsu Kameichi and his wife had gone to Korea where Kameichi drove an army truck as a civilian; five other households had given up sons to the draft or to wartime jobs. One draftee died on the Southeast Asia front, and two others returned but died in 1948 and 1952 of ailments probably incurred during their wartime absence. Though the community lost relatively few members, either temporarily or permanently, during hostilities, their absence created enough labor shortage to lead various households, at transplanting and harvest time, to revert to co-operative labor exchange of a sort that Niiike had almost forgotten before the war. The arrival of evacuees from the bombed and burned city did little to alleviate this labor shortage.

Japan's rural villages showed an astonishing capacity, crowded as they were, to absorb wartime evacuees. Niiike, where the problem occurred in more or less normal proportion, found ways to incorporate its refugees, but not without cost. Urban evacuation between 1943 and 1945 thrust three refugee households on the community, and repatriation from Korea after the armistice brought back the fourth. Thus suddenly food and shelter had to be spread among twenty more persons, almost a fifth more than before. Each of these households had a strong claim on the hamlet, for each was closely related to one of the five family lines and had forsaken the countryside only within the present generation. Two of the four had even retained a small bit of property leased to those who stayed home. But so small a stake did not go far toward giving shelter and land for livelihood. True to tradition, the community rose to the emergency as a whole, not merely as groups of separate kindred, to find a place for the evacuees. In earlier times, for example, Niiike had arranged things so that the prewar gap left by Iwasa Tsuyoshi when he migrated to Hokkaido was filled by the return from across the valley of Hiramatsu Teigo, nephew to Hiramatsu Mitsusaburō but no kin to Tsuyoshi. When the wartime evacuees arrived, they, too, got shelter and some land. Two built modestly on lots converted from dry fields, and one made shift with renovated storehouses. They retrieved their own rented fields and bought or rented enough other small parcels to establish themselves in farming, though continuing to be dependent in some degree on close relatives or neighbors for firewood, well water, or farm equipment. In 1950, their landholdings put them in the same class with newly branched households, averaging nine-tenths of an acre, about half the size of the per-household holdings for the community as a whole. This amount is considered to be about two-thirds of the minimum required to provide a living for a household unless supplemented by some other source. Hiramatsu Asae, a former detective from Osaka, and Kameichi, the truck driver repatriated from Korea, could make no use of their former skills but had to accept a scale of living so low that it was actually injurious to their health; Iwasa Tamaichi, a barber from Okayama City, though continuing his barbering in the country, has found this subsidiary income inadequate for the needs of his large family. The only evacuee household that lives at an approximately normal scale does so at the cost of a broken family. Hiramatsu Masao, employed as an engineer with a firm in Kobe, gets home for a brief visit only once in two or three weeks. Thus, despite community efforts to make adjustment, and despite their social integration after years of absence, the evacuee group lives under strained conditions. All have been counted officially as resident farmers, although the landholdings of two in reality were below the minimum (0.735 acres) to qualify them as farmers at the time of land reform.

For centuries Japanese farmers have worked persistently and vigorously for economic security. They have remodeled the landscape, harnessed the streams, and developed an intensive technology of cultivation. By the end of the Second World War, however, these efforts to achieve security through technology were seriously undermined by non-technological factors. Most important was the persistent drift of farm land into the hands of landlords, leaving a growing class landless and often tenants. Basic to this economic imbalance was the fact that Japan had virtually exhausted ts reserve of unreclaimed but cultivable land. Farm tenancy was a major and growing problem.

This is not to suggest that farm tenancy in itself is a troublesome or undesirable institution everywhere. Many of the most productive and prosperous farms of the United States, not to mention other countries, are operated by tenants who rent from absentee landlords. Under appropriate conditions, the person with capital to invest and the person with labor and skill to supply can form a mutually profitable team. One provides the land, and not infrequently buildings and equipment as well, while the other supplies the energy and know-how. Tenancy is a useful and flexible device for drawing capital into agriculture. But the system becomes onerous when the landlord alone is free to specify the terms and duration of the relationship. Land shortage creates such conditions, and extreme land shortage such as existed in Japan puts an enormous weight of advantage on the landowner's side. The tenant, unable to find unoccupied acreage elsewhere, has little choice but to accept and try to live with whatever conditions his landlord may choose to impose. In Japan and other densely populated areas of Asia and Africa, such land shortage, coupled with the absence of protective measures to equalize the balance between landlord and tenant, has been the critical factor intensifying the problem.

Japan inherited the problem of tenancy from long past. In feudal Japan the peasant was not legally bound to the soil as absolutely as in feudal Europe. Such a regulation was probably unnecessary because movement was so restricted by the scarcity of agricultural land. As Japan entered the modern period, landowners tended to be closer to the political center of gravity than the peasants, making it difficult to formulate or enforce measures limiting the power of the landowner and increasing the rights of the tenants. One effort made in 1926 to relieve the problem by legislation had only slight effect. Most of this was nullified during the succeeding nationalistic decade, when the official attitude toward the landlord-tenant problem was tempered by the landlord's greater capacity to contribute to armament and heavy industry. Rising farm prices during the war, coupled with work opportunities in war industries that drew many tenants off the land, brought a slight statistical improvement in the over-all tenancy situation. The percentage of tenant families and the percentage of tenant-cultivated land dropped slightly. But there was no basic change in the conditions making land tenancy a long-standing problem throughout the Japanese countryside.

The situation can be partially illustrated with some statistics.[1] In 1944,

[1] Figures are drawn from *Farm Tenancy in Japan* (Supreme Commander for the Allied Powers, Natural Resources Section, Report No. 79 [Tokyo, 1947]) and *Agricultural Programs in Japan, 1945–51* (Supreme Commander for the Allied Powers Natural Resources Section, Report No. 148 [Tokyo, 1951]). These reports furnish more detailed analysis of the problems sketched here and in some respects present a different viewpoint,

in Japan as a whole, the percentage of land worked by tenants ranged from 36 per cent of all cultivated land in some prefectures to 59 per cent in others. In Okayama Prefecture, tenants cultivated 43 per cent of all agricultural land. Viewed in another way, this meant that, with the exception of newly developed Hokkaido, 75 per cent of Japan's farm households held only 37.5 per cent of all cultivated land. Put another way, three-quarters of all Japanese farm families had less than the national "average" of about 2.5 acres per household, a figure arrived at by lumping large farms with tiny ones. At the other end of the scale, 3 per cent of Japan's agricultural landowners held 29 per cent of all cultivated land. Those who owned 12.25 acres (5 *chō*) or more cultivated only 30 per cent of their holdings themselves; the remainder was worked by tenants. By far the majority of tenants operated on a scale of less than 2 acres. The rental price, though differing by locality and type of field, varied usually from 50 per cent to 60 per cent of the main crop yield. The tenant ordinarily carried the costs of house, equipment, seed, and fertilizer, though taxes were paid by the landowner. In Okayama, as an example, only 30 per cent of all tenancy contracts were estimated to be in written form. Obligations such as division of costs and protection against being dispossessed without compensation, therefore, were not contractually fixed. They could be unilaterally determined by the landlord, whose absolute right to manage his own property was apt to be upheld in the rare cases that came to court.

Figures tell only part of the story. They miss the subtle play of power the landlord might exert over his tenants, the extra charges, services, and deference he might exact when his tenant was chained to one plot by perpetual debt, perhaps carried over from his father's generation. This power frequently extended to non-tenant farmers who, unable to pay for chemical fertilizer, were obliged to make compost from the sweepings of forests owned by such landlords. On the landlord's side, figures fail to point out the burden involved in the investment of money and effort to improve land, water controls, and cultivation practices. It was often landlords who reclaimed new fields from wasteland and sea bottom. It should also be understood that a very large proportion of "absentee landlords" were not great landowners but very small ones: shopkeepers, minor officials, and salaried persons who bought their lands as their sole source of income in old age. While a heavy indictment can be brought against the institution of tenancy and against the practices of individual absentee landowners, the case was not wholly one-sided.

As the Occupation opened, however, its officials were firmly determined to carry through a massive land reform. By late 1947, the data were gathered and the purpose crystallized into law, affecting paddy land, dry-field, and pasture holdings—but not the forest and wood-lot holdings—of all classes of landowners, part owners, and tenants. To reconcile execution of the land reform policy with the policy of local autonomy, as well as to permit adjustment to the special conditions of each locality, each prefecture was given considerable latitude for interpretation, and the plot-by-plot reallocations through government purchase and resale were made in each village by a locally elected land commission composed of tenants, independent cultivators, and landlords in proportions of five, two, and three. The ensuing transfer of land reduced the national tenancy rate to 10 per cent of all cultivated lands by the end of 1948. The ranks of independent but very small-scale farmers who owned all the land they tilled were greatly increased.

The limits set on ownership and rental acreage in Okayama Prefecture, although not precisely identical to those of other prefectures, show how the leveling process worked. The upper limit of land to be owned and culti-vated by one household was 4.9 acres (2 *chō*) unless the owner himself had been cultivating a larger acreage before the reform law went into effect. Additionally, one household might lease up to 1.71 acres (0.7 *chō*). Thus the maximum permitted to a single household was 6.61 acres (2.7 *chō*). This low limit spelled ruin for the Fujita Company, the private enterprise which had reclaimed and leased much of the new land in Kojima Bay area, for it was treated as a legal person and was forced to sell everything over the 6.61-acre limit. The reform also forced liquidation of the land assets, personal or corporate, of several owners holding as much as 1,000 acres by forcing them to sell at the government's near-confiscatory price of ¥2,400 ($6.66) per acre. We should note in passing that this economic loss was generally not great enough to reduce the high social, political, and economic status which these families held, thanks to their industrial and other investments. Nonetheless, as the Occupation intended, the reform opened the way to various social changes. In Kamo itself one-quarter of the cultivated land changed hands by order of the village land commission (see chap. 12). This commission also disposed of another 40 acres relinquished by the owners in lieu of paying new high taxes.

Landownership patterns in Kamo and Niiike show surprisingly little change, considering the over-all extent of land reallocation in the village. There had been no great landlords and few landless tenants. Niiike's people entered the land reform as small, independent farmers and emerged in the same condition. The same was true in many other villages on the coastal plain. Tenancy, as reflected in the prefecture-wide statistics, was concentrated in a few localities on the plain and spread more widely through the mountains in the northern half of the prefecture. Among the 550-odd farm families of Kamo, only four had owned more than 25 acres (10 *chō*). Land reform affected but a bare half-dozen households in Niiike; two had to sell, and four (including wartime evacuee families) were enabled to buy. The village land commission's job in carrying out the land reform law was clearly a delicate one. All but a very few of its cases in Kamo were of the borderline type found in Niiike. The Kamo land commission seems to have done its task thoroughly and conscientiously, whereas in many other villages social and economic pressures made the task too delicate to be carried out in the intended spirit. In Niiike we are concerned not with extremes of landlordism or tenancy but with small farmers who might rent a field or two to someone else or cultivate one or two leased fields in addition to those they owned.

Two land-short evacuees were able to buy small plots, since they were cultivating only slightly more than the one-third-acre minimum required to class them as "farmers," but the increment was not enough to give them very adequate income from farming alone. One of these two today works a field rented to him on an under-the-counter basis by a man living across the valley. Although the arrangement is satisfactory to both parties, the rent exceeds the limits permissible under land reform regulations. Two Niiike farmers lost land they owned but did not cultivate. One was Hiramatsu Isamu, whose land management leans toward cash cropping. For him, adjustment was relatively simple. The second was Hiramatsu Mitsusaburō, the Sensei of Niiike. His case is worth examining because, although a life-time resident and small cultivator in the village, he was one of the "molecular landlords" described in an Occupation publication as "salary earners, merchants, officials, money lenders or, as a supplement, hotel and brothel keepers." These are represented as "the most parasitic group living off the tenants. Their rented holdings are so small that even the rack-renting they practice is not sufficient to provide them with sufficient income."[2] This judgment seems strained in the case of the Sensei and many others like him in the villages of the Okayama Plain. Sufficiently educated to hold clerical or minor professional jobs, and unwilling, in consequence, to burden their children with their old-age support, these persons bought land as a sort of old-age insurance. The Sensei's holdings were less than four acres, lower than the maximum permitted for owned and cultivated lands. But he rented out more than the permitted one-third of an acre. Neither the Sensei, on account of his age, nor his adoptive son, holding a full-time job as teacher, could very well cultivate the total.

[2] *Farm Tenancy in Japan*, pp. 11–12.

The village land commission's ruling, therefore, reduced his rented acreage to one-third of an acre, leaving him with a total holding of 1.4 acres. About half of this was dry field or single-crop paddy land. The ailing Sensei, nearing seventy at the time of the land reform, has had to put in long hours since then, especially in the dry fields where he grows persimmons for sale. It was precisely such persons as the Sensei and his son whose orientations and aspirations were generally most in harmony with the objectives of the Occupation. It is thus one of the ironies of high-level planning that, while the co-operation of such people was being sought for local economic, educational, and other reforms by one section of the Occupation, they should be denounced as "molecular landlords" by another.

Despite his personal loss, the Sensei is among those who regard the land reform as generally successful. As a matter of fact, our survey of some 1,000 farmers throughout the Inland Sea region in 1952, four years after the reform, revealed that 65 per cent regarded the reform as successful while only 15 per cent thought it unsuccessful. The chief problem, as most of them conceive it, is not whether the reform was properly executed but whether its benefits can be expected to last. Various legal checks were instituted to prevent reversion to the old situation. For example, all land purchases have to be approved by the village land commission, written contracts embodying protections for the tenant have replaced the old-style oral arrangements, and, until 1950, land prices were frozen at a very low level. It is an open secret, however, that clandestine sales take place because of inability to pay taxes, poor management, and such things as covert pressure from still influential former landlords. Okayama's principal newspaper called attention at the beginning of 1954 to the rising rate of land sales within the prefecture.[3] In contrast to 250 known sales in 1949 and 3,300 in 1950, sales from 1951 through 1953 exceeded 10,600 per annum. The acreage involved rose from 76 acres in 1949 to 3,310 in the first three quarters of 1953. The article estimated that nearly 20 per cent of the newly independent farm households established in Okayama Prefecture by the land reform program had disappeared by the end of 1953. It concluded that the present high volume of land transfer presages a revival of extensive landlordism. Such a trend was not evident, however, in Kamo or its neighboring villages on the prosperous Okayama Plain.

[3] Unsigned feature article, *Sanyō News*, January, 1954.

7. *Niiike* AT WORK

The panorama of successive crops which continually unfolds across Niiike's valley floor from hillside to hillside is both beautiful in itself and a testimony to human ingenuity and labor. Few people work their land so carefully or intensely as the farmers of Core Japan. Niiike's farmers maintain two major crop cycles, each one varied and sharply contrasting with the other. Few Niiike fields know even a little rest, and no fallowing is tolerated unless dictated by poor drainage.

Through summer and fall, rice, the main crop, dominates the irrigated fields. The paddy fields come alive with activity in June as the men and women of Niiike set about plowing and irrigating in preparation for transplanting rice seedlings. The controlled flooding of the fields transforms the valley floor into a man-made marsh for the water-loving rice. By July most of the lowland fields are filled with neat straight lines of rice plants waving above the shallow water. But the rice has not yet crowded out all other crops. Occasional masses of dark green among the lighter green of the rice mark the mat rush (*igusa*) plantings nearing their maturity. But by late July these too are replaced by rice and the valley floor has become a sea of light green. Here and there a few small clumps of sugar cane or sweet sorghum tower over the rice. And, hidden by the growing rice, in the corners of many paddy fields are narrow plantings of vegetables. In late summer mat rush is set out in small seedbeds, to be transplanted later into the winter fields. By September the rice has reached full height, and the heads have formed. The entire valley is clothed in a monochromatic, intense green. Now the farmer's great concern is the typhoons that may threaten the ripening crops with violent winds and abrupt downpours. But the typhoon rains also relieve any threat of drought in early fall, when Ōbara Pond has been drained dry and irrigation water from other sources is at its lowest point. Finally, in October, the paddy fields are drained, and the green of the summer landscape gives way to the yellow and then brown of the harvest. The farmer watches the colors

145

closely: strong traces of white indicate the rice borer has been at work; excessive brown tells of fatal damage from typhoon winds. But at last, in between November's spasmodic drizzles, the rice is cut with small hand sickles and hung in sheaves to dry on wooden racks set up in the fields (see Fig. 25).

No sooner has the rice been removed than the earth in the drained fields is hoed and heaped into parallel elevated ridges to promote drainage and soil aeration. Winter crops are now planted, much of the acreage being devoted to subsistence crops. Winter wheat is grown for sale, but barley is important to Niiike farmers as a food supplement to rice. Rape seed is grown to make cooking oil. These crops all thrive on dry fields. But they vary in their tolerance of soil moisture, so the degree of drainage determines the fields in which each crop is planted. Some of the paddy fields, particularly those reclaimed in 1925, are so low lying and have so much surface water in the spring that they must lie fallow. A few fields are used exclusively for vegetables or the clover-like *renge*. In December and January the mat rush is transplanted into irrigated fields from the seedbeds. By this time the winter landscape has assumed a distinctive coloration, the soft brown of the unplanted patches serving as contrast to the vigorous green plants putting forth their winter growth across the face of the plain and on the adjacent slopes. The field colors are matched in mood by the variable weather of the Okayama winter, stretches of rainy, damp, and foggy weather competing with clear, crisp days of warm sunshine. Snowstorms and bad freezes are unwelcome and fortunately infrequent.

The spring that follows is by far the loveliest but also the busiest time of the annual agricultural cycle. The farmers are in the fields almost every day cultivating or fertilizing the rows of maturing winter crops, now grown tall enough to conceal the mothering earth. In April the green of the grains and rush forms a backdrop for an explosion of color, the brilliant yellow of the rape seed, the pink of the clover, the snow-white of the radish, and the multicolored display of wild flowers along the paddy field dikes and on the hillsides. Irrigation ditches are alive with frogs and the snakes that pursue them, while overhead the barn swallow swoops across the fields. Rice seedbeds are prepared in June. Small plots left vacant during the winter are plowed, irrigated, and planted. By this time spring harvest colors have replaced the floral brightness of April. Usually dry weather lasts long enough before the onset of the rainy season for the winter grain crops to be removed in quick succession, clearing the valley for the rice-growing cycle. Soon only scattered stacks of wheat and barley straw sit in the drizzle as a reminder of the winter crops. Work has already begun to prepare the fields for the rice seedlings (see Fig. 26 for spring crops).

FIG. 25.—Crops of the summer-fall season in Niiike. Comparison with Fig. 26 shows how extensively fields are given over to rice

ORCHARD

IGUSA SEEDED

FOREST

VEGETABLES

POND

DITCH

HOUSING AREA

OPEN

NON-NIIKE FIELDS

SUGAR CANE

RICE

ROAD

PATH

SCALE

0   100   200   300   400

FEET

N

RAPE
RICE SEEDED
ORCHARD
IGUSA
FOREST
VEGETABLES
POND
DITCH

HOUSING AREA
NAKED BARLEY
OPEN
NON-NIKE FIELDS
BARLEY
RENGESO
WHEAT
ROAD

N

SCALE

0   100   120   300   400
FEET

The intense seasonal cropping pattern familiar to the farmers of Niiike today is little changed from that maintained by their fathers before them. It is a system in which the production of food has been the primary concern, and its efficient scheduling leaves little opportunity for crop rotation or crop changes so characteristic of Western agriculture. Through trial and error over many generations, every Niiike family learned the varying capacities of its land, how well each field holds water, how much fertilizer it needs, how often it must be drained, and what crop it best produces. Some of the techniques and equipment Niiike farmers have used for generations. But coupled with their respect for tradition is a willingness to try what is new.

THE SEARCH FOR SUBSISTENCE

In allocating land to various crops, Niiike farmers are careful to balance their relative needs for subsistence and cash income. Once such a balance has been achieved, variation in the year-to-year schedule of crops is seldom attempted. The scarcity of land leaves no room for experimentation or for relaxation. In recent memory, however, a fairly drastic change was forced upon the Niiike crop system. This was when wartime and postwar food-control programs obliged the farmers of Niiike to discontinue the production of non-food crops. In their place were substituted dry grains, potatoes, and even some crops such as rape seed that were not grown in Niiike before the war. These changes were artificially induced and, when food controls were relaxed, prewar patterns quickly returned. Mat rush replaced dry grains and rape seed increasingly from 1949 until it resumed its prewar importance as a winter cash crop. But its production has not expanded to the point of crowding out winter-grown subsistence crops completely. Further expansion is inhibited by the nature of the rush market as well as by the farm household's need for food. Farmers know that much more rush production, when coupled with the increased crop being grown in others parts of western Japan, will result in overproduction and depressed prices. They are also aware that they must not go too far in sacrificing acreage planted to wheat, vegetables, and other foods which supply their daily needs.

Rice is the foundation of Niiike's economy. It provides an estimated 75 per cent of the buraku's staple food supply and a cash income at least sufficient to cover all major crop production costs. The farmer considers no other crop so basic to his existence. And no other crop demands so much of his attention. From planting until harvest, rice imposes on the people of Niiike the most demands for labor, special techniques, and tools.

Both ordinary (non-glutinous) and glutinous rice are grown in Niiike, and the acreage allotted to each fluctuates from year to year. Normally, however, ordinary rice is produced in much greater quantity than the glutinous. In 1950, more than 90 per cent of the rice planted in Niiike was of the ordinary type. Glutinous rice is more of a specialty crop, since it is in demand primarily for the preparation of sweetmeats. It is also a less dependable crop, since its stems are weak and the grain falls easily as it matures. Despite this drawback, a rise in market price will increase its acreage. Just before and during the first part of the war, the price of glutinous rice rose so high that it was planted in about half the Niiike paddy fields. Family preferences are also reflected in the amount of glutinous rice a farmer will grow: one likes it well enough to plant it in 30 per cent of his irrigated fields; others expand acreage only when market conditions warrant.

The rice cycle begins around May 1 with the preparation of seedbeds on small fields or portions of fields purposely left fallow during the winter. Farmers try to pick a seedbed site that is centrally located in relation to their paddy holdings to facilitate the transfer of seedlings at transplanting time. In Niiike, the seedbeds are usually grouped in small clusters on the plain or around Ōbara Pond, both major rice-growing sectors, and are planted when the main fields are still in dry crops. By the time the dry grains have been removed and the paddy fields plowed and irrigated, the rice seedlings are already a vigorous seven weeks old.

The seedbed is first plowed and irrigated. After remaining under water for three or four days, it is painstakingly worked with hand tools until it has a smooth, muddy consistency free of clods. Over this carefully worked surface, further subdivided into rectangular beds separated by narrow walkways, rice is sown broadcast. The seed rice has first been soaked in salt water for two days to cull out infertile grains. A mere 3 shō (4.7 quarts) of this selected seed provides seedlings for each chō (2.45 acres) of cropland. After being seeded, the bed's surface is usually blanketed with a thin layer of charred rice hulls before being flooded again. The charred hulls presumably conceal the seeds from birds, inhibit the sprouting of grass and weeds, and help concentrate heat during the germination period. A radical new seedbed technique being tried by one farmer involves planting the seeds in a well-worked dry seedbed under a thin mantle of dry manure, thus eliminating much of the labor involved in the preparation of irrigated beds. Scarecrows placed around the beds add a gay but practical note. These are of great variety and ingenuity: bamboo poles set in the ground dangle wads of straw over the surface of the beds; painted cardboard faces adorned with streamers are suspended on lines between bamboo poles; strips of aluminum foil strung from lines flap in the breeze; old clothes and hats stuffed with straw are set up in the beds; and even old electric light bulbs are suspended from slender pieces of bamboo. Seedlings appear by the middle of May. When three or four inches tall, they are thinned periodically to remove injured, diseased, or poorly shaped plants.

When the barley, wheat, and other winter crops have been harvested in late May and early June, the farmer must ready the main fields for rice transplanting. Generous amounts of compost and chemical fertilizer are added to the soil before it is plowed twice, irrigated, and the wet surface harrowed and smoothed. The rice seedlings are ready for transplanting between June 22 and 30. The plants, now eight to ten inches tall, are removed from the seedbeds, tied into bundles, and transferred to the empty paddy fields. The seedlings are then transplanted in rows by hand into the muddy earth. Usually three or more seedlings are placed together as a single planting, although a few Niiike farmers are experimenting with the technique of setting only one seedling to a spot. Transplanting is laborious and is done with utmost care. In the straight rows plantings are inserted every 0.7 foot; the interval may be slightly greater in poorer soil. Once the rows and intervals were measured by eye, but now notched sticks and precisely marked cords are used, exactness having proved important in increasing production.

Transplanting is hard on the back and a strain on the patience; it leaves everyone muddy and worn out. Yet there is a certain exhilaration which comes from the group work and the sense of accomplishment. All who are not absolutely infirm wade out into the mud, leaving only babies at home with a grandparent to baby-sit and keep the house safe. Even the school-age children, who normally are free from household or farm responsibilities, are granted a special leave from school and bend their backs in the paddy fields beside their parents. Sometimes members of the household who work in the city can stay home to assist. In many parts of Japan transplanting is a group or community function with many people working together in one paddy field, but in Niiike the job is done almost exclusively by the labor available in each household. In rare cases, households who have a labor surplus or who have finished their own planting will lend a hand, first to short-handed relatives and then to neighbors. This is a gesture of friendship in which money is never involved; the only repayment is meals, provided while work is in progress, and later a token of appreciation, perhaps some children's clothes, presented at an important ceremonial event.

In Niiike, transplanting is completed in a week or ten days. Momentary irrigation water shortages may slow the task somewhat despite the drizzly monsoon rains typical of late June weather. The eastern stretch of valley fields served by river water are irrigated and planted rapidly, but the upper fields which must depend on ponds fill slowly, and delays result, especially if the winter has been dry.

Paddy fields are weeded four times before harvest. The three weedings in July and August can be handled with a specially designed cultivator. The September weeding must be done by hand. Chemical fertilizer (ammonium sulphate, lime phosphate, and potash) is applied twice in decreasing amounts in July and August, and periodically the wooden water wheel or motor-driven water lift must be taken to the fields to keep an inch or two of irrigation water around the base of the growing plants. Finally, in mid-October the paddies are drained in preparation for the harvest. The community mobilizes its manpower in another intense labor period for cutting, drying, threshing, winnowing, and hulling the new rice. Children again join their parents in the still sodden fields, cutting and tying the rice into sheaves. The rice is hung to dry on racks made of poles set up on the dikes or in the fields. Off-and-on drizzles may keep the rice from drying properly for two weeks and endanger it through rotting, for the unthreshed harvest is too bulky to be brought under shelter. When the drying is complete the sheaves are ready to be taken down for threshing. Relieved of the rice sheaves, the drying racks are dismantled and stored for another year.

Before claiming their harvest Niiike farmers must fight a host of insect pests and plant diseases. Their battle is not yet won, but they now use insecticides and preventive measures unknown to their fathers. Niiike farmers are now so well aware of scientific agricultural developments that they no longer resort to the drums, noisemakers, and torches which two generations ago were used for insect control. The rice borer is the most persistent and destructive insect pest. This small moth larva bores into the rice stalk, causing it to droop and die. It attacks in two destructive waves, one between mid-May and late June and another about the end of August, when the rice heads are just beginning to form. In the past, the only practical method of combating the borer was the time-consuming one of cutting and burning the infected plants. In recent times tobacco dust has been used effectively, later to be superseded by DDT and BHC. The latter is a special insecticide developed by the Mitsubishi Company. Another effective control measure is the setting-out of fluorescent lights or kerosene lamps at night to attract the adult moths to puddles of insecticide placed beneath the lights. But Niiike does not use this method because, as one farmer explained, unless everyone in a region joins in setting out lamps, those who go it alone merely succeed in luring all the insects in the valley over to infest their own fields.

Despite the modern chemicals used by the farmers of Niiike, the rice borer and two destructive species of leaf hopper seriously reduce the rice crop every year. Several serious diseases, of which the rice blast is the worst, also attack rice. This blight can damage the rice plant at any stage of its growth but especially when the rice is in head. About the only preventive is a disinfectant soak for the seeds before planting.

The rice cycle is completed with the threshing and final drying of the rice. Threshing is done in the field or farm courtyards with small foot-powered or motor-driven threshers. The threshed grain is dried on straw mats laid out in the courtyards or edges of roads. When dry, the grain is hulled by one of the several co-operatively owned hulling machines. It is then ready for storage or for packaging to meet the government requisition or to be sold. Rice kept in the household for domestic use is stored in large galvanized iron containers. That which leaves the village is packed in straw bags. Rice straw is frugally saved for use in making rope, sandals, mats, and bags and as feed for cows.

The winter cycle of Niiike's double-crop system of cultivation is dominated by two major crops: dry grains and mat rush. The dry grains are considered important for subsistence and so are not thought of as income crops. Barley rather than wheat is the dry grain used in country-style cooking, either mixed with rice or boiled by itself, but wheat was given prominence during the war and postwar years as part of the government requisition program. Since the termination of wheat requisitions in 1951, it has continued to be grown but almost entirely for sale outside the community. Naked barley and bearded barley are grown on a small acreage each year. Much less cost and effort go into dry grain production than into rice production, for the three dry cereals play a correspondingly smaller role in the buraku economy.

Dry grain crops are planted in November immediately after the rice harvest. While the rice sheaves still hang over their drying racks in the field, the earth is hoed into straight ridges three feet apart and raised fifteen inches above the furrow. In planting, seeds are dribbled by hand into a shallow groove the length of the ridge, except where persistently poor drainage makes clump-planting necessary. Handfuls of rich compost are spread over the seeds to provide the fertility for a vigorous start. Soon bright-green sprouts push forth to brighten the winter landscape. Soil heaving during the winter often loosens plant roots, and the farmer, sometime in January, tramps along the rows to compact the earth with his foot. About the same time, he attaches a metal wing to his plowshare and goes out with his ox to reshape the ridges. The fields then rest until time for hand weeding with a scooped wire basket hoe in March and April. From then on, the grain grows without much attention except for fertilizing and control of rust, mildew, smut, and blight which may appear. The grain is harvested in early June after the rice seedbeds have been prepared. Barley ripens first, followed by naked barley and wheat, in turn, at about five-day intervals. Harvesting is done, as with rice, with a straight-bladed sickle, and the stalks are cut at the base rather than near the head. Then the threshing machines are pulled into the field, along with the motors to power them. For almost two weeks there ensues a hubbub of flying chaff, straw sheaves piled on dike paths, and houseyards crammed with mats of drying grain. But the work stretches out without being too demanding of time and effort, since the grain ripens a bit at a time and weather damage is unlikely. Eventually order is restored, as the threshed grain is stored away in large containers or bags woven of rice straw. Wheat and barley straw is carefully stacked in neat cylinders on unused land, eventually to serve as roof-thatching or fuel.

Also important as food crops to Niiike households are the vegetables and fruits which are grown in considerable variety throughout the year. Most vegetables are grown on a rectangular block of dry fields on the hill slope immediately on the eastern fringe of the buraku housing area. These fields have been kept in use after other hill plots were permitted to revert to forest during the 1920's when, through improvement, the paddy fields on the valley floor became more profitable for farming than upland fields. The eastern exposure of the area now retained for vegetable production provides sunshine and winter protection, but the land is relatively infertile and hard to work. It is used only because of its convenient location to the housing area and the lack of sufficient alternative space. Another stretch of unirrigated plots still exists around the fringes of the Ōbara Pond depression, but this land is inconveniently far from the housing area for vegetables and is gradually being converted into paddy fields by the construction of many small water storage ponds in the gently sloping valley sides. Vegetables are also grown on the valley floor. Here during winter and spring they compete successfully for space with dry grains. Even during the rice-growing seasons, vegetables can be found in an occasional corner of a paddy field. Irrigation embankments and partitions between fields are also carefully utilized as are diminutive patches in the housing area itself.

The main vegetable-growing area on the slope includes about twenty-five plots of various sizes, all small and owned, with one exception, by Niiike residents. The slope is steep, and plots must be partially terraced. The soil is sandy with a heavy clay base and very infertile without the addition of generous amounts of night soil. On this relatively uninviting base an intensive, dry-field multicropping system is in successful operation. No sooner has one crop matured and been removed than its place is taken by another. Three crops during the same year are common and every field bears at least two.

Spring and early summer bring the greatest variety of vegetables to the Niiike table, although every attempt is made to equalize the supply during the rest of the year. Early summer finds the hillside green with small patches of barley and naked barley; yellow-flowered rape; broad beans, peas, and other legumes; root crops such as edible burdock, white potato, giant white radish, onions, and carrots; fruits such as strawberries, tomatoes, cucumbers, and edible gourd; and such leaf crops as spinach, a type of cabbage, lettuce, and scallions. Space is not too precious for the farmer's wife to add a small cluster of ornamental flowers that she will offer later at the family graves. By late summer the dry grains are gone, but the fields are laden with soybeans, red beans, and cowpeas, the tangled green of growing sweet potato vines, sesame, eggplant, carrots, and watermelon. During the long winter, the dry fields are clothed with the green of leaf vegetables such as Chinese cabbage, spinach, edible chrysanthemum, and leek, and the winter planting of giant white radish. Two or three crops are particularly important for the food they provide at critical periods. The sweet potato, although it constitutes only 6 per cent of Niiike's food, as opposed to the 75 per cent made up by barley and rice, is an important staple, and virtually all the potatoes are eaten during the winter or in late spring when grain stocks are depleted and other vegetables are in short supply. The giant white radish is also important during much of the year, because both a summer and winter planting can be made. A few vegetables that cannot be raised on the hillside must be given space in the valley. Sugar cane needs more room than the hillsides provide, and taro and lotus root must have water. Cotton is one of the very few non-food items raised on the dry fields. Although its cultivation was abandoned some forty years ago, it was reintroduced under wartime emergency conditions. Three families continue its cultivation to provide small amounts of filling for cushions and quilts.

Vegetables are sometimes marketed through itinerant dealers, usually from Kurashiki City, but only when production outstrips family needs. At least a few families derive some cash every year from the sale of tomatoes, radishes, sweet potatoes, onions, leeks, and several kinds of beans. Hiramatsu Isamu, a graduate from a prewar farm school, has been the most active in growing vegetables commercially. With moderate success he has interplanted barley on a valley field with cucumbers in early spring. By the time the barley is harvested, the cucumbers are approaching maturity and can be harvested for sale in Kurashiki before the field is

156

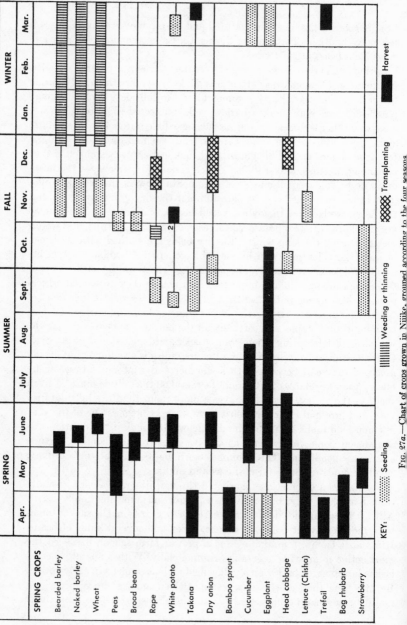

Fig. 27a.—Chart of crops grown in Niike, grouped according to the four seasons

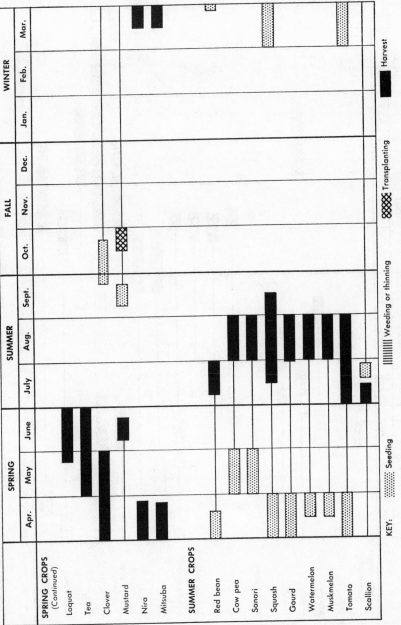

Fig. 27b.—Chart of crops grown in Niiike, grouped according to the four seasons

157

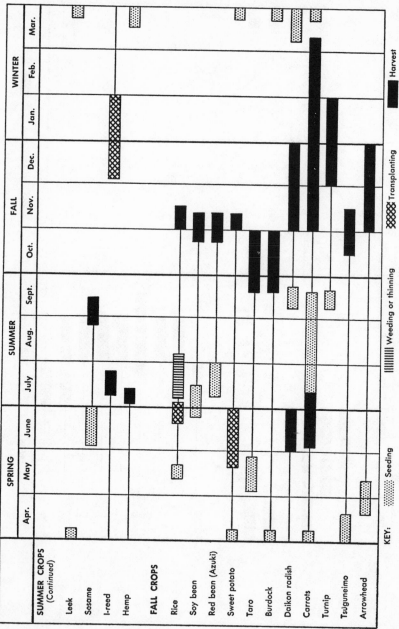

Fig. 27c.—Chart of crops grown in Niiike, grouped according to the four seasons

KEY:
▓ Seeding   ▦ Transplanting   ║ Weeding or thinning   ■ Harvest

SUMMER CROPS (Continued)

Leek
Sesame
I-reed
Hemp

FALL CROPS

Rice
Soy bean
Red bean (Azuki)
Sweet potato
Taro
Burdock
Daikon radish
Carrots
Turnip
Tsuguneimo
Arrowhead

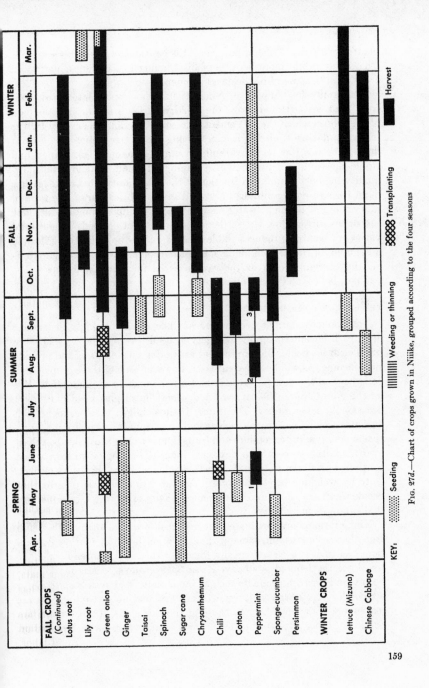

Fig. 27d.—Chart of crops grown in Niiike, grouped according to the four seasons

159

planted with rice. Others, however, still hesitate to follow his example. They admire him more because of his training in handling a variety of crops then because of his business acumen.

The family food supply in Niiike is further supplemented with fruit from the trees scattered across the unirrigated fields and around the base of the hill on which the settlement is located. Persimmons are by far the most popular fruit, although many young peach trees have been set out during the postwar period. Mandarin oranges, plums, figs, grapes, and edible chestnuts are also grown. A number of small, ill-tended and low-quality tea bushes supply a fraction of the community's tea needs. A few palm trees provide a fibrous bark used in the fabrication of one type of rain cape and a tough, water-resistant rope. Bamboo stands which dot the slopes surrounding the settlement serve a host of needs. One special variety of bamboo produces edible sprouts; others provide strong flexible poles used for roof thatch binders, props for young plants, fencing material, and carrying poles, or the raw material for baskets, fishing poles, handles, ladles, and many other items.

THE SEARCH FOR CASH INCOME

The Japanese farmer everywhere has become increasingly dependent upon cash income to supply a variety of needs beyond those met by the produce of his fields. Rice and wheat are major surplus crops and provide such income. As will be apparent later, however, sale of these crops yields little beyond the cost of fertilizer and other expenses of production. Nor do the minute quantities of fruit and vegetable surplus yield more than occasional pocket money. The farmer is thus obliged to experiment with various specialty cash crops such as mulberry, tobacco, peppermint, pyrethrum, and quality vegetables and fruits if he is to meet cash needs. Whatever his initial success with any such item, the farmer soon learns that continued profit depends on the ever changing whim of the urban market. Only by weighing production costs against estimated sale price can he decide whether to continue his current specialty or to switch to something that promises more return.

Niiike farmers are fortunate that mat rush provides them with a cash crop that is in constant demand though rather beset by market fluctuations. As rush is used universally for covers of the Japanese floor mats, the domestic demand is steady. Recently even an overseas market has been found for rush products such as table mats. Mat rush is suitable for a secondary crop because its growth pattern and labor requirements are reasonably complementary to those of the rice cycle. There are certain periods of labor overlap, but these can be taken care of by hired labor.

Though rush requires large amounts of fertilizer, it gives the highest return per acre of any Niiike crop. Furthermore the weaving of rush mats is not difficult. It can be performed in the household on hand looms, thus providing farm households with slack-season employment and additional income.

Mat rush thrives in the Okayama Plain climate. It likes the warm spring weather with many fine days, plenty of moisture in June, and a combination of clear weather and high temperatures about the middle of July. The sunny spring stimulates root growth, plentiful rain in June makes the stems grow rapidly, and July's dryness hardens the hollow stems and speeds drying after the harvest. The rush does best in a wet location and a well-consolidated clay soil. Thus in Niiike it occupies older fields near main irrigation ditches that fulfil these conditions. Reconditioned paddy land in the valley that is too poorly drained for dry grains is likewise useless for rush-growing. The sandy soils become muddy too rapidly and must be drained and hardened too often to make profitable operations feasible.

The cultivation of mat rush is not easy and requires exceptional skill on the part of the farmer. The rush is transplanted into irrigated fields sometime during December or January, but the seedlings for these plants must be started a year earlier. First, seeds are planted in a dry bed, or root cuttings from the previous year's crop are similarly prepared. Early in the following summer the root stocks are shifted to dike bank beds for a six-month period during which they multiply. During this period the root clusters are divided once and set out again until time for winter transplanting. Planting techniques are similar to those for rice. The small plants are set out by hand in evenly spaced rows in the wet fields prepared to receive the rush after the November rice harvest. This is one of the most disagreeable jobs in the Niiike work calendar, for the weather is bitterly cold and the water in the fields near freezing. Though irrigation water is temporarily drained off during transplanting operations and the farmer now usually has rubber boots to protect his feet from the mud, nothing but an occasional pause at a straw fire on the dike bank can relieve his fingers. Once transplanted, the plants turn a dirty brown and look dead and forlorn in the ice-coated fields. But the warm spring weather brings new green shoots that soon give promise of the eventual harvest.

Rush cultivation is exceptionally demanding of fertilizer. Large amounts of ammonium sulphate and liberal doses of compost are applied from three to five times during the growing period. Niiike farmers welcome the technical information supplied by the branch of the prefectural experimental station that specializes in rush culture, because the timing and quantity of fertilizer is a prime factor in eventual rush quality. Yet, n spite of scientific findings, long-established ways are not easily abandoned. For example, experts claim the commercial fertilizer alone is sufficient for the crop, while the farmer considers compost, which he has always used, essential. Whether necessary or not, the compost undoubtedly improves the soil for the subsequent rice planting and meanwhile contributes to the farmer's peace of mind.

Loss of rush harvest can occur during any stage of plant growth and harvesting. Some fields develop brown spots from fertilizer deficiency that can result in complete loss. Too liberal application of fertilizer causes excessive growth and loss of color in the spring. Rush has few natural enemies, but the sawfly that hatches twice a year consumes the tough stems with great relish and must be controlled with derris. Grasshoppers appearing around the middle of May also develop an appetite for rush but are controlled with insecticides or by burning off the dikes where they originate. Usually the damage from these two insect marauders is not serious enough to threaten the crop.

In May the rush begins a final period of vigorous growth and soon is so lush that many farmers cut off the tops to keep it from falling over prematurely. This also takes time and is bypassed in labor-short households. By the end of June the fields are a tangled mass of heavy green rushes from three to five feet long and remarkably uniform in stem size from root to tip. The rush harvest is a backbreaking and technically complicated operation. In the humid heat of July, the farmer must work his way into the tangled growth with his straight-bladed sickle, cutting a handful at a time at ground level. He then must straighten up, shake the heavy bundle of rush to free it of short ends, and place the bundle with others to form large sheaves. After being cut, the sheaves are further processed by dipping in a liquid solution of "drying clay," a sort of mud bath prepared from a fine clay imported from neighboring Hyogo Prefecture. This treatment controls drying and helps preserve the light-green color of the rush that is an essential market asset. After processing, the rush is spread out for drying. Vacant areas for drying are hard to come by, and the dipped rush, now a chalkish green color, is spread along roads and paths, among the houses, and in the already harvested fields. These are anxious moments for the farmer, who works with one eye on his task and the other on the sky trying to judge the weather, ready to gather all the rush under cover if rain comes. The rush needs two days of bright sunshine to cure properly, and even a short stretch of continuous rain can spoil the entire harvest. Luckily, such tragedy is uncommon. The bright sunshine of July co-operates, and the rush is dried and stored in the barn without mishap.

Not only is the rush harvest a backbreaking job in itself but it follows on the heels of the winter grain harvest and rice transplanting. For one-fourth of an acre the unremitting labor of four people for one entire week is needed to harvest the rush and to replant the cleared field with rice seedlings. Because of interruptions caused by bad weather, however, the fieldwork often occupies most of the latter half of July. As with rice plant-ing, each family is too busy with its own personal race against the weather to practice co-operative labor in the rush harvest. Until 1951 household labor was able to handle the busy July peak of work. Since then, rush acreage has been increased to the point that some Niiike households must rely on hired outside labor. Throughout the southern Okayama Plain the onset of the rush harvest attracts as many as five thousand experienced harvest hands from Kagawa Prefecture in northern Shikoku, who cross the Inland Sea by ferry. These workers find employment for ¥400–¥1,000 and as many as five meals per day, which makes them the highest paid farm workers in Japan. Kagawa workers come to Niiike, although part of the buraku's help is contracted in advance from the small surplus labor force found in the nearby shopkeeping buraku, Senzoku.

Some of the harvested rush may be sold to outside dealers for immedi-ate cash, but many households keep the bulk of it to weave into mat covers themselves. The consequent delay in receiving an income is usually offset by a slightly increased return. Looms are operated for the most part by women working in time snatched from household or field duties or when weather drives them indoors. The clacking of looms is a familiar sound in Niiike during summer and winter. Work on the loom is slow and hard, but the women put up with stiff necks and aching eyes in the small, dim loom-sheds, keeping their legs and arms in constant motion hour after hour. Once the inexpensive hand loom is bought, the only cash outlay involved in this home industry is the purchase of hemp cord for warp. Hemp can be grown locally but calls for so much work to cut and prepare that only Hiramatsu Hideo's family, which has a labor surplus of unmar-ried adults, grows its own hemp. Others use the relatively low-priced hemp imported from Tochigi Prefecture, where it is a principal cash crop. Usually it is purchased on credit from the dealer, who then deducts the cost from the price he pays for the finished matting. A full rainy day's work brings ¥120–¥180 (33–50 cents) profit above costs. Matting made of rushes long enough to form a single weft in the standard mat, three feet wide, brings the highest prices. Two inferior grades are made of short rushes that must be overlapped to attain the same mat width. Scraps also have value when made into rope or woven into baskets.

Because of seasonal fluctuations in the market price of matting, the farmer would do best to hold on to his mats until spring, when prices tend to rise. However, he must finish the processing before the spring work season and feels pressure to sell early to be able to buy needed clothes or equipment. The rush can be stored, but with the passage of time it loses its color and declines in value; it should be made into matting within a year after being harvested. Niiike farmers market their matting through local dealers or the village agricultural co-operative. Many local dealers have made their appearance since the war; before then, a large central market near Niwase handled most of the matting produced in the Niiike area. The farmers prefer local dealers because they advance hemp on credit and are but a few minutes' ride by bicycle from Niiike. But payment from the small dealers is often delayed, sometimes as much as two weeks after receipt of the matting. At the co-operative, payment is immediate, and regardless of market conditions the co-operative will always buy matting.

Besides raising mat rush, Niiike farmers engage in a number of other activities which yield cash income. Some farmers derive supplementary income by buying young oxen, using them for draft while they grow, and selling them after one or more years for beef. Niiike, like other lowland communities, is a mid-point in the journey of cattle from their origins in the mountainous interior to urban slaughterhouses. Cattle-raising is an economic mainstay of many mountain villages where plentiful forage is available. Calves raised in the mountain areas are sent to markets such as the one at nearby Kurashiki. Niiike farmers buy their oxen from dealers who come from Kurashiki. While in Niiike, the calves grow to maturity, are trained and used for work in the fields, and produce valuable fertilizer. When resold to the local dealers, they may bring profits as high as ¥10,000, plus the purchase price of another calf. After resale to the Kurashiki dealers the oxen are shipped by rail to slaughterhouses in the Osaka-Kobe area.

These cattle transactions take careful handling if they are to make a good profit for Niiike farmers. Seasonal price fluctuations usually result in lower prices in the fall and summer, and the shrewd farmer sells his animal in the winter when prices are highest and buys his calf later when prices have dropped. Heifers bring higher prices than bulls, probably because they are supposed to have tenderer meat, although young bulls are castrated to induce gentleness and improve meat quality. For the best price, a heifer should be marketed when about two years old; beyond that age, the price begins to drop. Tied as it is to urban markets, the meat business is very sensitive to urban economic conditions. For example, with the outbreak of the Korean War, Kobe beef prices rose, only to precipitate heavy sales and a subsequent drop in price. Several Niiike families have tried to break their dependence on outside dealers by breeding their cattle with a stud bull kept in a nearby buraku. But this has not worked well. The story is slyly told of the Niiike farmer who had his heifer serviced four times at the rate of ¥800 for each servicing but with no results and no refunds. And to top the farmer's misfortune, the animal had so aged in the process that it no longer brought a premium price on the market.

The most dramatic and potentially important departure from customary ways of earning cash income has been the experiment in dairying begun by one Niiike resident, Hiramatsu Isamu. Trained in the prefectural farm school like several of his neighbors, Isamu has continually displayed a vigorous initiative in trying new ventures. His first experiment was in 1935, when at the age of twenty-seven he became interested in commercial grape-growing as a result of his classroom instruction. He invested in a large hothouse with wooden sides and a glass roof in which he raised Muscat of Alexandria grapes during the summer. His profits financed two smaller hothouses for the cultivation of muskmelons four years later. Isamu's success with his hothouses continued throughout the war years but was terminated one dark night in 1947 when a thief stole about 10 per cent of his glass panes. At that time the reconstruction of bombed-out Okayama City made the panes a precious commodity. To avoid further loss, Isamu dismantled the greenhouses and sold the remaining panes in Okayama at high prices. With this money, his savings, and a large loan obtained from the agricultural co-operative, he purchased in 1949 his first milch cow, a registered Holstein thoroughbred. Subsequently, Isamu built up his herd to three Holsteins.

This was a major achievement in itself, but there was still much that Isamu had to learn before he could make a success of dairying. Thus, he was induced to join the Tsukubo-Kurashiki dairying co-operative. This move gave him access to professional guidance from prefectural and national dairying agencies with which the local co-operative was allied. Isamu also became a familiar figure in the agricultural co-operative office in Okayama, where he could secure specialized magazines and governmental publications on technical aspects of dairying. Here also were several advisers ready to give on-the-spot assistance on herd management, proper handling of milk, cow diseases, and milk marketing. The dairying co-operative registered his thoroughbred cows and sold Isamu sperm taken from prefecture-owned stud bulls at reasonable prices. This latter service is well received by Isamu and other dairymen. With cow-breeding conducted now almost exclusively by artificial insemination, herd quality in Okayama has improved.

Isamu appears to be doing well with his new enterprise, but dairying has also brought its problem. Cows are expensive (approximately $550 each); if they go dry temporarily, income is reduced but expenses continue. Furthermore, the market for milk in Japan is limited, despite the fact that postwar school lunches contain milk and have promoted a taste for milk among children. The market has been met, and discouraging price drops have induced more than one farmer to dispose of his cows, even at a loss, and to turn again to the more customary ways of making a living. Isamu has difficulty marketing his milk because the nearest dealer who pays acceptable prices is a fifteen-mile round trip away by bicycle. By now, Isamu on his bicycle with his milk can has become a familiar sight. Dairying has also forced Isamu to change his farming practices. Since there is no adequate pasture for his cows, he has become the first Niiike farmer to plant vetch for forage in his winter paddy fields; he grows corn and other cattle feed in dry-field plots and an increased amount of wheat in place of mat rush for use as fodder. He has built two small silos, resembling huge wooden tubs sunk half into the ground. Yet he must purchase additional supplies of wheat and barley bran for his cows from the village co-operative. Dairying has left Isamu less and less time for other farmwork, which has been shouldered by his wife. He still grows commercial rush but is the only Niiike farmer to sell his entire crop unprocessed. His household has no time for weaving.

The complete reorientation in farm management which dairying entails for many years discouraged others from following in Isamu's footsteps. In 1954, however, a national program to promote milch cow–breeding offered loans up to half the cost of cows at 7.5 per cent instead of the usual 12.5 per cent interest. Four Niiike households and nine others in Kamo village bought cows as a result. Isamu's example certainly had much to do with these decisions, for he was commissioned three times within a few months to travel north to Gumma and Chiba prefectures to purchase cows on behalf of these families.

Another cash-income project a few Niiike farmers have tried, which promises to become more important in the future, is the growing of specialty fruits. Fruits such as peaches, pears, and Muscat grapes are raised in quantity in the eastern section of the Okayama Plain. Niiike lies in an area where fruit has not been particularly popular. On the other hand, the high price of fruit in the postwar markets has been a stimulus to experimentation. Isamu's attempt to raise hothouse grapes was cut short in 1947. Since then, Hiramatsu Kumaichi has set out small grape arbors in two dry fields and a stand of peach and persimmon trees. Others were planning to raise fruits before our study period ended, and there has since been further conversion of dry slope to fruit orchards.

AGRICULTURAL TECHNIQUES

In his search for both subsistence and cash income, the Niiike farmer is constantly on the alert to improve his efficiency and the quality and quantity of his production. Farming techniques in Niiike are a remarkable combination of traditional practices and new, scientific methods. Older ways persist for the same reason new ones are taken up: someone believes that they contribute to high production under the prevailing conditions of small field size, low capital investment, and year-round use of the land.

The unbroken seasonal sequence of multiple crops taxes heavily the soil fertility in the fields of Core Japan. Although commercial fertilizers have become plentiful and other techniques of soil replenishment have greatly improved in recent years, the fields would have been worn out repeatedly over the generations but for the constant application of irrigation water and the long tradition of composting organic materials. The benefits of irrigation in improving soil productivity have already been mentioned. Compost in Niiike, where green cuttings are relatively scarce, is made from straw left from the rice and winter grain harvests. This is chopped into small pieces, mixed with cow manure and night soil, and consolidated in neat rectangular piles for patient aging, lasting six months at least. Compost is added in quantity to the wet fields.

The application of liquid night soil to the dry fields on the slopes is the secret of the copious vegetable growth which the poor soil supports. Every Niiike household saves its human wastes to be removed periodically to a submerged tub near the fields for aging. Water is added, and after the solid materials have broken down, the liquid is ready for application with a long wooden ladle. The amount of night soil available to each family decides how it will be used. If there is more than enough for composting and vegetable plots, the surplus is poured around young wheat and barley plants or sprinkled across a paddy prior to planting.

Niiike farmers all use commercial fertilizer to supplement compost. Before the war, fish fertilizer from Hokkaido and soybean meal from Manchuria were most common, but in the postwar years the chemical fertilizers, ammonium sulphate, lime phosphate, and potash, all manufactured by Japanese firms, have come into greater use. Ammonium sulphate, to insure good roots and a full head, is most generally needed for rice on the Niiike soil, the amount spread on each field being dictated by suggestions from government bureaus and the farmer's own sense of individual field requirements. As chemical fertilizer has become cheaper and more available it has become one of the heaviest cash-outlay items in the farm budget. It is secured either from the village agricultural cooperative or from town merchants, depending on which source is cheaper, although the co-operative is favored because of its credit policy and the fact that it will deliver the heavy sacks.

Improvement of seeds and insecticides is also a major concern in Niiike. The Niiike farmer by now has selected those varieties of rice and dry grains best suited to his fields from the many improved strains circulated by the prefectural experimental station and national seed companies. The principles of seed selection from the previous harvest are well understood, though there is some variety of opinion about the best method of seed renewal. Those who renew seed each two or three years privately criticize as penny-pinching the practice of getting new seed only once in ten or a dozen years. Occasionally the agricultural co-operative will have available a new strain of grain for trial on a voluntary basis. Niiike people are willing sometimes to purchase a small amount for experimentation. But, in general, they are content to put stock in seed strains that have been proved over the years, each man swearing by his favorites.

The Niiike farmer, in company with farmers throughout Japan, finds that he has easy access to scientific information on his agricultural problems. A central agricultural experiment station on the outskirts of Okayama City works to improve rice, dry grains, and some vegetables, while four specialized branches elsewhere in the prefecture experiment with fruits, commercial rush, white potatoes, and upland rice. Information from these research organs filters down to the farm areas through extension workers and formal publications. Bulletins are distributed through the village offices; radio programs provide data on weather and market conditions. During the Occupation a new method of disseminating information was introduced, namely the county-agent system, based in form and function on the American model. The agent nearest Niiike is at Sōja and serves five villages, among them Kamo. While he has visited Niiike and neighboring buraku on formal calls, most of his frequent contacts with the farmers are in his Sōja office. There, Niiike farmers join others in seeking advice; if they seem conservative about taking it, the agent's tendency to be over-impetuous in urging changes that fit government policy of the moment is somewhat to blame. A wide gulf still remains between the results of crop experimentation or the agricultural economist's plans for the rationalization of agriculture and the actual application of new findings and plans in rural areas.

Certainly the people of Niiike and the Okayama Plain rank high nationally in the speed with which they accept and apply the findings of science. Yet, in Niiike, as elsewhere, individuals vary in their reaction to innovation. At one extreme, there is the relatively well-educated young farmer who is willing to experiment with fruit-growing and dairying in preference to raising the customary crops of rice and dry grains. At the other extreme, there is the traditionalist, not necessarily less educated, who will reason: "I can't afford to gamble on newfangled farming—even if I liked the idea, which I don't." The bulk of farmers come between these extremes. They are rooted in tradition yet willing to listen, observe, and occasionally to depart from their established routine. Niiike fields are now plowed only once a year, in the spring after harvest of the winter-spring crops. Fifty years ago, they were plowed in the fall also. The change in practice is the result of advice from prefectural technicians and actual experiment by willing farmers that showed fall plowing was unnecessary. On the other hand, a typical example of reluctance to experiment was displayed after the war when the privately financed Ōhara Agricultural Experimental Station at Kurashiki was seeking volunteers to try out a revolutionary rice-planting system. The new system involved the direct planting of rice seeds in the drained paddy fields in late spring before the winter dry grains had been harvested. It promised the elimination of spring plowing, seedbed preparation, and seedling transplanting, some of the most labor-consuming steps in the rice cycle. Risks included possible slight crop decreases and greater vulnerability to insect attacks. Only one volunteer, the Sensei, turned up in Niiike. Others merely stood by to see the results of the experiment. Although the initial crop was successful, the second planting failed completely, thus reinforcing the skeptics' belief that it was wiser to remain aloof from such experiments.

The swift succession of specialized crops in the Niiike farming cycle demands a corresponding variety of tools and equipment. Here again tradition and innovation compete for the attention of the Niiike farmer. Many tools used today are unchanged since Tokugawa days, but they must prove their utility in the face of new tools developed outside the village. Though handwork is still preponderant, now appearing in Niiike are evidences of the search for technological improvement.

Hand tools are most common, cheapest, and, with their simple but effective traditional design, basic to farming activities in Niiike. Perhaps closest to an all-purpose instrument is the hoe. This is the farmer's favorite tool, whether for breaking tough clods and shaping the earth in his fields or for constructing and cleaning irrigation ditches. Other hand cultivating tools include straight-bladed sickles, shovels, scoops, rakes, clod-breakers, and spading forks, to name only some of the ones everywhere in evidence.

Many of the simple machines of the past, wheelbarrow, foot-pestle and mortar, stone mill, and water wheel, have not been improved significantly over three generations or more. Changing economic conditions have eliminated the flail, spinning wheel, and cloth loom, but nonetheless much work in the home and in the field is done with the simple hand tools to which time has added little except better iron blades. Some traditional tools have become the basis of new improvement. The best example of this is the metal, mechanical cultivator for rice. Shoved through the paddies on

Fig. 28.—Machines used in Niiike. *A*, foot-operated pestle and mortar, for cracking wheat and barley. *B*, wheelbarrow, an Inland Sea regional device; carts are used elsewhere. *C*, rotary mill for making wheat or barley flour. *D*, huller. *E*, polisher. *F*, all-purpose 4.5-horsepower kerosene motor. *G*, thresher. *H*, paddle-fan winnower, cranked by hand. *I*, hand cultivator operated by the all-purpose motor. All are portable single units except the pestle and mortar, which is stationary, and the huller, which must be dismantled before being moved.

a boat-like frame, it contains a rotating wheel with multiple prongs for catching and removing weeds. It appeared in the nineteenth century; its precursor was a simple, multipronged soil-scratcher without moving parts.

While most of the traditional tools and equipment still in use are extremely effective, others continue although it would seem they could be improved. For example, the right-angle blade attachment of the sickle requires two distinct motions for each stroke: a positioning motion and a cutting pull. However keen the cutting edge of the sickle, the hand fatigues quickly when using it. The horse and ox draft-harness commonly used in Niiike concentrates the pull on a saddle-frame which is cinched on the animal's back; a tight cinch is all that prevents this saddle and girth from slipping back to the loins, so load limits must be considerably lower than when the animal is fitted to the Western-style ox-yoke or the horse collar which brings the load to bear on the shoulders.

The tools and equipment of the West which might serve as alternatives are not beyond reach. Occasionally horse collars are used by carters in the city. Western-type tools are illustrated in magazines and appear in farm implement stores. But one looks for them in vain around the countryside. One might conclude that a considerable resistance prevents acceptance of a foreign tool even where its superiority is evident. But this simple conclusion seems overhasty, for several tools of American or European origin are now generally owned, though not heavily used, by the well-equipped Japanese farming household. Examples are: shovels with curved blade and D-handle (called *sukoppu*), the garden rake (*reiki*), and the American garden hoe (*jōren*). Since others equally available have been ignored, there appears to be a conscious selectivity in the pattern of adoption.

The tools of both Japanese and Western farmers are not random aggregations. Rather they represent unified systems closely integrated with agricultural techniques and patterns of behavior. Thus, motor habits suited to one Japanese tool are just as serviceable for others in the Japanese system, whereas they are not well accommodated to the tools of the West. Western tools, with few exceptions, require a work stroke that pushes outward from the body: the shovel and pitchfork throw out and up, the ax out and to the side, the saw and the plane push forward. Most tools of the Far East, including Japan, are pulling tools. Saw, plane, and adz are arranged to cut toward the body. Thus, it seems natural that the Japanese farmer's favorite tool is the hoe, of which six varieties are regularly used in Niiike. This also accounts for the design of the Japanese fork, which, in contrast with the Western pitchfork, is hafted so the blade meets the handle hoe-fashion. All four varieties of native fork used in

Niiike are thus adapted to a hoe stroke with pulling motion. Other favored field tools, as well as implements for carpentry and food preparation, are pulling tools. The ingrained habits of working with such tools will cause a Japanese to turn the blade of the Western scoop around on the handle. A laborer shoveling gravel into a truck lifts his load hoe-fashion on the reversed scoop blade, working comfortably with a motion which in half an hour would strain every sinew in a Westerner's body. Undoubtedly, it is this motor pattern that affects the selection of Western tools by Niiike farmers, for the Western hoe and rake that hang in every barn are pull tools; the scoop, discordant to the pattern, has very rare usage.

Very few of the tools used in Niiike today are made in the immediate locality, and none is made in the home. Some plows still in use were made by the small group of *Eta* outcasts comprising half the nearby buraku of Horen, among whom this was a hereditary occupation. The majority are factory products closely following the old style and are bought in Okayama City or through the farm co-operative. Manufacturers' trade-marks adorn other pieces of field and household equipment, and any machinery, of course, is factory produced.

A special word should be added about the Niiike plow, an extremely simple device, light enough to be carried by one man for long distances. It is essentially a two-piece instrument. A single wooden beam forms both handle and tip, and the base is shod with iron. A second beam extends to the singletree that is hitched to the ox. While this instrument has few of the refinements of the Western plow, it cuts a shallow furrow with precision.

The plow and harrow are the only important farm tools operated by animal power, usually by oxen. Despite the availability of oxen for draft purposes, it is surprising how little use is made of them in Niiike. Counting times when used only for a short while, the sleek black ox does not emerge from his stall more than 40–60 days during the year. Meanwhile, his owners work hard for his keep. They warm his drinking water. They must cut grass on the dikes and paddy borders, gather leaves from the forest, and perhaps raise some vetch to supplement his usual diet of chopped straw and bran. They bring his food to the stall and not the ox to the food, all this to insure collecting every bit of manure for organic fertilizer. The ox, of course, is indispensable for those few days when he is used, and the farmer who does not own an ox must hire one at plowing time. But it would be folly to pretend the ox fully earns his keep in a cost-and-profit sense. As a traditional symbol of a household's wealth, however, ownership of an ox is desired. In Niiike, thirteen houses own an ox, naming the creature, petting it, working it slightly, and grieving when the aging animal must be sold. Horses are rare on the Okayama Plain. More prevalent a generation or more ago, they are being replaced by oxen throughout Core Japan. Only in frontier areas, especially northern Honshu and Hokkaido, do they remain the principal draft animal.

The answer to Niiike's labor problem seems to lie less in an increased number of draft animals than in mechanization. Machines of varying complexity have invaded the village over the last half-century, paving the way for firsthand acquaintance with industrial production. Although in any single household there is still a strictly limited number of machines, the Niiike people are well equipped compared with farmers in many parts of Japan. One reason for this may be that they happen to be near-neighbors to villages along the reclaimed farmland of Kojima Bay, famous throughout Japan for their high degree of mechanization. The advanced application of machine power to agriculture in the latter villages results in part from the guidance and help of government and the leadership of the large landowning corporations, but, also, farmers have not been inhibited in this newly settled area by the pressure of surplus labor commonly found elsewhere. Today, however, even the older, crowded settlements of the plain, of which Niiike is one, have moved in the direction of mechanization. As a consequence, Okayama City has more farm-tool and machinery factories producing for the domestic market than any other city of Japan.

A synopsis of machinery used in Niiike is shown in Table 2. The list is particularly impressive when we realize that few if any of these machines were in use two generations ago. Some of these machines, such as the rope spinner, thresher, winnower, and huller had their traditional predecessors. It is the all-purpose kerosene motor and the various grain-processing machines introduced during the 1930's which should be thought of as the first major steps toward mechanization. The kerosene motors are remarkably effective in both yard and field. Simply made and cheap to repair, they are portable to any field and may even be attached to run a simple but cumbersome hand cultivator. Most often these motors are used to power grain-processing tools or to run water lifts for irrigation.

The new motor cultivator shown in the table epitomizes the present-day trend toward further mechanization. In 1953 in the prefecture as a whole five times more households used cultivators than two years earlier. Statistics for all Japan in that year showed one motor cultivator for every twelve households. Thus, if the effort to built cultivators small enough for the tiny fields of Japan and cheap enough for the farmer's slim purse is successful, the age-old character of farming may well change in Japan. Already, Niiike has begun to move in this direction.

AGRICULTURAL PRODUCTIVITY AND AGRICULTURAL CHANGE

In the above pages we have described the yearly round of farm activities in Niiike with its attending technology. We are now in a position to seek answers to some questions of a more general sort concerning the nature of Niiike's agricultural system. What is the actual balance between labor and productivity? What do we mean when we speak of the intensive quality of Niiike farming? How does it fit with the changing technological and economic conditions of Japanese society at large? Is the Niiike farmer actually holding fast to key elements of his system or is the use of machines

TABLE 2

MACHINES OWNED IN NIIIKE IN 1954

Machine	Number	Where Used	Construction	Remarks
Radio..............	21	home	5-tube sets common	
Sewing machine........	13	home		Loaned to non-owners
Bicycle*..............	35	road		Women's models included
Kerosene motor........	11	home, field	$2\frac{1}{2}$–$4\frac{1}{2}$ h.p., wt. 230 lbs. and up	
Mat-rush loom*........	23	home	Hand and foot operated	
Rope spinner..........	20	home	2 strands twisted on rotating, horizontal axle	
Grain thresher*†.......	14	field	Fan attached; a few treadle-type	
Grain winnower.......	20	home	Hand-cranked, inclosed fan	Separates poor quality grain as well as chaff
Grain huller†..........	4	home	Large machine, polishes grain between rubber rollers and sorts it	Owned by co-operative groups
Grain polisher†........	12	home	Helical screw in base of pottery jar	
Field pump†..........	13	field	Archimedes' screw in cylinder	
Motor cultivator.......	1	field	Kerosene engine, rotary blades of 2-foot beam, wt. 420 lbs.	Bought January, 1954.

* Some households have more than one such machine.

† Powered by separate, all-purpose kerosene motor listed above.

and the chemical fertilizers obtained from the industrial community around him committing him to changes that will revolutionize his life?

What we refer to as "intensive agriculture" should not be understood to mean merely "highly productive agriculture," for this is only one of various advanced agricultural systems which share the goal of high production. By "intensive agriculture" we mean a system adapted to a situation of perennial land shortage, which aims at high production *per acre of land.* Its productive rate *per unit of labor* is very low, in consequence, for it uses great amounts of manpower in relation to other elements of production. Seen another way, by relying on manpower intensive agriculture minimizes requirements for any form of energy other than human toil.

The data on rate of production with which we must work are approximate and must be used with caution, though they lead to fairly realistic conclusions. How much produce each farmer actually obtains from his land is one of his best-kept secrets. Intentional secrecy is not necessarily implied, for the farmer himself keeps no exact accounting of the yield of all his little patches of vegetables and rows of bean plants tucked away on the dikes among his staple crops. Yet he avoids revealing everything he does know, in these days of heavy income tax and government requisition quotas. Even the village records of field size and productivity on which we must base our analysis are surely downgraded and inaccurate. We use them, however, with the comfort that they at least provide a minimum account of rice and dry grains harvested in an average year.

According to the village records, the Niiike rice yield averages 52 bushels per acre, with a range of 44 to 59 bushels per acre. This yield is lower than for Kamo as a whole, mainly because many Niiike paddy fields are poorly drained. Yet it is a tremendous increase over the seed sown, amounting to 750–950 fold. Stated in terms of the basic economic unit, the average Niiike household of 5.6 persons harvests 84 bushels of rice from its land. Measured by *koku*, a standard unit of capacity (4.96 bushels) originally based on a one-year rice allowance for one person, the amount of rice Niiike's average household raises is 2.5 times what it requires for its own use. More accurate for present-day consumption, no doubt, is the present rice ration quota. If consumption is calculated according to the government's allowance for farmers, with the usual age variations, the average household's harvest appears to be just twice the amount consumed by the family, enough to leave some surplus beyond the requisitioned quota for free sale on the market or for sale at a bonus price to the government. Wheat and barley, which are calculated together in village records as "dry grains," yield much less than rice, though, when we recognize that in large part they comprise a second crop, the yield is still respectably high. The average yield is 22 bushels per acre, with a range of 20 to 27 bushels per acre. This amounts to about a 35-fold increase over the amount of seed sown. The harvest of the average household is 18 bushels, though many households have an actual harvest almost double that figure. Government ration allowances, calculated on the basis of 25 per cent dry grains to 75 per cent rice in the total nation, suggest that the household would consume slightly more than 11 of the 18 bushels, the remainder being available for sale on the market.

For both rice and dry grains there is good evidence to indicate that the

yield per acre of cereals has increased tremendously since the late nineteenth century when scientific farming began. The elders of Niiike claim
that in their youth rice yields were roughly one-half present yields, and
their contention is in line with the earliest survey of production made by
the village office in 1872.

Niiike's rice production, though slightly below the coastal plain average, is about 12 per cent higher than the prefectural average shown in
official publications. Okayama Prefecture as a whole is in the middle
range of rice productiveness for the country as a whole in recent years.
The national range, by prefectural units, is from 28 to 59 bushels per
acre. Surprisingly, the lowest extreme for the country is in southern
Kyushu, the highest is in the north, owing to the rapid rise of productivity in northern prefectures as chemical fertilizers have come into wider
use since World War II. The latter yields are from fields which support
but one crop a year, lying fallow during the winter. The total grain crop
through the year is greater in Okayama.

There is strong evidence that actual production in Niiike both in yield
per acre and in size of the total harvest per household is considerably
larger than the official figures we have just used. Current estimates of
land productivity date from 1949, when the government set up local committees at the buraku, ōaza, and village levels to make parcel-by-parcel
evaluations of paddy productiveness. The resulting figures, representing
compromises between the farmers' figures and the estimates of their
neighbors who served as committeemen, surely understate the yields just
as earlier assessments as far back as feudal times did. Gossip of rather
circumstantial character suggests that the actual yield in some cases may
be nearly double the official figure. The figures for total harvest per household may be low for another reason: inaccurate records of field size. It is
a rare field that is smaller than its recorded size; throughout Okayama
Prefecture, fields may range from 10 per cent to 50 per cent larger than
listed. Such discrepancies are apt to be greatest in long-settled villages
where no surveys have been made since the inadequate ones of 1871 and
1890. Measurements are most correct where rectangular fields have been
laid out recently, as in the section near Niiike that was improved and
redivided in 1925. In a sample of seven irrigated fields in Niiike, measured
carefully to check their size, the average cultivated surface was found to
be 14 per cent larger than the recorded size. Such discrepancies rise only
partly out of subterfuge on the part of the owner, for an attitude of lenien-
cy is clearly apparent on the part of the government officials.

Out of the various uncertainties in the foregoing data about rate of
production emerges the conclusion that yields are, if anything, actually

higher than claimed. And even the lowest firm estimate of rice and dry grain productivity in Niiike, 52 bushels per acre of rice and an added 22 bushels of wheat for many of the same acres, is among the highest in the world. This calls for systematic analysis of the intensive agricultural techniques which produce such spectacular results. First to be inspected are the basic materials of the craft, the plants and animals.

Rice is the sort of crop that is especially suited to intensive cultivating methods. Its yield rises startlingly when it is given detailed attention and adequate nutriment; no other grain will fill as many straw bags per acre under ideal growing conditions. It is widely grown, on this account, where farm households have exceedingly small units of land in proportion to the labor available. Intensive cultivation is not limited to rice or any small group of crop plants, of course, for selection is made from a wide variety, each crop being carefully chosen for the special features of a small patch of ground, but crops that have low yields or low money value per acre are relatively rare. Irrigated crops are particularly common. Standing irrigation water itself enriches the soil through its nitrogenous bacteria, and it facilitates the absorption of almost limitless quantities of chemical and organic fertilizers. Thus, plants that flourish in standing water are favored under intensive cultivation.

Animal raising is held to a minimum. Land shortage accounts particularly for the rarity of grazing animals. On arable land, crops grown for direct human consumption are much more efficient than natural vegetation or fodder crops for grazing animals. Small creatures that require little space or that feed on garbage may be raised, but, where wasteland has disappeared, sheep, goats, cattle, and horses are kept low in number in order not to outrun the meager natural fodder on dike banks and other uncultivable patches. Niiike's chickens take up only a few square meters of houseyard and eat largely scraps. The oxen, though large beasts with large appetites, are not too numerous to feed on dike bank grass; their use is not for food, however, but for their draft energy. To estimate the significance of this energy requires consideration of all the forms of energy put into cultivation.

Three sources of energy are available: the farm worker himself, his draft animals, and power machinery. By far the largest amount of work is accomplished through human energy in Niiike and other intensive agricultural communities. Moreover, the labor per unit of land throughout Japan, according to official figures, has increased from year to year as crop yields have risen; over and above changes brought about by seed selection, planting and cultivating methods, and increase of fertilizer, the rising harvests have exacted a greater toll of working hours. The direct contrary has been the case in the extensive farming system of the United States, where mechanical energy has gone far toward supplanting the human energy invested in crops. In Japan, in 1949, the average acre of rice took 870 man-hours of labor throughout the period of crop growth; the average acre of wheat required 636 hours. The United States figures of man-hours per acre, between 1945 and 1948, according to the same source, were 26 man-hours for rice and only 6 man-hours for the still more highly mechanized growing of wheat.[1] Rice and wheat in Japan, then, require, respectively, over 30 times and over 100 times the amount of human effort that they consume in the United States. The contrast, though variable, runs in the same direction in the case of other staple and commercial crops.

Niiike's hand-tool cultivation, though costly in man-hours, is cheap in total expenditure of energy. Again, the American comparison is illuminating. The contrast is clear if all sources of energy, animate and inanimate, are considered as if converted engineer-fashion into their equivalent in horsepower. American 50-bushel-per-acre rice farming has been calculated to use 806.5 horsepower-hours per acre; Japanese 50-bushel-per-acre rice farming uses only about 100 horsepower-hours per acre. The Japanese energy input, 90 per cent of which is human labor, thus, is only one-eighth of the total American input.[2]

Each mode of cultivation is linked to a total economy. America is rich enough for its rice growers to own costly capital equipment, in the first place. More than that, however, its total production system provides great quantities of energy for every type of productive operation, whereas Japan must accomplish work on low amounts of mechanical energy per worker as well as on a minimum of capital equipment. American agriculture saves human energy, Japanese agriculture uses it in high quantity.

In sum, the traditional pattern of intensive cultivation develops in a situation of land shortage. It is strongly marked by selection of plants capable of high quantity production in small areas and by minimum use of grazing animals even for farm work, let alone for food. The total of human labor per unit of harvested crop or per unit of land is very high. But two innovations in Niiike, at least, appear to fly in the face of tradition as we have defined it. Five households bought dairy cows, even devoting staple crops to feed them. In several instances, householders have decided to buy larger kerosene motors, which consume more fuel, and, finally, in 1954 Hiramatsu Hideo bought the first power cultivator owned

[1] *Nōrin Tōkei* ("Farm and Forestry Statistics") (Tokyo: Ministry of Agriculture and Forestry, 1954).

[2] William Frederick Cottrell, *Energy and Society* (New York: McGraw-Hill, 1955), pp. 138–41.

within the community. Higher energy input was cheerfully undertaken with no clear promise of a rise in the yield of any single crop. Of what significance were these moves?

A clear and definite answer is hazardous, considering that prosperity and postwar dislocation of traditional farm practices through government crop requisition formed the immediate background to these innovations. There has been for some time, moreover, year-to-year fluctuation in secondary crops and marketable crops, as experiments and fads have been undertaken to increase cash income. The critical point, however, seems to be the release of manpower. Niiike already has "surplus" manpower, as we know both from repeated assertions that "our house could cultivate twice as much as we do now, if we could only get the land," and from the number of persons who hold jobs outside the community or spend hours weaving mat covers. The labor which is "surplus" in farming can be invested productively in other activities. Caring for dairy cattle, a time-consuming activity, is one such activity, justified if the calculation is correct that milk and calves will bring more profit than the grain which is fed to them. This is a risk operation; hence relatively few are now attempting it. Working at outside jobs carries less risk and discommodes the household very little through most of the year. At harvest time, however, any saving of man-hours is an advantage, particularly since increased plantings of market crops such as mat rush have developed a heavy-labor harvest that overlaps with the dry grain harvest and the rice transplanting. Machinery such as a cultivator may stand idle for most days of the year yet be worthwhile if its use to prepare fields for rice transplanting reduces the manpower squeeze intensified by the new emphasis on money-making crops. Such changes mark a readjustment of farm schedules but not a transformation of the intensive pattern of cultivation. Only as city jobs draw the sons and daughters of Niiike completely away from the community or give them lifetime occupations will the reduced farm population need to rely more on machinery used in the extensive farm pattern.

NON-AGRICULTURAL OCCUPATIONS

Early each morning several young men dressed in dark suits emerge from their homes in Niiike, wriggle their feet into ready-laced shoes, mount their bicycles, and peddle off to the train station, where they leave for their salaried jobs in Okayama City. These commuters are the main contingent of persons working full time outside the buraku. Their jobs represent one of two solutions to the double problem of acquiring cash income and putting surplus labor usefully to work. Only two households out of twenty-four in Niiike can keep all their working members busy regularly in the fields; most, in fact, would need up to twice their present acreage to make the most of their labor force. Part-time, subsidiary work at home is one current solution to the problem; weaving mat covers on the hand loom standing in the workshed is a standard way of filling odd hours, and caring for chickens and dairy cows may also be viewed as subsidiary home occupations that augment cash income. The second solution is to hold a salaried job, either temporary or permanent. Twelve households in 1954 had at least one member so employed; the number fluctuates with the season or the year but is unlikely to go below eight. Table 3 lists the jobs or positions held in April, 1954, by the sixteen persons from

TABLE 3

Iwasa Toshio (M, 25) . . . . .Grain mill, Takamatsu
Hiramatsu Misao (M, 19) . . . . .Grain mill, Takamatsu
Hiramatsu Hajime (M, 37) . . . . . . .Grain mill, Takamatsu (part time)
Hiramatsu Kōichi (M, 25) . . . . .Ice plant, Niwase
Hiramatsu Michinobu (M, 39) . . . *Grammar school, Misu
Iwasa Takeshi (M, 28) . . . .*Farm agency, Kurashiki City
Hiramatsu Hideo (M, 48) . . . .*Post office, Kurashiki City
Hiramatsu Katsurō (M, 23) . . . . . . .Chamber of commerce, Okayama City
Hiramatsu Shigemi (F, 19) . . . . . . .Knitting school, Okayama City
Iwasa Katsumi (M, 25) . . . .*Prefectural office, Okayama City
Iwasa Yoshio (M, 28) . . . .*Railroad motor shop, Okayama City
Hiramatsu Teigo (M, 41) . . . .*Savings office, Okayama City
Hiramatsu Yukuji (M, 22) . . . .*Prefectural office, Okayama City
Iwasa Tamaichi (M, 57) . . . .*District office barbershop, Kojima City
Iwasa Tamae (F, 23) . . . . .Department store, Kobe
Hiramatsu Masao (M, 50) . . . . .Engineering firm, Kobe

these twelve households, beginning with those located closest to Niiike. Each person's age and sex are shown following the name. Jobs which were on the payroll of the prefectural or national government are starred (*).

In a fully developed household, a second son almost invariably holds such a job after finishing school; the first son also may work outside until he begins to consider marriage seriously or finds that household circumstances require him to turn to fieldwork. In branch households (see chap. 9) composed only of a young couple and a child or two, the husband usually works outside to get half or more of the household income and helps his wife in the fields on weekends. Iwasa Takeshi, Iwasa Katsumi, Hiramatsu Teigo, and Hiramatsu Yukuji head four such small households. Fully developed households are headed by Hiramatsu Hajime, Hiramatsu Hideo, Hiramatsu Misao, and Iwasa Tamaichi. But the first of these works only at slack season, and the last two are evacuees who, as a matter of choice, would not be normal residents of Niiike. Outside work usually is not favored or needed by mature households. Several girls have held temporary jobs before marrying; but, although many girls commute outside to attend a sewing school, only Tamaichi's household, overburdened with girls and continually at the bottom of the income distribution, has sent its girls out to permanent jobs. Woman's place is in the home or fields.

Government offices, above all, absorb surplus labor from communities such as Niiike. As Table 3 shows, half the outside jobs are on the government payroll rather than in private business. Salaried jobs for the slack season are not numerous. However, the grain mill at Takamatsu which was employing three men from Niiike offers such slack season employment. What is remarkable for a village that regards itself as purely concerned with farming is that fully half of the households augment their income on a year-round basis with non-agricultural, salaried jobs.

A great many occupational specialists are scattered through the countryside, in communities like Niiike, where their services are quickly available to buraku of the vicinity. They may or may not farm much, but almost all have a truck garden at least. But only one person has practiced a non-agricultural occupation within Niiike. This is the barber who, evacuated from the city of Okayama during the war, salvaged one chair and other equipment and offered his barbering services to people in the vicinity only because he could not by any means support his large household on the scraps of land he was able to obtain for farming. Given the opportunity to return to barbering in Kojima City in 1953, he took it even though the post was too far for daily commuting and meant that his time at home would be restricted to weekends. His job, and that of another househead, Masao, who works in Kobe as an engineer, approach the category known as *dekasegi*, well developed in the Inland Sea region. Persons who engage in *dekasegi* must live away from home to be near their jobs but contribute a sizable portion of their income to the homestead. Their over-all contributions to the economy of their households is a significant feature in the high level of Inland Sea village income.

Beyond the immediate economic influence of these non-agricultural workers on their households, notice must be taken of the ties their community forges with life and events in the city. Niiike cannot be isolated from the city as long as such jobholders spend a good part of their daytime lives in the city. On the other hand, though some of the younger members of this salaried group seem tempted away from farming, the greater number would return immediately to farmwork if circumstances permitted. The group as a whole is not being alienated from rural life.

Subsidiary activity in the household seems an older phenomenon than does commuting to salaried jobs outside, a practice developed in the last quarter-century. However, village records of 1879 show a fairly large number of girls employed in the spinning mills of Kurashiki, which were among the largest of local enterprises in Japan at that time. The mills now employ larger numbers than ever, but the management has found its labor relations best served by girls brought from more distant areas, such as northern Kyushu, and local girls are not employed there now as spinners.

LEISURE AND CEREMONY

A description of Niiike at work would not be complete without a word about the pattern of leisure activity of the farming households. Leisure is now available to the people of Niiike as never before. Various laborsaving machines and the electric light bulb, which has extended the day, have been primarily responsible for bringing about this change. Amusements, too, have increased for the farmers with the coming of the newspaper and magazine, the radio, and, to a minor degree, the cafés and movie houses in Okayama City. The individual habits of leisure and amusement vary greatly for the inhabitants of Niiike but are tending, generation by generation, to orient the villagers toward the city and the nation. Thus, the villagers find themselves leaving behind in yet another way a part of their traditional way of life.

Until a generation ago a major emphasis in ethnographic studies of Japanese villages was placed on traditional folk customs and activities. Even today the more remote rural communities of Japan maintain a highly varied and localized folk life distinguished by characteristic festivals, ceremonies, clothing, folk songs, and games. Niiike today has lost much of this distinctive quality about its community life. One of the last vestiges of traditional folkways, which, too, has begun to vanish in Niiike, is the use by the women of the customary blue and white cotton farm clothes at rice-transplanting time. The men long ago went into machine-made shirts and khaki trousers. Nonetheless, behind the cycle of agricultural activity there is still a strong reliance on the customary practices which unite leisure with ceremony.

When the Niiike farmers as a community interrupt their daily round of work in the fields, it is not for rest as such but usually for another sort of activity, for a calendrical ceremonial occasion. Days set aside for rest are rare. The seven-day week provides no day of rest except to school children and those with salaried jobs in the city, who get their day or day-and-a-half weekend holiday as part of the new tradition. On the farm, where an

annual rather than weekly cycle is observed, ceremonial activity continues
to pervade most non-working days, providing a change of rhythm and
tempo and a shift of purpose that gives relief from the monotony of labor
in the fields.

Ceremonials have the overt objective of renewing ties with the world of
the spirit. But at the same time they serve the double purposes of satisfying the individual's need for a change of pace and the community's need
for reinforcement of solidarity. A great many Niiike people today may be
neutral to if not skeptical about the supernatural functions of ceremonies
at the village shrine. For one thing, they have been through a full course
of science-oriented, naturalistic public schooling; and though schools before the end of World War II were permeated with compelled worship of
the emperor as the great spiritual guardian of Japan, defeat in war dealt
a blow to such faith in divinity. But they are fully and clearly aware of
the individual and social benefits of shrine ceremonial and consider these
functions desirable regardless of the state of their religious convictions.
Consequently, there is concerted participation in the calendrical ceremonials, although the attitude often seems practical rather than mystical,
especially among younger persons.

A few of the annually recurrent ceremonies that absorb the leisure hours
of the Niiike community conflict with the schedule of field labor. Most
of these involve only single households and are part of the Buddhist cult
celebrated in connection with the Buddhist temple. The greater number
of ceremonies by far involve more than single households and usually occupy the whole community. They occur in rhythmic alternation to periods
of heavy work. They are spaced along the calendar in a cycle that gives
form and meaning to the passing seasons, just as does the unending cycle
of crops. The harmonious pulse of work alternating with ceremonials offers
us, in fact, an explanation of the otherwise mystifying neglect of certain
ceremonies that are almost identical in form and purpose to others which
are heavily stressed. As Table 4 shows, the calendrical ceremonies clearly
fall into five or more groups when they are compared on the basis of objectives and forms, irrespective of their order on the calendar.

Of the five groups, the most recent is the set of dates fixed by the government as national holidays. These are observed by banks, schools, and
business firms throughout the nation, often by closing for the day, but
they get little or no attention from farmers. The seasonal ceremonies in
the second column are seven: a quartet of festivals for all the four seasons
and a trio of prayer days that serve as prelude to three of the four festivals. New Year's and the Fall Festival are two of Niiike's primary ceremonial occasions, whereas the others are minor. In a third group are fes-

tivals fixed on odd-numbered days of the same odd-numbered months and symbolized by flowering plants appropriate to each date. The system originated in China; the Japanese borrowed it long ago and make of the Cherry Blossom Day a flower-viewing day of nationwide popularity; the Bamboo Day, or *Tanabata*, is moderately important to children in Niiike and elsewhere; but Niiike and most of Japan tend to ignore the remainder. Children are the ones primarily concerned with the next group,

TABLE 4

PRINCIPAL POPULAR CEREMONIES IN NIIIKE

Month	Official Calendrical Holidays	Traditional Calendrical Ceremonies			
		Seasonal Prayers	Flower Festivals	Children's Festivals	Ancestral (Buddhist) Ceremonies
1.....	New Year 1* Adult Day 15*	New Year 1–15 Prayers 9–11†	Seven-grasses 7		
2.....					
3.....	Equinox 21*		Peach 3 Cherry 15*†	Girls' Day 3	Equinox 21*
4.....	Emperor's Birth- day 29*				
5.....	Constitution Day 3* Children's Day 5*	Spring Prayers 1–11† Spring Festival 14*† Summer Festival 14†	*Shobu* (Iris) 5	Boys' Day 5	
6					
7			*Tanabata* (Bamboo) 7		*Bon* (13–15)
8					
9.....	Equinox 23*	Fall Prayers 10–11† Fall Festival 12–13*†	Chestnut 9		Equinox 23*
10.....					
11.....	Culture Day 3* Labor Thanks- giving Day 23*			Seven-five- three Day 15	
12.....					(Clean graves)

* Solar dates; all other dates are lunar, hence a month or so late by solar calendar (e.g., New Year is in early February).
† Dates which vary with locality, convenience, etc.

though these festivals began as calendrically spaced rituals of purification for women or for all persons; only Girls' Day (alternatively, Doll Day) gets much attention as a holiday in Niiike, though the decorations that announce the approach of Boys' Day usually are in evidence. The fifth set is distinguished by being associated with the Buddhist temples and the cemetery rather than with the village shrine; on these days the households of all the communities of the nation join in venerating their respective ancestors and, while *Bon* has grown to become a three-day holiday, a fair amount of attention is also given to the other three occasions, as also to other Buddhist ceremonies of veneration that recur on dates which differ from one household to the next and so are not listed in Table 4.

The aim of all the traditional ceremonies except the Buddhist occasions is to preserve and promote harmony with nature. Harmony, as represented in the dependable ripening of the crops, the health and continued fertility of the members of the community, freedom from the natural disasters of plague, flood, and conflagration, is achieved in considerable part by common-sense, practical measures but also by appropriate activities at the shrine. These activities are undertaken not so much in the spirit of appeal to a personalized deity as in the same matter-of-fact spirit that animates the transplanting and cultivation of crops, the tending of the hearth, or the mending of dikes and ditches; they are ceremonies which ritually channel the spiritual force that flows from the shrine out over the area it protects, and which, at the same time, by purifying each member of the community makes him fit to stay in touch with this beneficent spiritual force. Conceived as action relating man to nature, the ceremonies form a fitting counterpoint to the labor activities that have the same end.

When we match the ceremonial calendar against the crop calendar, as in Figure 29, we find there are three outstandingly important ceremonies: New Year's at the turn of the year, *Bon* in midsummer, and the Fall Festival in mid-autumn. The first two follow the two major work peaks of harvest and replanting, the last arrives just before the commencement of the all-important rice harvest. Other ceremonies tend to cluster in the slack work months of February through April and August through October, whereas the months between are either devoid of ceremony or have ones of minor importance.

What calls for further attention, however, is the fact that the harmony is not complete. Discords of various sorts occur that we should not expect, considering that the matching of a traditional round of ceremonies to a traditional round of crops has been in progress for many centuries. These discords in the system appear in several ways: conflict between work schedule and a ceremony that should have importance in view of prevailing modes of thought and custom (e.g., Boys' Day, which is curiously muted in comparison with Girls' Day if we consider the relative social superiority given to boys); celebration of one ceremony by a solar calendar date while its counterpart is set by the lunar calendar; and, as mentioned above, the variable amount of emphasis given to ceremonies that are systematically related to each other. Why have dates not been shifted, harmonized on one consistent calendar, be it solar or lunar, or otherwise adjusted to resolve these apparent discords and achieve full consistency?

One important answer is that changes either in social and supernaturalistic orientation or in the patterns of work have been taking place. Adjustments have been made, some of which are of temporary effectiveness, and further adjustments may be brought into the cycle. But the cycle is a living, changing thing with tensions as well as harmonies and will become static and fixed only if the ceremonies lose their connection with the total life of the villages, as they have begun to do in the cities of Japan. The discords and tensions, then, bring us back to forces that are at work to change the focus and pattern of community life.

The solar calendar, which Japan officially adopted in 1873, gives fixed

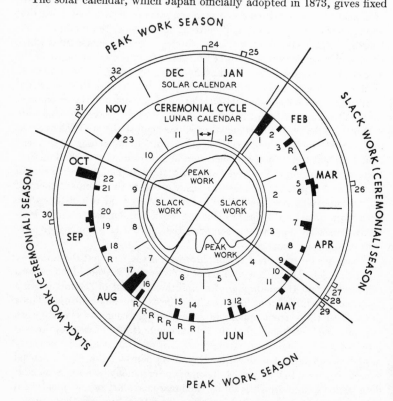

Popular Festivals. Length of line indicates importance
Orientation to lunar calendar　□ National holiday
Orientation to solar calendar　R Community rest day

Numbers next to festivals and holidays refer to numbers in text

Fig. 29.—Ceremonial and work cycles in Niiike. Note that important ceremonies occur during broad periods of relative leisure unoccupied by heavy farm work.

dates to the national holidays commemorating events and issues of national importance. The local community can do nothing to shift these dates, which are uniform over the entire nation, but neither the dates nor the purposes of the official holidays have any direct bearing on farm life. As a group, therefore, they are ignored in rural hamlets such as Niiike even though newspaper, radio, and school holidays or special events bring them to everyone's notice.

In the city all ceremonial dates have been shifted to the solar calendar. Throughout the countryside, however, the lunar calendar, a reckoning of twelve months of twenty-eight days each, appropriate enough to the village of several generations ago when everyone could see the moon but few could read a written calendar, is the standard basis for local ceremonies. Because of this, the same ceremony in the city comes about a month earlier than in the country, because the Japanese lunar first month happens to begin near February of the international solar calendar; and the gap varies from year to year because the lunar calendar of twenty-eight-day months crawls ahead of the solar calendar until, every five years, an extra intercalary month brings it back in harmony with the change of seasons. The rural preference for the lunar calendar reckoning of ceremonies is not unreasoningly conservative but stems from the general harmony between work and ceremonial dates created long ago on the basis of the lunar calendar. This harmony would be seriously upset if, say, lunar New Year were shifted to the accepted solar New Year.

The solar calendar has had its most direct influence on the rural ceremonial cycle by making possible the shift of traditional local ceremonies to the solar calendar if convenience warrants it; thus half-days of rest that are declared for the buraku by the Youth Association every fifth day during heavy rice cultivation in July now follow the solar calendar. In Niiike, the all-important Fall Festival and the less important Spring Festival have gone to the solar calendar equivalent of the tenth and fifth lunar month, respectively. We have no certain explanation of the Fall Festival shift, but it may have occurred with the advent of double cropping, for the planting and cultivating of dry grains during and immediately after rice harvest, as well as the increased quantity of harvested rice, extended that work-peak period across what may once have been a breathing spell for a thanksgiving ceremony in the late lunar tenth month. There is some evidence, according to Japanese scholars, that the Fall Festival, now a pre-harvest festival everywhere, was a thanksgiving after the harvest in ancient times. The reason for the shift in the Spring Festival date is clear simply from inspection of the work schedule, for it now fits into the very beginning of the year's highest work peaks, from late May through July.

During this period conflict with the work schedule presses on a cluster of ceremonies, increasingly so since the mat-rush harvest has come to fill July, and it does not answer the problem entirely to shift each one a month earlier. If the Boys' Day, the Spring Prayers, and the Summer Festival cannot, like the Spring Festival, eventually be accommodated on their equivalent solar calendar dates, they face demotion to the low status of other ceremonies of early summer which are now too minor to be listed in Table 4.

In general, a non-Buddhist festival day is marked by two events: a visit to the shrine by the househead or a delegated member, with or without the family, and generally in company with representatives from every other household; and the serving of some special food. Other events such as dancing and the playing of special games may occur, either as a necessary part of the festival or simply because the occasion offers the opportunity. The day itself is the climax and the termination; although the village may have been decorated for it as much as two or three weeks in advance, the decorations are taken down and stored away on the night that ends the festival.

CATALOGUE OF ANNUAL CEREMONIES

Calendrical order of ceremonies is followed below (see Fig. 29). The ceremonies are divided into two groups, traditional and official. The latter comprises national legal holidays, some of which date only from the end of World War II. The former are those observed in Niiike; phrases such as "all communities" identify widely popular ceremonies, but even widespread ceremonies may occur on different dates elsewhere.

TRADITIONAL CEREMONIES

1–3. NEW YEAR (*shōgatsu*); lunar first month, days 1–3; 4–6; 7, 9, 11, 15; Shinto and Buddhist. *Purpose:* to welcome the new year, renew community ties, and pray for welfare (Shinto); to venerate ancestors (Buddhist). *Persons:* all adults and children of all communities. *Preparation:* clear away debts, clean the house, tidy up graves; place straw ornaments or a pine branch at the entrance to the house by the last day of the old year (*o-misoka*). *Activities:* (1) feasting at home, a round of goodwill visits nearby, a visit to the shrine; (2) trip to parents or relatives paid by bride or daughter who lives away from home; venerate ancestors at home and at graves (Buddhist); (3) work resumed with intermittent days of rest; a soup of "seven spring grasses" is served on the first rest day, and ceremonial hoeing in the rice seed beds (*yarebo*, or *yae-ho*) used to be practiced; on the fifteenth, all ornaments are burned in a community bonfire (*tondo*). *Foods:* glutinous rice cakes (*mochi*), including large cakes pyramided on a mirror; a special soup (*zōni*); tangerines and oranges. *Note:* its protracted and intense activity makes the New Year one of the top three celebrations. It is one of five seasonal occasions called *sekku* that fall in odd-numbered months on days of the same number: first, third, fifth, seventh, and ninth. *See* Nos. 7, 12, 16; the Chestnut *sekku* (ninth month, day 9) is not observed in Niiike.

4. LITTLE NEW YEAR (*ko-shōgatsu*); lunar second month, day 1; Shinto. *Purpose:* to rest. *Persons:* all adults and children of all communities (optional). *Preparation:* none. *Activities:* rest and a special meal with New Year foods. *Foods: mochi, zōni.*

5. NIRVANA-MEETING (*nehan-e*); lunar second month, day 15; Buddhist. *Purpose:* to celebrate the Buddha's passing to Nirvana, spoken of as "Buddha's death." *Persons:* adults (optional). *Preparation:* none. *Activities:* visit the temple for special services sometime during the day. *Foods:* none. *Note:* celebrated mainly by temples of Shin sects on varying dates. For Niiike, it is celebrated only at Sōrenji, hereditary temple of the Hiramatsu lineages.

6A. EQUINOX (*higan*); solar March 18–25; Buddhist. *Purpose:* to venerate ancestors. *Persons:* all persons of all communities, by households. *Preparation:* tidy up the family graves and arrange leafy branches of *shikimi* tree; set out ancestral tablets in the house, with offerings in front. *Activities:* venerate ancestors at home and at graves each day, if possible, near evening; set out bits of uncooked rice and water; have "ascetic" supper on the equinox or the last day. *Foods:* offerings of rice and water; "ascetic" cooking prohibits the use of salt, fish, flesh, eggs, or sake. *Note:* equivalent ceremony at autumnal equinox, at New Year, and at *Bon* (*see* Nos. 2, 17, 20).

6B. EARTH SPIRIT FESTIVAL (*Jijin matsuri*); day-of-the-dog nearest the vernal equinox, March 21; Shinto. *Purpose:* to celebrate the Earth Spirit's rise from the earth. *Persons:* household representatives of the community, in most communities. *Preparation:* collect a small bit of rice from each house for communal meal. *Activities:* rest, especially (in theory, not practice) avoiding any work that disturbs the earth; toward evening, representatives assemble at inscribed votive stone of the Earth Spirit to pray (Buddhist style) and offer "red rice" balls and ceremonial sake (*miki*). Give children rice balls while representatives share a simple communion meal. *Foods:* rice balls of "red rice" (steamed rice mixed with red beans); ordinary sake, called *miki* because dedicated to ceremonial use. *Note:* a parallel ceremony occurs near the autumnal equinox (*see* No. 19). Both may be called *shanichi*.

7A. DOLL DAY (*hina matsuri*) or Girls' Day; lunar third month, day 3; Shinto. *Purpose:* amusement of children, especially girls. *Persons:* girls of the household below adolescence, in all communities; boys may join. *Preparation:* a stand is set up with stepped tiers, covered with red cloth, on which are displayed special dolls representing an ancient imperial court; also other decorations including special rice cakes and "red rice" balls. *Activities:* children dressed in finery visit each other's houses, play various games, eat special foods. *Foods:* rice cakes made in a pyramid of four to six diamond shape layers, alternate layers dyed green or red (*hishi mochi*); "red rice" balls; sweet, slightly fermented rice-gruel (*amazake*); any party food. *Note:* this ceremony was first popularized in the nineteenth century.

7B. MOUNTAIN-CLIMBING (*yama-agari*); lunar third month, day 4; Shinto. *Purpose:* amusement on a picnic. *Persons:* children of the community, accompanied by male youths. *Preparation:* packing picnic lunch. *Activities:* children dressed in finery and the youths climb the highest nearby hill about midday; the children eat their picnic lunch, the youths add sake-drinking. *Foods:* any picnic foods, plus sake. *Note:* picnicking and sake-drinking are important in Flower-viewing (*hana-mi*), a nationally observed ceremony, undertaken during cherry blossom season. Has lost its original import, of bringing the Mountain Spirit down to give fertility to the irrigated fields during their growing season.

8. GREAT KISHIMO FESTIVAL (*Kishimo-taizai*); lunar third month, day 17, though the "proper date" is solar April 3 or 4; Buddhist. *Purpose:* to worship Kishimo, a converted demoness and protectress of children. *Persons:* parents of any community (optional). *Preparation:* temple priest posts notice of visiting lecturer on community bulletin board. *Activities:* attend temple to hear lecture and services. *Foods:* none. *Note:* Performed only at the Hiramatsu ancestral temple, Sōrenji; this ceremony gets little attention in Niiike.

9. PRAYERS (*gokitō*); lunar third month, about day 9, but set by agreement; Shinto. *Purpose:* to insure health and welfare of the community. *Persons:* household representatives of the community. *Preparation:* host household fixes the date, collects a pint of rice and ¥5 from each house, obtains inscribed slips of paper from the temple to impale on a stick at roadside at each end of the community. *Activities:* representatives assemble at Kōjin shrine for prayers, followed by a meal at the house having the hostship (*yaku*). Prayers ask for welfare of each household, the community, and (in this generation) the nation. *Foods:* fish is emphasized in the meal. *Note:* One of a trio of annual prayers (see Nos. 13, 21).

10. DAIKOKU FESTIVAL (*Daikoku-sama no matsuri*); lunar fourth month, day 3; Buddhist. *Purpose:* to honor the abbot Daikoku, apostle of Nichiren doctrines in western Honshu. *Persons:* households of Nichiren faith (optional). *Preparation:* none. *Activities:* prayers and offerings of food and dedicated sake at stone with Nichiren inscription; those so inclined spend the night at nearby temple associated with Daikoku, hearing sermons and praying. *Foods:* children receive rice balls, *mochi* cakes, etc., to eat after these foods have been offered. Men drink the offertory sake.

11. SPRING FESTIVAL (*haru no matsuri*); solar May 14; Shinto. *Purpose:* to insure welfare of the community. *Persons:* household representatives of the community, with those of other communities. *Preparation:* Youth Association members raise banners at center of housing area, at beginning of the

day. *Activities:* Representatives assemble in early evening at Kōjin shrine on top of Tsukuriyama tomb, some with offerings. *Food:* dedicated sake (*miki*) and *mochi* as offerings. *Note:* One of three seasonal festivals (see Nos. 15, 22), less important than the third (fall) festival.

12A. BOYS' DAY; literally, *tango* Seasonal Day (*tango no sekku*); lunar fifth month, day 5; Shinto. *Purpose:* amusement of children, especially boys. *Persons:* boys of the household below adolescence; children in general. *Preparation:* large "wind-sock" banners in shape and color of orange or black carp are flown from pole in yard for two or three weeks; a pair of large vertical banners picturing a mounted warrior is raised at yard entrance for a similar length of time; decoration of the *tokonoma* inside the house includes a warrior helmet or warrior dolls on a stand, a toy tiger with a bobbing head, and *kintoki* dolls (with character for "gold" [*kin*] inscribed on bib). *Activities:* children visit among homes, are given special foods to eat. *Foods: mochi* cakes wrapped in a large oak leaf; balls of "red rice"; other sweets and cakes. *Note:* most houses, pressed by fieldwork, do little other than preparations listed above.

12B. IRIS SEASONAL DAY (*shōbu no sekku*); lunar fifth month, day 5; Shinto. *Purpose:* prophylaxis against illness and disaster. *Persons:* household representatives of the community, in all communities. *Preparation:* nosegay made of *shōbu* (a type of iris), miscanthus, mugwort, and a moss. *Activities:* nosegay is placed on eave above main entrance to the house; *shōbu* is placed in the bath stall. *Foods:* none.

12C. OX-SPIRIT DAY (*ushi no kamisama no hi*); lunar fifth month, day 5; Shinto. *Purpose:* to insure welfare of household oxen. *Persons:* representatives of ox-owning households in the community (optional). *Preparation:* none. *Activities:* at a time individually convenient, offer cakes and ceremonial sake at an unmarked ox-spirit stone in hillside group of stones. Tie *shōbu* garland around ox horns before leading ox to stone: leave garland at stone. *Food:* ordinary cakes and dedicated sake. *Note:* some say the proper date is lunar fifth month, day 15. In part because of overlapping ceremonies on day 5, the ox-spirit ceremony is all but completely ignored.

13. PRAYERS (*gokitō*); lunar fifth month, about day 9 but set by agreement; Shinto. *See* No. 9 (Prayers) for description. This is the second of the three annual community Prayers.

14. DISEASE SPIRIT FESTIVAL (*Yakujin matsuri*); lunar sixth month, day 6; Shinto. *Purpose:* to ward off illness from everyone in the community. *Persons:* household representatives of the community. *Preparation:* none. *Activities:* representatives gather at inscribed Disease Spirit stone in hillside group of stones, light tapers in the lantern, offer cakes and dedicated sake (cakes are then given to the children). *Foods:* none apart from offerings. *Note:* this ceremony has been all but completely ignored since World War II.

15. SUMMER FESTIVAL (*natsu no matsuri*); lunar sixth month, about day 14 but set by agreement; Shinto. *See* No. 11 (Spring Festival) for description. The basic pattern is also like that of No. 22 (Fall Festival).

16. TANABATA; lunar seventh month, day 7; Shinto. *Purpose:* amusement and instruction of children. *Persons:* mainly children of grammar-school age, of all communities. *Preparation:* children select tall sprigs of bamboo, attach colored paper slips on which they have written a character or a poem, according to ability; also attach decoratively cut slices of new eggplant and cucumber, set the sprig up in the front yard or against the front wall. Lay out festive foods under the tree. *Activities:* after eating the festive foods at evening, children take the poem-bamboo to a stream (a pond in Niiike, in default of a convenient stream) and toss it, decorations and all, into the water. *Foods: dango* (sugary rice cakes, originally of sorghum), vermicelli soup and "red rice," with evening meal. *Note:* Associated with a Chinese star-story known as "The Herd Boy and the Weaving Girl."

17. BON, or *urabon;* lunar seventh month, days 13–15; Buddhist. *Purpose:* to venerate the ancestors. *Persons:* all persons of all communities by households. *Preparation:* clean the house, tidy the family graves, and arrange *shikimi* branches in the *tokonoma*, set out the ancestral tablets on a white cloth, together with a display of rice cakes, *mochi*, and the best vegetables in season. May set up a covered wooden stand outside with small rice offering for unattached ancestral spirits. *Activities:* paper lantern hung out in front of the house each evening. Prayers to the household ancestors, everyone in the house participating, are followed by a stroll to the graves to make rice and water offerings. On evenings of the first and third days, young boys light small fires of pine roots along the road to welcome the visiting ancestral spirits and to speed their departure. A selection of offerings is put into a small straw boat on the last evening. Household representatives bring the boats, a lighted candle set in each one, to a bonfire built where boats used to be floated down an irrigation ditch; the boats now are burned. Up to sixty years ago, young people of both sexes performed special dances, which now are skipped. On *bonrei* (day 16) women and absent relatives go to native place to pay respects to the household ancestors. *Foods:* No special dishes except favorites, but should conform to ascetic prohibitions of salt, fish, flesh, eggs, and sake. *Note:* one of the year's three big ceremonies (see New Year, No. 1–3, and Fall Festival, No. 22).

18. NICHIREN FESTIVAL (*Nichiren matsuri*); lunar eighth month, day 12; Buddhist. *Purpose:* commemoration of Nichiren, founder of the Hokke sect. *Persons:* all households of Hokke sect in the community (optional). *Preparation:* collect a small bit of rice from each house for offerings. *Activities:* household representatives assemble before stone inscribed with Nichiren sutra and recite the sutra in unison as the leader sets time by ringing a bell. Make offerings of rice and water; give children rice balls. *Note:* Because

activities duplicate those for *Shanichi* (see below), except for the particular stone at which ceremonies are aimed, this Nichiren ceremony tends to be cursory.

19. SHANICHI, or Earth Spirit Festival (*Jijin matsuri*); day-of-the-dog nearest the equinox, September 22; Shinto. *Purpose:* to accompany the Earth Spirit's returning into the earth. *See* No. 6B (Earth Spirit Festival), a parallel vernal equinox, ceremony for description.

20. EQUINOX (*higan*); autumnal equinox, September 22; Buddhist. *See* No. 6A for description.

21. PRAYERS (*gokitō*); lunar ninth month, about day 9 but set by agreement; Shinto. *See* No. 9 for description and No. 13 for the second of this trio of annual prayers.

22. FALL FESTIVAL (*aki no matsuri*); Solar October 12 and 13; Shinto. *See* No. 11 for basic description. Of four seasonal festivals (New Year, Spring, Summer, and Fall), the first and last are primary holidays of the year. More elaborate than the Spring Festival, this festival includes: *Preparation:* Youth Association sets up a covered wooden arch across main road in which candles burn at night; in addition they raise banners. *Activities:* paper lantern hung out before each house; in fine clothes, people do much visiting, feasting, and drinking of sake within the community and with friends nearby.

23. MEMORIAL SERVICE (*eshiki*); lunar tenth month, day 12; Buddhist. *Purpose:* to commemorate all the dead. *Persons:* Nichiren sect members (optional). *Preparation:* prepare *mochi* cakes. *Activities:* visit a Nichiren temple for prayers at various spots pertaining to the dead. Offer *mochi* cakes to households not of Nichiren faith. *Foods: mochi* cakes (given away). *Note:* participation is slight, confined mostly to a few elders of Niiike.

OFFICIAL PUBLIC HOLIDAYS (ALL BY OFFICIAL, OR SOLAR, CALENDAR)

24. NEW YEAR'S DAY (*ganjitsu*); January 1. *Purpose:* to celebrate arrival of the New Year. *Activities:* none in Niiike. *Remarks:* the present holiday, new since 1946, replaces three former occasions all of which centered on ceremonies performed by the emperor; Worship-in-Four-Directions (*shihō-hai*) on January 1, New Year Ceremony (*genshisai*) on January 3, and New Year Banquet (*shinnen-enkai*) on January 5. Many offices now close for three days, January 1–3.

25. ADULTS' DAY (*seijin no hi*); January 15. *Purpose:* to honor youths who have just reached adulthood. *Activities:* Kamo officials sponsor a meeting for youths, which some young people from Niiike may choose to attend. *Remarks:* the present holiday was first declared in 1946.

26. VERNAL EQUINOX (*shumbun no hi*); March 21 or 22. *Purpose:* to honor nature and enjoy all living things. *Activities:* celebrated in Niiike as Equinox

(*higan*); *see* No. 6, above. *Remarks:* the present name, new since 1946, replaces Spring Imperial Ancestor Worship Ceremony (*shunki kōrei sai*) on the pre-1946 official calendar. A prewar holiday for women that was abolished in 1946 without replacement was the empress' birthday, March 6.

27. EMPEROR'S BIRTHDAY (*tennō tanjōbi*); April 29. *Purpose:* to honor the present emperor on his birthday. *Activities:* none in Niiike. *Remarks:* the present name, new since 1946, replaces the same holiday, with the same purpose, named *tenchō setsu*. The death anniversary of the Emperor Jimmu (*Jimmu tennō sai*), honoring the legendary founder of the imperial line, was formerly celebrated on April 3. It was abolished in 1946 without replacement.

28. CONSTITUTION MEMORIAL DAY (*kempō kinembi*); May 3. *Purpose:* to commemorate the granting of the postwar national constitution. *Activities:* none in Niiike, unless someone chooses to attend the oratorical meeting in the Okayama civic auditorium. *Remarks:* the present holiday was first declared in 1946.

29. CHILDREN'S DAY (*kodomo no hi*); May 5. *Purpose:* to honor all children. *Activities:* None in Niiike, although spring Prayers on the lunar calendar (*see* No. 9) may coincide with this or the foregoing two holidays, depending on the year. *Remarks:* in the city, where people observe the solar calendar, this is the new name, since 1946, for the traditional Boys' Day (*see* No. 12).

30. AUTUMNAL EQUINOX (*shūbun no hi*); September 23 or 24. *Purpose:* to worship the family ancestors. *Activities:* celebrated in Niiike as Equinox (*higan*) (*see* No. 20, above). *Remarks:* the present name dates from 1946. It replaces Autumn Imperial Ancestor-Worship Ceremony (*shūki kōrei sai*). The Harvest Thanksgiving Festival (*kanname sai*) set on October 17 prior to 1946, marked by the emperor's dispatching of rice to the great shrine at Ise, was abolished in 1946.

31. CULTURE DAY (*bunka no hi*); November 3. *Purpose:* to honor cultural activities. *Activities:* none in Niiike, unless someone chooses to attend the speeches and dance and music performances in the Okayama civic auditorium. *Remarks:* the present holiday, new since 1946, replaces the Commemorative Festival for the Meiji emperor (*Meiji setsu*) celebrated prior to that time.

32. LABOR THANKSGIVING DAY (*kinrō kansha no hi*); November 23. *Purpose:* to honor laborers and their work. *Activities:* none in Niiike. *Remarks:* this holiday, new since 1946, replaces the second Thanksgiving Festival (*niiname sai*), marked by the emperor's partaking of new rice, and the simultaneous celebration of the emperor's enthronement (*daijōe*). One further prewar holiday abolished in 1946 without replacement was the death anniversary of the Taishō emperor (*Taishō tennō sai*), father of the current reigning emperor, on December 26.

8. *Income* AND EXPENDITURE

In the previous chapter we have described Niiike's economy in terms of the cycle of work and the many varieties of productive enterprise in which her farmers are engaged. In this chapter we will attempt to analyze Niiike's economic balance, tracing quantitatively the productive factors that provide income in cash or credit and balancing these against costs and other elements of investment and consumption. The treatment, though unavoidably incomplete in details, will demonstrate more specifically what we have already observed in general terms, namely, that Niiike, as an up-to-date community in modern Japan, has been able to diversify its economic base and to adjust reasonably well to the economic problems and opportunities of modern Japan.

Income from sources other than agriculture and the processing of home-grown rush now constitutes almost a quarter (23 per cent) of Niiike's measurable net income. In the main, it is the salaries of men at work in town that provide this important fraction. The remaining three-quarters of Niiike's net income derives from agriculture or the processing of agricultural products. Rice, although primary, contributes only 37 per cent of the community's total net income. Mat rush and its processing bring in another 31 per cent, while wheat, barley, vegetables, fruit, livestock, and firewood account for the remaining 9 per cent.

The rice, wheat, and barley harvests (43 per cent of total net income) provide staple food plus just about enough money or credit to cover fertilizer and other costs of production and to pay most taxes. Rush and its processing is the main source of income for the ordinary and special cash costs of living. Thus, rush prices on the open market together with the availability of outside jobs largely determine the community's standard of living during the year. Taking all income from crops and other sources together the community as a whole does somewhat better than break even in years of reasonably good harvests and markets. After taxes, there is a small cash surplus, which usually is left as credit in the agricultural co-operative, to provide for such extraordinary expenses as marriages, illness, or funerals—which every provident househead must foresee—or to be invested someday in tools, land, or a new house. These are the main features that emerge from a close look at the structure of the community's economy and within it the economy of the Niiike farming household.

SOURCES AND TREATMENT OF DATA

At this point, we should note again the difficulties that beset any attempt to obtain and analyze statistical figures dealing with economy or finance. First, the very nature of farm life is not conducive to exact bookkeeping. Whenever the housewife plucks a few vegetables from the garden for the family pot or decides to use today's eggs in soup instead of selling them, these potential items of production and consumption are lost from the record. Nor is any account kept of family labor, be it hard work in the field or a half-hour spent chatting with neighbors and holding the nose rope of the ox while it grazes along the road.

Another problem is the long-standing social convention in a farm village that makes money matters private, not to be exposed, probed, or inspected. Farmers dealing with outsiders are understandably reticent, even in speaking about non-pecuniary matters such as soil fertility, acreage, insecticide, and fertilizer in terms which might lead to monetary conclusions. Generations of tax agents representing highly exploitative regimes have been looking into just such matters, to the disadvantage of the producer, who is convinced that at best his costs of production, being more elusive than his returns, are undervalued. Again, any public statement of an individual farm's worth is very apt to affect relations with neighbors, whether the results are better, worse, or no different from what they expected.

The people of Niiike necessarily have been our principal source of information on these matters, if only because their experienced estimates are better than available records. They made a serious effort to assist this inquiry and showed a rather remarkable sophistication in such bookkeeping concepts as income, expenditure, interest, depreciation, and overhead —a sophistication sharpened, no doubt, by practice on complex annual income-tax forms.

We were able, with their help, to observe at two levels how Niiike makes a living. First, a systematic inquiry was made in 1951 by Charles F. Remer, professor of economics, into the sources of income throughout the year for the buraku as a whole and into the uses to which income was put. Household economy as seen from this approach is the economy of a hypothetical average household. This approach is supplemented at a second level by a review of the cash accounts kept by one of the community's medium-sized households during 1950. At both levels, certain factors cannot be accurately accounted for and, hence, do not appear in the resulting balance sheet. There is, for example, no estimate of labor as a component of production costs, and there is no account of farm produce consumed at home, except for rice, a major staple. Since home-consumed produce—consisting mainly of barley, vegetables, fruit, and some eggs—would appear both as a component of income and a component of expenditure, failure to compute it probably does not significantly distort the balance sheet but simply lowers the totals, making this record not directly comparable with, for example, the records of urban families where cash figures would represent more completely production and consumption. Labor does not cancel out so simply. Save for a few special purposes, it does not involve any cash outlay by members of the community.

Again, the above-mentioned record of a single household's accounts, which consists simply of the housewife's day-by-day notes of cash transactions in one of the few Niiike households that keep such books, besides providing no record of labor or the amount of home-consumed produce also fails to note credit transactions through the local agricultural co-operative. The co-operative served as agent for the government in the requisitioning of produce, which in 1950 included rice, wheat, barley, and rape seed for oil. Probably 40 per cent or more of the household's total annual income for that year consisted of credits on the books of this co-operative, only 60 per cent or less passing as cash through the farmer's hands. Thus total income does not balance with total expenditure in this incomplete record. Nevertheless, while we cannot directly compare this household record with the more complete per-household average derived from the all-buraku study, its detailed breakdown of cash income and expenditure is an important supplement.

In 1951, the period of inquiry into the buraku economy, Niiike had 23 households and a population of 127 persons. The average household size at that time was 5.52 persons, slightly less than the average three years later. Landholdings of Niiike households were computed as totaling 52.2 acres (21.5 chō or 215 tan). This figure was used where necessary in computing costs and agricultural production but is almost 17 per cent below the total of 62.7 acres derived from a field-by-field survey of some 435 parcels traced to Niiike households. Parcels registered in the name of absent or deceased persons account in large part for the discrepancy. Field rentals may add a second slight source of error. Niiike people appear to rent a trifle more land from others than outsiders rent from them, but the net gain of acreage from rental is small. Most of the uncounted acreage in the smaller total, moreover, consists of wood lot, the least productive category of land, as the comparison of figures in Table 5 shows. In addition to the uncertainty concerning how much land is cultivated in Niiike, neither assessment shows how much of the cultivated acreage produces two crops annually. Effective paddy field acreage is larger than the acreage shown above, thanks to Niiike's double-cropping techniques. In sum, these considerations indicate that the landholding figures given above are a minimum assessment of land resources.

TABLE 5

Two Assessments of Landholding in Niiike

Description	Area Reported in 1951 Survey of Buraku Economy (in Acres)	Area Determined in 1951 Field-by-Field Census (in Acres)
Paddy field	34.1	36.4
Dry field	4.9	6.4
Wood lot	13.2	19.9
Total............	52.2	62.7

BURAKU INCOME[1]

The buraku as a whole derives income from cultivation of dry fields and irrigated fields, from wood lots, from animal products, from household processing, and from salaries earned outside. Each of these items may be considered separately. To discover how much Niiike makes from cultivation, the gross product must first be balanced against costs of production to obtain a net product figure. Costs differ for specific crops but can be calculated for each main category of crops without serious error. As to costs of tools and machines, the same tools are often used to cultivate or process crops in different categories and so enter separately into the production costs of such categories. For convenience, however, their depreciation is here treated as a unit and charged entirely to the production costs of rice, the crop for which they are most important.

GROSS AGRICULTURAL PRODUCTION

Dry-field minor crops.—Niiike households sell some of each of the following crops grown on their dry fields: sweet potatoes, red beans, soybeans, and fruit (persimmons, peaches, and grapes). Wheat and barley grown in small amounts on the dry hillside fields need not be considered here but can be considered with the far larger amount grown as an unirrigated winter crop in the paddy fields. An estimate of the quantity of dry-field produce sold is quite difficult, for this goes out of the buraku

[1] The calculations of Niiike's income and expenditure for 1950–51, which follow here, are set forth in tabular form in Table 7 on p. 204.

piecemeal. It is usually sold by the housewife to a peddler bicycling through the back roads of the countryside or is taken by the househead on his bicycle to one of the Kurashiki produce dealers. Since selling among the community's households is rare, almost all sales represent money entering the buraku from outside. Niiike's gross product for the crop year 1950–51 in this category was:

Sweet potatoes	¥48,400
Soybeans	19,665
Red beans	5,422
Fruit	25,000
Total	¥98,487

The total of ¥98,500 thus represents our estimate in round figures of the gross product in minor crops of Niiike's dry fields.

Wheat and barley.—To meet their government requisition quota for dry grains, Niiike farmers harvested seventeen acres of wheat and barley in 1951. The government prices, based on a scale of four grades, made up their gross income from dry grains. In later years, when requisitions were lifted from these crops, the farmers gave over much of the wheat acreage to mat-rush cultivation in the paddy fields and to fruit on the hill plots, for either rush or fruit is a better money-maker than wheat. An undetermined quantity of barley is consumed at home. If the common claim is valid that, through the year as a whole, the boiled "rice" of ordinary meals consists of at least one-third rolled barley mixed with two-thirds rice, the home-use quantity is considerable. In the absence of more precise information, it has not been possible to make allowance for the portion consumed at home. The portion of the barley crop requisitioned or sold has, therefore, been regarded as the total gross product. This procedure probably introduces some underestimation of gross income in this category, which may be balanced to some extent by a slightly generous calculation of Niiike's savings rate as reported below. With this qualification, we estimate Niiike's gross product in wheat and barley for the crop year 1950–51 at ¥271,000.

Rice.—Despite the various measures taken by the government to keep strict account of rice production—witness the apparatus of land fertility indexes, damage estimate committees, requisition inspection teams, quality grading of hulled and unhulled rice, and elaborate quota-setting procedures—the apparent precision of the official production and requisition statistics is misleading. They probably fall appreciably short of actual production, though we cannot say how far short. The year 1951 was a good crop year. At planting time a quota was assigned for each house to deliver to the government. This was based on the expectation of a normal harvest and was so calculated as to leave the household enough rice for its own consumption needs. In 1951 this quota was not subsequently revised upward, though any surplus above the quota and household needs could be sold to the government at a bonus price. Such surpluses were, of course, supposed to be reported but might well be diverted to the black market or other destinations. We have no evidence that very much Niiike rice went to the black market. In 1951 the local official figures indicate for Niiike a rice harvest averaging 46.6 bushels per acre. We consider this to be low but, in the absence of a more reliable estimate, have used this figure in the following calculations. In 1951 Niiike's 34 listed acres thus produced at least 1,584 bushels of rice, of which 803 bushels were requisitioned by the government, leaving 781 bushels for home consumption. Of this harvest, 820 bushels were rated as third grade and 764 bushels as fourth grade, the respective official prices for which were ¥1,112 and ¥1,080 per bushel (in terms of Japanese measures, the prices were ¥5,508 per *koku* and ¥5,358 per *koku*, respectively). Niiike's gross income from rice computed at official prices thus amounts to ¥1,736,960, or ¥1,737,000 in round figures.

Mat rush.—More important than dry grains as a winter crop in the irrigated fields is the mat rush, for it is sold on the open market by each grower and may bring a good cash price. The market for rush, historically quite unstable, has in general tended to be good in postwar years, especially the earlier ones when the entire nation was rebuilding. More recently, increasing production in new regions of the country has seriously threatened the farmers' returns from this difficult crop. The price of rush varies also with its length. It falls into four standard grades. Prices for the best grade during 1951 ranged from ¥700 to ¥250 per *kan* (8.27 lb.). Rush must be coated with clay ("dyed") before drying to achieve the "natural" color prized by its purchasers. The prices quoted above are for the "dyed" product. Rush was grown on 4.16 acres of Niiike land in 1951. The gross product from this is estimated at ¥975,000.

Firewood and lumber.—Besides their private holdings of wood-lot acreage, Niiike people in common with the other buraku of their ōaza hold half an acre of wood lot in common. Since this wood is used only for cremation fires at funerals, for which the user pays a small price, it contributes nothing to buraku income. The remaining holdings only occasionally provide a small bit of lumber, mostly for domestic use, and no lumber was reported sold in the year under study. Part of the pine needles, underbrush, and wood for fires gathered from these wood lots is sold, however. Four Niiike households with inadequate wood lots of their own buy a part of this, but most goes outside of the buraku. Only the latter is considered in our estimate of Niiike's gross production, which amounts to ¥20,000.

Animal husbandry.—The chicken population of Niiike holds fairly steady in spite of house-by-house fluctuations. In 1952, Hiramatsu Hideo's household turned to poultry as a major sideline, selling eggs rather than the white Leghorn chickens, but this event postdates our economic survey. Few eggs are eaten; they are sold to peddlers and bring in a small but steady income to about three out of four households. Milk from Hiramatsu Isamu's lone milch cow was sold in 1950, except for a fraction, to an outside creamery. The plow oxen produce no milk, so contribute productively only when a calf is born, trained, and sold when mature. Except for a few rabbits raised briefly by Hiramatsu Ai's teen-age sons, no other economically productive livestock exists in Niiike. Thus eggs, the milk of one dairy cow, and the sale of a couple of young oxen during the year contribute to a modest gross product in this line, which we estimate to be ¥138,000.

EXPENSES OF PRODUCTION

In determining expenses of production, labor costs should be included as well as an allowance for depreciation of equipment and for outlay for materials and supplies of all kinds. However, Niiike's people do practically all their own work, rarely hiring help even for the rush harvest. Money is paid out for labor only on special projects, such as house-building, which do not enter into our costs of production. Labor costs are not, therefore, included as an item of expense in these calculations. When the remaining expenses are deducted from the gross product figures established above, the remaining figure or net product represents the return for the labor of Niiike's households.

The principal expenses in connection with dry-field vegetable and fruit crops are fertilizer, much of which is night soil, costing nothing, and insecticide sprays. The cost during the 1950–51 crop year is estimated at ¥60,000. For the dry grain crops, wheat and barley, the main expenses are fertilizer, seed, and fuel for threshing. In the first category manure-straw from the ox-stalls costs nothing, but chemical fertilizer is used at an estimated rate of ¥4,000 per acre (¥1,000 per *tan*). Seed costs ¥480 per acre (¥120 per *tan*) and threshing-machine fuel ¥120 per acre (¥30 per *tan*). For the seventeen acres of wheat and barley harvested in 1951 the total expense of production is estimated at ¥78,200.

The cost of production of rice is relatively difficult to estimate. In connection with the calculation of 1950 income for tax purposes, the government allowed up to ¥1,700 per *koku* (4.96 bushels) of rice for production costs. Applied to Niiike's 34 acres of rice in 1951, this allowance amounts in round figures to no less than ¥544,000. Our independent estimate of the costs of production—including seed, insecticides, fertilizer, fuel, and depreciation on machinery—indicates that this official allowance is probably appreciably higher than actual cost. Much rice fertilizer is chemical and is purchased through the farm co-operative. In 1950–51 we estimated its cost to be approximately ¥210,000. Seed and insecticide were reported to cost an additional ¥11,000. The cost of kerosene used as fuel is difficult to compute for one crop for a single year but is thought to have been in the neighborhood of ¥110,000. In the present instance the depreciation of machinery is, for convenience' sake, charged entirely to rice cultivation. The people of Niiike suggested an annual depreciation rate of 5 per cent as reasonable. This was then applied to the machinery owned in 1951. Depreciation on the machines listed in Table 6 thus amounts to

TABLE 6

Equipment	Unit Cost	Cost	Depreciation at 5 Per Cent
Kerosene engines, 12.....	¥20,000	¥240,000	¥12,000
Screw pumps, 8..........	2,000	16,000	800
Threshing machines, 11...	15,000	165,000	8,250
Hulling machines, 2......	60,000	120,000	6,000
Polishing machines, 11....	2,000	22,000	1,100
Total...............	....	¥563,000	¥28,150

¥28,150; but an additional allowance must be made for simpler tools and equipment (winnowers, plows, etc.) and for storage structures. It is not unreasonable to suppose that the total should amount to at least ¥40,000. In addition, imputed interest may be allowed at least to the investment in machinery, if not to that in buildings and land connected with cultivation, since their worth does not represent a similar outlay of cash. Computed at 5 per cent of the value of the above machinery, this amounts to ¥28,150 or in round figures to another ¥28,000.

Thus, when the costs of rice production are considered in detail, the total outlay for fertilizer, seed and insecticide, fuel, depreciation, and interest on machinery amounts to at least ¥399,000. This sum is still appreciably below the official allowance of ¥544,000 for 1950. One concludes, therefore, that either the estimates obtained in Niiike were too low or, as seems more likely, actual production costs in Niiike are below the national average. The fertility of the land and availability of irrigation water lend credence to such an assumption. Nevertheless a substantial area of doubt remains, and we have, on balance, preferred to adopt the official figure of ¥544,000 as representing the cost of Niiike's rice production during the crop year 1950–51.

Mat rush requires an extraordinary amount of fertilizer, costing on the average about ¥24,000 per acre (¥6,000 per *tan*) for the year. On the 4.16 acres (17 *tan*) planted to rush in 1951, the fertilizer actually cost ¥102,000. Clay to coat the rush before drying cost about ¥6,000 per acre (¥1,500 per *tan*). The actual outlay was ¥25,500 for the whole crop. The expense incurred in producing mat rush for sale totaled ¥127,500.

No meaningful estimate has been possible of the cost of gathering fire-wood. As to costs for livestock, chickens are fed in part with purchased feed, and young chickens are bought and raised for egg production. Some silage materials are purchased for the milch cow. The expenses represent-ed by these items were not ascertained in total, but household estimates appear to justify an allowance of ¥100,000 for their cost of production.

NON-AGRICULTURAL INCOME

Two sources of income apart from crops are important to Niiike house-holds: *tatami* covers woven in the household as a side occupation and work outside the community for salary or wages.

An upright loom or two for weaving the three higher grades of rush into covers for *tatami* is standard equipment in almost any house in this section of the coastal plain. Children acquire some skill at the loom before they reach adolescence. Everyone finds a certain amount of spare time for weaving, but most of the covers are woven by women. Unlike villages supplied with higher voltage electricity, Niiike has no power looms but works entirely on hand looms, so there is no cost for electricity. The loom itself, made of wood, is quite cheap (about ¥3,000) and durable, so its depreciation is slight. Materials are the major expense—the rush which forms the weft and hemp twine for the warp. A skilful weaver can make five mat covers in a day of ten hours. A mat cover of the long, first-grade rush sells for ¥180, whereas the same amount of unwoven rush would bring only ¥90. Practically all households use their own rush and pay only for the hemp used (about ¥30 per mat). The added value for two hours' work on first-grade rush thus amounts to about ¥60. *Tatami* covers of second- or third-grade rush bring lower prices and are more difficult to weave. They provide income at the rate of ¥40–¥50 per mat. The value added by a year's production of mats within Niiike is estimated at ¥138,000.

In addition to such work within the community, eight men have full-time jobs outside Niiike, and two or three others work during agricultural slack seasons at the grain-processing mill in Takamatsu and elsewhere. Among the full-time outside workers, Hiramatsu Masao, an engineer in Kobe, returns home only on one or two weekends each month, while his wife and sons cultivate the fields. The Sensei's adopted son teaches school in Sōja; Hiramatsu Hideo works in the Kurashiki post office; and most of the others commute to government offices, the railroad yards, or machinery and motor manufacturing companies in Okayama City. Most of this employment is clerical, at a modest rate of pay ranging in 1951 from ¥6,000 to ¥10,000 per month. The combined income from these outside jobs was estimated to be ¥740,000 at the time of our survey.

TOTAL INCOME

We are now in a position to estimate in rough terms Niiike's total income from agricultural and non-agricultural sources. The figures are summarized in Table 7.

TABLE 7

SUMMARY OF ANNUAL INCOME AND EXPENDITURE FOR NIIIKE
BURAKU DURING THE CROP YEAR 1950–51

INCOME

	Gross Product	Expense	Net Product	Percentage of Net Production	Average per Household per Month	Average per Household for Year
Agricultural:						
Dry-field minor crops....	¥ 98,500	¥ 60,000	¥ 38,500	1.7		
Wheat and barley.......	271,000	78,200	192,800	8.2		
Rice...................	1,737,000	544,000	1,193,000	51.2		
Mat rush..............	975,000	127,500	847,500	36.4		
Firewood..............	20,000		20,000	0.9		
Livestock.............	138,000	100,000	38,000	1.6		
Subtotal..........	¥3,239,500	¥909,700	¥2,329,800	100.0	¥ 8,441 ($23.45)	¥101,296 ($281.38)
Non-agricultural:						
Tatami-cover weaving (added value)........			138,000		500 (1.39)	6,000 (16.67)
Salaries and services.....			740,000		2,681 (7.45)	32,174 (89.37)
Total net income....			¥3,207,800		¥11,622 ($32.28)	¥139,470 ($387.42)

EXPENDITURE

Direct taxes..............		¥ 480,000		¥1,739 ($ 4.83)	¥20,870 ($ 57.97)
Savings..................		350,000		1,268 (3.52)	15,217 (42.27)
Rice held back from requisition..................		569,500		2,161 (6.00)	25,935 (72.04)
Total................		¥1,426,500		¥5,168 ($14.35)	¥62,022 ($172.28)
Balance for cash expenditure		¥1,781,300		¥6,454 ($17.93)	¥77,448 ($215.14)
Total annual expenditure...............		¥3,207,800			

Net agricultural income for the entire buraku amounted to ¥2,329,800 ($6,471.67) during the crop year 1950–51. The average share of each of the twenty-three households comes to ¥101,296 ($281.38), or ¥8,441 ($23.45) per household per month. When these figures are increased by the addition of non-agricultural income, it emerges that Niiike's total net income in this year was ¥3,207,800 ($8,910.56). Distributed among twenty-three units this yields an average total income of ¥139,470 ($387.42) per household, or an average monthly income of ¥11,622 ($32.28) per household.

These figures should not be construed too literally. They represent the writers' best estimate of the community's income during a twelve-month period in 1950–51. The highly complex nature of the Japanese farm economy, the lack of accurate community or household records, and the constant intermingling of cash and kind in the local exchange system make a really accurate survey almost impossible. It is interesting to note, however, that the estimates of average household income obtained from this survey accord remarkably well with similar figures obtained independently from the district's tax records (see Table 20, p. 375) for the years 1949 and 1952. In view of the steady improvement of economic conditions in this area and Japan as a whole during these years, it would be expected that the 1950–51 figure for average income would fall roughly midway between the 1949 and 1952 figures, as it does. Needless to say, the community's average income has increased markedly in more recent years, as the tax records will show.

BURAKU EXPENDITURE

Items of community and household expenditure are in most instances even more difficult to determine accurately than are those of consumption. By aggregating such known or estimable items as direct taxes, savings, and the value of rice retained for household consumption and by subtracting the total so obtained from the community's net income, it is possible, however, to compute roughly the balance remaining to the community for cash expenditures.

Niiike's tax bill varies with changes in government tax policy. The tax records are analyzed in chapter 12. For 1950, Niiike's direct taxes were reported to total approximately ¥480,000 ($1,333.33). Other taxes are paid, of course, on salt, tobacco, sake, and other consumer goods, but it has not been possible to include them in the present estimate. The community's twenty-three households thus have a direct tax bill averaging ¥20,870 ($57.97) for the year, or ¥1,739 ($4.84) per month. This accounts for slightly less than 15 per cent of Niiike's net income.

Nearly all of the households in the buraku keep their savings in the form of credit in the Agricultural Co-operative Association. The exceptions, so far as could be determined, are negligible. A few keep ready cash in the house, and some buy postal savings or have money out on personal loan, but there is a remarkable lack of interest in depositing savings in city banks. Past experience may partly account for this. Prewar savings, other than those kept in the local co-operative, were either frozen or made difficult to withdraw until the postwar inflation had pushed prices so high that Hiramatsu Hisa, when she finally drew out her postal savings, had just about enough to buy some sweets on her way home. Until the last few years, moreover, year-end credit balances at the co-operative were apt to be very low, so a person with savings in a bank would have to make an inconvenient trip to the city to withdraw money for fertilizer, seed, and insecticide at planting time. Personal checks of the American type are not a part of Japanese banking practice.

The accounts kept at the co-operative have been examined to provide a check on the amount of savings reported in the economic survey of Niiike's 1950 income and expenditure. Unfortunately, even though the

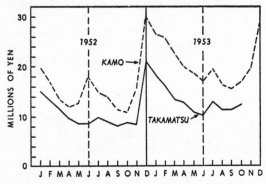

Fig. 30.—Fluctuation of the total credit balance of members of the agricultural co-operative associations in Kamo and in Takamatsu, 1952 and 1953. Note that the over-all trend in these years is upward and that main peaks occur just after the rice harvest.

local co-operative holds almost all savings, they are entered as credit. The credit balance fluctuates so greatly that an attempt to compare it against the reported savings to verify Niiike's rate of saving is severely handicapped. Figure 30 shows fluctuations in the credit accounts of the 502 members of the Kamo Village Agricultural Co-operative Association during the calendar years 1952–53. The rice harvest in November produces a sharp, high peak of credit at the end of the year, which is preceded by a low point. Immediately after, the harvest accounts drop rapidly as people pay their bills to start the new year right. The wheat harvest in June also increases credit but to a minor degree compared with November. The records of the neighboring Takamatsu Co-operative exhibit the same phenomenon, as Figure 30 shows.

Where Niiike is concerned, our economic survey reported the total 1950 savings to be approximately ¥350,000, an average of ¥1,268 per household per month or ¥15,217 for the year. This amounts to about 11 per cent of the community's net income and seems improbably high. Niiike informants possibly interpreted "savings" to mean minimum credit balance during the year rather than a savings gain over the preceding year. In 1952, according to the accounts summarized in Figure 30, the credit of the average member of the Kamo Co-operative ranged from ¥21,000 to ¥61,000. A minimum credit balance of ¥15,217 per member for the less prosperous year of 1950 would not seem implausible. Yet to mistrust Niiike informants, who may have been reporting savings held elsewhere in addition to their credit gain during 1950 at the co-operative, may be unjustified. It must be kept in mind that each household must normally expect to shoulder the periodic cost of weddings (¥20,000–¥45,000), funerals (¥25,000–¥35,000), memorial services for various ancestors (¥2,000–¥4,000), major house repairs such as rethatching the roof (¥35,000), and the like. Any number of such expenses over a decade would be impossible without a considerable rate of savings. With these qualifications then, we accept a 1950 savings rate for Niiike of ¥350,000.

On deducting these estimates of direct taxes and savings from the community's net income, we get a balance of ¥2,377,800. Not all of this is in cash, however. An important exception is rice for household consumption. The buraku appears to keep about half of its rice crop, worth about ¥596,500 at the requisition rate, for this purpose. This amount is equivalent to an average of ¥25,935 ($72.04) per household for the year, or ¥2,161 ($6.00) per month.

These three items of ascertainable community expenditure during 1950 —direct taxes, savings, and rice withheld for home use—total ¥1,426,500 ($3,962.50). If apportioned among the 23 households, they yield an average annual expenditure for these purposes of ¥62,022 ($172.28), or ¥5,168 ($14.35) per household per month. By deducting these totals from the buraku's total net income, one may approximate the amount of cash remaining to the community to cover all other expenses during the year. This amounts to ¥1,781,300 ($4,948.06) for the buraku as a whole, or ¥77,448 ($215.14) per household for the year. The monthly sum would be ¥6,454 ($17.93) per household. It is with this balance that Niiike's households must pay for clothes, most prepared foods, equipment, education, and entertainment, all of which is acquired outside the buraku.

ONE FAMILY'S FINANCIAL PROBLEMS

The foregoing sections give some statistical insight into Niiike's financial circumstances in 1950–51. They fall far short, however, of conveying what such conditions mean in human terms. What thought do the people give to increasing their income? For what do they spend their available cash, and what standards of judgment do they use? What wants go unsatisfied for lack of money or credit? Answers to these questions are bound to vary widely, depending on household circumstances and outlook. We hesitate to offer generalized answers. Perhaps the following letter received from a young woman living near Niiike in Nishi Kamo buraku will serve this purpose.

I deeply enjoyed seeing the motion pictures of the wheat and mat rush harvests in Niiike. And now, a year later, we have finished the dirty and painful job of harvesting mat rush again. Next comes the sorting of the rush, or, as some call it, "the jewels of our sweat," into four grades, going from top-grade *naga* to *roku*, *tobo* and *kuzu*, according to the length. Most farmers usually sell their top grade to get money and use the *roku* to weave mat covers. If they have extra time and labor, they weave the *tobo* into matting also, but sell the *kuzu* for pocket money. These can be sold to brokers or the village co-operative.

The dealers call the mats woven of *roku* "Mid-whiskers" and the ones woven of *tobo* "Short-whiskers." Through the prefectural office that handles mat rush products, the covers are often taken to the big cities where they get to the consumers as *tatami*.

Farmhouses which have power looms make up their top-grade rush into mat covers and sell them. But most people sell through mat rush brokers to weavers who have lots of machines and do weaving as their primary business. Recently, many things have come to be made of rush—table-centers, various sorts of baskets, coverings, and the like which are quite new to people like me.

The income from rush pays the greater part of a farmer's living expenses. Not counting households in which someone is working for a salary, the money from the requisition of rice and wheat hardly pays for taxes and fertilizer in a purely farming household. So we use the money gotten from selling the top-grade mat rush for current living expenses, and weave *tatami* covers to cover the expenses of *Bon*. Then, since the Fall Festival is soon upon us, we decide whether to sell a little more of the rush crop as is or to dig in and weave more covers.

But much depends on the size of the family, the acreage cultivated, and the living standard. Suppose, for example, that in each of two households, A and B, there are three able-bodied persons, but that A has seven children, while B has only two. There will be a considerable difference between these houses in the amount of staple grains requisitioned, after the rice for the farmer's family has been taken out, even if cultivated acreage is the same. Living expenses, as well, will be very different for the two families on account of the number of children. So A's household gets very little money from the rice requisition, and after he has spent the mat-rush money for living expenses he may or may not have a little cash left at the end of the year, while B's household is able to pile up some savings year after year. Some people, to be sure, save money by cutting living expenses to the bone, never going to see people or having them over, not eating enough food, and living so miserably that people ridicule them. There are more ways of handling things than one can imagine.

In my own household, we grow 2.7 acres (11 *tan*) of rice, 1.7 acres (7 *tan*) of spring crops, and 0.4 acres (1.6 *tan*) of rush; in all, we have 2.94 acres (12 *tan*) of paddy and upland fields. My family is made up of my father (54) [and mother], myself (25), my six younger sisters, and two younger brothers—eleven in all. The oldest of my sisters has studied dressmaking and can earn a little money, but only during the slack season, so it is not enough to buy clothes for herself. My second oldest sister is a clerk in a bank. The next two children are in high school, the following two in middle school and primary school, and the next is in kindergarten.

Their school tuition alone amounts to considerable money, so the upshot is that our credit for requisitioned crops written down in our co-operative savings book gets cleaned out before each harvest, whether of wheat or rice. Besides, the cost of the fertilizer we buy from the co-operative is drawn from our account, so we can't take it all out in cash. So, as soon as the seeding is over we have to sort out the mat rush and sell some of the top grade to get money for taxes. Then we turn quickly to weaving mat covers before the *Bon* festival season begins, and while we are still at it summer vacation ends, school starts, and [the children] begin needing some money every day. It just seems that no matter how hard we work at weaving mat covers, we can't catch up.

If there is a little cash left over, it goes into furniture or farm tools we've looked forward to ever so long, or into the first new bicycle in many, many years, or into clothing for the family. Whenever there are ancestral memorial services they, too, add to the expenses.

It's always a matter of trying to cut down on everything not absolutely necessary in order to have some balance left. . . . So when I wonder where the wedding money will come from if marriage arrangements are finally settled for me, I feel I'd better stay at home as I am. But my people probably won't listen to this idea, so I'll be married to someone of our social level.

Even so, things might turn out so that I may someday have to earn my own living. When I think of this, I would like to learn some sort of skill to provide against a rainy day. Up till now, as oldest daughter, I have spent all my time just working in the fields since graduating from Youth School (Seinen Gakko) and have gotten no skill or craft to give me confidence in supporting myself. Because I have been feeling gloomy about it, I asked my parents if they could let me learn to use the wool-knitting machine which has come into fashion recently. That was during the winter slack season, and I thought I could go study for the three months from March to May. But their response was, "We would like to have you go to school, but we just don't have the money for it now. Not until next year's mat-rush harvest, anyway." So I said no more and waited until we got this harvest in.

Now, this year too, after the harvest is in, we have to weave more mat covers. The knitting machine alone probably costs four or five thousand yen, and over and above that I would need tuition, train fare, and other things. Knowing the family's financial situation I can't insist that I want to go to school. So I have resigned myself with the thought, "Well, it's better to work to improve things here and now than hope for something in the future. It will work out somehow."

Even though I know I shouldn't let myself get tied down by everyday things, my aspirations keep getting crushed. Once in a while I resolve to read a book for a few moments at night, but I'm so tired from the day's work that before I know it I fall asleep. Through the day there may be a few minutes to sit down for a look at the paper, but there is absolutely no time for reading books. An old saying goes, "Tend to the crops while the sun shines and leave the books for rainy weather." But if women on the farm have a rainy day, they are swamped with work clothes to be mended.

ONE FAMILY'S FINANCIAL RECORDS

The household of Hiramatsu Kumaichi, whose six members make it of average size, has furnished us with a record of their cash transactions during 1950. This took the form of a simple cashbook, kept largely by Kumaichi's wife. There are gaps where she simply forgot to make entries or was too busy to do so. May and June seem to fall in this latter category. Or again, other members of the family occasionally forgot to tell her about their expenditures.

Despite such shortcomings, Kumaichi's cashbook confirms most elements of our analysis of Niiike's financial circumstances. It throws no light on savings, but tax payments and the household's total cash outlay for consumption approximate very closely what Table 7 would indicate was probable for one of the buraku's more well-to-do households. It is interesting to note in Table 9 how considerable a portion (14.8 per cent) of this relatively well-off household's income was spent on food. Much of this went for fish, small portions of meat, cakes or cookies, and fruit. Clothing, another sizable expense, is lower because most purchases were of cloth to be sewn up at home. School expenses are considerably higher in other families with older children. This household, with only one kindergarten child, spent almost nothing in this category in comparison with others reporting amounts as high as ¥30,000 annually.

Kumaichi's household was well off in terms of land, especially in fields that produce rush. However, none in the family was working outside, so no salary income was received. In this and several other respects, its income and expenditure patterns differ more or less importantly from those of other households in the buraku. Exact records are kept by few, but inspection of estimates of expenditure drawn up for us by each household suggests that the proportions for each category are not normally very different from those emerging from Kumaichi's cashbook. Some discrepancies do emerge, however. Other households' estimates of their expenditures for food often exceed the 14.8 per cent of monthly expenditure noted by Kumaichi, rising in some cases to 20 per cent or more. Many spend slightly more on clothing. All but five record payments for insurance. Since cheap health insurance was not offered by the government until 1952, most of these payments in 1950 were probably for fire or life insurance or both. Though Kumaichi's household had what they regarded as extraordinary dental expenses during late summer, other households seem to have an almost similar proportion of medical expenses.

The cash income of Kumaichi's household is charted in Table 8. It should be noted that their income from rice and dry grains does not appear on this record, since it remained as credit on the books of the co-operative. With this exception, however, the cashbook does give an excellent indication of various matters. One is the extraordinary importance of mat rush as the principal source of cash income with which to meet the family's normal living expenses. Note, for example, that some rush was sold in November, surely to tide the household over the last few weeks before the rice harvest was delivered to the co-operative to restore the credit balance. Rush is not infrequently kept on hand, as this transaction suggests, as a form of savings in kind.

To show what sort of day-by-day expenses occur, the pages of the cashbook itself are much more informative than the monthly summary presented above. Expenses and receipts for February, 1950, are, therefore, listed in Table 10 in direct translation from the original. Each month's record has its own peculiarities. It will be recalled that February is the month of the lunar New Year marked by an unusual amount of feasting and entertainment. Contributions for community prayer meetings are also unusually numerous because of the holidays. The sale of glutinous rice noted in the income column is also related to the New Year festivities. Kumaichi sells it to households which do not grow their own to make *mochi* ("rice cakes"), for the holiday. The traditional obligation to clear away all debts before the old year ends probably accounts in large part for the sizable sale of mat rush only a month after his sale of a still larger amount.

Apart from February's special expenses, several other features of this account are worth attention. Food expenses, in February as in other months, consist mostly of very small purchases of fish, processed foods, and fruit. Cases of bartering vegetables to a peddler for foods he has for sale are not noted in this record. Sugar is bought on ration and, since this household uses little, appears in other months' accounts as an item sold to someone else. In connection with pay for work done, it should be noted

TABLE 8

MONTHLY TOTALS IN YEAR OF RECORDED CASH INCOME, 1950

Source	Per-centage	Annual Total	January	February	March	April	May	June	July	August	September	October	November	December
Mat rush sale	75.9	¥64,130.00	¥57,160.00	¥4,990.00	¥597.90	¥142.75	¥730.00	¥530.00	¥418.50	¥438.50	¥191.00	¥529.00	¥1,250.00	¥496.00
Egg sale	6.5	5,345.35	682.20	628.00	600.00	548.00	691.50	110.00			300.00	80.00		200.00
Vegetable sale	5.6	4,608.00		2,040.00									730.00	
Wood sale	2.4	2,000.00	1,200.00		510.00	950.00							800.00	
Tatami cover sale	0.1	150.00										150.00		
Pay for services	1.8	1,665.00	186.00	205.00		300.00								
Other	7.7	6,514.00		3,420.00	680.00		70.00				72.00	77.00		1,016.00
Total	100.0	¥84,412.35	¥59,228.20	¥11,283.00	¥2,387.90	¥1,940.75	¥1,491.50	¥640.00	¥418.50	¥438.50	¥563.00	¥1,529.00	¥2,780.00	¥1,712.00

TABLE 9

MONTHLY TOTALS IN YEAR OF RECORDED CASH EXPENDITURES, 1950

Paid Out for	Per-centage	Annual Total	January	February	March	April	May	June	July	August	September	October	November	December
Labor and service	8.6	¥9,188.10	¥1,126.00	¥77.10	¥4,351.00	¥408.98	¥710.00	¥235.00	¥560.00	¥1,723.00	¥1,800.00	¥632.00	¥1,300.00	¥2,420.00
Farm supplies	7.3	7,759.98	235.00	160.00	1,235.00	144.00	280.00	335.00	90.00	305.00	505.00	1,065.00	160.00	150.00
House supplies	4.1	4,371.00	309.00	1,198.50	102.00	158.00	168.00	203.00		168.00	161.00		234.00	52.00
Electricity	1.9	2,071.00	196.00	242.00	103.00	158.00	158.00	93.00	105.00		59.00		210.00	224.00
Reading and radio	1.4	1,490.00	859.00	843.00	63.00							57.00		
Food	14.8	15,821.50	1,940.40	1,444.50	996.50	1,421.00	770.00	915.00	1,246.00	1,364.00	2,032.00	1,905.50	815.00	1,500.00
Clothing and cloth	11.0	11,718.40	510.00	2,187.00	1,280.00	952.00	1,069.00		270.00	3,315.00	170.00	2,370.00	1,330.00	800.00
Medical and dental	9.7	10,309.00	150.00	90.00	1,339.00	660.00					3,150.00	370.00	975.00	100.00
School	1.2	1,249.00			416.00	475.00	88.00	45.00	65.00		80.00		80.00	
Ceremony, fees, gifts	4.3	4,570.00	850.00	455.00	510.00	550.00	215.00	60.00	485.00	823.00	152.00	270.00	225.00	540.00
Recreation and tobacco	3.0	3,231.50			732.50	572.50	9.50	40.00		210.00	90.00	555.00		512.00
Child recreation, candy	0.6	661.00	88.00	160.00	95.00	143.00	45.00			20.00	30.00	80.00	21.00	
Travel and bicycle	0.8	821.00		110.00	110.00	60.00	200.00			180.00		140.00		
Taxes	29.1	31,099.30	8,305.00	5,286.00		109.00	132.00	510.00	3,615.00	1,932.00	3,996.00		5,730.00	1,994.30
Other	2.7	2,922.00	50.00	209.00	194.00	1,395.00	125.00			169.00	120.00	104.00	98.00	148.00
Total	100.0	¥106,782.28	¥13,818.40	¥11,907.10	¥11,562.00	¥7,051.48	¥3,859.50	¥2,216.00	¥6,436.00	¥10,209.00	¥12,346.00	¥7,548.50	¥11,218.00	¥8,610.30

TABLE 10

Itemized Account of Income and Expenditure Recorded for Hiramatsu Kumaichi's Household, February, 1950

Date	Income Item	Yen	Expenditure Item	Yen
Feb. 1........			Fried bean curd	30
			Matches	18
2........	Eggs	200		
5........	Glutinous rice	3,400		
7........	Eggs	45	Tobacco, etc.	446
			Chikuwa (fish)	40
8........	Sweet potatoes	480		
9........	Eggs	54	Medicine	30
			Notebook	45
			Cloth for haori	670
			Candy	50
			Bottle for *kamidana**	75
			Suit buttons, boy's	19
			Chopstick box	23
11........	Sweet potatoes	480	Fish	50
	Broad beans	600	Tangerine	90
			Dressmaking book	230
			Farm magazine	65
			Nori (edible seaweed)	55
			Playing cards, child's	30
			Fish	50
			Eraser	5
			Towels ×4	134.50
			New Year ornament (seaweed)†	55
			Shikibi (for graves)	70
			Stone mortar, pestle	800
12........			Oil	195
			Newspaper	53
			Cloth (using rice bonus)‡	1,368
13........	Sweet potatoes	480	Pond guard fee	7.10
	Pay for work in Niiike	85	Bean curd	30
	Sold rags	20		
	Eggs	75		
15........			Haircut	30
			Fried bean curd	58.50
			Hoji§	5
			Pond guard fee	70
16........			New Year ornament, for shrine	164
			Sugar	140
			Thanks token (for shrine)	50
17........			Cakes	75
			Bleach, for rice	50
			Ball bearings, for motor	160
			Geta (footgear)	80
			String	60
			Candy	70
20........	Eggs	77.50	Roof tiles	118
			Medicine	60
			Watch repair	170
			Light bill	232
			Income tax, installment	5,000
			Fish cake	40
			Bike parking fee	10
			Prayer offering‖	5
			Bike repair	100
			Gokito#	20
			Tax	286
23........	Eggs	75	Cakes	50
	Pay for water-gate repairs	120	Toy	10
			Fish	45
25........	Eggs	101.50	Cakes for *kanki***	16
	Sold mat rush	4,990.00		
	Total	**¥11,283.00**		**¥11,903.10**

* Spirit-shelf in house.
† Front-entrance ornament.
‡ Over-quota delivery of rice receives bonus price.
§ Periodical services for ancestor on death anniversary.

‖ Probably contributed on visit to shrine or temple.
Periodical community prayer meeting.
** Monthly community prayer meeting.

that fees paid out for the pond guard, for example, are hardly more than token payments (though assessed by a household's amount of irrigated acreage), and money received for similar community services, such as labor by the household or his son on the village water gate, is also reimbursed at a purely nominal rate. The cost of other labor, however, is not high in comparison with materials. Note, for example, that one could not quite buy four notebooks with the money paid to a jeweler for watch repair.

February's notations, like those of other months, are surely incomplete. Judging from internal evidence, the housewife has entered her own expenditures rather meticulously, whereas the two men in the house have remembered only occasionally to tell her of their expenses (only one haircut is noted and no expense for sake is shown despite the holiday season). This record, therefore, cannot be regarded as a complete accounting of the household's income and expenditure.

LABOR AND INVESTMENT

In the foregoing sections we have found it particularly difficult to set a value on labor. Actually its value varies, of course, with season and tasks. In slack periods, weaving mat covers is an occupation which repays the labor expended at a rate of about ¥30 an hour. Approximately the same amount is paid to carpenters and other hired help in building (¥300 a day for about ten hours' work), but meals are given in addition. However, in heavy work periods labor is worth twice as much.

Many farm areas in Japan have difficulty in scheduling their activities so as to keep a fairly even work load throughout the year. Niiike certainly has work cycles, but the mat looms always offer an opportunity to make profit from spare time. This sort of secondary occupation is very much desired in rural Japan but is often lacking. Niiike and its neighbors are fortunate in this respect and in their access to outside jobs. They suffer little from that widespread rural problem—"concealed unemployment" or "underemployment." This refers to the condition of persons, usually relatives of the household, who are ostensibly at work on the farm but are not actually needed for their labor. Niiike would have this problem were it not for the mat looms and outside jobs.

Here lies the key to the buraku's tendency to invest in farm machinery despite having ample manpower for traditional hand cultivating. The hillside behind the community was once covered with dry fields. These were abandoned when rush-growing became profitable. Labor was needed on the rush at times that precluded the simultaneous cultivation of these dry fields. Given mechanized plowing and perhaps mechanization of the harvesting of rush, wheat, or rice, Niiike's people might be able to plant commercial crops on the hillside or to branch out in other ways without having to hire labor during the harvest or transplanting periods. Increasingly close communication with the city, whether for its jobs or for its markets for commercial crops and processed goods, has been instrumental in giving Niiike choices of how to invest its labor. Niiike's positive interest in mechanization today is a step toward acquiring the freedom to make these choices rather than have some of them ruled out by the demands of the present harvest schedule.

Finally, it should be noted with respect to Niiike's financial circumstances that most of the detailed data upon which the present chapter rests date from the year 1950–51. The community's economy, of course, did not stand still thereafter. The succeeding several years were on balance good to the people of Niiike. The community's income rose steadily in both apparent and real senses. Perhaps the best rough guide to the degree of improvement is found in the tax statistics (see chap. 12). They indicate that if an average household income was ¥139,470 ($387.42) in 1950, it had probably risen to about ¥160,313 ($445.31) in 1952 and ¥233,895 ($649.71) in 1956. The real value of this increase was somewhat offset by inflation, but a very substantial improvement was still involved. After 1956, outside capital in large amounts opened the way to a veritable economic revolution for the people of Niiike, as described in the Epilogue, chapter 15. Mechanization and other improvements in the sources of income transformed the situation, creating a "new Niiike" at least in the economic sense. The study of this transformation is a matter for the future. The materials in this chapter, which chart the various factors of income and expenditure of farm economy under relatively constant conditions, establish a background for such a study.

9. The Household

The household is the fundamental social unit of the community. There is no enduring group of smaller size. It is the elemental unit in situations within the buraku or outside of it, for activities usually are undertaken either by single households or by larger units made up of households. Almost every larger group of the community is regarded as an assembly of households. Thus when a meeting of a larger group is held, usually only a single person from each of the several households attends. But this person is a delegate. The household rather than the person is the participant. In Niiike, having been told "everyone will be there," we attend a mass meeting called to discuss festival plans or the schedule for irrigation and find that the gathering consists of no more than a couple of dozen persons. But this number is, truly, the whole community, one from each household, for "everyone" really means "every house." Seldom does any man, woman, or child think of himself or another person apart from his role as a member of his house (*ie*). The *ie* looms above the individual identities of its members to a degree that is hard to overstress.

Outside the community the same habit of thought is reflected. Ask a man, "How large is that buraku across the valley?" He answers, "About sixty houses." An official at the village or prefectural office can give a more exact answer, but it is still a count of households. Pressed to tell how many persons live there, he usually goes to various records to make a special count. A short cut now is available in a rice-ration list of persons, but such lists do not predate World War II and have not altered habits of thought. Virtually all personal records are filed by household, vital statistics among them; no separate birth or death register is kept for individuals. In the eyes of the government, a man's birth, marriage, or death are events not so much in his own life as in the career of his household. Vital statistics are recorded in the household register or *koseki*, in which each household is given a page of its own. Notations of births and deaths are kept on such household pages, and names of brides or adopted persons are written onto the page of the household that takes them in after they have been crossed out on the register of their house of birth. The *koseki* and other government registers, thus, demonstrate that officially the household is a substantial entity and that persons do not count for much by themselves.

A distinction must be drawn at this point between household and family. Each household is a discrete economic unit, operating as such in production, in consumption, and—in fact, if not on the official record—in ownership of land and chattels. While the core of the household is a group linked closely by kinship, non-kindred may be included. At present every household in Niiike consists entirely of persons related through descent, marriage, or adoption—the last being a rather frequent tie. Notwithstanding this kinship linkage, it is not precisely accurate to speak synonymously of "household" and "family." The latter term may denote one couple and their children, in a narrow sense specified by the designation "nuclear family"; or else, alternatively, "family" may be used in a wider sense, in reference to persons who are of common descent but who may be dispersed through marriage or adoption to separate residence in the same or different communities. Both uses differ from the concept of "household" which includes all co-residents, including servants and workers, whose activities contribute to the maintenance of the house as the elemental economic unit.

As in English, although two words exist, one for "house," *ie*, and one for "family," *kazoku*, they are now used almost interchangeably. The history of these two words is of some interest. The word *kazoku*, a compound of two characters literally signifying "house-belongers," was devised by the nineteenth-century Japanese scholars for use in translating from European languages and has since then crept into common usage. Its identity with the English "family" is a consequence of its origin. Through many centuries, however, the one word *ie*, "house," served the Japanese quite adequately to communicate all meanings in this area of social affairs. The word *ie* (and its humble and honorific synonyms of different form but identical meaning) has a range of connotations corresponding closely to the varying meanings of our word "house." It may refer to the physical structure, the domicile; to the residents of the domicile, the household; or to the family line as in the English "House of Windsor" or "an honorable house." It is at this last, broader level that *ie* acquires the rich shading of social and ethical value implications important to Japanese society.

The pre–World War II Japanese constitution and civil code, by giving the legal household head almost autocratic and absolute authority not only over persons quartered with him but also over members of the legal household unit who lived elsewhere, tended to blur the distinction that existed in fact—and that we draw here—between household and family. Supporters of the constitution's doctrine of a strong "family system" poured forth streams of literature idealizing the "house" and "family" in the broadest sense. This literature conveys the impression that Japan as a whole is indifferent to the smaller unit, the household. But we will not comprehend the variety of interpretations and emphases in different segments of Japanese society unless we preserve the conceptual distinction between household and family, the persons who are co-residents and those who comprise a more scattered kin group. It is the household that is the subject of this chapter. The family will be dealt with in the following chapter.

HOUSEHOLD ORGANIZATION AND COMPOSITION

It is possible to think of a household as an economic entity or as a kin group. Most households are both at once in Niiike. The members of a household act together as a unit for production and consumption. They also are kindred, linked together by consanguine, affinal, or adoptive ties. Ideally, the household has patrilineal continuity, each generation being linked to the next in a genealogical succession through men. The eldest male born to the house stays in the house all his life to serve as head and connecting link between his male predecessor and successor. Others are not lifelong members; some are born in the house but leave after maturing, while the rest join the household only as adults, by marriage or adoption. There are, thus, three categories of permanence. The category to which any person belongs is determined almost automatically by the position he occupies within the household, as the accompanying chart shows. Eleven stand-

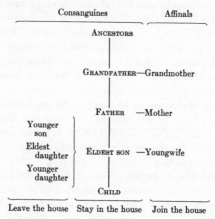

ard positions are shown, each with a kinship designation. Only nine of the positions need be considered in detail; the ancestors, though real enough in a symbolic sense, are not physically present, and the position of daughter is roughly uniform regardless of elder or younger status. The nine positions to be considered are: grandfather, grandmother, father, mother, eldest son, youngwife, younger son, daughter, and child. These are functional positions, not merely descriptions of relationship and some have interchangeable functional designations, e.g., "househead" for "father." Should new persons come into the household who have a different actual kin linkage (e.g., a niece) or no link at all (e.g., a neighbor's kinsman), they tend eventually to be treated in terms of one or another position named here and to be given the title, as well. These positions are the various parts of a unit, the household. Several places may be temporarily vacant, but as members enter they are accommodated by being fitted into vacancies.

The household positions relate persons not simply to other persons who happen to be co-residents but to the household as a unit. Responsibility for particular functions goes with particular household positions. It simply does not occur to a person, usually, to co-operate by casually exchanging functions according to the convenience of the moment; an attempt to do so is apt to have ulterior motives and may create a very difficult and awkward situation. Even persons of the same sex and nearly similar age cannot readily exchange functions. For example, if the daughter were to accept the youngwife's duty of closing the house up at night, she would not only confuse the division of duty but compromise the status of both of them. Particular tasks go with particular positions because they symbolize the status that is clearly linked to the position. Hence, when a position particularly critical to basic functions within the household, such as housewife, becomes vacant, a daughter, a househead's sister, or another available person may take over the housewife functions; but the normal consequence is that her household position changes correspondingly and she is given the new title along with the new functions. The unmarried eldest sister living in the house of Hiramatsu Hideo, whose wife died some years ago, is less often referred to as "eldest sister" than as "housewife," for she performs most of the housewife functions necessary to the household.

Though various examples of shifted positions might be cited, only one is so common as to be taken for granted. This is the adoption of a marriageable but often unrelated young man as eldest son by households that have produced no sons. This adopted eldest son takes on a role identical to that of an inborn eldest son, except that he marries the eldest daughter of the house instead of a girl from outside. Thus the vital matter of patrilineal continuity is safeguarded.

The everyday phrases that are used to refer to persons in the community provide constant reminders of their household positions. Everyone has his personal name, chosen to avoid duplicating the name of any other person living in the community, and this name is used under the proper circumstances. But it is more usual to refer to one's neighbor by his household position coupled with some term that identifies his house. One hears, for example, a mother speaking to her small daughter:

"Ma-chan, has West-Grandmother gone across to the store yet?"

"No, she went out to see Eldest-Sister-Uphill first."

"Well, go tell her that Grandfather-Within wants her to bring him something from the store."

In this brief colloquy, the child Machiko hears her own personal name in its diminutive form but recognizes the other persons referred to by their household designation. The household is the first consideration and the individual person achieves social existence only as one of its designated members.

Distinctive qualities of each household position appear in the following brief paragraphs, which treat first the men from oldest to youngest, continue with women who are born in the house, and proceed to women who normally arrive as adults. The appropriate Japanese kinship terms are not included at this point, for these exist in various alternative forms that connote the relative status of the speaker as well as designating the kin connection. The subject of kinship terms is given special attention later in the chapter.

Grandfather.—This position is assumed gradually and has some variability. Retirement from a full work load and full authority to a routine of light tasks and advisory functions marks the step-by-step assumption of the role, though the title often comes, in compliment, with the birth of a first grandchild. Full retirement is a formal matter, involving official transfer of headship and, usually, of title to property as well as gradual relinquishing of the role of household representative to community functions. In Niiike, most grandfathers never go through formal retirement, even though past sixty, the traditional age of retirement. A grandfather merits respect, but in addition his ties with other household members become warmer as his exercise of authority diminishes. Skilled handcrafts, menial tasks, and some baby-tending become his main economic functions.

Father (househead).—The position of househead carries greatest overt authority, prestige, and responsibility. His nearly absolute legal authority over all household members is now diminished under the postwar constitution and laws, but great ultimate power over household organization, budget, and co-residents' behavior still is granted to him by custom, if not by law. As chief worker and main custodian of household welfare, he finds his relations with other members almost inevitably marked with reserve and lack of intimacy, for his power isolates him, and his own attitudes tend to be colored by his perception of each member in terms of cost and profit to the household.

Eldest son.—This heir-apparent position gives its incumbent a full share of loyal affection from the household and prestige among outsiders but also brings responsibility as a curb to his prerogatives. Of all male children, eldest son is most apt to have ties of warmth to his father, as well as a sense of security within the household. This security, at times, makes him placid and unaggressive, compared with his younger brothers. After as much schooling as circumstances and household policy permit, he assumes a full share of heavy work and gradually takes over management, eventually to become househead.

Younger son.—Once his schooling is finished, the younger son is expected to help the household either in fieldwork at home or from a wage or salary job off the farm. But eventually his relation to his natal house must be severed either through marriage-adoption into a house without male heirs or through a move to separate residence in the city. A third and rarer possibility is that of setting up a separate household as a branch from his natal household. This action avoids sharply severing ties to the natal household but is possible only if landholdings and finances permit. If his fate is not yet determined when the eldest son succeeds to headship, the younger son becomes by definition the younger brother but without essential change in his functions or problems.

Child and baby.—Though the baby's future is fixed by custom according to his sex and order of birth, all babies tend to receive much the same warm affection during infancy. As they become active children they come to perceive their differentiated relation to the household. Preschool training, which emphasizes awareness of the household as an entity, comes from both mother and grandmother and develops very strong and warm maternal ties. In school itself, all children to the age of twelve receive similar instruction but are treated with clear sex distinction. The child's relation to his schoolteachers is almost the only one in which he may figure as an individual rather than a household member. This aspect of the relation perhaps greatly enriches the teachers' influence and prestige.

Daughter.—A daughter has no permanent place in her natal house and very little chance to continue life in her native village, for eventually she marries elsewhere. One daughter may stay home, however, if her household lacks male heirs and adopts a man to become her husband and the household heir. In later years of school and before her marriage, the daughter helps with housework and may make several years' full labor contribution, but she does so to qualify for the marriage that will take her away, at high cost to the household. Thus, any warmth of personal relations is balanced by her low position as an ultimate deficit member of the household.

Youngwife.—Upon marriage to the eldest son, the youngwife comes into the household as a rank outsider from a distant community and must undergo the ordeal of proving her worth and her supreme loyalty. Hard work, circumspect behavior, and fertility—above all, fertility—save her from being "sent home" and raise her from a low and insecure position to one which, though inferior to all other permanent members, carries security, respect, and affection. Her warmest ties tend to be with her children, whose existence validates her position; her most strained relations are with her mother-in-law, the housewife, who must train the newcomer to the ways of the house and eventually share with this intruder or lose to her the affection of her own child, the eldest son.

Mother (housewife).—Heavy responsibility balanced against very few prerogatives traditionally marks this position. The housewife carries the main or entire burden of housework while sharing in the field drudgery as well. Despite her supposedly low position of authority, however, her position as mother as well as housewife often brings much behind-the-scenes managerial authority. She meets and serves all guests, deals with tradesmen, manages a good deal of the budget as surrogate for the household, and guides the children in many policy matters.

Grandmother.—As the youngwife arrives and develops her position, the mother gradually comes to be grandmother. Whether she moves or is pushed into this new position is an issue that has become a classic example of interpersonal tension: wife versus mother-in-law. If and when this struggle is resolved, the woman who gracefully accepts the position of grandmother has the most tranquil position of all women. Her outside origin has long since lost its stigma; her duties have shrunk to light field and house chores, often with doting attention to her grandchildren uppermost; and, while she shifts responsibility for work and policy enforcement to her successor, she retains affectionate relations with her husband, her son, and her grandchildren.

Ancestors.—Ancestors are conceived as being merged with the compassionate Buddha, yet at the same time they are potentially present and spiritually active in affairs of the household. They seem not to be pictured with any individualized characteristics of sex, age, or other human features, but their spiritual nearness is real enough to provide a sense of security and to remind the current generation of its debt to its forebears. This debt is paid through working for the welfare of the household. Chief symbols of the continual presence of the ancestors are the small gilded tablets (ihai), inscribed with the names of each ancestral generation, set in the butsudan. Each year, the midsummer Bon ceremony celebrates the three-day visit of ancestral spirits to the household.

The nine positions just described for the living members as a rule cover any person who is likely to be a member of a household. Seldom, of course, does any household have all these positions filled simultaneously, for its actual membership fills only part of the complete household pattern. Households grow and diminish as their members arrive and depart. Ideally, however, households grow toward the fullest expression of this pattern, as will be seen when the actual composition of Niiike's twenty-four households is examined. Their variation in number and composition may best be understood after examining Figure 31, in which all the quantitative variations are represented as four classes (A, B, C.1, C.2) presented as four stages in the development and maturation of the complete or type-household.

In Stage A, the eldest son, who will be called Yoshio for the sake of clarity, is entering adult life as a fully productive household member, working side by side with his father, the househead. His bride, the young-wife, has established herself by bearing the first grandchild but works largely under the direction of Yoshio's mother. His sister, still in school uniform, will leave the household when she marries between age twenty-two and twenty-four but meanwhile tends the baby and helps in the house or fields. The household, at this stage, consists of six persons.

In Stage B, Yoshio's father has died, so Yoshio now serves as househead. There are no collaterals (sisters or brothers) above the age of young children. The eldest son, heir apparent, is learning farming by doing it, even while finishing the compulsory school years that his junior siblings are beginning. As in Stage A, there are six members in the house, but these represent three generations of direct descent.

In Stage C.1, the main household has not only Yoshio and his wife but also the adult eldest son and his bride, the youngwife, to carry on the labor of the fields, in so far as the grandmother can take over baby-tending. Between Stages B and C, we see that family affairs have prospered enough to keep the younger son in the community by establishing a branch house (Stage C.2); farming alone does not provide a full living for the branch house, however, so the younger son, married and househead of the branch house, commutes to a salaried city job while his wife carries on the day-to-day job of cultivating. Had affairs prospered less, the younger son would have disappeared from the community, as his aunt, Yoshio's sister, did when she married earlier. To extend this household cycle further, one need only picture the changes that will bring the young couple of the parent house of Stage C.1 to headship and imagine the gradual maturation of the new branch house as its members increase through a couple of generations.

Thus, households of different size and shape can be regarded as phases in the recurrent maturation of a single pattern. Our inquiries around

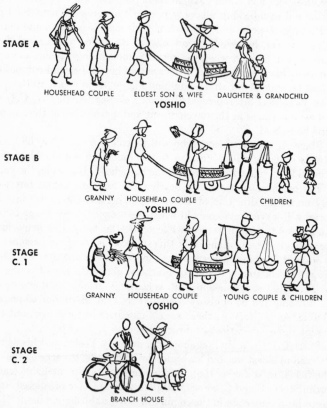

Fig. 31.—Four categories of household membership in Niiike, treated as stages in the development of a single, hypothetical household. Change through time may be followed by tracing Yoshio's position in each stage.

Niiike indicate rather conclusively that the villagers hold this view. But it is true that the various stages of development are not equally represented at any given time. To take a different view of the household composition, in 1953 there were from two to nine members in each household of Niiike, households with seven members being the most common. The average household size is 5.37 members.

Figure 32 shows that a small proportion of houses is occupied by only a single nuclear couple. More frequent than such single-generation houses,

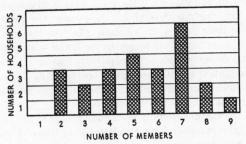

Fig. 32.—Niiike households, showing the number of households of each size

TABLE 11

Composition of Niiike Households

	Composition	Number of Households
Group A.1	Nuclear family.............	7
2	Lone parent and children....	2
Group B.1	Nuclear family, grandparent(s)................	11
2	Lone parent and children, grandparent(s)...........	1
Group C	Nuclear family, grandparent(s), great-grandparent(s)	1
Group D	Nuclear family with adult siblings, grandparent(s)...	2

or even than two-generation houses, are houses in which three or four generations of a single descent group live together. This situation may be analyzed with the aid of Table 11, which shows four principal types of composition. In this table, the designation "nuclear family" is understood to include a married couple and any of their immature children.

The nuclear couple taken as the baseline is not necessarily the titular househead and wife; it is whatever couple is most centrally located among the generations represented in the household. Taking as an example the six-member house of the Sensei, Hiramatsu Mitsusaburō, in which he and Masano are the elderly househead and housewife, Sadako and Michinori are daughter and adoptive husband, and Reiko and Masako are granddaughters, the computation used here has treated the younger couple and their children as the nuclear family. The Sensei's house falls into Group B.1.

In Niiike, the modal type of household is clearly that of Group B.1, the group represented by the Sensei's house of grandparents, parents, and children. Next most numerous is the small household comprising a couple or parents and children (Group A). Relatively few persons live long enough to see their great-grandchildren; the four-generation household (Group C) is uncommon. Also rare is the house with unmarried adult siblings of the nuclear couple or their parents (Group D). Note that such a house, by definition an extended family because of having collateral relatives as permanent members, differs functionally from the lineal household which we have pictured as the modal type.

In Niiike, the extended family is an oddity. One of the two households that fall into this category is that of Hiramatsu Hideo, a widower whose brother and two sisters perhaps stayed to take care of his children when his wife died but have passed the proper age of marriage or have stayed single because of personal and family troubles. In the second such household, the collateral relative is a mentally defective brother who cannot be sent away in marriage or for work because of his incapacity. These extended families, then, have come into being by accident, not by plan, and are no more part of the expected pattern of households in Niiike than are the three households designated by the term "lone parent" (Groups A.2 and B.2), which were broken by the early death of the wife or husband.

Thus, instead of a range of types, Niiike presents two frequent types and certain other exceptional households. The two types are in contrast, however, one being the large household comprising three or more generations of direct descent, the other being the small nuclear-family household. If most or all nuclear households are likely to develop eventually into multigenerational units, as was suggested above in the analysis of household development, their current numerical prominence is to be discounted as evidence that the type is desired or ideal. Almost everyone in Niiike does seem oriented toward the larger family and speaks warmly of having grandparents in the house.

Wider data, it is true, suggest an alternate interpretation. On a nationwide scale, Japanese sociologists have pointed to figures suggesting that Japan over a long period has had a high proportion of nuclear-family households. Their contention is based mainly on data gathered as a special project of the 1920 census, which produced a count of generations and degrees of kinship represented in rural and urban households of a large, nationwide sample. Assuming that two-generation houses were, in fact, nuclear-family houses, they found that the proportion in the total national sample was 54 per cent; this figure is not far below the proportion of 60 to 65 per cent nuclear families estimated for the United States. Moreover, although studies from subsequent censuses were not possible owing to lack of appropriate data, the proportion of two-generation houses was higher in cities than in rural areas in 1920 and has been taken as an indication of a trend toward the small-family norm running parallel with increasing urbanization, in Japan as in the United States. As the sociologists have observed, these conclusions run contrary to the assumption implied by the concept of *ie*, for the ideal of strong family solidarity should find expression in the prevalence of large, multigenerational households. Therefore, they are led to conclude that the *ie* ideal is being weakened and altered in Japan as a whole, especially in areas under urban influence.

With this sociological interpretation as background, it is enlightening to examine the small-family phenomena, not only in Niiike, but in a variety of nearby communities. All these communities carry the imprint of wartime dislocation. Four households in Niiike moved in as wartime evacuees from the city, and each one falls in the nuclear-family group. Four of the remaining five in this group are true branch households, of which two were formed after the war. An elderly, childless couple comprises the one remaining household. Nuclear-family households, then, appear to have been far less numerous in prewar days than now. Accordingly, as the individual circumstances are perceived, it is difficult to accept the nuclear family as a stable, normal type of any importance in Niiike. Much the same is true of neighboring rural communities whose circumstances are like those of Niiike. In them, also, the proportion of minimal-size households is larger than before the war, because they, like Niiike, acquired evacuee households from the city during the war and have formed branch households in the few prosperous postwar years. But the proportions of each household type suggest that a three-generation house is the only modal type.

The prevalance of nuclear-family households among evacuees from the city, on the other hand, suggests that this type is, indeed, common in the city. Table 12 compares household groupings in Niiike with figures obtained from a house-to-house survey in two larger communities in Takamatsu, three miles away in the direction of the city. Though Takamatsu is classed as a town, many of its households live primarily or entirely by farming. Others are shopkeepers or hold similar urban occupations. Takamatsu is intermediate between city and country in its occupations.

When farm households are separated from others in the two Takamatsu buraku, Inari and Harakozai, and compared with Niiike, a consistent shift in proportion of nuclear-family households asserts itself. Niiike, most rural in character, has the lowest percentage of small households; the farmers of Inari and Harakozai, rural in occupation but living among shopkeepers, have a large proportion of such households. The shopkeeper households include the greatest percentage of the nuclear-family type. Interestingly enough, the commercial people of Inari, many of whom run small inns or restaurants for the hordes of annual visitors to the famous Inari shrine of their community, have a notable reputation

TABLE 12

HOUSEHOLD COMPOSITION IN NIIIKE AND IN TWO
BURAKU OF TAKAMATSU (PERCENTAGE)

		FARM HOUSEHOLDS			SHOPKEEPER HOUSEHOLDS	
HOUSEHOLD TYPE		Niiike (n=24)	Inari (n=88)	Harakozai (n=110)	Inari (n=54)	Harakozai (n=81)
A.1	Nuclear family...................	30	42	40	52	61
2	Lone parent and children..........	8	26	15	20	7
B.1	Nuclear family, grandparent(s)......	46	22	25	18	27
2	Lone parent and children, grandparent(s)...	4	6	9	6	1
C	Nuclear family, grandparent(s), great-grandparent(s)...............	8	1	1	..	4
D	Nuclear family, adult siblings, and others...	4	3	10	4	..

locally for clinging to family connections. Yet this insistence on the tradition of *ie* does not prevent their forming small families. The conclusion seems clear that urban occupations promote a rising proportion of nuclear-family households, whereas the relatively larger household of lineal descent is, as Niiike illustrates, the characteristic rural type.

HOUSEHOLD WORK ROUTINES

Allocation of tasks in Niiike is clearly associated with each person's household position which sets relatively strict limits on what he may do or be expected to do. Men almost never touch household chores such as cooking, dishwashing, or housecleaning. Women, on the other hand, are expected to get their special tasks out of the way as quickly as possible and then help with work in the fields. Few ordinary tasks are considered beyond the strength of women; yet when there is a choice between mat-weaving and fieldwork, the housewife weaves and the household does the heavier fieldwork.

A large portion of baby-tending falls to grandparents, especially grandmother, who spends much time keeping babies from under foot. She may take on other work she feels able to do, to free the housewife for the field tasks that consume so many hours. Grandfather, likewise, shares in work that is not too arduous, but he also is likely to plait baskets, straw sandals, or rainwear as needed by the household members or their neighbors. School-age children are not put to work with any great consistency, on the premise that their time must be devoted to their studies.

The tempo of life varies considerably for the various members of the household. Grandparents can savor their retirement from the most strenuous jobs. Children do not yet know that life is arduous and demanding. The househead works steadily through the day in the irrigated fields with the main crops or, as the occasion requires, in the dry fields, but he is relatively free in the evening. The housewife is the first one up in the morning and the last to bed at night. Of all the members of the household, she has the most insistent and continuous demands on her time and is least free to work at a leisurely pace. Even in her work, however, there is little air of rush and bustle except at peak seasons, and the work tempo of other members is steady but moderate during most days of the year.

The summary of one day's activities in the household of Hiramatsu Isamu (Table 13) follows a representative three-generation household through an ordinary day in late spring after the rice has been transplanted. This synopsis, gathered by a combination of observation and interview, represents an ordinary day rather than a particular day. Households with different membership vary from this schedule to a certain degree, but the allocation of tasks to specified positions remains much the same.

Nowhere is a work plan consciously set up for the following day or for the week to come. Isamu's household is partly exempt from this judgment for, as described in chapter 7, Isamu has set his cap for cash marketing and so manages a variety of vegetable crops as well as dairy cows that require a distinctive work schedule. His case serves by contrast to emphasize that the basic work schedule of most houses is set by community consensus, based on identical schedules for major crops. The possibility of each household planning its work in detail and particularly of setting a schedule of work hours, recreation hours, and visiting hours simply does not occur to most persons. The lack of a close schedule permits easy interruption of work in case visitors arrive or a meeting is called, while rigid planning would be considered both unusual and less sociable than custom expects. Hence, little incentive exists for altering the round of customary activity.

On the other hand, so completely do irrigation and other community-wide matters set the habit of community scheduling that throughout the

TABLE 13

DAY'S WORK SCHEDULE OF A REPRESENTATIVE HOUSEHOLD OF NIIIKE IN JUNE, 1950

	Grandmother (Age 62)	Father (Head) (Age 42)	Mother (Housewife) (Age 38)	Girl (Age 16)	Five Children (Ages 1–13)
5:00 A.M.			Rises, washes / Slides outer doors open / Heats ox feed and water / Cooks breakfast and rice for noon and night / Offers rice at shrines		
5:30	Rises, washes / Helps get meal / Takes baby on back		Prepares school lunches / Cleans oxshed / Helps children dress		Baby wakes
6:00		Rises, washes / Checks water in nearby field / Feeds chickens		Rises, washes	Rise (boys latest) / Wash
6:30		Breakfast			
7:00	Breakfast		Breakfast	Breakfast	Breakfast / Leave for school / Play in schoolyard
7:30	Helps with dishes / Takes baby on back for walk out of sight of mother	Takes weeder to paddy, weeds, with pauses for tobacco pipe and water	Washes dishes / Tidies house	Leaves for school / Plays in schoolyard	
8:00			Sweeps yard / Starts laundry / Buys from peddlers / Sells eggs / Finishes laundry / Goes to weed dry field, cuts grass for ox, feeds ox	In class	In class
10:00			Works at loom		
11:00			Helps get lunch		
12:00 P.M.	Begins to get lunch / Lunch	Returns for lunch / Lunch	Lunch	Lunch in school / Returns to class	Younger starts home / Younger dawdles on way home / Lunch
12:30 P.M.	Rests, plays with baby / Takes baby on back, to pick up kindling	Rests, plays with baby / Receives village message board, reads and passes it next door / Goes to paddy field with fertilizer			
1:00		Scatters fertilizer	Washes dishes / Begins mending (or goes to fields)		

TABLE 13—Continued

	Grandmother (Age 62)	Father (Head) (Age 42)	Mother (Housewife) (Age 38)	Girl (Age 16)	Five Children (Ages 1–13)
2:00 P.M.	Weeds dry field Gossips while baby naps	Resumes weeding Changes field			
3:00	Takes wakened baby on back				
4:00		Changes field	Turns from mending to mat loom	Out of class Talks with friends Lingers at magazine shop and strolls toward home	Out of class Play in schoolyard
4:30	Resumes strolling on hill			Chores: sweeps yard, hauls bath water, starts bath fire	Return home Play at home
5:00		Cuts grass for cow Returns home			
5:30	Tends bath fire	Smokes, chats First in bath		Chats Starts homework Third in bath	
6:00	Helps get supper		Begins to get supper		In bath by age Supper
6:30	Second in bath	Supper		Supper	
7:15	Supper		Supper Last in bath with baby		
7:45	Washes dishes	Reads newspaper Hears radio, choosing programs	Rolls out bedding Hears radio, mending clothes	Helps roll out bedding Closes outer doors (at dark) Resumes homework	Younger goes to bed Older start homework Older go to bed
8:00					
8:30	Goes to bed	Goes to bed			
9:00			Goes to bed, leaving light burning	Goes to bed, reads before sleeping	
9:30					
10:00					
10:30–			Tends children if they wake		
11:00–					
5:00 A.M.					

year one sees all manner of incidental activities begin and end on exactly the same day for a particular set of buraku, as though on command. On one day nearly everyone starts to cut wood for winter, on another day everyone begins airing and beating the *tatami* house mats, on yet another day everyone starts plowing. The clockwork of seasonal ceremonies for the community sets the general pattern and reinforces the habit of abiding by a community-oriented pattern which leaves little encouragement for planning by each individual household.

As has been mentioned in chapter 7, work is set by crop needs, not by the seven-day week, which now is firmly established in government and city occupations. Everyone is aware of the day of the week, for the children are home from school on Saturday afternoon and Sunday, some peddlers and small buyers make their rounds weekly, and, finally, everyone follows the weekly routine of radio broadcasts. Yet household and field-work routines are unaffected by the seven-day cycle. It is a thing of the world outside the village. Within the community, it is the season which most influences the work schedule.

HOUSEHOLD HIERARCHY

The household more than any other social unit in Niiike has a hierarchical pattern of organization. Governing the relations of each member to every other member, there is a recognized order of obligation and privilege that places each person measurably above or below everyone else. Strictly speaking, however similar the position or role of members may appear at any moment, there are no equals within one household. This is not to say that the pattern of hierarchy is uniformly and rigidly observed. People often tend to behave in ways contrary to hierarchical postulates, not only in Niiike, but in all the more well-to-do agricultural communities of the Core Zone of Japan. Niiike, thus, is located in a geographic belt or region where the principle of graded privilege falters. Yet this weakening of hierarchical patterns, as will be shown later, occurs mainly outside the household. Whatever principles are substituted in other affairs, the household itself is the main stronghold for unequal or vertical relationships, whether in Niiike, the Core Zone, or any other part of rural Japan.

Three principles govern household hierarchy: males are superior to females; elders are superior to juniors; and those born in the household are superior to those born elsewhere. In theory, personal qualities or individual abilities or defects have no bearing on status; no amount of profligacy or incompetence should be permitted to alter the position established automatically by the three principles. In practice, to be sure, status is not so fixed by ascription that achievement cannot alter it. But the rule stands that each member of the household has a specific grade of privilege and responsibility. The rule is ingrained from infancy by household practices and is reinforced by religious doctrines and legal codes, described below, which date many centuries back.

Within the house itself, every room is conceived as having an "upper" and a "lower" end; at gatherings of any degree of formality persons are seated by descending status from the upper to the lower end. The seating of the household at mealtime, according to etiquette that differs in particulars from one region to another, places the househead on the "upper" side, his male offspring ranged close to him, while the youngwife, whose status is lowered by her female sex, her relative youth, and her birth elsewhere, sits "below" everyone else—close to the cooking and food-storage area, for this is at the "low" end of the house. To the eldest male belongs first turn in the evening bath, while the water is hot and fresh, and others follow in order of importance; sooner than break the fixed order, children are kept up late at night or are excused from bathing when an elder is out late in the evening. In feeding and clothing children, in assigning chores and privileges, or in a myriad of little things down to fine-shaded subleties of politeness in speech forms used between household members, hierarchy can be expressed so unmistakably that even a very dull child perceives and internalizes the principle. These customs do not exist purely for their own sake, of course, nor do they merely symbolize an otherwise abstract principle. Their function is to develop awareness in each person that his comfort, security, and freedom continually must be measured against the greater responsibilities and privileges of those who are ahead of him, whether the matter be a place to sit, a time to bathe, or the deeper-cutting matters of authority over the household budget or disposition of his future. People in Niiike often are halfhearted in observing the lesser symbolic customs or find good enough reason to alter them in their own household, even though they are perfectly well aware of their existence. On occasion, they handle even the most fundamental household problems in ways that do not hold to the principle of vertical obligation, though it continues to be recognized as the ideal.

The family system has been buttressed in Japan by an interpretation of obligation or duty that stresses one's responsibility upward toward his seniors or superiors. In Niiike, one hears relatively little of such an interpretation. As an illustration, the word *on*, which literally refers to a fief or precious gift granted from a superior, in more recent times has often been applied to the favor bestowed on a child by his parents in rearing him; the child's obligation to repay this *on* is unending and without limit, it is asserted. Various lines of evidence including projective test data convince us that, in Niiike, few people conceive of any bond stronger than the bond to their parents. Their phrasing, however, almost invariably is in terms of love and affection, not in the harsher terms of obligation for an *on*. They *want* to look after their parents, because of fondness for them. A closely related obligation is that of *giri:* one's obligation, as member of a respectable house or rank or class, to live up to the standards of that house or rank or class and to do nothing to discredit it is *giri*. The people of Niiike occasionally interpret certain situations in terms of *giri*. An adopted son, they say, may feel obliged to work harder and, upon succeeding to householdship, probably will be more lavishly generous than a natural son lest he be thought to undervalue the *giri* proper to his adopted home. The community's good name is upheld by inviting the neighborhood to catch fish in its irrigation pond when it is drained, whereas to attempt to profit by selling the fish would "break *giri*." In such ways, *giri* is recognized, but it is by no means a word on everyone's lips.

Like any other community in Japan, Niiike is familiar with the traditional ideological systems that have given explicit, positive support to the vertical orientation of loyalty and obligation of which household hierarchy is one expression. Whereas the local Shinto worship in Niiike carries little or no expression of hierarchy and tends to stress an orientation toward communal mutuality, the net effect of Buddhism, Confucianism, and State Shinto has been to reinforce household hierarchy and to repress all conflicting loyalties. The supporting voice of Buddhism was first heard in Japan more than a dozen centuries ago; many sects have diverged since then, but all unite in teaching their followers to love and venerate their ancestors. Confucianism, known in Japan even before Buddhism, gradually gave to the Japanese a code of values which stressed the wisdom and superior judgment of one's elders. After the beginning of the seventeenth century, Confucianism was widely sponsored as the official ethic of Japan. Its doctrines as interpreted by the Tokugawa and Meiji regimes, spelled out the different degrees of loyalty owed in each of five relations: obedience of younger to elder brother, of wife to husband, of child to parent, of friend (vassal is implied) to friend, and of subject to ruler. In each of these pairs, the burden is one-sided and bears upon the lower member. As scholars have pointed out, Japanese Confucianism, in working out these relations, succeeded in reaffirming family obligations while building over them the rationale of higher duty to one's lord. Thus an explicitly hierarchical concept grew out of the more diffuse and undifferentiated early concept of upward obligation, for a step-by-step intensification of obligation led upward through the household and beyond it to the ruling house.

Precisely similar logic dominated State Shinto, which was concocted out of selected bits and pieces of native religious practices and mythology by nineteenth-century supporters of the Meiji emperor; its doctrine emphasized, as the paramount duty, loyalty to the emperor and represented him as the most divine being of a divine race, whose position at the peak of a pyramid of superiors made him, in larger scale, like a father over a household. This code colored the schooling of every Japanese up to the end of World War II and was designed to supplant as far as possible the communalism of local Shinto shrine worship, which handicapped governmental centralization and was negative to the basic principle of vertical orientation.

Apart from the religious doctrines enumerated here, Niiike and the other communities of Japan, from 1880 to 1945, were made answerable to the civil law which in unequivocal detail supported a rigidly patriarchal mode of household organization and control.

Each of these many voices that have surrounded the villagers for so many decades or generations has borne a message of hierarchy, countered only in part and locally by the egalitarian tendencies of unorganized Shinto. But each voice has sounded from outside the confines of the village. A practical-minded villager, if his practical interests conflicted with the hierarchical principle, might conceivably shrug off religious preachments and find ways to circumvent the law in managing his own affairs. This has not been commonly done. In the last analysis, hierarchy has lived in villages such as Niiike primarily because it has been appropriate to local conditions of life.

Hierarchy in the household finds concrete support in economic conditions, among which landholding is foremost in the farm community. Everyone in the household depends for livelihood on the fields that were acquired and kept productive by previous generations and that are now held by the household. He and his forebears have a claim on household loyalty through the land. Furthermore, this acreage is normally too small to support more than one of his children, and the resulting differential claims to inheritance lay the basis for differential relations of these children to each other and to their parent. Precisely what form and stringency these relations take, and whether they will be ultimately hierarchical, depends on factors such as the availability of alternatives for livelihood apart from succession to the land, and the possibility of escape from dependency in ordinary times and in crisis. Hierarchy in some form is implicit in almost any part of agricultural Japan, where unclaimed cultivable land is almost non-existent. But its character and pervasiveness differs, under the canopy of uniform doctrines, precisely because conditions of land tenure and inheritance vary.

Niiike normally expects that the eldest son will be sole inheritor of the homestead, its chattels, its crop land, and the ancestral tablets. Legal title often is transferred before his father dies, the act of transferring title becoming at the same time his father's act of retirement. By this time the eldest son has a wife and one or more children and is fully active in farmwork. His wife and babies share the parents' home, though one or the other couple may sleep and eat in a separate room, called *hiya* or *hanarebeya*. But the old man may put off making official transfer until he dies. Or he may shift parcels to his son piecemeal or withhold them, especially if he anticipates some tax benefit; several households, to minimize taxes, never have reregistered certain parcels of land from the name of their deceased forebears.

Inheritance of personal effects such as heirlooms, trinkets, and clothing hardly rises as a separate question, for almost all these items are thought of as belonging to the household. Thus, the dolls exhibited on Girls' Day, pieces of art or jewelry, or luxury clothing, though they are in the care of the housewife, stay in the storehouse and, in effect, are handed from mother to son's wife (her successor as housewife) rather than from mother to daughter.

The rule of male primogeniture, which, as we have said, is the ideal or norm of inheritance, makes sisters and younger brothers dependent on the first son for their own future, if it is not settled during their father's life. Even though they usually leave the household eventually, they need money from the household to get properly married or to establish themselves elsewhere. Authority, thus, concentrates in the household head whether he is father or brother to other members. Until the end of World War II, the national constitution and civil law gave almost absolute authority to the household head and stipulated the sort of succession by the eldest son which we have described here as normal. Succession is one of the most completely revised portions of the postwar civil code, for, by contrast, the new laws vest the right to a third of the estate in a widow with dependent children and otherwise give *all* offspring equal rights to inheritance. Nothing actually prohibits primogeniture if all children are grown and the consent of all parties is obtained, but the law is widely believed to require that each survivor get an equal share regardless of his willingness to concede it to the eldest brother. Compliance being out of the question, if any inheritor is to have a useful patrimony, the farmers continue their established practice of unitary inheritance with the uneasy conviction that circumstances are forcing them to break still another one of the nation's laws.

The preference for male primogeniture or for unitary inheritance, thus, has not been suddenly altered even by the presumption that the law forbids these practices. On the other hand, these norms have not by any means created an inflexible pattern in Niiike, as we see when specific cases are examined. The case histories of all households in the village provide thirty instances of household succession in the last six decades; fifty-four men were involved, counting elder and younger natural sons and inheritors adopted from outside by households without natural sons. Whereas seventeen eldest sons inherited in standard fashion, seven did not, and six houses had no natural son to succeed to the patrimony. In six cases, the principal or sole inheritor was a younger son. These cases serve to illustrate alternative modes of inheritance and provide an insight into the forces that shape social orientations.

It will be noted that no instances appear of inheritance by a woman. Inheritance of property and succession to headship by women have been avoided, though they were not impossible even under the prewar civil code. The accepted principle is that the property of an established household belongs truly to the household itself, so whoever holds the legal title is only the trustee, according to custom. A woman holding custody would wish to marry, however, whereupon the property, like her own fealty, would be swallowed up in her husband's house. She would have to do obeisance to her husband's household's ancestral tablets, not to those of her natal house. She would take the name of her husband in place of her inherited one. No one, then, would carry on her original household, and it would become extinct. In recent memory, only a few cases of any descent of property to females have occurred in Niiike, none of them constituting succession to an established Niiike house. Widows, it is true, have managed their houses until their sons reached maturity but without taking legal possession; so that title to the property has gone from deceased husband directly to the son.

How best to keep the household going is the ultimate question before which all else is subordinated. The problem is faced by any couple with no boy child. Adoption is the accepted solution. Persons unfortunate enough to have no children at all usually start by adopting a young girl, if possible from the husband's paternal relatives, and thereafter find a husband whom they also adopt. Those who have a daughter of their own adopt as son and heir the man who becomes the daughter's husband. As the girl comes to the age of marriage, her parents employ go-betweens to look in other villages for a suitable junior son who will move into the girl's house, marry the girl, and be simultaneously adopted as heir. An alternative procedure noted elsewhere in Japan, including Inland Sea fishing villages, is to adopt a father's brother's son or another boy in the paternal line at an early age and have him marry the household's daughter after he reaches maturity. The adopted bridegroom (*muko-yōshi*), no matter how selected, loses all connection with his natural family in exchange for this chance to make his living. He assumes the family name, worships the household ancestors, and manages the household as if he were the natural eldest son. His life has its difficulties, of course, for he has to work a bit harder and do a bit better than any natural son merely to prove that he deserves the position. In Niiike, an adopted groom's performance is judged as strictly as a youngwife's.

TABLE 14

SUMMARY OF THIRTY CASES OF INHERITANCE

Disposition	Eldest Son	Junior Son	Adopted Son	Cases
Full succession...................	14	5	7	26
Major inheritance................	3	1		4
Minor inheritance (branch)........	0	4		4
Emigration:				
As adoptive groom.............	2	6		8
Overseas.....................	2*	4		6
To city......................	2	3		5
Incompetent....................	1			1
Total persons involved.......	24	23	7	54

* Returned to the community from overseas to form *pro forma* branch houses.

While Niiike adopts its girls young and from within the paternal lineage, as noted above, to insure solidarity, it seems to feel that solidarity is preserved adequately when men as inheritors are adopted even after they have grown to maturity in an entirely unrelated family. Wives, after all, are brought in under the same conditions. Adopted husbands are no great rarity for, as Table 14 shows, seven out of thirty, or more than a fifth, of the cases of succession were solved in this way.

A household fortunate enough to have two natural sons and a surplus of land and other resources at the same time need not hold to the rule of unitary inheritance for they can set up a branch house for the second son. Iwasa Takeshi's case is typical. After a long period of saving and planning, his father registered a house lot in Takeshi's name. Then his father helped Takeshi and the carpenters build a new house while go-betweens looked for a suitable bride. When Takeshi married, he moved into the new house, receiving his share of crop land, the total investment taking about a third of the resources of the parent house. This amount is high for some parts of Japan. Even so, it rarely, if ever, makes the branch house self-sustaining from farming alone. So Takeshi, like most younger sons, has to keep a job in the city which gives him economic independence. Branching is more often wished-for than achieved. However, it is branch-house formation that accounts for the gradual, steady growth of the settlement from eighteen houses in 1870 to twenty-four in 1954, once evacuee accretions are written off against an equal number of households that became extinct. The "boom" quality of postwar years is evident from the fact that three new branch houses were formed in 1949, 1953, and 1954.

The adoption of bridegrooms or the occasional formation of branch houses are practices which merely supplement primogeniture. But as Table 14 shows, the primogeniture rule was actually violated in seven out of twenty-four cases, for seven eldest sons did not inherit. These exceptions are important for what they have to teach about Niiike society. Three cases throw light on the power of the housewife in household affairs: Hiramatsu Sakutarō left home because he could find no wife his mother would tolerate. In the cases of Hiramatsu Kantarō and Hiramatsu Tadashi, both had a stepmother and a young half-brother who was her son; the stepmother preferred her own son even though he was the second in line and managed to get the eldest son sent away for adoptive marriage while her own son succeeded to the headship of the house. Three other elder sons were affected by the lure of the city or the land of promise overseas. Iwasa Ishita and Hiramatsu Tokujirō went to America and, though their younger brothers inherited in their absence, each returned with enough savings to build a comfortable house and buy fields, resuming a position in the community as a branch house. In the last case, the eldest son was mentally deficient and incapable of normal life; he had no brothers, so his parents adopted a groom for the eldest daughter. Yet the parents in this case, as in all the exceptional instances reviewed here, were careful to give the appearance of first-son inheritance on the official village records by putting a token parcel of land in the name of the first-born as "successor"; the official records, however, do not tell the true story.

Niiike's actual inheritance practices, thus, are seen to be more varied and flexible than appears on the surface or on the records. Considering that in the prewar years, when these deviations occurred, the national code of civil law stood unambiguously and inflexibly in favor of primogeniture, a practice supported also by Buddhism, Confucianism, and State Shinto, these deviations speak impressively not only for the inclination of the village to dispose of its affairs to suit the particular local circumstances but also for its capacity to do so despite close governmental supervision.

We have little detailed information from other rural communities in

Japan to indicate how prevalent such autonomy may be, for most studies use the data of official records in the village office which, of course, cover over unauthorized deviations from the law. The practices detailed for Niiike seem in no way exceptional among communities around the Okayama Plain and may perhaps prove to characterize the patterns of Core Japan in general. In the northern prefectures of Honshu, by contrast, studies show that younger sons are set up in branch houses more rarely and more penuriously. Little land is given them, and, lacking nearby cities in which to earn supplementary salaries, they must rent parcels from the parent house, thus reinforcing the bond of subordination already forged. No evidence appears of the major or total inheritance being given to younger sons in such regions.

Our survey has revealed some of the reasons that have led to division of patrimony and to rejection of the eldest son. But perhaps we should return to the preferred form, primogeniture, and ask what the forces are that lead to prevalence of unitary inheritance by the eldest son. What has produced a system that so firmly excludes women from functioning as custodians of property; that makes division of property and prerogatives so rare; that favors first-born males at the expense of others? Is it perhaps that the system is part of ancient rural tradition?

A glance at the historical evidence provides us with but a limited answer. Most such evidence deals only with the ruling nobility, warriors, and officials of earlier days, groups whose family interests and practices differed markedly from those of the peasantry. Whether in medieval times when great families and their vassals met in battle, or in the succeeding period when the powerful Tokugawa house extended its rule from the capital at Edo through consanguine and marital ties of kinship as well as ties of vassalage, legislation for the upper class concerning descent and inheritance was inspired first by the need to regulate power positions, to control their transfer and prevent their dissipation at the whim of a parent. Even before the Tokugawa regime the predominantly military character of most positions restricted succession to males; the immediate predecessors of the Tokugawa rulers bound together into an indivisible whole the rights which till then had been separately inheritable, so that succession to position entailed also inheritance of household name, real property of rice fiefs, and the privilege of conducting rites for the household ancestors. Primogeniture was required, for inheritance by the first-born son carried the least risk of leaving a critical post in the hands of an immature successor. To avoid gaps in the male continuity, the practice of adopting male heirs (*yōshi*) was well established, and the practice of branch-house formation was a standard one. Such practices, suited to the requirements of a martial elite, became the basis of the civil code embodied as national law under the Meiji constitution and applied downward to all commoners as well as to the classes of privilege.

In contrast to the detailed information concerning the upper classes, we have little factual documentation concerning the rural peasantry before the mid-nineteenth century. But if we are tempted to surmise that commoners quickly adopted the model set by the upper class, either because of the force of social prestige alone or because of the combination of legal and religious doctrinal pressure, we find strongly contradictory evidence from cases officially recorded in the early years of the Meiji regime as well as from subsequent studies of village society. Prior to issuing the civil code, the Ministry of Justice in 1880 published a work entitled "Collected National Civil Customs" (*Zenkoku minji kanrei ruishū*), detailing, among other practices, actual inheritance cases of the period. Besides male primogeniture there were abundant instances of almost every form except inheritance by the widow. The eldest daughter, the youngest son, a chosen son, all sons, or all children, or even a younger brother turned out to be inheritors. To a limited extent regions tended to show particular patterns of inheritance customs. The interpretation best supported by detailed community studies of a later date is that each locality tended to have its own pattern and to vary from others in the region because of its own distinctive requirements for efficient management of household economic resources. However interpreted, the patterns of rural inheritance were far from a mirror image of upper-class practices in the 1870's. Patrilocal residence prevailed, in that girls from other communities were brought to live in their husbands' homes; the cultivated fields of the household thus generally descended in the male line; but the daughters and especially the younger sons were by no means rigorously excluded from receiving part or all of the patrimony.

Since the early Meiji period, if this spotty sampling of evidence is close to representing the actual situation, there has been a growing tendency among farmers to favor the elder son exclusively as successor. Junior sons have had less chance to be chosen as heir. Now, as in the Meiji period, household continuity through males is a supreme consideration. To assure this continuity, the household should have a second son as contingent heir in case of incapacity or death of the first son before he has produced children of his own. Hence, it is not decrease in the number of junior sons that accounts for the shift to exclusive primogeniture. Rather, it may be the rapid growth of cities with their industry and labor market since the

Meiji period that has opened an alternative to inheritance which was all but lacking in Japan before then. Niiike's boys have had this alternative, and many have taken it.

The thirty known cases of inheritance in Niiike reach back to the middle years of the Meiji regime. Excluding the seven cases settled by adoption of men from outside the buraku, there remain twenty-three cases which, one way or another, made provision at home for twenty-seven of Niiike's sons. But nineteen other sons, during the same period, had no place in their household. Go-between negotiations placed eight of them as adoptive grooms in nearby villages. But the largest number, eleven, left to make a living in the city or to try their fortune overseas.

How successful migration has been is another question. The fortunes of these men have varied. The war, with evacuation and repatriation, brought back two from the city and one from Korea to lead an impoverished existence in the postwar village. America drew not only junior sons but also two eldest sons. No doubt they followed the lead of a junior son whose emigration predated our records but whose success in America can be measured by his own son's eminence as a physician in Los Angeles. The junior sons who emigrated to America stayed there; their success has been only moderate for America, but they own cars and homes that would not have been dreamed of back home. The two eldest sons saved enough from their laborers' jobs in America to move back to Niiike, buying land and building houses of modest elegance there, so that they may be considered successful even though they missed inheriting the household farm.

Had the period been the early nineteenth century instead of the post-feudal late nineteenth and twentieth centuries, some of the junior sons who were third to fifth in order of birth might have starved or have been killed in infancy; others would have been adopted elsewhere; one or two would have been able to form a branch house; but more would have spent unrewarding lives as unmarried "uncles" (ojibun) in their natal homes, potential nuisances or threats to household harmony. Since Japan began her process of rapid industrialization, however, the fast sprouting cities have added a not unattractive career. Sons who migrate cityward are removed from any competition with those who stay home. Under these circumstances, parents might feel less pressure toward choosing the most competent or most aggressive as successor and instead could follow the more rigid, automatic selection of the elder son as demanded from above by the government. Hierarchy, already established but flexible under pre-Meiji conditions, was strengthened by the capacity of cities to absorb excess males from the farm. Even so, in Niiike, as we see, hierarchy among brothers has not become immutably rigid.

KINSHIP TERMINOLOGY

The terms for addressing or referring to relatives present two note-worthy features. First, these kinship terms form a system very much like that of English but with slight differences that underscore the differences in actual behavior among close kindred. Second, a rich range of variation in etiquette is prescribed and made possible by alternate forms and by prefixes and suffixes that imply respect or familiarity. To suggest a comparison, it is as if the use of "dad," "papa," etc., as alternatives to the English term "father," were more explicitly prescribed for given situations and accompanied by similar variants for all other common English kinship terms.

The terms by which Niiike people ordinarily address their relatives or refer to them follow the system of standard Japanese. Individual terms have dialect forms—e.g., *otōn* for *otōsan*, "father"—but the usage of these terms, despite their difference in sound, is the same as that of standard Japanese. The system which these terms form is basically like the English system for relatives who ordinarily are outside of the household; it is a bilaterally symmetrical system, applying the same terms to collateral relatives, relatives in ascending generations, and affinal relatives, without distinguishing between paternal connection and maternal connection. To illustrate concretely, any uncle in Niiike is *oji*, any aunt is *oba*, any cousin is *itoko*, any nephew is *oi*, and any niece is *mei;* in the second generation upward, each grandfather is *ojii*, and each grandmother is *obaa*. For relatives by marriage, compound terms comparable to the English "brother-in-law," etc., are available; these also refer symmetrically to both paternal and maternal connections. These affinal terms, however, are rarely heard, for it is much more common to refer to in-laws descriptively, e.g., "my daughter's husband," instead of with the compound term, in this instance "son-in-law."

Within the circle of closest relatives, Japanese differs from English terminology in one significant respect: relative age is specified in the terms used for all siblings. There is a one-word term for elder brother, *ani;* one for younger brother *otōto;* one for elder sister, *ane;* and one for younger sister, *imōto.* One cannot refer to all one's brothers or all one's sisters with a single term, except by using a formal compound of Chinese derivation that means literally "older-younger brother" (*kyōdai*) or "older-younger sister" (*shimai*). The term *kyōdai* is sometimes used to signify all one's siblings, irrespective of sex, but it is not frequently heard; *shimai* is very seldom used; thus, terms expressing age-difference are the ones that are heard every day. The age-distinction which is thus built into the terminology reflects actual behavioral discrimination, for siblings do have differential rights to inheritance and other privileges, the eldest being favored over junior siblings. Brothers and sisters are conditioned to anticipate unequal treatment through the everyday kinship terms they learn as they first begin to prattle; so when they actually receive unequal treatment, as they do in fact, they are not impelled to question it.

Whereas terminology and practice coincide within the household, where kin relations are the dominant relations, the kindred outside the household who are terminologically equivalent are not treated in similar fashion in actual practice. Male kinsmen in the father's line are much the most important to men and their wives. Yet these persons are not terminologically distinguished as a group from male kinsmen in the mother's line. This is no violation of the logic that relates language to social reality, however, for there are linguistic labels other than kin terms which set such male paternal relatives apart. First of all, they share a formal family name—Hiramatsu or Iwasa, in Niiike. The importance of this is set forth in chapter 10. Second, they are the kinsmen who actually live in Niiike, whereas other kindred are scattered elsewhere, and so, instead of a kinship label, they have a residential label: *mura no hito*, "a person of (our) village," or *Niiike no hito*, "a person of Niiike." Kinship as such is subordinated to other sorts of relationships outside the household, and kinship terms are not needed to identify groups with common interests. What the kinship system does accomplish that is highly important, in view of the economic and property-holding functions of the household, is to segregate all more distant kin from those within the household, "peeling off" collateral relatives, affinal relatives, and others from the immediate, small lineal-descent group. The tenure and disposal of property and goods, or the identification of the common-budget group, is simplified by the fact that there is no terminological identification of more distant kinsmen with members of the household. The property concepts of English-speaking households are generally similar, so it is not surprising that English kinship terminology also distinguishes between the close circle of immediate relatives and more distant kinsmen. Among most peoples of the world whose economic lives are predicated on ownership of property, in fact, similar kinship systems prevail, in contrast to tribal societies where property and goods are held and distributed communally and where quite distinctive systems of kinship terminology apply terms of close relationship not only to members of the immediate household but to wide circles of relatives. In some localities of rural Japan, communal ownership of pasture, forest, and even of cultivated fields persisted until very recently; those localities display at least a few non-standard kinship terms that designate large collectivities of relatives. Since such localities, as known at present, seem to be few and scattered, they do not require detailed attention here.

Attention may be turned at this point to the various forms which the people of Niiike, in addressing or referring to kinsmen, used to connote different degrees of respect or familiarity. In almost all instances, persons address only those who are their seniors by a kinship designation; when addressing kindred below their own age level, they use the person's given name (or a diminutive or nickname) instead of the kinship term. A similar habit prevails among English-speakers, for a son addresses his father as "dad" but is addressed in return more often by his given name than by the term "son." In contrast to English usage, however, as observed above, variant forms implying respect or familiarity exist for all the common, standard Japanese kinship terms used in Niiike, not for just two or three; the shadings of deference are richer than in English; and the prescriptions concerning which term must be used in a given situation are more exact and inflexible than in English. One special characteristic, true of Japanese speech in general, is that women invariably use terms of greater respect than men. A frequently voiced complaint of older persons against the young is that they don't know etiquette, the proof of which is their failure to use proper kin terms of address, reference, and respect; the new system of schooling is often condemned for this failing.

Kinship terms of *address* appear in the first two columns of Table 15; one addresses one's own kindred with the familiar terms in the left-hand column but uses the standard terms to address another person's kinsmen. Kinship terms of *reference* are shown in the second and third columns; reference to another person's kindred requires the standard terms (i.e., address and reference terms are identical for kinsmen of other persons), whereas one uses the formal or impersonal terms shown in the third column to refer to one's own kindred, thereby giving humble connotations. Terms in the fourth column are alternatives describing the functional position within the household and may be used to refer to and, in most cases, to address another person's kindred.

Several peculiarities of Table 15, from the English-speaker's viewpoint, become clear when it is recalled that the household rather than the individual person is the point of reference for use of kin terms. Thus, within one's own household, one's personal relation to elder brother or elder son is less significant than his position as presumptive heir within the house; hence, father and siblings alike tend to refer to him by the same term; the three other son-brother or daughter-sister positions are similarly treated. As in our own homes, parents may address or refer to each other by parental terms, which their children also use, instead of by spouse terms, thereby reflecting the household position. The use of the alternative terms which comprise the fourth column of Table 15 again illustrates the conception of the household as the main point of reference, since these terms explicitly describe function within the household rather than kinship as such.

TABLE 15

KINSHIP TERMS OF ADDRESS AND REFERENCE FOR HOUSEHOLD MEMBERS

	ADDRESS	REFERENCE		FUNCTIONAL‡
	Familiar*	Standard†	Formal‡	
Grandfather..........	Jiichan	Ojiisan	Sofu	Inkyo (retired)
Father...............	Tōchan	Otōsan	Chichi	Shujin (head)
Son (indiscriminate)...	Personal name§	Musukosan	Musuko	
Elder son............	Personal name; sibling term‖	Chōnansan	Chōnan	Chōnan (1st son)
Younger son.........	Personal name	Jinansan	Jinan Sannan etc.	Jinan (2d son) Sannan (3d son) etc.
Elder brother........	Niichan	Oniisan	Ani	
Younger brother......	Personal name; sibling term	Otōtosan	Otōto	
Daughter (indiscriminate).............	Personal name	Musumesan	Musume	
Elder daughter.......	Personal name; sibling term	Chōjosan	Chōjo	Chōjo (1st daughter)
Younger daughter	Personal name	Musumesan	Jijo Sanjo etc.	Jijo (2d daughter) Sanjo (3d daughter) etc.
Younger sister........	Personal name	Oimōtosan	Imōto	
Girl.................		Ojōsan		
Child...............	Botchan (boy); personal name Jōchan (girl); personal name	Okosan (indiscriminate) Kodomosan (pl. indiscriminate)	Otoko-no-ko (boy) Onna-no-ko (girl)	
Baby...............	Bōya (boy) Jōchan (girl)	Akachan		
Grandchild..........	Personal name	Magosan	Mago	
Youngwife..........	Personal name#	Oyomesan Waka-okusan	Yome	Yome (bride) Waka-fujin (young-wife)
Husband............	Personal name#	Shujinsan Dannasan	Otto	Danna (master) Shujin (head)
Wife (housewife)......	Personal name#	Okusan	Tsuma (Kanai)	Shufu (housewife) (-fujin) (Mrs.)
Mother.............	Kāchan	Okāsan	Haha	Shufu (housewife)
Grandmother........	Bāchan	Obāsan	Soba	Inkyo (retired)
Ancestors...........		Hotoke-sama	Senzo	Senzo (forefather)

* May carry honorific prefix o-; -chan is a diminutive used either by a child in reference to others or by adults in reference to children. Chan may be replaced by san.

† o- omitted in more familiar usage; sama may be substituted for san and is more respectful.

‡ Readings of characters in official documents, used in speech to specify one's own (not another's) relatives precisely.

§ Personal name most commonly used, especially in addressing one's own children.

‖ The sibling term is also frequently used by parents in referring to their children.

Husband uses omae or kimi ("you," familiar) to wife; wife uses anata ("you," respectful) to husband, or each uses personal name.

Functionally, households are related to households rather than persons to persons. One may address a close relative such as uncle or aunt by the appropriate kinship term, but in speaking to others about these kinsmen

Readings of characters in official documents, used in speech to specify one's own (not another's) relatives precisely.

one more commonly identifies the household and the position held in it by the relative in question. More distant relatives are addressed as well as referred to by their household position. Persons who have no kinship connection at all are addressed or referred to by their household position probably more often than by their personal name. In effect, kinship nomenclature is more frequently heard in Niiike than in the ordinary American community, but it consists merely of the few terms for close lineal kindred and is treated as the nomenclature for positions within a house. The household as a prime unit, rather than its several members as independent individuals, associates with other unitary households in outside affairs, to which we now turn.

10. Community AND KINSHIP ASSOCIATIONS

While the household is clearly the fundamental unit of the social and economic life of Niiike, the collectivity of households is itself an integral communal entity. When acting as a political unit, the people of Niiike refer to themselves as a buraku, but action as a social community is undertaken in the name of the co-operative group, or *kōjū*. This term of religious origin probably was first applied to those occasions when households functioned together as a Buddhist congregation. Today, it is the term which most aptly connotes the sense of "community" which unites the people of Niiike. Joined in the *kōjū*, the people of Niiike perform many important co-operative social functions. Although community life extends beyond the *kōjū*, the communal sentiment thins out quickly beyond this small face-to-face group. Associations linking the people of Niiike to wider and larger communities on the mura level and beyond are conceived as different from *kōjū* associations. In the world beyond, distinctive and limited functions or relations are undertaken by distinctively named associations. None has the multiplicity and diffuse functions of the *kōjū*. In successively wider associations, particularly at the mura or prefectural levels, functions become more narrowly and explicitly administrative.

One outstanding characteristic of the *kōjū* as it functions in Niiike is the equal-level relationship between households upon which it is based. This quality is reiterated in other types of association in the Okayama area but is by no means characteristic of all Japan. Other regions, especially those of later settlement, still show strong signs of hierarchical interhousehold relationships which contrast sharply with the pattern in Niiike.

In ordinary daily dealings the households of Niiike relate as neighbors and peers. The basic pattern of equal-level relations is concretely visible in the simple method of spreading news or instructions throughout the

248

community. For instance, when it becomes necessary for the mura office to communicate with the people of Niiike, announcements, requests, or instructions, usually in mimeograph form, are sent to the house of the elective head of the buraku, the *burakukaichō* or "buraku-meeting leader." He circulates a board carrying the notice by passing it to his immediate neighbor, who reads the notice, then passes it on to his next neighbor. The board goes from house to house along a constant route, known as the *iizutae kōro* or "passing-the-word route," until it has made the full round and returns to the leader's house. The route normally is followed in a counterclockwise direction, but rush notices are received in two copies to be passed in both directions at once.

In using this method to pass messages, the mura is utilizing an already established informal custom important to the conduct of internal buraku affairs. Inquiry into the origin and significance of this custom reveals that it is closely associated with certain religious practices of the community. On the twelfth day of each lunar month, the buraku gathers at one of its houses, for the recitation of prayers and religious texts, one representative from every household. The host serves an evening meal, which is followed by the religious service. At its conclusion it is customary for the elders to initiate discussion of matters of collective community interest. Any sort of village affair may be aired in this informal forum. Decision, if any, is by consensus. The responsibility for playing host to this traditional religious and social meeting shifts regularly from house to house each month in counterclockwise direction along the precise route used to circulate mura notices. The host does not bear the expense of the meal but only the responsibility for serving it; he collects about a pint (three *gō*) of rice and ¥5 from each house beforehand as well as getting ¥20 from the buraku funds. Besides these meetings and meals, an identical assembly is held for the four main seasonal festivals and the special prayer days held three times a year about the ninth day of the third, fifth, and ninth lunar months. The ceaseless cycle of rotating responsibility for playing host omits no house, demeans no house, glorifies no house, but apportions an equal share of responsibility and prestige to every house in turn as host.

Throughout the Okayama Plain similar religious meetings are held each month, the meeting date varying from group to group. The texts and prayers used in the religious part of the meeting are always those of a particular Buddhist sect, usually that of the village majority, but the majority sect is different in different villages. Theoretically, households of a sect other than that of the village majority would have no reason to attend if the meeting were solely religious. But each household feels it

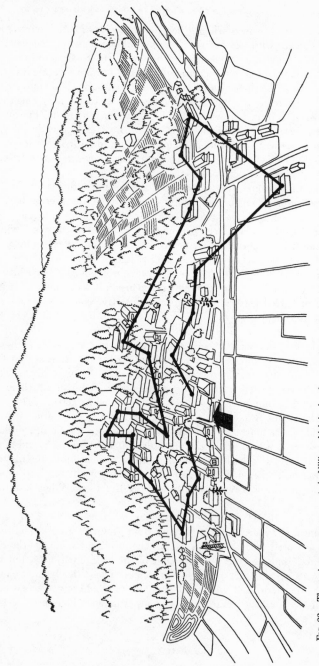

Fig. 83.—The customary message-route in Niiike, which is also the route for transfer of responsibility of hostship for ceremonies. Arrow shows starting point of route. Note that one house (*upper center*) is omitted.

important to join with neighbors in this traditional religious gathering in order to discuss local affairs afterward. Sometimes a family may change its sect to that of its village majority. In these meetings the buraku residents reaffirm their collective unity. The occasion is called *kanki* or prayer meeting, while the group itself is called *kōjū*. Though taking its name from such religious gatherings, the *kōjū* is a functioning unit of much more than ceremonial significance. In Niiike it is the co-operative work unit, the mutual assistance unit, the unit of management, protection, and solidarity of the *buraku;* in other words it is the primary organization that takes care of problems outside the scope of the single household. Let us glance first at the religious responsibilities other than the monthly gathering which the *kōjū* undertakes. The *kōjū* handles the contribution of money or labor to maintain and repair the inter-buraku shrine and conducts community worship there as a unit. Near the road behind the buraku meetinghouse is a row of three upright stones, two of rough form, the third inscribed in characters of elaborate ecclesiastical form giving the special prayer of the Nichiren sect; farther up the hill two still more modest upright stones and a stone lantern mark a second ceremonial spot. These are the two locations at which persons from all twenty-four households assemble for prayers on certain ceremonial dates. Even when the people of Niiike join with neighboring communities for ceremonials which take place at the Kōjin shrine across the fields, the *kōjū* representatives gather first at one of these two spots within the buraku to offer preparatory prayers.

Most of the occasions on which the *kōjū* functions, however, are secular. Greeting a newly arrived bride or giving assistance at a funeral both require the participation of every household. Newer activities, such as making contributions to the Red Cross, Community Chest (Red Feather Campaign), and Save the Forest Organization (Green Feather Campaign), are also organized by the community as a whole. The *kōjū* members pool their contributions to be handed over to the mura office and are more apt to agree on a standard amount to be given by each house than to let each determine its own contribution. The *kōjū* also, in its political guise of buraku-meeting group, informally manages the postwar crop requisitions. Requisiton quotas, by law, are set for each household individually on the basis of its cultivated acreage. The *kōjū* will treat the sum of individual quotas as a collective responsibility, however. By this we mean that, in case of the failure of one member to meet his quota, the deficit is made up by the remaining members so that the *kōjū* (or, from the government point of view, the buraku) quota will be filled.

Several seasonal activities are undertaken by the *kōjū*. The two important traditional tasks are cleaning local irrigation ditches and clearing the local paths and roads. Because these are not merely practical tasks but also are definite expressions of communal solidarity, their performance takes on a certain air of ceremony. Ditch-cleaning prepares the ditches for the continual use made of them during the rice-growing season. Just after the winter wheat harvest is complete, or in years of late harvest just before it begins, the buraku engineer designates a date and has the word passed from house to house along the *iizutae* route around the settlement. On this day, after breakfast, each household sends one person, with hoe and sickle, to the crossroads that marks the heart of the community. Under the engineer's direction the group divides in two and spreads out along separate ditch systems to scoop out accumulated mud and cut away the overgrowth of grass. As they arrive at the traditional point separating Niiike's portion of the ditch system from that of neighboring buraku, each group shifts to the next system. With occasional rest periods and a pleasant amount of talk and joking as they work, their task is wound up about noon, when they disperse. Up to the postwar austerity period, the engineer would expect the group to gather again at his house in the evening for light refreshments and conversation, but this amenity had not been resumed by 1954.

Repair of the roads and paths follows the same pattern but is undertaken after the typhoon season has done its damage so that everything will be in order again before the Fall Festival date arrives. In place of the househead, his adult son or a woman may come to work as household representative; provided only that each house is represented, the sex and age of the workers is of no account in road repair.

Less traditional than ditch-cleaning and road repair is the now abandoned annual chimney-sweeping and house-cleaning instituted by the Japanese government several generations ago. On the appointed day, set by the *kōjū*, though subject to the convenience of the police, everyone would drag his floor mats out to the front yard for beating, spread his quilts out for airing, and the Youth Association of *kōjū* young men would make the rounds wielding chimney-sweeping equipment. After checking the results to insure that the group collectively would pass muster, the *kōjū* then waited for the police to arrive and make their official inspection. Now, one sometimes hears regrets about the postwar abandoning of mandatory house- and chimney-cleaning because, although police inspection to get the required sticker posted on the doorpost was unpleasant, many households now omit the house-cleaning altogether and go into the Spring and Fall Festival seasons in untidy fashion.

Sometimes a partial group takes action in the name of the *kōjū*. For example, Ōbara Pond serves whatever land its water will reach, whether owned by Niiike people or not, but it is considered to belong to Niiike, and its management is always in the hands of this buraku. The pond guards are Niiike men whose land depends in part on pond water; two at a time take the duty, their assignment being determined only within the Niiike *kōjū* although their token pay comes from the *ōaza*, the larger political unit which is the lowest level official irrigation management organization.

Another partial group acting for the *kōjū* is the Youth Association, *Seinendan*. Boys join when they are fifteen or sixteen and leave somewhat after marriage, at about twenty-five or twenty-six, though some do not leave this fraternity until they are as old as thirty-five. Only the households with young men of appropriate age are represented, of course. There is no corresponding girls' organization in Niiike in modern times, although some parts of rural Japan retain a traditional girls' as well as youths' organization, each with its own gathering place, often the home of a tolerant-minded widow or widower. The gathering of young men is of long-standing tradition at the *kōjū* level and once had the name *Wakashū-gumi* ("Young fellows' group"). The present young men's group has a formal status of more recent origin as a branch of the Mura *Seinendan*, Village Youth Association. In prewar Japan, these associations were organized as part of a national federation and thus were tightly organized for central government manipulation. Since the end of the war, the Youth Association has been relatively autonomous at the mura level. As part of the larger village organization the young men of Niiike send representatives to a village meeting for discussion of policy and become mildly involved in civic good-works projects, chief of which is sponsorship of an annual athletic meet. But the traditional functions within the buraku are ones they generally deem more important.

The Youth Association supplies the initiative and most of the labor force for many tasks connected with the community's ceremonial life. If shrine repairs are needed, its members round up contributions and provide the labor, trying to make a showing as good as or better than the parallel youth associations of five other buraku that use the same shrine. They set up the banners and structures that grace the village during the major Fall Festival; they construct the tableaus, contributed one from each buraku, at the festival celebrated every third year at a nearby hilltop shrine, Kōshingu; and they set out the small red-and-white flag that announces the traditional rest period, *shiromite yasumi* or "planting-finish holiday," in the afternoon of every fifth day between rice transplanting and the end of the weeding period.

In addition, the Youth Association takes primary responsibility for helping any member of the *kōjū* who is specially shorthanded or ill at a busy season, in case his closer relatives cannot take care of him. They also patrol the village in pairs for five nights or more in the cold of the lunar New Year, when the newly filled rice granaries are considered to be in special danger from thieves. Those waiting for or finished with their watch lend moral support from the buraku assembly hall, where conversation, song, and a bit of sake shared around the brazier make the nights shorter. In the old days, when insects threatened the crop, the youths would organize and lead a procession through the fields, two carrying and beating a drum, the others bearing tall paper banners with prayers inscribed by the priests. In time of drought they would gather wood and lead another procession to the nearby hilltop to build a great bonfire and pray for rain.

A sense of fellowship among young men who are not yet burdened with household responsibility helps to keep this association lively. Tangible reward for their effort comes in the form of food and drink in the evening following one of their activities, but their own contributions buy the food for such feasts, which are never elaborate.

About one generation ago the Niiike youths amalgamated their organization with that of nearby Ōyama buraku to provide better for entertainment. The accomplishment was easy because each buraku has an almost identical schedule of activities. Thus, the Youth Association is not literally confined to the single buraku, having several extra-buraku connections. Except for the occasional member with some political ambitions, however, the outside ties mean very little as compared with ties formed within the buraku.

The fire brigade, *Shōbōdan*, is formally set up in the same pattern as the *Seinendan*, with the Niiike contingent constituting a branch of the mura organization, and the mura brigade subordinated under higher level organization that sets policy and rules. Its membership is almost identical to that of the Youth Association. As fire brigade members they are in charge of the buraku fire-fighting equipment, a water pump and hose. Their uniform is a workman's loose jacket, *happi*, dyed with a standard design and label. In the absence of professional fire departments, these volunteer brigades are important to rural communities, and the higher level organization provides a useful chain of command and communication to assemble adequate forces against a serious village fire or forest fire. For this reason, as well as because brigade membership provides another occasional opportunity for an evening meal with sake, participation is relatively eager and enthusiastic.

There is one group at the *kōjū* level in which membership is by a woman representative from each household. The Women's Association, *Fujinkai*, was formed by government mandate in the late 1930's for the purpose of influencing women's attitudes and activities. Some meetings are at the buraku level, others at the mura. Theoretically the women attend as *kōjū* members, one from each household. Attendance at mura meetings is light and sporadic. Moreover, women have little sense of autonomy within their buraku organization and no tradition of women's activity within the *kōjū*. They are shy and hesitate to involve themselves; they know that overzealousness will bring criticism from their men and their neighbors. Niiike is expected to elect one committeewoman and one vice-committeewoman to the Kamo association each year; the women carefully rotate each post and seek to avoid election unless it is clearly their turn to make the sacrifice. The Women's Association is the weakest of all *kōjū* organized associations.

These activities of the *kōjū* as a social unit are typical of rural Okayama and many other communities in neighboring areas. It should be noted, however, that the identity of *kōjū* and buraku is not always as close as in Niiike. For various reasons, it appears that *kōjū* cannot grow beyond a certain size and still be manageable. Hence, when more than about sixty houses comprise a single cluster, whether or not they constitute a single buraku, they usually are split into two or more *kōjū*. Occasionally a *kōjū* contains persons of only one or two lineages, but more often the division is spatial, all neighbors on one side of a dividing line forming one *kōjū* regardless of kinship ties or lack thereof, and all neighbors on another side forming another *kōjū*. The Youth Association, and the Women's Association to somewhat lesser degree, also tend to form according to *kōjū* rather than the sometimes larger buraku. Occasionally the matter of just how the line is drawn to limit *kōjū* offers some interesting insights. Two examples of this are found within the immediate experience of Niiike.

As has been mentioned, there is a small sawmill-residence close to Niiike, on the auto road. Along the same road, but farther from Niiike, is the new house built by Iwasa Eikichi. Because the post office address of each is in the same series of numbers that runs through Niiike and continues to Ōyama, the two houses might be identified with either buraku so far as the Kamo village office is concerned. But Eikichi, though removed spatially from Niiike, remains in its *kōjū*, whereas the sawmill owner belongs neither to Niiike nor to Ōyama. This man moved his family to the sawmill from Horen buraku which, though close by, is in Misu village rather than Kamo; he retains his Horen *kōjū* membership. Actually Horen has two *kōjū* even though it is a small buraku. One is composed of households

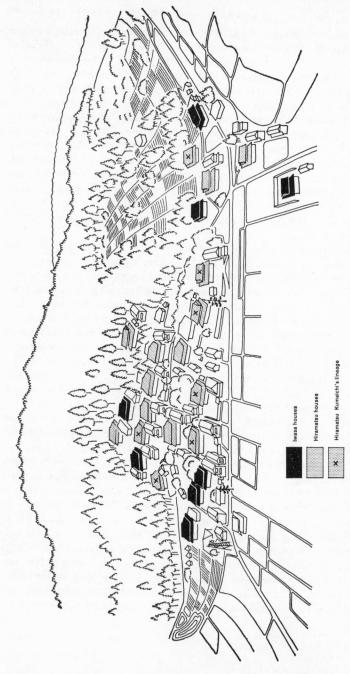

Fig. 34.—Iwasa and Hiramatsu houses in Niiike, showing also the location of houses in the largest Hiramatsu lineage, headed by Hiramatsu Kumiachi

whose ancestors were *Eta*, the outcasts formerly prohibited from associating with ordinary persons; the other comprises the remaining eight houses of ordinary ancestry. The sawmill owner belongs to the latter *kōjū* even though he is a legal resident of Kamo and is physically separated from his *kōjū*. His case shows that *kōjū* affiliation, a social matter, need not conform to administrative affiliation and does not require absolute physical contiguity.

A different example illustrates the degree to which *kōjū* or community membership may be considered voluntary. The careful reader will have noted in Figure 33 that one house is not included in the transmission of messages. This house is in the midst of the community, is the parenthouse of one Niiike lineage, but is not fully part of the *kōjū*. The househead, Hiramatsu Hideo, since childhood has been known as having a forthright and blunt character. His wife died while his two children were still quite young. His two sisters and younger brother, whose marriages he would be expected to arrange, still live with him and his elderly mother, and his children now have grown almost ready for marriage themselves. Tadashi, his elder brother, married outside Niiike instead of inheriting the household lands according to custom but later established himself in Niiike by inheriting from a childless aunt. Hideo's relations with others in Niiike may have become more difficult after his brother's return; in any case, he became known as a cranky, unneighborly person. Various accumulated frictions flared in 1949 when, in the course of the fixing of fertility ratings for every field in the community, Hideo contested but lost the decision about one tiny parcel of his land which the buraku assembly voted to rate higher than he thought proper. So he formally withdrew from the buraku assembly and virtually shut himself off from communication with the rest of Niiike. As tempers cooled somewhat, the majority of the community became anxious to welcome him back but waited in vain for an opportunity. By participating in path- and ditch-clearing, Hideo has made it moot whether his withdrawal was from the *kōjū* altogether or only from its political facet, the buraku assembly; but his household has not participated in funerals or other occasions directly with the *kōjū*. Thus he remains in but not of the community.

In withdrawing from the neighbor-group, Hideo was, in a sense, calling on one of the most extreme sanctions of community life: ostracism. In Japan the procedure for formal ostracism is called *mura hachibu*, "village eight-parts." The etymology refers to cutting off most (80 per cent) of all relations with the village. A community council which, after solemn council, declares a *mura hachibu* thereby excludes one of its members from all normal contact with the rest of its members. This ostracism deprives the offending household of support in crisis and, depending on local conditions, may greatly handicap the everyday processes of making a living. It is, therefore, a severe penalty not lightly invoked. The villagers say no household within memory has ever been subjected to *mura hachibu* in Niiike. Of course, Hideo's withdrawal was not *mura hachibu;* the community did not reject him, he rejected the community. Nonetheless, Niiike was profoundly disturbed by the open rupture of monolithic solidarity and took little comfort from the fact that Hideo, though head of a parent house, got no support from his lineage, who sided with their neighbors. The basic issue was and is the principle of overt unanimity. The breaking-off of communication is not absolute; several women exchange occasional visits with the women of Hideo's house, and Hideo himself, after a year's abstinence, joined in the road-clearing that most explicitly symbolizes *kōjū* communality. His continued separation is an inconvenience mainly to the mura office, which must send one copy of every notice to Niiike and a separate one to Hideo. Hideo himself lives comfortably without help from his neighbors. He not only has sizable acreage and enough household manpower to cultivate it but holds a salaried job in the Kurashiki post office as well. His case tests the degree to which economic and social circumstances compel neighborliness. The resources of a number of other households in the community are adequate to allow their taking an independent course opposed to community opinion, but they would not only suffer loneliness but risk long-term goals as well, goals such as making suitable marriages for their household members. In a strict sense, to suppress individual wants for the sake of *kōjū* solidarity is voluntary, not compulsory; but the penalties and risks of a contrary course are considerable.

Before leaving the *kōjū* and *kōjū*-wide associations we should note again three significant *kōjū* characteristics. First, the *kōjū* has a long tradition reaching into the immemorial past. Similar neighborhood organizations are an important feature of village life almost throughout rural Japan. Though certain areas have a quite distinct pattern of organization, notably in the northern quarter of Honshu as will be discussed below, the *kōjū* is a widespread and typical mode of rural organization. Of various regional names, *kōjū* is the term used around the Inland Sea. Second, the *kōjū* has a multiplicity of functions—economic, social, and ceremonial. It is the many and diverse functions of the *kōjū* that make it the most important social unit in village life second only to the household. Third, the *kōjū* is organized on the explicit assumption of equality of membership with no implications of differential status. Among the *kōjū*-wide associations we have discussed, long tradition, multiplicity of function, and equality of membership are emphatically characteristic of the Youth Association and the fire brigade. On the other hand, the Women's Association lacks long tradition, having been recently imposed from without; it is weak in multiplicity of function; but it certainly has complete equality of membership. Thus, equal-level relationships are dominant in Niiike as a community. They are characteristic not only of *kōjū* and *kōjū*-wide associations but of smaller associations within the community as well.

SUB-KŌJŪ GROUPS

The organizations which identify Niiike as an interacting local community are those which stem from the *kōjū*. Within the buraku, however, there are informal voluntary groups of a size smaller than the *kōjū* as a whole. Most of the small informal groups in Niiike develop according to the convenience and needs of their participants for co-operation in labor, borrowing money, or sharing equipment. These teamwork groups, when named at all, usually are known simply as *kumi* ("group, team"). The members may be near relatives, close neighbors, or age-mates. Co-operation among relatives is most common but only slightly more so than co-operation for identical purposes among unrelated households. Houseclads who happen merely to live close to each other, to be the same age, or to share some common interest may get together for a variety of purposes. Few occasions for interaction are exclusive to a group of related households. In fact, there is at present only one such exclusive activity in Niiike, a primarily symbolic one, the periodic memorial services to an ancestor of one or another household. All other co-operative activities have some examples of unrelated participants.

Co-operation in labor and the sharing of equipment may be undertaken in many ways. The simplest sort involves the sharing of wells and baths. Three households have no well at all, and wells on the western side of the village are not fully adequate the year round. Almost a quarter of the houses have no baths, and even those that do sometimes share a bath to save firewood or straw used in heating the water. The households thus joined are those of brothers or parent and son in certain cases, of unrelated neighbors in others. Again, co-operation occurs in house-building or repair. When Iwasa Takeshi moved and rebuilt his house, those who helped him happened to be exclusively kinsmen. Specifically, they were his father, uncle, elder brother, and, occasionally, his first and third cousins. This listing, by individual relationships, is more simply expressed, in the Japanese way, by saying that two branch houses gave occasional help to their parent house in setting up a new branch house.

Another example of labor-sharing occurs in fieldwork. In the old days, a number of households, sometimes the larger part of the *kōjū*, would join forces for the arduous labor of transplanting and harvesting. During the labor shortages of World War II several households did work together, and the practice is still not uncommon in the countryside; but in Niiike joint labor groups of this sort have passed out of existence, with some sighs for the passing of a fine old tradition. Also gone into disuse is the custom of feasting and drinking that used to wind up a period of co-operative labor. Households now work separately for the most part. An exception is Hiramatsu Isamu and his children who regularly help his elderly and arthritic uncle, Tokujirō, in transplanting and harvesting his main crops, without charge or obligation. But by and large the extra hands in Niiike fields today are most likely to be transient laborers hired for the mat-rush harvest or friends and age-mates from some nearby buraku whose help will be reciprocated. Stable labor groupings, in short, no longer are customary.

Also out of fashion are the informal money-raising groups, *tanomoshi-kō*. Formerly, interested households joined in a financial pool contributing a mutually agreed-upon sum of money; the common fund would then be lent in whole or in part to one of their number for a fixed period at a set interest rate. After repayment, the group might dissolve or might continue to lend capital to other members. Such groups were not necessarily confined within the buraku. Recently restrictive government regulations and easier credit arrangements through the agricultural co-operative have put an end to *tanomoshi-kō* in this region, with a few minor and almost surreptitious exceptions.

Another type of co-operative group nowadays declining in importance is the *kō* organized for the purpose of sending one or more members each year to one of the great shrines or temples of the nation. Like the money-raising groups, these operate by pooling funds. The recipient is chosen by lot and, in the case of the *Ise-kō*, travels to the great shrine at Ise, 200 miles east. The *Daikoku-kō*, sends its members to the Izumo great shrine 130 miles north on the Japan Sea coast. Enthusiasm for trips to these shrines, which were of key importance to the cult of State Shinto, reached a peak during the prewar and wartime period of nationalism but has withered in postwar times. Elderly Niiike pilgrims setting out in 1953 and 1954 have gone to Buddhist temples important to the village sect, Nichiren. Rather than organize *kō*, they have had their expenses paid by their own households. Similarly, expenses are paid by the travelers themselves on the not infrequent trips taken by young men who join together in groups of three or four of about equal age to visit some shrine such as Kompira in Shikoku. One suspects that these men prefer Shinto shrines to Buddhist temples on their quasi-religious trips because proper form for temple pilgrimages would require them to eat their food saltless and abstain from drinking sake. No special name dignifies the group that goes off to a shrine, partly because the men are rather frankly out on a lark. What this amounts to is that people no longer feel it necessary to form special organizations to support travel but nonetheless choose their traveling companions from within their own buraku.

In contrast to subgroups just listed, which often are temporary and decreasing in importance, mutual ownership groups remain stable by virtue of the equipment they share. Our best example comes from the shared ownership of the bulky, expensive rice-hullers. Of three rice-hullers in the buraku, two are owned jointly; eight houses share the first, four houses the second. The third was bought outright by Hiramatsu Isamu, who, although already a shareholder in the first machine, apparently in this as in other matters of farm management felt uncomfortable at not being his own master. The two sharing groups are both composed predominantly but not exclusively of kindred households. Eight houses banded together in 1936 to buy the first rice-huller in Niiike. Six of the householders were from Hiramatsu lineages, two were Iwasa brothers. For several years the group hulled their own rice and, for a fee, that of other households. Then three non-owner Iwasa households joined by a non-owner Hiramatsu decided to buy a machine of their own, making it available to non-owners for a small fee just as the first group did with their huller. The third machine, as noted, was purchased by Isamu for his individual use. Except for Isamu, no co-owner has withdrawn or been added to these machine-owning groups in the twenty years since the first purchase.

LINEAGE TIES IN NIIIKE

An examination of the composition of the two rice-huller co-operatives raises an interesting question concerning the relationship of lineage to the formation of subgroups in the buraku. In each case the co-owners live sufficiently scattered through the village that proximity could not have been the sole motivation. The first group to own a huller is predominantly of Hiramatsu households, perhaps because their slightly larger harvests led them to an earlier appreciation of the machine's utility or because they had more money to spend. But some say that friction over the use of this huller led to the formation of the second group, which is predominantly of Iwasa households. In short, cleavage between surname groups can be read into the composition of these joint-ownership groups, though the mixture of ownership shows that other considerations as well must have been involved.

Of all the subgroups formed in Niiike only those that own the rice-hullers have any approximation to the most troublesome cleavage line in Niiike, the division between surname groups. Otherwise, subgroup memberships for one function tend to cut across groups formed for a different function, thus inhibiting factionalism. The very diversity of groupings makes these special associations work to reinforce the over-all sense of community. The membership of the various smaller-than-*kōjū* associations crosscut each other to such an extent as to prevent the emergence of a stable subgroup which feels itself distinct from the village itself. No single cluster of persons or households share enough functions to feel themselves more closely tied to each other than to the community as a whole.

But there are other reasons for the pervasive sense of unity within the community, for the feeling of the closeness and permanence of village life. An emotional habit of harmony is born of life-long association with the fields, houses, and people of the buraku as a whole. Most of the men and some of the women were born in Niiike. It is where the household ancestors have lived for generations back. As children, the villagers walked to and from school with age-mates who were in the same room at school and with whom they played at home. In adulthood they pass each other daily on their continuing rounds of work. True, some persons are housebound, and others may not cross paths on their errands for days or weeks at a time. But these coincidences are irrelevant to the long-range fact that all the households are constantly and unavoidably thrown together day after day in the close quarters of the buraku. They are together in mutual company and help through all the vicissitudes of life, in earning a livelihood, forming opinions, reaching decisions, in recreation, worship, sickness, and death. Common interests and outlook, joint organization and activity pervade almost every major experience in life.

But despite these harmonious aspects of community association, and despite the fact that the villagers themselves insist that they live in close-knit unity without schisms or cliques, this is not the whole picture. It is only a village fiction that everyone likes everyone else in Niiike. Everyone's mutual best interest is served by minimizing factions, but, obviously, any people living so close together cannot eternally suppress their differences. When such differences appear in the open they tend to follow certain deep-cutting lines.

There are five lineages (called *kabu*, "stock," or *kabu-uchi*, "within-stock") in Niiike today. Three carry the Hiramatsu surname. These number seven, five, and four households and total sixteen households or two-thirds of the community. The two remaining lineages carry the Iwasa surname and number four households each. Each lineage has a central parent house (*honke*) and branch houses (*bunke*) which are descended either from the parent or from earlier branches.

Lineages may decline or even disappear. Kamo records show that in the past fifty years five households have disappeared from Niiike. One was an impoverished household, the last of a Hiramatsu lineage which became extinct for lack of male heirs, its daughters having married outside the

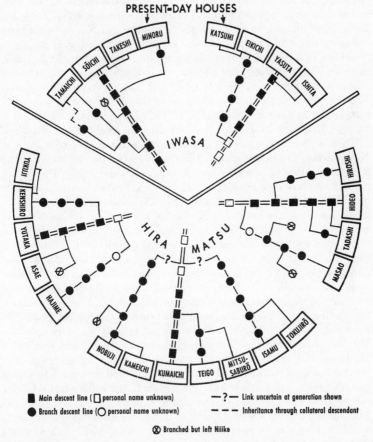

FIG. 35.—The five lineages of Niiike, showing the accepted ancestral links among the houses of each lineage.

community. A second household, belonging to the largest Hiramatsu lineage, lost its land and finally moved to Okayama City. No longer a neighbor, this household has lost contact with Niiike except for an occasional visit from the Sensei or another villager on a trip to the city. The remaining three were Iwasa households; one, unrelated to any other, emigrated to Hokkaido to the far north and eventually was followed by the other two households. The emigration to Hokkaido, in effect, canceled two lineages in Niiike except on the village records. It is interesting to note, incidentally, how the virtual impossibility of transferring household records, until the end of World War II, led to the official fiction that household events in Hokkaido and elsewhere were happening in Niiike. From older village records we see that a century ago Niiike more nearly resembled most of the communities surrounding it today in having a sprinkling of unrelated households among its lineages. But the fact that there are none today seems to suggest that having the support of relatives within a community is a definite advantage for survival and prosperity. And the lack of any unrelated additions to the community suggests, also, that lineage connections contribute to the corporate unity of the community. It retains its own kindred but does not easily accept outsiders.

There is no evidence to show any connection among the five lineages in Niiike today. The shared names, Hiramatsu and Iwasa, are attributed to a common place of origin rather than to common kinship. The former home of all three Hiramatsu lineages, according to tradition, is Hiramatsu buraku in neighboring Shō mura; the two Iwasa lineages are supposed to have come from the buraku of Madokoro, a mile distant from Niiike in Kamo mura. No one in Niiike today has any known relatives in either place. It is presumed that several unrelated houses came initially from each locality. During the two and a half centuries of the Tokugawa regime, farmers and other commoners were prohibited from openly using surnames, though, in fact, some were used secretly. When this edict was lifted in the nineteenth century, many people assumed local place names, eminent family names, or others at will; hence, names shared frequently need not imply relationship. From temple records we learn that the Hiramatsu surname was in use, presumably at the present locality of Niiike, as early as 1685. (The temple records, not being official government documents, might record a surreptitiously used surname.) But these records merely list deaths within the parish, so tell us nothing of lineage connections. For that matter, the connections among the several households of any one lineage today have to be taken on faith in oral tradition for, in contrast to farmers descended from samurai or nobility, whose written genealogies are family treasures, farmers of commoner origin in this region have in their possession no written record of their family line. The oral tradition goes back, with gaps, about five generations. This span is just too short to account positively for the earliest branches of each lineage. Hence, the matter of connections within lineages as well as the separate descent of each lineage in Niiike must be accepted on the basis of tradition for want of evidence either to support or negate tradition (see Fig. 35).

Interconnected or not, the five lineages within themselves contain related households, and there is no unrelated household in the village. Therefore, everyone in Niiike has close kin in the village in addition to the members of his own household. But in the conduct of daily affairs the villagers act as if kinfolk were no more dear to them than neighbors who have no claim of relationship. They go to some lengths to avow and demonstrate that their feeling about each and every household is as if all were in one large family. Equal treatment for everyone is the rule. Each person's close kindred are also his neighbors, and he tends to group all neighbors together, treating them as fellow members of the community who are on close and intimate terms irrespective of degrees of kinship. The other side of this picture is that relatives who live outside the community are emotionally distant. Ties to them are as thin as to any outsider and are rarely renewed. Niiike and other rural communities in this respect differ from urban and upper-class groups. The people whose elite standing gives them social prestige and economic advantage tend continuously to renew ties with distant kindred. The people engaged in business in the cities, similarly, ignore community boundaries in keeping track of relatives. Theirs is not the closed community within which every neighbor is as close as if he were an immediate kinsman. The people of Niiike, however, do maintain this attitude among themselves.

For example, when Hiramatsu Yoshio died one morning after two months' illness from a sudden cancer, this sorrowful crisis for the household of which he was grandfather was shared by both relatives and neighbors. The role of Yoshio's kin within Niiike was not distinguished from that of non-kin neighbors except, perhaps, for sitting a little longer with members of the bereaved household. Yoshio's kin from outside Niiike converged from their distant homes upon the house of their deceased relative only to play the role of guests under no requirement to be active in this family crisis. Yoshio's sisters, his only blood relatives iving outside the community, may never previously have met his wife's parents, who represented relatives by marriage. In any case, this bereavement brought them in touch with Yoshio's household for the first time in months or even years. At the end of the funeral, each returned to his or her own household elsewhere. But Yoshio's kin within Niiike behaved as one with other neighbors, all of whom were involved in this family affair as much or more than relatives living scattered among other buraku.

The fact that scattered members of the line of descent, such as married sisters or adopted brothers, have little contact with each other or with their natal households follows logically from the conception of the household as a unit of solidarity. Kinship links are links between houses, as the Niiike people see it, not person-to-person bonds. The households are the real units of larger kinship groupings. Therefore, the woman who leaves her natal household for married life elsewhere thenceforth reckons the relatives of her new household as her own closest kindred. Even though linked only through marriage, she is part of her husband's household and puts ahead of her own parents and siblings all persons in all the houses related to her husband's house. Her parental house quickly loses close contact with her as, similarly, with anyone else who is absorbed into an alien, unrelated house. Though such persons continue to be called "relatives" in the formal sense, their functioning ties are with the new kindred, not with the house they were born to. This accounts for the very minor role played by most relatives outside the village. The few exceptions stand out by contrast. Hiramatsu Isamu and his sister visit each other fairly frequently, and this seems remarkable, not because she lives so far away (less than three miles separate their homes), but because she is seen at all in Niiike, where she was born.

But if kinship is given little regard in daily affairs, it rises to the surface at times of crisis. At such times, the people draw together in their lineages and act as though the lineages were related. The Hiramatsu line up on one side, the Iwasa on the other. In time of crisis the relationship which matters most is not the literally demonstrable lineage but the general principle of lineage, or *kabu*. The kinship principle, once brought into action, then looms dominant over all alternatives. A most dramatic example occurred during our study, in 1950, and brought to the surface cracks in the community solidarity which otherwise might have longer escaped our attention. An unsolved attempt at murder shattered village harmony and split kinship cleavages wide open. This unprecedented crime of violence was extraordinarily painful to every member of the community, not only because it stained the previously unimpeachable record of gentle tranquility, but because it remained unsolved and kept the buraku in turmoil long afterward. To us, this event is particularly interesting because of the way in which it demonstrated that kinship ties, though overlain by the patiently woven bonds of harmonious community life, are never quite broken.

The murder was attempted on the night of May 2, 1950. Iwasa Takeshi, age twenty-four, was sleeping alone in his new branch house, built slightly apart from the rest of the settlement. He had moved to it in February together with his attractive bride of five months with whom he had been living hitherto in his parents' crowded home. On this night she was absent on her first postnuptial visit back to her own parents' home on *Mugiu-rashi*, a traditional free day before the wheat harvest. For this reason Takeshi was in the extremely unusual position of being alone overnight. Past midnight, some person entered the house through the single window which happened to be unlocked. He picked up a heavy cultivating fork from its place in the entry, struck one blow on the sleeping man's head, then set the fork back on the dirt floor of the entry and departed through the window. Nothing else was disturbed. Takeshi, his head gashed and his cranium broken in two places by the prongs of the heavy fork, lay unconscious and in a spreading pool of blood until his mother found him when she came to cook his breakfast at six o'clock the next morning. Soon police were on the scene. Not until several hours later was it permitted to take Takeshi, still unconscious, to the hospital in Okayama City, members of the Michigan group of observers serving as ambulance drivers. In the hospital, blood transfusions and other medical attention helped Takeshi to recover so that several weeks later he was able to return to the village.

Meanwhile every attempt was made in Niiike to solve the near-murder. Uniformed police, plain-clothes men, and trained dogs were able to turn up only very slight clues. There was one unidentified fingerprint on a chest of drawers. A cheap pocket mirror and comb found outside the one window might have been planted as a false lead. How had this window been unlocked when usually all the house was shut tight? Takeshi himself could give little help. He had not awakened to recognize his assailant, knew of no particular enemy, and could find none of his possessions stolen. The motive was elusive. An alarmed burglar, a jealous rival, any person who envied Takeshi for having a pretty wife and a new branch house might have done the deed. Police investigators are never welcome in Japan, and they learned little for their trouble. Months and years later, they were still unable to list suspects or even to guess whether the assailant was an outsider or, perhaps, from within Niiike itself.

Among the villagers fear and suspicion grew. If a potential murderer had struck once, he might strike again. First, Takeshi's parents, then several other households, purchased large, pedigreed watchdogs. Everyone double-checked his locks each night. Children using toilet facilities at night had to be accompanied by an adult. For all anyone knew, one of his own neighbors might be harboring murderous thoughts. The village solidarity that ordinarily welded together all twenty-four households began to weaken. Subdued resentments flared into the open. Reasons were conjured up for suspecting one person after another. The conviction grew that the murderer was in their midst. As tempers flared, accusations first were mumbled in veiled terms, then written in anonymous letters to each other, and finally sent in signed letters to the police. The police came to be embarrassed less by scarcity of clues than by altogether too many leads founded on circumstantial or ancillary evidence or on unfavorable testimony as to character. The community drew apart into two camps, the Hiramatsu and the Iwasa, and each picked its most likely suspect from the opposite side—a man older than Takeshi, unmarried, and likely to be seriously unhappy. Old animosities rose to the surface quite apart from the search for the murderer. The leading Hiramatsu househead, Kumaichi, went to the police—a shocking step in itself—to accuse an Iwasa neighbor of stealing his fruit. Frictions between kin-aligned groups so disturbed the village that Takeshi made up his mind to emigrate.

But time passed. There was no renewed violence. Takeshi resumed his work; and demands on the community to co-operate in work and ceremony reasserted themselves. Wounds to house and lineage pride began to heal even as Takeshi's head wounds had healed. Gradually the cleavage closed again and Niiike regained its community-centered equilibrium.

We are not able to end this real-life murder story in proper style with the culprit brought to book, for the case remains unsolved. But the story reveals a great deal about the inner structure of the buraku and the conflict between the mutually co-operative kōjū organization that binds all the households together and the kinship solidarity that splits them into two groups. Here is tension between two unreconciled principles, the principle of unity among neighbors and that of unity among kindred. It is important to recall that in a different crisis, the dispute ending in Hideo's withdrawal from the kōjū, neighbors united without mention of kinship. But in the murder crisis, neighbors turned kinsmen, abandoned their neighborhood solidarity, and fell back on kinship, even on kinship of the undemonstrable ties among lineages. The situation raises several questions. If kinship ties have a value, why are they usually suppressed? Have they always been so suppressed? Is there no way to give full weight to kinship regularly while maintaining community solidarity? These questions are not easily answered and must lead us to a further study of kinship patterns in Niiike as well as in other parts of Japan.

KINSHIP HIERARCHY AND COMMUNITY ORGANIZATION

The conflict between equal-level *kōjū*-type relations and the kinship bases of community organization reveals the changing pattern of rural social organization in Japan. The nature of this change is best understood if we consider more carefully the other alternative to the *kōjū*-organized community, namely, one in which kinship is the dominant force. Characteristic of the kinship-centered community is the hierarchical arrangement of its households and the way in which fictive kin relationships draw in those who have no lineal connection.[1] Japanese sociologists have used the term *dōzoku* ("common kin") to describe this kind of group, consisting of a hierarchy of households linked by kinship or fictive kinship ties.

Stress on *dōzoku* relationships is characteristic of the northern part of rural Japan and of southern Kyushu, that is to say, of the Frontier Zone. Not many entire communities of northern Japan are incorporated into a single kinship body. More often two or three *dōzoku* make up the community, each occupying or competing for position in an inter-*dōzoku* hierarchy, while the constituent households of each are linked to each other in an intra-*dōzoku* hierarchy. An extreme example of *dōzoku* organization is found in Ishigami mura, a community in northern Japan. This community, first described by Professor Kizaemon Ariga of Tokyo University, is often referred to as a model of the *dōzoku* type. Its example has stimulated much of the thinking about the nature of rural society in Japan and serves as a useful comparison to Niiike.

Ishigami mura, in Iwate Prefecture, near the northern tip of Honshu, lies inland on the eastern slope of the central mountain range of northern Honshu. Here the winters are long and cold, the summers cool. Each year only 130 to 150 frostless days normally are expected. With so short a growing season, even prime land provides only one annual crop of grain. Moreover, there is a conspicuous absence of heavy fertilization, of a well-developed irrigation system, and of other practices of intensive farming considered normal around Niiike.

Ishigami comprises thirty-seven households which constitute a single farm community on the order of Niiike. But its organization, by either

[1] Confusion about the nature of adopted kinship ties may be avoided if it is recognized that three quite different types exist, each being exemplified under appropriate circumstances in Japan: (*a*) ties relating single persons to each other (example: godparent-godchild); (*b*) ties relating one or more persons to a group (example: adopted son–adopting family); (*c*) ties relating households to each other (example: *dōzoku*). The last-named type, though rare or absent in the Occident, appears in a variety of situations in Japan, e.g., landlord-tenant, or main store–branch store relations. When the respective househeads, owners, or managers "personalize" and perpetuate their relations through formal declaration of kinship, the bond simultaneously affects all the close kindred living in the household of each. The leading house as such has the "parent role" (*oyabun*), dependent households have the "child role" (*kobun*), and the members of each, respectively, carry either *oyabun* or *kobun* relationships to each other.

genealogical or fictive kinship ties, places one household as the *ōya* ("great house") and the other thirty-six households on a hierarchical gradient downward from the *ōya*. Though its inhabitants have arrived at different times and in various circumstances, the entire community regards itself as a single kinship group (*dōzoku*). The *dōzoku* hierarchy is accepted as the natural and inevitable pattern for almost all human relations.

The *ōya* is, indeed, the "great house," at the apex of the community. Its household is the direct descendant of the first settler, a former samurai warrior of the Nambu domain who returned to farming. The *ōya*, when studied prior to the land reform, still controlled virtually all the surrounding arable land, though most of it was let out under various arrangements to other members of the community. For itself the *ōya* farmed only 3.3 acres of rice land and 5 acres of dry field. While such amount would be huge around Niiike in the Core Zone, it is not great in this northern area of relatively extensive farming. The principal occupation of the *ōya* today is the production of lacquer ware. In this activity the household operates as a small family factory. The *ōya* roof shelters not only the household, his mother, sister, wife, daughter, five sons, and the wife and child of his eldest son but eight servants as well. The servants constitute two nuclear families—a couple and their three young children, and a man with his adoptive son and the latter's bride. These twenty persons made up the *ōya* household at the time of Professor Ariga's study. *Ōya* members from time to time move out to other positions in the community but always look back and up to the *ōya*.

Each of the thirty-six non-*ōya* households is related to the *ōya* in one of three ways. Figure 36 presents the relationships schematically. In order of prestige, *bekke* (7 households) are junior sons of the *ōya* (5) or other *bekke* (2) and genealogically linked to the *ōya*. *Nago* (27 households) are tenant farmers with only assumed kinship ties to the *ōya*, *tsukuriko* (2 households) are also tenant farmers but rather looked down upon as latecomers, having been in the village for only fifty to a hundred years. The manner of establishing households and the obligations involved vary with the class of relationship. *Bekke* households, the junior sons of the *ōya* or of other *bekke*, branch away and receive a small bit of farm land, a house and lot, furniture, and tools. They are not obliged to give either rent or service to the *ōya*. *Nago* households are all land-renters but may be one of three classes. *Nago* A households (9) have only a simple tenant, land-rental relationship either directly with the *ōya* (4) or indirectly through *bekke* (5). *Nago* B households (15) were established by former hired hands of the *ōya* or, sometimes, *bekke*. *Nago* C households (3) are those of former *ōya* household servants for whom their master arranged a marriage, built a house for them to rent, and gave them land to cultivate, permitting them to keep a fixed portion of the harvest and to divide the remainder into two parts, giving the principal part to the *ōya* as rent. As former servants, *Nago* C enjoy deep affection from the *ōya*. All *nago* are obliged to render the *ōya* two days' service in each of such activities as plowing, harrowing, transplanting rice, weeding, harvesting, and processing. *Tsukuriko* households (2) were established when the *ōya* permitted them to immigrate to Ishigami and rented land to them to cultivate in

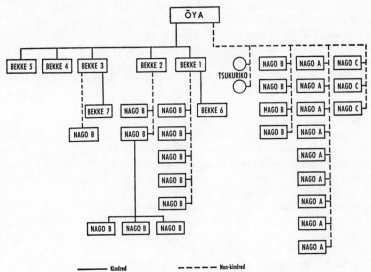

FIG. 36.—Organization of the *dōzoku* of Ishigami in northern Japan, showing consanguine and other relationships among the various categories of membership in the hierarchical structure.

return for a fixed amount of harvest and service. Since their original admission to the community was under the patronage of the *ōya*, the *tsukuriko* give service in gratitude and in different amount from the *nago*. Within each class of relationship the houses whose relation began earlier have higher standing than later comers. Altogether, each household is tied by economic dependence to its founder and ultimately to the "great house."

Hierarchy in Ishigami goes beyond the economic relation just described, for it is re-enforced by social and sentimental subordination as well. *Bekke* are the most nearly self-sufficient households, but they, nonetheless, consult the head of the *ōya* before reaching important decisions and are careful to invite the head to visit them on all their own ceremonial occasions.

For all households the "great house" is the principal social and ceremonial center. Its family ceremonies and festivities are public occasions attended by all. To it come the genealogical branch members for ancestral commemoration ceremonies. The *nago* who is ready for marriage comes to consult about choice of bride and terms of marriage and finally to have his wedding ceremony performed in the "great house."[2]

Work, social activities, and ceremonial life in Ishigami mura call on the people for co-operation and joint enterprise, just as in Niiike. But whereas Niiike co-operates on a basis of equality, these people of the north work together within the frame of enduring and pervasive hierarchy. There is no place in their social scheme to incorporate a new member as an equal, for gradations of obligation are implicit in every interaction between households. Economic patronage and social sponsorship from above and services and obedience from below are exchanged according to the position of each party on the ladder of real or fictive kin descent. Consequently a position on this ladder must be assigned to any newcomer to establish the nature of responsibility between him and his neighbors.

Niiike and its neighbors on the coastal plain have no *dōzoku* with the rigid, particularized vertical structure seen in Ishigami. This is not to say they know no hierarchy, however, for, wherever kinship linkage carries any weight, hierarchy tends to make an appearance. The vertical structuring of kin groups in Niiike is apparent even on brief inspection. Within the household we already have outlined the hierarchical positioning of members, i.e., male, older, and first-born persons have higher status. In a broader context, within a lineage, households also have differential status. The parent house, headed by first sons born of first sons has highest status; no matter that certain of the "sons" were adopted, for this fact is forgotten after a couple of generations. The branch houses, established by junior sons, are subordinate to the parent house, though superordinate to any of their own branches. As between lineages the same pattern is carried over even though Niiike lacks concretely defined kin linkages among lineages. Of the three Hiramatsu lineages, the largest and perhaps oldest in residence is given precedence and an implied seniority: the head house, Hiramatsu Kumaichi's, is known as the "head house among head houses." The branches of this dominant lineage, though inferior to the head, are not necessarily inferior to the head houses of the two other Hiramatsu lineages. The two Iwasa lineages follow a similar vertical structuring though of a more faintly impressed pattern. Iwasa Sōichi's household is the "head house among head houses."

---

[2] Summary of Kizaemon Ariga, *Nihon Kazoku Seido to Kosaku Seido* ("The Japanese Family System and the Tenantry System") (Tokyo, 1943), pp. 84–92, 118–25.

In a still broader context, the broadest in Niiike, the Hiramatsu group enjoys a certain elevation, albeit slight, over the Iwasa group. The Hiramatsu houses outnumber those of the Iwasa two to one. But their superiority is not merely one of numbers. They usually are presumed also to have been first to settle in the locality. They have a slight but definite edge in amount of land owned per household and in occupancy of the choicest fields. As to house sites, the leading Hiramatsu lineage occupies the central group of houses in the lower row, convenient to the main road, whereas Iwasa houses are at one side or inconveniently up the hill (see Fig. 34). Though Iwasa men have held various community posts of responsibility, none has yet served as buraku head. Thus in numerous slight but measurable ways the position of the Hiramatsu is superior to that of the Iwasa. On both sides, allusions are made to an earlier day when the Hiramatsu families were more explicitly superior, a day, we note, when there were fewer paths to economic strength. But even today, however subdued the degree of superiority may be, the relationship is still that of a slight elevation on the Hiramatsu side.

As we look beyond Niiike into the surrounding countryside, we see that some aspect of inferiority or superiority is implied in every situation that bears on descent and relationship. The traditionally important houses in Kamo, on the one hand, are houses descended from hereditary village officials of the Tokugawa regime whose offspring were constant holders of office in the new village organization of the nineteenth and early twentieth centuries. On the other hand, as has been noted earlier in the case of Hōren buraku, there are lineages or entire buraku in the neighborhood whose status in premodern times was that of outcasts, *Eta*, and whose children are still blamed (often with justice) for most of the pranks and vandalism of the neighborhood, while the adults are accepted only with reservations. Family line is a main determinant of all these varied status positions.

In Niiike, although villagers speak of both genealogical and fictive kinship relations as having been important in the past, today there are no fictive relationships in use except that of adopted son. Nor have fictive relations been characteristic of Niiike or other communities in the vicinity for as long as people now living can recall. They know well enough what such relationships are; indeed, the terminology is part of the vocabulary of most Japanese. They know of several types of "godparenthood," particularly the *kaneoya* relation established with a child a few years before puberty and ceremonially renewed at the transition to marriageable status at age fifteen to seventeen, because such was the practice of their grandparents. But, as the Niiike people see it, "godparenthood" is old fashioned and folkish; *oyabun-kobun* groups are associated with the proletariat and gangsters of the city; and the assumed relationships through which unrelated households are absorbed into a rigid *dōzoku* are oddities of villages in the mountains behind them, known mostly from hearsay. They themselves have no use for artificially extended kinship relations. Presumably, they get along without fictive ties for the same reason they subdue their genealogical ties. Both imply verticality of relations, subordination under superiors, a hierarchical order established by birth. Achievement brings few or no direct rewards under such kinship hierarchy. If Niiike were like Ishigami, for example, its Sensei, Hiramatsu Mitsusaburō, who represents a branch house rather than the main house in his lineage, could not rise, whatever his achievements, to the position of prestige and leadership he actually does occupy in Niiike. Niiike favors patterns of mutual, equal-level relationship and, at least outside the household, avoids stress on vertical relationships as much as possible. In this stress on equal-level relationships, the *kōjū* of Niiike illustrates the preferred pattern of association that typifies rural areas of Core Japan.

What lies behind these differences between such communities as Ishigami and Niiike? Japanese scholars who have made extensive studies of hierarchical organization conclude that economic dependency lies at the root of social and ceremonial subservience of the sort found in Ishigami. Our information supports this conclusion. It should not be assumed, however, that unequal distribution of wealth of itself creates the necessary conditions for pervasive hierarchical patterns. Members of a *kōjū* or similar association in Core Japan may include both relatively rich and relatively poor farmers, all co-operating in patterns of equality. The critical question for conditions favorable to hierarchy is how poor are the poor. If the poorer members of a group are very close to the lower margin of existence, hierarchy becomes a form of life insurance. If any small setback such as a below-average harvest poses a calamity threatening starvation, patronage may be welcomed on almost any terms. Tenants or small landowners who are hard pressed to keep alive under the best of circumstances are in no position to refuse subservience to the house that can help them through hard times. Over the years the habit of dependency hardens and becomes accepted as life's natural course. Any malcontent who attempts to renounce his traditional obligations may find his community mobilized against him, his neighbors being motivated not by love for their mutual patron but by the necessity for quelling any disturbance impeding the smooth functioning of their community. So long as a substantial number of households in a community have little more than subsistence, while a few households have the power given them by surplus, so long the *dōzoku* can perpetuate itself.

But in Niiike and most of Core Japan the margin above mere subsistence is considerably wider than in Ishigami and the Frontier Zone generally. In Niiike, by canny double-cropping and skilled techniques, a farmer with only a small bit of land can provide a fair bulwark against minor crises. Furthermore, in times of poor crops he can step up household processing of goods or work at a salaried job to bolster family income. Under such circumstances the security of kin-based hierarchy is less attractive than the freedom and flexibility of equal-level organization. Economic independence fosters attitudes of equality and mutuality. The organization of the *kōjū* and similar associations among farmers of the Core Zone reflects the relative independence of the participants. In the past, apparently, there was more vertical organization in Niiike and the Core Zone than there is today. But the favorable conditions for agriculture probably have long been a deterrent to the development of such extreme hierarchy as that of Ishigami mura and the Frontier Zone. Urban-industrial influence in the area today gives farmers in the Core Zone more economic latitude than ever before, further reducing the poverty that is the best environment for rigid hierarchy.

Of course, the Niiike household must still meet emergencies, often too severe to handle alone. But no one in Niiike need prepare for these crises by serving a patron. The villagers meet emergencies by household groups. Sometimes they fall back on old kinship groupings, as in the case of the attempted murder. But increasingly they rely on the collective resources of neighborhood groupings not only for daily intercourse but for emergencies as well, as in the case of funerals, accident, illness, or crop failure. The *kōjū* and the various smaller *kumi* or teamwork groups of Niiike offer a collective cushioning against diaster. Of course, the corollary of such collective security is that no household may escape the exacting demand of good neighborliness, upon which Niiike lays such stress, unless it is in a very strong economic position. Such, for instance, was Hiramatsu Hideo's. But no household need be totally subservient, and the member of a community of equals seldom thinks of his position as one of bondage, for this aspect of his situation is obscured by the local prestige that personal achievement can bring and by reassuring security that comes from having the guaranty of support and comfort from all one's neighbors.

ŌAZA ASSOCIATIONS

Community associations discussed thus far have been largely those within Niiike, but there are, of course, many associations which reach outside the buraku as well. Beyond the buraku, Niiike's widening relationships start with the ōaza, where their intensity and intimacy is already greatly diminished, and extend to the mura and still larger units. It should be remembered that, in Kamo, ōaza boundaries are almost exactly those of the Tokugawa mura and represent the area of widest co-operative interaction of those days. The importance of ōaza and mura boundaries and the influence of the historical past is strongly apparent in Niiike's associations with other buraku. Within a quarter-mile radius of Niiike there are five buraku. One might expect all of them to be closely associated. But one of them, Horen, lies across the mura boundary. Although Horen people work in fields scattered among those of Niiike farmers, Horen children wander at play over the same hillside the Niiike children play on, and one Horen house, as noted earlier, is actually in Kamo next door to Niiike, still Horen and Niiike have no community relations. Niiike turns toward the buraku within Kamo while Horen joins other buraku of Misu. The mura boundary, which a century ago was the boundary of a fief, is a social as well as political barrier to interaction. Relations between the two communities are not unpleasant, but the two buraku share no common organization.

To certain nearby buraku in its own mura, however, Niiike is strongly bound. One of the strongest extra-buraku bonds comes from the continuing demands of operating a mutual system of water supply. Niiike and ten buraku of the northwestern third of Kamo mura (see Fig. 37) are bound by mutual dependence for their primary water supply on the Ichinohi feeder ditch from the Twelve-Gō Canal system (chap. 6, pp. 132–38). The eleven buraku concerned, involving 1,392 persons, are divided into two ōaza just as the ditch serving them divides in two shortly after leaving the main canal. The upper branch feeds the five buraku of Upper Shinjō ōaza (which includes Niiike) while the lower branch serves the six buraku of Lower Shinjō ōaza. Today all eleven buraku are collectively responsible for the maintenance of their feeder ditch. Each buraku has additional water resources. Niiike, for example, has Ōbara Pond, which it manages by itself, and nine Niiike houses get a share of water from Taishō Pond. But since almost every house in the village has some dependence on canal water, the buraku as a whole takes great interest in the feeder canal. The same is true of other buraku. Ordinary cleaning and maintenance is done by each buraku as a part of *kōjū* ditch-cleaning activity each spring. Beyond this, the water-users pay a fee for "engineers" to manage the water and to hire men for occasional repairs. Though sent to the mura office and disbursed there, the money is treated as an ōaza account. The "engineers," two local farmers, are considered ōaza employees, one for each ōaza. For small repair jobs, the engineer merely calls on the buraku most involved to supply needed labor. For major repairs, he recommends that the mura hire laborers to be paid from the ditch fees in the ōaza account.

Another bond uniting the community is religious. Eleven buraku—the same eleven as those above except that Suenaga is replaced by Nagada to the east across the Ashimori River—are bound together informally to worship at Upper Kamo shrine and keep it in good repair (see Fig. 37).

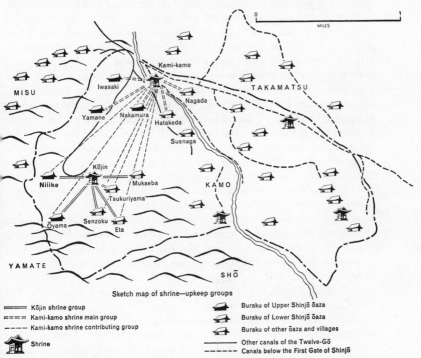

Sketch map of shrine–upkeep groups

═════ Kōjin shrine group	Buraku of Upper Shinjō ōaza
═ ═ ═ Kami-kamo shrine main group	Buraku of Lower Shinjō ōaza
─ ─ ─ Kami-kamo shrine contributing group	Buraku of other ōaza and villages
Shrine	———— Other canals of the Twelve-Gō
	─ ─ ─ ─ Canals below the First Gate of Shinjō

FIG. 37.—Buraku affiliated with Niiike as *ujiko* of Kōjin and Upper Kamo shrines, showing how closely this network matches the course of irrigation ditches leading from the First Gate of Shinjō on the Twelve-Gō Canal.

This relationship has historical origins. Though the river now separates the shrine and Nagada buraku from the other buraku, several bits of evidence suggest that the river formerly had a more easterly course so that the shrine and all eleven buraku were together on the west side. In such case, the eleven buraku would all have been joint users of the Twelve-Gō Canal branch as well as joint worshippers at the shrine.

Another shrine important to Niiike is the shrine to Kōjin (usually regarded as a hearth deity) erected on the crest of Tsukuriyama, the great prehistoric tomb on the valley floor near Niiike. Though actually a branch shrine of the small, rather auxiliary Kōjin shrine built in the shadow of the larger Upper Kamo shrine mentioned above, the branch is a much more elaborate structure than its parent. The Tsukuriyama shrine is the size of a large room, with assembly grounds and a stone torii gate. It has become the principal local shrine (*ujigami*) for Niiike and is important to the five other closely located buraku (see Fig. 37) largely because it is more convenient to visit than the parent shrine clear across the river. These six buraku, thus, belong to two shrine groups; their main attention is given to the nearby Kōjin shrine on Tsukuriyama, but they also make donations to the Upper Kamo shrine for maintenance and repair. One may guess at the history behind these practices. In general, shrine-worship groups appear to represent ceremonial consolidations of farmers linked by irrigation problems into common-interest groups. The Upper Kamo shrine group must have formed with the creation of the Twelve-Gō irrigation system, if not earlier. Niiike, whose people are almost exclusively concerned with the branch Kōjin shrine, may have come into existence only after the river, by shifting its course, cut the original shrine and one buraku away from the main body of buraku. The six buraku that worship at the Kōjin shrine, incidentally, have common drainage problems centering on a main drainage ditch and dike which do not concern the other five buraku of the combined ōaza. Since 1946, worship at Shinto shrines has no official compulsion. But until the end of the war, in order to promote the state cult, villagers were virtually required to participate in worship at officially designated Shinto shrines. Upper Kamo, Kamo, and Hachiman were the three shrines designated for Kamo mura. But the Kōjin shrine, though omitted from the official list, continued to be most important to the six buraku whose neighborly relations were cemented by common worship there. As joint worshipers they form an *ujiko* ("children of the *uji*"), the social body under the beneficent guardianship of the local spirit.

Upper Shinjō ōaza, in which Niiike is located, serves as a co-operative entity in other ways. A small patch of wood lot is owned as common land by the ōaza. This wood lot is just large enough to provide the fuel for cremation of the dead. Each lineage has a hereditary relationship with a certain outcast family to cremate its dead, and these families do the actual cutting of wood in the common wood lot. The ōaza also holds title to the crematory ground. There is also an ōaza command level for the fire brigade and Youth Association, though this serves only for liaison between mura and buraku and has no part in forming policy. Finally, the ōaza is shown by marriage records of the nineteenth century, when marriages were made nearer home than today, to have been an exogamous community; that is, marriage within the ōaza was frowned on, even when completely unrelated persons were involved. To be sure, brides are still sought outside of the ōaza and, in fact, outside of a still wider area, but today the sense of restriction is phrased in terms of kinship, not in terms of locality.

MURA ASSOCIATIONS

Kamo mura has become increasingly important in the life of Niiike in the years of ferment and continuing crisis which Japan has experienced since 1937 and particularly since 1947. Mura government, as the agent of higher professional bureaucracy, has been called on to carry out a growing number of functions having a direct, constant, and highly important bearing on the daily lives and fortunes of its inhabitants. At the same time, the average farmer's legal capacity to participate in and direct the policy and actions of this government has been substantially increased. As a consequence, most persons have a distinctly heightened consciousness of the importance of local government to themselves and their households. They may not yet be strongly resolute in participating meaningfully in the local political process, but they are more interested in this sphere than seems to have been the case before the war. Some of the old mistrust remains, but farmers are no longer so inclined to regard the government of their mura as an institution essentially marginal to their wants and welfare.

Favorable attitudes toward the mura are engendered by its community roles which are important to the farmers. In most cases, these are more formal and more recently established than the roles held by ōaza and buraku. The link to past tradition is perhaps strongest through irrigation. The mura collects irrigation taxes, part of which go to the Twelve-Gō Canal Association, and also serves as the active representative of its inhabitants on the committee that manages the canal. This committee is composed of the mayor, or his representative, of each of the thirteen participating villages and towns. Kamo mura has a special additional role, for its mayor is ex officio head of the Six-Gō Canal organization that manages the lower half of the Twelve-Gō Canal and is personally in charge of the critical water gate at Iwasaki.

Grammar-school education is conducted by the mura. In addition, in 1940, Kamo mura united with Oishi mura and the two adjoining towns of Takamatsu and Makane to build and support a junior high school (new since the postwar renovation of the educational system) and a high school.

Each mura has its own P.T.A. (referred to as "pee-chee-ay" rather than with a translated title), which is organized within the mura for grammar-school problems but joins the other three in concern for mutual problems of junior and senior high schools. Education is almost universally regarded as important, but the high degree of interest is not matched by an equal show of participation in school affairs on the part of adults. No opportunity to participate was open until the P.T.A. was formed after the war. One of the younger fathers in Niiike for several years has held office in the P.T.A., but most of the thirteen eligible households leave participation to the mothers, who merely attend the meetings. From a third to half of them attend most meetings, which in part inform them of school policies and activities and in part attempt adult education.

The Women's Association (*Fujinkai*), described earlier as being composed of one woman from each house of the *kōjū*, has its official existence at the mura level. Each buraku elects a committeewoman and a vice-committeewoman every year. The mura association then sends a representative to the prefectural federation of Women's Associations. The Women's Association is no longer a tool for mobilizing nationalist sentiment and obtaining volunteer service on projects of interest to the government, as it was from its inception in the 1930's to the end of World War II. It conducts lectures and demonstrations on cooking, housekeeping, and other feminine subjects, and one of its two main annual meetings is given over to a pleasure trip to some shrine or scenic spot paid partly from organization dues. Nevertheless, most Niiike women give the mura association no more than token attention; half of them were absent, for example, from the important fall meeting in 1954. Though their participation is good when compared with other buraku of Kamo, few Niiike women have ever taken one of the excursions; perhaps ten women attend a lecture-demonstration on culinary matters, but attendance dropped to three from Niiike when the lecture subject was birth control.

For the men of Niiike, as they take on the responsibility of managing the farm, the farm co-operative becomes the most important mura organization. It provides fertilizer, seed, and tools at discount and, if necessary, on credit; it collects the requisitioned crops for the government and may act as agent in selling other crops; and it is by far the most important of all savings and loan sources. Even under the postwar policy of mura autonomy, the co-operative finds itself doing the government's work in collecting, recording, and shipping the requisitioned crops, for little compensation, but it is much less a tool of higher government than it was before 1945, the end of the war. Members must buy at least one ¥5,000 share, but are now quite free to join or stay out. The new freedom not to join, in the early postwar period, was rather widely popular; but now over 90 per cent of all farm households in the Kamo area have memberships, some holding two or more shares. Price discounts and the convenience of being able to leave harvest money as credit and to borrow money without security are clear incentives to join. Though details of the operation of this co-operative may be left for later discussion, some idea of its significance is conveyed by the total credit balance. During 1952 and 1953, which were relatively good years, the credit balance ranged from a pre-harvest low of ¥11 million to a post-harvest peak of ¥31.5 million ($30,555 to $87,500). Divided by the number of members in the Kamo co-operative and converted to dollar equivalents, this range would represent a rise from $60 to $175 credit for the average member.

As indicated, among Niiike community activities the Youth Association and the fire brigade are strongly connected to the mura which for them is the policy-making, nearly autonomous level of organization. The mura collects modest dues from the young men of the various buraku and budgets expenses of equipment and activities.

Relatively few formally organized associations extend beyond the mura. Of these, the Twelve-Gō Canal Association has been mentioned. The administration of the joint junior and senior high schools is another instance. The co-operation of the four mura involved is voluntary, but the majority of people in each community have been unwilling to go further. The prefectural government, in connection with the recent drive for amalgamation of rural villages, has recommended that several mura join together as a single *machi* ("town") to gain a larger financial base than any has at present. But this suggestion was resisted until 1956, when it became clear that higher government would force through a merger in any case.

UNORGANIZED EXTRA-BURAKU COMMUNITY RELATIONS

Niiike has a number of informal relations with other communities largely for the purpose of obtaining a variety of goods and services. Niiike shoppers can buy a number of items such as food, salt, and incidentals at the two small general stores at Senzoku buraku, five minutes away across the fields. But for more ambitious household purchases they must go two miles to Harakozai buraku in Takamatsu-chō, just beyond the border of Kamo mura. Few people come to Harakozai stores in Takamatsu from farther away than Niiike; Takamatsu is the primary shopping area for medium and minor purchases for two mura, Kamo and Oishi, and Takamatsu-chō itself. Table 16 presents a summary of both goods and services available to Niiike shoppers in Takamatsu. Those of

Inari buraku in Takamatsu-chō are listed separately to the right of Harakozai figures. The two buraku are considerably different, for Harakozai, along the railroad track, is the main shopping center of Takamatsu, while Inari, a mile up the valley, is a group of inns, restaurants, and souvenir shops to serve the many visitors from all over the Inland Sea who come, principally at New Year's, to the large Inari shrine on the hill above. Though Niiike people avail themselves of Inari buraku services only to a limited extent, still the area offers a touch of increasing cosmo-

TABLE 16

SUMMARY OF GOODS AND SERVICES AVAILABLE IN HARAKOZAI
AND INARI BURAKU OF TAKAMATSU

Goods	Harakozai	Inari	Services	Harakozai	Inari
Fish market..........	3	..	Physician............	1	..
Food and drink........	3	..	Midwife..............	1	..
Tobacco, sweets.......	11	2	Dentist..............	3	..
Sake mfg.	1	..	Moxicautery	..	1
Soy sauce mfg.........	3	1	Barber...............	1	1
Noodle maker.........	..	1	Beauty parlor	3	..
Clothing	5	..	Cleaning, dyeing......	2	..
Stationery, books......	4	..	Knitting teacher......	1	..
Drugs...............	2	..	Photographer.........	1	..
Hardware............	7	1	Cafe.................	3	10
Farm tools...........	2	..	Hotel................	..	10
Motors..............	2	..	Movie, show	1*	1*
Seed, fertilizer	3	..	Pinball game.........	..	1
Fuel, sand...........	1	..	Fortuneteller.........	..	2*
Lumber mill..........	1	..	Watch repair........	1	..
Souvenirs............	..	17	Radio repair	2	..
Votive items.........	..	4	Bicycle repair	3	..
Wheelbarrow maker ...	1	..	Metal goods repair....	1	..
Rush products........	4	..	Tinsmith.............	1	..
Bamboo weaver.......	..	1	Stonemason..........	1	1
			Carpenter...........	1	..
			Rice polisher.........	1	..
			Grain processor.......	1	..
Total............	53	27	Total...........	29	27

* One temporary in each case.

politanism. Figures 38 and 39 show the arrangement and type of goods or service offered in the stores of Harakozai and Inari.

The habit of going by bus or train to Okayama City to spend a day shopping has become strong enough in the postwar years so people tend to make medium as well as major purchases there. Okayama City department stores offer a wider selection of goods and at lower prices. However, department-store purchases have to be paid in cash. A long-established system of receiving credit from Takamatsu merchants until harvest time keeps the shopping habits of many people from shifting more strongly to Okayama City. The family's small purchases often are picked up by Niiike junior and senior high school pupils on their way home from school in Takamatsu. Figure 40 shows the degree to which various businesses in Takamatsu, as roughly estimated by their proprietors, mirror in reverse the work and slack cycle of cultivation, with the wheat and mat-rush harvest in June and July, the rice harvest in November, the slack season and *Bon* festival of late summer, and the Fall Festival.

For their more serious ailments the people of Niiike go to the Kibi Hospital in Takamatsu-chō, which is staffed by five physicians, one of whom is a gynecologist. This hospital is the primary facility for the people of

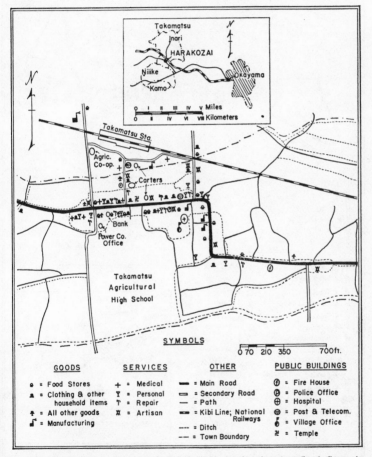

SYMBOLS

0 70 210 350   700ft.

GOODS	SERVICES	OTHER	PUBLIC BUILDINGS
● = Food Stores	+ = Medical	▬ = Main Road	ⓕ = Fire House
▲ = Clothing & other household items	⊻ = Personal	▭ = Secondary Road	ⓟ = Police Office
♣ = All other goods	⊤ = Repair	— = Path	⊕ = Hospital
⌁ = Manufacturing	⋈ = Artisan	▰ = Kibi Line; National Railways	⊖ = Post & Telecom.
		---- = Ditch	⌀ = Village Office
		—·— = Town Boundary	⧓ = Temple

FIG. 38.—The shop area at Harakozai, showing the various goods and services offered. Comparison with Inari (Fig. 39) shows the contrasting character of these two commercial areas of Takamatsu.

284 VILLAGE JAPAN

Takamatsu-chō and of Kamo and Oishi. Recently, since the attempted murder in Niiike, villagers have been equally inclined to get treatment from the Okayama University Hospital in Okayama City. A mura sponsored midwife lives near the mura office. Expectant mothers visit her for a five months' checkup; the midwife visits the patients' homes for delivery. Dental service is provided by two dentists in Takamatsu, each in his own private office. The few women in Niiike who have had their hair

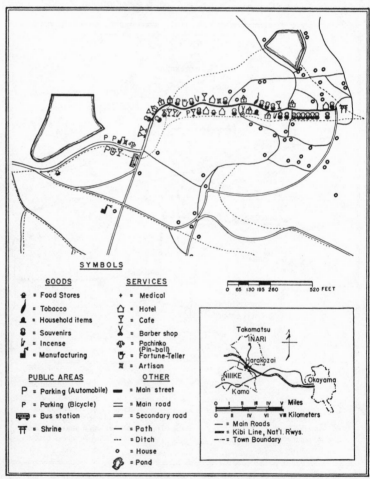

SYMBOLS

GOODS
- = Food Stores
/ = Tobacco
- = Household items
- = Souvenirs
- = Incense
- = Manufacturing

PUBLIC AREAS
P = Parking (Automobile)
P = Parking (Bicycle)
- = Bus station
TT = Shrine

SERVICES
+ = Medical
- = Hotel
Y = Cafe
- = Barber shop
- = Pachinko (Pin-ball)
- = Fortune-Teller
- = Artisan

OTHER
- = Main street
= = Main road
= = Secondary road
- = Path
--- = Ditch
o = House
- = Pond

0 65 130 195 260   520 FEET

Takamatsu
INARI
Harakozai
NIIIKE   Okayama
Kamo

0 I II III IV V Miles
0 II IV VI VII Kilometers
— = Main Roads
- = Kibi Line, Nat'l. R'wys.
-·-= Town Boundary

FIG. 39.—The shop area at Inari, showing the predominance of recreational services and groups

permanent waved have also gone to Takamatsu. As already noted, the men's haircutting is done by Hiramatsu Tamaichi in Niiike.

SUMMARY

We have said that the people of Niiike feel their main attachment to their buraku and are not merely less intimately attached to their mura but regard it with a certain amount of suspicious reserve. Under present-day circumstances, this attitude may seem unjustified. Kamo even, apart

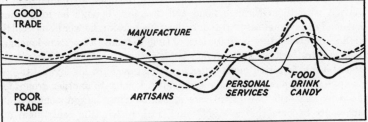

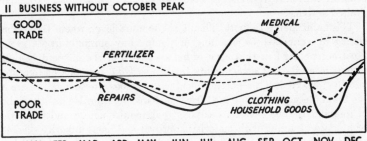

FIG. 40.—Business cycles in Harakozai, compiled from the estimates of all shopkeepers and service people. Note how the cycle of farm work and leisure is reflected, directly or inversely, in the amount of activity in most enterprises.

from its political role, offers activities and associations in which almost anyone may find a place. It also acts or may act as the agent for its inhabitants and serves many of their needs. It represents them in the large irrigation community and in the secondary-school community, and it is their spokesman at higher levels of government. Two considerations, however, may help us to understand why the mura has not yet assumed the mantle of primary community and may not do so for some time to come.

One consideration is that the size and structure of the mura throws the participating farmer into diverse associations that conflict with deeply ingrained habits of social relations. He is habituated to being with the same familiar persons in one situation after another, one activity after another, through most of his life. As a child he walked to school and back with the children who were his chief playmates; as he grew up, he was with the same persons in the Youth Association, the fire brigade, the *kōjū*, the buraku assembly. These persons were his wedding guests and helped him through personal or family crisis; he rejoiced with them at the shrine and later over the sake cups when the crops were abundant or worried with them through flood and drought. Though he might find personally congenial associates outside of his buraku, he would have little chance to develop ties, both for lack of time to follow his personal inclinations and for lack of any common organization. Except in the rare case when kinship is pitted against neighbor relationships, his loyalty to one group does not have to be balanced against loyalty to another group, for the persons in the two groups are identical. Thus buraku-centered attachments become the habit of mind, rather than the centrifugal attachments that characterize groups whose members hold diversified and separate ties apart from the one that brings them together for a particular, limited activity.

This habit makes rapport difficult at the mura level, where the farmer sitting in committee or assembly or joining any special-purpose group must accept the fact that each of his associates of the moment has unshared interests and attachments to diverse *kōjū*, common-age groups, and the like. He is ill prepared to deal with persons whose loyalties are in the main unknown to him or at least unshared by him. He has the habit of unanimous consensus on decisions that require action and lacks the techniques of acting with majority approval and open minority dissent, although these techniques are in the rule book, as they must be when diverse interests and associations lie behind decision-making. So he approaches participation in mura affairs as a mariner approaches uncharted waters.

The second consideration is the newness of the mura organization. Until the end of the war, the mura was primarily an agency for expressing the will of outside government to the local inhabitants. Its interests were those of the prefectural and national government, which were indifferent to local needs and wants if not actively antithetical or hostile to them. Compromises reached at the mura level between local and outside interests tended increasingly to favor the outside government as mobilization of national effort to national ends grew in the period of military expansion and all-out war. The end of the war and reorganization of the mura have not fully changed the situation, for the mura still must do much of the work of prefectural and national government and enforce their laws. The mura, at best, has a dual character. It is not simply one of a series of graduated spheres of control beginning at the buraku and reaching up to the national capital. It is a meeting point of two opposed systems of control which adjust to each other in uneasy compromise. The memory of dominance by the outside system remains, and the fear that the mura may soon again become the tool of a resurgent national government, despite all legal checks, is a very real deterrent to wholehearted participation in mura affairs.

11. The Life Cycle

Traditionally, Japanese folk culture has had strongly marked age grades. At one time, for example, boys shed their childhood name for a permanent one, changed their hair style, and were ceremoniously given an adult cap at specific ages, especially in the elite ranks. Though this custom is long outmoded, other ceremonious signs of the transition from one stage of life to the next are well known, though regionally varied. In Niiike some of these are no longer observed, and others are treated very lightly. Perhaps the dominant reason for such neglect is to be found in changing social conditions. The very nature of age grades is undergoing a gradual and subtle transformation that drains the significance from some of these ceremonies, leaving them empty symbols. Other ceremonies, however, such as weddings and funerals, are brighter, more splendid, and more expensive than ever before in living memory. This change, too, is traceable to social conditions.

It should be clear that age grades themselves, and the points at which a person moves from one to the next, though often in rough correspondence to the processes of biological maturation, are determined not by physiology but by external social conditions. Contrasts between Japanese age divisions and those, say, in the United States are better accounted for through distinct social and cultural circumstances in each nation than through the slight physical differences between the two populations. Recent physiological studies are reported to show that in characteristics such as bone ossification, muscle control, and sexual development, Japanese children mature somewhat more slowly than American children. This fact, though interesting in itself, has little or nothing to do with age grades, which are cultural phenomena providing for the assignment of individuals to various social groups according to their assumed level of maturity. The traditional divisions once developed in harmony with particular sociocultural conditions and now tend to change with these conditions. Formal schooling, for example, clearly establishes an age grade with subdivisions for the primary and secondary levels. Unknown in older times, this is superimposed upon the more traditional age-grade divisions, affecting them but not immediately erasing them. Young people now marry when they are six to eight years older than their grandparents were at marriage, in part because of schooling. Though this change is clear and definite, some current features of Niiike life may not create permanent alterations of age-grade patterns but instead may be evanescent reflections of postwar turmoil. What seems to be an emergent "teen-age" division, for example, is not at all clearly developed yet in Niiike and may tend to fade away as conditions become more settled. Thus, although our consideration of contemporary Niiike must give attention to such possibly emergent patterns, these must be understood to be superimposed upon an older pattern of age grades. These are traditionally defined in terms of

TABLE 17

TRADITIONAL AGE GRADES AND THEIR ASSOCIATED CEREMONIES

Age Grade	Terminating Ceremony	Age of Transition
Newborn..................	Shrine presentation, *miya mairi*	31 days (boy) 33 days (girl)
Infant, *akambo*...........	Belt shedding, *himo otoshi*	3 years
Child, *kodomo*............	Presentation of clothes, *hankō* (boy)	16–17 years
	Tooth blackening,* *kanetsuke* (girl)	14–16 years
Young adult:		
seinen.................	Marriage,† *kekkon*	23–25 years
wakashū.................	Inheritance,† *sozoku*	variable
Adult, *otona*..............	Retirement,* *inkyo*	60 years
Oldster, *toshiyori*..........	Funeral, *sōshiki*	death
Ancestor, *hotoke, senzo*......	Memorial services, *tsuizen kuyō*	to fiftieth anniversary of death

* Ceremonies in disuse or rarely performed.
† Ceremonies without a fixed sequence.

the distinctive roles of their members, male and female, and the ceremonies of transition that terminate each grade (see Table 17).

As noted in the table, neither the so-called tooth-blackening ceremony for girls nor the retirement ceremony has been practiced regularly in the remembered past. Retirement is a clear-cut, ceremonious event especially in villages of Frontier Japan, but grandfathers in Niiike, as throughout Core Japan, withdraw gradually and unceremoniously from houseadship; their successors only gradually come into full control. In consequence, the borderline between young-adult and adult status is left fuzzy. Thus, marriage itself rather than having a son or succeeding to headship of the household seems to confer the badge of maturity. As these comments indicate, our data are uncertain about some age-grade borderlines. If our interpretations are correct, this reflects a growing uncertainty—or lack of concern—about traditional age distinctions on the part of Niiike people themselves. Nonetheless, as compared with an outside society rather than with its own more rigid past, the age-grade pattern in Niiike is quite sharp and readily serves as a framework for considering the life cycle.

BIRTH AND INFANCY

Great paper kite-banners in the shape of carp and brightly colored, flying from a pole in the yard during the Boy's Festival, proclaim to passersby the pride of a house where a boy has been born within the last half-dozen years. Every household wants a boy or two to guarantee continuity in the next generation, even though some mothers may prefer to bear a girl early enough to use her help in caring for later children. Having a boy as the first child is considered most fortunate. But, as proof of the mother's fertility, even a girl baby is welcome. The birth of twins causes no fear or alarm, except on the part of the occasional person who remembers the ancient concern that providing food and care simultaneously for two infants might be a real hazard to the survival of both. Though the birth of a defective child, in the words of one granny, "would not happen unless there was something evil" in the household, the idea of not keeping such a child alive is shocking to most persons.

For almost thirty years, Niiike mothers have gone to the government-certified midwife of the village for prenatal instruction. Government bulletins on pregnancy are also available. Instead of reckoning ahead to fix the probable date of delivery, pregnant women have a system of counting back three months less seven days from the end of their last menstruation. After an initial visit to the midwife in the fifth month of pregnancy, they walk over for a checkup several times at increasingly frequent intervals in the last months, provided that these trips do not impede the farmwork. For the most part, they smile at old prenatal precautions such as a taboo on eating shrimp "lest the baby be born with a crooked back"; but a mother-in-law, if she gets very nervous about the welfare of her son's unborn child, does sometimes draw on folk hygiene without reference to the midwife's instructions or even contrary to them. Her will in such matters is apt to prevail, whether the prospective mother feels the same way or not. The expectant father often makes a trip to the nearest shrine of Kannon (Kuan Yin, a bodhisattva) to pray for a safe birth and a healthy baby. The midwife's instructions have no reference to magic or supernatural powers and are very similar to prenatal recommendations usual in the United States—foods rich in vitamins and calcium, sleep, and rest. Rarely is fish eaten in sufficient quantities to offset a calcium deficiency, however, and mothers usually have trouble with their teeth.

The mother-to-be cannot be spared from usual tasks. Hiramatsu

Chiyoko, age 37 when her third child was born, for example, stayed at work in the paddy right up until her final pains began. The mother-in-law and, at least for the first birth, perhaps the woman's own mother are on hand to help the midwife. The older women, fussing about the patient as she lies reclining and ready for delivery, remember their own much different experience in childbearing. In the old days the mother-to-be knelt in a back room of the house (some parts of Japan used a separate shed for parturition), grasping a low table set before her and mindful that she must restrain any outcry that would call attention to her pain or to the polluting process of labor. Even today there persists the custom of burying the afterbirth at a well-trodden spot in or near the house. For boys, the spot is just inside the threshold; for girls, it is in the yard just beyond. The umbilicus, after it withers and falls off, is wrapped neatly in a paper inscribed with the baby's name and becomes a memento carefully laid away in a safe spot until death, when it is put into the coffin. Childbirth, because of its association with blood, traditionally carries a ritual pollution that makes the mother's glance poisonous to the world. She should not go into the yard for seven days nor outside the compound for thirty-one days following the birth of a boy infant, thirty-three in the case of a girl. Today, actually, the new mother usually returns to housework after three or four days and may be back in the fields not very long afterward. However, on the thirty-first or thirty-third day, having passed the period where her presence would defile the shrine, she dresses the baby in a fine red costume given by her own parents and takes it there for the simultaneous purpose of asserting her own purification and of introducing the baby as a community member. This is called *miya mairi*, "the shrine visit." After making a small offering of money and burning a few sticks of incense (elsewhere more appropriate to temples than to shrines), mother, baby, and grandmother go home and eat a holiday dish of rice with red beans to complete the ceremony. This is the first of the age-grade ceremonies. Alternatively, the naming ceremony may be considered the introductory age-grade ceremony.

Every household in the buraku offers its congratulations within a day of the birth and, on the seventh day, when the mother is first supposed to leave her bed, the child receives his name at a simple ceremony for family members only. Anyone may suggest a name, but the final choice is the prerogative of the household. As a symbol of continuity, one character of the grandfather's name often appears in a boy's name (e.g., Eiki-chi, the grandfather, passes the "Ei" character on to Eisaku, his grandchild) perhaps with a different reading to avoid too close duplication. Adopting the maternal grandmother's name for a girl is a custom that is known but little practiced. In any case, the written characters of a boy's name should signify some happy or admirable quality. For girls, seasonal names, flower names, or other attributive names, followed by the terminals -*ko*, -*no*, or -*e* (e.g., Haruko, "spring-girl"; Matsuno, "pine-girl"; Shizue, "calm girl") are very common. The giving of boys' names in one of the standard forms indicating birth order (e.g., -*tarō*, "eldest"; -*jirō*, "second"; -*saburō*, "third"; -*shirō*, "fourth") is less common in Niiike than elsewhere. Invitations to naming ceremonies go to relatives in the shape of small gift boxes holding the festive boiled rice-and-red-bean dish, on top of which is a card with the child's name. A similar card is pinned to a stake in the yard to inform other visitors. Few persons outside the immediate household attend naming ceremonies, especially for second or subsequent children. They are quite simple. The baby—perhaps Eisaku, if a boy, or Haruko, if a girl—lies swathed in fine clothes given by the wife's parents. At its head, the father sets a tray bearing various dishes of food and, on a separate dish, a small stream pebble symbolizing endurance. The group eats a simple meal, and the ceremony is ended.

Eisaku, if a first-born son, starts life under two favorable conditions: his birth has settled the permanence of his mother's marriage, which might have been dissolved at any time up to her pregnancy, and has insured the perpetuation of the household. These are two very concrete reasons for the close care and warm affection that now envelop him, interrupted only by the call of outside work upon his mother. He spends much time in the arms of mother and grandmother and even more lashed close to the back of one or the other by a long strip of cloth. Though the outside observer may wait with bated breath for the bobbing head of a sleeping infant to snap its slender neck at the next jerky movement of his busy mother, the sensation of being carried on the back, recalled by persons when they muse on their infancy, is not one of discomfort but of warmth and pleasurable accommodation to the rhythm of bodily movement. Grandfather occasionally straps Eisaku to his back for a walk. Of all the household members, father has least actual physical contact with his child, except at night, when he shares his quilts not only with his wife but with the nursing infant who sleeps with them.

Eisaku receives attention whenever he cries, even though the women's magazines kept around the house may recommend scheduled feeding, bathing, and attention (a mode inspired from America but a decade or more delayed). When crying begins, someone picks the baby up, and soon the breast is offered.

Infant mortality seems to have declined greatly within a short generation. The death of children is not easily traced. Children above the age of two are listed in the village office records and, if they die, they receive more or less full funerals. Things are simpler, however, when an infant dies. The body is not cremated but buried in a rough box under a field stone or a roughly dressed stone marker. The bereaved household attending the simple rite offers bits of rice and water and may strew a few pathetic wild flowers over the stone, but no one tends the grave in later years, and all record of the fleeting existence of the baby is apt to vanish.

Some reduction of child mortality through disease has come about through immunizations carried on in the schools. All the school children are vaccinated against smallpox and tuberculosis and are given diphtheria shots. But their mothers' increasing awareness of health and sanitation requirements has helped to reduce serious illness as well. Summer is regarded as the most dangerous season, as well it might be with unrefrigerated fish brought by bicycle from the coast and other circumstances conducive to food spoilage. There is little possibility of avoiding intestinal parasites, but sulfaguanidine, santonin (a vermifuge), and other drugs are widely used to cure diarrhea and worms in children as well as adults.

Accidental injury or death becomes a concern as soon as the child begins to crawl. Young Eisaku or Haruko spend much of their waking and sleeping hours lashed on someone's back as a precaution against their falling from the edge of the raised floor to the ground in a moment of inattention. At the same time, if the child is being carried, he is unable to damage the paper panels or other parts of the fragile house. Another spot considered dangerous within the house is the toilet, which, opening at floor level, offers no barrier to the inquisitive crawler who might fall through. Toddlers and preschool children are less constantly under the parents' or grandparents' eye but are likely to be in view of some older person of the community. Broken arms from falls from bicycles or into ditches and bites from the poisonous snakes that occasionally turn up in the fields have occurred frequently enough to keep people generally alert when youngsters are around, and children are stringently (but fruitlessly) warned against wandering to the river. But the danger of serious accident is small by comparison with the risk of death through illness.

Niiike's conceptions of childhood illness overlap interestingly at one point with the category of discipline and child-training. Starting with the assumption that children are naturally good and obedient, many parents fear their child is ill when, as often happens about age two or three, he has a protracted spell of temper, disobedience, and fretting. This distemper is blamed on a kind of worm infestation. When santonin or other patent drugs fail, the parents often resort to a traditional cure, taking the child by bus or train to a practitioner of moxibustion and acupuncture (hari-kyū). Both practices, derived from Chinese medicine, try to cure muscular and internal ailments by applying treatment to one or more of some five hundred prescribed points on the body: e.g., the angle of the thumb with the hand to alleviate eye-ache or various spots on chest and back for chest pains. For acupuncture the operator carefully inserts a fine wire needle of silver into the body or limb, guiding its direction by feeding its one- to four-inch length through a slender tube; he jiggles the wire a bit, then withdraws it. The practitioner's second technique, moxibustion, is the burning of a small pinch of dried artemesia flowers (Eng. moxa, Jap. mogusa) laid on the patient's bare skin at a spot chosen according to diagnosis of the ailment. The glowing material, ignited by a length of punk, burns for half a minute or more, raising a blister and creating a scar, especially if the treatment is repeated. Moxibustion is the technique used to relieve a fretful child of his "worm."

This painful therapy can be practiced at home by whoever feels competent to treat himself or others. Equally well, it can serve not so much for cure as for punishment of naughtiness. Some parents burn moxa on their young children as a standard, though severe, punitive measure. One mother tells how her husband used moxa on their little girl after she played in clay against orders, applying the moss while the mother held the child fast. Other parents use moxibustion only as an ultimate and extreme disciplinary measure. Once is usually enough for their children. Some observers of the Japanese scene have seized on this "cruel and unusual" punishment as a standard by which to measure the severity of Japanese parental discipline. But we must remember that a child in Niiike is aware of the therapeutic intent of this treatment and of the solicitude and sympathy of parent for child which often invests the whole process with an utterly different psychological aura. He has at least some chance of perceiving moxa treatment as an act of love, however painful it may be.

Until well into the toddling stage, a child "does not understand" attempts to train him, so Niiike people do not hold it against a youngster if he fails to follow instructions nor do they blame him for disobeying. Actually, of course, many principles and habits are instilled in the baby before the age of "understanding," and the real consequence of the Niiike point of view, which contrasts with the common American view of child-training as a continuing process from early infancy, is a minimum of early punishment or negative discipline. Before his mother gets around to conscious discipline, the child may have behind him one or two more age-grade ceremonies. The first of these ceremonies is the birthday anniversary at the end of the first full year of life; the second is the belt-shedding ceremony on the fifteenth day of "November" (actually, the eleventh lunar month, arriving about January) of the child's third year.

In Niiike, actual birthdays pass unnoticed except for the first one. One cannot avoid relating the neglect of this very personal and individual occasion to the social scheme as a whole, for the whole essence of Niiike ceremonial life is to reflect the group—household, community, age grade, etc.—rather than the individual persons who are submerged in the group. Hence, it is fair to illustrate the growing sense of personal individuality by noting that Niiike people are now well aware of the Euro-American custom of birthday celebration, and some toy with the idea of adopting it as many of their city neighbors do. None, to our knowledge, has actually begun to celebrate birthdays, however.

Recent official requirements now force people to count their total elapsed years of age. Previously, however, Niiike people followed only the traditional Japanese age-count that pays no attention to birth dates. This regards the child as being one year of age from birth. Moreover, the lunar New Year begins a new year of life for everyone. Generally speaking, the Japanese age-count (*kazoedoshi*) fixes a person's age one year higher than the official or Euro-American count of total elapsed years (*mannen*), but the gap may be greater, for a January child reckoned as being barely a month old in February by *mannen* reckoning is already two years old by *kazoedoshi*, having been one at birth and having turned two at the lunar New Year. Perhaps birthday celebrations will wait until the habit grows of reckoning each person's age from the date of his birth, if such an individualistic custom ever can take root. The first birthday celebration is quite simple, in any event. At best it is a household occasion on which "red rice" (rice boiled with red beans) is served at mealtime to denote festivity. A few relatives or close neighbors may drop in to renew their congratulations, directing them as much to the parents and grandparents as to the baby.

The belt-shedding (*himo otoshi*) ceremony comes on the same day for every household with a three-year-old by traditional age-count. *Himo otoshi* is the local folk name for a nationally popular November 15 ceremony known as *shichi-go-san* ("seven-five-three") when mothers take their children aged seven, five, or three, to visit the shrine in their most colorful costume. Though *himo otoshi* is celebrated within the home as well as by a visit to the shrine, it takes everyone aged three simultaneously to a new age grade and is more elaborate than the individual birthday anniversary. Outgrown baby clothes are replaced by an outer robe and inner robe (kimono and *naga juban*) cut in the shape of adult clothing and large enough, when tremendous tucks at waist and shoulders are let out, to fit a child of fifteen. The mother's parents send a fine set of such clothes, including especially, for girls, the first broad sash and, for boys, a soft, narrow sash to replace the short cloth ties or cloth belt of infancy. The ceremony gets its name from the shedding of this infant belt. Other relatives, neighbors, or friends also may give clothing, which in recent years has been Western-style shirt and short pants for boys or blouse and skirt for girls, their standard costume from now until they change to junior high school uniforms. Red rice, the only ceremonial dish, is served to family and any visitors. Sometimes during the day the women of the household, with or without the men, parade the child in his brave new Japanese costume to the community shrine for purificatory worship. The child carries a gift box containing some of the red rice as an offering and may also have a bit of money to put in the shrine's offering box. The shrine visit concludes the ceremony.

Training of children beyond the toddler stage is a conscious goal of Niiike parents and grandparents. They have certain well-defined goals to which they direct their efforts. The points of emphasis and timing often differ from those commonly seen, for example, in America, but even more in contrast are some of the techniques. Loud-voiced commands, repetitious and detailed instruction, scolding or tongue-lashing, and physical beating are relatively rare and disapproved in Niiike homes. Those who finished school before the end of the war or had military service are no strangers to violent discipline, for cuffing and slapping of students and army trainees were an accepted part of the routine. Moreover, no one denies or seems repelled by the tradition, scarcely past, that permitted a superior to manhandle his inferior or gave free scope to roughness on the part of officials such as the police. Physical and verbal violence in these situations seems to fit a pattern of official or outside authority. But it is not an important part of parental authority. For one thing, these methods embarrassingly draw attention of outsiders to friction in the home; for another, nagging is disapproved lest it "sour" the child. A mother angered at her child may pinch him painfully. A father pushed past endurance will cuff the child on the head, but only rarely. Physical contact is used more often as a positive method of instruction than as punishment. As the very young child sprawls on the floor, grandmother uses her hands to shape the infant's limbs into the proper kneeling posture or bobs the child's head from behind to produce a polite bow. Into his teens this child, if slow to bow, will get his cue from the guiding hand of an adult. Parents demonstrate how to do things by setting an example and by guiding the child through the proper motions more than by giving verbal instructions. Explanations are given to older children, to be sure, and various cue words and commands for younger children are made familiar by repetition: "dirty," "quietly, now," "be gentle," "quickly," "stop it." But these usually come out in a quiet tone of voice. Much more important, it seems, is teaching by showing, by handling and manipulating the child in patterns that in a sense continue the infant's kinesthetic familiarization with the postures and motions of work and rest absorbed through his body as it lies strapped to the back of his mother and grandmother.

Cutting the child off from physical and social contact is an effective and customary sort of coercive discipline. This is the reversal of the process of socialization and indoctrination by touch described above. A misbehaving and fretful child finds himself ignored and psychologically isolated from those around him. Deprived of attention in this fashion, he may continue to misbehave for a time, but, time and again, instead of seizing upon the moment to follow his own inclinations, the child goes to his mother or grandmother for comfort. The lesson taught, his mother does not rebuff him long. Seeking reconciliation, a child of four or more may whine until his mother gives him a few moments nursing at her breast as a sign of being accepted again after his misdeeds. Sweet foods and candy, though not constantly on hand, also serve to make peace between mother and child.

From the point of view of disciplinary constraint, this training is permissive. Many aspects of the child's daily life have little if any compulsion. Boys and girls learn pretty much at their own speed to take care of their toilet needs (mothers encourage their children to take initiative in this by about two, perhaps, but leave them diapered for up to a year longer), to dress themselves, to handle their own chopsticks, to spread and fold away their own bedding, and to develop other independent abilities. Weaning ordinarily is gradual and unforced. As children shift to solid food they show passing likes and dislikes, but the child who develops strong food prejudices simply goes hungry; so he finds it difficult to adopt this sort of fussiness as a way of monopolizing his parents' attention. Regular chores are rarely required of children until they reach their teens, apart from baby-tending, which may be assigned to a girl. No one sets a small-change allowance for his children; mother hands out sweets or gives enough money to buy some candy when pestered at the right moment or long enough. When a child gets sleepy during the day or at night, he simply falls asleep on the soft mat floor at the edge of the room if his bed is not prepared. He is not expected to keep regular bedtime hours, nor is he excluded from special occasions at night on account of the hour.

The child must learn early and well, however, to obey and conform to certain inflexible rules. Obedience is easier, perhaps, in that these are rules for a way of life followed by everyone he knows, not rules made especially for children. Many express the pattern of hierarchy. Speech is one example. No one cares greatly whether his children, in their early years, speak in standard Japanese or in the local dialect forms, but they should be able as soon as possible to control the precise shades of politeness conveyed by particular choices of words and word endings. So parents and grandparents tend to use polite forms in addressing their children, to familiarize them with these forms, and are distressed when the boys, especially, drift into speaking roughly and abruptly to adults as well as to their age-mates. As a simple example, mothers of other houses are *okāsan* to the child, so his parents refer to his own mother similarly or, eliding the honorific *o-*, say *kāsan*. In speaking of his own mother to others, however, the child should use the humble form *haha;* occasionally the children confuse these forms or, worse, forget themselves in the house and let slip the uncomplimentary *ofukuro* ("bag"). The complaint is that this happens more often since the "freedom" of postwar years began. Boys in Niiike do not develop the deferential habit of doffing their caps when addressed by elders or strangers, as do children in many other communities. But they do learn their place in the status system. They do not thrust themselves obtrusively into a conversation among adults. They feel free, however, to torment girls and younger children; and, when forming gangs or acquiring cronies as they reach school age, they know better than to include certain children from nearby Horen who happen to be of outcast status.

These generalities, of course, ignore the plain fact that no two children are treated quite alike. The consistent tendencies described here need qualification in specific cases—for example, in the distinction between treatment of eldest sons and younger sons. Niiike at this period has too few youthful pairs of brothers to permit detailed examples of treatment less systematically observed elsewhere but permits inferences to be drawn from the differences among adult siblings. The eldest son, unless he is a fool or wastrel, has the best chance for an assured but preplanned life. As heir apparent, he is gratified and protected with fewer denials than his younger brothers face. When mature, he is perhaps more accustomed to being served and obeyed; but he may also be more pompous, duller, and stodgier than his younger siblings, who win their place through personality and initiative rather than through inherited position.

A little girl faces more numerous and restrictive compulsions than does her brother. She should be more careful to use polite speech and should answer politely when spoken to. She must sleep in the approved posture, lying on her back without spread-eagling. She is called on at least occasionally to help with housework or baby care. She learns that girls are not merely different from boys but inferior to them. In going to school, by herself or with other girls, she never walks directly ahead of any boys. At meals she gets her food only after the boys have been served and, in using the bath, must wait until the boys have finished. In general, she must fend for herself when her mother is preoccupied with her brother's troubles. Boys are protected and deferred to. They can openly vent their aggressive impulses against a sister or even their mother under circumstances where a girl would be reproved. While the little boy's mother helps him tenderly across an open ditch, she is likely to leave the little girl to find her own way across. Through many such experiences the little girl learns to solve her problems by herself or not at all, to swallow reproof without outward resentment, to gain her ends often by indirect means without losing her demeanor of shyness and self-denial. She can tease and torment a boy, even under the unseeing eyes of a parent, but must expect reproof if he complains. In resentment, then, perhaps she will hide his cap or free his captive cricket but with no prospect of openly gloating over her revenge.

We may doubt that the little girl, either now or later on, resents her discriminatory treatment as being unfair. As she is bound to see it, the way others behave toward her and expect her to behave is simply part of being female, as is the way she wears her hair or dresses or plays games, and, unless she is an unusual creature, she does not resent being female. The new talk about equality of the sexes may set an adolescent to wondering, these days, but not her small sisters. This traditional regimen for girls carries certain advantages, of which no one seems actively conscious. Whereas the pampering and protecting of boys may well encourage in them a basic and lifelong dependence under the cover of self-will and even arrogance, the little girl grown to adulthood is more likely to find in herself a reservoir of inner strength and stamina and a habit of self-reliance under the cover of deference, which she will surely need in her woman's role, just because from a very early age her upbringing developed these inner resources.

FORMAL EDUCATION

Eisaku and Haruko look forward delightedly to entering school and proudly sport the leather and cloth knapsack their mother buys, which is their badge of school-age. Neither wears a uniform to kindergarten or for the first couple of elementary school years, for uniforms have been made optional as a step away from regimentation. Yet children like the school uniform, and mothers find it saves argument about getting a skirt and blouse "just like Masako's." So uniforms come on the scene about halfway through the six years of lower school and continue through the three years of middle school and three years of high school.

Of the twelve years of public schooling provided locally, in a 6-3-3 sequence, the first nine years are compulsory by law. Throughout Japan a surprisingly high number of children actually finish the ninth year, even where scarcity of funds places schools so far apart that some pupils can reach the nearest school only by walking perhaps six miles over mountain roads after a long bus ride. Niiike's children are relatively well favored. Each administrative village around Kamo can afford its own six-year elementary school, so that children walk, at most, no farther than the distance Niiike's children cover, a mile and a quarter each way. For Niiike's older children, it is a half-mile farther to the middle school (seventh to ninth grades) and high school (tenth to twelfth grades), which are near the railroad station in Takamatsu and are supported jointly by four villages or towns: Kamo, Oishi, Takamatsu, and Makane.

A mother usually goes with her five-year-old child to kindergarten on the first exciting day. Before long, however, each child jumps up from breakfast to join a friend or a group of the same age as they leave the housing area to take shortcuts across the fields to school unattended. From the earliest grades on, boys walk separately from girls.

Just across the Ashimori River, the children pass the village office which fronts on the bare school playground and troop into the long frame school building at its front entrance, where they leave their tennis shoes or geta. In their home room they sit on fixed, straight, wooden seats, facing simple desks, two to a seat, girls and boys not only together in the same room but carefully seated "coeducationally" as recommended by American advisers during the Occupation reform period. All rise and bow as the teacher enters, receiving a nod as a signal to sit down for class to begin.

An overhauling of the educational system since the end of the war has brought changes in subject matter and teaching methods as well as in the administrative organization of schools. Younger teachers, who include both men and women, for the most part favor the curriculum changes. These leave basic subjects such as arithmetic and language subject to standards set by the central Ministry of Education but give local option in the choice of textbooks and permit much local autonomy in the handling of the new social studies course. This last course combines history and geography with the study of contemporary living. Each locality is encouraged to draw on things familiar to the children in their own locale for its social studies course. Thus, Kamo children may use a textbook emphasizing the history and environment of Okayama Prefecture and the Inland Sea, and their classes frequently go out on field trips, trooping along the dusty roadside in pairs after their teacher. Much diminished are the former history hours of memorizing lists of emperors, famous battles, and national glories from the mythical founding of the empire to the present, for school policy tends now to de-emphasize the nationalism that formerly dominated all schooling. Changes from the pre-war curriculum are marked even in the hours given to exercise, drawing, and music. Coeducational square dancing and organized games replace the sex-divided marching and physical exercises that once had every school child in Japan simultaneously bending and swinging arms to in-structions broadcast each morning from Tokyo; and songs such as "The Sparrows' School" now take the place of ones such as "The Soldier" or "The Rising Sun Flag."

Most drastic of the changes, and most controversial among officials and parents, is the elimination of the prewar course in ethics (shūshin). This important pre-surrender course used history and legend moralistically to inculcate reverence for the emperor, loyalty to one's superiors, and pride in acts such as serving as a soldier. What has bothered many parents since this course was abolished is the lack of any explicit moral instruc-tion in school. In their opinion, whether the morality taught in school is nationalistic or otherwise takes second place to the duty of the schools to teach morals, especially in the troubled times postwar Japan faces. Yet a good many other parents agree with Hiramatsu Michinobu of Niiike, who as a teacher considers the social studies course to be broad and flexible, giving teachers an opportunity to emphasize a system of human values. Controversy about re-establishing an explicit morality course is by no means limited to Niiike or to the tradition-minded countryside; it remained a national issue in 1957.

The children go through a lower school curriculum that closely parallels a modern American grammar school curriculum in teaching method and subject matter for such basic skills as counting and reading, although certain aspects of arithmetic and the Japanese writing system set up dis-tinctive hurdles. The principal of the Kamo lower school, on several occa-sions since the establishment of the postwar curriculum, has made the rounds of the buraku with several of his teachers to explain teaching objectives to the assembled parents—rather, to the mothers, who attend as members of the P.T.A. His outline of arithmetic shows the following goals—first grade: counting to 100, adding and subtracting single digits; second grade: fluency in adding and subtracting two-digit numbers, counting by twos, by fives, and by fifties; third grade: counting to 1,000, using the clock and calendar, using the metric system; fourth grade: multiplication by single digits, area measurement, decimals; fifth grade: fractions, long division, volume measurement, graph and map reading; sixth grade: consolidating decimals and fractions, multiplication and division. From the third grade onward, children learn to use the abacus. Their skill with this device eventually replaces their skill at mental calculation to such an extent that, in later life, many adults cannot make change at a store or add two-digit numbers without an abacus in hand. Not only must children by the sixth grade deal with Japanese traditional measurements in addition to the metric system; they must also learn historical dates and spans of time in a double system, one using the continuous chronology of the Christian calendar, the other using the variable regnal years of each of the emperors since recorded history began. Their schooling is even more beset with difficulty in the case of language and reading, for they have to handle two sets of syllabic signs, fifty in each set, which are taught from the first grade on, in addition to two thousand or so of the more complex characters that become an everyday adult necessity for reading newspapers, magazines, bulletins, or letters. Knowledge of about seven hundred characters is expected of sixth-grade pupils. The Latin alphabet is taught as an added subject, and a few English phrases are taught from the third grade on. The spoken language presents separate teaching problems, the first of which is familiarization with standard Japanese in the place of dialect forms which the children bring from home and into which they lapse on the playground outside the schoolroom. A second problem is training in comprehension of formal announcements and speeches, where custom prescribes the lavish use of compound words rarely heard in conversation. The children take tests for comprehension of standard conversational Japanese as distinct from dialect and take separate tests for comprehension of the more stilted Japanese of radio and official communications.

Though the children undergo periodic tests, they almost invariably are promoted each year and so stay with the same group of schoolmates, with whom they form friendships that endure through life. Teachers in lower and middle school almost never inflict on a child the shame of failure, which would be reflected on the child's family and buraku, so the slow children pass through school at the same rate as the bright ones. This concern for the social aspects of education, a tradition that coincides with American educators' views promulgated in the postwar revised school system, tends to go considerably farther than its American counterpart. Every participating child, for example, gets some sort of prize at the annual athletic meets, art contests, rhetorical contests, or other competitive occasions. Five or six highest prizes are usually given, but no one, however poor, goes unrewarded, unless specifically for punishment.

Together with this curb on incentive to excel, the opportunities for independent and constructive thinking are limited by the sheer burden of rote learning imposed, for example, by three systems of arithmetic notation (Japanese, Arabic, and Latin), and four systems of script (*katakana* and *hiragana* syllabaries, the Latin alphabet, and Sino-Japanese characters). Teachers show undeniable zeal to produce more capable pupils under the new system than was possible under the pre-surrender system of centrally dictated, regimented and nationalistic education. But, unless backed with more skill and training than most teachers get, they are heavily handicapped under these conditions in lower schools. In the middle school, past the stage of rote memorization, there is more time for students to write compositions, edit a mimeographed school paper, organize student committees on school affairs, and even undertake investigative projects, though many simply carry over the complacent habits of learning by rote. But shortage of equipment, especially for science courses, and impoverished school libraries handicap the middle and high school levels. Homemade maps and apparatus are used, but much learning is confined to books when it would be more effective in the laboratory. Each school now has a sixteen-millimeter projector for films circulated by the Ministry of Education or for films circulated by other ministries for adult education assemblies. But the high school has too few sinks and Bunsen burners and chemistry supplies to go around, even for the boys, who make up about 60 per cent of the total enrolment of five hundred.

Though the limited facilities and the tradition of promoting dullards at the standard rate might serve to encourage a casual attitude toward school, the reverse is more often true. Children take their schoolwork very seriously. They are assigned heavy loads of homework from about the fourth grade on and stay with it until late at night without protest from their parents, who avoid giving them chores that will interfere with study. They study intensely for the graduation examination. This zeal does not have to be generated within the school system itself. It comes ready made. In consonance with the tradition of respect for learning, both parents and children in Niiike look on schooling as a primary avenue for bettering one's self and one's family, and their urge to achieve betterment is strong. Though little public attention is given to poor performance, autobiographical accounts show how deeply chagrined the children are who find book learning difficult.

Niiike children have managed to get a surprising amount of schooling, averaging considerably more than the required minimum for the past several generations. As Figure 41 shows, even the oldest men are likely to have had eight years of schooling, though this amount became compulsory only after their day. More recently, girls as well as boys have usually reached the twelfth grade. But women, thirty-five years and more ago, may have had no more than fourth-grade education. Education for women, at one time, was either a dispensable luxury or considered positively undesirable. More recently, however, girls have been supported in

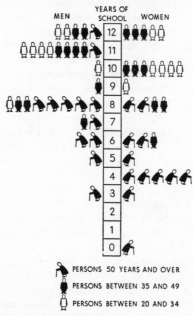

FIG. 41.—Schooling of Niiike men and women, showing each sex separated into three age groups. Younger persons have had slightly more years of schooling all together than older persons, the increase being most notable in the case of women.

school well beyond the minimum period, though, on the average they still have somewhat less schooling than the boys. Some persons in the older group had no public school to attend but went either to the traditional classes conducted by priests in the temple or to a subscription school established in the village shortly after the fall of the feudal shogunate in 1868. The younger generation, with public schooling that charges tuition only in high school and at higher levels, are finishing high school and even going on to the farm school which is conveniently located near the high school in Takamatsu. Four men between the ages of twenty and forty-five are graduates of the farm school's two-year course. Two boys from Niiike, between 1953 and 1956, entered the University of Okayama, one of the low-cost prefectural universities established by the central government in 1948, on the pattern of United States state universities. These college students ride the train to town along with other commuters to Okayama City, spending about an hour each way, thus acquiring their college education without losing touch with their home community.

The route from public elementary school through high school since the war is "single track," identical for all children of either sex, regardless of status or objective. They proceed from lower school (six years) to middle school (three years) to high school (three years). Theoretical restrictions on high-school entrance rarely hold a pupil back, because middle-school graduates almost invariably meet the standard. Beyond high school there are trade schools, of which Niiike boys choose the farm school in Takamatsu or the business school in Okayama City; or there is the prefectural university for professional education including teacher-training. Entrance examinations of considerable rigor set enrolment limits at the universities, less so in the prefectural universities such as Okayama than in the major universities such as Tokyo and Kyoto, which accept only 10 to 20 per cent of those examined. This system is much more simple and uniform than the "multiple-track" system of education of prewar Japan (see Fig. 42). Almost from the first grade, under the old system, the nature of the school which a child entered would narrowly determine the character and limit of his education. Schools were specialized to produce different qualities of citizens; a person's chance for professional training or for holding office was determined by his type of schooling as well as by the social and economic position of his family. The former school system, modeled on European originals, frankly reinforced class and occupational distinctions. The present system attempts to cancel them out, in so far as a uniform educational program can do so.

Much controversy surrounds portions of the new education system: its 6-3-3 sequence of schools, the "single-track" uniformity of education, coeducation through high school, the course of social studies. As to how Niiike people regard it after eight years of experience, though each person has his own ideas, the consensus seems similar to that set forth by a feature article from the local newspaper, the *Sanyō Shimbun*, for January 8, 1954, portions of which are summarized here. Mention of "problems of virtues taught in social studies classes" in this article is a veiled reference to the controversy over reinstating a course of ethical instruction like the banned *shūshin* course mentioned earlier.

Coeducation shocked many adults, who were raised on the maxim: "Separate children by sex after seven." Parents of seventh to twelfth graders worried about sex and adolescence problems, but no great harm came of it, and children placed with the opposite sex got a competitive spirit and improved marvelously. Girls' achievement rose astonishingly under the stimulus of classes with boys, and classes as a whole did better. Some parents and brothers, however, comment that girls are becoming "unfeminine" in language and manner.

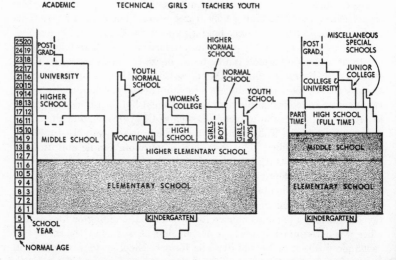

MULTIPLE TRACK SYSTEM
(THROUGH WORLD WAR II)

SINGLE TRACK SYSTEM
(AFTER WORLD WAR II)

Fig. 42.—*At left*, the school system of Japan through World War II, showing five separate tracks of specialization beyond the elementary level. *At right*, the school system of Japan since World War II, showing development of a uniform single-track system permitting individuals to transfer to new specialties even after secondary schooling.

The 6-3-3 system, as against the older system aimed at selective education, is considered successful. The compulsory middle school system has produced students no whit inferior to scholars of the old-time middle school. But in eight years many opinions have formed about social studies. Viewed as a course foisted on Japan by Americans, it has many points of conflict with other parts of school. A national Curriculum Review Committee has felt that local history as well as problems of virtues taught in social studies classes need modifying but not abolishing; an Education Ministry report makes similar recommendations. But the teachers themselves are against these reports. And parents admittedly do not understand the content of the social studies course, nor such things as its avoidance of religion. The course stands at the crossroads. Girls, for example, in high schools with electives, are reluctant to choose social studies but commit themselves to domestic science. If enrolments continue to be low at this level, the government may elect to standardize the content of this course [to insure its acceptance].

Niiike children go further with their schooling than children in many other parts of rural Japan primarily because of the higher standard of living in their locality. This makes schools more numerous and accessible and allows young people more years for learning before they must contribute to the household income. The practical advantages of schooling, moreover, can well be realized in this urbanized area where cash crops and city jobs play a part in household economy. It is not surprising that the majority of these children show a strong positive interest in school. But this same sort of enthusiasm is reflected all over Japan, including isolated rural areas where attendance is difficult and advantages more nebulous. One reason seems to be that the school environment offers an entirely novel and exhilarating social situation. In school, for the first time in his life, the child associates with others who are neither kindred nor close neighbors. Among them he makes his way as an individual; his personal qualities count for as much as his household connections, or more. Attachments grow both among age-mates and between pupil and teacher. The boy is apt to find his way into a gang that expresses its intimate solidarity innocuously by inventing scurrilous nicknames for disliked teachers or, less harmlessly, by hazing younger, unattached boys. Such playground gangs were much more prominent and powerful features of school during the militaristic decades. Their structure today seems considerably less centered on the strong, self-willed leader. The girl, less gang-minded, nonetheless finds close friends with whom she exchanges dozens of secret letters. Though some of these age-mate relationships continue throughout school and carry on into adult life, they are no stronger than the children's relations with certain teachers. The child is often wondrously sensitive to the casual opinions of a teacher, partly because this is one adult who treats him as an individual in his own right and partly because the teacher is the one person in official, respected status with whom personal, affectionate relations are possible.

Affection is mixed with respect of a sort that prevents the child, if he considers himself unfairly graded, from going directly to the teacher to protest against a low mark. This respect is shared by the parents as well, for they have almost unquestioning faith in the superior wisdom of teachers and rarely defend their own opinions, if they have them, against the teacher's viewpoint brought from school by their child. As long as their primary goals and values harmonize, the weakened position of parents in this triangular relation of parent-child-teacher goes unnoticed, but it helps to account for otherwise puzzling phenomena. Until the end of the war, teachers had an extraordinarily potent role in promoting nationalistic sentiment, as dictated by the central government. Postwar years have seen certain celebrated incidents in scattered parts of Japan in which left-wing, politically active teachers have successfully moved their pupils in a nearly unanimous body to strike in defiance of their parents and the school board. Partly because the prewar and postwar incidents have completely opposite political coloration, parents see little connection between them. Prewar nationalistic indoctrination, though unfortunate, at least was in the line of duty, whereas postwar left-wing teachers are considered to be misusing their office and so should be prohibited from expressing any political opinion in school or out. In neither case is the weakness of parental opinion as opposed to teacher opinion brought into question. Parents in large part habitually disavow responsibility for forming the child's viewpoint outside of the home, as is evidenced by their frequent pleas to revive the course on ethics in the schools. Behind their attitude is the view that teachers, like other public officials, are not just ordinary persons subject to human frailties and errors in spite of their training but are members of a superior class who are trusted to live up to the standards which qualify that class for leadership and authority.

YOUNG ADULTHOOD

Americans have come to regard the teen-age years as a special period of turmoil and problems, of moods switching between ecstasy and despair, of special gangs or clubs and sudden fads. Especially in America, teen-agers have their own slang, their own styles of music, clothing, books, magazines, and foods. Some of these are self-generated, some appear in response to their demand, some are foisted on them by sophisticated merchandisers who have perceived them to be a distinctive consumer group. Teen-agers are indubitably a distinct age group in America. But all these elements are echoed only dimly in Japan as a whole and are almost altogether lacking in Niiike. The eighteen or twenty adolescent boys and girls there have no proverbial collective temperament or other peculiarities. They are obviously maturing biologically, emotionally, and mentally, but the process for most of them is placid and stable and attracts very little notice. They are not brought together in any recognized age-group organization for adolescents, unless we so consider the Youth

Association (*Seinendan*) for boys; but its functions suggest a different interpretation. The marked contrast between the general rule in Niiike and the prevailing pattern in the United States arouses the suspicion that something more is involved than biological development, which seems much the same in Japanese and American youngsters. We suggest the following interpretation.

Adolescence, as has often been said, has an in-between quality. It paves the way from childhood to adulthood. Biologically and psychologically it is a period of recognizing one's self anew as male or female and discovering how to deal with other persons, whose roles through adult life also will be partly sex-defined. This process is one of individuation, of discovering one's self as a distinct individual. In American society, persons who become the most highly individuated as adults find themselves well adapted to the expectations of their society. The well-adjusted American is expected to make up his own mind, by and large, about his own marriage, occupation, place and style of residence, general mode of living, and innumerable other matters. In fact, neither he nor anyone else can forecast very far ahead the decisions and choices to be thrust on him as a consequence of his life in a very mobile society. His ideal role is an autonomous, individually distinctive role. His teen-age period can be viewed as preparation for it. The teen-ager demands autonomy or finds it thrust upon him. It is up to him to choose whether to join the Boy Scouts (or Girl Scouts); he must find his own date for the movies or dance, he picks his own hobby, and decides whether or not to take a part-time job to pay for it or other expenses. Of course, his autonomy and initiative are not limitless but, on the contrary, tentative and subject to ups and downs. He will want privileges and will accept responsibilities, but in proportions somewhat different from those offered by parents and others. These disagreements bring conflicts, and so does his own uncertain control over himself in his partial autonomy.

Adulthood under traditional circumstances in Niiike sets requirements quite different from those we have supposed for Americans. Rather stringent limits on individual initiative and autonomy are perhaps most significant in this connection, for when there is no frequent call for either capacity in the adult there need be no period of training for the adolescent. Birth and circumstances give the ordinary adult in Niiike little choice over where he will live, how he will make his living, or who will be his associates. The choice of whom he marries and when is much less his own than his parents'. Other choices are similarly limited. Tradition in any case presents a relatively fixed mold of appropriate behavior for such standard roles as farmer, parent, neighbor, in which unanticipated situations are relatively infrequent. The step from childhood to adulthood is simplified by this fact.

Whether or not adolescence takes its shape from the requirements of adult life in as clear-cut fashion as we have suggested here, the traditional pattern of life for the adolescent boy and girl in Niiike carries almost no hint of "teen-age" characteristics comparable to those familiar in the United States. The years between twelve and eighteen do not form a unit, but are broken in the middle; the earlier half belongs to childhood, the latter half to adult life. Children's games and activities continue to be played up to the age of about fifteen. Within a year after this age these erstwhile children are grouped with young adults and carry on essentially adult types of activities.

Boys' games occupy youngsters from late pre-school age to about fifteen, except that the youngest of the group are ruled out of baseball, volleyball, and other organized games that require much open space, for the reason that the school playground, the only flat space that is not filled with crops throughout the playing season, is too far from home for them to join in. They may be taken in summer to nighttime wrestling (*sumō*) contests for boys, however. The hills, fields, and ditches nearer home are haunts of all boys out "doing nothing," that is, climbing rocks, catching crickets or fish and crayfish, or chasing each other in local varieties of cops-and-robbers. In these wanderings they sometimes try a test of spunk (*kimodameshi*, "liver-testing"), in which, especially on a summer night, one team tries to terrify another by grisly stories before sending them to retrieve an object from a cemetery or other lonely spots—ghosts are not too unreal at this age. In stay-at-home hours, they often play *patchi*, a game with cards gotten from packages of candy, in which the player slams a card forcefully down among his opponents' cards lying on the ground and is entitled to collect for himself any of their cards that are flipped over by the blow. Girls may be admitted as on-lookers, or even as players, to this sort of game. Most boys would not be caught dead playing the games that are popular among girls, however. The girls leave the playground to the boys after school, come directly home to call to their mother, "I've come back!" and then play in or near one of the more spacious yards. One group gathers for a favorite ball game in which the girl with the ball bounces it in time to the words of a song, then gives a slanting bounce at the end of the last line so she can catch it in the back folds of her short skirt. Another group plays hop-scotch, using glass taws. A third, with an elastic rope, lets each girl in turn try vaulting or cartwheeling over the rope, which two other girls hold first at knee height, then at hip, waist, shoulder, and head height;

sprawling, rather than touching the rope, loses the turn. Neither in connection with these games nor for any of the ceremonies or festivals that are regarded as mainly for children do Niiike's youngsters have any formal age-group organization such as is still maintained for children from about five to fifteen in a few parts of rural Japan. Their groups are small and informal and vary in membership from one day to the next. Fifteen-year-olds play along with the six-year-olds and ten-year-olds.

At the age of about fifteen (sixteen by Japanese age-count) boys get ready to join the Youth Association. Girls have no equivalent association in Niiike, though some parts of rural Japan preserve a Maiden's Group (*musume-gumi*) for girls above fifteen, the counterpart of a Youngster's Group (*wakashū-gumi*) for boys which has generally become the formal and official Youth Association. Nor, in Niiike do girls go through a coming-of-age ceremony. In more traditional localities, at a formal party for family and relatives, the girl receives a kimono for fancy occasions and, in ritualistic echo of the old-time cosmetic custom that gives the ceremony its name, "Iron-applying" (*Kanetsuke*), may even have her teeth blackened temporarily. Niiike appears to have given up this girls' ceremony long ago. But for a Niiike boy, usually before he joins the Youth Association, his household observes the *hankō* (a local name), a party for family and relatives where clothes are given to the boy. The important traditional garment on this occasion would be the final two pieces of formal adult apparel, the *kamishimo*, consisting of a waistcoat with broad, stiffened shoulders (*katai*), and full, skirt-like trousers (*hakama*). Today one rarely sees this out-of-date costume except on the stage or occasionally at a funeral or ritual occasion. So the gift clothing at today's *hankō* is more often the Western-style wool suit, with shirts and accessories. The ceremony itself is increasingly neglected, for the boy needs to go to town to be fitted for his suit, which makes the ceremonial of giving it to him rather anticlimactic. The occasion often slips past with no performance of this coming-of-age ceremony

Thus, the only symbolic act which brings the boy into traditional adult society today is his joining the Youth Association. Almost half the members, of course, have not yet reached legal adult status of twenty-one years of age. Viewed from the age of its members alone, the Association might be considered a teen-age rather than an adult group. Its members, however, occupy themselves with activities that are essentially adult, and they obviously are out to show that they are young men, not boys, in the amount of sake they drink and the sort of songs they sing at their parties.

But what we have described is only the older, more traditional part of the picture. Conditions that have existed for only the last five or six decades have imposed a different sort of age-group pattern onto the adolescent years, whereby boys and girls reach full adulthood later than did their grandparents. One of these conditions is schooling that lasts ten to twelve years for the majority of boys and girls. Along with this has come a delay in age of marriage. Grandfather married when he was perhaps seventeen and grandmother fifteen; but youngsters since their time have been in the classroom at those ages and in no position to marry until in their twenties. Formal schooling thus has imposed a new sort of age grade extending through most of the teens. Though this has not erased the older pattern, in a sense it competes against the older pattern, for it creates an interlude between childhood and adulthood that is a sort of teen-age.

Although the boy in this period may begin to be aware of girls, he has no real opportunity to show interest in them. He is increasingly separated from them in class and has to watch his step outside in order not to start gossip. There is very little free time and almost literally no room for privacy in the countryside, and tongues are ever ready to wag. "Just let a boy give a girl a lift home behind him on his bicycle, and all the grannies around here will have them married within a week," was the rueful joke of one of the boys in his early twenties. A hobby, perhaps model planes or study of engines, is a safer and more likely preoccupation than girls. Evidence of various sorts, including psychological data, suggests in any case that boys right up to marriage age feel more drive to establish themselves among males than among females. Overt homosexualism is rare, it seems; in psychogenetic terms, phallicism, consisting in competitively demonstrating one's maleness to other males, better describes their orientation. But the eldest son now begins to feel the pressure of responsibility to his household, for his parents want him to know farming well and expect him to spend more time helping his father. Perhaps, in mild resistance to this cut-and-dried future, he dreams briefly of becoming a truck driver or mechanic instead, but conscience is strong and his closest approach to rebelling against his parents is to develop a sudden interest in studies and insist on taking the entrance examination to enter farm school after graduating from high school, or to insist on temporarily taking a commuter's job outside the community. His younger brother is in not too different straits, for, although his future is less clearly settled, it offers only limited possibilities. He, too, is under some pressure to develop, in school and out, the fairly standard skills that will enable him to acquit himself well as an adult.

Whereas men, reminiscing over their own lives, frequently conclude that the years just after marriage have been the most richly satisfying period of their lives, the high point for girls is the period before marriage. This period, colorfully termed the "Green Spring Period" (*Seishunki*) in Japan, is romantically associated with girls. The girl about to finish school is relatively carefree and alive to the world about her. With her senior class, both in middle school and in high school, she takes an early summer trip to a famous scenic spot, perhaps as far away as Osaka or even Kyoto. The excitement of this week-long excursion of boys and girls is an important and joyous memory through the rest of life. Even those whom war jobs or military service sent to much more distant places in later years remember their graduation trip vividly. Before graduating, the girl, especially, is likely to discover in literature a world of imagination that sets her to improbable dreaming—girls read a great deal during these years, both in the Japanese classics and in translations. She will work hard to be praised by her teachers for her talent at calligraphy, drawing, or sewing. She is free, for a space, to see herself and the world through her new-found emotions: she romanticizes her friendships with other girls and develops an inordinate fondness for autumn, "because it is a sad season." The overtones of this last sentiment are not necessarily borrowed from the precious melancholy that invests classical Japanese literature. It may be a more personal sentiment, anticipating the marriage that will put an end to this period. The girls have few romantic notions about marriage, for what they see all about them shows that their wedding will bring them into a life of hard work and difficult adjustment, especially on the farm. Most girls in the middle school come from farm households and will have farmer husbands, but their attitude toward this future may be gathered from a questionnaire which asked, among other things, whether or not they anticipated marrying a farmer. Less than 6 per cent of two hundred girls responding answered that they would choose a farmer as a husband.

This response, perhaps, should be taken with just a grain of salt or at least be viewed in the context of the postwar years when a reassessment of values has been taking place throughout Japan, and voices have been lifted on every side to advise youth and women of their constitutional and legal guaranties of human rights. Young people are having new horizons of individual choice opened to them by law. These vistas of a bright new life are almost blinding in contrast to the rocky path of self-control and obedience along which youth was sternly guided in the prewar decades. It is hard for young persons to judge how far these legal rights, such as the right to an equal share in inheritance or the right to free choice in marriage or the right to reside where one pleases, are still hedged about with economic and social restrictions. Those who have a number of years yet before reaching the critical choice between the freedom of striking out for themselves and the security of conforming to parental guidance tend noticeably to be most vociferous in their demands for self-expression. The middle-school questionnaire results may be an instance of this premature rebellion.

The girls who thus declare their distaste for becoming farm wives, however, seem to represent more than merely a temporary postwar disequilibrium, for this restiveness is in keeping with the teen-age frame of mind outlined above (with the United States as the model) and is by no means an isolated instance of this frame of mind. The boys and girls of Niiike and the nearby countryside are, perhaps, several years behind the youth of Japanese cities in adopting the forms distinctive of teen-agers, but a few show signs of falling into this pattern. Several boys nearing their twenties and earning money at outside jobs disturb their parents more than a little by the money and time they spend on movie magazines, by their visits to the movie in the city, and by their fondness for the latest popular songs learned from the radio. No boy from Niiike has yet adopted the clothes and the long hair of the *anchan* (child talk for "elder brother") who are the urban and fishing-town equivalent of the United States' zoot-suit stratum, but a few surreptitiously have tried the permanent waves and hair perfume favored by the *anchan*. A number of the girls, after careful study of the style magazines, have discovered and taken to wearing just the styles of sweater or blouse and skirt that catch the urban teen-age fancy. Such phenomena may be superficial and external. But a few young persons are beginning to show deeper stress. Hiramatsu Shigemi, graduating with high grades at eighteen, wanted to become a typist; talked out of this, she compromised on attending a weaving school in Okayama City, rather than the more conventional sewing class near home. She not only faced the neighborhood's disapproval of her "running loose" in the city, but took a temporary job in Hiroshima after finishing her course. And yet, wavering between bold self-assertion and traditional maidenliness, she tended to assume that at the proper time she would accept her parents' choice of a husband, who would probably be a farmer. She toys with the idea of marriage after a romance but is afraid it will not work out. Most restive of all the incipient teen-agers in Niiike at the time, this girl's relatively mild attempt to break loose shows that the development of the teen-age pattern among Niiike's adolescent youth is not yet at the point of causing critical tensions.

In the years that precede marriage, even the boy who expects to succeed his father may work for pay at some job outside of Niiike for a time. Most of his salary or wage, as we have noted, is regarded as household income. Military conscription, an outstanding concern in a young man's life throughout the previous generation, is eliminated by the new constitution's controversial clause renouncing war; and no one from Niiike has taken up the chance to join the enlarged "Self-Defense Force." But this is the time when a younger son, in a household that holds enough acreage to consider creating a branch house, can scrape together savings for building the new house and getting himself well started after marriage. Neither Niiike nor the region in general has seen much development of the Four-H clubs that have begun to flourish in Japan. The spirit and goals of these clubs are rather along teen-age lines, encouraging initiative and competition among their members in farming and other affairs more than do the tradition-oriented Youth Associations, which draw from the same age level. It is the Youth Association rather than the Four-H which interests the youth in the Niiike area.

Probably no boy comes to his marriage completely lacking in sexual experience. There are girls on call at the inns clustered near the Inari shrine just east of Takamatsu or, until recently at any rate, in licensed houses of prostitution in the city of Kurashiki. It is an easy matter to try these out in the course of a Youth Association gambol or with a few cronies, except that such things cost money. However, even apart from the cost, there is a double handicap that keeps most boys from becoming at all familiar with sex through this avenue. Adults disapprove any repeated expenditures on drink and sex. More than this, the lifelong experience of Niiike boys and girls with regard to most aspects of sex has certified it as an undercover subject, not fit for open consideration. Half-comprehended confidences from age-mates and older boys or girls provide almost all the information a youngster acquires, for parents tend to avoid the subject altogether. Niiike, like every community, has had its rounder every generation or two but, unlike some other communities, has shown little patience with these persons. Given these attitudes, and considering how quickly word gets around, most boys are unlikely to repeat their visits to prostitutes very often; nor, as we have mentioned, is there much opportunity to consort with girls of the locality.

Some say that virginity in a girl is of little importance, as such. This merely means, however, that an unsuccessful first trial at marriage does, not handicap a girl's later changes merely because she is no longer virginal. The girl is not especially watched or guarded against receiving sexual approaches before marriage. Circumstances simply make it unlikely that she will be out of the public eye enough to have any premarital sexual contacts without immediate damage to her reputation and chances for marriage. In this respect the opportunities of several girls commuting to school in Okayama City, including the restless Shigemi mentioned earlier, are quite unprecedented in Niiike. Other exceptions occur, of course, and various cover-up techniques are known. Sometimes a mother who already has a daughter nearing twenty will reveal herself to be "pregnant" despite her age and eventually add a new baby to her grown-up brood. Alternatively, a girl may pay an extended visit to relatives far away. The stigma of sexual misbehavior today plays havoc with a girl's marriage chances. Public opinion possibly was much more tolerant a few generations ago, but little evidence of it remains. Niiike has shifted a world away from the lusty folk tradition—still alive in some localities—of *yobai*, boy and girl liaisons in which any red-blooded boy might wrap his face in a towel for disguise and sally forth to slip secretly into his girl's bed at night. Changing conditions have taken the initiative in matchmaking away from the young people and given it to their parents, and the signs of its returning are still slight.

The search for a marriage partner is almost completely divorced from the questions of heterosexual interest and compatibility implied above. The outstanding qualifications for a wife are those set by the household; she should be healthy, able and skilled at housework and (if possible) farming, good natured, and docile. A girl's family, similarly, looks for a healthy, hardworking young man who is a good bet economically. These are merely the first-order requirements. The search for a proper spouse may take a long time. So in order to reach a decision before the twenty-fifth year, the boy's or girl's parents, perhaps a couple of years earlier, approach some couple, usually elderly and gregarious, who are known to have been successful as go-betweens (*nakōdo*, or *baishakunin*), and ask them to help find a suitable match.

The arranged marriage to which the go-betweens' services lead is known as the *kikiawase-kekkon* or *miai-kekkon*. Each term refers to a critical aspect of the procedure. The go-betweens soon show up with, say, four or five prospects, from which the most promising one or two are selected. Then parents and go-betweens begin the *kikiawase* or "asking about," a surreptitious but exhaustive inquiry into the health, financial welfare, personality, and background of the unsuspecting candidate and his or her family. The parents look over photographs and hear the go-betweens' report, usually laying the possibilities before the youngster who is at the center of it all before reaching their tentative decision. Then the go-betweens openly approach the parents of the favored youngster, who have been completing a *kikiawase* of their own. If all goes well, the plotters arrange an inconspicuous meeting between the two households to give them, especially the two central figures, the chance to look each other over. This meeting, the *miai*, is artfully "accidental," usually taking place in some public spot, such as the main department store or the old castle garden in Okayama City, or is hedged with some plausible excuse of business in order to avoid embarrassment to anyone if the negotiations should not go through.

The alternative to this arranged marriage is the free or romantic marriage (*jiyū* or *ren'ai-kekkon*), planned and carried through by the two who fall in love. The form has long been familiar through Western literature and movies, but through well-publicized suicides and other tragedies of frustrated lovers it has come often to imply not only marriage based on mutual attraction but also marriage in defiance of parents. Though a group of Niiike men once estimated that as many as one in ten of the current young couples got acquainted before the go-between machinery was set in motion to bring about an arranged marriage, they forbear to call such marriages love-matches because of the conflict implied by this term.

One quite practical reason for calling on go-betweens regardless of how affairs stand is that this procedure provides an extremely full dossier of pertinent information. The secrecy surrounding the *kikiawase* investigation—or the *miai* that follows—is a convenient fiction, of course, for the inquiries among neighbors and friends are too searching and detailed to be kept truly under cover. In connection with health, the family history with regard to certain maladies—leprosy, insanity, venereal disease, tuberculosis—is specifically examined on the presumption that these afflictions are hereditary. Other illnesses and weaknesses are noted, of course, especially those on the paternal side, down to and including color blindness. Family affluence is studied, to get just the right balance between households and kindreds (the girl should be slightly poorer, so she will not be tempted to put on airs, but not too much poorer, for then her parents will have trouble making gifts of the quality required for her children's age-grade ceremonies). The whole range of paternal relatives of the prospective bride or groom is studied for education, social reputation, and official record; maternal relatives are gone over more lightly, for at best they will be only remotely involved in future interfamilial intercourse. On the paternal side, is there any connection with outcasts, with criminal or undesirable occupations, with unpaid debts or *kōjū* altercations? Who are their friends and connections; who are their enemies? Are there kinship connections that make the match undesirable? What zodiacal animal is associated with the birth year of each (everyone knows that girls born in the year of the sheep are unlucky, especially when marrying boys born in the year of the tiger)? Almost any sort of information may turn out to be relevant to the decision. Skilled go-betweens must be gossipy but tactful to get all the information, and they must be good at evaluating hearsay and know when to gloss over things that might harm a good match and when to undersell a match they consider hazardous. They are held lastingly responsible for the marriage as much as are the parents on either side.

The people of Niiike say that, when youngsters rush into a romantic marriage, they fail to look dispassionately at all this information, even if it is available to them. Their rashness would be foolish though no worse, perhaps, if only their own future were thus put in hazard; but their entire household and kindred are involved, and to compromise their house (*ie*) is an act of impiety. This is their practical reason for distrusting any but the conventional arranged marriage. People can point to a case or two in Niiike in recent years that failed to work out and trace the failure to its roots in an initial romantic attachment. Iwasa Toshio's father, for example, perhaps influenced by his own younger years spent in America, allowed Toshio to bring as his bride a girl he met while working in town. His father did insist on using a go-between. But in spite of this precaution the girl went back home within about six months. Toshio, presumably chastened, was willing on his second trial to take a girl whom he saw for the first time at a *miai* arranged in time-honored style by the go-betweens. Other youngsters, incidentally, who have been weighing the merits of romantic marriage in their own minds, see Toshio's as a test case proving their parents' point that the arranged type of marriage is more satisfying all around.

One can know entirely too much about the prospective spouse's family, of course. Therefore a match within Niiike itself, such as the one between Kameichi and Tomoko, second son and second daughter of different Hiramatsu lineages, is a very rare thing. In most cases, people say, a marriage inside the community does not get started on its own merits, but is overshadowed by all that each house knows about the other. But Kameichi's marriage, understood to be in prospect from the time he was about eight, at least preserved balance by matching him—he was from the leading lineage—to a girl from a slightly subordinate lineage. In any case, their migration to Manchuria took them out of immediate village affairs. All other marriages have followed the rule of village exogamy, that is, marriage outside of the local community.

Village exogamy has been a long-held custom, but its pattern has changed over the decades, owing mainly to improvements in transportation. When we locate the original home of each bride and groom (adoptive son) who came to Niiike before 1900 (Fig. 43), we see that the rule of exogamy applied not only to the buraku but to the ōaza as well, which had been the administrative village through Tokugawa times. Almost all brides and grooms were brought from buraku other than those of Upper Shinjō ōaza. To use nearby examples, no brides came from Yamane, 400 yards east of Niiike and in Upper Shinjō, but several came from Ōyama, 250 yards south but in Lower Shinjō. But, at the same time, the average distance between bride's or groom's original home and Niiike was only 2.9 miles or slightly over one *ri*. In that day, when one traveled on foot

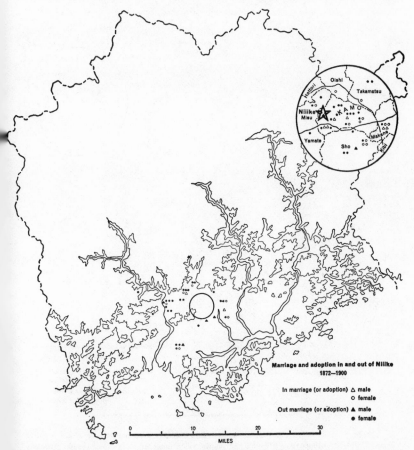

Fɪɢ. 43.—Homes before marriage or adoption into Niiike or after marriage or adoption out of Niiike, 1872–1900.

or perhaps hired a ricksha, a distance of one *ri*, the accepted measure of half a day's walk, permitted brides and their mothers to visit each other on ceremonial occasions without having to arrange for an overnight stay. Visiting customs have not changed greatly since great-grandmother's day but the railroad and bus have changed matters. A glance at Figure 44, locating the original homes of brides and grooms since 1925, and at the summarizing table (Table 18, p. 322), shows dispersion over twice the

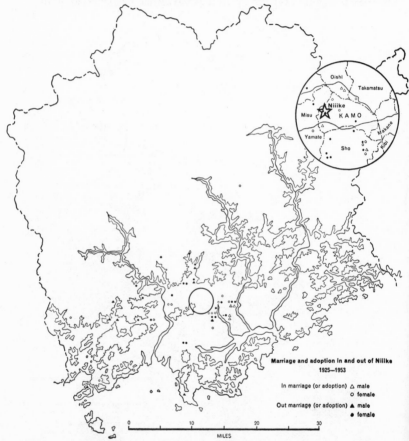

Fig. 44.—Homes before marriage or adoption into Niiike or after marriage or adoption out of Niiike, 1925–53. Comparison with Fig. 43 shows wider range in more recent years, especially decrease in marriage and adoption within Kamo; but the tendency persists to confine marriage and adoption to localities in the coastal plain.

pre-1900 radius. Thus, Niiike people seem to choose from as wide a field as railroad and bus permit, as long as customary visits are not made awkward.

The maps show the degree to which marriages are concentrated on the coastal plain, although Niiike is within easy view of the foothills. Figures 43 and 44, showing marriage and adoption into and out of Niiike, disclose that Niiike people are willing to take spouses born in hill villages but send almost no one there in exchange, for the upland communities are regarded as poor and behind the times. Several other tendencies are evidenced in these maps. Villagers of old Bitchū, including those of Niiike, rarely marry across the old boundary line with persons from Bizen, even though the only obstacle today is one of sentiment. There is one notable exception, however. Niiike households do tend to choose girls from farm households inside the limits of Okayama City, which is in Bizen, and to send girls there as well, apparently because communication with the city is good. Their motive certainly is not to make a match with a city girl as such, for city girls are alleged to be incompetent at many tasks of the farm housewife; instead, it is a farm girl who is sought, even within the city boundaries. Finally, a good many marriages take place between Niiike and the village of Shō to the south, a tendency accounted for by the fact that Hiramatsu lineages originally came to Niiike from Shō. It is of some interest that each of these tendencies is almost equally clear in the case of marriages before 1900 and marriages since 1925. The range of marriage has increased over the decades without significant alteration of the patterns of searching for brides and grooms.

Recalling the feeling of division that separates the Hiramatsu from the Iwasa lineage groups, it may be asked in what way this division influences the selection of brides and grooms. Except that Hiramatsu lineages have ranged slightly more widely than Iwasa lineages and favor their village of origin, Shō, no significant differences are perceptible. As far as community affiliation is concerned, neither avoids communities favored by the other, though they seem not to marry into identical lineages.

A marriage area roughly similar in character—commencing outside of the local village, as this is historically defined, and extending only a limited distance outward—surrounds every rural community in Japan. Each community's marriage area has its own particular characteristics. Various studies have shown, however, as one might expect, that the more isolated and strictly rural communities tend to hold most strictly to village exogamy and, at the same time, not to reach outward as far as do communities of shopkeepers and businessmen. The implication supports our conclusion with respect to Niiike's change through the decades, that habits of transportation and communication do much to broaden the intermarriage zone. Summarized in the following table (Table 18) are the results of surveys of two buraku that are incorporated in Takamatsu, Niiike's shopping town: Harakozai, a buraku of farmers and general shopkeepers; and Inari, a buraku of farmers interrelated with keepers of souvenir shops, restaurants, and inns. The Harakozai shops supply only the local countryside, but the clientele of the Inari resort comes from all over the Inland Sea region to visit the famous shrine. In the table, farmers from Niiike, Harakozai, and Inari have been grouped together; those whose main occupation is other than farming are shown as a separate group. Average distances to the original homes or marriage destinations

TABLE 18

DISTANCES BETWEEN ORIGINAL HOMES AND MARITAL HOMES FOR
NIIIKE AND TWO NEIGHBORING BURAKU

	Cases	Okayama (km.)	Inland Sea	All Japan	Total Average Distance (km.)	Outside Japan
Farmers:						
Into Niiike, 1872–1900........	18	4.70	.....	.....	4.70	..
From Niiike, 1872–1900.......	11	4.14	.....	.....	4.14	..
Into Niiike, 1925–53..........	45	8.77	.....	.....	8.77	..
From Niiike, 1925–53.........	43	7.28	10.89	.....	10.89	..
Into Harakozai (1900?–53).....	75	6.78	10.78	.....	10.78	..
Into Inari (1900?–53)..........	84	12.05	14.71	43.33	43.33	1
Shopkeepers:						
Into Harakozai (1900?–53).....	88	9.26	15.75	35.33	35.33	4
Into Inari (1900?–53)..........	44	13.87	33.40	.....	33.40	..

are given in kilometers, first for marriages within Okayama alone, then for all marriages made in the Inland Sea region, then for all Japan. The cumulative average also is shown. Marriages made outside Japan are enumerated, but no attempt has been made to compute their distance figures, which would be meaningless.

A striking distinction appears between the range attained by shopkeeper families and the range characterizing farm families other than those of Inari. Farmers show a much more limited range of marriage than do persons engaged in business. The apparent inconsistency of Inari farmer marriages is explained through the close kin connection of these households with the Inari shopkeepers, most of whom are branch houses from the farms, whereas the Harakozai farmers have no such connection with their shopkeeper neighbors, most of whom moved in from the outside. Other studies have shown that, just as farm households tend to seek farm girls as wives, so families in other occupations, in the course of cultivating business ties within their occupation, reinforce such ties through inter-marriage. In Inari, both main and branch houses, which is to say both farmer and innkeeper houses, share economic interests and stand to gain mutually by seeking brides among families engaged in *mizu shōbai* ("water business": occupations that offer recreation and services to travelers) all over western Japan. These matches have greatly extended the average distance of marriage.

Although parents gradually have ranged more widely to find spouses for their children, it is still not easy to find just the right match. It may happen that, having found a girl whose character and family meet all the requirements, the Niiike parents realize that her brother also will be a good match for their daughter. Without further search, both children can be satisfactorily married, through what amounts to an exchange of offspring between households. Also, though wedding costs are not greatly altered, neither household needs to be so concerned over the bridal gift of money (*yuinō*) described below, for each receives a *yuinō* and offers one simul-taneously. Out of about 110 marriages into or out of Niiike in the last three generations, in which detailed relationships can be traced, twelve exemplify such an exchange, that is, on six occasions a Niiike house has simultaneously acquired a son's wife and unburdened itself of a daughter to a particular house outside. In three more cases (involving six mar-riages), the exchange has involved brothers from a single house marrying sisters from another, Niiike providing the brothers in two instances, the sisters in one. Usually one brother goes as an adoptive groom so that the girls' house as well as the boys' house gains a young couple.

Even more commonly, however, marriage to a cousin has solved the problem of wife-hunting, being "the safest way to make sure the marriage is even." Cousins usually have less adjustment to make in a new house-hold; so people still marry cousins if they think their own house is espe-cially troublesome to adjust to, even though they frequently have heard of the Western conviction that first-cousin marriage may be biologically harmful. Since far back, they have regarded the offspring of brothers (patrilineal parallel cousins) as more truly kin to each other than the offspring of sisters (matrilineal parallel cousins) or than cousins whose connecting relatives are different in sex (cross-cousins). As we might expect in a society emphasizing descent through males, marriage between patrilineal parallel cousins is most rare. Out of the 110 marriages referred to above, thirteen are known to be cousin marriages. Cross-cousin marriage is most common; there are eleven instances, in two of which the spouses were cousins once removed. The two other cases involved matrilineal parallel cousins. In the closest approach to the marriage of persons whose parents are brothers, the parents were only half-brothers, having the same mother, but different fathers. This seems to have removed the sense of incest that besets a marriage between descendants from common male ancestors. Curiously enough, although the differentiation drawn in Niiike between different stripes of cousins fits the patrilateral bias of Japanese kin reckoning in general, and cousin marriage is common enough in almost any part of Japan, the preferences shown where data are available are not necessarily for cross-cousin marriages. Older people usually scrutinize closely the question of possible kinship between two candidates for marriage. Yet, needless to say, several generations of marriage between cousins, marriages with mother's more distant relatives, and brother-sister exchange, can create a veritable maze of marital and descent cross ties—all of which reinforce the sense of a funded investment in solidarity between the houses concerned.

Within five days from the *miai* when the two families first meet, the go-betweens look for a decision. A reversal is still possible until the amount to be paid to the bride's house as *yuinō* is settled and a date is fixed. However, serious preparations begin that will culminate in the next stage, the ceremony with its feasts and the exchange of cups between bride and groom that binds the marriage. September is favored for weddings, when the demands of work in the fields are slight. In any case, an engagement period lasts from a month to six months and, these days, the couple may be able to meet several times to get acquainted. But even though things go smoothly right up to the wedding ceremony, the suspense lasts beyond it until the marriage is registered officially at the village office, a final step which may wait for as long as a year, for married life starts off with an explicit period of probation. Thus, as the main task of the go-between ends, a period of mixed tension and elation opens for both households.

The prospective bride and groom stay in the background while their parents, without yet meeting each other, agree through the go-betweens on the amount of money that should come from the groom's side as a bridal gift called *yuinō*. In the early 1950's, a time of fair prosperity, the Niiike house would want to pay at least ¥10,000, since the amount will soon become an open secret and reflect on household honor (*giri*) but would probably be unable to give more than about ¥30,000. Thereafter, unless the marriage is that of a second son for whom a branch household is to be set up, the boy's parents' expenses are confined mostly to providing a wedding feast and perhaps buying a full-dress suit with swallow-tail coat for the groom to wear at the ceremony. The girl's parents pay out much more in preparation than they receive in *yuinō*.

A wedding kimono embroidered from hem to thigh and its accessories is a costly item. The bride, moreover, should bring with her at least the seven traditional items of clothing and household goods. Iwasa Toshiko, marrying in 1949 before the period of postwar shortages was over, brought not one but two large veneered chests of drawers, one filled with her clothing, and two clothing chests rather than one. A geta-box holding her footgear, a sewing stand, a mirror and stand, and a washtub completed the six items apart from clothing, and several small extras were added. All this cost half again what her family received as *yuinō*.

On the wedding day, set by astrological reckoning, the bride must rise early to put herself into the hands of the professional hairdresser hired by her father. It takes several hours to adjust the heavy wig done in the *takashimada* coiffure for brides, shave her face and neck, apply a dense, flat coat of white powder, blacken her eyebrows, and draw a tiny bow of lipstick on her mouth, help her don several layers of garments under her embroidered kimono, wrap her long sash and tie it with the special knot for brides, and adjust the white bride-band ("horn-screen," *tsuno kakushi*) modestly across her forehead and hairline. Thus disguised and encumbered, the bride waits for a hired car to arrive about ten o'clock, bringing the groom in his morning-dress coat and the go-betweens in black, formal kimonos. They visit for up to an hour at the house, while the bride's mother serves light refreshment of sake and, perhaps, fish. If the bride has planned to observe the optional symbolic custom of changing clothing from virginal white to melancholy black to red, she retires now to don black for her departure from her parental home; the red costume she will take along to wear after the ceremony. The bride's baggage, if it has not been sent the day before, meanwhile is dispatched to the groom's house, and before long the groom and go-betweens take the bride to the car. Her father or mother (rarely both) and several of her father's relatives ride in a second car, or the first vehicle returns for them. Tears of sentiment may flow in the second car as the girl leaves her home and native village, but custom permits the bride no show of expression under her white mask of powder as she goes off to a new life in a community she may never have seen before.

Though everyone will be in a state of nerves waiting for the bride to arrive in a community the size of Niiike, only adults from the groom's lineage gather near the house in the early afternoon to welcome her. Men are in dark suits or formal black kimonos; most women wear kimonos.

The bride, like a spring-wound doll, steps out of the car and walks slowly after the groom into his house, followed by her own relatives bringing the sake, broiled fish, and other foods her parents contribute to the feasting. Sliding doors are thrown open to the main room for everyone's entrance. In an atmosphere of solemn and restrained cordiality, she is greeted by her new parents and introduced to their kinsmen. Then she is led from house to house around the community by her father-in-law to be introduced to every house in the *kōjū*, while her viands are added to the feast prepared by the groom's mother and her helpers. Before she returns for the feast to begin, she must walk across the fields to the shrine to be introduced as a new member of the community and to pay her respects there.

Generally at this point the bride and groom, seated again in the main room with their go-betweens, perform the *sansankudo* ("three and three nine times") that binds the marriage. The brief ceremony is directed by one of the go-betweens or, if a priest from the temple is present, by him. A special stand is set on the floor bearing three nested, flat cups. The maiden selected as pourer goes through the motions of pouring sake in each one successively, once for the groom and once for the bride; each makes motions of emptying the cup in three sips. The nine sips completed, a tray of food is set before each. Though neither actually touches the food, it is the ritual of drinking and eating together in public that makes the two man and wife.

The wedding banquet, served on individual red lacquer trays, begins ceremoniously with the first round of sake poured by a preadolescent girl, chosen for the honor by the groom. Stiffly solemn at first, the assembled relatives begin to enjoy themselves after downing a few of the thimble-size cups of sake. Conversation warms, led especially by the go-betweens from their seats of second highest honor flanking the young couple before the *tokonoma*, for they are practiced conversationalists and, moreover, can arouse humor and good spirits by their veiled allusions to the difficulties overcome in promoting this match. Mild jollity flows around the stiff, doll-like figure of the bride without touching her, for she must sit expressionless and motionless, seeming too overcome to touch her food. Nor can the groom relax yet or eat, for his duty is to play attentive host and fill each sake cup before it is emptied.

After nearly an hour, the bride goes into the rear room to rest (sometimes to reappear in a red kimono, her final costume for the ceremony); women gradually take their leave to tend children or households. But the men linger to turn the affair into a real party with toasts (when toasting, two persons exchange cups and pour for each other), more food, jokes, and songs. The groom's part in the wedding ends finally when rice is served to signify the end of the meal, and the men wend their jolly, unsteady way home.

Should a widow or widower remarry, the banquet is less ornate and expensive, but parents attempt to maintain high standards for the first weddings of all their children. Most feast costs are borne by the groom's household. At about ¥1,000 per person for food plus sake, the bill for a modest gathering of fifteen may run up to ¥25,000 even in Niiike where drinking is extremely moderate. A final cost is the gratuity to the go-betweens, fixed at 10 per cent of the *yuinō*, or ¥2,000–¥3,000, which is given them when the new couple, a few days afterward, pay their first visit of thanks.

Honeymoons of a week or so have become stylish in recent years. But the new couple may not be able to afford a trip even to a modest inn and will merely spend the week at home without going to work. In the latter case, no conflict arises with the traditional third-day visit paid by the bride to her native home, accompanied by her husband, his father, and the go-betweens. An astrologically favorable day is chosen, so the visit may actually be a week after the wedding. They take along fish and sake as a present and stay only a little while.

Through the next year, there are seven to nine traditional occasions, set according to the lunar calendar, on which the new bride may return home briefly without exciting gossip that her marriage has collapsed. These are frankly regarded as days of relief from strain for the bride. If the wedding occurred in fall, as many do, her permitted visits are in the following order:

Lunar Month	Occasion	Meaning	Remarks
September	*Aki no matsuri*	Fall Festival	Pay respects to shrine of native place
November	*Akiyasumi*	Fall rest	Slack season after rice harvest
January	*Shōgatsu*	New Year	Important; may stay home overnight or longer
March (solar)	*Higan*	Equinox	Respects to ancestors (grave-clearing)
March	*Haruyasumi*	Spring rest	Coincides with Girls' Day, the festival of dolls; used to take rice cakes home to commemorate first setting-up of the dolls in her new home
May	*Mugiurashi*	Wheat-ripening	Precedes busy wheat harvest
June	*Ashiarai*	Foot-bathing	Feet are "muddy" from transplanting
July	*Bon*	Ancestor festival	Pay respects to own ancestors
September (solar)	*Higan*	Equinox	Respects to ancestors (grave-clearing)

An adoptive bridegroom goes through almost identical wedding arrangements except that the entire Youth Association should be invited to the banquet, for he is expected to become a member. Such a groom's task of adjusting to a strange household's ways are similar to those of a bride. He does not have the same privilege of returning home, however. The bride may actually get no more than half of these vacation days but has the right to each one in theory. Not so the adoptive groom. The rationale, as the mother-in-law of one adoptive groom explained it, is that a man's work gives him contacts outside the household, and he is less the victim of loneliness than the girl, who must stay quite isolated within the house.

Life is relatively unchanged for the new-married eldest son, who goes on living at home as before and carries on with his work. His parents continue to spread their quilts in the back room at night; he and his bride occupy either the small inner room or the larger main room, being separated from the parents in either case by the fusuma, opaque paper sliding doors. Especially if the house is crowded with younger siblings, an effort is made to arrange a room apart from the house, a *hiya* (*hanarebeya* is the standard word form), where either the older couple or the younger couple will sleep, as convenient. Eventually, on retirement of the father, separate cooking arrangements may be set up.

The emotional impact of marriage, moreover, may well be slight. The young man has not acquired his mate as a companion and object of sexual love but as an addition to the team in house and fieldwork, a person who will look after his wants and relieve his discomforts much as his mother has always done. He is likely to see his wife as an alternate mother and, indeed, opens himself to unhappiness if he lets himself develop a more romantic view and then has to give the girl up.

A younger son, of course, experiences more change, if he is moving into a new branch house. He now has an independent responsibility in the *kōjū* and buraku meetings but deals with completely familiar persons in his new roles of husband and householder. If he is marrying and being adopted into a household elsewhere, his problems are much like those of a bride, though rather less wearing. Toshiko, coming as a bride from a mountain village, had no experience with mat-rush cultivation. She was taken aback to find that the women worked so hard, that they would get up early to start work at the *tatami*-cover looms and would work until it was too dark to continue. She thought, "What a terrible place I have come to. All they do is work—no time for enjoyment—no time even to take care of their children." Then, too, the Niiike people seemed very wary about spending their money. And they used such polite speech that she was ashamed to speak to any of them. She learned to enjoy remembering the correct things expected of her and liked the task of keeping track of all the special occasions to give gifts or compliments. But for a long time she was very lonely. Almost a year after her marriage she did not even know who lived in about twenty of the two dozen houses in Niiike. The birth of a son changed all that.

Loneliness is an emotion almost all young wives have in common. Women recalling their own early days of marriage again and again comment on how lonely they felt. There is actual physical isolation from others in the community, especially from girls in similar circumstances, for all new brides must stay with their housework, which leaves no time for sociability and may cut down their sleep to an average of about five hours a night. When a visitor arrives, the bride is brought to be introduced, but proper decorum requires her to keep her eyes down, scarcely glancing at the visitor, let alone conversing freely with him. The others within the household, of whom one is with her constantly, are in essence sitting in judgment on her every word and action, for, no matter how kindly they regard her, their first duty is to see that she has the stuff needed for the household's welfare. Her isolation, thus, is psychological as well as physical.

The youngwife's position within the community is seen from the viewpoint of a still unmarried farm girl living near Niiike in the following translation from a letter to the authors:

Generally speaking, there is not much chance for a bride who has come from another village to get on friendly terms with the villagers. A farmer's bride usually first sees her husband's house on the day of the wedding. In her wedding dress, she is taken by her husband's aunt to be introduced to the local deity (*uji-gami*) and any small shrines (*hokora*) in her hamlet, and she pays a courtesy visit to the neighbors, the relatives (*kabuuchi*), and members of the *kōjū* on the wedding day or the following day. After that, through shyness, she avoids going out as much as possible. The villagers are very eager to get a look at her, but she is all the more inclined to hide at home.

But while she is there she has many chances to meet the near neighbors and first gets on good terms with them. And then when harvest time comes, she has to go out to work with the family and begins naturally to exchange greetings with the people in the neighboring fields and to talk with them. But when the women's association meets, she does not go as long as her mother-in-law is there. Even if she has no mother-in-law, the bride who has just arrived is not very eager to join the assembly. This is why she is slow to become familiar with the villagers and village affairs. Even if villagers catch sight of her in a temple or shrine at festival time or visiting the graves at the *Bon* festival, they merely learn that she is the wife of so-and-so, and—far from greeting her—it turns out that they watch her furtively from a respectable distance. So it really may take several years before she gets on friendly terms with the villagers.

Although a law for registration [of marriage] has been passed recently, things are just as they always were, and it is usual for the bride to be registered only when she is about to have a child. The reason is that the family are thinking of a separation in case she doesn't fit into the family ways and does not suit them. Besides, I have heard that it wouldn't do to register the bride right away because if she is divorced after registration, half of the family property will now be taken for her.

The curiosity of the villagers, of course, centers on the question of whether this marriage will endure. With remarkable consensus, the people of Niiike and the rest of Japan agree that the duration of a marriage depends mainly on the bride's relation to her mother-in-law. Data derived from our psychological tests, combined with what has already been said about the social situation, cast some light on this situation. Her husband feels at home among things that may be strange or distasteful to the bride. The codes drilled into him require him to consider the *ie* ("house") and to side with his parents in any clash of opinion. His life experiences give him an emotional attachment to his father as an exemplary model or image and to his mother as a warm and sheltering person, making it difficult for him to achieve detachment or to incline toward his wife's side. In spite of this, it is true, people call a husband who never takes his wife's side *ita basami* ("board-scissored") because he is passively squeezed like clothing between two pressing boards. The projective tests indicate that a young man viewing the matter hypothetically often may feel he should assert his individual wants and try to keep a disapproved wife but, should the crisis come, his parents in the end probably will prevail, for they do have the greater authority. His father often is in sympathy with the new bride's problems, but his role makes him aloof and, by never touching women's work, he has to argue from weakness in favor of the bride. The groom's mother has two reasons to be critical of the bride: she herself went through a similar introduction to the ways of the home years before and became, perhaps, a stouter proponent of household ways than anyone else in the process; and she may find it hard not to resent sharing or losing the love of her son, which has been one of her few satisfactions through married life. For the wife's role competes with her own in many respects; she is a younger mother intended to comfort and serve her husband in a maternal role. If she wins him, the mother may well be the loser.

The mother, thus, is apt to have the "We do it this way" attitude toward her new daughter-in-law's housework. She may look through the newcomer's clothing chests and select garments suitable for festivals, reject ones that are too gay, or confiscate those needed for someone else in the household. In serving meals, she may skimp on the bride's portion to encourage economical self-sacrifice. Though the bride can give up and go home, a sincere girl will work hard, avoid joking, and put up with much bossing, for she knows that even the most warmhearted of mothers-in-law is occasionally guilty of hazing. Her chances of remarriage after a failure depend very much on how hard she tried to succeed.

The nagging and bossy wife (*kaka-denka*), too blunt to rule domestic affairs by indirection, is often the classic harsh mother-in-law. Shizu, mother of three daughters and two sons, Sōtarō and Masaji (the names are fictitious), was a strong-willed woman. As second son, Masaji at eighteen was sent as an adoptive groom to a nearby hamlet before Sōtarō's marriage was arranged. The first girl brought to Niiike as Sōtarō's bride was unable to stay. A second girl and a third girl tried but failed. On the fourth try, a match was arranged with the daughter of Shizu's sister, Sōtarō's cousin, overruling the objections of Sōtarō's mild father. But this girl, too, soon was told to pack up and return home. Sōtarō, however, convinced after the fourth impasse that, if his mother could not stomach her own kin, she would not tolerate any girl permanently, left home rather than cancel his marriage. With Kiyo, his cousin-wife, he rented a room near the village office where he was working. His mother flew into a fury and send him a quilt, a water bucket, and one *tō* (about four gallons) of rice in symbolic disinheritance. Peacemaking efforts by the head of the parent house accomplished no more than to get for Sōtarō the three-quarters of an acre originally allotted to Sōtarō's father, a second son, when he formed his branch house. The house and its remaining $2\frac{1}{4}$ acres were left without an heir. To meet this problem, Masaji's marriage was dissolved, and he was brought back to become the successor in due time. The search for brides started all over again, with the same result as before, Shizu could tolerate none of the brides who came. Two girls in succession were sent home. Now Masaji, modifying his brother's stratagem, built a new house immediately in front of his parent's house before he took a third bride. By creating a separate hearth in this way, he turned the trick, for his third bride stayed, ending the long turmoil. Officially, his elder brother inherited the patrimony by virtue of his three-fourths acre of land, while Masaji's new residence was a branch house. Actually the reverse was true. Masaji inherited the larger acreage, took care of his parents and the ancestral memorial tablets, and had the responsibility of arranging marriages for his three sisters.

No doubt the mother-in-law gets more than her share of blame for marriages that prove incompatible, just because of well-known stories such as the one here recited. Mother-in-law trouble nonetheless looms large, and nearly half of the first attempts at marriage fail. Figures are uncertain, for men tend to gloss over or forget their early failures, but even though the marriage is not officially recorded until clear sailing is in prospect, the village records for Niiike show that six of the present twenty-four house-heads have divorced and remarried. In four other houses, at least, the bride whose name finally was registered was the second or third girl taken into the house.

Under prewar laws, legal annulment of a registered marriage could be initiated from either side, although it was far easier for the husband and his family to win their case. The provisions for a contested divorce differed from those for an uncontested one. However, if a woman could not see that it was "beautiful" to obey her husband and wanted to break a marriage after it was registered, there would be little chance that his family would conquer their aversion for courts and law and oppose the divorce. Court and lawyer fees would be high in any case. All divorces in Niiike seem to have been uncontested and, except in one case, to have been initiated by the husband. The grounds are not recorded, and, according to village remembrance, all were really based on incompatibility or on willingness to dissolve a marriage legally to let the wife inherit property from her natal family, though ill health might be alleged officially. Recently, there has been only one divorce resulting from barrenness of the wife. This case is unusual, for a wife who works hard and gets along with the household usually need not fear being returned home for failing to bear children. Successors are indispensable but can be acquired through the familiar practice of adoption.

Everyone hopes the new wife will get pregnant within the first year or so. But the various members of the household have rather different, personal reasons for wanting a baby to arrive. For the prospective grandparents, a child insures household continuity and validates their good judgment in choosing a fertile bride. For the husband, even the birth of a daughter settles his marriage and gives him added standing in the community. For the bride, a child of her own is vastly important. Some women say they first began to like their mothers-in-law when they saw their air of tenderness with a new baby. Common love for the child brings the mother truly into the family circle. More than this, her own child is one dependent creature whom at last she can love unreservedly without fear of being hurt in return. The new mother becomes touchingly devoted to the child—to a male child all the more because he will be with her as long as she lives. Her own emotional drives reinforce the established custom that women exist to serve men, and she gladly spends her time giving her boy child every maternal solicitude through his infancy, childhood, adolescence, and adult manhood. She lets him nurse at the breast long past walking age and, at each successive stage of his life, caters to his new wants and softens his sorrows to the limit of her ability. When he is grown, she still will pick up his clothes, check to see that he has his tobacco and matches when he leaves the house, and wait up for his return. The same protective relation, the same reluctance to have him do for himself any household service she can do for him, extends to her husband. Coupled with her sexlessness in dress and manner before the men of the house, this maternalism sets the boy's image of what a woman should be in the house. The magic is applied to any woman he respects.

It seems likely that most women sublimate in love for their children a considerable part of the drives that might otherwise be expressed in sexual relationships. There is much to inhibit rich sexual partnership between husband and wife. Both come to the marriage with little instruction, and whatever sexual experience the boy brings is usually wrapped in the context of parties and hired sex partners who are trained to take the initiative in foreplay and performance. The house is small and crowded. Unless a *hiya* ("separate room") is arranged, the house offers almost no privacy for intimacies, nor is there much possibility of wandering unobserved on the hill or in the fields. The expected pattern of daily behavior, during the first year especially, tends to curb any show of affection, caresses (kissing is regarded as a paraphrase of the sex act), or sense of humor in the husband and virtually bans all sexual allurement on the part of the girl. The outstanding thrill, some say, comes from concealment. Therefore, the investigator gathers (in the absolute absence of candid statements), the sex act itself usually is a brief, businesslike affair with a minimum of foreplay. The husband, after waiting in the quilts at night for the rest of the household to settle into slumber, grasps his wife and satisfies himself as quietly and inconspicuously as possible, releasing his tensions and settling his duty to posterity at the same time. It probably does not occur to him, if he is acquainted with geishas and girls in the inns, to apply his experience there to relations with his wife or any similar respectable woman.

Men in Niiike, their minds on the movie version of American customs, tend to be touchy and defensive about their patterns of marriage and relations between the sexes. They equate the period following the *miai* with the American period of engagement before marriage during which the couple come to know each other. They justify parent-arranged marriage with considerable practical recognition that economically and socially healthy conditions help, not harm, romantic emotion. One returnee from America pictured the church minister as a go-between who is paid for his services and stays on hand to smooth out subsequent rifts in the match. Men also assert that passion, not merely affection, ties husband and wife together in Niiike. As evidence, they claim that the community, in condemning a married philanderer, takes offense at his heartless treatment of his wife rather than his squandering money. Whether he can afford the expense of his extramarital activity is the business of his household, not of anybody else.

Until very recently, every external encouragement was given to having large families, and no concern with limitation or planning of children appeared on the surface. A complete reversal of policy at the national government level has marked the postwar period. Very active campaigns are now being waged to develop convenient birth-control methods and to inform all levels of the population about them. Magazine and newspaper articles are frequent and detailed; Welfare Ministry lecturers occasionally address Women's Association gatherings; and midwives are put through a course and given pamphlets on contraception. Abortion is openly recognized as a method of birth control. In 1952, after a not-too-satisfactory experience with a law permitting abortion upon recommendation of a committee of physicians, a eugenics protection law was added to the civil code which permitted any gynecologist to perform an abortion on his own cognizance. The conditions were extremely permissive: evidence of inheritable mental disease or physical deformity among relatives to the fourth degree, leprosy in either spouse, physical danger to the mother, economic hardship to her household, or conception resulting from rape. By including the provision concerning economic hardship, the law permitted women everywhere to terminate pregnancy by abortion. What woman could fail to convince a sympathetic gynecologist that adding a child to her household would create hardship?

From 1952 on, abortion has figured prominently in a sudden, sharp decrease in the rate of births in Japan, a drop so marked as to require drastic revision of all previous population forecasts. Country wives have utilized the discretionary economic provision of the law just as have women living in cities. Should women from Niiike seek abortion, they may choose among seven gynecologists within a four-mile radius. The nearest gynecologist serves on the staff of the Kibi Hospital, a small hospital to which patients come mainly from the towns of Takamatsu and Makane and the villages of Oishi and Kamo. Through the courteous co-operation of its staff, a summary of its obstetrics records is available. These records surely understate rather than overstate conditions, for women may visit any other nearby gynecologist or go farther away to the hospitals of Kurashiki or Okayama City. However, if we make the unlikely assumption that all women from the four communities named came to this hospital for their abortions through 1952, and compare the total of 142 abortions against the 186 births registered in the same communities in the same year, it is clear that at least 43 per cent of local pregnancies ended in abortion. The ratios for each community, shown in Table 19, vary considerably. From Makane—which is close to Okayama City and has a high proportion of suburban residents—more women may go to the city hospitals for abortions than go from the other communities. This would distort the apparent ratio. The Takamatsu ratio for 1952 more nearly reflects comparable national estimates for the year 1953, when the number of abortions performed in Kibi Hospital also rose. But Makane's low ratio of abortions and low total of births, as compared with the other three communities, may also reflect a trend generally noted in Japan for persons in urban

TABLE 19

BIRTHS AND ABORTIONS IN THE NIIIKE AREA IN 1952

Place	Births	Abortions	Percentage of Known Pregnancies Resulting in Abortion
Kamo..............	55	29	35
Oishi..............	37	21	36
Makane............	30	12	29
Takamatsu.........	64	80	55
Total..........	186	142	43

communities to use contraceptives as well as abortions to control births. More recently, this trend has been apparent in the countryside as well.

Niiike people, like others in Japan, recognize the dangers of abortion even under ideal conditions. It is inconvenient, moreover, for the mother to leave the household for a week or so in the hospital. However, though young and middle-aged people often have clear opinions about an ideal family size (between three and four children in a house), legalized abortion and contraception as alternative means of holding to this ideal are new to them. From the figures cited above we may assume that they, as other Japanese, turned first to abortion despite its inconvenience and danger. Contraception should have been favored first, if the traditional Buddhist prohibition against taking life had much significance, but aesthetic and practical considerations seem to have been stronger than this religious scruple. Men were likely to grumble at the newfangled contraceptive measures their wives were trying or urging them to try, for all of them either dulled the pleasure or interrupted the mood of lovemaking. Many women were too embarrassed by the matter to read or ask about the various methods of contraception, even apart from their reluctance to annoy their husbands. Though the midwife in Kamo was their closest source of advice, her report is that very few women had openly come to ask instruction by late 1954, and, being a countrywoman herself, she found it embarrassing to volunteer the information taught to her in a course on contraceptive practices. Contraception consequently lagged behind abortion as a means of limiting births. But in 1954 the barriers began finally to break down, it seems, as evidenced by the wry amusement shown by Hiramatsu Asae when, after confidently denying that anyone used contraception "in a country village like ours," he learned from his wife that he was behind the times and that she knew of its use in several households.

ADULT LIFE

After it becomes clear that the new bride is in the house to stay, her young husband gradually assumes his role as a fully mature adult. This role comes by steps which are not fixed in order, however. He eventually gives up commuting, if he married while holding a salaried job, and takes over the main burden of work in the fields—though Hiramatsu Hideo is one fully mature man who still holds a post-office job in Kurashiki, having enough other persons in his household to do the fieldwork. He leaves the Youth Association, but stays active with others his age in the fire brigade, although there have been men who stayed in the Youth Association long after marriage. Landownership is gradually put in his name, or sometimes fathers keep the land in their own name until they are well along in their sixties, or even until they die. Both son and father may simultaneously hold shares in the agricultural co-operative association as long as each can describe himself as a farmer, whereas membership in the equivalent prewar organization was by households and was itself one mark of maturity.

Typically, the fully mature adult owns the fields of his house, spends his days working in them, is official household head, acts as host and representative of his household for various kōjū activities, and has one or more children. Few men move into this role at the same age or by the same path, however, and the absence of any particular ceremony to mark, for example, his becoming househead as his father retires makes it quite impossible to locate any precise point at which, leaving the ranks of junior adults, he reaches full maturity. He simply grows into this position by gradual steps, and people bit by bit stop counting him as one of the youths or wakai hito.

Conditions outside the household in the postwar era differ drastically from those of prewar days. Inflation with its threat of financial catastrophe, government requisition of staple crops, agricultural land reform, increasingly complex income tax regulations, intensified concern with cash crops, and considerably more involvement in village government and its committees than ever before—all these matters have kept a latent sense of crisis in the air. People have reacted in different ways. In some households, the elder househead has been glad to let his son take over household affairs early because of his own uncertainty in the atmosphere of national crisis, while in others the older man has delayed giving over his authority, with the thought that his experienced hand is more needed while storms threaten. This contrast in reactions to national and local affairs has done much to obscure the dividing line between young and mature adults. Moreover, it certainly has made it more difficult to be immersed completely in the affairs of Niiike alone. The demands of household and buraku affairs are no less compelling than before, and hard work in the fields is still the first remedy for most problems, but men listen perhaps more carefully to the radio, skim less casually through the newspaper, and find affairs outside the buraku rising in conversation more persistently than before. Among the younger wives, at least, are some who follow the radio and newspaper almost as much as the men. Where they once rarely ventured beyond their own fields, they are beginning to get used to going not only to Women's Association or P.T.A. meetings but even to the city by train or bus for shopping.

Older men and women appear to have aged quickly after entering their forties, partly because their unrelieved physical labor with its special features such as tramping knee-deep in water throughout a wintry day bends their backs and knots their hands in arthritis, partly because they make little effort to cling to the appearance of youth. These elders do not fear and despise old age but accept it with some gratitude for the compensations it offers to offset their increasing physical infirmity—the maturing of plans for household continuity, the loosening of pressures of work and responsibility, and their respected status as grandparents. Two sorts of occasions, the first rarely observed in Niiike, illustrate the happy view adopted toward growing old. The first is a family affair. In his sixtieth year a man (or woman) dons a bright red costume—a color most improper for men at any other time—as a symbol of becoming a child again, that is, of regaining the carefree existence of an infant. Household and friends join the new "child" in a party. The second occasion is a party offered by the village each year in honor of all of its citizens who are seventy or over. Besides food and drink served at the school, speeches extolling the elders mark the occasion.

Many younger persons entering their forties, it is true, seem much more to be approaching their prime rather than leaving it behind. Between their generation and that of their parents there have been marked improvements in hygiene and public health, raising the initial life expectancy for Japan as a whole to about 68 for women and 64 for men as against 43 for women and 42 for men thirty years ago. Dental and medical care, in addition to improved medicines available at home, have postponed the onset of physical deterioration for younger persons just as they have put off the imminence of death for the elders.

Illness, nonetheless, is an ever present concern, as projective testing of personal attitudes and orientations shows. Habituated to modern concepts of disease and infection, Niiike people by and large use modern ways of treating ill and injured persons. They put iodine and bandages on cuts, take patent drugs for intestinal parasites, and practice a loose sort of quarantine against infectious illnesses. They try to eat fish and other perishable foods fresh and to throw away spoiled parts. They take precautions not to use night soil on table vegetables in the ground and since the war have attacked houseflies with much success, using DDT. Everyone has colds during the winter, and children have sniffly noses well into summer, without much special care being taken, yet the women at least worry about complications. Summer illnesses are most worrisome and are perhaps most frequent. A check made on one August day showed one or more persons in five houses in bed with high temperatures from sunstroke and virus infection, while a September check showed a differently diagnosed virus infection afflicting four houses. Yet most adult deaths do not arise out of complications from a minor illness but come from serious organic ailments—embolisms, liver disease, cancer—and, above all, from tuberculosis, which is still the big killer throughout Japan.

DEATH

When Hiramatsu Yoshio, aged sixty-four, died at home of the cancer that had kept him in bed since late autumn, preparation for his funeral began immediately, even before the doctor was brought to certify his death, as required by law. It was winter and cold, so there was less haste for cremation than in the hot weather of summer, but custom urged nonetheless that the funeral be finished before evening the next day. However, a funeral is one of life's major ceremonies, for like the wedding it serves the double purpose of readjusting personal relations among household members and of displaying through its magnificence the household's sense of self-respect and status. To make elaborate preparations in so short a time is beyond the capacity of the members of a single household, so every house in the *kōjū* organization participates in some way.

Unlike people in towns and cities, the people of Niiike do not like to leave things to professional undertakers. Yoshio's funeral was taken care of entirely by the Niiike *kōjū*.

Since Yoshio's death was not unexpected, Hiramatsu Isamu, as head of the *buraku* assembly and *kōjū* leader, was quickly on hand and, as each household sent someone to express sympathy, he consulted with the group to arrange a timetable and distribute tasks. Had he been away, the head of Yoshio's lineage might have assumed the lead instead. While a couple of helpers went to dig a small grave for the cremated remains in the cemetery, others began making a coffin and bringing materials for the funeral cortege out of storage. Still others went in pairs by bicycle to notify the priest in the temple, the cremator hereditarily linked to the family, and the village office, to report the news by telegrams to all distant relatives and friends, and eventually to purchase funeral materials and food for the funeral banquet. Women quickly set about preparing clothes for the corpse, making ready to cook food, and helping the family clean house for the expected crowd of visitors.

Once housecleaning was finished and most decisions were made in preparation for the following day, all the members of the household and his closest relatives, with wives, children, and grandchildren, donned old clothes, made belts of straw, and gathered silently in the main room, where the body had been moved and laid out, the head to the north. Quilts covered the body, but no one followed the vanishing custom of laying a knife across the quilts to ward off bad luck. On a low table at the head of the pallet was a bowl with burning incense and candles, a bell, and a jar holding sprays of the shiny-leafed *shikibi* plant associated with Buddhist death ritual. People of the *kōjū* who were not busy with assigned tasks stood outside chanting a sutra. These close kindred had the mournful duty of *yukan*, the ritual of washing and dressing the corpse.

Since the priest had not yet arrived to recite the *makura-gyō*, or "pillow-reading," the oldest man present began intoning a Nichiren chanted prayer. One by one, in order of age and close kinship, each person took a swatch of cotton soaked in alcohol (replacing the warm water formerly used), dabbed it at the body and then used a white cloth to dry the spot. Adults guided the children through this ceremony to prevent their becoming squeamish. The hair was carefully combed, not shaved off as it used to be, and the fingernails were cut. Everyone who had washed the corpse then put his own nail parings into the *zuda-bukuro* ("pilgrim's bag"). Into the same bag went some money, including six imitation *mon*, an old type of coin, to pay the spirit's ferry fare on the road to the next world, and particularly personal articles such as the deceased's tobacco pipe.

The bag was hung about the neck when the family finished dressing the body—this time using Yoshio's best clothes instead of the traditional *kyō-katabira*, "death costume." The traditional garb, made specially of white cloth, would all be put on or tied in reverse: a robe with the Nichiren common prayer written by the priest down the back, armlets, leggings, gloves, a boat-shaped cap, *tabi* with the soles removed, and straw sandals with white strings on the feet. Yoshio's own clothes, on this occasion, were similarly lapped over in reverse. By this time, the large box to serve as a coffin was ready, and helpers brought it into the room. It was made to receive the body in a sitting position, about three feet square at the base and three and a half feet high. Each person, before the lid was nailed on, dipped a leaf torn from the *shikibi* sprig into a bowl of water and moistened the lips of the corpse, in a gesture of final parting. Then the lid was nailed down, a small cross of sticks was nailed to the face side, and the coffin was placed in the *tokonoma*. By this time it was evening. The people of the *kōjū* dispersed, and the kinfolk, who remained, settled down to spend the night in a wake.

As the night grew chilly, quilts were brought out. People now and again came to the door to offer their condolences, mumbling uselessly how untimely this death was, and were thanked by Yoshio's wife and Yutaka, his heir. Those sharing the vigil spoke to each other of their memories of Yoshio and his virtues and sought other appropriate topics of conversation, but words faltered as the night wore on. First the children, then the adults, one by one, dropped off to sleep.

Everyone again was very busy next morning preparing for the two main parts of the funeral, the *tachiba*, or departing meal for visitors, and the *sōshiki*, or funeral proper. Some relatives or friends, because of bus schedules, had already arrived the night before and stayed at the next-door houses. All the shoji, or sliding panels, were now removed and piled to one side to make a large sitting area for these early arrivals. Others began arriving near noon, soon making a crowd that began to overflow into nearby houses.

Before many persons gathered, two men were stationed at the entrance. One was to make an exact notebook record of the *kōden* ("incense gifts") and the givers. This task is of utmost importance at any funeral, for the list is a concrete testimonial to the number of sorrowing friends and relatives, and, further, it becomes a memorandum for this household to use in the future in deciding the proper amount to contribute to a funeral in the families of any of the visitors. Accordingly, every name and gift must be entered scrupulously. The duty of the second man, who received name cards, was to announce each visitor to the family, thus preventing embarrassment if the survivors should happen not to know one of Yoshio's acquaintances.

The *kōden* brought by the visitors, in a few cases, included rice or other foodstuffs. In decline for some years, this custom has hardly revived since the wartime and postwar period of food shortage, however, and most gifts were of money, in amounts varying between ¥20 and ¥500, in envelopes which were kept by the recorder while the food gifts were ranged in good view along the edge of the veranda. Each visitor, after lighting incense in a stand on the veranda, stepped up to the main room where the coffin rested in state to be served the *tachiba*. In the case of relatives, a full tray of food, without fish or liquor and supposedly without salt (the ascetic cuisine of monks), was set before them. Others were handed, in substitute, a gray-bordered envelope holding ten ordinary postcards and inscribed "Seed of Tea" (meaning, approximately, "a gratuity"), before they moved on toward the crowd in the rear rooms.

Somewhat past the appointed hour, the priest began the funeral service that preceded the procession to the crematory. For this service the coffin was moved from the *tokonoma* into the room, where the priest faced it as he sat looking north, the direction associated with death, with several nuns at his left. The relatives, seated at his right in a row, and the visitors, seated behind the relatives and overflowing into the yard, followed him in reciting a sutra and then listened as he rose to deliver the requiem intrusting the departed into the care of the Buddha. To close this ceremony, the priest lighted incense in a bowl set before the coffin, and each nun and mourner rose and did likewise, one by one. Then all gathered in the yard, while men of the *kōjū* slipped the coffin into the bier with its carrying poles and the priest and elders assigned each item of paraphernalia to its proper bearer and gave him his or her place in the cortege. Children hovered around impatiently while their elders, the men in black monogrammed kimonos and the women in flower-enlivened dark kimonos, moved around in conversation and covertly inspected each others' fine dress. Just before the procession began, each woman draped over her head a cloth or put on a special white, boat-shaped headgear. Up to a decade ago, headclothes cut like miniature kimonos were worn.

Some seventeen to twenty standard positions are designated in a funeral. Since every position designates the order of relationship to the deceased and those near the coffin show who is to inherit, considerable care is taken to see that each person carries the correct object and walks in the correct place. Yoshio's cortege offered no particular problems. Men from the *kōjū* walked first, carrying white paper lanterns, a large artificial flower made of colored paper, and tall banners inscribed with Yoshio's name and several Sanskrit characters. The priest came next, setting the rhythm for the procession by striking a jangle-tipped staff on the ground. Then followed a dozen relatives, singly or in pairs, carrying tall hexahedrons and lanterns hung from the tip of long bamboos, *shikibi* sprigs, lighted candles, an incense bowl, a book of sutras, a scrap of cloth from the corpse-clothing, and a tray of coin-shaped cakes for offerings. Yutaka, the heir, and his sister—in the place of his wife, who was dead—preceded the coffin. Yutaka held a ribbon that led to the peak of the coffin and carried a tray of household ancestral name-tablets; his sister bore tea for offering at the crematory. A son-in-law brought up the rear, carrying a bamboo from which a paper parasol hung over the coffin before him. Behind this ribbon-strewn procession, the train of relatives, neighbors, and friends strung out along the path, several carrying footgear for the coffin bearers and members of the bereaved household, whose special sandals were to be left at the cremation ground. Yoshio's wife stayed home, according to custom, where she would not have to witness the cremation. Just as the procession moved off, someone brought Yoshio's rice bowl from the house and broke it in the yard, leaving the fragments on the ground. The procession took the shortest path to the crematory ground of the ōaza, about a quarter of a mile away (in some localities the procession winds around to pass every house). There the coffin circled thrice around the farther of two platforms and was set down. Offerings of tea were poured, and the inner coffin was slipped out and set on the pyre. A few men stayed to witness the entire cremation, for stories abound of corpse-robbing on the part of cremators, who are hired from among the *Eta* outcasts in the village. The rest of the procession returned, receiving thanks from two of the *kōjū* men stationed en route, the relatives going to the house for a brief meal before leaving for home, where custom prohibits their cooking again that day. The *kōjū* helpers were then fed before the exhausted members of the household were finally free to cook their own ascetic, saltless meal.

Next morning the cremator arrived to take Yutaka and other relatives to pick fragments of bone out of the now cold ashes. Two persons using special chopsticks picked out the remains, beginning with foot bones and ending at the skull under the cremator's direction. These burned bones were brought back in a small box. Meanwhile Yutaka's mother and married sisters were busy wrapping small gifts of food to give in thanks to the *kōjū* members, the priest, and relatives who would again come to help bury the ashes in the cemetery seven days later. The priest at that time would give a death-name for the deceased, eventually to be inscribed on a stone monument. Characters of varying value appear in such a death-name, depending on how zealous the dead person had been on behalf of the temple—or, some say, depending on the size of gratuity offered at this point. For the first two nights, *kōjū* members would come for prayers, and throughout the seven days the members of the household would stay at home in mourning, receiving repeated visits from each house in the *kōjū*. Actually, tasks such as addressing printed postcards of thanks to all who had brought funeral gifts and opening and counting these gifts, together with housecleaning and airing the clothes of the dead father, would give little free time. Since food again is served to seventh-day visitors, the women would probably be kept busy at home until after the ceremony and would slip up to the cemetery later to pay their own respects.

Yoshio's funeral itself ended on the seventh day. Payments for food and the services of priest, nuns, and cremator by this time amounted to about ¥10,000. A large expenditure remained, amounting to about ¥25,000, for the gravestone. Minor costs would accompany each of the memorial services: one on the forty-ninth day and others on the third, fifth, seventh, thirteenth, twenty-fifth, and fiftieth annual anniversaries of the day of death. Someone from the household would make offerings to the grave each seventh day during the first forty-nine days, at which time the priest would come to the house to read sutras to the family and a small group of relatives gathered at an extemporized altar before the *tokonoma*. The same ceremony would be repeated on subsequent memorial anniversaries.

Thus Yoshio, after sixty-four years of life as eldest son, husband, father, and grandfather, became one of the venerated ancestors. His life-name on one side of the ancestral tablet, his death-name on the other, will remain in the cabinet of ancestral tablets. Each memorial anniversary will remind his descendants of their obligation to him as a person; each mid-year *Bon* festival will bring his spirit again to the village to rejoice in his descendants.

TWO AUTOBIOGRAPHICAL ACCOUNTS

To complete this outline of the life of persons in Niiike, autobiographical sketches of their own lives written by two grandmothers are presented below. They touch on subjects discussed earlier but contribute their own intimate, personal reactions. Each was written only after urging by the American researcher made it difficult to refuse. Though introspective writings have an honored place in Japanese literature, it is not easy for proper countrywomen to expose their feelings to public view. Each account complements the other. The first deals mainly with its author's experiences as a mother; the second stresses her working life as a farm wife.

I am fifty-five years old, the housewife of a farmer's household. I was born in 1895 in Ishima-son, near Okayama, the youngest child among one boy and three girls, in a farmer's house.

I was beloved by my parents and sisters and passed a pleasant childhood. In the spring after I turned seven I entered Ishima Primary School with my hair done in a plait tied with a ribbon and wearing a brown *hakama* skirt for the first time. I was by turns full of joy and shyness. At that time school pupils had narrow-sleeved garments with sashes and aprons for everyday wear, and on special days we wore black garments with a crest and long, figured sleeves.

In the winter of my thirteenth year, my father built a new house. I came home from school and found my family busily pounding rice for rice cakes in two mortars, side by side, singing loudly "From the High Mountain!" The next morning carpenters came early and raised a big house with the help of villagers and relatives. They fixed shelves when only the main posts were raised, decorated them handsomely with various masks, wheel fans, and *gohei* [purificatory cut-paper pendants], and beside them they set crates of rice cakes sent in congratulation by relatives. And then everyone [of the family], dressed in haori and *hakama* with family crest, divided into groups to toss the big, square rice cakes down from the four corners and to throw smaller cakes with all their might out and down. People from the village and nearby jostled each other catching these rice cakes. I too climbed up and threw the cakes to my friends down below as hard as I could. It was such fun. I can still see them gathering the cakes up.

Eight years of school life were ordinary, perhaps, but constantly happy. After I finished school I went to a girl's sewing school in Okayama City and studied the art of sewing, and on Sunday I used to study flower arrangement and the tea ceremony with some friends. In these three years before graduating I cherished the dreams that girls have. Then there followed a dreamlike period when I helped with housework at home and learned women's skills. In those days girls liked to wear their hair in either the *momoware* or *shimada* style.

In the spring after I turned twenty, my aunt arranged my engagement, and in October of that year I was married into the Hiramatsu family. At that time a bride used to ride off in a ricksha, her hair done up with combs, hairpins, and a red *kanoko* ornament. These were the days before the revamping of the rice fields [here], and I had a sinking feeling, wondering what sort of place I was being taken to as I was brought [for marriage] farther and farther west from Okayama and over the hills. The day after the wedding my mother-in-law took me to visit the village shrine and to greet our near neighbors. I remember how a man who looked like a shopkeeper said, "Why, this bride has come from near Okayama City!" because at that time when the roads were bad there was quite a difference in dress between Okayama City and here.

The next year, with the prefectural government's assistance, revision of the rice fields was started. There was a continual commotion, involving everyone, young and old, men and women alike, some moving dirt in trucks, others pounding their thousand strokes [on the rocks and dirt]. This took three or four years to finish, as I remember. Even as rustic as these parts are, they are now incomparably more pleasant and easier to farm than in the old days.

At first the new family ways were strange, but I learned to get along in the family and finally became used to the life and felt at home. Three years after my marriage my first daughter Kazuko was born, and everyone came around for congratulations. We had a big feast to celebrate the seventh day [after birth]. On the thirty-first day I dressed the baby in the *ubugi* [baby's kimono] which my family had sent and took her to the shrine to pray for protection that she might be strong and grow up to be a fine girl.

My days were happy as I cared for the baby, seeing her get affection from all the family as she grew up carefree. When she turned three, we held the *himo otoshi* ceremony for her; again, everyone came to congratulate us, and my family sent a set of festival clothes (*haregi*) for her. Our family here also made various things for her, and as I watched her going off to the shrine with her grandmother, wearing her long sleeves and high *pokkuchi-geta* I felt her as lovable as any doll.

When my first daughter was six, my first son was born and all the family were overjoyed to have a boy child—above all, my father-in-law. But just as we were busy preparing for the seventh-day celebration, he caught a slight cold and suddenly died the day before the celebration. We went through the funeral service in deep grief. The following autumn my favorite elder sister passed away, leaving three children behind her. For some time I was so heartbroken over her death that I lost my energy and couldn't go about my work. And then my second daughter was born and then died within sixty days. How bitter and thankless life seemed then.

But from that time on I watched over our single daughter as I would over a tender plant. When she was eight, she entered Kamo Primary School, and I for my part enjoyed helping her with her homework at night. We had an especially severe drought when Kazuko was in the second grade. Then my father-in-law, who never was sick and was as fine as ever in the morning, had a stroke when he went out to weed the rice, fainted, and died just as the doctor arrived. I shall always regret that he died without even a single day's gentle nursing.

My daughter Kazuko was always well and finished her six-year course without any serious illness. She then started to attend the Sōja Girls' High School. She used to put on her uniform and go over the hill daily four kilometers to school with her friends, while I would pray that she would get safely home. Five years passed quickly as an arrow, and after her graduation she went to study dressmaking, and learned how to keep house along with flower arrangement and the tea ceremony. When she was finishing these lessons, my mother-in-law took to her bed and died after half a year of fruitless treatments.

At about this time I went up to Mt. Washiu on the annual outing of the Women's Association. We rode there in sections in eight big busses and spent a pleasant spring day. I have lived always surrounded with mountains, and the view down to the sea from the mountain top is still an unforgettable memory. I wish now sometimes that we could go out and refresh ourselves drinking in the sea air.

When my daughter was twenty-two, we adopted a son [for marriage], with my relatives serving as go-betweens. This fall was in the middle of the war and men were being called up to the colors. Our adopted son was working for a company in Yamaguchi Prefecture, and our daughter also went there. My husband and I were shorthanded and terribly busy at harvest time and worked with might and main from early in the morning till the stars were out above us without time to have a leisurely meal. In the meanwhile we got a pretty grandchild, and I went visiting in Yamaguchi two or three times.

Living in the country, we seldom ride on a train, so I felt the trip to Yamaguchi was very long. I was taken on a tour of such famous places as Miyajima and the Kintai Bridge in Iwakuni City, and the trip to beautiful and picturesque Itsuku-shima shrine by ferryboat is a lifelong memory.

The war news was being reported in each day's newspaper and radio. This was 1945, the year of the air raid on Okayama City, which makes me shiver just to recall it. As my relatives lived near Okayama City, I worried greatly about them. They were all burned out of their houses. I was relieved to think that my own family would be all right, for they lived away from the center part of Okayama City. But they took a direct hit and three children were burned to death, and the family made a narrow escape with no more than the clothing on their backs, and their house was burned right down to the foundation. Their distress is beyond my power to describe. This was one of the worst things in my life.

Two families from Okayama City evacuated to our house here, and at the war's end, my daughter and her husband came home, so that we had a big family all of a sudden and had a truly hard time getting along, since foodstuffs were so short then. In due time, however, the world returned to its senses. My relatives went one by one to build their houses at their old homesites; I have three grandchildren; and all the household is now happily together to try to raise our level of production. Bus service recently has been opened between Okayama and Sōja, so that traveling is much pleasure when there is time to spare in taking the grandchildren with me to Okayama.

Formerly their black hair was as dear to women as their lives, but young girls these days actually go to get a permanent, and, in the city, ballroom dancing has become the rage. Even the social studies class that started in Kamo-son this year has dancing as part of its recreation activities, which is a great change from the past.

In April of this year we were surprised to see a strange car stop here, a thing which never had happened before. At that time I heard Mr. Eyre speaking Japanese. Although I have often seen foreigners in Okayama City, I had never before spoken to one directly and was very impressed at hearing his good Japanese. Since then we have come to expect the visits of these scholars almost every day.

Niiike hamlet, since I came here, has been a peaceful and calm farming village.

However, it was on the night of Constitution Day (May 3), a windy and rainy night, that a thief took advantage of the housewife's absence and broke into the most newly built home in Niiike, seriously wounded the husband, and fled, leaving us peaceable villagers in a state of alarm. Since then most of us have gotten watchdogs, but as the criminal is still at large, he has put us all on edge.

The other day I went to see our grandchildren's athletic meet and saw housewives joining in social dancing and the hundred-meter race, practices which leave me with open-mouthed astonishment as compared with the old days. Up till now, farm housewives would stay at home and be more than busy with cooking and other housework, but now they go out in ever larger numbers. I hope young women of today will bring back new knowledge to improve our living.

I have tried to write about my life just as it happened, uneducated though I am. I shall be very happy if my writing will be of any help.

WRITTEN BY IWASA KIKUNO, BORN IN NIIIKE, WIFE OF SŌICHI, OCTOBER, 1950

I was born on December 1, 1897, and entered Kamo Primary School on April 1, 1905. I finished the six-year course in April, 1911. At that time only the six-year course was compulsory education, and the two-year higher course was added in 1913.

As my father's health was not very good, I started helping him with farming as soon as I finished my six-year course. In my spare time, I studied Japanese dressmaking. When I was about eighteen, farmers were wearing kimonos with sleeves. They worked with their sleeve ends tucked into a shoulder-harness belt [tasuki], shielded the back of their hands with handguards [tezashi], and wore leggings.

Formerly we had to weed fields bit by bit with a field hoe in summer. Looking back now, I can hardly believe how hard we worked then.

In growing wheat, we had to plow two or three times before sowing the seed. We would then cultivate, weed, and cut the wheat, harvesting it ear by ear and then threshing it on the "thousand tooth" and drying it on rice-straw mats. When thoroughly dried, the ears were beaten with the flail, sieved, winnowed in the winnower, and put into straw bags.

In rice-growing, harvest time is in November. The ears were removed on the "thousand tooth," spread out, about nine shō per straw mat, dried for four days, then hulled in a pottery mortar. Only about three hyō (six bushels) could be hulled at once. We usually worked till about 11:00 at night. We threshed by daylight and hulled at night. At that time it used to take more than forty days to finish the round of harvesting, hulling, and wheat-planting.

I was married in April, 1916, when I was twenty years old and my husband was twenty-four. On March 12, 1917, my first son Masayoshi was born; my second son Kiyoshi was born on October 3, 1919; my first daughter Yukiko on January 1, 1923; my third son Takeshi on March 12, 1926. I had four children. But my first son Masayoshi fell sick and died when he was six. I have never felt deeper grief. For a while afterward I did not work, I grew weak, and took no joy in anything. But after four or five years, I more or less forgot my dead baby.

My third daughter Yukiko had been born in the meantime, and I finally got too busy to think of my dead child. I really feel the world has no sorrow more terrible than the death of one's own child.

There were no electric lights at that time. It was about in 1924 that we got electricity for the first time, and life began to be more convenient. Even if we got home after dark, the rooms were bright enough to work in, whereas when we had no electricity, we had to put up with it and go to bed in the dark. So the world changes.

Farming tools have changed, too, in these twenty years. For instance we now have weeders, motors, threshers, irrigation pumps, rice-cleaning machines, straw-rope machines, and so on. Farming has become easier than before. As against the old days, I think particularly of weeders, threshing machines, and hulling machines. But of things that have not changed as culture has advanced, I think of rice-planting, where no machine can yet be used. We transplant rice by hand. But wheat-planting has been so changed that I can't imagine there is much room for more improvement.

The thirty-eight years from when I was sixteen to my present age of fifty-three are like a dream. There has been a terrific rise in prices since prewar days, up to one hundred times, they say, and some things have gone as much as two hundred times higher.

What gives farmers the most trouble is taxes, and second is the high price of clothes. Rice prices are low, but fertilizer costs are high. We work from early in the morning till late at night, but if we forget to pay attention for a moment when our hands are full, we end up in the red. So the world changes.

On another subject my son Kiyoshi, when he was twenty, passed the physical examination for conscription and entered the First Infantry Regiment in the Imperial Guard in Tokyo on January 10, 1940. This was the first time my boy had been away from home, and I worried about him. I wondered how he was when it got cold. While he was away, I arranged for my daughter Yukiko to be married. A year later my husband passed the conscription physical examination and entered the Fukuyama Regiment. Then the Pacific War began and I worried all the more. And then my third son Takeshi went into the Navy. And I worried so terribly about my boys that I couldn't get to work.

But while I was worrying, the war ended. On August 19, 1945, Kiyoshi came home, right after the armistice. And then my daughter's husband returned safely; and Takeshi got back on October 20.

I was no end relieved to see both boys home.

Soon after their return we got a bride for my first son and planned to set up a branch family for Takeshi, the third son, and built a new house on October 11, 1949. On December 26, 1949, he got married, and I was much relieved to have him set up in his own house, on February 11. I felt then that my job was finished.

On May 3, 1950, he was sleeping alone, when somebody stole into his house and seriously wounded him in the head. At that time you, Dr. Beardsley, took him to the Tsuda Surgery in Okayama University Medical College. Really thanks to you, he got well after a twenty-one-day treatment in the hospital.

12. The Community AND LOCAL GOVERNMENT

It is in some ways misleading to use the term "government" with respect to a rural community like Niiike. To a Westerner, "government" conjures up associations with constituted authority, the rule of law, and similar formal institutions. Government in this sense does, of course, exist in Japan but primarily at the village, prefectural, and national levels. In the buraku the sphere of formal legal relationships is to a large extent left behind. One enters a world where considerations of law, though present and felt, are remote, partial, or tangential to much of the business of daily community life. Again, the intimate reciprocal political relationships among the buraku, ōaza, and village pose a further problem. Any attempt to describe the governmental structure and activities of the buraku as an isolated unit would be inexcusably artificial and frequently unintelligible. Some preliminary understanding of government at the ōaza and village levels and its relations to the buraku is necessary.

BACKGROUND AND LEGAL STRUCTURE

Originally the individual buraku was in both social and legal senses the elemental community of rural Japan, known as the mura or village. By the Tokugawa period, however, gradual and piecemeal processes of growth, division, and combination into larger units had occurred until the mura came to be composed of a number of buraku. The ōaza of Japan after the Meiji Restoration are frequently identical with these Tokugawa mura. The Law on the Organization of Cities, Towns, and Villages of 1888 usually amalgamated several of these ōaza to constitute the present villages. During this process, the buraku, although continuing as the elemental *social* unit of rural Japan above the household level, moved progressively farther and farther from its original status as the elemental *legal* unit of rural Japan. In Tokugawa times, it was merely a sublegal component of the then-village, the present ōaza. After 1889 the buraku

349

became, technically speaking, an extralegal subunit of the fundamental unit of rural government, the modern village.

This remoteness from any legal personality becomes even clearer when one places the buraku in the total context of local government in Japan. According to the present law the major civil divisions of Japan immediately subordinate to the national government are the prefectures, variously known in Japanese as *to, dō, fu,* or *ken.* Regardless of name, all now have basically equivalent powers. These prefectures are subdivided geographically into cities *(shi),* towns *(chō* or *machi),* and villages *(son* or *mura).* The distinction among these is primarily one of population. All are legal entities, and within any one prefecture the sum of their areas equals the total area of that prefecture. Japan lacks the distinction between incorporated and unincorporated areas with which we are familiar. Consequently, Japanese cities, towns, and villages differ from our own comparably named settlements mainly in the sense that they are not compactly or contiguously built-up areas. This is, of course, less true of towns and cities than of villages, but, even so, cities are likely to include extensive tracts of distinctly rural and agricultural land, and towns are certain to. These units—prefectures, cities, towns, and villages—constitute the ordinary major and minor civil divisions of contemporary Japan. There was formerly a further unit, known as a *gun,* intermediate between towns and villages, on the one hand, and prefectures, on the other. Though stripped of its legal personality in 1923, the *gun* continues to exist in popular speech and usage and to serve a variety of administrative and statistical purposes.

The village is thus the lowest regular legal unit of public organization in Japan. According to the Local Autonomy Law of 1947, its formal powers include extensive police jurisdiction; the preservation of the safety, health, and welfare of inhabitants; the construction and maintenance of roads, bridges, canals, and irrigation systems; the establishment and management of public utilities plants, schools, libraries, museums, hospitals, jails, etc.; extensive taxing powers; investigative authority; and a variety of other powers. This list seems to indicate a broad sphere of local autonomy, but, in practice, the extent of the autonomous powers wielded by any village is drastically curtailed by a variety of legal, traditional, and political factors.

Below the village one encounters in rural areas the even smaller units of *ōaza* and *aza* or *koaza.* These now have no legal personality but are essentially units for the registry of landownership and title, somewhat comparable to our surveyors' townships and sections. As has already been indicated, however, in the speech, attitudes, and traditions of the farmer the ōaza possess considerably more importance than is indicated by their legal status. The still smaller units known variously as *aza* or *koaza* never have enjoyed a comparable social importance and today serve purely as units for the convenient registry of land titles and boundaries.

Against this background the remoteness of the buraku from the sphere of law and formal political structure begins to become apparent. Since the Restoration, buraku have had no legal identity; they are not what the Japanese technically call "public bodies." In fact, from 1947 to 1952 they were positively illegal. This requires a bit of explanation. Between 1889 and 1937 the rural buraku had been largely ignored in terms of law and formal political organization. After the China Incident, however, the national government began to tighten its controls over economic and social life at all levels. In the buraku this trend first manifested itself in the field of agriculture with the establishment of the *nōka kumiai* ("associations of agricultural households") and later of the *nōji jikō kumiai* ("associations for the furtherance of agricultural affairs"). By 1940 these had expanded into a net of so-called *burakukai* (literally, "buraku meetings" or "buraku assemblies") organized in all the buraku of Japan. Each of these possessed a *burakuchō*, or leader, and functioned as an important unit in Japan's wartime crop-requisitioning, rationing, financial, and morale-building programs. In the opinion of the Occupation authorities, they also had served as a vicious, exploitative, national intelligence system and a tyrannical means of enforcing collective responsibility for, and control over, the activities of individual citizens. It seems probable that there is considerably more truth to such accusations when they are leveled against the block associations (*tonarigumi*), the wartime urban equivalent of the *burakukai*. But the Occupation made no such distinction, and in 1947 both the *burakukai* and the block associations were made illegal and continued so until the general recision of the so-called Potsdam Ordinances in 1952. However, this five-year interdiction of *burakukai* had little effect on actual practice in rural Japan. They continued to exist, to elect or otherwise to choose certain buraku officials, and to perform an astonishing variety of collective functions. Such a pattern of association was found too useful and convenient by both buraku inhabitants and local government officials to be readily displaced, although the *burakukai*'s identity was usually disguised by the adoption of misleading new names.

BURAKU ORGANIZATION AND FUNCTIONS

The organizational pattern of buraku varies considerably from place to place in terms of officials, the manner of their selection, frequency of assembly meetings, and so forth. But one factor remains constant and of fundamental importance: the prime constituent element of all buraku is the household; individuals have only a secondary significance. Buraku may or may not represent an extended family (in practice it is difficult to ascertain the older relationships because farmers had no surnames prior to the Restoration), but, in either case, they are usually organized into households composed of members of two or three lineally related generations. In Niiike there are twenty-four such households which serve as basic units of representation within the buraku.

The precise forms of community organization reared upon this foundation of households in Niiike has varied over the years. Written evidence is almost entirely lacking at this level, but the most reliable informants agree that prior to 1934 the only buraku-wide organization with any continuing responsibility for making decisions on matters of community interest was a monthly religious meeting known as *kanki* (see pp. 248-51). At this time all members of the buraku were adherents of the Nichiren sect of Buddhism, and they were in the habit of meeting regularly on the twelfth of each month (by the lunar calendar). These meetings rotated on a monthly basis from house to house within the buraku. Although they were essentially religious gatherings, it was customary at the conclusion of the prayers and ceremonies to bring up for consideration and decision all matters of community interest. The eldest member present would initiate these discussions. Decisions were taken by consensus, and it seems that the matters considered covered much the same range of subjects of local interest as is true today, with the exception of such wartime and postwar phenomena as rationing and crop requisitions. No more formal organization of the group was felt to be necessary or desirable.

In 1934 an event occurred which gradually led to the splitting-off of these deliberative functions of the *kanki* and the institution of more specialized and systematic provision for making community decisions. Since the Meiji era there had been officially sponsored agricultural associations known as *nōgyōkai* scattered throughout rural Japan and operating through the village offices. This system was revised in 1934 and its organization extended to the buraku level. So-called *nōka kumiai* ("associations of agricultural households") were established in all buraku, and these were supposed to function under the direction of the town and village *nōgyōkai*. The general objectives of these *nōka kumiai* were vaguely stated to be the improvement of agricultural conditions, the rationalization of the economy, and the general advancement of rural civilization. Actually it seems doubtful that these new associations accomplished very much, but they were responsible for the introduction into Niiike and other buraku of a more formal type of intra-buraku organization. There seems also to be a feeling that they were instrumental in heightening the spirit of solidarity and co-operation within the buraku and in facilitating its co-operative purchasing arrangements. In 1940, with the international situation far more taut, the *nōka kumiai* were renamed *nōji jikō kumiai* ("associations for the furtherance of agricultural affairs"), and their responsibilities were broadened to include a role in the new national crop-requisitioning program. This increased both the activities and importance of these buraku organizations.

With the introduction of the *nōka kumiai* in 1934 the older religious meetings known as *kanki* gradually came to share some of their community decision-making powers. Henceforth the agricultural association became a second forum within which decisions of general import were taken, whether they concerned agricultural matters or not. At first the *nōka kumiai* did not meet regularly and the *kanki* meetings continued to discuss common problems, but after 1940, with the increase of buraku responsibilities attendant on the crop-requisitioning program, the need for special buraku meetings became more frequent and the *kanki* lost more of its deliberative functions. Today, although it continues to provide a regular monthly forum for the discussion of community affairs, the *kanki* increasingly shares this function with a more specifically political gathering. Technically this should be known as a *burakukai*, but actually in Niiike this term is seldom used. Such a buraku assembly is generally referred to as the *kumiai* ("association"), the *shūkai* ("assembly"), or more often the *jōkai* (literally the "regular" or "ordinary" meeting). Meetings are irregular and highly informal, occurring in Niiike about once a month.[1] They are held whenever there is enough collective business to necessitate a gathering. They are almost invariably held at night so as to interfere as little as possible with working schedules and meet normally in the *kōkaidō* or buraku meeting hall. Thus, with the regular *kanki* meetings, the inhabitants of Niiike usually have two occasions per month for the collective discussion of community affairs.

Membership in the *burakukai* is based on household units, and each family has a single vote in decisions on buraku business. In theory each household should be represented by its head, but frequently the head does not care to attend meetings (they are generally considered very dull), and some other member of the family—a son, wife, or daughter—goes in his stead. Membership tends to be stable. The very small size of Japanese farms, especially since the postwar land reform, makes it almost impos-

---

[1] Such meetings seem to be somewhat more frequent in Niiike than in many buraku of the Okayama area. Elsewhere they may be held as seldom as once a year, interim business being conducted by an informal system of household-to-household liaison.

sible to divide the average existing farm and still retain a viable economic unit. Branch households may be created by families possessing above-average landholdings, thus slightly increasing the total number of households in a buraku. But the number of farms and farm households tends to remain constant, though there are shifts among the merchant and non-farmer populace. The general rule is that all households in a buraku are members of the buraku association. Membership is no longer compulsory, but such is the cohesiveness of rural society that it is very unusual to find families that do not participate in the conduct of collective business.

The crude records kept by the *kumiai* in Niiike indicate that since 1937 four new households have joined and three have resigned from the association. The additions were attributable to the return of former residents from the cities in the difficult years immediately following the war or to the establishment of new branch houses. Two of the resignations were due to households moving out of the buraku. The third resignation was the interesting and unusual case of Hiramatsu Hideo's voluntary withdrawal from the association as a result of prolonged and bitter quarrels over the proper fertility assessment of a tiny plot of rice paddy (see pp. 257–58). The family had been rather unsocial to begin with, and their new status apparently made little difference in terms of casual contacts with their neighbors. They continued to participate at least in collective road-maintenance work. In general, there seemed to be grounds for believing that both sides to this quarrel were somewhat embarrassed and unhappy about so overt an instance of disharmony within the community and that the self-isolated household would eventually be taken back into the fold.

Buraku assemblies discuss and decide a large variety of matters of common concern. The manner in which they arrive at these decisions is quite different from that to which we are accustomed in the West. The traditional means of taking group decisions in Japan is by the joint techniques of recommendation (*suisen*) and consensus. In rural areas this practice still flourishes, as indeed it does at every level including the national. The chairman or presiding member will announce some item for consideration. Following a certain (and not infrequently exhaustive) amount of discussion, one of two things will happen. Either the chair, without a vote and often without any overt statement of individual stands on the part of the other participants as far as an outsider can see, will announce the consensus of the group; or some member will make a positive recommendation of a course to be followed and the chair will then announce the adoption of that recommendation in the absence of objection. Seldom does anyone proclaim his disagreement with such an announced consensus, although some members may, in fact, dissent strongly from it.

Japanese concepts of propriety place a heavy premium on the appearance of unanimous conformity, and it would be considered radical and improper, particularly in rural areas, to oppose openly a publicly declared course of action. In a personal sense, it would raise immediately the question of the "face" of the individual whose recommendation was challenged; in a larger sense, it would publicly acknowledge the existence of a serious rift in the solidarity of a group which attaches extraordinary importance to the outward preservation of a common, harmonious, and undifferentiated front. It is obvious that neither of the above processes has much in common with the use of the open or secret ballot in the West. Both place a premium on conformity; they weight meetings and decisions in favor of conservative and accepted courses of action; they give considerable power to the person presiding, not so much as an individual, but as an agent of a normally conservative community; and they require an open, positive, and extraordinarily courageous stand by anyone who would oppose the recommended decision.

The Japanese are familiar with occidental voting techniques and use them in public elections, in the national Diet, and in a few other contexts. In many situations, however, they seem to prefer the older and more familiar methods of recommendation and consensus. These methods can, of course, be used for the "railroading" of decisions, but more frequently they are used in such a manner as to produce endless indirect discussion which gradually clarifies the areas of agreement and disagreement and ultimately suggests an acceptable compromise. As a matter of fact, in Niiike it is difficult to conceive of a situation where this system of decision-making could long ignore or ride roughshod over any significant segment of minority opinion. But the securing of such a consensus by no means guarantees the loyal support of all participants for the decision taken. The conflict is often simply removed from the floor of the meeting to less conspicuous areas, where bitter, secret opposition and sabotage are quite possible.

To what matters does the buraku assembly apply these techniques of decision? What are its functions? In a formal sense they are very simple and of narrowly local significance. Their most important function is the selection of certain buraku officers, a headman and a vice-headman. This selection is usually made by secret ballot, the only instance of such voting encountered at the buraku level. They also discuss and make recommendations or reach decisions on such matters as requests for the reassessment of the productivity index of land owned by members; minor reclamation projects; the collective purchase of prize goods made available by the government as a reward for the fulfilment of crop quotas; the time to carry out the collective spring housecleaning; the date and arrangements for certain religious or traditional holidays; the holding of collective entertainments such as the recitals of old tales known as *naniwabushi;* and a variety of other matters of local concern. Niiike's assembly has discussed all these matters at one time or another. A similar sampling for other buraku assemblies shows a wide variety of subjects depending on the circumstances and customs of the particular buraku. Usually, however, buraku assemblies meet in order to learn from their headman or other officials about programs when the village office either wants to request their action or co-operation or simply wants to have them informed. The matters involved are almost always prosaic and routine but are still of considerable practical consequence.

Most of Niiike's collective business is transacted by its officers, particularly by its headman. This office seems to have existed in a formal elective sense only since 1934. The term of office, at first two years, was reduced to a single year as the duties became more numerous and time-consuming. During this period Niiike has had eleven different headmen. One individual, however, has served on five different occasions for a total of approximately eight and a half years.

Although the post of headman is an honor and a mark of general confidence, it is generally assumed with real reluctance. It takes time which many farmers can ill afford to give, and it obliges its occupant to initiate action or make public recommendations that are certain to incur the ill will of at least some members of the buraku. By our notions, however, the headman's responsibilities are not onerous. He appoints for limited terms certain other buraku officials, such as a treasurer, a purchasing agent, field guards, or irrigation-system tenders. He presides at meetings of the buraku assembly. He is responsible for planning and making recommendations in respect to certain aspects of the crop-requisitioning program. He represents the buraku in a ceremonial or collective capacity on the few occasions when such services are necessary. He formally notifies the people of births, deaths, and accidents within the community and may take the lead in any collective actions made necessary by these events. But by far his most important and time-consuming function is liaison with the village office. One of the principal reasons the national government established the buraku on a legal basis from 1940 to 1945 was the administrative utility of having in every community a definite headman responsible for communicating to the people information about all relevant official programs. Village and town mayors and officers still find him useful for the same purpose, especially in relation to the continual complexities and troubles of the tax, rationing, and crop-requisitioning systems. Consequently, the headman must frequently walk or bicycle to the village office to listen to the explanation of new regulations or programs and then return and explain these to the families of the buraku.

Under present circumstances, it is highly incorrect to regard these headmen as petty tyrants or corrupt and grasping bosses. In the first place, they have practically no formal authority. In the second place, the collective decisions and actions of buraku, while they may be initiated by the headmen, are usually the product of extensive group discussion and some kind of consensus. Headmen usually function as group representatives and liaison officers. Their formal leadership functions are negligible.

The roles of the remaining buraku officers do not require extended comment. Niiike also has a vice-headman (*fuku-kumiaichō*) who plays a significant part only in the absence or illness of the headman, and whose office is elective for the same term. The treasurer (*kaikeikakari*) is appointed by the headman. He collects, two or three times a year, the small payments made by every household to defray the buraku's expenses and receives and records the contributions which families traditionally make on such felicitous occasions as marriages or the birth of a son. There are also several buraku purchasing agents (*kohankakari*), appointed by the headman and responsible for obtaining rationed or scarce incentive or prize goods made available by the government to buraku that fulfil their crop-delivery quotas and for several other matters in connection with the crop-requisitioning system. Finally, there are appointed "officials" responsible for operating and maintaining the local irrigation facilities and for the inspection of roads, paths, and bridges. This completes the roster of buraku "officials" who might be said to possess community or, in a loose sense, governmental functions.

Such a brief description is very likely to convey an impression of greater formality and artificiality than the homely facts of Niiike's community organization actually justify. The people themselves for the most part do not regard this as "government." Its essential functions have developed naturally over the centuries in response to the elementary demands of group living in an agricultural society. The basic needs for some measure of collective planning and activity with respect to local irrigation facilities and roads, liaison with the village or other higher political agencies, agricultural work schedules, community religious observances, holidays, and recreation have existed as long as Niiike. The buraku's people chose to cope with these fairly simple needs through a type of highly informal co-operation which operated effectively enough even through the strenuous years of Japan's modernization and early industrialization. It was only the dawn of the somewhat ineffectual wartime attempts at making totalitarian the national structure of Japan which finally dragged the buraku, Niiike included, into the arena of more formal and extensive governmental activity. The justification for this innovation imposed from above was found in the national rationing and crop-requisitioning programs, the spiritual mobilization campaigns, and the exigencies of wartime and postwar public finance.

As far as the people of Niiike are concerned, they seem to have responded to these new involvements with the loyalty expected of Japanese but also with considerable suspicion and dismay. They did as their political superiors bade them and as a consequence, from 1934 on, the organization of community "government" gradually became more explicit and formalized. Fundamentally, however, the buraku maintained to a surprising degree its traditional cohesiveness and in-group attitudes toward external contacts and tended to meet its complex new responsibilities by much the same techniques of group discussion and consensus that had prevailed for centuries. The overlay of elective headmen and appointive treasurers, purchasing agents, and so on was more an embellishment than a replacement of the older system. In an internal sense it does not indicate any signficant incursion of law, formal organization, or legally coercive relationships into the buraku.

VILLAGE ORGANIZATION AND FUNCTIONS

Niiike is merely one of the thirty communities or buraku which compose the village of Kamo. It is intimately linked to the village in such matters as local finance, social and economic services, justice, political behavior, and leadership. These subjects cannot be discussed intelligibly with reference to Niiike alone. They must be set against the larger backdrop of the village scene.

For this, we must examine the village as a transitional unit of organization occupying a point midway between the traditional world of the buraku and the legally oriented world of formal politics and government. It partakes of the characteristics of both but is fully identified with neiher, although it is undoubtedly drifting more and more within the orbit of the latter. Owing to its artificial and relatively recent origins and the fact that it is necessarily closely associated with and responsive to many vexatious, extralocal, and hence suspicious influences, the village does not command the unrelieved loyalty and trust of its inhabitants. It is commonly regarded with reserve and some apprehension. On the other hand, as the most localized agency of modern government it has become progressively more intimately involved in a variety of activities that seriously affect the well-being and daily fortunes of the inhabitants, so much so that its organization and activities cannot be ignored or avoided. The average inhabitant of Niiike and his fellows in other buraku therefore regard the village as an established and important, if not wholly trustworthy or welcome, part of their universe. It is a social unit in which they feel personally and collectively involved, with a degree of reality and continuity far different from what they feel toward the prefecture or the nation. This attitude has probably been intensified by postwar economic and political programs at the local level.

As the village is a formal unit of government, the major patterns of village organization in post-constitutional Japan have always been prescribed by law. Structurally speaking, few major changes were made in the system of village government between 1888 and 1946. Throughout this period and down to the present, village administration revolved about the mayor (*sonchō*), vice-mayor (*joyaku*), and the village assembly (*sonkai* before 1947 and *songikai* since), plus a varying staff of subordinate functionaries. Prior to the Occupation-imposed reforms, however, the village lacked any significant autonomous powers. It was merely the last link in a chain of command running from the village through the prefectural governor to the all-powerful national ministries, particularly the Home Ministry, in Tokyo. In practice, however, throughout most of the period preceding the China Incident the impact of such drastic centralization seems to have been greatly modified by the quieter nature of the times and the more passive and less pervasive characteristics of politics and administration. Under normal circumstances the village governmental scene was quiet and surprisingly free from overt external intervention, so long as the local authorities performed satisfactorily the routine tasks imposed upon them by the agencies of national government.

National intervention became much more pronounced during the mid-1930's, as a function of what later came to be called the National Mobilization Movement, aimed at rationalizing and tightening up the entire apparatus of governmental control. At the village level this trend was felt particularly in the economic and morale-building spheres. Both involved new and expanded functions for village administrative authorities and connoted more extensive and effective intervention and supervision from higher levels of government than had normally been common. The economic and social impacts of the Second World War intensified these developments, while the stresses and shortages of the subsequent defeat and the Occupation increased the scope and penetration of nationally administered economic programs involving village and buraku participation. The villages of Japan have thus not yet seen any return to what many of their middle-aged and older inhabitants still nostalgically regarded as the quiet normalcy of the years of Taishō and early Shōwa.

The hectic years of would-be Japanese totalitarianism were followed by the even more frenetic years of Allied Occupation and "democratic" innovation. Though utterly different in conception and aim, these latter years resembled the earlier "totalitarian" period in the breadth and depth of their impact on all levels of Japanese government and society. The economic stringencies of the war period and the attendant need for broad rationing and requisitioning programs, ultimately administered at the village level, was if anything more severe in postwar days. The spiritual and social fabric of village life was torn and strained by the multiple shocks of defeat and foreign military occupation. Added to all this, there now came the Local Autonomy Law with its well-intentioned but somewhat naïve attempt to decentralize political authority and thereby, its authors hoped, to consolidate and strengthen the grip of the new "democratic" institutions on a bemused and dubious Japan.

This law, formally enacted in April, 1947, and still valid in large part, replaced the extreme centralism and authoritarianism of the prewar Japanese law with elaborate legal provisions for as thoroughgoing a system of local autonomy as is readily imaginable outside a federal or confederate state. Wherever possible, technical authority and responsibility were transferred from the national ministries in Tokyo to the cities, towns, and villages, leaving to the national government and the prefectures only those functions held to be necessarily supralocal in nature. The whole system reflects a typically American distrust of remote authority. In practice, however, the degree of local autonomy conferred by this law was so drastically curtailed by a variety of legal, traditional, and political factors that Japan continued to have, in fact, a moderately centralized government.

The village governments established by the Local Autonomy Law may best be described as miniature semiparliamentary systems, revolving primarily about the offices and interrelationships of a village assembly and a mayor. Both mayor and assembly members are elected by universal adult suffrage for four-year terms. This represents a departure from the prewar appointive system whereby the mayor was nominated and in effect chosen by the village assembly, although technically the appointment was made by the prefectural governor. While both the mayor and the assembly are directly elected by the people, their offices are interdependent in a parliamentary sense. The mayor has the power of dissolution, and assemblies can interpellate and vote lack of confidence with the usual results. The complement of village authority is filled out by a considerable number of officials, boards, and commissions, chosen in different ways for different terms and invested with a great variety of authority.

The village assembly of Kamo is now composed of sixteen members, an increase of four over the pre-1947 twelve. Although technically elected at large from the entire village, actually, since all members owe their seats to the support of one or more specific buraku, there is a system of informal but quite rigid election constituencies within the village. Dissolutions are uncommon, and members usually serve their full four-year term. They are eligible for re-election, and prior to 1947 it was considered normal for the same individuals to be more or less continuously re-elected. So far it is difficult to say to what extent this practice will be duplicated in the more unsettled and fluid conditions of the present. Of the sixteen members of the Kamo assembly in 1954 one was serving a fourth term and eight others were serving their second. Small annual salaries and expense allowances attach to membership. All members are farmers and male, although more or less sincere but vain efforts were made to induce one or more women to run in the 1947 election.

The Kamo assembly, obliged by law to meet at least four times a year, actually has been meeting some ten to thirteen times. Normal sessions are open to the public, although no unofficial visitors had been known to attend prior to visits by members of the Michigan field team. The meetings are presided over by a chairman elected by the members from their own number, and minutes are kept by two secretaries. The atmosphere is friendly and informal, and discussion on the more important items is likely to be detailed and prolonged. The mayor is present and takes a leading part in the presentation and explanation of practically all items on the agenda. He does not vote. Decisions, which are supposed to be taken by majority vote, are actually arrived at by "negative consensus," the characteristically Japanese process described above in connection with the buraku assembly.

The law gives village assemblies very considerable powers. They debate, adopt, modify, or rescind all village ordinances and regulations; they approve all items in both the ordinary and extraordinary village budgets; they authorize any borrowing of funds; they review and approve the audit of all village expenditures; they consent to the mayor's appointments to designated official positions; they create a variety of committees; and, through their investigatory and budgetary powers, they may exercise a sort of general, after-the-fact supervisory influence over practically all aspects of village government and administration. It would be seriously misleading, however, to take such statutory prescriptions of the Kamo assembly's authority at face value. In practice, the assembly does, in any significant sense, very few of the things the law says it is supposed to do.

Legally speaking, the assembly's primary responsibility is the enactment of village ordinances (*sonjōrei*) and regulations (*sonkisoku*). Actually it has little to do with such matters. Most village ordinances and regulations are originally drafted as model legislation by the Local Government Section of the General Affairs Department of the prefectural government. These drafts are then passed on to the village mayors who, with or without the assistance of their staffs, examine them, make minor adaptations to local circumstances, and then submit them to the assembly for consideration and formal enactment. All of Kamo's ordinances and regulations have originated in this manner, and all have been adopted without change by the assembly.

A second major function of village assemblies is the approval and enactment of the budget. In point of legislative time consumed, this usually bulks larger than any other assembly activity. Again, however, the assembly plays a largely passive role. Budgets are drawn up by the vice-mayor and first secretary of the village office under the policy supervision of the mayor. This draft budget (as well as the four or five supplementary budgets which have become common) is submitted to the assembly for its approval. Even in a small village like Kamo it is a technical and involved document, about which the mayor knows far more than the average assemblyman. The budget is usually presented and explained orally, section by section, by the mayor, who answers questions and explains the background and necessity of particular items as he goes along. In Kamo the assembly members are certain to ask a great many questions; one session attended by the writers took all of three legislative days. Considering this volume of questioning and the heat occasionally developed, the amazing thing about these budget sessions is the fact that almost invariably the budget is then approved without change.

In these important respects, as well as most others, the role of the assembly is distinctly subordinate to that of the mayor. In Kamo at least, open opposition to his projects or desires is relatively rare. Occasionally, however, problems provoking serious controversy have come up, and the assembly or some of its members have asserted their position against that of the mayor, though apparently with considerable reluctance. There have been several issues of this sort during the past few years. Two of the most serious have been specifically financial in nature, one concerning the assembly's reluctance to approve added levies on their constituents to pay Kamo's share of improvements on a co-operative irrigation system which would be of substantial benefit only to the other villages concerned, the other involving similar reservations in respect to the mounting expenses of a village drainage project. Also controversial has been the issue of where to locate a projected village meeting and recreation hall. On this sort of question the normal passive solidarity of the assembly is quite likely to break down, and its individual members play a relatively active and assertive part. Even then, however, the competition involved is probably more among individual members and groups of the assembly, each desiring to locate the new institution in or near his particular buraku, than it is between assembly and mayor. In most normal contexts it seems accurate to say that the mayor tends to dominate the determination of Kamo's finances in general, and the budget in particular, while the assembly usually plays a quite passive and ineffectual role.

If, then, Kamo's village assembly does not legislate and usually does not exercise significant financial authority, what does it do in its four mandatory and several extraordinary sessions during the year? In general the answer may be summed up in two phrases—it discusses and it approves. The fact that it receives all its ordinances and regulations ready-made from the prefectural government via the mayor and accepts these without substantial change in no wise inhibits discussion of this legislation. Furthermore, this discussion is by no means uncritical or abbreviated. The particular ordinance under consideration is dissected with care, and certain portions of it may be forthrightly questioned. In the end, however, the draft ordinance will almost certainly be enacted. A good deal of time is also consumed by similar discussion of the items in the annual budget and several supplementary budgets. Beyond this there are a number of appointments to commissions and committees which fall in whole or part within the assembly's sphere of responsibility, transfers of funds within budget titles to be approved, local tax matters to be discussed, and questions to be settled concerning the place of deposit of village funds or whether or not to borrow money to meet short- or long-term village needs. In most of these cases, however (with the possible exception of some appointments), the assembly tends to ratify proposals made to it by the mayor.

This does not mean that the assembly's activities are so much waste motion. Appearances notwithstanding, local political decisions in Japan are seldom arbitrary or unilateral; the assembly really contributes more to the substance of most decisions than is apparent from the above-described procedures. It serves as a public symbol of community participation in the political process, a service not to be minimized in a society which so values both the appearance and the fact of solidarity in public action. The assembly also acts as a means of publicizing and focusing popular attention on items of political interest or importance. In Kamo it does this not through any group action or formal publicity but through the informal contacts of its individual members with their constituents. Interaction at this level is an important way of formulating public and legislative opinion within the village. Finally and perhaps most important of all, discussions in the Kamo assembly serve as a guide to administration.

There is a canny recognition shared by both mayor and assemblymen that it is the manner in which a law or ordinance is administered rather than its formal contents that really counts. One not infrequently gains the impression that the assembly is enacting a measure in the precise form in which it has been received largely to placate the offices of the prefectural or national government which originated it and, in a sense, to protect the position and "face" of their mayor, who must work and get along with these extra-village authorities. Thus they adopt the measure without change, but the assembly's discussion serves as a guide to the mayor in its administration. The same is often true of items which the mayor himself originates, such as the budget. The assembly indirectly but effectively demarcates the areas in which it desires or will tolerate effective administration of the letter of the law vis-à-vis those where it would prefer partial or merely ritualistic enforcement. Examples of this are difficult for the outsider to detect, but the authors were able to isolate a number and strongly suspect the existence of many more. For instance, many of the village committees mentioned below (see p. 371) were established essentially to placate the prefectural government and have done little or nothing since. Again, the prefecturally and nationally sponsored regulations governing the pay and allowances of village staff members are actually observed only to the extent that suits local convenience and standards. Where mayoral-assembly relations are concerned, the assembly has on a number of occasions enacted measures backed by the mayor only after making clear their disapproval of particular portions thereof and their understanding that the mayor would not activate these, at least without coming back again to the assembly for special approval before doing so.

The ostensibly formalistic activities of the Kamo assembly are thus neither so shallow nor so meaningless as superficial observations might indicate. As a matter of fact, in general, it does not seem too far-fetched to suggest that few additional claims can be made for the actual political functions of many contemporary legislative bodies. In these days of growing executive initiative, most of the world's legislatures at all levels find themselves performing less and less the classic functions of a legislative body. But any analogy with occidental experience breaks down on the point that Far Eastern legislatures have never performed what the West regards as classic legislative functions. This variation in tradition makes for an important difference in practice.

The village office carrying the highest prestige is that of mayor. There is not the slightest doubt on this score in the minds of the villagers, although most of them seem to believe that in general the quality of their mayors has deteriorated since the Occupation-sponsored reform of local government. Kamo has had only ten mayors since its establishment as a village in 1889, of whom six have served more than one four-year term. One, the venerable Tada Kōshirō, served continuously from 1893 to 1913. Practically all occupants of the post prior to 1947 held it on an honorary basis, drawing no salary, and their actual administrative responsibilities appear to have been nominal. The office was habitually accorded to persons of outstanding local families, of notable character, or of great wealth. Such qualifications apparently appealed to the villagers, since one frequently hears disparaging comparisons between the salaried, civil-servant type of occupant of the office in postreform days and their more traditional and illustrious predecessors. Under the old system the actual functions of the office were usually performed by the vice-mayor, who was normally a professional bureaucrat. Since 1947 Kamo has had two mayors, one a former vice-mayor, the other principal of the local elementary school at the time of his election. Both were popularly elected, the former without opposition, the latter only after a three-way contest with his predecessor and another local notable.

The office of mayor is now a full-time position, carrying with it, in 1954, the modest base salary of ¥20,500 per month. As official positions go in Japan, the job seems to be fairly arduous. It demands a combination of character (which includes family reputation) and what we would call personality, with a broad variety of professional talents. The average villager wants a man of maturity and dignity, possessed of as many of the traditional Japanese virtues as possible. High among these he ranks sincerity (*makoto*), politeness, and a humane interest in the problems of his fellows. The extent to which a superior "character" offsets in the public mind any number of professional failings or incompetencies is one of the more remarkable aspects of Japanese politics. Beyond this, present-day mayors play a leading role in the guidance of village government, which, while not inordinately complex or technical by modern standards, requires extensive knowledge. In a village like Kamo, the mayor should, for example, have a thorough practical knowledge of the problems of farming and irrigation; he should have a fair amount of training and ability in the field of local public finance, since fiscal problems bulk very large in his work; he should also be as familiar as possible with the labyrinthine technicalities of Japanese public administration at the local level. Such knowledge was not necessary in the older and quieter days when the vice-mayor did most of the work. As a consequence, one not infrequently finds that mayors at the village level now ascend through the subordinate ranks in the village office, and particularly from the positions of vice-mayor and treasurer. As of 1950 about half the village mayors of Okayama Prefecture had previous experience in village offices. This phenomenon may prove temporary, however. During the early days of the Occupation's purge of local officials, many villages capitalized on the experience, availability, professional inconspicuousness, and neutrality of vice-mayors by electing them to replace their purged wartime mayors, as in Kamo, where the purged Namba Shigeo, who had occupied the office since 1938, was replaced by the vice-mayor. As Occupation activity and supervision waned, however, some reversion to former practices became apparent. In the absence of reliable national statistics, it is difficult to say how pronounced this is, but the mayor again may often be chosen for reasons not primarily related to professional administrative experience and competence. When this happens, the vice-mayor is usually an experienced bureaucrat who assumes actual control of the staff and day-to-day operations of the village office, much as in the prewar pattern.

The specific functions of Kamo's mayor are numerous and time-consuming. He is ceremonial head of the village. He drafts and presents to the assembly all village ordinances and regulations, although these usually follow models devised by the prefectural government. He prepares the village budget; consults with prefectural officials about the availability of tax revenue; presents the budget to the assembly and explains and discusses its many aspects. He administers the crop-requisitioning program. He represents the village on the regional irrigation co-operative, and he acts as liaison with the prefectural government and with the mayors of other villages and towns. He also receives visits from villagers having favors to ask or complaints to make and directs the work of the village office staff.

The most important of the eleven members of this staff are the vice-mayor (*joyaku*) and the treasurer (*shū'nyūyaku*). Both are nominated by the mayor and approved by the village assembly. All other staff members are appointed by the mayor without such approval. There are individuals in charge of: land and requisition matters (*kangyōkakari*); taxation (*zeimukakari*); health insurance (*kenkōkakari*); family records and census (*kosekikakari*); public health (*eiseikakari*); public welfare and statistics (*kōseikakari* and *tōkeikakari*); and agricultural affairs (the clerk of the *nōgyō iinkai*). The *kenkōkakari* has an assistant, and a combined janitor and servant fills out the roster. All these are full-time positions with salaries ranging in late 1954 from ¥5,700 to ¥17,700 per month plus allowances. Normally all such village employees are residents of the village, and the mayor makes a conscientious attempt to distribute such jobs as equably as possible among the village's buraku. Although not particularly remunerative, such employment does carry with it the prestige of public authority.

There are no officials concerned with police or fire-fighting functions on this list. In both respects Japanese practice differs somewhat from our own. Until 1954 at least, two separate police forces existed in Japan, the autonomous police and the National Rural Police. Villages with a population of less than five thousand could, if they so chose, maintain their own autonomous police force. In practice few villages elected to do so, and their police protection was supplied by the National Rural Police operating locally under the direction of a Prefectural Public Safety Commission. This was the case in Kamo, and the village authorities, therefore, had no direct responsibility for the protection of the peace. This situation continued under somewhat more centralized control following the abolition of all town and village autonomous police forces in 1954. Fire-fighting is generally regarded at the village level as a co-operative responsibility. In Kamo all men between the ages of seventeen and thirty-five automatically belong to the *shōbōdan* or fire-fighting organization and turn out to operate the village's scanty equipment in the event of fire.

In this survey of the governmental structure and functions of the village of Kamo, certain aspects of the mayor's true position and authority must now be made clear. There is little doubt about the leading role played by the mayor or his immediate subordinates in the planning and administration of village affairs, but the mayor and his staff also operate subject to a number of handicaps and controls which make it difficult to regard them as truly autonomous agents in any meaningful sense of the word.

For example, there is no doubt in the mind of the mayor of Kamo that his most difficult and time-consuming task is the local execution of the crop-requisitioning program. Since the 1950 crop year, only rice has been requisitioned, but previously barley, wheat, rape seed, soybeans, potatoes, and other vegetables were included. Prefectural quotas are established by the national government. The prefectures in turn allocate their quotas among the villages and towns subject to their jurisdiction. A village committee sets individual quotas for all producers of rice in accordance with a complicated productivity formula. In a lowland, rice-farming village like Kamo, practically every household is vitally affected by such measures. The day-to-day administration of this highly controversial program and the handling of most of the continual and bitter complaints attendant thereon fall to the mayor. But in discharging this onerous function the mayor has little freedom of action. His hands are bound at every turn by the detailed specifications of the Crop Requisition Law. Usually the most he can do is recommend action to the local requisition committee, which must in turn obtain permission from a prefectural committee before any action is possible.

Mayors do have more independent authority in the administration of village property. Where Kamo is concerned, however, the significance of this power has decreased with the decline in the amount of property owned by the village. It once owned sizable plots of forest and undeveloped land, but today it owns only such public buildings (with land) as are necessary for the conduct of village affairs—the village office, primary school, fire stations, isolation hospital, etc. Consequently the scope and importance of the mayor's managerial authority in this sphere has been correspondingly diminished.

The mayor's role in the administration of public works, which in rural Japan means primarily the construction and maintenance of roads and irrigation systems, is also limited. Any sizable project of this nature is both too costly and too complicated for a village to carry out by itself; the village applies to the prefectural and national governments both for a grant-in-aid and for technical advice and assistance. Almost complete prefectural and national control invariably accompanies such assistance. Also, irrigation projects customarily involve a number of villages co-operating through a special irrigation district or association, sharing costs and administering the system through a joint intervillage committee, and this limits the degree of autonomy exercised by any one village or mayor.

Again, relief and public welfare, although administered locally, are now controlled primarily from the prefectural or national levels, where standards of public assistance for the aged, indigent, and invalid are set. The manner of their administration is also largely dictated from above, and this control is reinforced by the fact that a significant proportion of the necessary funds comes to the village in the form of national and prefectural subsidies. The mayor's role in these fields is, therefore, largely administrative within variously prescribed limits. Much the same situation prevails in the field of education. Theoretically, local educational policy has until recently been determined by elective boards of education, but it is difficult to tell how effective such boards are, and there is reason to believe that the professional staff is usually in control. Where peace preservation is concerned, Kamo, as we have seen, falls under the jurisdiction of the National Rural Police, where the mayor has no authority.

Furthermore, the mayor's domination over the assembly is not so significant as it may appear on the surface. Very seldom is a mayor chosen who is not the candidate of a majority of the village assembly. Assembly members are the most influential politicians of the village, and in a very real sense the mayor owes his office to their support. He is generally reluctant to take steps which would seriously offend any significant element in his assembly. As a result of this and the general closeness of basic views and feelings prevailing in the small rural communities of Japan, there is a decided tendency for mayors and their assemblies to share the same viewpoint on many matters of political concern to the village. This solidarity is reinforced by the ubiquitous Japanese practice of holding elaborate private discussions and negotiations before permitting a matter of any importance to reach the stage of public consideration. The intent of such informal preliminary conversations is, of course, to prearrange an attitude or solution acceptable to all or most parties concerned. While sometimes failing to produce the desired result, this device appears to operate successfully to a degree which would not be possible in most modern occidental societies.

Such factors as these, plus the related facts that village administration in Japan actually is a part of a very complex and technical national administrative system about which the average farmer-assemblyman knows little and that the mayor is either a technician himself or is speaking for a trained technical staff, inclines the assembly to accept the mayor's proposals in the great majority of cases. However, a not inconsiderable number of instances in which disagreements with their assemblies have led either to the dismissal or resignation of the mayor testify to the basic strength of the village assembly's present position and to their readiness to use their authority if pressed far enough. Such disagreements do not, however, represent the normal pattern.

Finally, it is worth noting that there exist significant practical restrictions on the mayor's freedom of action regarding his semilegislative activities, that is, the ordinances, regulations, and financial bills which he drafts for presentation to the assembly and which are usually accepted without change. It has already been explained that he usually just copies, and perhaps adapts slightly, model ordinances and regulations sent to him by the Local Government Bureau of the prefectural government. Similar but much less extensive and explicit controls over a mayor's freedom of action are often exercised, particularly in the financial field, by a combination of two organs, the so-called *Chihō Jimusho* and the prefectural and *gun* associations of town and village mayors known as *Chōsonchōkai*. The *Chihō Jimusho* are branch offices maintained normally on a *gun* ("county") basis by all prefectural governments. Through these the prefectural government decentralizes some of its administrative and control functions and maintains far closer, more continuous and effective liaison with and supervision over the activities of town and village governments than would otherwise be possible.

The mayors' associations are organized primarily on a *gun* basis and secondarily on a prefecture-wide basis. There is also a national association. All mayors of towns and villages in a given *gun* belong to their local association and attend monthly meetings presided over by the chief of the *Chihō Jimusho*, a prefectural official. Membership in this association is not compulsory, and the association has no legal authority to dictate any course of action to its members. Nevertheless, it is used as a device for concerting policy on the local level. Major policy decisions are made at the monthly meetings of the prefectural association and passed on to the *gun* meetings which occur later in the month. These *gun* meetings then apply the decision of the higher organ to local circumstances and adopt it as their policy. The participating mayors are in no sense obliged to abide by these decisions, but the writers have been told by several mayors that they always do. In this manner the mayors of all villages in a given *gun*, and to a lesser extent in each prefecture, agree in advance on such matters as the percentage of their villages' revenue that they will allot in their budgets to village assembly or personnel expenses, the salaries that they will pay for certain jobs, the rate at which they will set such village imposts as the bicycle and cart taxes, the amount of their contributions to the support of certain prefectural or regional associations, supplementary allowances for teachers, and other similar matters. This procedure obviously circumscribes the village mayors' independent initiative.

There emerges, then, from these observations on the mayoral office of Kamo a picture of an official far less powerful and autonomous in fact than either the Local Autonomy Law or the normal subservience of the village assembly described earlier would have led one to expect. It is quite erroneous to assume that, since the village assembly usually subordinates its legislative and financial functions to mayoral control, the mayor is a free agent and the true fount of local autonomy. In actual practice all the above-described legal and extralegal limitations and controls on mayoral authority by the prefectural and national governments and their agents leave the village mayor with a not very significant residue of autonomous power. He remains the most prominent and the most potent agent in strictly local government, and, in a secondary sense, he plays an important administrative role. But the fact is that village governments do not really have any very important degree of autonomy.

VILLAGE AND COMMUNITY ORGANIZATIONS

The picture of village government would be seriously incomplete if we were to stop with a description of Kamo's elective and appointive officials. There are also many committees, boards, co-operatives, and groups with some sort of public function. Kamo has no less than twenty such organizations. Some of these, like the irrigation co-operatives, the fire-fighting organization, or the Youth Association, have traditional foundations extending back for centuries; others, like the Women's Association or the Agricultural Co-operative Association, antedate the Second World War by some years; the majority, however, are recent in origin and closely connected with the wave of change and reform instigated by the Allied Occupation, and all share the quality of governmental sponsorship, support, or overt participation. Most important are the irrigation co-operatives, the Agricultural Co-operative Association, the Agricultural Commission, and the already-mentioned fire-fighting organization. All deal with matters of lasting or current importance.[2] Kamo also participates officially in five multivillage irrigation co-operatives (*yōsuikumiai*), some of which are centuries old (see above, pp. 132–38).

The Agricultural Co-operative Association (*Nōgyō Kyōdō Kumiai*) dates back to the co-operatives established at the end of the last century. In the early 1930's and 1940's such organizations underwent a process of expansion and combination at the hands of the national government until they were established in all farming villages throughout Japan. The co-operative is still organized on a village basis, and practically all farm households belong to it. Members pay a small initiation fee upon joining, ¥5,000 at present, in return for which they receive a single share. The co-operative has never been known to pay a dividend. At present the Kamo co-operative has 499 regular and 3 associate members. Twenty-one of the regular members are from Niiike. Its affairs are administered by a board elected by all members for a three-year term. It consists of fifteen directors and five auditors. The directors select a full-time head of the co-operative. There is also a staff of eleven full-time employees in the office and store.

The co-operative serves several purposes. It makes bulk purchases at wholesale prices and sells the items so acquired to members at a small markup to offset operating expenses. The major articles involved in such transactions are fertilizer, seed rice, insecticides, farming tools and machines, clothing, soap, and other articles of daily use. The stock of such

---

[2] See Paul S. Dull, "The Political Structure of a Japanese Village," *Far Eastern Quarterly*, XIII, No. 1 (February, 1954), 182–86, for a more extensive discussion of these and similar organizations in Kamo.

items on hand in January, 1954, for example, amounted to about ¥1,300,000. In rural areas, under the crop-requisitioning system of post-war years, the co-operative is also usually the sole government-accredited rice dealer. In Kamo this means that the farmers must sell their quota of requisitioned rice to the co-operative, which stores it in its own ware-houses and resells it to the government. An important part of the co-op-erative's income is derived from charges assessed against the government for the storage of its rice.

The co-operative further performs banking functions. Kamo's farmers normally find it convenient to leave all or a considerable part of the price they receive for their requisitioned rice on deposit with the co-operative, where it draws interest at the favorable rate of 4.1 per cent to 7.1 per cent per annum. Similarly, the co-operative is the normal source of agri-cultural credit in Kamo. Members may obtain from it both unsecured and secured loans repayable with interest at the time of rice delivery. Interest for unsecured loans ranges from 6.5 per cent to 13.8 per cent (low rates in Japan), the rate depending on the purpose of the loan. In June, 1954, a fairly representative period, the Kamo co-operative had total deposits of about ¥20,000,000 and outstanding loans amounting to approximately ¥5,000,000. More than half its members (259 out of 502) borrowed money in 1953. It was claimed that none of these was from Niiike, though some of the buraku's inhabitants have negotiated and repaid small loans in the past. Apparently recent loans have most commonly been drawn to obtain cash for the purchase of fertilizer. The co-operative has a few old and overdue loans on its books, but it seems never to have considered recourse to legal or other forced means of collection. The co-operative itself may in times of need borrow from the Okayama Prefectural Federa-tion of Co-operative Credit Associations (*Okayama-Ken Shin'yō Kyōdō Kumiai Rengōkai*) on relatively favorable terms.

Although the Agricultural Co-operative Association still plays an im-portant part in the lives of the inhabitants of the village of Kamo, it was even more important during the years of acute wartime and postwar shortages. Many economic and financial regulations have now been re-laxed, and alternative sources of supply and finance are increasingly available to the farmer. A number of agricultural co-operatives have failed because of undercapitalization, restricted credit facilities, and mis-management. Also the selection, variety, and quality of items stocked by the co-operative stores has often failed to please the membership. As a result the average farmer today regards his village co-operative with something less than complete faith and support, although he continues to use it.

The Agricultural Commission (*Nōgyō Iinkai*), formed recently by amalgamating older agencies, also performs important semigovernmental functions, such as administering the land reform and crop-requisitioning laws. Although the redistribution of land under the former was practically complete by 1949–50, other aspects of the program required continuing administration. Beneficiaries had to be protected in their new holdings; the remaining tenants also had new rights to be enforced and maintained; practically all subsequent attempts to sell or otherwise dispose of agricultural land had to be scrutinized to see that they conformed with the letter of the law; and the government's attempts to consolidate scattered agricultural holdings in the interests of more efficient production had to be administered. Only rice remains on requisition, but this is Japan's principal and most prized crop, and the ultimate determination of precisely what amount of rice must be sold at fixed prices to the government by each farmer is made by the Agricultural Commission.

The Agricultural Commission in Kamo consists of eighteen members elected by the heads of all village households that cultivate land. The commission meets about ten times a year. While it has all the usual difficulties with the setting of local rice quotas, always a sensitive matter, its land reform problems are perhaps less severe than those in many areas. Kamo had no really large resident landowners before the reform; the largest held about 10 *cho* (24.5 acres). Some 83 cultivating landlords and 18 resident but non-cultivating landlords lost land in the reform. Added to these were some 216 small absentee landowners holding an average of about 2.6 *tan* (ca. ⅔ acre) apiece. A total of 111.4 *cho* (272.9 acres) of agricultural land—approximately half from absentee owners and half from resident non-tilling landlords or landlords who held more than the 2.7 *cho* (6.61 acres) maximum—were actually involved in the reform program. This represents about one-fourth of the village's total agricultural land. This is not to say that a number of bitter struggles over land did not develop within the village; they did, but not on the scale encountered in many villages throughout Japan.

There is also within the village an astonishing number (sixteen to be exact) of less important committees and groups with either semigovernmental functions or a distinct public interest. These are too numerous to describe in detail, but they range all the way from an association of buraku headmen to the P.T.A. Three men and one woman from Niiike were serving as officers of such groups in 1954. Given the traditional rural characteristics so prominent in Kamo, it comes as something of a surprise to discover so rich an endowment of modern-sounding, not to say textbookish, organizations as, for example, the Social Welfare Investigation

Committee or the Town Meeting Committee. Many of them have sound permanent or temporary functional justification in village needs and practices, but one wonders about the need for and durability of others. In these dubious cases, the initiative came from above and outside the village. Postwar Japan has been characterized, especially during the Occupation years, by a tidal wave of hastily improvised laws and administrative measures aimed at effecting some aspect or other of vaguely defined and ill-understood democratic goals. At both the national and local levels these were often intended to increase the degree of popular participation in and control over governmental processes, particularly in the fields of education and social welfare. As a consequence the village offices of Japan have found themselves more or less continuously bombarded with orders or requests to constitute and staff this or that new committee. Since compliance is customary in such situations and since, in any event, many of these committees seldom met and less frequently accomplished anything, the village officials were only moderately reluctant to acquiesce to these demands; besides, they created honorary appointments which might be of some local political value. In such an atmosphere, popularly constituted committees have multiplied at the village level; but only those dealing with a subject considered to be of immediate local importance by the people seem to have any prospect of amounting to much.

LOCAL TAX STRUCTURE AND TAX BURDENS

Tax obligations constitute an important aspect of every farmer's relationship with his government. From his viewpoint, the tax burden is heavy and never ending and is inequitable in important respects. It significantly affects not only his household budget but his attitudes toward government. In other words, a reasonably factual understanding of the local and national tax systems is essential to any rounded picture of village communities in Japan.

A description of the local impact of Japanese taxation is complicated by the fact that the entire system was drastically overhauled in 1950. Thus two quite different systems of taxation prevailed in Niiike and Kamo during the period with which we are concerned. A preliminary account of the principal features of both systems is therefore essential.

Japanese taxes may be classified in various ways, for example as national or local, depending on the identity of the levying authority, or as direct or indirect, depending on their incidence. For the period 1948–54 the principal taxes might be listed as in Table 20. The relative importance of these taxes as revenue-raising devices—and, from the farmer's standpoint, their relative burden—has changed since the tax reforms of 1950.

In general, however, the total yield from national taxes far exceeds that from local taxes, and personal income taxes—the national income tax, the local inhabitants tax, and the local enterprise tax—are by far the most important taxes upon individuals. The corporation and inheritance taxes have usually contributed far smaller proportions. The yield from the land and house taxes has also been notably small in postwar Japan, owing

TABLE 20

NATIONAL TAXES Direct	LOCAL TAXES Direct
Income tax (*shotokuzei*)	Inhabitants tax (*jūminzei*)
Corporation tax (*hōjinzei*)	Real property tax (*kotei shisanzei*)‡
Inheritance tax (*sōzokuzei*)	*a*) Land tax (*chiso*)
Gift tax (*zōyozei*)*	*b*) House tax (*kaokuzei*)
Transportation tax (*tsūkōzei*)	Enterprise tax (*jigyōzei*)‡
Revaluation tax (*shisan saihyōkazei*)†	
Wealth tax (*fuyūzei*)†	
Negotiable instruments transfer tax (*yuka shōken itenzei*)	

Indirect	Indirect
Liquor tax (*shūzei*)	Admissions tax (*nyūjōzei*)
Soft drink tax (*seiryō inryōzei*)	Real estate acquisitions tax (*fudōsan shuto-kuzei*)*
Sugar tax (*satōshōhizei*)	
Commodity tax (*buppinzei*)	Amusements, eating, and drinking taxes (*yūkyō inshokuzei*)
Textile tax (*orimono shōhizei*)*	
Transaction tax (*torihiki takazei*)*	Liquor consumption tax (*shushōhizei*)*
Tobacco tax (*tabakozei*)	Electricity and gas tax (*denkigasuzei*)
Gasoline tax (*kihatsuyuzei*)	Automobile tax (*jidōshazei*)
Customs tax (*kanzei*)	Cattle tax (*gyūbazei*)*
Other minor miscellaneous taxes	Electric pole tax (*denchūzei*)
	Telephone tax (*denwa kanyūzei*)*
	Irrigation tax (*suirichiekizei*)
	Bicycle tax (*jitenshazei*)
	Cart tax (*nigurumazei*)
	Dog tax (*inuzei*)
	Other minor miscellaneous taxes

* Abolished in 1950.
† Newly instituted in 1950.
‡ Part direct and part indirect.

largely to the failure prior to 1950 to readjust their bases to take the currency inflation adequately into account. Where indirect taxes are concerned, the major revenue producers are the tobacco and liquor imposts, followed normally by the admissions and amusements taxes.

The tax revisions of 1950 were basic and far-reaching. Two primary motives seem to have underlain these changes. The first was to supply

Japan with a modern integrated tax system as a sound basis for her future fiscal needs. The second was to provide more adequate and more independent revenues for the prefectures and municipalities of Japan and thus to advance the Occupation's goals of local autonomy and democratization. These objectives were sought in a variety of ways. We will here consider only those which significantly affect the inhabitants of Niiike.

Where the personal income tax is concerned, the effect of the 1950 revision was to decrease the average rates and increase the exemptions. The net effect of these changes was to lower the burden of this tax on average incomes by approximately one-fourth to one-third, or more, of the pre-1950 rate. The reductions were inversely related to income, being most sizable for smaller incomes and less appreciable as income increased. Basic exemptions and deductions for dependents have also increased steadily since the 1950 revisions. By 1953, for example, the basic exemption was ¥50,000, and the deduction for each of the first three dependents had been raised to ¥20,000. At the same time strenuous attempts were made by the lawmakers to tighten up the administration of the income tax law. The net effect of the revision for the average farmer, therefore, was likely to be a significant reduction in the burden of the national income tax. None of the other principal national taxes, such as the corporation, inheritance, or wealth taxes, is of direct major concern to the inhabitants of Niiike.

Among local taxes, the 1950 revisions of the real property, enterprise, and inhabitants taxes are those which most affected farm villages. All of these had existed in slightly variant forms prior to 1950. But all had been basically prefectural taxes, the rates for which were set at the national and prefectural levels. Towns and villages then simply imposed local surtaxes—usually at identical rates—upon these prefectural imposts. A most inflexible structure of local revenues resulted, and the entire system operated along lines intentionally subversive of any meaningful fiscal autonomy for Japanese towns and villages. The 1950 reforms attempted rather drastic changes in this situation. The rates of all three taxes were increased to provide more adequate local revenues. At the same time they were made strictly local taxes in all respects, with the inhabitants and real property taxes becoming exclusively city, town, and village perquisites, while the enterprise tax was awarded solely to the prefectural level of government.

Before 1950 the inhabitants, or head, tax was computed at the village level on a complex and somewhat variant basis involving annual determinations of rate and system of allocation at the national, prefectural, and local levels. Within a given prefecture its major components were a flat per capita element plus a component usually graduated according to income, though other standards were also used. Since 1950, the tax has become a municipal impost. The per capita element remains and in 1953, for example, varied from ¥300 to ¥900 depending upon the size of the community concerned. To this was added a second component, based on the individual's taxable income during the preceding fiscal year. Since this tax is primarily proportional to income, it is also a crude indicator of the relative prosperity of farm households.

The present real property tax derives historically from two older components—the land tax and the house tax. The former was levied on all privately owned land in accordance with a complicated system of determinations of its prewar annual rental value (*chintai kakaku*). The scale of rental value was determined by the tax division of the Ministry of Finance and was generally revised every ten years. The tax itself was a set multiple of the land's rental value and was assessed by the prefectural government with the municipalities adding a surtax of equal amount. In Kamo during 1949, for example, the combined prefectural and village land taxes amounted to 600 per cent of the prewar rental value of land. This sounds very high, but in fact, since the tax base made no allowance for subsequent inflation, the rate and the yield were both low. The pre-1950 house tax was similarly assessed and administered. It bore on buildings of all types and was based on a comparable system of rental values. Its actual burden was also light in terms of inflated postwar values.

The 1950 revision consolidated both these taxes as a real property tax and altered them in several important respects. In the first place, the new tax was allocated exclusively to the municipal level of government —cities, towns, and villages. Second, it was expanded to include all depreciable assets—machinery as well as land and buildings. And third, the tax base was shifted from annual rental value to capital value. The rates were appreciably raised. Because of the postwar absence of a free market in farm land, however, special and more lenient provision was made for the assessment of the capital value of arable lands. As a consequence the revised tax is not yet a heavy burden on the farmers, although the basic assessments of capital value—and hence the tax rate—are scheduled to increase in rural areas.

The present enterprise tax also existed prior to the 1950 reforms. Then essentially a prefectural tax to which the municipalities added a surtax, it was divided into two categories, "first class" and "second class." The first-class tax was levied on the profits of wholesale and retail businesses, and industrial, commercial, and financial concerns in general. It was in effect a surtax on the national income tax. Its rates were high and exemptions small. It bore with particular severity on small businesses. The second-class enterprise tax applied to agriculture, fishing, and forestry. It was considerably less onerous, since the rates were lower and income derived from the production of staple foods was exempt. The revisions of 1950 freed the farmer entirely from the enterprise tax, in consideration of increases in his land and house taxes and of government control of the market price of agricultural products. The tax was retained for businesses, however, and was made into an exclusively prefectural tax. Its base was shifted from business profits to a rather complex calculation of the annual "value added" by a given firm to the materials and equipment which it acquired from outside sources. For this reason the enterprise tax is often referred to as the "value-added tax" (*fukakachizei*).

In rural districts there is also an irrigation tax levied independently by town and village assemblies. All proceeds are earmarked for the maintenance and repair of the local irrigation system, and the tax is levied directly on the cultivators of irrigated land.

In 1948 the National Health Insurance Law of 1938 was amended to apply to the citizenry in general. As a consequence, some 116 villages in Okayama Prefecture, including Kamo, decided to participate in the health insurance plan. This is supported primarily by a special tax separately enacted by each participating village. The amount of the tax is proportional to the degree of medical coverage desired and to the average costs of medical care in the area in past years.

These then are the major taxes having a regular and direct effect upon the inhabitants of Niiike, either before or after the revisions of 1950. As has been noted, there are also various minor taxes, both direct and indirect. Some of these will be noted in the ensuing description of the impact of the tax system on the households of Niiike.

Owing to the variety of minor taxes involved and the incompatibility of others in their pre- and post-1950 forms, it is difficult to give a consistent total picture of the impacts of the national and local tax systems on Niiike during the period of our concern. If, however, for the sake of simplicity and consistency, we restrict our present account to the six major taxes concerned—the personal income, inhabitants, enterprise, real property, irrigation, and health insurance taxes—a relatively accurate over-all picture will emerge.

The caveat "relatively accurate" in the above statement must be kept firmly in mind. The only generally accessible records of tax obligations and payments in rural Japan are those maintained by the village offices and the local branches of the national tax authority (*zeimushō*). The writers have examined these official records. No one seriously believes, however, that they represent a full and accurate statement of farm income. A number of the more important taxes are self-assessed, that is, they are based upon the individual farmer's estimate of what his production, and consequently his income, was for the past tax year. Several difficulties ensue. To begin with, the average farm household keeps few and cursory records, if any at all, of its economic activities. Its members often honestly do not know all the details of their income status. Second, Japanese farming is a highly complex sort of operation normally involving the cultivation by a given household of a considerable number of small scattered parcels of land with varying productivity indexes and a variety of crops. Double-cropping and intercropping are common. Income from secondary occupations, such as the sale of mat rush, is particularly difficult to check. Thus, to verify the accuracy of a farmer's estimates of his income is both complicated and time-consuming. Third, the present-day Japanese farmer is no different from and no more scrupulous than his fellow sufferers the world over in his attitudes toward tax officials and tax payments. In the changed economic and social circumstances of postwar Japan, understatement of tax obligations and tax evasion in general have become endemic. Certain portions of the population have greater opportunities to evade their tax obligations than do others: the business and fishing groups have acquired particularly bad reputations,[3] and the record of the farming class is none too good. The question of how much on the average the farmers of a given area understate their income is hard to answer. In Okayama estimates from tax officials and farmers willing to discuss this sensitive matter ranged from 10 to 30 per cent or more. A tendency toward regional patterning was also apparent, the grosser forms of misrepresentation being more common in the poorer northern sections of the prefecture. The reputation of Kamo was relatively good—its farmers might normally underestimate about 10 or 20 per cent. Here again the facts would be very difficult to check.

With this caution then, let us examine the tax returns of the inhabitants of Niiike in the pre-reform calendar year of 1949 and the post-reform calendar years of 1952 and 1956. Together the experience of these years yields considerable insight into both the relative incomes and the tax burdens of the buraku's households. It should be noted that, while in theory the income and most other taxes are levied on individual incomes and properties, in practice the officials usually calculate taxes on a house-

[3] A veteran tax official in an Inland Sea fishing area gave it as his considered opinion that a truly extraordinary fisherman, a veritable paragon of civic virtues, might in a particularly weak moment declare for tax purposes as much as 50 per cent of his actual income from fishing. A more normal procedure would be to declare approximately one-third of it. Similar stories are frequently heard about business practice, while those about farmers show them to be usually somewhat less evasive.

hold basis, if the individuals concerned are living in the same house and fall within the third degree of relationship. The government increases its tax revenues in this manner. It should also be understood that Japanese practice about keeping official records up to date is, by American standards, very lax. For the purpose of taxation and other official records, the listings of household income and ownership are subject to numerous vagaries. Income earned, for example, may be attributed on the books to a deceased household head for years after his demise. The situation is further complicated by the propensity of long-absent members of the community to maintain it as their residence-of-record. For reasons of this sort—and there are a few other factors which are not susceptible to overly close scrutiny by outsiders—the tax rolls are frequently in somewhat imperfect accord with the actual community situation. The following tax table (Table 21) is arranged by households in descending order of admitted affluence, based on their personal income tax returns for the calendar year 1949. Information with respect to actual tax payments was not available in a few cases.

Table 21 demonstrates in rough, relative fashion a number of interesting facts about the income and tax status of Niiike's households during this period. To begin with, the spread of admitted incomes is quite broad, ranging from highs of ¥254,300 ($706), ¥301,840 ($838), and ¥487,200 ($1,353) to lows of ¥32,942 ($91), ¥69,588 ($193), and ¥66,900 ($186) in 1949, 1952, and 1956, respectively. Second, the financial status of Niiike's farmers has been improving in a monetary sense, though the real gains involved, while appreciable, have been seriously qualified by the inflationary condition of the economy. Third, Niiike's average household income in two of the years concerned accords quite closely to the declared average for the village of Kamo as a whole. The average income for the village in 1949 was ¥122,649, and in 1952, ¥178,756. A comparable figure for 1956 village income was not available. The figures for the entire jurisdiction of the Kurashiki tax office show that Niiike, until recently at least, tended to fall somewhat below the average in reported household income. The average figure for the Kurashiki division in 1952, for example, was ¥187,238, compared to Niiike's ¥160,313. Finally, it should be noted that the remarkable increase in income shown by the 1956 figures is in some part a result of the program of mechanization and improvement recently undertaken in the community by the Asia Foundation.

The effects of the tax revisions of 1950 also emerge quite clearly from the table. Most notable is the amount of tax relief extended to farmers by these changes. The figures in the last three columns do not, of course, represent the individual's total tax burden. They leave out of account

TABLE 21

NIIKE'S TAX RECORD FOR 1949, 1952, AND 1956

Households	Reported Income			National Income Tax			Inhabitants Tax		
	1949	1952	1956	1949	1952	1956	1949	1952	1956
Hiramatsu Hideo	¥254,300	¥301,840	¥487,900	¥80,900	¥25,300	¥29,560	¥3,158	¥6,480	¥24,840
Iwasa Eikichi	249,000	234,100	381,500	51,803	15,200	21,900	2,738	9,874	8,980
Hiramatsu Kenshirō	226,780	195,700	209,393	57,226	no tax	6,350	2,738	5,199	5,320
Iwasa Yasuta	162,200	184,490	299,592	34,700	2,000	8,150	2,104	7,135	9,780
Hiramatsu Kumaichi	149,600	194,675	318,457	35,100	7,600	19,750	2,316	6,083	11,400
Hiramatsu Isamu	145,900	89,100	280,600	26,300	no tax	no tax	1,472	1,098	7,850
Hiramatsu Hiroshi	141,897	160,350	272,762	28,300	no tax	8,950	2,104	4,953	7,660
Iwasa Sōichi	140,706	186,440	239,886	34,700	1,000	no tax	2,738	7,854	6,440
Hiramatsu Kinjirō (Hajime)*	133,500	135,070	205,400	......	no tax	no tax	1,262	......	4,520
Hiramatsu Yoshio	128,412	144,900	......	24,700	no tax	......	1,894	4,757	......
Hiramatsu Mitsusaburō (Michi-yuki)	126,575	183,780	255,531	9,575	no tax	19,000	1,682	4,546	7,730
Iwasa Kakuji (Minoru)	122,500	130,650	176,440	27,900	3,400	600	1,788	5,291	3,650
Hiramatsu Tadashi	116,800	139,300	212,396	21,900	2,200	no tax	1,682	4,301	4,810
Hiramatsu Nobuji	113,900	132,610	271,650	20,775	1,200	8,750	1,578	3,283	8,910
Hiramatsu Teigo	107,000	135,400	265,200	7,550	no tax	no tax	1,368	2,622	7,310
Iwasa Ishita	82,600	205,950	282,200	15,615	3,600	15,300	1,262	4,127	4,680
Iwasa Takeshi	71,460	148,400	212,800	7,675	9,200	450	no tax	3,734	5,470
Hiramatsu Asae	57,451	73,600	167,600	6,000	no tax	no tax	904	2,184	3,210
Hiramatsu Kameichi (Tomo)	42,200	......	66,900	350	no tax	no tax	610	......	no tax
Hiramatsu Tokujirō (Hisa)	35,810	......	112,600	525	no tax	no tax	820	300	1,490
Iwasa Tamaichi	35,000	69,588	121,700	no tax	no tax	no tax	378	534	580
Hiramatsu Ai	32,942	......	172,700	no tax	no tax	no tax	610	600	710
Hiramatsu Jun†	......	......	184,865	......	......	1,350	......	......	3,660
Iwasa Katsumi†	......	......	182,200	......	......	no tax	......	......	3,880
Averages for households paying a tax	¥121,660	¥160,313	¥233,895	¥25,873	¥7,070	¥11,683	¥1,676	¥4,247	¥6,495

* In parentheses are the names of individuals who have succeeded to the headship of the household concerned by virtue of the death or retirement of their predecessors.

† Households so marked have been recently established as a result of branching from the main family.

TABLE 21—Continued

Households	Real Property Tax 1949	Real Property Tax 1952	Real Property Tax 1956	Irrigation Tax 1949	Irrigation Tax 1952	Irrigation Tax 1956	Enterprise Tax 1949	Health Insurance Tax 1952	Health Insurance Tax 1956	Total Tax Payments 1949	Total Tax Payments 1952	Total Tax Payments 1956
Hiramatsu Hideo	¥2,028	¥5,076	¥9,560	¥1,208	¥2,890	¥1,760	¥3,240	¥1,410	¥1,750	¥90,534	¥41,156	¥67,560
Iwasa Eikichi	1,396	3,068	7,500	755	1,806	820	2,970	1,383	1,990	59,662	31,231	41,280
Hiramatsu Kenshirō	1,610	3,997	5,690	1,321	2,989	970	4,060	1,960	3,110	66,955	14,145	21,440
Iwasa Yasuta	1,484	5,202	8,210	885	2,116	1,410	no tax	1,892	4,770	39,173	18,345	32,320
Hiramatsu Kumaichi	1,702	4,115	7,080	1,102	2,640	1,680	3,120	1,702	4,660	43,340	22,140	44,580
Hiramatsu Isamu	1,172	2,420	4,310	492	1,184	560	6,660	1,466	4,230	36,096	6,168	17,380
Hiramatsu Hiroshi	1,344	4,248	6,790	988	2,244	1,470	5,040	1,709	4,260	37,726	13,154	29,100
Iwasa Sōichi	1,520	4,772	8,490	1,154	2,010	1,110	3,720	1,828	3,030	43,832	17,464	20,300
Hiramatsu Kinjirō (Hajime)*	796	336	4,370	696	1,826	900	4,140	....	....	....	....	12,820
Hiramatsu Yoshio	1,434	5,094	....	844	2,036	....	7,920	2,575	....	36,792	14,462	....
Hiramatsu Mitsusaburō (Michiyuki)	1,584	....	5,170	398	....	640	1,350	228	1,780	14,589	....	34,320
Iwasa Kakuji (Minoru)	1,280	2,276	5,330	760	3,036	1,120	2,340	1,555	2,550	34,068	15,558	13,250
Hiramatsu Tadashi	1,306	2,669	8,070	913	2,190	1,330	1,800	1,338	2,360	27,601	12,698	16,570
Hiramatsu Nobuji	1,128	2,874	5,400	648	1,702	1,130	6,090	1,212	3,910	30,219	10,271	28,100
Hiramatsu Teigo	994	994	640	234	562	410	1,260	957	no tax	10,696	5,135	8,360
Iwasa Ishita	1,128	3,516	5,080	598	1,426	890	900	900	1,890	19,503	13,569	27,790
Iwasa Takeshi	no tax	1,132	4,650	no tax	766	490	no tax	142	no tax	7,675	14,974	7,510
Hiramatsu Asae	668	2,036	no tax	442	1,058	660	450	896	2,640	8,464	6,174	11,160
Hiramatsu Kameichi (Tomo)	214	379	4,110	251	602	360	no tax	....	no tax	2,505	....	360
Hiramatsu Tokujirō (Hisa)	1,068	3,443	1,540	419	472	550	1,080	....	1,910	2,832	....	8,060
Iwasa Tamaichi	244	714	5,060	74	180	300	no tax	1,107	2,580	696	4,215	5,000
Hiramatsu Ai	676	2,013	3,170	425	816	610	no tax	658	1,780	1,711	4,087	8,160
Hiramatsu Jun†	....	....	no tax	....	....	870	no tax	....	2,520	....	....	11,570
Iwasa Katsumi†	....	....	....	....	....	360	....	....	no tax	....	....	4,240
Averages for households paying a tax	¥1,146	¥2,874	¥5,303	¥ 693	¥1,645	¥ 887	¥3,302	¥1,306	¥2,968	¥29,269 (24)‡	¥14,078 (9)‡	¥20,488 (9)‡

‡ Parenthesized figures represent the percentage of reported income paid in taxes.

the admissions, bicycle, transportation, amusement, and liquor taxes as well as a variety of others. The impact of these on the frugal and abstemious citizenry of Niiike is relatively small, however, and the total picture is not seriously distorted by their omission. One notes that, whereas the average Niiike household was paying approximately 24 per cent of its reported income in taxes in 1949, this figure had fallen to about 9 per cent in 1952 and 1956, a very significant drop. Despite the incomplete listing of taxes paid, it seems quite likely that the average tax relief afforded Niiike by the 1950 revisions was close to 50 per cent. Probable increases in tax rates and tightening of tax administration may affect him adversely to some degree, but the Japanese farmer at the moment is in a more favorable tax position than ever before in the modern history of his class.

The table also reveals the changed incidence of the tax system. The national income tax was hit hardest by the reforms, its yield in Niiike dropping on the average from 88 per cent of total tax payments in 1949 to 50 per cent and 57 per cent in 1952 and 1956, respectively. To some extent the relief afforded by this major decline was offset by a compensatory increase in the principal local taxes, but a very sizable bonus remained for the taxpayer. Autonomous local tax revenues did increase significantly, though via-à-vis local needs they remained critically deficient.

A word must also be said about the actual payment of taxes in Kamo. It is generally agreed that before the war the local farmers were more or less model taxpayers in at least the sense that they met their tax obligations speedily and in full. Tax default or serious delinquency was quite unusual and was an occasion for shame and loss of face. This situation has changed drastically in postwar Japan owing to a variety of obvious economic and social factors. The degree of change varied, however, depending upon the area and the type of taxpayer concerned. The record of Niiike and Kamo in general has continued to be good. Until 1949 tax payments were practically 100 per cent in Kamo. In that year they slipped to about 90 per cent, that is, some 10 per cent of the payments due were uncollected at the end of the tax year (payments are usually made on the instalment plan throughout the ensuing year). In 1957 Kamo was nevertheless still meriting its reputation as a model village. Collections have averaged 90 per cent on obligations due for the tax years 1953 through 1955. For the sake of perspective, this situation may be contrasted with that of a neighboring fishing and commercial jurisdiction where the tax delinquency rate in 1949 was 57 per cent for the inhabitants tax and an incredible 98.5 per cent for the first-class enterprise tax.

Finally, a word might be said about local attitudes toward the taxation system. It is particularly difficult to distinguish fact from fancy on such a sensitive and emotion-generating subject. In general one is tempted to say that no matter what changes are made in the tax system or what degree of relief is afforded the taxpayer, it is regarded as poor gamesmanship to admit to satisfaction with one's remaining tax obligations. This is probably particularly true in discussions of the subject with outsiders. In Niiike the tax revisions of 1950 were publicly acknowledged by comments and attitudes compounded, in minor part, of a reserved and wary pleasure at the diminished total burden and, in major part, of disbelief that such relief represented more than a temporary aberration in national policy and of speculation about when and how the earlier rates might be restored or increased. The prevalence of such views in agricultural communities rests upon a complex base. In part, the attitudes reflect the centuries-old experience of farmers with their rulers. Farmers have traditionally been a grievously exploited segment of the population, and, in spite of recent significant improvements in their circumstances, they are still far from convinced that the day of the common man has dawned in Japan. Probably of greater current importance, however, is the widely shared conviction—rational or not—that they are unfairly treated by the tax authorities in comparison with other economic groups in the population. Business and urban elements, they feel, are in general less heavily taxed than they are. In addition, they believe that businessmen in particular dishonestly evade large portions of their tax obligations and that the government is largely indifferent to or even abets such practices. Most serious of all, perhaps, is the bitter conviction that tax revenues are unjustly expended by the government in the sense that a completely disproportionate share is spent for urban improvements, industrial subsidies, etc., while the crying needs of the countryside receive distinctly secondary consideration. The farmers feel that there has been very small correlation between the proportion of the national revenues which they have provided and rural improvements of direct and tangible benefit to them. Historically there is considerable truth in all these views. Governmental practice in these respects has changed significantly in recent years, but popular attitudes and the prevalent mythology among the farmers have not yet altered accordingly. The people of Niiike, therefore, probably do not consider that even the revised tax system is equitable or that they are getting value received for their tax yen.

LOCAL FINANCE

In describing the community life of any political or social group it is always instructive to examine the financial aspects of their collective activity. In the present inquiry this may be done very simply for Niiike, but the fiscal affairs of the village of Kamo are considerably more complex.

Perhaps the best insight into Niiike's finances can be gained by examining the buraku's very rudimentary written accounts. Before the war the buraku treasurer kept a considerable amount of cash on hand, usually some ¥5,000–¥6,000, a large figure before devaluation. Because the buraku's inhabitants kept little or no cash on hand, the buraku treasurer paid many of their bills and was reimbursed at New Year's. During the war this practice ceased, and today the treasurer usually maintains a balance of only ¥2,000–¥3,000 in devalued currency in the local Agricultural Co-operative Association's bank. This small fund is derived from two principal sources: a levy of ¥60 per household collected by the treasurer in three instalments each year and contributions customarily made by inhabitants of the buraku on such felicitous occasions as marriages and adoptions. Such gifts have ranged from ¥20 before the war to a maximum of ¥1,000 on the occasion of a recent marriage. The fund is used to maintain the buraku hall, to pay for collective entertainments or feasts, and to purchase occasional group gifts. Actually the authors have been reluctantly responsible for the largest single items of expense in recent years, since the buraku has on several occasions insisted on entertaining them. Aside from infrequent special subscriptions to funds for the bulk purchase of fertilizer, work shoes, and such items, this is the extent of joint financial activity within the buraku.

The village budget is perhaps the best source of information on the finances of Kamo. In recent years this has been an exemplary document, its style and contents prescribed by national law. It covers a fiscal year beginning April 1, and its six-column format gives major titles, subdivisions thereof, estimates of revenue or expenditure for the current fiscal year, revenue or expenditure for the preceding fiscal year, amount of increase or decrease, and a brief explanation or justification of the particular item whenever necessary. This apparent precision is decidedly misleading, however; there are many pitfalls for the uncritical investigator. To enumerate a few: The investigator must be sure that he has gathered all village budgets for a given fiscal year. In these days of inflation and general financial uncertainty, the formal budget is seldom more than a wistful prayer. There are certain to be supplementary budgets (tsuika yosan), and probably quite a few of them. Kamo, for example, had five in fiscal 1949, and five, six, seven, and six, respectively, in the ensuing fiscal years. Also, the comparative data given for revenue and expenditures during the preceding fiscal year are largely meaningless, since, at the time a given budget is compiled, firm figures for the preceding year are still unavailable and only estimates are used. Third, certain items in the budget seem habitually to be treated with some freedom and used for purposes not evident from the document itself. It is not that the budget is dishonestly compiled or administered, but there is a tendency to regard it as a sort of externally imposed nuisance to be used more for purposes of public record and display than for actual administrative control. Finally, during the period we are treating, the local financial picture was greatly altered on the revenue side, and comparisons have been made complicated and difficult by the adoption of the Revised Local Tax Law, which made significant changes in the sources of village funds and attempted to increase local fiscal autonomy.

For many years before the Revised Local Tax Law of 1950, the structure of local revenues had not undergone any basic changes. In 1949, for example, Kamo's total budgeted income amounted to ¥5,380,815. Official accounting practice attributed 72 per cent of this sum to tax sources, 24 per cent to national and prefectural grants-in-aid, and 4 per cent to other village sources, such as income from village enterprises, property, rents and fees, and contributions. These categories are, however, most misleading. Of its so-called tax income Kamo had more or less independent control over only 17 per cent. Earmarked taxes represented another 13 per cent. The balance, by far the larger part of the village's tax revenues, was derived from surtaxes on various prefectural taxes (on which Kamo had little freedom to vary the rates) and the so-called locally apportioned tax, which was in effect another grant-in-aid from the national government. Beyond this, if one examines that share of the village's 1949 revenues properly assignable to grants and subsidies, it emerges that Kamo was dependent on Okayama Prefecture for a further 16 per cent of her total revenues and the national government for another 31 per cent. Thus a total of 47 per cent of her 1949 revenue was being drawn directly in the form of grants from external and largely uncontrollable sources. This fact alone represents a degree of financial, and consequently of political, dependence which went far to render the 1947 grant of local autonomy largely illusory.

In the succeeding fiscal years, 1950–53, the sources of village revenue were considerably altered by the adoption of the Revised Local Tax Law aimed at increasing the financial autonomy of the various units of local government. Under this law, village taxes fall into two main classifications, ordinary (*futsūzei*) and earmarked, or special purpose (*mokutekizei*). At this level the latter category is concerned almost exclusively with irrigation taxes, a small part of the total revenue which need not concern us here. The category of ordinary taxes is far more extensive and complex.

In addition to such minor components as taxes on bicycles, wagons, electricity and gas, mineral products, lumbering, and personal service, this class includes two major taxes: the inhabitants tax (*jūminzei*) and the real property tax (*kotei shisanzei*). Between them these now supply the greatest part of village revenue. As has been noted, the villages have gained considerably greater control over these tax sources than was the case earlier.

Dependence on prefectural and national tax sources and subsidies has not been completely eliminated. Villages continue to obtain certain grants and subsidies from the prefecture, and they still receive an important national subsidy, the so-called equalization grants (*heikō kōfukin*) which replace the earlier locally apportioned tax. Such grants are intended

TABLE 22

REVENUES OF KAMO FOR THE FISCAL YEARS 1949 AND 1951–53

Source	1949–50	1951–52	1952–53	1953–54
Ordinary taxes:				
Inhabitants..............	¥ 671,190	¥ 2,775,000	¥ 2,649,827	¥ 3,365,000
Real property............	1,449,923	2,667,000	2,520,414	3,044,080
Other...................	243,396	303,000	424,266	359,000
Earmarked taxes:				
Irrigation................	499,440	562,000	746,954	1,315,127
Prefectural and national grants and subsidies:				
Equalization grant.........	1,243,000	899,000	1,606,000	1,673,000
Other national grants......	408,800	967,000	10,248	356,500
Prefectural grants.........	865,066	592,000	1,127,277	993,393
Other revenues*...........	....	2,625,988	2,251,286	2,680,697
Total...................	¥5,380,815	¥11,390,988	¥11,336,272	¥13,786,797

* This category was said by village officials to be abnormally high in all these years owing to the carrying-over of large unexpended surpluses from the preceding year.

roughly to equalize throughout the country the discrepancy between locally available revenues and needs. Consequently the proportion of village revenue coming in this form varies widely with the level of productivity and prosperity of the areas concerned. In northern Okayama Prefecture, for example, a relatively poor area, an average of 30 per cent of village revenues is provided by equalization grants. In the more prosperous southern regions of the same prefecture, this figure is only about 10 per cent.

The revenues of Kamo during the fiscal years 1949, 1951, 1952, and 1953 are set forth in much simplified form in Table 22. Because the village was amalgamated in 1955, the 1953 budget is the last complete budget available for Kamo.

Table 22 shows that village revenues have more than doubled since the 1949 figure of ¥5,380,815 and that their sources have also been considerably changed. Table 23 shows the sources as a percentage of total revenue, making clear the changes brought about by tax reform in 1950. Since all tax revenues in the three latest years are derived from levies at least theoretically under local control, it is evident that, in a technical sense, the fiscal autonomy of Kamo has been substantially increased. The question of whether this has meant an equivalent or even significant increase in actual village autonomy is far more complex. The authors doubt that it has.

On the expenditure side of Kamo's budget, while the major items have remained constant since 1949, their costs have increased enormously. A few examples are set forth in Table 24. It will be noticed that the 1951–

TABLE 23

SOURCES OF KAMO'S REVENUE FOR THE FISCAL YEARS 1949
AND 1951–1953 (PERCENTAGE DISTRIBUTION)

Source	1949–50	1951–52	1952–53	1953–54
Taxes........................	49	55	56	59
National and prefectural aid....	47	22	24	22
Others........................	4	23	20	19

TABLE 24

SELECTED ITEMS OF EXPENDITURE IN THE KAMO BUDGETS
FOR THE FISCAL YEARS 1949 AND 1951–53

Item	1949–50	1951–52	1952–53	1953–54
Village assembly	¥ 132,710	¥ 231,000	¥ 321,501	¥ 435,200
Village office	1,356,761	2,392,000	2,607,340	2,796,883
Police and fire	68,720	234,000	288,015	423,980
Public works..........	602,282	693,829	1,589,536	3,785,255
Social welfare..........	538,741	1,111,000	462,724	425,550
Education.............	885,606	4,074,129	2,184,172	2,360,500
Others................	1,795,995	2,656,030	3,294,374	3,447,472
Total*............	¥5,380,815	¥11,391,988	¥10,747,662	¥13,674,840

* It will be noted that only the 1949 expenditures balanced with income. This is due to the general vagaries and inexactitudes of Japanese statistical and accounting practice which are baffling and never ending. In the majority of these cases one suspects that any excess of revenues over expenditures was treated as a floating contingency fund and transferred as a credit to the following year's revenues.

53 totals are more than double those of 1949, and individual items in some instances have increased more than sixfold. In general this is attributable to two facts: first, with tax reform, local governments assumed new and more extensive obligations for education, public works, police and fire, social welfare, etc.; second, the rapid inflation of these years is reflected in the increased cost to the village of practically all services, materials, and other items.

It is only when one considers the foregoing account of Kamo's finances in conjunction with the present and foreseeable village and regional needs, on the one hand, and probable future economic conditions in Japan, on the other, that a more meaningful picture emerges. Compared with her immediate neighbors, Kamo, while not unduly prosperous, is reasonably well off. Even so, her fiscal capacity falls far below village needs. Available educational facilities are felt to be seriously inadequate; roads and bridges obviously stand in need of improvement and extension; official salaries continue low. In every direction there is urgent need for additional revenue, but none is in sight. It was essentially for this reason that projects for amalgamation with several neighboring villages were long considered, although, even after the realization of amalgamation in 1955, Kamo's prospects do not appear bright. One hesitates to speak with any assurance or optimism of the financial future of Kamo; in terms of the existing desires and expectations of the people, the village still lacks an adequate fiscal base.

Such conditions lead one to speculate about the future of the attempts at fiscal decentralization in Japan, bearing in mind the fact that a very appreciable degree of financial self-sufficiency is probably essential to the development of any significant or enduring measure of local autonomy. If they are to be valid, such speculations cannot confine themselves to the village scene. One must consider the financial capacity and prospects of the country as a whole, as well as the trend of major political developments. It is noteworthy that the prefectures, more than any other unit of government, have paid the price, in terms of revenues under their own control, of the increase in the fiscal self-sufficiency of the cities, towns, and villages. Naturally they object strongly to this and have long been bringing strong pressure upon the central government to rectify it. Their protests reinforce the more or less continuous opposition of the national authorities to any very extensive measure of financial decentralization. From the beginning most of them fought against the acceptance of the recommendations, and it is doubtful that they ever became reconciled to them. The Japanese traditions of national control and centralized administration are very strong in the financial sphere, as elsewhere. Demands for a pronounced diminution of local autonomy in practically all spheres have figured conspicuously in the movement for the revision of the so-called MacArthur Constitution. When one combines these pressures for recentralization in the financial field and revisionism in general with the essential financial weakness and inadequacy of the great majority of local jurisdictions in Japan, it seems quite probable that the central government will succeed in the not-too-distant future in recapturing an appreciable part of the fiscal controls taken away by the reforms. Even that inadequate degree of fiscal underpinning provided the local autonomy movement by the reforms will be further reduced and the process of recentralization correspondingly advanced. Given so small a country, so precarious an economic situation, and so urgent a need for effective national planning in the financial sphere particularly, the swing of the pendulum seems inevitable.

DISPUTES, CRIME, AND THE COURTS

Until the end of the war, both Niiike and Kamo were quiet places with few disputes acrimonious or conspicuous enough to attract official attention and practically no serious crime. There were a few bitter private and family enmities, but they seldom gave rise to illegal acts or required police intervention. Since 1945, however, the nation's troubled circumstances have produced what many Japanese regard as a major breakdown of popular morals and a crime wave of unprecedented proportions, most serious in the cities but reaching into the villages as well. Although by American standards the dimensions of this "crime wave" in the Kamo area are negligible, the Japanese, applying other standards, are often quite shocked by it.

Kamo, having no autonomous police force of its own, falls within the jurisdiction of the National Rural Police Station for the Kibi district with headquarters at the city of Sōja. This is one of the largest police districts in the country, serving some twenty-eight villages with a total population of approximately 83,000. It is seriously understaffed and has personnel to man only about one-third of these villages regularly. Its official records reveal no serious crime in Kamo during the period 1934–45. Since then, there have been four major crimes, a number considered excessive by the police in relation both to other villages in the area and to Kamo's peaceable and law-abiding reputation in the past. There was an armed robbery in 1946, two cases of rape of middle-school girls in 1949–50, and one attempted murder in 1950. In all cases save the last the offender was caught and sentenced to prison. In the entire Kibi police district there have been but two murders, both solved, since 1946.

In addition to these four serious crimes the village police records reveal a number of minor offenses and convictions. Between 1945 and 1954, Kamo's 3,434 inhabitants provided 49 reported cases of illegal sales of rationed foodstuffs, the most common offense. The next most frequent offense was gambling, 23 cases being reported during the same years. There were also 17 burglaries in the village during this period. All other offenses were of a distinctly petty nature.

Since August, 1945, there has been but a single civil suit involving a resident of Kamo. This was a matter of a disputed inheritance heard by the Family Court in Okayama City (*Okayama Katei Saibansho*), a special branch of the District Court. Divorces in rural areas are not usually matters for the courts. Marriages are frequently not entered on the family register (*koseki*) kept by the village office for some time after the wedding, often not until the birth of the first child. Since the marriage itself requires no civil ceremony or notice, it has no official status until the proper *koseki* entry is made. Most separations occur during this unofficial stage and are completely private arrangements with no official intervention whatsoever.

Once a marriage has been entered on the family register, its formal dissolution must be similarly recorded. In Kamo there were four "formal" divorces in 1948 and five in 1949, and only one of these involved a visit to the Family Court. The rest occurred as a result of discussions between the husband and wife, with the families of course playing a part. Both principals then signed a simple statement of their agreement to divorce and took this to the village office, where it was recorded on their family register and a notice sent to the legal affairs section of the prefectural government. Generally the wife would in such cases take back her dowry with her to her family home, and the husband would ask for the return of his bride price (*yuinō*). The husband has a traditional right to the custody of all children, if he cares to exercise it. Unless the case goes to court, there is normally no alimony paid in such separations.

Niiike proper has been generally regarded as a peaceable and law-abiding buraku. Although there is little serious crime in the Kamo area, buraku with reputations for vicious and unruly behavior such as pilfering neighbors' crops, petty thievery, evasion of crop-requisitioning quotas, flagrant black-marketeering, or excessive drunkenness are not uncommon. One of Niiike's neighboring buraku has such a reputation. But Niiike's people are well behaved and meet their private and collective obligations in a satisfactory manner. They drink little and then only at festival times. This generally good reputation has been marred only by the previously described attempt on the life of Iwasa Takeshi in 1950 (see above, pp. 266–68).

This section would be incomplete without some mention of the legal and judicial facilities available to the people of Niiike and the village of Kamo. In a physical sense these lie outside the village, and, although seldom or never used, they do provide its inhabitants with a final means of settling disputes. There is a Summary Court (*Kan'i Saibansho*) at Okayama City with jurisdiction over the village of Kamo, which handles petty crimes and small suits. More serious cases go to the District Court (*Chihō Saibansho*) at Okayama City, which has prefecture-wide jurisdiction. The Family Court is a branch of this. There is also a regional court of appeal, known as the "Higher Court" (*Kōtō Saibansho*), at Hiroshima with jurisdiction over the five prefectures comprising the Chūgoku area. Highest of all is the Supreme Court in Tokyo.

But very seldom and then only with the greatest reluctance do the people of Kamo make use of these courts. When apprehended in any of the criminal offenses described earlier, they were, of course, haled before one or the other of them for hearing and sentence, but this was involuntary. Only a matter of the greatest personal or family importance could induce them voluntarily to seek the assistance of the courts in the decision of a dispute, and then only after they had utterly exhausted all alternative means of settlement. Public disputes between community members are disapproved. The community values its harmony and solidarity and dislikes seeing these breached in any serious fashion, especially if the breach is so conspicuous or flagrant as to draw the attention of neighboring communities and thus expose it to shame and ridicule. Such affairs challenge both the reputation and the cohesiveness of the community and are not viewed lightly. Probably, one must be brought up among the incessant, intimate contacts of a settlement group such as Niiike fully to understand the force of this view.

But the Japanese farmer is neither so naïve nor so impractical as to believe that disapproval can eliminate disputes. Certainly Niiike and its neighboring communities provide instances of both intra- and extra-buraku quarrels of every degree of bitterness and seriousness, from accusations of petty thievery of persimmons through the circumstances leading to the self-imposed ostracism of Hiramatsu Hideo's family and the centuries-old friction between Hiramatsu and Iwasa, to the possibly connected attempt on the life of Iwasa Takeshi. The community accepts the inevitability of such rifts, but at the same time it seems to demand two things of its disputants. First of all, overt displays of ill-feeling and hostility should be avoided; and second, the settlement of disputes should be attempted through the traditionally approved technique of mediation.[4] Mediation is the manner in which Japanese farmers have settled their disputes for centuries. Still the approved means of settlement, it derogates from the use of the court system. Also, being completely local in operation, it is a means of reinforcing the community against outsiders and thus contributes to community cohesiveness and self-containedness.

Various more practical considerations sustain and reinforce the predisposition toward local mediation. Historically the farmer's experience with

---

[4] In respect to the former of these demands, there does seem to be some difference between the willingness to display ill-feeling toward residents of other buraku and toward co-residents of Niiike, whether Hiramatsu or Iwasa. The authors rather early heard slighting remarks and veiled accusations by Niiike people against residents of other buraku, but it was a long time before they became privy to any intra-buraku discord.

the formal institutions of Tokugawa justice probably did not breed confidence in the courts. There are similar deterrents today. To go to court one must employ a lawyer, and the cost of lawyers is prohibitively high. Lawyers are commonly regarded as interested primarily in maximizing their fees and are generally suspected of prolonging and complicating cases to this end. The financial risks of bringing a civil suit are considerable, particularly if the judgment goes against one. And, anyway, the humble farmer simply feels ill-at-ease and out-of-place in the formal and official atmosphere of a courtroom. All of these are circumstances hardly conducive to the free or effective use by the villager of judicial process as a means of settling his disputes.

Of the considerable number of persons with whom we discussed such matters, many summed up their views by quoting the old adage *chūsai wa toki no ujigami* ("Mediation is the god of the times"). Despite such feelings, however, it was generally held that as a last resort for the solution of their most desperate problems they might with great reluctance and trepidation go to court. When pressed as to the possible nature of such problems, most could conceive of little that could induce them to take so desperate a measure, save the most vital questions affecting the boundaries of agricultural land or irrigation rights.

The villagers' attitude is of particular interest when considered against the elaborate measures taken by the Allied Occupation to "reform" the entire Japanese legal and judicial systems in an attempt to make them perform political and social functions similar to those in Anglo-American societies. It proved quite feasible to make the statutory and organizational changes desired, but, in so far as the residents of Niiike and Kamo are concerned, such reforms can have little practical effect where the people display so pronounced an aversion to judicial process in any form.

Particularly relevant to a consideration of the courts as the guardians of private versus official rights is the matter of so-called administrative suits. These are actions brought by citizens against the government to secure redress for some alleged invasion of their rights stemming from a public or administrative action. Under the prewar legal system it was both difficult and expensive for citizens to bring such suits against the government. Actions could be brought only in a special court in Tokyo and were relatively few. Since the war this procedure has been much simplified. The District Courts (*Chihō Saibansho*) in each prefecture have been given original jurisdiction over all administrative suits. In Okayama Prefecture, the decisions of the District Court, located in Okayama City, are appealable first to the Higher Court at Hiroshima and ultimately to the Supreme Court in Tokyo. Despite greater accessibility, the number of administrative suits in Okayama Prefecture remains small, as Table 25 indicates. (The "New Suits" category in Table 25 is analyzed in Table 26). Okayama Prefecture had a population of 1,689,800 in 1955, and it is somewhat remarkable that in a period of nine years this many people found only 241 occasions on which it was necessary to bring suit against their public officials and agencies.

TABLE 25

ADMINISTRATIVE LITIGATION IN OKAYAMA
PREFECTURE

Year	Suits Carried Over	New Suits	Suits Settled
1948.......	6	61	26
1949.......	41	46	36
1950.......	51	32	40
1951.......	43	8	13
1952.......	38	16	12
1953.......	46	24	20
1954.......	50	21	18
1955.......	53	15	15
1956.......	53	18	16

TABLE 26

NATURE OF "NEW" ADMINISTRATIVE SUITS IN OKAYAMA PREFECTURE

Year	Land Reform Suits	Tax Suits	Election Suits*	Others†
1948...........	52	5	..	4
1949...........	36	3	..	7
1950...........	12	5	2	13
1951...........	5	2	..	1
1952...........	4	4	4	4
1953...........	8	3	2	11
1954...........	3	6	2	10
1955...........	3	1	..	11
1956...........	3	5	..	10
Total........	126	34	10	71

* This category was broadened to include the entire sphere of suits pertaining to "local autonomy" in 1952.

† Prior to 1952, this category included for the most part suits against local mayors and assemblies often involving attempted recalls or dissolutions. Since 1952, such items have been classified as "local autonomy" cases. The residue are suits on such matters as nationality, fair trade, city planning, labor administration, etc.

Where the government is directly involved, as it is in these administrative suits, the above-noted hesitancy to take formal legal action is reinforced by the age-old submissiveness of the Japanese before the governing elite, by the assumption that the government is separate from and wiser than the people, and by the feeling that it is not only radical but also probably dangerous and futile to challenge the government openly. The courts are not trusted as a means of settling disputes with the government and its agencies. Aggrieved individuals do try to obtain redress, but their attempts are far more likely to take the form of direct or indirect approaches to and pressures on particular public officials to secure their intercession and assistance. This is the traditional pattern of action, and although it may slowly be changing, for the present, in Okayama, the courts are of only marginal significance as guardians of popular rights against administrative abuses.

VILLAGE AMALGAMATION

Kamo's career as a separate political entity ended on January 1, 1955, as a result of its amalgamation with two neighboring jurisdictions—the town of Takamatsu and the village of Oishi. Sweeping programs for the amalgamation of units of local government are not new in Japan. The history of local government in post-Restoration Japan begins with experimentation along these lines, culminating in the massive amalgamation program embodied in the Law on the Organization of Cities, Towns, and Villages of 1888. There was no further amalgamation on a national scale until after the Second World War. In the villages at least, the Meiji amalgamations have not been forgotten, and one frequently hears comment and speculation about the present amalgamation plans couched in terms of the experiences of the 1870's and 1880's.

Throughout Japan the national and prefectural governments have been urging villages and towns to amalgamate into larger units. The legal authority for this goes back to Article 7 of the Local Autonomy Law of 1947 and to the Law for Expediting the Amalgamation of Towns and Villages (*Chōson Gappei Sokushinhō*) of September 1, 1953. The latter, valid for only three years, sets forth specific procedures to be followed and anticipates the establishment of new towns and villages having populations of at least 8,000 and areas of not less than 30 square kilometers. The procedure is simple. Amalgamation of towns or villages into a new town or village requires only the consent of the assemblies concerned plus a perfunctory approval by the prefectural assembly. Where the creation of a new city by such methods is involved, the preliminary consent of the prime minister is necessary.

The basic reasons for the current emphasis on amalgamation are also simple. The needs of the average rural town and village, whose area and population have been substantially unchanged since 1888–89 in most cases, have outgrown their fiscal capacity, especially since local autonomy has given many expensive new functions to local government. Where available tax and revenue bases are inadequate, amalgamation seems a reasonable and desirable solution. A similar argument is advanced in the administrative field, where it is claimed that amalgamation will permit reductions in staff and improvements in efficiency. But political motivations are inevitably present in projects for amalgamation. Any such change entails the disruption and realignment of long-established political affiliations. For this reason amalgamation is likely to be regarded with distaste and apprehension in the localities concerned. It is precisely this disruptive effect, however, that recommends amalgamation to certain prefectural and national officials. They anticipate that the realignment of sociopolitical affiliations attendant upon amalgamation will facilitate breaking the hold of certain dominant individuals and families on their local followers. In the new and larger jurisdictions they hope that the status and strength of such persons will be diluted and eroded to an appreciable extent, thus assisting in the destruction of the old order in the countryside.

Table 27 shows how far the amalgamation program has gone in Okayama Prefecture. The steady decrease in the number of villages matched by

TABLE 27

AMALGAMATION IN OKAYAMA PREFECTURE

Year	Cities	Towns	Villages	Total
1936......	4	56	319	379
1940......	4	58	312	374
1948......	5	60	302	367
1950......	5	69	293	367
1951......	5	71	283	359
1952......	7	72	256	335
1953......	9	67	192	268
1954......	10	67	155	232
1955......	12	67	43	122
1956......	12	69	24	105

a corresponding increase in the number of towns and cities well illustrates the pace at which village amalgamations have proceeded.

Where the village of Kamo was concerned, two projects were discussed. The first, sponsored by the prefectural government and the village office, envisaged the amalgamation of Kamo with the neighboring towns of Takamatsu and Makane and the village of Oishi. The second, which for a time enjoyed more popular support within Kamo itself, advocated amalgamation with the village of Shō only. The first plan would produce a large, compact unit of a diversified economic nature with desirable characteristics from the standpoint of transportation, communications, educational administration, etc. It would, however, involve the merging of Kamo, which was relatively prosperous, with three other less prosperous units, and the people of Kamo feared that this might entail an increase in their taxes and a lowering of their present level of public services. Shō, on the other hand, like Kamo, was a prosperous agricultural area with which Kamo had traditional affiliations and, if amalgamation was necessary, many of the people of Kamo preferred this plan. It would, however, have formed a long, narrow unit difficult to administer and with poor communications.

Despite this initial lack of public enthusiasm and support within Kamo, both the prefectural and village governments were convinced of the necessity for amalgamation. They embarked on an educational campaign calculated to convince the people and, more directly, the members of the village assembly of its desirability. The pressure, although not intense, was steady and resulted in late 1954 in approval by the local assemblies concerned and by the prefecture for the amalgamation of Kamo with the town of Takamatsu and the village of Oishi. These new arrangements went into effect on January 1, 1955, at which time Kamo disappeared as a separate political unit and became a part of the enlarged town of Takamatsu.

13. The Community

Niiike, considered as an isolated and self-contained unit, provides very few occasions for the operation of processes which might be called "political" in any but the most rudimentary sense. These have to do almost exclusively with the taking of collective decisions and the selection of buraku "officials," particularly the headman. Since these offices are seldom overtly sought and since their functions are largely routine and their powers negligible, they do not really exemplify the operation of political processes in a very meaningful sense. The community, in terms of the conduct of its internal affairs, is not, therefore, what might be described as a "politicized" unit. It is only when we view Niiike and other such communities in the wider context of village, prefectural, and national politics that we can appreciate the political role of the buraku. In a general sense it is no exaggeration to say that an accurate comprehension of this role is fundamental to an understanding of the political process in Japan as a whole.

TRADITIONAL ATTITUDES TOWARD POLITICS

The level of *effective* political interest is still low in the Japanese countryside, and traditions or experience conducive to the development of positive attitudes toward politics are just beginning to develop. These people are only eighty-odd years removed from the Meiji Restoration. Before that lay unbroken centuries of experience with oligarchic governments whose attitude toward any popular (particularly peasant) participation in the political process is well summed up in the old saying *kanson mimpi* ("officials honored, the people despised"). Since 1868 the forms of government have been greatly altered and the scope of popular participation substantially increased. But only with the advent of universal manhood suffrage in 1925 was the average male citizen permitted any formal voice in the selection of even so carefully controlled a part of the national decision-making apparatus as the lower house of the Diet. In other words, in spite of the real and important changes in the political process since the Restoration, effective political interest continued to be manifested by relatively small, though slowly increasing, segments of the population. Participation by the masses, especially the rural masses, was largely formalistic and, in any positive or sustained sense, ineffectual. To be sure, this situation seems to have occasioned no general sense of injustice or grievance on the part of the farmers. Although there were sporadic, unfocused outbreaks from time to time, caused primarily by depressed economic conditions, by and large the farmers continued to feel that government was something done to and for them by their betters, not a process in which they themselves played a positive or responsible part. There was little in their class experience and background to substantiate any other attitude toward politics at either the national or local level.

The general tenor of the nation's constitutional and legal institutions reinforced such popular attitudes until 1945. Thereafter, the Allied Occupation was responsible for a statutory revolution which almost completely inverted the emphasis of the older legal substructure of the political process. At all levels and in all fields the formal institutions of government now became geared to the facilitation and accomplishment of "American democratic" rather than "Japanese oligarchic" political objectives. As had been foreseen, this created a profound discordance between the formal and the informal aspects of the political process, between politics as depicted on the statute books and politics as envisaged and practiced by the people. It is quite true that some political practices were quite readily adapted to the new forms and that some portions of the population—and these highly vocal—seized upon the new institutions with positive enthusiasm. But the piecemeal and selective aspects of the process of adjustment have not been adequately understood abroad. The widespread persistence and strength of the informal institutions, of the older attitudes and practices, and the manner in which these have managed to subvert in significant part the glittering new formal trappings of democratic process to ends which are little different in effect from those emerging in prewar Japan are often overlooked. The political role and activities of the people in Niiike and Kamo well exemplify this phenomenon.

POLITICAL PARTICIPATION

POPULAR POLITICAL INFORMATION

To appreciate the political role played by the people of Niiike and Kamo, it is first necessary to distinguish between *abstract* interest in or information about politics, on the one hand, and *effective* interest or participation in the political process, on the other. The people of Niiike, while for the most part lacking any very impressive fund of precise political information, are abstractly interested and generally informed about politics to a rather surprising degree. All except four families have radios and listen to them regularly, especially to news programs and commentaries. While not all subscribe to newspapers, the majority see and read them regularly, particularly the local *Sanyō Shimbun*, a major regional paper published in Okayama City. Several subscribe to Japan's large metropolitan dailies, *Asahi* and *Mainichi*, as well. At least one takes *Diamond*, a rather sophisticated journal featuring economic and political commentary and analysis. Some seven families also subscribe to *Ie no Hikari*, a popular rural magazine of general scope. In view of these regular sources of outside information and contacts with regional, national, and international affairs, it is difficult to regard Niiike as in any way isolated or backward from the standpoint of communications.[1] The people know what is going on, they are interested in major developments outside the village and the area, and they frequently discuss such matters among themselves. This is particularly true of major political events concerning Japan. In 1950, for example, the nature of the projected peace treaty and the course and implications for Japan of the Korean affair or, in 1954, the bribery scandals in Tokyo and the hydrogen bomb experiments in the Pacific were common subjects of buraku conversation.

THE VOTING RATE

Between political information and interest, on the one hand,.and political participation, on the other, there exists a broad gap which is scarcely peculiar to the Japanese farmer. It is the degree, not the fact, of political inertness on the part of the average farmer, of the lack of what we have called effective interest, which distinguishes the citizen of Niiike and Kamo. This is not manifest in a high abstention rate at election times, a sign of political apathy so often encountered in the United States. As a matter of fact, if one were to judge by the voting record alone, the village of Kamo would certainly appear to be far more politically interested and active than the majority of Western communities. Some 85 to 95 per cent of its electorate votes in village elections, and a somewhat smaller percentage votes in prefectural and national elections. Table 28 provides comparable statistics for Kamo, Tsukubo *gun*, the area immediately surrounding Kamo, for Okayama Prefecture, and for Japan as a whole. These figures, especially the national ones, well illustrate the descending scale of popular

---

[1] While the level of political information in Niiike is high, it is not completely out of line with that prevailing among heads of households throughout the Inland Sea area as a whole. The following figures may be of some interest: In the area as a whole 72 per cent listen daily to the radio (82 per cent in Niiike) and 77 per cent read newspapers daily (90 per cent in Niiike).

electoral interest in Japan. Unlike the West, local assembly and mayoral elections tend to draw more popular participation than do any others. This is particularly true in the rural areas, which almost invariably show a higher voting rate than do cities. The reasons for this are related to such factors as greater community cohesiveness in Japan, particularly in rural areas; the prevalence of the belief that it is socially proper (indeed semi-obligatory) to vote; and the greater popular responsiveness to social pressures reinforcing this attitude. The efficacy of these factors decreases as the election becomes more remote from the local level, at first slightly at

TABLE 28

PERCENTAGE OF ELECTORATE VOTING, 1947–53*

Election	Kamo	Tsukubo Gun	Okayama Prefecture	Japan
Village assemblies:				
1947	85	85	84†	81†
1951	94	96	95†	91†
Village mayors:				
1947	No election‡	71	79§	89§
1951	95	96	94§	90§
Prefectural assembly:				
1947	83	85	84	82
1951	91	92	88	83
Prefectural governor:				
1947	69	72	71	78
1951	91	92	88	83
House of Representatives:				
1947	65	62	66	68
1949	82	74	76	74
1952	82	78	79	76
1953	77	75	75	74
House of Councillors:				
1947	63	54	56	62
1950	83	81	77	72
1953	....	75	67	63

* Comparable figures for more recent elections are not available owing to the amalgamation of Kamo with neighboring jurisdictions on January 1, 1955.

† Includes town and city assemblies as well.

‡ No election was necessary, since the only candidate was unopposed.

§ Includes town and city mayors as well.

the prefectural level and then much more markedly at the national level. Also, elections for the House of Representatives bring out a higher vote than those for the House of Councillors, a fact probably attributable to the greater importance attached to the former in general repute as well as in the campaign activities of the political parties. In the light of such figures one must conclude that voting rates by themselves are not a meaningful positive index of effective political interest in rural Japan. Two other areas of political activity—direct legislation and informal pressure groups—may then be examined as indicative of the degree of effective popular political participation.

DIRECT POPULAR LEGISLATION AND CONTROL

The Local Autonomy Law of 1947 grants the people reasonably extensive rights of direct control over the governmental process. While lacking provision for direct use of the initiative and referendum, this law does empower any group of citizens numbering one-fiftieth or more of the total number of registered voters in the village, acting through a petition to the mayor, to bring about the mandatory and prompt submission to the village assembly of popularly initiated projects for the enactment, amendment, or abolition of almost any village ordinance or regulation. The village assembly must then consider such projects, although it is under no legal obligation to take the action requested in the petition. This qualified right of popular initiative is, moreover, reinforced by other popular powers. One-third or more of the local registered voters can force the holding of a special election to determine whether or not the assembly shall be dissolved or the mayor recalled from office. By a similar petition they can also force the assembly to decide whether or not other high officials of local government should be discharged.

In practice, these rights are seldom invoked. In Okayama Prefecture during the six years 1948–54 the total number of villages varied from 302 to 155. During this period the records show but eight attempts by voters' groups to bring about the dissolution or resignation of village assemblies (of which four were successful); one attempt to procure the recall or resignation of a particular village assembly member (successful); and eight attempts to force the recall or resignation of village mayors (of which five succeeded). Normally, other channels of popular political activity at the village level are more important.

PRESSURE GROUPS

Organized pressure-group activities are of little importance in Kamo. Practically all formally organized interest groups—the P.T.A., various agricultural and irrigation groups, merchants' association, town meeting, etc.—were established as a result of prodding from above, and they function, if at all, in close association with the village office. No instances are known of systematic pressure by such groups on the village assembly or village officials.

Occasionally one does encounter isolated instances of group activities intended to influence the decisions of village officials. In Kamo in recent years these have invariably been due to serious dissatisfaction with some aspects of the local agricultural program, primarily the crop-requisitioning system. Niiike was involved in one such instance in 1948. The community quota of requisitioned crops that year seemed to all its inhabitants to be unprecedentedly and unaccountably high compared to quotas of neighboring buraku. After considerable hesitation, they decided to send a delegation to the mayor to protest. The group waited upon the mayor, who subsequently reviewed the matter with the village crop-requisition committee. A mathematical error in computing Niiike's quota was discovered, and the mistake was rectified. The villagers agree that this was a most unusual action for Niiike to take, even though it was justified in the end.

Thus, instances of sporadic and unsystematic pressure-group activity do occur in Kamo, but they are rare, and extreme provocation is necessary to stimulate this form of collective protest. All demonstrations known to the authors have been against rather than for something; they have been occasioned by some urgent major grievance, the removal of which was considered imperative. No examples have been encountered at the village level of agitation by pressure groups for positively formulated programs.

One need not seek far for the explanation of such phenomena. Popularly based pressure-group activities of an organized sort are a function of what might be termed a positive attitude toward government, of the tradition and belief that ultimately it is the people in a broad sense who do or should govern. In Niiike and Kamo, government continues to be regarded as something that is done to and for rather than by the average citizen. For this area, therefore, the dearth of pressure-group activities is normal. This is not true everywhere in rural Japan, however, and in other areas one does encounter farmers' or teachers' unions working systematically for the realization of social and political programs.

Despite the absence of systematically organized, positively oriented pressure-group activities in Kamo, there are informal ways of representing public or private opinion to the local governmental authorities. The village is small and cohesive, a circumstance which facilitates personal contacts and diminishes somewhat the need for formal pressure-group activities. An individual with a serious grievance or a project amenable to local governmental treatment can do one of several things. Simplest and most normal is to create a favorable climate of opinion within his own buraku concerning his grievance or project. If he obtains general support, the matter will then come to the attention of either the buraku's representative in the village assembly or the village office in a relatively anonymous fashion. This, of course, is a form of low-grade pressure-group activity, but it is of a distinctly unorganized and unspecialized variety. Again, a person in such a situation might take his problem directly to either his local representative in the village assembly or to the mayor. Such action is uncommon, indirect representation being favored, but it does occur.

In general, it is misleading to describe in specialized institutional terms the manner in which village authorities become aware of, and make allowance for, group and individual desires of a political or administrative sort. The situation is most un-Western. One should understand, to begin with, that very few meaningful decisions can be made at the village level. As a consequence, a village assembly or village office is not a particularly appropriate or fruitful focus for pressure-group activity. The important decisions are made at higher levels. Second, within the restricted sphere of decisions which can be locally made and locally influenced, specialized channels and organizations for the exertion of pressure have not yet developed to an appreciable extent, although their beginnings are increasingly apparent throughout the countryside. This lack of specialized articulation does not mean an absence of group and personal pressures. These do exist in abundance, but they tend to function through a sort of social osmosis more congenial to the traditional preference for indirection rather than along the more conspicuous or systematic lines familiar in the United States.

POLITICAL LEADERSHIP

There exists within the village of Kamo a group of persons who might be regarded as the community's "political leaders." Applied in its Western sense, however, the term is misleading. The circumstances and techniques of political leadership in rural Japan differ from their occidental analogues in a number of respects. These should be made clear.

One must first realize that the Japanese traditionally place a low value on conspicuous personal leadership in politics. Relatively few great individual political leaders emerge clearly from Japanese history; men such as Oda Nobunaga, Hideyoshi, and Ieyasu are therefore the more remarkable. Generally, patterns of group leadership have marked Japanese politics at all times and all political levels. In fact it sometimes seems as if the decision-making system had been devised for the dual purpose of negating "leadership" in the usual, individualistic, Western sense of the word and of hopelessly obscuring individual responsibility for any given decision. This Japanese characteristic was well illustrated by the anonymity and fantastic complexity of the national decision-making apparatus revealed at the Tokyo war crimes trial and is clarified in several recent studies of Japan's decision to end the war. At the local level it is apparent to anyone who has extensive dealings with Japanese officials or observes the manner in which political decisions are taken in the Japanese countryside today.

The system works mainly through advance discussions and private prearrangements among subgroups, broad participation, extensive discussion, compromise settlements, and at least superficially unanimous consent to the decision reached. The general procedure has already been described (pp. 354–55). We need only note here that the mechanics of the system are such as to minimize strong or conspicuous leadership. Taking clear or forthright stands in public—or even, apparently, in smaller and more private groups—is not traditionally approved in Japan. It is likely to raise the sensitive issue of "face" and to render compromise settlements more difficult. The system has resulted in the emergence of leadership techniques not qualitatively different in many respects from those recently attributed to the talented "organization man" in the United States. One "leads" from within the group by persuasion and indirection to a greater extent than is customary in Western politics. Notable exceptions occur, particularly in Western-style committees and legislative bodies which include left-wing representation, but the older patterns are more common. Leadership does exist in rural Japan but it is a subtle and elusive phenomenon.

There are, to be sure, few occasions in a village like Kamo for the exercise of political leadership on a significant scale. The numerous qualifications of any meaningful degree of local autonomy have already been described. Not much of a political nature remains for the local leaders to decide, and much of what does is cut and dried. Social and economic leadership is thus more important than political leadership in the village.

In rural Japan, however, one does not usually distinguish among a community's social, economic, and political leaders. They are the same people. Their status and influence is general rather than circumscribed and specialized as is characteristic in societies such as our own. Persons in political power tend also to have—by modest local standards—prominent economic and social status. Within these limits then, what are the common characteristics of political leaders in Kamo?

The village leaders are, to begin with, local. It is hard for an outsider to achieve a position of leadership in a Japanese village. The direction of migration is normally from the villages to the cities—except in times of major economic depression or readjustment such as the recent postwar period. Relatively few strangers enter the villages as permanent settlers. Those who do come usually do so as *yōshi* or adoptive sons, a low-grade status that involves a political handicap (see pp. 232, 238). Thus it is the native sons who—despite occasional exceptions, such as a recent mayor of Kamo who was a *yōshi* from Mitsu *gun*—usually furnish the local leaders. Other things being equal, one might add to this qualification a corollary, "the more local, the better." It helps to be of an old and well-established family. The people of Niiike are relative newcomers in Kamo;

their buraku has been there for only two and a half centuries or so. The area is used to Niiike now and has long accepted its people. But assimilation is a slow process in Japanese villages, and strangers may well be at a competitive disadvantage for several generations.

Second, the local leaders are men possessed of some leisure. Political leadership takes time, in a Japanese village as elsewhere. One must attend meetings, cultivate support, and talk to people. The average farmer has little or no spare time to devote to such non-essentials. Those who do become village leaders must therefore either be relatively prosperous or have somehow freed themselves from the obligations of full-time farming. The latter is normally possible within the village only through regular employment in the village office or the agricultural co-operative. Occasionally a man with enough land and with grown sons to work it also achieves a degree of emancipation.

Third, it is of prime importance that the local political leaders have extensive personal knowledge of farming techniques and problems. Kamo is a farm village and its principal concerns arise from farming. Anyone aspiring to a position of leadership must demonstrate his understanding of such problems to the local citizenry. In practice almost all Kamo's political leaders either are farmers themselves or have had almost lifetime connections with farm villages and farmers and are well acquainted with their ways and needs. A recent mayor who was a professional school-teacher and administrator represents the only significant departure from this rule, and he had a good working knowledge of farm problems.

Fourth, local leadership is still usually a perquisite of middle-aged or elderly men. Despite the postwar reforms, women have still not taken a place in village politics. In fact, in 1955 they represented only one-half of 1 per cent of the total membership of Japanese town and village assemblies. Younger men are also at a political disadvantage. Age is traditionally revered in Japan and has long been associated with both wisdom and political power. Young men aspiring to political leadership must first cope with the handicap of youth. They also are likely to have less leisure to devote to politics. There is evidence, however, that since the war younger men have gradually been becoming more assertive and more politically active and influential at the village level. Still, the typical local leader in Kamo and throughout most of Japan is from forty-five to sixty years old. The national average falls in the early fifties for those actually serving in town or village assemblies.

Fifth, a better than average lineage or ancestry is helpful in achieving local political status. The descendants of former samurai families, village headmen, or similar pre-Restoration or Meiji local functionaries enjoy some competitive advantage, provided they have the other necessary qualifications. To some extent such an advantage may be based on local regard for the traditionally superior status of members of such families. Probably more important is the practical consideration that such families have long been active in the management of local politics. They are able to combine useful political connections in neighboring villages and at higher political levels with some degree of political knowledge and experience. These are usually significant advantages in the average villager's eyes, especially the existence of useful connections. Politics at this level is still largely a personal rather than a programmatic process. An aspirant for political leadership normally joins someone, not something. It helps to have established personal or family connections.

Finally, it should be noted that local leaders usually have no formal political party affiliation. In Kamo and elsewhere, the majority, when they run for office, do so as independents. In 1955, for example, 98.2 per cent of all candidates elected to village or town assemblies claimed to be political independents. This is true in the sense that they do not hold formal membership in any party and usually run for office without sponsorship or support from any organized party. Many, however, actually do have a general political orientation which, in Kamo and rural Japan as a whole, is normally conservative. In the 1955 local elections, for example, of some 43,168 "independent" candidates elected to town and village assemblies, only about 7.5 per cent could be identified as having socialist or proletarian party orientations. Most of the remainder were probably conservatively oriented. One of the more formidable problems faced by left-wing political parties in Japan is the difficulty of developing favorably disposed village leadership groups from very small beginnings.

In Niiike and Kamo the local political leaders seem to follow quite closely the above-outlined pattern. Hiramatsu Mitsusaburō, known as Sensei, is undoubtedly Niiike's outstanding political figure. Since his retirement from the village assembly in 1947, Niiike does not have a leader of any real prominence. His temporary successor on the village assembly was very much an aspiring amateur who has yet to attain local recognition. In an informal way, Sensei continues to exercise an appreciable amount of political influence, especially within the buraku. He meets almost perfectly the foregoing specifications. He is a descendant of an old local family of better than average lineage; he is aged and venerable; he is technically a political independent though conservatively oriented; and he has, relatively speaking, a fair amount of leisure and had more before war and land reform reduced his economic circumstances.

At the village level, Kamo's political leaders may be identified in terms of their present positions and careers. Since the abandonment of honorary mayorships after the war, village mayors have all been active political leaders. So have about half the members of the village assembly; the other half fall in the category of aspirants to leader status, not yet firmly established or recognized throughout the locality. Among the seven or eight assemblymen who may be said to have arrived politically, four are generally considered to be of prime importance. These four are farmers and all but one have served more than a single term in office: two were first elected in 1942, while a third, who is chairman of the assembly, has held office since 1937. He is one of the most influential political leaders in the village. The fourth, though elected for the first time in 1947, comes close to being a professional politician in the Western sense of the term. He is a former mat-rush merchant, now a farmer. To this list should be added several technically "retired" and elderly men who have served in prewar assemblies and who are occasionally referred to in hushed tones as political "bosses." These men—the authors knew three and heard of two or three others—had had long careers of service on a variety of village committees. They were, moreover, rather prominently identified with one or the other of the two national political factions important in this area—that of Inukai Ken, son of the redoubtable Tsuyoshi (see p. 424), or the opposition group headed by Hoshijima Jirō and Hashimoto Ryūgo (see p. 426). Finally, among the top local political leaders, should be mentioned the chairman of the village's Agricultural Co-operative Association. This is a politically critical position in many villages. Its occupant is strategically placed in terms of extensive contacts with practically the entire population, of insight into every family's economic status and problems, and of ability to influence the crop-collecting and valuation procedures as well as the local credit system. The holder of such a post is almost inevitably a political leader.

A list of twelve to sixteen individuals thus covers the more important political leaders of Kamo, a village of somewhat over 3,500 people. There are gradations of importance within this group, of course, and some of the villagers would claim that the mayor, the chairman of the co-operative, the chairman of the assembly, plus some two or three of its members, and perhaps three of the so-called bosses—a total of nine men—constitute the really central group. It is very hard to evaluate such claims from the outside, however, and it therefore seems wiser to us to offer the broader, if less discriminating, estimate of twelve to sixteen persons as constituting the first rank of local political leadership.

It should be understood that even this degree of local political status is not particularly impressive. Politics is a part-time activity for these men, most of whom continue to operate their own farms. They do, however, play a leading part in the preliminary discussions and compromises leading up to the taking of those political or administrative decisions which can be made locally. When election time comes around, they become particularly active on behalf of themselves and those with whom they are affiliated at higher levels. Most, if not all, of them have connections with prefectural politicians, usually members of the prefectural assembly, and with either the associates of Inukai Ken or those of Hoshijima Jirō and Hashimoto Ryūgo at the national level. In this sense they represent the village end of the web of political relationships stretching downward from the national and prefectural levels. So far as possible, they organize and deliver the Kamo vote for the candidates they support.

All these top local leaders are conservative in their prefectural and national political affiliations—with the possible exception of one recent mayor. There is a left-wing vote in the village, amounting, for example, to some 18 per cent, 15 per cent, and 32 per cent of the respective totals in the 1949, 1952, and 1953 House of Representatives elections. This goes largely to the Labor-Farmer and Socialist parties but has included on occasion some forty-odd Communist ballots as well. Despite this, local politics is conservatively organized and oriented. No outstanding left-wing leaders could be identified within the village, though individual supporters of the Socialist or Labor-Farmer tickets at the national level could be.

There are, of course, lower levels of political leadership to be found within Kamo. The twelve to sixteen top leaders have associates spotted about in some of the village's thirty buraku. The top leaders' strength is usually based on their own buraku and perhaps a few neighboring ones as well, or on their own ōaza. Their associates are apt to be politically interested individuals of some status in their respective buraku. Often they are relatives or friends of the top leaders, rather than assistants or inferiors, and they do what they can in a quiet and inconspicuous fashion to assist the leaders. Lower-level as well as top-level political leaders in Kamo seem to fall into the previously sketched categories—middle-aged or elderly farmers of better than average family and economic circumstances, long established in the village, nominally political independents but actually conservatively oriented in their political views and affiliations.

THE LOCAL ELECTIVE PROCESS

VILLAGE ASSEMBLY ELECTIONS

Against this background of information about traditional political attitudes, popular political participation, and local political leadership, we may now turn to a consideration of the political process as manifested in

Kamo's local elections. Under the postwar system all members of village, town, and city assemblies are popularly elected. These offices, unlike their intra-buraku counterparts, are regarded as eminently desirable and as conferring considerable prestige and status on their occupants.

In rural areas such as Kamo, campaigns for assembly seats are waged primarily along buraku lines and secondarily along family lines. All buraku are anxious to place at least one of their own members in the village assembly to represent their interests in respect to the apportionment of local taxes; appropriations for the maintenance, repair, or extension of irrigation systems and roads; remission or reduction of crop-delivery quotas in the event of poor harvests or natural disasters; and a variety of similarly unglamorous but locally important matters. Where Niiike is concerned, the achievement of this goal raises the following problems.

In local assembly elections all members are chosen at large, the village functioning as a single electoral constituency. Kamo's thirty buraku have populations ranging from 17 to 327, with the average about 112. In recent years the size of the village electorate has ranged from 1,971 to 2,133, of whom 85 per cent to 94 per cent actually voted in the first two postwar assembly elections. Prior to 1947, when the village assembly had twelve members, this meant that a successful candidate had to poll about 135 votes; since 1947 and the increase in the size of the assembly to sixteen, somewhat more than 100 votes are necessary. Actually, since the vote is not distributed equally among the candidates and since there may also be two or three unsuccessful contenders for the sixteen seats, a somewhat smaller quota of votes insures success. In the 1947 election, for example, the successful candidates polled from a high of 169 to a low of 70 votes, while in 1951 the range was 141 to 77.

Under these circumstances Niiike has found itself in an uncomfortably marginal position. It usually has about 70 votes. Even though its residents vote as a bloc behind their buraku candidate, it still would lack some 65 votes of controlling a seat under the old assembly system and some 30 under the present one. Niiike, therefore, has had to work out informal co-operative arrangements with other buraku in order to assure representation of its interests in the village assembly.

The manner in which this has been accomplished serves as one example of the continued vitality and practical utility of ōaza bonds. Niiike has always in recent times co-operated with other buraku located in Upper Shinjō ōaza. Under the old twelve-member system it was customary for the five buraku comprising the ōaza—Nakamura, Iwasaki, Yamane, Ōyama, and Niiike—jointly to present two candidates. These were normally furnished by Nakamura and Niiike, the two largest, and dutifully supported by the voters of the other buraku. Thus the ōaza made the most effective use of its votes and obtained reliable control of two seats in the village assembly. Under the sixteen-member system introduced in 1947 it became apparent that the ōaza commanded enough votes to acquire three seats, one for each of its largest buraku. In the early postwar years the system revolved therefore, where Niiike was concerned, about co-operation with Ōyama buraku, its closest neighbor. Ōyama had about 30 votes, which it usually cast in support of Niiike's candidate in local assembly elections. In more recent times and under slightly different circumstances, the arrangement has been expanded to include Yamane buraku as well.

In actual practice two aspects of the above system stand out. In the first place there is a strong tendency for a given buraku to vote as a bloc in any election of village assembly members. This is not absolute, but the authors found few deviations in Kamo or elsewhere. When they do occur, they may be attributable to intense personal dislike for the candidate by one of his fellow residents, to a severe ideological split in the community, or—and this is more common—to the overriding strength of family obligations. If a resident of one buraku is confronted with a situation in which both a relative living in another buraku and a fellow resident of his own buraku are running for office, he will probably vote for the relative in preference to the neighbor. In Niiike, for example, a recent member of the village assembly was quite certain that he got practically all of Niiike's votes. The sole exception he knows of was that of a resident who had a relative running from Kurozumi buraku. In this case the person concerned had indirectly informed the Niiike candidate in advance that he would reluctantly have to vote for his relative.

Second, the system operates with remarkable precision. Frequently the advance calculations of candidates are so accurate that no election is necessary; the number of candidates and the number of seats are precisely equal. This is a tendency apparent at the local level throughout Japan. There have been only three general elections of members of city, town, and village assemblies since the war—in 1947, 1951, and 1955. In each of these an average of only 1.3 candidates has competed for each seat in a town or village assembly. This contrasts with averages of 3.0, 2.2, and 2.3 candidates, respectively, for each seat in a city assembly. The figures for Okayama Prefecture are very similar. In Kamo there have seldom been more than two or three unsuccessful candidates, a high point of five being reached in the 1951 assembly election. There also is appreciable popular sentiment within a given buraku or ōaza against the candidacy of more individuals than that buraku or ōaza knows that it can elect. The people want the fullest possible representation in the assembly for their own unit and fear that any excessive candidacies within their unit would split their vote and perhaps redound to the benefit of other districts. This feeling is a significant check on the number of candidates advanced in such elections.

Personally conducted and hard-fought campaigns in our sense of the word are unusual and when encountered in the villages are a sign of the presence of strong internal dissension or "radical"—Communist or doctrinaire socialist—elements within the community. The average villager regards a seat in the village assembly as a mark of honor and prestige and would undoubtedly like to achieve such status. Yet any attempt on his part to gain such a position by unduly overt or active means, such as a real campaign, would make him an object of ridicule. He would be involved in obvious public issues of "face," and, contrasting sharply with his more passive opponents, he would probably lose the sympathy and support of the conservative majority. The various campaign techniques appropriate in the individualistically organized societies of the West are thus not approved in the more family-centered and cohesive communities of rural Japan.

The "campaign" of Niiike's representative in the 1947 election well exemplifies these points. Hiramatsu Mitsusaburō, a long-time member of the village assembly and one of Kamo's most honored elders, had decided not to run again. This left one of Upper Shinjō ōaza's seats vacant. Traditionally it would go to a Niiike man and, with the increase in assembly membership to sixteen, it seemed certain that Niiike and Ōyama jointly could control it. Under these circumstances Hiramatsu Tadashi decided to run. It is not certain whether the decision originated with him or whether he was urged to be a candidate by friends and neighbors within the buraku. Probably it was a combination of both. The self-arranged political draft is a common phenomenon in Japan. In any event the first public indication of Tadashi's interest was his refusal to run. Eventually, after a careful and very cautious analysis of his chances—veiled conversations with leading residents of Niiike and Ōyama and perhaps with a few relatives living elsewhere in the village—Tadashi was prevailed upon to run. His notification of candidacy was signed by the headmen of both Niiike and Ōyama.

Tadashi's advance calculations were interesting and apparently typical of local practice. He made no secret of the fact that he would not even have considered running if he had felt there was any possibility of losing. His analysis of his chances was ultra-conservative. He felt that a minimum of 80 votes would elect him. As it actually turned out, 70 would have been enough. He felt certain of receiving a large majority, though not all, of Niiike's 70-odd votes and Ōyama's 28, plus perhaps another 10 to 20 from relatives in Eta and Yamane buraku. Under these circumstances, as Tadashi said, his chances looked excellent.

His ensuing "campaign" can hardly be called such, although, given the conditions described, any campaign effort seemed unnecessary. Apparently he visited his relatives in other buraku to request their support, though probably in a veiled and indirect manner. Within Niiike his entire public campaign seems to have consisted of an appearance at a meeting of the buraku assembly where, at the headman's urging, he delivered himself of the following resounding statement: *"Kondo tatte imasu kara, dōka yoroshiku onegai shimasu"* ("Since I am standing [for election] this time, please do what you can"). Otherwise he spoke to no one directly about his campaign, and no one worked overtly in his behalf. The headmen of Niiike and Ōyama did, however, pointedly inform their people of Tadashi's candidacy, and on election day a few of his more ardent supporters asked their neighbors "not to waste their votes," that is, to go to the polls and vote, but they made no mention of Tadashi. Needless to say, Tadashi was elected to office by a safe majority.

VILLAGE MAYORAL ELECTIONS

The selection of a village mayor differs somewhat from "contests" for seats in the village assembly. Mayoralty campaigns focus the ambitions of all the village's buraku on a single office, the most important of all local offices. A somewhat different approach is necessary, and the problems involved, under the postwar system at least, place a greater strain on traditional techniques. Under the system prevailing prior to 1947, the mayor had in effect been chosen by the village assembly without any direct expression of popular opinion. The office was then regarded as largely honorary in nature. These circumstances were more conducive to the functioning of the traditional Japanese techniques of private discussion and compromise.

Under the present system contests are more common at this level, but, even so, there are a surprisingly large number of instances where no election is necessary because of general agreement on a single candidate or where, if an election is held, it is a heavily one-sided contest. The figures for all of Japan indicate that in 1947 there was an average of just two candidates for each mayoral post at the town and village levels. Comparable figures for the 1951 and 1955 local elections were 1.9 and 1.8, respectively. Furthermore, in the latter two years no mayoral elections at all occurred in 37 per cent of Japan's towns and villages because there was only a single candidate for the office.

Mayoral campaigns are similar to those of village assemblymen. A candidate seldom advances his own candidacy; he is drafted, although the draft may have been preceded by discreet but intensive prompting and ground-laying on his part. Campaigning, by local standards, will probably be more intense, though the personal part played by the candidate may still be negligible. Probably the campaign will be managed in his behalf by a small group of local leaders operating through buraku and family units and connections. The men most likely to take such action are the members of the village assembly, the top officials of the village agricultural co-operative association, or any village residents of outstanding prestige and status. As we have seen, the membership of these three groups is usually identical, or at least it overlaps markedly.

There have been but two mayoral elections in Kamo during the period 1945–56, the first in 1947 and the second in 1951. The village was amalgamated prior to the 1955 local elections. The first of these was no contest at all; indeed, owing to the lack of opponents, no election was held. The victorious candidate, Migaki Yoichi, had been *joyaku* or vice-mayor of the village since 1936. He was not a native of Kamo but had come there from Mitsu *gun* at the age of twenty-four as an adoptive husband. He attended an accounting school in Okayama City and after graduation served as a bank clerk in several communities in Okayama and Hiroshima prefectures. He fell ill in the early 1930's, however, and was obliged to return to Kamo, where he spent three years recuperating from his illness before going to work in the village office in 1936.

Migaki claims that he had no intention of running for mayor in 1947 but that his friends and supporters literally drafted him. The former mayor, a widely revered man, had fallen victim to the Occupation's general purge of local officeholders and had to be replaced. Migaki, as vice-mayor and a longtime worker in the village office, was thoroughly familiar with local procedures and needs, and he was available. His "campaign" was organized by two former headmen of his buraku, while Migaki himself had only to sit quietly by and benefit from their discreet activities. So effective were these that his recommenders included ten of the twelve village assemblymen, the headmen of all the village's buraku, and an assortment of other local notables. It is small wonder that no one cared to challenge the choice of such an assemblage. Consequently no election was necessary, and Migaki became mayor. Apparently the determining element in this "campaign" was the practically solid support of the former village assemblymen. Migaki was their candidate. Thus, in effect, the intentions of the Occupation had been thwarted, and the village assembly informally selected the mayor in 1947, as they had done in more formal fashion under the previous system.

Once in office, Migaki had a difficult time. His predecessor, who had been purged, had commanded almost universal respect and admiration throughout the village, and Migaki was regarded as a distinct comedown. Further, the years 1947–51 were probably more trying and difficult from the standpoint of village administration than any similar period in modern Japanese history. Given the social and economic consequences of defeat and occupation, the rationing and crop-requisition program, increased taxes, etc., it would have taken a master politician to remain in an agricultural village's good graces. Even though these problems and difficulties were generally recognized, Migaki still bore some of the blame for them in the popular mind. Beyond this, he was subject to a number of more specific criticisms. The most common of these, widely believed throughout the village, alleged a lack of courtesy on his part toward the average villager. He was said to be amiable and courteous toward the wealthy and important but abrupt and short-tempered with others. He also had difficulties with the staff of the village office which led to a brief strike in 1949 aimed primarily against Migaki. This engendered further ill-feeling. Some held that he was unduly influenced in his decisions by a small local politician from his own buraku. Others criticized his part in committing the village to what was regarded as an overly expansive and expensive drainage project in one sector of the village. He was held to be honest, however, and it was an open question in the minds of many whether anyone else could have done a much better job in these trying times. But there was little positive enthusiasm for the man or his record.[2]

Under these circumstances it is not surprising that Migaki was opposed when he tried for a second term in 1951. His opponents were a well-known political figure, also from the west side of the village, and a teacher in the local primary school who had had political experience. For Kamo the campaign was a hot one, though still largely covert and traditional in organization. The victory went to Namba Shizuo, the schoolteacher, who polled 878 votes to Sadahiro's 570 and Migaki's 483. The villagers in general claimed that Namba won because he was a "new face." By this they meant that both his opponents were professional politicians regarded as participants in past failures and scandals. Namba was new and untouched by such associations. A number also mentioned the favorable impact of

[2] It might be remarked parenthetically that the authors found Migaki Yoichi unfailingly friendly, obliging, and helpful. To them he seemed a capable and intelligent man struggling with a bewildering array of new and complex problems, the real difficulties of which were not generally appreciated by the villagers.

Namba's status as a teacher. His position of "sensei" apparently was in his favor. Some even claimed that the P.T.A. worked successfully in his behalf. The more politically sophisticated among the villagers also pointed out that Namba was from the more populous eastern side of the village of Kamo, while his two opponents were from the western side. There is some sectional feeling within the village, and the split in the western vote operated in Namba's favor.

THE NATIONAL ELECTORAL SYSTEM

A far more extensive insight into the dynamics of politics and political attitudes in rural Japan is to be gained from an analysis of the strategy and tactics of prefectural and national election campaigns as seen in the Kamo area. Elections for local office are almost completely self-contained affairs where the community's needs can still be met by modifications of the traditional techniques of compromise, co-operation, and prior agreement. Elections at higher levels, especially those for seats in the House of Representatives, are quite different in nature and conduct. They mark the major point of contact between the villagers and the national political process. As such they provide an extraordinarily interesting opportunity to observe political attitudes and behavior within the village at the point where it touches the world outside. But here, too, techniques have been evolved which make use of the old behavior patterns. Before describing the village in these respects, some general information about the Japanese election system may prove helpful.

The average citizen in Japan has more or less regular opportunities to vote in elections for the following major offices: assemblymen and mayors of cities, towns, and villages; assemblymen and governors of prefectures; members of the lower house of the national parliament, or Diet (the House of Representatives); and members of the upper house (the House of Councillors). There is also a variety of special types of elections and referendums which need not concern us here. All the above offices carry four-year terms, barring an earlier recall or dissolution through parliamentary process, except the House of Councillors, members of which serve six-year terms with half the membership elected every three years. Elections for prefectural and local offices are normally held every four years, but elections for the House of Representatives have always been far more frequent. From 1945 to 1956 there were no less than six general elections to the lower house, all but the first occasioned by dissolutions. The inhabitants of Kamo thus have regular opportunities to exercise their franchise. They have had occasion to vote in three local, three prefectural, four House of Councillors, and five House of Representatives elections, a total of fifteen major elections in the ten-year period, 1947–56. Since the new constitution specifies universal suffrage for adults of both sexes of the age of twenty or over, practically all adult inhabitants of Niiike and Kamo have been eligible to vote.

The Japanese system of election administration is extremely complex and directs the political process along unusual lines. It is best exemplified by the general elections for the House of Representatives. For this purpose all Japan is divided into 117 election districts. Okayama Prefecture has two such districts, each returning five members to the lower house. Kamo falls in the second Okayama district, which comprises roughly half the prefecture. This election district is in turn divided into a large number of polling districts (there are three in Kamo alone) and a smaller number of counting districts, usually one per village, as in Kamo. Japan thus utilizes what is technically known as the multimember constituency electoral system. This is greatly complicated by its combination with the single, non-transferable type of secret ballot. Each elector, in all elections save those for the House of Councillors, casts but a single vote; yet his election district, in the case of Kamo's voters, returns five members to the House of Representatives. The problems such a system creates for candidates and practical politicians are numerous and difficult.

Most serious contenders for seats in the House of Representatives are sponsored by one or the other of the major national political parties. Two problems confront the local manager of such parties. He must maximize the total number of votes polled by his party's several candidates (in Okayama's second district major parties usually run from two to five candidates), and he must insure that these votes are distributed in such a way as to elect the largest possible number of his party's candidates. If such a distribution is not obtained, the dynamics of this multimember, single non-transferable vote system are such as to draw off votes from a party's weaker candidates in favor of its stronger ones. The stronger ones may thus amass a sizable surplus of votes over and above the quota needed to insure their election. From the party's standpoint these are not only wasted votes; they are positively dangerous, because they reduce the support of the party's weaker candidates and render them susceptible to defeat by rival candidates from other parties. Thus the practical party politician has to worry about vote distribution in addition to his other problems.

Elections are also complicated by the extremely stringent regulations governing campaign tactics. Practically every aspect of campaigning is rigidly controlled in what is said to be an effort to minimize the advantages of large financial support and to equalize the terms of competition among candidates. Such matters as the following are precisely specified by law: the beginning and duration of the campaigning period; the identity and number of those permitted to campaign in a candidate's behalf; the types and, on radio and television, the number of speeches which a candidate or his supporters may make; the amount of money which may be spent by a candidate or his supporters for campaign purposes; the number, color, size, and distribution of newspaper advertisements, posters, election cards, and other publicity media which any candidate may use; the number of autos, trucks, or other vehicles that may be employed; the type of contacts which campaigners are permitted to make with the public (house-to-house canvasses, for example, are absolutely forbidden).

Under such circumstances the politician's life is not a happy one. Indeed, from the standpoint of practical politics, it would be an almost impossible one, if any substantial amount of attention were paid to these regulations. In practice, they are as freely and widely circumvented as the Hatch Act and similar legislation in this country. This is particularly true in respect to political campaign funds. Most candidates will admit quite freely in private conversations that few if any candidates, themselves included, even come close to observing the legal regulations governing maximum expenditures.

Few of the essential attributes of this electoral system have changed since the inauguration in 1925 of universal male suffrage and the creation of medium-sized election districts returning three to five members. The major formal changes in postwar years have been the expansion of the suffrage to include women and the lowering of the voting age from twenty-five to twenty. These have more than doubled the size of the prewar electorate, but the mechanics of the system continue relatively unaltered. Election management and administration have, however, undergone profound changes. In prewar days the system of election administration was notorious for widespread political intervention by the Home Ministry, prefectural governors, and the police; for blatant discrimination in favor of approved candidates; for the often insurmountable obstacles placed in the path of left-wing candidates; and for the prevalence of bribery on both petty and grand scales. A great deal has been attempted and much accomplished in postwar years to render election administration far more impartial. Systematic, large-scale political intervention has been virtually eliminated; complaints of police bias in the enforcement of campaign regulations, while not lacking, are relatively scarce; and the enormous expansion of the suffrage has gone far to render direct bribery of voters impossibly expensive and impractical. The major complaints today are those familiar in the West as well: the greater availability of campaign funds to conservative candidates and the general evasion of the maximum limits placed on campaign expenditures. The new and non-political election management commissions have accomplished much since 1947.

KAMO'S ELECTORAL RECORD

Against this background we may examine the record of Kamo in the four general elections of members of the House of Representatives held from 1947 to 1954. It is necessary to focus attention upon the village rather than upon Niiike proper, since this is the smallest unit for which separate election statistics are available.[3] House of Representatives elections are chosen in preference to House of Councillors or prefectural elections because they have been more numerous and because they provide the best index of party and crude programmatic affiliation available in rural Japan. The village record may perhaps best be explained in tabular form. For the sake of local comparison, statistics are also provided for Tsukubo *gun*, the area immediately surrounding Kamo, and the second election district of Okayama (five seats) in which Kamo is situated.

Space precludes a detailed analysis of the social and political characteristics of the parties and groups listed in this table. Suffice it to say that the Liberal and Democratic parties were, during these years, the principal representatives of what the Japanese themselves regard as "conservative" or "right-wing" interests, while the Right- and Left-Wing Socialists, Labor-Farmer party, and the Communist party represent progressively more radical views. They are usually collectively characterized as "proletarian" parties in Japan.

It is obvious that the voters of Kamo overwhelmingly favor conservative candidates (so-called independent candidates in this area have invariably been conservatives). In 1953 Kamo gave 68 per cent of her vote to conservative candidates. For the 1952, 1949, and 1947 elections the proportions were 85 per cent, 82 per cent, and 57 per cent, respectively. These figures give a reasonably accurate picture of the extent of conservative political allegiance within the village. Only in 1947 and 1953 did left-wing candidates make any significant inroads into the conservative monopoly. On these occasions five left-wing candidates split 36 and 32 per cent, respectively, of the village vote. However, the 1947 election was the first under the present system and was atypical in several other respects. The high Socialist vote that year does not seriously detract from Kamo's status as a conservative stronghold. In their best year, 1949, the Communist party polled only 49 votes or 3 per cent.

[3] The writers do have some data of this sort for Niiike, gathered by interviews and questionnaires, but they are incomplete and of uncertain accuracy. Questions about how a particular individual voted fall within the sensitive area in rural Japan, and many villagers interpret the principle of "secrecy of the ballot" as precluding even the voluntary revelation of how they voted.

The last column of Table 29 also shows how accurately the Kamo vote mirrors that of Tsukubo *gun*, the area immediately surrounding the village. Only when one dilutes the rural conservative preponderance by the addition of the urban vote within the second Okayama district does any significant decrease in the conservative majority appear. Even then, the conservative majority increases steadily from 56 per cent in 1947 to a high of 78 per cent in 1952.

Other aspects of the voting statistics for Okayama's second district are also of interest. The number of candidates standing for election to the

TABLE 29

ANALYSIS OF LOCAL VOTE BY PARTY AFFILIATION IN FOUR
GENERAL ELECTIONS BETWEEN 1947 AND 1954

ELECTION AND AREA	LIBERAL (*Jiyūtō*)	DEMOCRATIC (*Minshutō*)	SOCIALIST* (*Shakaitō*)		LABOR-FARMER (*Rōnōtō*)	COMMUNIST (*Kyō-santō*)	MINOR PARTIES	INDEPENDENTS	TOTAL VOTE	CONSERVATIVE VOTE AS PERCENTAGE OF TOTAL VOTE†
			Right-Wing (*Uha*)	Left-Wing (*Saha*)						
April 19, 1953:										
Kamo	1,091			251	272				1,614	68
Tsukubo *gun*	18,640			5,634	3,502				27,776	67
Okayama District II	218,143			57,349	73,011				348,503	63
October 1, 1952:										
Kamo	1,257			22	125	31	26	228	1,689	85
Tsukubo *gun*	20,512			1,166	1,923	427	565	3,720	28,313	85
Okayama District II	250,955			23,419	36,868	8,997	9,974	39,665	369,878	78
January 23, 1949:										
Kamo	389	913		34	118	49	83	37	1,623	82
Tsukubo *gun*	9,474	13,057		1,147	2,071	1,345	1,668	3,089	31,851	80
Okayama District II	124,545	78,638		14,039	31,541	26,193	56,831	8,286	340,073	62
April 25, 1947:										
Kamo	520	271		495		45	62		1,393	57
Tsukubo *gun*	10,800	5,509		8,292		1,366	2,110	51	28,128	58
Okayama District II	111,046	57,674		81,595		15,985	34,563	677	301,540	56

* The Socialist party split into left and right wings in October, 1951. Thereafter each wing put up its own candidates.

† Conservative vote equals Liberal vote plus Democratic and independent votes. During this period independent candidates were uniformly conservatives.

House of Representatives, for example, in general declines steadily during the period 1947–55. Here again the preponderance of conservative and especially Liberal party candidacies is noteworthy. Since 1947 the Liberal party has been the only serious contender for political primacy within the district. Their success is best indicated by the ratio between the number of their candidates and the number of seats won, a remarkable 78 per cent. One of the successful Democratic candidates later joined the Liberals, so the party record is even better than Table 30 indicates.

Also, local voters tended to return the same political representatives to office for several terms. During these five general elections twenty-five seats in all were at stake. These were occupied by only eight men. Of these, one, Hoshijima Jirō, was elected on all five occasions; Inukai Ken, Hashimoto Ryūgo, and Nakahara Kenji were each elected four times;

Kondō Tsuruyo won on three occasions; another man served two terms, and the other two but a single term. During this period the party allegiance of several of these successful candidates changed. One Democrat and one independent formally joined the Liberal party; one Socialist became a member of the Labor-Farmer party.

One other aspect of the voting record requires consideration: the distribution of the total vote for any one political party among its several candidates. This problem concerns the Liberal party particularly, as it habitually puts up anywhere from two to five candidates for the second district's five seats. The optimum allocation of the party's votes among these candidates is the supreme test of campaign management. Let us

TABLE 30

NUMBER OF CANDIDACIES AND NUMBER OF SEATS WON IN HOUSE OF REPRESENTATIVES ELECTIONS IN OKAYAMA'S SECOND DISTRICT, 1947–55

Party	1947		1949		1952		1953		1955		Total Number of Candidacies 1947–55	Total Number of Seats Won 1947–55	Percentage of Successful Candidacies
	Candidacies	Seats Won	Candidacies	Seats Won	Candidacies	Seats Won	Candidacies	Seats Won	Candidacies	Seats Won			
Liberal	4	2	3	3	4	4	4	3	3	2	18	14	78
Democratic	4		1	1			1	1			6	2	33
Socialist	3	2	1								4	2	50
Right-wing									1		1		
Left-wing					1		1	1	1	1	3	2	67
Labor-Farmer			1	1	1		1	1	1	1	4	3	75
Communist	1		1		1						3		
Minor parties	2	1	4		2						8	1	13
Independents	1		1		1	1			1		4	1	25
Total	15	5	12	5	10	5	6	5	8	5	51	25	

consider then the records of the several major parties running more than a single candidate in the general elections of 1947–55.

The 1947 election, it will be remembered, was the first to be conducted under the present system. Times were still politically chaotic, and this is reflected in the relatively unsystematic internal distribution of the several party votes. Thereafter the Liberal party, the only one supporting multiple candidacies, distributed its support with almost optimal skill. In 1949 the mean vote for Liberal candidates was 41,515 and the average deviation of the actual vote from this only 2,930. In 1952, the corresponding mean vote was 62,738 with an average deviation of 6,278; in 1953 the figures were 54,538 and 2,682, respectively; while in 1955 they were 52,766 and 4,487. Given a total Liberal vote amounting to as much as 275,492, the average deviations from the mean of perfect distribution ranging from 2,682 to 6,278 are a remarkable tribute to the skill of the party's campaign managers.

PRACTICAL POLITICS: THE TRADITIONAL PATTERN

While the electoral record of Kamo and its surrounding areas set forth in the preceding section is of interest in its own right, it also poses a great many related questions of equal or greater concern. Many of these focus on an area which may be loosely subsumed under "practical politics." In the broadest sense this treats of such matters as the geographic analysis of party support and its extent and sociopolitical characteristics with particular reference to the ways in which party managers strive to exploit and utilize these factors to their partisan advantage. Herein lie the

TABLE 31

DISTRIBUTION OF PARTY VOTE AMONG CANDIDATES IN
OKAYAMA'S SECOND DISTRICT IN HOUSE OF
REPRESENTATIVES ELECTIONS, 1947–55

Election	Liberal	Democratic	Socialist
April 25, 1947:			
Candidate 1..........	58,405*	17,478	34,816*
Candidate 2..........	31,797*	17,175	31,316*
Candidate 3..........	16,691	13,439	15,463
Candidate 4..........	4,153	9,582	
January 23, 1949:			
Candidate 1..........	45,911*		
Candidate 2..........	41,370*		
Candidate 3..........	37,264*		
October 1, 1952:			
Candidate 1..........	70,611*		
Candidate 2..........	67,423*		
Candidate 3..........	57,486*		
Candidate 4..........	55,435*		
April 19, 1953:			
Candidate 1..........	57,291*		
Candidate 2..........	57,144*		
Candidate 3..........	52,669*		
Candidate 4..........	51,039		
February 26, 1955:			
Candidate 1..........	56,424*		
Candidate 2..........	55,839*		
Candidate 3..........	46,035		

* Successful candidates.

secrets of the ancient art of practical politics, and it is through their comprehension that one gains insight into the true dynamics of the political process in rural Japan. In discussing these matters, however, we find again that it is impossible to confine our attention to so restricted an area as Niiike or Kamo. Both the character of available statistics and the nature of the process itself require a wider view. This is presently provided by the second election district of Okayama Prefecture, which controls five seats in the House of Representatives (the first and second election districts are shown on Figure 45).

Okayama's second district had 479, 852 qualified electors in 1953. Thirty-three per cent (157,503) of these lived in the six cities of Kurashiki,

Okayama Prefecture
First and Second Election districts

SECOND ELECTION DISTRICT

FIRST ELECTION DISTRICT

Atetsu Gun¹

Niimi City

Atetsu Gun¹

Jōbō Gun

Takahashi City

Kawakami Gun

Kibi Gun¹

Kibi Gun¹

Sōja City

Kamo

Tsukubo Gun

Okayama City

Shitsuki Gun

Oda Gun

Kibi Gun¹

Asaguchi Gun

Kurashiki City

Ibara City

Kojima Gun¹

Asaguchi Gun¹

Tamashima City

Kasaoka City

Kojima City

Kojima Gun¹

Tamano City

INLAND SEA

```
———————  Prefectural boundary
– – – – –  Second Electoral District boundary
· · · · · · ·  City and gun boundaries
ᵒᵒᵒᵒᵒᵒ  Kamo Village Boundary
— ·· — ·· —  Extent of prefectural jurisdiction over islands in Inland Sea
¹  Indicates Gun split by creation of new cities
```

Fɪɢ. 45.—The second election district of Okayama and its subdivisions

Tamano, Kojima, Tamashima, Kasaoka, and Ibara, while 67 per cent (322,349) resided in the rural areas included in the nine counties (*gun*) of Kojima, Tsukubo, Asaguchi, Oda, Shitsuki, Kibi, Jōbō, Kawakami, and Atetsu. Actually the cities contain within their boundaries sizable rural areas, and the figures therefore considerably overstate the urban proportion of the population. This is also true of the three cities, Sōja, Takahashi, and Niimi, established since 1953. Historically, it is also of interest to note that the present-day boundaries of the second election district—minus the Kojima and Tamano areas—coincide almost precisely with the traditional boundaries of the old province (*kuni*) of Bitchū. This constitutes the western and smaller half of Okayama Prefecture. It is primarily rural and agricultural with population most heavily concentrated in the plains on its southern fringe and becoming progressively lighter northward through higher ground to the mountains.

The second district has had an interesting political history. Its political traditions and heritage are different from those of the greater part of Okayama's first election district, which is composed in major part of the former province of Bizen. In Tokugawa days Bizen was controlled by the Ikeda family and under their guidance achieved considerable prosperity and sociopolitical stability. The second district, comprising former Bitchū, was quite different. It had been split prior to the Restoration among some thirty-one small feudatories, exclusive of temple lands. These usually had no outlets to the sea or to the major overland routes save through Ikeda territories and were frequently hard pressed to preserve their position against their larger and stronger neighbor. This tended to develop a rugged individualism among these smaller fiefs, which was subsequently reflected in the voting statistics for the second district. The support of particular politicians has often been concentrated in small districts, the limits of which sometimes correspond roughly to the boundaries of the earlier fiefs. Such areas of political support are known as *jiban*, perhaps best translated as "bailiwick," meaning one's special political domain. Niiike, Kamo, and for that matter all of Tsukubo *gun* fall within one of the oldest and best-known *jiban* in modern Japan—the so-called iron *jiban* originally built by Inukai Tsuyoshi during the 1890's. This is still a salient factor in the political record and attitudes of the villagers of Kamo. To understand it, one needs to know something about the story of its founder, Inukai Tsuyoshi, widely known as Bokudō.[4]

Inukai Tsuyoshi was one of Japan's most famous party politicians.

---

[4] The story of Inukai's life and political career is admirably told in Joseph L. Sutton, "A Political Biography of Inukai Tsuyoshi" (unpublished doctoral dissertation, University of Michigan, 1954, 277 pp.). The present account is based upon this.

Born in Niwase, a town in Kibi *gun*, Okayama Prefecture, in 1855, he shares only with Ozaki Yukio the distinction of having been victorious in every general election from the first in 1890 to the eighteenth in 1932. At the time of his assassination in May, 1932, he was serving as prime minister of Japan. Within Okayama Prefecture he was renowned as the creator of a political machine which almost completely dominated both the local and national aspects of prefectural politics from 1890 until his first "retirement" from politics in 1925 and which continued to exert major control until his death in 1932. Upon his death he was able to pass on a portion of his original *jiban* as a legacy to his son, Inukai Ken. Many of the voters of this area, including those of Kamo, continue today to give their loyal support to the son of their old favorite. It is the techniques by which such steadfast support at the polls is elicited that are of concern here.

One must understand first that a *jiban* is a personal, not a party, appurtenance. It is gained, belongs to, and is lost by an individual politician. Traditionally, if an individual is solidly intrenched in his *jiban*, he is completely safe from party discipline at the polls. If he chooses to switch his party allegiance, the local voter usually assumes that he had good reason for doing so. Regardless of party policy, he can go his own way in so far as the majority of issues are concerned. In practice, such freedom is not, of course, absolute; there are other ways of disciplining recalcitrant Diet members than at the polls. But this political independence is extensive enough to form an important part of the background of the constant schisms and regroupings which have characterized party politics in Japan. So peculiarly personal a possession is the *jiban* that in the most mature examples, such as Inukai's, it can in major part be lent to someone else or even passed on at death by a sort of testamentary procedure. At election time in 1902, for example, Inukai wrote to his follower Kojima Kazuo: "I gave half of my constituency [*jiban*] (this half includes Kayō and Shimomichi *gun*) to Nishimura Tanjiro. I am holding the other half, plus two *gun* in the Bizen area."[5] And, as has already been mentioned, Inukai Ken, the son of Tsuyoshi, simply inherited the heart of his present *jiban* upon the death of his father.

The formation and proper maintenance of a *jiban* is a complicated and time-consuming task. To use the Japanese expressions, one "nurses" a *jiban;* one "feeds" its stalwarts. The actual techniques vary with the time and the sociopolitical circumstances of the area concerned. The organization and methods of the older Inukai, although unusual in some respects, are still widely admired by professional politicians in Japan and may well

[5] *Ibid.*, p. 129.

serve as a sort of prototype of the traditional *jiban*. They help also to illuminate current political attitudes and practices in the Kamo area.

The primary goal of an organization of this type is the delivery of votes, particularly in prefectural and national elections. This requires the construction and maintenance of appropriate political machinery of a most elaborate sort. Inukai's organization was hierarchical. At its summit was Inukai himself directing operations, sometimes locally but more often from Tokyo, where he spent most of his time. He had only two chief assistants throughout his entire career. Technically they were known as "campaign managers" (*senkyo jimushochō*), but actually they worked continually, serving as liaison agents between Inukai and his *jiban* and maintaining its strength and vigor on a day-to-day basis. Until 1923, Inukai Gentarō held this post; thereafter it was filled by Uchida Yatarō.

Also at the top level was a group composed of Inukai's best-known and most important protégés (*kobun*), usually men from Okayama who were closely associated with him in the House of Representatives. The *oyabun-kobun* or master-follower relationship is very common in Japanese politics, in proletarian as well as in the more traditional conservative parties. The closeness of the bond, the extent of the obligations, and the quality of the obedience flowing from such a relationship usually far surpass those commonly encountered in analagous Western associations.

Inukai's group was composed of such individuals as Hoshijima Jirō, Nishimura Tanjirō, and Takakusa Miyozō, whose careers as prefectural and national politicians were launched and subsequently directed by Inukai. In time these individuals came to have recognized *jiban* of their own. Hoshijima's, for example, lay in the extreme southern part of the second election district, centering in Kojima *gun* and portions of Asaguchi *gun*.[6] In important part, however, they owed the acquisition of these *jiban* to Inukai's aid and benevolence—in some instances to his outright gift of a portion of his own expansive *jiban*, as in the above-cited case of Nishimura Tanjirō. Such persons functioned then, in their own and Inukai's behalf, among the top echelon of the local political machine. For many years a small group of them under Inukai's direction almost completely dominated general elections and themselves occupied the second district's seats in the House of Representatives. This tight control survived unimpaired until about 1925, and major elements of it persist today in the *jiban* of Inukai Ken and Hoshijima Jirō.

Below this top level one finds a more extensive array of political figures functioning primarily at the prefectural level. For many years in Okaya-

---

[6] Hoshijima was born in Kojima *gun*, the son of one of the prefecture's wealthiest families. His early political career was greatly aided by his family connections with wealthy and important spinning and weaving interests in this area.

ma, Inukai's machine included a considerable majority of the prefectural assembly. One participant characterized this parliamentary body as "practically an Inukai fan club." It was common then and still is for members of the prefectural assembly to be drawn from among the most influential politicians of the area. It was also traditional that many of these men in turn possessed a *jiban* of their own, particularly in the extensive rural areas of the prefecture. In general these were somewhat more fluid and shifting units than the *jiban* of Inukai or Hoshijima, but this control insured a politician's own election to the prefectural assembly, while combinations of these second-level *jiban* furnished the constituent elements of the primary *jiban* which functioned in national elections.

Below the prefecture one begins to approach the "rice-roots" level of informal political organizations and activity. Here one encounters the men reluctantly termed "big bosses" by a number of the authors' informants, several of whom fell in this category themselves. The term "boss," or "political boss" (pronounced *bosu*), is opprobrious in Japanese as in English, and one quite uniformly finds it avoided by those who are personally associated with such activities. Instead, most seem to prefer such circumlocutions as *chihō no seijika* ("local politician") or, better yet, *chihō no yūryokusha* ("locally powerful or influential persons"). There were, for example, ten such important political leaders in Kibi *gun* alone before the Second World War. Each of them controlled a definite district, known locally as his *nawabari* (literally, "roped-off place" or "domain"). An average *nawabari* consisted of two or three villages, a large one of five or six towns and villages. In their areas the politicians invariably served in some official capacity, in almost all cases as assembly members, town or village mayors, or leaders of the agricultural or business co-operatives and associations. They were men of great political experience, usually acquired through years of service in such posts. Beyond this, and more important, they possessed status and prestige and were considered outstanding community leaders by the local populace. Herein lay the basis of their authority, which normally does not seem to have rested on either coercion or corruption. In short, they were generally regarded as, first, sincerely interested in the well-being of the community and its inhabitants; second, familiar with the esoteric mysteries of politics and administration and skilled in their manipulation on behalf of the particular community concerned; and, third, well rounded in their abilities beyond the specifically political sphere.

Directly beneath these "big bosses" were either smaller political leaders operating on an even more local level or the terminal links in the organization, the men who were in actual contact with the rural voter, known in this part of Okayama simply as *yūryokusha*, or sometimes, more colloquially, as *kui* (literally, "stakes"). Such men were found in every buraku: sometimes one to a buraku, sometimes more than one, in which case they might be in competition with one another for the support of the buraku inhabitants. Within their buraku these *kui* were certain to be men of recognized status by virtue of family connections or their own achievements. Furthermore, in an essentially apolitical rural world, they were individuals possessed of some political information, contacts, and perhaps even experience.

Besides this chain of "bosses" there were other lines of local influence and contact at Inukai's disposal. Prominent among them were the major commercial associations in Okayama. For many years, the textile interests, fishermen, and dealers in mat rush had been organized in separate associations on a prefecture-wide basis with numerous local branches. Inukai early appreciated that these could serve as excellent channels of political influence and took over their control. For a time he himself served as chairman of the mat-rush association, subsequently turning the post over to his son Ken. He installed his protégés, Hoshijima and Takakusa, as chairmen of the textile and fishermen's associations, respectively.

Also in prewar Japan the priests of some Shintō and Buddhist sects, especially Kurozumi and Nichiren, were active politically through their numerous shrines and temples. Inukai maintained close and cordial relations with both, to his considerable political advantage. He also cultivated the support of the *Eta*, the outcast group, a most unusual and daring step for a Japanese politician. His protégés further organized in his behalf a network of so-called *Bokudō-Kai* (Inukai clubs), devoted to developing a cult of admirers and, incidentally, of political supporters. They published a regular magazine and maintained a junior auxiliary which stretched far beyond the boundaries of Okayama. There was even a branch in Seattle, Washington.

We are dealing, then, with a political machine, well and intricately organized on a variety of fronts and, incidentally, from an organizational standpoint little different from Western political machines. How and with what efficiency did this machine fulfil its purpose, namely, to deliver the vote?

In general the way it operated in what many informants obviously regarded as "the good old days" was this: When a general election was announced, the prefectural and regional political leaders aligned themselves behind a particular candidate. In Inukai's *jiban* such alignment was almost automatic. The majority of them were his loyal followers. In less committed areas, the choice was usually not difficult. The range of practicable alternatives was small. The entire system had a conservative bias, and there were as a rule only two or three major conservative parties in the arena plus a scattering of independent but conservative candidates. The individual "boss" at the higher levels was likely to have some affiliation with one or another of this small group of local conservative candidates. This might be based on an *oyabun-kobun* relationship, on participation in an established *jiban*, on family ties, on common village or regional bonds, or on a variety of such relationships. In almost all of these money would play a part but, in this area, usually not a predominant one.

It must not be forgotten that the average prewar politician owed much of his political influence to the fact that he was an "honorable" man, a man of outstanding character in the traditional sense. Such a role was not readily compatible with outright bribery. There were, to be sure, "floating bosses," influential individuals with no established political allegiance, who made a practice of more or less openly selling the votes they controlled to the highest bidder. In marginal elections their influence could be critical and would be eagerly sought, but the traditional politician looked upon such types with contempt and disapproval. In the words of one indignant and allegedly semiretired "big boss": "They give the profession a bad name." In Okayama the old province of Mimasaka, comprising the far northern parts of the present prefecture, is generally regarded as a contemporary stronghold of such "floating bosses."

This is not to say, however, that sizable sums of money did not pass from candidates to local political leaders in almost all cases. Even Inukai, solid as his local support was and parsimonious as his campaigns were, is said never to have managed to stay within the legal maximum set for campaign expenditures.[7] The money that was paid, in many instances at least, was not given or received as a bribe. It was rather "expense" money, broadly interpreted. This money was variously known as *mae-gane* or *ato-gane*, depending on whether it was paid before an election or after—often six months after. A solidly established "boss" with a good credit rating could pay after the election. The six-month interim allowed the statute of limitations for election offenses to take effect.

Even in a well-established *jiban* the expenses of a campaign were formidable. There were travel and living expenses during the campaign for the whole hierarchy of practicing politicians. It was professionally essential that the top men be freehanded with their followers, not only during

---

[7] Inukai's thriftiness in such matters became practically legendary. The writers encountered, for example, good-natured complaints that he did not even supply *waraji* ("rice-straw sandals") to replace those worn out in his service by his campaigners. It was customary to do so.

campaigns, but throughout their association. Entertainment costs (*kōsai-hi*) were an important item. Campaign directors and workers were lavishly feted at banquets as elaborate and plentifully endowed with *sake* (and, at the more elevated levels, with *geisha*) as the candidate's resources would permit. Then there were the normal costs of printing, publicity, and general propaganda attendant upon modern elections. Before such onslaughts, sizable campaign funds literally melted away. Among the more traditional local politicians there was little left to use as direct bribes to individuals at any level.

A politician's reward came later and in more subtle ways. For the more important figures there were lucrative sinecures as advisers to business firms interested in maintaining good political relations. More common were payoffs in the form of public works projects and improvements, roads, bridges, irrigation facilities, etc., for the communities represented by the "boss" concerned.

Once having selected their candidate for a particular election on grounds compounded of principle, traditional association, and financial advantage, the "big bosses" would set the local campaign machinery in operation. Word would go out from each to his affiliates and subordinates identifying the candidate of his choice. Sometimes this seems to have taken the form of a command, more often of a more elaborate and reasoned appeal calculated to convince the smaller "bosses" concerned of the wisdom of his choice. Expense money would be distributed and entertainment would get under way. The local politicians would then embark upon the practice known colloquially in Okayama as *kuiuchi*, literally "the driving of stakes," hence the name *kui* or *kue* ("stakes") for the local *yūryokusha* or persons of influence. This involved visits to their *kui* in each buraku to explain the merits of their candidate and secure the indorsement and support of the *kui* during the campaign. At this time also, some money might change hands. In Kibi *gun*, for example, one of Inukai's strongholds, it was customary to pay an ordinary *kui* from ¥20 to ¥30 in the old days, perhaps as much as ¥100 if he were more important. This payment was euphemistically known as *meishigawari* ("in place of a calling card"). It would in all probability be used for local entertainment and bolstering the "face" and position of the *kui* concerned, thus reinforcing his political influence and utility. Such house-to-house calls for campaign purposes, known in Japanese as *kobetsu hōmon*, are strictly forbidden by the election law. They are officially regarded as a particularly insidious form of campaigning technique subject to all sorts of dangerous exploitation. Despite this, the smaller "bosses" or their followers regularly made such visits.

Having made the rounds of the local *kui* and having ascertained the extent of their support, the local leaders were in a position to determine with great precision how many votes the particular area would produce for their candidate. Under normal circumstances each *kui* knew exactly how many votes he could influence or control. Long before the election, therefore, the "big bosses," having received this information, were in a position to inform their candidate's campaign manager of the minimum number of votes he would poll in that election district. If additional votes were still needed, the campaign manager could then undertake expensive negotiations with "floating bosses" or others of less than steadfast allegiance, preferably suborning the votes from the most dangerous rival.

This formidable apparatus of usually reliable "bosses" and *kui* underlay the remarkable ability of the major parties to apportion their support among several candidates with optimal efficiency. Had it not been for the existence of some such system, Japan's combination of multimember constituencies with the single non-transferable vote would have spelled electoral chaos and ruin for the major parties. As it was, however, the campaign managers for the several candidates usually run by any major party could readily caucus, decide how many votes recognized party candidates *in toto* could command, which individuals were running weakest, and how many additional votes they needed. Often these could be supplied from the surplus vote for the party's strongest candidates. Particular "bosses" would simply be asked to have their *kui* transfer the votes in particular locales from the stronger to the weaker party candidate.

Before the war this system operated with wondrous precision. Inukai Tsuyoshi was returned to the House of Representatives in eighteen consecutive elections between 1890 and his assassination in 1932. The system operated for years in the almost exclusive interests of the group known in the second district as the "Big Five." Besides Inukai himself—replaced by his son Ken after 1932—the "Big Five" included Hoshijima Jirō and Kotani Setsuo of the Seiyūkai party and Ogawa Gōtaro and Nishimura Tanjirō of the Minseitō party. Between the introduction of universal manhood suffrage in 1925 and the outbreak of the Second World War there were five general elections in Japan. In each of them the second district had five seats to fill. On every occasion save two (the 1930 and 1932 elections) all five of these men were elected. On those two occasions other Inukai stalwarts temporarily acquired seats, one at the expense of Kotani, one at that of Nishimura. During this entire period, the electoral strength of these five was so unchallengeable that their total competition at the polls numbered only six other individuals, whose vote was usually small. Only two of these six represented a left-wing or "proletarian" party. The remainder represented various degrees of conservative opinion, especially the Seiyūkai political party. During the years 1925–41 Okayama's second district consistently ranked as a prime bastion of Seiyūkai strength, largely because Inukai supported this party after 1925.

A more precise insight into the operation of the prewar *jiban* system may be obtained from an examination of Tables 32 and 33. These set forth and analyze the electoral records of the two Inukai, father and son, and of Hoshijima Jirō in the five general elections held between 1928 and 1937. The wartime election of 1942 is omitted because it is atypical on a variety of counts.

TABLE 32

GEOGRAPHIC ANALYSIS OF INUKAI TSUYOSHI'S AND INUKAI KEN'S SUPPORT, 1928–37*

Area	1928	1930	1932	Average Percentage of Vote Polled 1928–32	Percentage of Total Support Contributed 1928–32	1936	1937	Average Percentage of Vote Polled 1936–37	Percentage of Total Support Contributed 1936–37
Kurashiki City .	†	2,017 *(43)*	2,420 *(48)*	46	8	1,790 *(31)*	1,708 *(31)*	31	7
Kojima *gun*	156 *(0.8)‡*	455 *(2)*	1,083 *(5)*	3	3	1,981 *(8)*	1,233 *(6)*	7	7
Tsukubo *gun* . . .	7,255 *(47)*	7,722 *(63)*	7,822 *(64)*	58	41	5,391 *(42)*	5,202 *(43)*	43	23
Asaguchi *gun* . . .	116 *(0.7)*	546 *(3)*	1,516 *(8)*	4	4	2,433 *(14)*	2,272 *(12)*	13	10
Oda *gun*	78 *(0.6)*	290 *(2)*	709 *(5)*	3	2	4,009 *(27)*	3,479 *(24)*	26	16
Shitsuki *gun*	29 *(0.4)*	108 *(1)*	250 *(4)*	2	1	1,582 *(21)*	1,548 *(22)*	22	7
Kibi *gun*	5,176 *(43)*	6,935 *(54)*	7,686 *(61)*	53	35	5,581 *(42)*	5,675 *(45)*	44	24
Jōbō *gun*	797 *(11)*	692 *(9)*	1,542 *(20)*	13	5	221 *(3)*	399 *(5)*	4	1
Kawakami *gun* .	64 *(0.9)*	197 *(3)*	391 *(5)*	3	1	1,030 *(13)*	717 *(9)*	11	4
Atetsu *gun*	9 *(0.1)*	88 *(1)*	104 *(1)*	1	1	385 *(4)*	288 *(3)*	4	1
Total	13,680 *(5)§*	19,050 *(3)*	23,523 *(2)*			24,403 *(2)*	22,516 *(3)*		

* Inukai Ken ran for the first time in the 1936 campaign. His father was assassinated several months after his victory in the 1932 election.

† Kurashiki City had not yet been established.

‡ Figures in parentheses indicate the percentage of the total vote in this jurisdiction polled by this candidate.

§ Figures in parentheses in the "Total" row indicate the candidate's competitive ranking in terms of number of votes received in the entire second election district.

The solidity and concentration of a strong prewar *jiban* is well illustrated by the section of Table 32 devoted to Inukai Tsuyoshi. In the three general elections held between 1928 and 1932 he polled an average of 58 per cent of the vote in Tsukubo *gun* and 53 per cent in Kibi. These two jurisdictions—plus the city of Kurashiki to a somewhat lesser degree—constituted his *jiban* and supplied throughout these same elections no less than 76 per cent of the total vote which he received—84 per cent, if Kurashiki is added. The stability of his support in Tsukubo was particularly noteworthy. The contribution of other jurisdictions was negligible. It is this fact which more than any other characterizes the old-style *jiban* —a high concentration of support in a quite sharply delimited area with votes falling off rapidly beyond its boundaries.

The prewar *jiban* of Hoshijima Jirō displays this same characteristic in even more marked fashion, owing in part to the fact that Hoshijima was not at that time a figure of prefectural and nationwide standing comparable to Inukai. As a consequence, his following tended to be somewhat more local. It was in fact concentrated in the large and populous area known as Kojima *gun*, where he polled an average of 52 per cent of the vote in the five general elections between 1928 and 1937. Adjacent areas in Asaguchi and Tsukubo *gun* and Kurashiki City also contributed smaller but reliable percentages of their vote. Of the total number of votes he received over these years, 65 per cent came from Kojima *gun* alone, a figure which rises to 90 per cent if the appropriate adjacent areas of Asaguchi and Tsukubo *gun* are added. No other jurisdiction contributed more

TABLE 33

GEOGRAPHIC ANALYSIS OF HOSHIJIMA JIRŌ'S SUPPORT, 1928-37

Area	1928	1930	1932	1936	1937	Average Percentage of Vote Polled 1928-37	Percentage of Total Support Contributed 1928-37
Kurashiki City.	*	344 (7)	614 (12)	953 (16)	705 (13)	12	3
Kojima *gun*....	10,414 (53)†	11,395 (53)	12,447 (55)	10,623 (45)	12,247 (56)	52	65
Tsukubo *gun*...	610 (4)	611 (5)	1,443 (12)	2,925 (23)	2,755 (23)	13	9
Asaguchi *gun*...	3,083 (18)	3,116 (18)	2,416 (15)	2,720 (15)	2,363 (13)	15	16
Oda *gun*.......	42 (0.3)	391 (3)	418 (3)	618 (4)	468 (3)	3	2
Shitsuki *gun*...	37 (0.6)	219 (3)	49 (0.7)	168 (2)	133 (2)	2	1
Kibi *gun*.......	86 (0.7)	101 (0.8)	257 (2)	339 (3)	321 (3)	2	1
Jōbō *gun*......	40 (0.6)	257 (3)	345 (5)	71 (0.9)	181 (2)	2	1
Kawakami *gun*.	104 (1)	481 (6)	453 (6)	172 (2)	121 (2)	3	2
Atetsu *gun*.....	17 (0.2)	72 (0.8)	158 (2)	118 (1)	64 (0.7)	1	1
Total......	14,433 (3)‡	16,987 (5)	18,600 (4)	18,707 (4)	19,308 (4)		

* Kurashiki City had not yet been established.

† Figures in parentheses indicate the percentage of the total votes in this jurisdiction polled by this candidate.

‡ Figures in parentheses in the "Total" row indicate the candidate's competitive ranking in terms of number of votes received in the entire second election district.

than 3 per cent of his total support, while most yielded less than 1 per cent. This is a classic example of the traditional *jiban*.

When Inukai Ken ran in place of his assassinated father in the 1936 and 1937 general elections, the old *jiban* underwent some revision. Tsukubo and Kibi *gun* were still its heartland, giving an average of 43 per cent and 44 per cent of their votes to young Inukai and providing 47 per cent of his total support during this period—54 per cent, if Kurashiki City is added. This still represents a marked loss as compared with his father's performance in these same two areas—a drop of about 2,000 votes per election in Tsukubo *gun*, for example, or from 76 per cent to 47 per cent of the total support contributed. The famous "iron *jiban*" was thus not completely heritable. Both Nishimura Tanjirō and Hoshijima Jirō made appreciable incursions into it. His losses were compensated for, however, by the younger Inukai's success in expanding the areas from which he drew substantial support. An examination of Table 32 will show that Ken was considerably stronger than his father in such areas as Kojima, Asaguchi, Oda, Shitsuki, and Kawakami *gun*. This broader patterning of support proved to be a forecast of postwar experience in these areas.

The traditional *jiban* system could operate effectively only as long as the average rural voter was willing to take the political advice of his local *kui* or "boss." The question becomes then, why was the average rural voter so dependable in his electoral activities? One reason was the traditionally apolitical attitude of the farmer (see pp. 398–99) reinforced by the relatively little political information available to him. Lack of communication made the prewar village an appreciably more cloistered unit than it is now.

Added to this is the fact that for centuries Japanese rural communities have for certain purposes been hierarchically organized. Some family or individual, perhaps more than one, was regarded as having superior status, and served as informal community leader. His advice or approval was likely to be sought for any decisions of a suprafamily sort taken by persons within the community. This general social practice could readily develop a specifically political aspect such as the *kui* system. And the growth of such a system of seeking and taking political advice would be materially assisted by the villagers' very lack of political experience. To them politics must have appeared an esoteric and mysterious field where decisions were better left to the greater wisdom of individuals in whom were combined trusted local status and wider worldly knowledge and contacts.

It is often alleged that this "boss" system of politics in prewar Japan rested ultimately upon widespread bribery of the voters through the payment of sums said to range from ¥1 to ¥5 per voter. There is some truth to this charge. Undoubtedly there was substantial bribing of voters in some elections and some areas of Japan, but this does not seem to have reached critical proportions in Okayama Prefecture, although it was probably more prevalent in Mimasaka than elsewhere. A number of persons knowledgeable in such matters were consulted, and in general they discussed bribery of voters quite freely and dispassionately. Their consensus was that paying the individual voter indicated a very low level of professional accomplishment on the part of politicians. Their major points were these: First, bribery of voters is too expensive save in close contests. The advent of universal manhood suffrage in 1925, by enormously extending the franchise, rendered such a practice too costly for the average candidate. Second, any moderately intelligent boss in a rural area should be able to influence the vote of his constituents by more subtle and less expensive techniques. Third, overt bribery was "un-Japanese" and would seriously compromise the regard in which the local voters held their leaders. Finally, it was a dangerous precedent. Once begun, the voters might expect such payments regularly. This was simply not practicable.

Direct bribery does not seem to have been a primary factor in the popular support of the "boss" system. There were important economic motivations which did play a part in its effectiveness. These had more to do, however, with community and collective benefits than with individual profit. The farmers felt that the local politicians were well-connected persons who enjoyed privileged access to the prefectural assembly and prefectural offices, perhaps even to Tokyo, and that it paid to support such persons. As one informant said: "We supported Inukai. Consequently, when he was in power, important roads were built in our district." Here lay the practical economic foundations reinforcing the sociopsychological supports of the system.

A complex apparatus of management and manipulation affected the entire electoral system from popular roots through "big bosses." It was probably more solidly intrenched, more prototypical in form and manifestation, in Okayama Prefecture than in most other areas of prewar Japan. It is difficult to sum up so elaborately articulated a system of campaign management, and perhaps the best attempt was made by a highly successful local "boss." "In winning elections in the Japanese countryside," he said, "the most important factors are: *jiban* ['bailiwicks'], *kamban* [literally, 'signboard' but here 'face' or 'prestige'], and *kaban* ['bag,' i.e., a money-bag]." The authors cannot improve upon this.

PRACTICAL POLITICS: POSTWAR DEVELOPMENTS

One cannot understand practical politics in present-day Okayama without a firm grasp of its traditional basis. It is for this reason that the prewar system has been described in such detail. The most salient political fact about Okayama's second election district today, as about all Japan, is the competition between the old ways and disruptive new sociopolitical forces. Defeat and the Occupation have acted as catalysts for a number of political forces which operated less intensively and in more restricted areas in prewar Japan. Recent political developments can best be explained by reference to the base point of local political organization and practice in the days of Inukai's dominance. Postwar developments stem largely from patterns of disruption and change intelligible only in terms of this point of departure. It is most important to note, however, that the political effects of this process of change have in no sense been catastrophic or revolutionary. Appreciable adjustments have taken place, but the continued strength and vitality of the old system is astonishing. With significant modifications it continues to dominate the local scene today. This is no doubt more true in Okayama's second district than in Japan as a whole, but essentially the same factors operate in both cases.

The second district has a staunchly conservative voting record in the five general elections held between 1947 and 1957. An average of 65 per cent of the district's vote went to conservative candidates. If one excludes the atypical 1947 election, the figure is even higher, amounting to 67 per cent. Only eight men shared the occupancy of the twenty-five seats in the House of Representatives at stake in these five elections (five per election). This is a record which compares favorably with that of the five prewar elections, where seven men monopolized the twenty-five seats at stake. One may ask then, what constitutes the change? Statistically the district is still a bastion of conservative strength. Changes exist, however, and are significant despite their piecemeal and emergent nature.

The most conspicuous political change has been the expansion of the alternatives presented to the voter. In the five prewar elections only two candidates represented the so-called proletarian parties which stood for some form of socialist political solution. Together they polled a total of 16,189 votes. In the five elections between 1947 and 1957, on the other hand, there have been eighteen left-wing candidates, who have collectively polled in a given election from 69,284 to 135,467 votes. Furthermore, they secured seven of the twenty-five seats at stake during these years. In each Diet, except that installed by the 1952 elections, representatives of left-wing parties have held at least one of the second district's five seats, and on three occasions they have held two. This is a respectable showing in such a solid constituency and a distinct threat to the conservative majority.

In addition, the local *jiban*, famous throughout Japan for their "iron" quality, their steadfast adherence to a single candidate whatever the vagaries of national politics, have begun to contract, to split their vote, and to show other signs of "left-wing deviationism." Let us take two of the best-known and most solid *jiban* in this area and all Japan as examples and see what has happened to their vote in the years 1947–57. The two concerned belong to Inukai Ken and Hoshijima Jirō. Both men, during this period, were nationally prominent leaders of the Liberal party.

An examination of Table 34 in conjunction with Table 32, which sets forth Inukai Ken's prewar electoral record, will make clear several important facts about present-day patterns of political support in Okayama's second district. First, the trend toward the gradual decay of sharply defined *jiban* and a concomitant widening of support, noted with respect to this candidate's performance in the 1936 and 1937 elections, has continued. No one jurisdiction has on the average given him more than 35 per cent of its votes, as compared with 44 per cent before the war. To compensate for this, he has quite regularly polled more than 15 per cent of the total vote in eleven constituencies and more than 20 per cent in six. The contrast with his father's record in this respect is particularly compelling. Expressed in terms of total support for Inukai during these

TABLE 34

GEOGRAPHIC ANALYSIS OF INUKAI KEN'S SUPPORT, 1949–55*

Area	1949	1952	1953	1955	Average Percentage of Vote Polled 1949–55	Percentage of Total Support Contributed 1949–55
Kurashiki City...	4,264 (23)†	4,122 (14)	4,807 (16)	5,567 (11)	16	8
Tamano City....	3,238 (19)	1,716 (9)	1,823 (10)	2,785 (10)	12	4
Kojima City.....	2,110 (16)	2,127 (16)	2,051 (17)	2,510 (17)	17	4
Tamashima City.	..........‡	1,326 (10)	2,009 (10)	2,423 (11)	10	2
Kasaoka City....	....	2,246 (18)	2,094 (18)	3,467 (16)	17	3
Ihara City.......	....	....	4,349 (26)	3,010 (18)	22	3
Sōja City	....	....	....	3,615 (20)	20	1
Takahashi City..	....	....	....	2,052 (13)	13	1
Niimi City.......	....	....	....	959 (6)	6	1
Kojima gun......	5,061 (12)	3,511 (8)	3,629 (9)	2,496 (10)	10	6
Tsukubo gun.....	13,057 (41)	9,325 (33)	9,213 (33)	8,409 (34)	35	16
Asaguchi gun.....	8,391 (15)	5,384 (12)	3,364 (10)	3,805 (14)	13	8
Oda gun........	9,454 (21)	5,231 (15)	5,147 (17)	4,209 (18)	18	10
Shitsuki gun.....	4,807 (25)	4,923 (24)	1,258 (24)	880 (16)	22	5
Kibi gun.........	12,806 (36)	8,384 (22)	8,040 (22)	4,990 (21)	25	14
Jōbō gun........	5,010 (24)	3,155 (14)	3,045 (14)	1,449 (10)	16	5
Kawakami gun...	5,750 (29)	3,717 (17)	3,749 (19)	2,269 (17)	21	6
Atetsu gun.......	4,690 (20)	2,319 (9)	2,566 (10)	944 (7)	12	4
Total.......	78,638 (1)§	57,486 (3)	57,144 (4)	55,839 (3)		

* Inukai was not a candidate in the 1947 election.

† Figures in parentheses indicate the percentage of the total votes in the jurisdiction concerned received by this candidate.

‡ Blanks indicate that the city concerned had not been incorporated as of this date.

§ Figures in parentheses in the "Total" row indicate the candidate's competitive ranking in terms of number of votes received in the entire second election district.

1949–55 elections, the figures indicate that none of these jurisdictions has contributed more than 16 per cent; the prewar high was 24 per cent. Despite this diffusion of support, there can be no doubt that the younger Inukai's political patrimony—Tsukubo and Kibi *gun*—continue to constitute by far the most important single elements in his contemporary *jiban*. Between them they have provided no less than 30 per cent of his total support, while, if one adds the adjacent areas of Kurashiki City and Asaguchi and Oda *gun*, this figure mounts to 56 per cent. One can still discern then a distinct geographical core of Inukai strength in this south-western section of the prefecture.

The reasons for this process combining decay and diffusion of traditional support patterns are complex; prominent among them are the following: There has been a large increase in the size and some change in the composition of the second district's voting population, partly owing to war-induced internal migration and the introduction of female suffrage. A comparison of the total votes cast for Inukai before and since the war will indicate this; the voting population has increased in all these jurisdictions by more than 100 per cent. Large numbers of these new voters in

TABLE 35

GEOGRAPHIC ANALYSIS OF HOSHIJIMA JIRŌ'S SUPPORT, 1947–55

Area	1947	1949	1952	1953	1955	Average Percentage of Vote Polled 1947–55	Percentage of Total Support Contributed 1947–55
Kurashiki City.	2,130 (12)*	1,193 (6)	5,158 (17)	4,314 (15)	11,739 (22)	14	8
Tamano City...	4,208 (31)	3,328 (19)	4,615 (23)	3,679 (20)	6,747 (24)	23	8
Kojima City...	.........†	3,910 (30)	5,008 (38)	3,756 (31)	4,513 (30)	32	6
Tamashima City	....	....	2,713 (21)	2,598 (13)	3,968 (18)	17	3
Kasaoka City..	....	....	2,249 (18)	1,787 (15)	4,675 (22)	18	3
Ihara City.....	....	....	....	2,573 (15)	3,264 (20)	18	2
Sōja City.....	....	....	....	....	1,370 (8)	8	1
Takahashi City.	....	....	....	....	3,037 (19)	19	1
Niimi City.....	....	....	....	....	2,138 (14)	14	1
Kojima gun....	17,951 (36)	12,858 (31)	17,155 (40)	13,502 (34)	10,539 (41)	36	25
Tsukubo gun...	7,178 (25)	3,554 (11)	3,752 (13)	2,868 (10)	3,812 (15)	15	7
Asaguchi gun...	7,539 (24)	3,783 (7)	8,590 (19)	4,886 (15)	5,044 (19)	17	10
Oda gun.......	7,485 (27)	1,571 (4)	7,148 (21)	5,300 (18)	5,310 (23)	19	9
Shitsuki gun...	3,311 (21)	1,085 (6)	2,765 (13)	537 (10)	822 (15)	13	3
Kibi gun.......	2,082 (7)	1,074 (3)	1,259 (3)	1,037 (3)	2,545 (11)	5	3
Jōbō gun......	158 (0.8)	1,439 (7)	2,717 (12)	2,031 (9)	2,223 (16)	9	3
Kawakami gun.	2,895 (16)	1,762 (9)	2,012 (9)	1,669 (8)	2,045 (15)	11	4
Atetsu gun.....	2,682 (14)	1,708 (7)	2,282 (8)	2,132 (8)	1,978 (15)	10	4
Total......	58,405 (1)‡	37,264 (4)	67,423 (2)	52,669 (5)	75,769 (1)		

* Figures in parentheses indicate the percentage of the total vote in the jurisdiction concerned polled by this candidate.

† Blanks indicate that the city concerned had not been incorporated as of this date.

‡ Figures in parentheses in "Total" row indicate the candidate's competitive ranking in terms of number of votes received in the entire second election district.

the old Inukai *jiban* have been less susceptible to the appeals of traditional loyalty. There have also been notable changes in campaign organization from the standpoint of communication. With the widespread ownership of radios, the general circulation of daily newspapers, better roads, and vastly improved rail and bus schedules, it is now physically possible for the candidate and his assistants to campaign far more extensively and effectively than used to be the case. When one adds to this the postwar appearance of left-wing candidates as feasible political alternatives and a growing feeling that new faces and solutions are necessary to cope with the problems of a "new Japan," considerable light is cast upon the changes which have occurred in the pattern of Inukai Ken's political support. Such developments are of general incidence and have affected Hoshijima Jirō in much the same way.

Formerly, in the years 1928–37, Hoshijima drew some 65 per cent of his total support from Kojima *gun* alone, and 90 per cent from a combination of this area with adjacent sections of Asaguchi and Tsukubo *gun*. Comparison of this with his postwar record is somewhat complicated by the creation of three new cities in the area since the war, but, if their vote is combined with that of the older rural areas, changes similar to those affecting Inukai Ken may be seen. In the five elections held between 1947 and 1957, Hoshijima drew only 39 per cent of his combined vote from the area of former Kojima *gun* and some 61 per cent from the present equivalents of former Kojima *gun* plus Asaguchi and Tsukubo *gun*. In terms of his share of the vote in such areas of strength, his best postwar jurisdiction is still Kojima *gun*, where in the five elections concerned he polled an average of 36 per cent of the popular vote. This contrasts with 52 per cent before the war. Again, such losses have been adequately compensated by increased postwar support in other areas. Before the war he was able on the average to poll 15 per cent or more of the vote only in Kojima and Asaguchi *gun*. Since the war he has quite regularly bettered this figure in five additional jurisdictions. Even with such diversification of support, however, the Kojima area and its environs definitely continue to be the heartland of Hoshijima's *jiban*.

In both cases, therefore, one can discern distinct areas of greatest and most reliable support for the two men, areas which, incidentally, overlap and interpenetrate to a certain extent. In both cases these core areas have in recent years furnished 50 per cent or more of their total vote. Note, however, that this is still far below what they need for election, and both men are critically dependent on a wide scattering of units throughout much of the second district. A contemporary *jiban* is already less than self-sufficient.

A closer examination of the figures in Tables 34 and 35 in conjunction with those of Table 36, which sets forth a similar geographical analysis of the support for Nakahara Kenji, reveals several additional points of interest about the contemporary status of *jiban* in this area. Nakahara is chosen for this purpose because he represented first the Socialist party (in 1947) and subsequently the left-wing Labor-Farmer party. He exemplifies the "proletarian" challenge to the intrenched conservatives. Furthermore, he has been distinctly successful, winning in four of the five elections under consideration.

The table shows that Nakahara, too, draws some 49 per cent of his support from three *gun* and one city similarly concentrated in the southwestern part of the prefecture—Asaguchi, Kojima, and Oda *gun*, plus the city of Tamano. Thirty-one per cent of this support derives from Asaguchi and Kojima *gun* alone, which thus provide for him, as for Hoshijima, a sort of electoral heartland. The overlapping concentration of support for these candidates—two conservative and one left-wing—in the southwestern section of the prefecture is not adventitious. This section constitutes by far the most populous part of the second election district, and a candidate with connections or opportunities of any sort in the area is bound to develop them to the utmost. From the conservative viewpoint

TABLE 36

GEOGRAPHIC ANALYSIS OF NAKAHARA KENJI'S SUPPORT, 1947–55

Area	1947	1949	1952	1953	1955	Average Percentage of Vote Polled 1947–55	Percentage of Total Support Contributed 1947–55
Kurashiki City.	801 (5)*	1,427 (8)	2,279 (8)	5,634 (19)	4,687 (9)	10	7
Tamano City...	5,127 (33)	3,095 (18)	3,064 (15)	6,418 (35)	4,075 (14)	23	10
Kojima City...	.........†	1,272 (10)	1,490 (11)	2,959 (24)	2,130 (14)	15	4
Tamashima City	....	....	2,842 (22)	7,505 (37)	5,201 (24)	28	7
Kasaoka City..	....	....	945 (8)	1,978 (17)	2,718 (13)	18	3
Ihara City.....	....	....	....	2,258 (14)	1,654 (10)	12	2
Sōja City......	....	....	....	....	1,195 (7)	7	1
Takahashi City.	....	....	....	....	2,409 (15)	15	1
Niimi City.....	....	....	....	....	2,204 (15)	15	1
Kojima gun....	9,071 (18)	4,834 (12)	4,895 (11)	9,463 (24)	3,148 (12)	15	14
Tsukubo gun...	1,678 (6)	2,071 (7)	1,923 (7)	3,502 (13)	2,099 (8)	8	5
Asaguchi gun...	10,615 (21)	7,244 (13)	6,496 (14)	8,677 (27)	4,391 (17)	18	17
Oda gun.......	3,256 (12)	2,262 (5)	3,591 (11)	5,975 (20)	3,565 (15)	13	8
Shitsuki gun...	949 (6)	735 (4)	913 (4)	495 (9)	439 (8)	6	2
Kibi gun......	1,064 (3)	3,667 (10)	3,137 (8)	5,845 (16)	3,038 (13)	10	7
Jōbō gun......	534 (3)	1,733 (8)	1,908 (8)	4,386 (20)	2,001 (14)	11	5
Kawakami gun.	530 (3)	968 (5)	1,242 (6)	2,886 (14)	1,381 (10)	8	3
Atetsu gun.....	1,191 (6)	2,233 (10)	2,143 (8)	5,030 (19)	1,705 (13)	11	5
Total......	34,816 (2)‡	31,541 (5)	36,868 (6)	73,011 (1)	48,040 (4)		

* Figures in parentheses indicate the percentage of the total votes in the jurisdiction concerned received by this candidate.

† Blanks indicate that the city concerned had not been incorporated as of this date.

‡ Figures in parentheses in the "Total" row indicate the candidate's competitive ranking in terms of numbers of votes received in the entire second election district.

the disconcerting and ominous development is that a left-wing candidate has been able to make substantial inroads so consistently in what had been a reliable conservative stronghold. That this could happen on such a scale is an indication of the decay of the traditional *jiban*.

This decay can also be illustrated in other ways. Table 34 indicates, for example, that even in Tsukubo and Kibi *gun*, Inukai's support has been steadily declining. Hoshijima's experience in his own bailiwick, Kojima *gun*, has been essentially similar. Another way of demonstrating the same phenomenon is by comparing the competitive standing of these men with that of other candidates in terms of total vote polled in their areas of greatest strength. Table 37 provides such an analysis.

Inukai, it appears, has consistently polled more votes than any other candidate only in Tsukubo *gun*. In his four other areas of greatest strength, his voting support has on the whole waned, and an increasing number of competitors have fared better than he has. Hoshijima's record is more spotty, but he too has consistently stood at the top of the list in only a single area, Kojima *gun*.

These phenomena are of great interest in their own right. They indicate an appreciable decrease in conservative strength in one of Japan's staunchest conservative areas, and they mark the gradual emergence of a left-wing opposition which ultimately could bring about great changes on the Japanese political scene. But these are long-term and slow-moving trends which are, furthermore, subject to future interruption, diversion, or distortion in terms of their political consequences. It is easy to overestimate their importance and wise to keep well in mind the fact that

TABLE 37

COMPETITIVE STANDING OF INUKAI KEN AND HOSHIJIMA JIRŌ IN
THEIR FIVE AREAS OF GREATEST SUPPORT, 1947–55

Area	1947	1949	1952	1953	1955
Inukai:					
Tsukubo *gun*	..	1	1	1	1
Kibi *gun*	..	1	2	3	1
Oda *gun*	..	2	3	3	2
Asaguchi *gun*	..	3	5	6	4
Kurashiki City	..	1	3	4	5
Hoshijima:					
Kojima *gun*	1	1	1	1	1
Asaguchi *gun*	3	6	2	3	1
Oda *gun*	1	7	1	2	1
Kurashiki City	3	7	2	5	2
Tamano City	1	1	1	2	2

they have not yet interfered to a critical extent with the traditional conservative control of Okayama's politics and that there is small prospect of their doing so in the forseeable future.

Yet underneath all these surface manifestations of political change, some developments of less obvious but potentially far more enduring significance have taken place. Ultimately the breakdown of these famous *jiban* and the growth of a new opposition is symptomatic of rather extensive changes in popular attitudes and loyalties. These trends were discernible in sections of Japan's populace decades before the Second World War, but it is particularly noteworthy that now they are also occurring in so conservative and rural an area as Okayama's second election district.

CHANGING POLITICAL ATTITUDES

The most significant political changes in contemporary rural Japan are those of attitude. The farmer's traditional attitude toward politics has already been described, and we have seen that under normal circum-

stances he had no positive or responsible part to play in the public decision-making process. Politics was a field in which things were done to or
for him, not by him; such matters were regarded as a sort of natural
monopoly of his superiors. They alone had the knowledge and experience
to act in this sphere. It is this fundamentally apolitical attitude that is
changing in rural Japan. An appreciable number of individuals—but far
from all—are acquiring gradually and piecemeal more positive political
attitudes. The symptoms and evidence of this development are to be
found in a number of phenomena already discussed—the erosion of traditional *jiban*, the discontent of "bosses" with the postwar political situation and their diminished number and power throughout the countryside,
the increasing support for "proletarian" parties and candidates, the political activities of farmers' unions, co-operatives, etc. All these are signs of
an extensive ferment which has important political consequences.

The causes of such developments are less obvious, however, and require
some comment. First is the effect of the war itself. In modern times, lost
wars have a generally disruptive effect on the national way of life. Defeat
and its sorry economic and social consequences pose embarrassing questions about the traditional political structure and processes which brought
the country to such a pass. This has been true in Japan as well as in Ger-
many. Many who would not normally have reacted in such a way were,
under the abnormal stresses of defeat, brought into the ranks of the social
questioners and the actively dissatisfied.

A number of other more specific and sometimes more intense forces are
also changing rural political attitudes and behavior. The traditional family system, under attack for many decades, has received particularly serious blows since the war. The continued cityward migration of second and
third sons and of daughters for whom there is no mutually satisfactory
place on the tiny family farm is, of course, the basic force disrupting the
family circle and weakening its bonds. This process has long been under
way. The postwar revisions of the civil code's inheritance sections promoted by the Occupation have tended to weaken the system still further.
The traditional pattern of primogeniture was abolished and provision
made for the division of estates among the surviving spouse and children.
Fractionalization of family holdings menaces the pattern of intrafamily
hierarchy, upon which the strength of the family organization has always
rested, and endangers the stability of the entire system. Although these
provisions have been widely evaded, their very existence is a threat to the
structure and functioning of the traditional family system. The "equal
rights for women" clauses of the new constitution and their implementing
legislation have a similar tendency.

The accelerated breakdown of the family system is politically significant in several ways. In the first place the ethical basis of governmental authority in traditional Japanese society rested foursquare upon the family system. Popular morality, political morality included, depended on the family unit and its relationship to community and state. Encroachments upon the family system have resulted in a concomitant decay in popular morality, which occasions prolonged and heartfelt laments in the villages of Japan. Second, the old techniques of political exploitation and control, such as the "boss" system, were organized on a family and community basis. The process of family disintegration attacks them at their very foundations. Finally, this decay of the family system accelerates the social and behavioral shift from an almost completely collective or family basis to a considerably more individualized basis. Politically this means substituting more individual and self-conscious political attitudes and behavior patterns for the traditional family-oriented and group-oriented ones. This process is of fundamental political importance.

Land reform has been another potent factor in changing rural political attitudes. Japanese traditional society was built on an agricultural economy characterized, in recent times, by a very high tenancy rate. The economic dependency of tenants on the good will and support of their landlords perpetuated distinctly hierarchical relationships in the countryside. Under this system the sociopolitical authority of landlords increased, while the farmers sank further into political passivity and apathy. It was this system that land reform attacked at its roots. Vast amounts of land were taken from the landlords with but token compensation and sold at nominal prices to tenants and small landholders. As a result, tenancy was reduced from approximately 46 per cent of the cultivated area to 11 or 12 per cent. In short, the system of land tenure was fundamentally altered, and much of the economic underpinning of the older system of rural sociopolitical relationships was suddenly removed. The class of small rural freeholders was greatly enlarged, and their group potentialities for developing new and freer political attitudes were considerably enhanced, temporarily at least.

So drastic a change in the land-tenure system naturally resulted in very strained class relationships. Most landlords were outraged but politically helpless; former tenants were delighted and determined to do what they could to protect and perpetuate their new status. For long-term results this would obviously require organization and political action. Consequently, the farmers, particularly the beneficiaries of land reform, found themselves impelled by the very dynamics of land redistribution to be more aware of politics as it affected the retention of their new holdings.

At the local level the agricultural land commissions often became arenas of bitter political strife between former tenants and landlords. On the broader prefectural and national scene all political parties rapidly became aware of the potential importance of this enlarged interest group among rural voters and tried to enlist their support. The left-wing parties in particular made strong bids for the votes of former tenants and frequently attempted to organize them for political purposes. The former tenant began to display a lively interest in the stand which particular political parties and candidates were taking on issues affecting land tenure, rural credit, etc. The group was acquiring new political attitudes and taking the first steps toward implementing them.

Other factors support this trend. Although their immediate effect has often been grossly exaggerated, the long-term effect of most of the Occupation's political reforms has been to reinforce and expand prewar tendencies toward individualizing and "politicizing" Japanese society. The purge, for example, removed many national and local leaders from the political scene long enough to permit new figures to emerge. The multiplication of elective offices, lowering the voting age, and extending the suffrage to women contributed to the partial breakdown of the older mechanisms of political control and facilitated the development of new political attitudes and behavior patterns. The enormous expansion of unions, including peasant unions, usually under left-wing leadership and possessed of distinct political programs and ambitions, has had a similar effect. In fact the forces making for change in political attitudes and behavior affect all levels of society in postwar Japan.

All these forces are present and felt in Niiike and Kamo, although in a strictly political sense both are somewhat unusual in their steadfast adherence to the persons and *jiban* of the Inukai, father and son. Also they were less widely affected by land reform than many other villages. It is perhaps the more significant, therefore, that one encounters so many signs of changing political attitudes in so traditional a setting. Although Inukai Ken continues to be the favorite, his supporters have decreased in numbers. One hears criticism of the extent to which he allegedly neglects his *jiban* and takes its support for granted. Unfavorable comparisons with his father in this respect are heard in the most traditional and loyal circles. Support for particular left-wing candidates, especially Nakahara Kenji of the Labor-Farmer party and Yamazaki Motoo of the Left-Wing Socialists, has increased markedly within the village. Even the Communists have been able to poll a handful of votes. Statistically more notable, perhaps, is the extent to which other conservative candidates are attracting support within the village. All these developments bespeak the change in local political attitudes. In Niiike and elsewhere throughout the village people are becoming better informed about politics, more interested in it, and, most important of all, aware that they have, as individuals, more than a single political choice. It is this dawning awareness of the existence of political alternatives, followed by a slowly increasing readiness to cast votes for other than the intrenched holders of local *jiban*, which has both present and future political significance.

Despite the potential importance of such developments, however, their current significance should not be exaggerated. These changes in political attitudes and behavior remain minority and piecemeal manifestations in Niiike and Kamo. They in no reliable sense indicate the probability of any very sizable increase in the local strength of left-wing parties and candidates. As a matter of fact, considering the enormous stresses to which postwar Japanese society has been subjected, the continued strength, resiliency, and adaptability of the traditional sociopolitical order and processes are most impressive. Politically, as otherwise, Niiike remains an essentially conservative community.

14. *Religious* INSTITUTIONS AND CONCEPTS

The calendar of annual festivals and ceremonies outlined earlier (see chap. 7) links in a single procession of events two quite different and separate systems of religion, Buddhism and Shinto. These are the two traditional faiths of Japan in general and of Niiike in particular.

Buddhism, originating in north India, passed to China somewhat before the Christian Era and arrived in Japan still later, about the sixth century A.D. Though changed and immensely variegated in its journey and in the centuries of development since its introduction in Japan, it remains a systematic and deep philosophy for scholars of Buddhism or even for the priests of local temples.

Shinto is of a different nature. The beliefs and practices of Shinto do not fall together in a closely reasoned philosophy, for the name conveniently covers all the heterogeneous religious phenomena native to Japan and not imported from elsewhere. Though these do share common features, they are of great regional diversity. Parts of this immense but unsystematized reservoir of legend and cult were exploited and reworked in the nineteenth century into an organized, highly nationalistic state cult, controlled and financed by the central government. This so-called State Shinto has been abolished as an active organ since the end of World War II. There are also in Japan indigenous evangelistic sects, some of great popularity and large membership, which are misleadingly grouped under the term "Sect Shinto," though their doctrines owe as much to the inventiveness of their founders of the last few generations as they do to the lore of traditional Shinto. Neither State Shinto nor these evangelistic sects play direct roles in Niiike today, but we will examine each briefly, State Shinto for its role in the recent past and the evangelistic sects because they are part of the contemporary environment. Since there is one Christian family in Niiike, Christianity in the community also merits attention. Primarily, however, the consideration of religious conceptions, sentiments, and practices must deal with village Buddhism and village Shinto.

446

The modifier "village" is used advisedly, since the lay farmer approaches Buddhism quite differently from the priest or scholar, foregoing most of its philosophical subtleties. Buddhism to the layman is a means of venerating his household's ancestors and of understanding and linking himself to the afterworld. Every temple (tera) near Niiike, or throughout Japan for that matter, is supported by its parishioners mainly for its services on behalf of the ancestors. Whatever else the priests and nuns concern themselves with is of little moment to the ordinary person. Hence, Buddhism has one character in its colleges and monasteries but has a different character in the villages. Unlike Buddhism, Shinto has no colleges; it is centered in the villages themselves. Moreover, Shinto, as distinct from Buddhism, is a religious system for the community as a whole, not for each household, and the role of the Shinto shrine (miya) in the local village is to insure well-being in this present-day, real world. The great majority of annual festivals described in chapter 7 relate to the Shinto rather than to the Buddhist system of belief, being community-wide and aimed at welfare here and now rather than in the afterlife. Besides this village Shinto, there are Shinto phenomena that concern individual persons or groups in special occupations, and higher-level Shinto organization exists for the nation and its leaders; though these have a conceptual relationship to village Shinto and the shrine, they are not identical with it and must be considered separately.

Religion, thus, is extremely varied, with organized and unorganized aspects, Buddhist and Shinto aspects, and intra-village and supra-village aspects. All these aspects fall together in a comprehensive and articulated religious life for the people of Niiike, as represented in part by the yearly round of ceremonies. This religious life in many respects is quite unlike the patterns of Christian faith, which have come to be synonymous with religion in most of the Western world; Westerners trying to understand Japan frequently question what constitutes religious interest and religious zeal among Japanese. Such questions are pertinent here but are best considered after the various aspects of religion have been examined.

SUMMARY COMPARISON OF VILLAGE BUDDHISM AND VILLAGE SHINTO

The ordinary village in Japan combines Buddhism and Shinto in its religious life. Some persons claim adherence to Buddhism alone, and others, who probably are fewer, participate only in Shinto, but these, together with the fairly large number (mostly living in cities) who profess no religious inclination at all, are a minority among the millions who participate simultaneously and equally in Buddhism and Shinto. More accurately, many villages tend to stress their Shinto activities and to neglect

Buddhist affairs, while many others give precedence to Buddhism. The people of Niiike are of the latter group, though their zeal for Buddhism still is not extraordinary by comparison with other adherents of their Nichiren sect, which is noted among Buddhist sects for its evangelistic fervor. Despite these leanings, each person in Niiike, except the members of the single Christian household, accepts the beliefs and practices of both Buddhism and Shinto within the community and uses each for its separate purpose without any sense of conflict or division of loyalty. It is quite remarkable, considering the many generations during which Buddhism and Shinto have lived together in villages such as this, that the two systems have remained separate. Though there is some intermixture and compromise, there is no confusion between the two. Anyone is able to distinguish the Buddhist from the Shinto matters in his life, whether he is considering religious structures and paraphernalia, the proper persons to participate on various occasions, the appropriate modes of worship and ceremony, or the conceptions of supernatural or otherworldly matters pertinent to each religion. A brief sketch of these features of Buddhism and Shinto will show how distinct the two are and how each complements the other in serving the religious wants of people in the community.

VILLAGE BUDDHISM

However different the priestly philosophy of Buddhism may be from the layman's view, priest and farmer need each other and are linked through the temple (tera). Most Buddhist worship in Niiike is done at home rather than in the temple, and the priests (Bon), who live in their temples, make the rounds of homes to assist in the ritual. But every household belongs to a particular temple, and its members are free to go there at any time. It will be recalled that the people of Niiike, who are all in the sect founded by Nichiren (1222–82), belong not to the closest such temple, Honryūji at Yamane, but to more distant ones across the Ashimori River: Hiramatsu households to Sōrenji and Iwasa households to Renkyūji, a circumstance unusual among members of a single sect in one community. Neither temple is elaborate. The visitor might take either one for an ordinary, though large, tile-roofed house inside a walled compound, except that he will notice a large bell sheltered under a roofed structure just inside the gate, and beyond it in the yard he will see the gravestones of a cemetery. Also, the main hall, where there is an elaborate gilt altar, is likely to have a distinctive tile roof or at least a curved gable over an arched entrance. Features of this sort, generally with Chinese antecedents, identify even a simple Buddhist structure; they are greatly multiplied in larger temples, which are impressive with their enormous tile roofs drooping over complexly bracketed supporting timbers and with all their buildings arranged in foursquare symmetry inside a walled compound.

Buddhist worship, whether in the temple or at home, utilizes bells, drums, and wooden sounding-boards; candles flicker and incense smolders; the worshipers rub rosaries wrapped around one hand as they read or recite sutras (verses) from a book of scriptures. Many of their aids to worship are strikingly parallel to those of Christian ritual, though of course the ancestral tablets before which the people pray at home or the images that face them in the temple are distinctive of Buddhism.

Temple affiliation is a family affair by tradition, though no longer by compulsion. Few persons ever shift from their family's sect and, even in these days of high mobility, few families ever transfer affiliation from their ancestral temple, though its cemetery may or may not hold their ancestors' graves. This is especially true in areas of relatively stable population, such as the countryside around Niiike. When enrolment in a temple was made compulsory three centuries and more ago, many persons not otherwise affiliated probably registered at the nearest temple, but some have shifted residence since then, and parishes of various temples have become interspersed, since each parish is linked to its temple on the basis of family line rather than proximity. In Niiike as elsewhere people living side by side call on different temples because their forefathers chose or were assigned to these respective temples. Personal conscience or personal choice has little bearing on one's temple or even sect of registry because each person worships or performs ceremonies not for his own sake but for that of his household ancestors, just as his own descendants will do in turn for him. Since his efforts are in behalf of his forebears, he tends to be content with the temple that satisfied them.

Buddhist thought and worship in the village have almost exclusively an otherworldy orientation, focused on the ancestors and their relation to divinity, as represented in the Buddha. A most important set of ceremonies, recurrent over a period of half a century, follows each funeral to assist the soul to its ultimate destination: mergence or identification with the Buddha. (Like other Japanese nouns, the word *hotoke*, meaning both "ancestor" and "Buddha," implies neither singular nor plural, so that questions of the individuality of ancestors are unlikely to rise.) It is the responsibility of descendants to perform these ceremonies, generally at home before the ancestral tablets, as well as to take care of the actual graves. In turn, the ancestors, who are thought by some to have traversed a dangerous path across chasms and rivers to arrive at Buddhahood (or, alternatively, Paradise) return each year at *Bon* festival time to rejoice that their descendants are doing well. Almost all important Buddhist ceremonies of the village worshipers are based on this conception of the supernatural. Passing recognition is given to other elements of Buddhist doctrine: the village observes an annual festival commemorating the enlightenment of the Buddha, thus recognizing his existence as a transcendent person, not a divinity, some six centuries before the Christian Era in India; food offerings never include liquor, fish, or other flesh, and some old persons still abstain from eating meat (but not fish or poultry or eggs) in acceptance of a ban against destroying life; the serious person tries to gain merit during his life rather than merely intrusting his fate to his descendants, his success appearing when, at death, the priest assigns a posthumous name of greater or less merit (the name often is measured, frankly, in terms of contributions made to the temple). But these and a great many other points of doctrine fade in comparison with the importance given to reverence of the ancestors and the Buddha as deity—or deities. Village Buddhism is concerned with the afterlife, each person acting in behalf of his own forebears.

VILLAGE SHINTO

More Shinto ceremonies take place at a shrine (*miya*) than at home. The congregation is one of neighbors. The shrines are quite unlike temples (*tera*) in construction and in arrangement. The architectural design of buildings usually follows ancient Japanese tradition without Chinese influence. Simple post and beam construction, without bracketing, and grass or cedar-chip thatching, instead of a tile roof, are characteristic. One enters or approaches the open side of the shrine under the eave rather than at the gable end, but one looks up to the gable peak for the telltale projection of the edge boards in a cross against the sky that characterizes most shrines. Even without this mark, a shrine is distinctive in the arrangement of its structures, which are not symmetrically grouped in an inclosure as are those of a temple but are strung out along an axis. A special gate or arch (torii) marks the entrance to the axis, standing with its uprights supporting the typical double horizontal beam across the path. Approaching the Kōjin shrine on the crest of the Tsukuriyama mound-tomb, where Niiike people most often worship, one walks under a small stone torii at the base, climbs the hill, and steps under a second torii into an open area. In this area is the single small building which is the shrine. Near it is a large stone trough (actually a Tomb period sarcophagus uncovered during the 1925 revision of fields) where worshipers may rinse their mouths and hands in ritual cleansing. Rice-straw ropes (*shimenawa*) with interwoven tassels of cut white paper (*gohei*) are strung across the torii, across the shrine front, and elsewhere, to insure purity; and worship, to be effective, requires that one be cleansed of ritual pollution while on the shrine precincts or in a sacred area. The torii-to-shrine axis of Kōjin points in the direction of its shrine of origin, Upper Kamo shrine. For most shrines a distant peak, a grove, or other landmark to which the shrine axis points is really the sacred point of worship, though only the more knowledgeable persons among the worshipers may keep this in mind. The shrine is set at a respectful distance from this point (and, incidentally, at a place convenient for the worshipers to assemble), and sacredness within the precincts diminishes as one goes from the main structure (*honden*) toward the torii. Larger shrines have supplementary buildings such as a roofed platform (*haiden*) for offerings and dances between *honden* and torii, and, when important enough to have a permanent guardian (*kannushi*, or *shinkan*) and staff, the shrine precincts may be filled with homes and outbuildings as well.

Shrine worship is comparatively barren of paraphernalia. When a guardian officiates, he passes a whisk of *sakaki* wood and white paper *gohei* over the assembly in exorcism of pollution, and worshipers may signal their presence by shaking the tassel of a distinctive bell, shaped like a sleigh bell. Several sorts of ancient woodwind and percussion instruments make up a band for large shrine ceremonies. Containers for food offerings (sake and fish are welcome) are generally of wood, quite different in shape from Buddhist offering stands and plates. Sake is more than a mere symbol of good living; one drinks sake, whether in driblets or in quantities, to animate one's self and so more easily achieve rapport with the spirit being worshiped. For this reason, the young men serving at ceremonials perform their roles half drunk. In contrast to sake, which pleases the spirit, both sex and blood outrage the spirit. It is important that girls who assist in ceremonies be virgins, and preferable that they withdraw after reaching puberty. The phallicism that pervades some shrines does not violate this principle of sex-pollution, apparently, but abstractly symbolizes fertility rather than sex. Most integral to the shrine is a material symbol kept in the *honden*, through which the spirit of the place is made manifest. This is the *shintai* ("divine embodiment"), and may be almost any object—a mirror, a sword, a necklace, a stream cobble, a statue— or it may be nothing at all.

Though the Kōjin shrine, as has been pointed out earlier (chap. 10), is a branch from the Upper Kamo shrine, and other cases exist of main and branch shrines, dependency relationships are not so regular and systematic as the mother-daughter sort of relation among temples of a Buddhist sect. A small shrine (more properly, the spot toward which it is oriented) exerts a mystic beneficence over its local vicinity. A larger, or more important, shrine covers a larger area with its influence and so spreads over the domains of numerous smaller shrines. People from Niiike go to the small Kōjin shrine, not merely because it is conveniently close, but because it has a more immediate relation to them as members of a smaller group. But they (together with worshipers at other small shrines) are under the protection of larger shrines: mura shrines, shrines of the former provinces, regional shrines, and national shrines. There is Upper Kamo, which is one of the three mura shrines; there is Kōshin, an unofficial shrine on the hill overlooking the Iwasaki water gate, which had a Buddhist origin though it is Shinto now; there is Kibitsu Jinja, the ancient shrine of the entire province; and there is the Great Shrine at faraway Ise, which is one of the shrines for the entire nation. These various shrines represent no clear pattern of organization. None has genuine organizational connection with the others; at any given level there may be one or several shrines; and the levels of size or importance are not clearly defined. Shrines differ from the hierarchically organized Buddhist temples in all these respects.

The comments above apply particularly to the shrines built for *ujigami* or tutelary spirits, which are the ones giving general protection to an area and all that it contains—crops, beasts, birds, and people. The congregation of an *ujigami* shrine includes everyone who resides within the area, and the traveler in the area enjoys the shrine's protection and beneficence almost as a tourist is protected by the laws of the city or state he is visiting. The group which comes together for worship at an *ujigami* shrine, then, is the entire neighborhood or community. Kōjin shrine is the *ujigami* of Niiike, Ōyama, Senzoku, Tsukuriyama, Mukaiba, a joint irrigation group of buraku with several other common interests. Upper Kamo at a slightly higher level is a more remote *ujigami;* at still higher levels, the provincial and great national shrines are tutelaries over the populations of the one-time province or the entire nation. At each level, persons share an interest in the shrine because of where they live, not because of family (as is the case with temple affiliation) or through personal choice (the theoretical basis for American church membership). The spirit identified with an *ujigami* shrine is supposed to promote welfare and prosperity and to ward off any natural calamity or disaster, including flood and drought, sickness and blight, accident and fire.

The Shinto *ujigami* shrine, unlike the Buddhist temple, is concerned with affairs of the present natural world. There is no doctrine concerning afterlife or ancestors, no sense of punishment or striving for merit, but only a concern for performing ceremonies on the proper occasions and for preserving purity at time of worship (which keeps menstruating women and postpartum mothers, among others, away from the shrine). One is led to ask in what form the supernatural is conceived, since shrine affairs differ so sharply from those of the temple. The word "spirit" has been used here for the Japanese word *kami*, ordinarily translated "god." The anthropomorphic connotations of the latter word seem misleading, where the *ujigami* of the local community is concerned, for this *kami* is a force or spirit without visible or imaginable form. In most respects, *kami* seems no more than magical power inherent in an object or locality. But it does take on some aspects of personality. At festival times it moves, for example, from its remote resting place to the *honden*, where it invests the sacred objects (*shintai*) with its force; these may then be put in an ark on a litter (*mikoshi*), and the young men of the congregation, shouldering the poles of the litter, either carry it on a drunken tour of inspection around the community or transfer it to another place where the ceremony of worship is performed. It can be pleased, and the purpose of offerings, songs, and dances performed at the ceremony is to amuse and please the *kami*. It can also have male or female sex, though scholars believe this sort of attribute does not ordinarily antedate the influence of Buddhism. The *kami* of certain shrines are without doubt deifications of actual or legendary heroes (e.g., Kibitsu Hiko at Kibitsu shrine near Niiike), and others are deified ancestors of historically eminent family lines (a prime example is the Naiku shrine at Ise for Amaterasu, divine ancestress of the imperial line). But, in spite of such cases, the predominant Shinto supernatural forces and spirits are thought of as never having had earthly, corporeal existence, in contrast to the conceptions of village Buddhism, where once-living ancestors are the pre-eminent supernatural beings.

Shinto and Buddhist worship together offer a satisfying combination for the religious wants of the villagers which, most of them feel, neither religion could offer by itself. Shinto, full of the pleasure of living, lends its assurance of health and sunny prosperity; it is a shield against adversity for the living. Buddhism, with its gentle knowledge of the all-compassionate Buddha, provides comfort in the presence of death. In Shinto, the worshipers reaffirm their community ties to each other; in Buddhism, they consolidate their family ties. Thus the two most basic and precious axes of social relationship gain recognition. For external crises of illness, poverty, and harm to one's property, one turns in general to Shinto for relief; internal and personal crises of body or spirit may be comforted or cured through Buddhism. In these respects the two systems of religion complement each other and articulate to provide a comprehensive religious life for each person. Neither contradicts or precludes the other. Hence both are practiced at once.

BUDDHIST CEREMONIES

Except for a very few ceremonies, notably a funeral, almost any Buddhist ceremony can be performed at home without the assistance of a priest. The housemead or an elderly relative is able to conduct the prescribed ritual for the assembled family. The ceremony is enhanced by the presence of a priest; for one thing, his learning enables him not only to select the most appropriate Sanskrit prayers but to read them directly from the difficult Chinese characters used to transliterate them in the book of sutras. A memorized prayer will do, however, and even children know the most characteristic prayer of the Nichiren sect that begins: "*Namu myō hō rengei kyō . . .*" ("Glory to the sutra of the lotus of truth").

A memorial service for the dead is the most common occasion for a Buddhist service in the home. This may be the *hōji*, performed for a particular ancestor on the forty-ninth day after death, then on the anniversary in the first, third, fifth, seventh, thirteenth, twenty-fifth, and fiftieth years (most people stop after the thirteenth); or it may be a *tsuizen kuyō*, for all the ancestors. For the former, which are the more important, each house of the lineage sends a member to the house where the ceremony takes place. Five such relatives—six, counting the baby one of the three women was nursing—gathered at noon at Hiramatsu Tokujirō's house, for example, for a service to his father. All were dressed in kimonos of somber color or in formal black garb with crest (*montsuki*). Preparations had been made in the main room. The ancestral tablets for the father and mother had been brought from the *butsudan* and set on the highest of three temporary shelves in the *tokonoma*, an incense bowl before it. A candle and a jar of *shikibi* leaves flanked tiny pedestaled dishes with food offerings on the next shelf below. Fruit and special cakes rested on the lowest shelf. The everyday floor cover, or *goza*, was removed, and on the *tatami* near the *tokonoma* were a rosary, a larger bowl for burning incense, a bowl bell and its striker, and a wooden sounding-board. Books of sutras were on a reading stand. After waiting half an hour in vain for the priest, the host invited his guests to move from the anteroom to the main room for the ceremony. Facing his five kneeling guests, he thanked them for coming, then asked his neighbor, the Sensei, to conduct the service. With only a brief, polite demurral, the Sensei took up the striker, tapped the bell twice, paused, then tapped the bell twice again to call the ancestor's attention; then, holding the rosary, and with a slow, regular beat on the sounding-board, he led the group in the most familiar chanted formula.

At this point the priest arrived to read more sutras and conclude the service by again striking the bell. The housewife then served a formal lunch without salt, fish, or sake on individual trays. (For her guests' sake she had boiled the soup with fish, but for religion's sake she had taken the fish out before serving.) After the meal, the group went to the cemetery to leave the offerings of food at the graves while the priest continued to read scripture aloud. Finally, all returned to the house for tea before being thanked by the host and departing to their homes about three o'clock.

Four times each year, during the calendrical festivals of New Year, *higan* (at each equinox), and *Bon* (in mid-August), the memorial tablets of all the household ancestors come out from the *butsudan* to the *tokonoma* to be honored in a ceremony essentially like the *hōji* for a single forebear just described. These four occasions have the appearance of annual community festivals, for every household goes through the ritual within the same few days; hence to point out that these ceremonies are essentially for the household and close kindred, just as in the case of the *hōji*, rather than for the community as a whole, may seem a quibbling sort of distinction. It is this point, however, that defines these dates as Buddhist rather than Shinto ceremonials.

Of these four ceremonials, people enjoy and treasure *Bon* most of all, for the ancestors are present as spiritual guests for its three days. Its essentials are no different from those of New Year's and the two *higan:* the house and the ancestral graves are made spic and span, the ancestral tablets are set out in the *tokonoma*, food offerings are placed before them, and prayers are chanted there after supper before the family proceeds to the cemetery to place pinches of rice before each headstone, pour a little water on each, and say more prayers. But *Bon* comes off with more of a flourish. It comes when the moon is full during the hot, leisurely weather of August, when children and their parents alike are in good mood for donning their best clothes and paying leisurely visits around the neighborhood; everyone can expect married daughters and other close relatives to come home for a day no matter how far the journey; as a welcome to visitors, each house is thrown open to the warm evening breeze and has a large paper lantern aglow on the veranda. Unlike many villages, Niiike does not kindle small fires with pine-root faggots in front of each house on the first and last evenings to welcome and send off visiting ancestral spirits, but people conceive of the spirits as being with them throughout *Bon*, taking part in the family meals, enjoying the incense-like smoke of pine-root fires kindled at the cemetery, and rejoicing in the display of rice cakes and seasonal fruits and vegetables arranged afresh each day in the *tokonoma.* Formerly more than now people set up little trays on stakes (*mizutanabata*) in their front yard, offering rice and water there for any homeless, wandering ancestral spirits whose descent line has become extinct. Formerly, also, young people practiced several weeks in advance to put on a well-drilled, complex, costumed dance that would fill at least one of the three nights; but, like villages all over Japan, where the *Bon* dance once was a high point of the year's festivities, Niiike has given up its *Bon* dance entirely.

Children stay up late on the last night of *Bon*, however, for the picturesque last act of *Bon*, the ceremony of straw boats. Though this rite should be performed at midnight, people generally start earlier, about 10:00 P.M., for the sake of the children. From the fruit and vegetable offerings in the *tokonoma*, the househead fills to overflowing one or two boat-shaped baskets he has made from rice straw. He lights a candle in each basket and carries it out of the house to a designated point beside one of the main drainage ditches. Other households from Niiike converge on this point with their candle-lit baskets, and, while one of the elders recites a prayer, everyone lays his baskets on a straw bonfire there. The children always tag along to see the bright sight. Until notions of sanitation strengthened in recent years, the people used to float each candle-lit boat away in the shallow irrigation ditch to symbolize the ancestors' leave-taking; this made a very pretty scene but left a straggle of garbage to rot in succeeding days wherever the boats stranded along the ditch; so, by *kōjū* consensus two decades ago, a bonfire was substituted for the older tradition. At about the time Niiike's bonfire blazes up or dies down one sees other bonfires in the fields, one near each buraku in the vicinity, for almost all have abandoned the older custom.

The lunar calendar governs *Bon* (seventh month, thirteenth to fifteenth day) and New Year (first month, first to third day), so they normally come, respectively, in August and February of the solar year, whereas the same festivals in the city and its closest fringe of villages go by the solar calendar. The equinoctial festivals of *higan*, of course, are necessarily calculated by the solar equinox in both city and country. A few other ceremonies, all celebrated on lunar calendar reckoning, are Buddhist in nature. All are almost defunct, or, since the temple rather than the village households sponsors them, are attended only by the most pious persons, which is to say by elderly persons who are beginning to fret over their own approaching death. *Nehan'e* (second month, fifteenth day) commemorates the enlightenment of the Buddha (or, as the village description puts it, "the day Shaka-sama died") with prayers at the temple. *Kishimo Taizai* (third month, seventeenth day), a ceremonial date almost ignored in

Niiike unless children go to a special sermon by the priest at the Hiramatsu family temple, celebrates the legendary conversion to Buddhism of a child-eating female demon, Kishimo, who now has become a kindly patron deity for children. Three other festivals are regarded locally as being especially linked to the Nichiren sect: the Daikoku festival (fourth month, third day) celebrating the abbot Daikoku, who propagated the sect's doctrines through western Honshu (not Daikoku, the wealth god of Chinese legend), is celebrated at an overnight service in a temple west of Niiike, which some elderly women find time to attend; the Nichiren memorial day (eighth month, twelfth day) is marked by a service at each temple of the sect; and *Eshiki* (tenth month, twelfth day), a memorial service for all departed souls, has a temple service. Niiike people stay at work, making no holiday of these three days; but a ceremony they perform toward evening of the Daikoku and Nichiren festivals shows interestingly how Buddhist and Shinto observances may overlap.

The ceremony occurs near the village assembly hall, where Niiike has a memorial stone inscribed with the common formula, *"Namu myō hō rengei kyō,"* standing adjacent to a memorial stone for the abbot Daikoku and a stone for Jijin, Shinto spirit of the earth. These stones once stood in separate spots but were grouped together some years ago, presumably because the ceremonies for each are identical. One person from each household arrives shortly after supper, dressed in ordinary clothes. Instead of sitting in the formal kneeling posture in the dust, all squat in the open space before the stones and accompany an elder (usually the Sensei) in Buddhist prayers while incense and candles burn. Children meanwhile drift in around the fringes of the group, for, as soon as the prayers are finished, the Youth Association officers open up the assembly hall and hand each child a package of rice cakes, cookies, and fruit; the children snatch these and rush home to share them with the rest of the family. The two dozen adults then sit down in the assembly house to a common meal arranged for them by the Youth Association, which draws on buraku funds for the costs. The prayers, whether offered to the Buddhist saints or to the Shinto spirit, are Buddhist, of course; but it is a Shinto characteristic for representatives of the community, after jointly performing a ritual, to end it by eating together. The villagers often comment on this mixture, of which they are fully aware: "Most other Buddhist sects don't like to mix things. But we use the Nichiren prayer because we know it best and eat together because it makes us feel good as a group." No one is disturbed either by the syncretism of these ceremonies or by the lack of it in other ceremonies.

SHINTO CEREMONIES

A sample taken from the many strictly Shinto ceremonies illustrates their clear-cut contrast with Buddhist ceremonies in concept and procedure. It may be well to comment on the relation of this sample to the whole complex of ceremonies that are considered Shinto in nature, for at first glance the list (chap. 7) seems endlessly diverse and heterogeneous. Only when a dozen and more ceremonies are perceived as variations on one or two themes does the sample which is selected for illustration reveal itself to be representative rather than arbitrary and partial. We have spoken of the entire community as the social group for Shinto ceremonies. Several other principles underlying Shinto ceremonies should be recognized. First, persons who are absent from ceremonies are nonetheless as fully benefited and almost as fully responsible for the success of the ceremonies as are the actual participants. As in other social matters, the household rather than the person is the basic social unit, so that its entire membership participates as often as one member is present to represent the household. Children participate most actively in certain festivals (Girls' Day, Boys' Day, *tanabata*, parts of the New Year sequence); older boys and young men predominate in one or two (a triennial Kōshin shrine festival and the Cherry Festival or *yama agari*); and househeads or their delegates are central figures in the greatest number. But, in all cases, the active persons stand for those they represent as well as for themselves. Second, festival days often have a free and easy schedule which makes the import of the ceremonies difficult to grasp for persons accustomed to congregational modes of worship. One might almost say that, so far as the villagers are concerned, they join in the festival but do not create it. Like the American Halloween, a festival gradually ripens without notable fuss or planning beforehand until, on the designated day, it blooms in the ceremony people have waited for. The ceremonial day itself ends things. There is no lingering into succeeding days. The day of a shrine festival usually is free of work, or partly so; each household often is free to choose its own convenient hour to go through a necessary part of the ceremony, and its participating representative as well as others in the house spend the rest of the day at their own affairs. The congregation may not literally be an assembly of persons unless a number of households happen to select the same moment. Worship consequently rarely is marked by the emotional fervor that mass congregations would tend to arouse; but this is not to say that the person who goes through ritual in perfunctory fashion is not serious about it. Third, food is important to a shrine festival in the sense of communion. Different special dishes are associated with different ceremonies (though most include rice), and a few ceremonies have no special food, but eating or the drinking of sake is important to the completion of ceremony. By eating together, either in someone's home, at the assembly hall, or elsewhere, the participants reinforce and symbolically express their unity and common purpose; moreover, the food they consume has a mystical link with the spirit to which the day is dedicated, so eating is an act that puts the worshipers in mystical rapport with the spirit. These three features thus are essential aspects of a Shinto ceremony: the principle of vicarious participation in a community ritual; the sense of community participation even in the absence of a congregation; and the achievement of mystical or symbolic rapport through consuming dedicated food or liquor. So much do ceremonies gain a family resemblance to each other through these common features, that, without detailed historical or comparative information, it is often difficult to disentangle the distinct festivals which in the course of time have come to be celebrated on the same day and so have merged in all but name, such as Boys' Day, referred to equally as *tango sekku* and as *shōbu no sekku* (Iris Festival).

As important as any Shinto ceremony is the one called "prayers" (*gokitō*), which recurs in almost identical fashion three times each year. All three *gokitō* once were scheduled on the lunar calendar, in the third, fifth, and ninth months, the date supposedly falling between the ninth and eleventh according to the wishes of the household principally responsible. The fifth-month ceremony, for reasons not quite clear but related to the agricultural busy season, is now usually celebrated on June 9, 10, or 11; that is, it has been attached to a fixed place in the solar calendar but shifted to June (the sixth month) to keep it near the fifth lunar month. The ninth-month *gokitō* is even less fixed at present, being on the lunar calendar one year, on the solar calendar the next, depending on which date seems most convenient to the households of the *kōjū*. Celebrated by solar date in 1950, it was postponed nine days until September 20 to make it coincide with a similar ceremony (*shanichi*) so that no one would lose too much time with two holidays. No one took amiss such cavalier juggling of dates, since the matter was settled by common consent, nor did this free variation incline anyone to qualify his assertion: "*Gokitō* are celebrated here between the ninth and eleventh of the first, fifth, and ninth months!"

Some household heads expected to be busy in the late afternoon of September 20 and arranged to have their wives participate in their place, or went to Kōjin shrine in the morning. Few put in a full day's work, though there were no other hints of festivity through the day. One Youth Association member, acting for his group, brought from the temple a *fuda* (see below) impaled on a stick, which was set in the ground at the crossroads and left there to protect the community. As the sun dropped low in the sky, about five o'clock, household heads or their surrogates changed clothing and walked in pairs and larger groups, dressed in somber-hued kimonos, across the fields and up the slope of Tsukuriyama to the shrine, where they set out small bowls of sake and "red rice." After a brief wait, the priest from the temple, Honryūji, arrived to lead the prayers. It would be more proper, the people grant, to have a Shinto specialist as paid shrine guardian, especially in view of the government's long decades of effort to dissociate Buddhist from official Shinto worship. The six buraku have not felt able to afford a guardian for Kōjin shrine since the war, however. And they add, "We Nichiren people don't object to saying Buddhist prayers at the shrine, anyway." The priest, on arriving, rang a bell near the shrine several times, then stepped before the shrine. As each person had done earlier, he clapped his hands three times to announce himself to the spirit and stood for a moment in silent prayer on the front step of the shrine, hands clasped. Then, with the group from Niiike standing quietly around him, he began a prayer for the welfare of the nation (an innovation just preceding World War II). There followed a prayer for a good harvest, then one asking that the village be kept in prosperity and safety, and, finally, a prayer that health and well-being come to every household. To conclude the prayers, the group stepped, one at a time, before the shrine, gave three hand claps, and bowed to the spirit. The entire group then descended and went to the house of Iwasa Ishita, whose turn it was to play host (to "hold the *yaku*") following the monthly prayer meeting (*kanki*) (see chap. 10). Here the housewife had used an *ad hoc* levy of a pint of rice from every household to prepare a joint dinner. Her guests first waited for offerings to be made to the household spirit shelf (*kamidana*), then sat down to dinner, filling the main room and anteroom. They ate only sparingly of the boiled and baked fish, the shrimp, and other dishes, for the custom is to wrap up in paper or a wrapping cloth (*furoshiki*) all the uneaten food on one's plate and take it home for the rest of the family to share—both as a gesture of family courtesy and to offer communion to all. The leisurely dinner and light conversation ended the *gokitō* ceremony. The host knelt in the anteroom beside the step and exchanged bows and thanks, hands on the mat, with each person: "*Gokurō sama de gozaimashita*" ("It was a task [on your part]"), ending with a quick, polite intake of air through the teeth.

A few of Niiike's festivals have a more openly gay air than *gokitō*, though to call the community at any time exuberant would stretch the meaning of this word. Most persons rate the year as having two festive peaks apart from *Bon*: New Year, which occurs in February of the solar calendar and the Fall Festival, celebrated on a solar schedule, October twelfth and thirteenth. A contagion of holiday feeling runs through the entire countryside for some days before New Year, for, unlike the *gokitō*, the festival is celebrated universally at the same time—except in the city, where the people are a month and more past their solar New Year spree. The house is cleaned, bright holiday clothes are made ready, and sake and the ingredients for special dishes are laid in before *misoka*, last day of the old year. The rice harvest is gathered and processed, and debts should be cleared away before starting the new year; but exceptions have been made since the war, especially for long-range farm improvement loans from the Kamo Agricultural Co-operative Association. Fathers help their children weave and fasten to the front of the house or gate an elaborately furled and tasseled straw ornament, attaching a large orange as center-piece. A few children may receive artfully ornamented wooden paddles and shuttlecocks from doting parents or relatives, though this is a bit spendthrift for Niiike. They are sure, however, to be able to gorge on gummy rice cakes, toasted or combined with fish and vegetables in the dish called *zoni* ("I put away fifteen bowls of *zoni*"—a modest boast), for more than half the houses keep large pine-log or stone mortars especially for pounding the glutinous rice for these cakes. Holiday reigns between the first and third days; food and sake are continually on hand for guests, and parents take their old folks and children for prayers (like those of *gokitō*) at the shrine and for visits to neighbors, friends, and relatives. More distant trips are planned between the fourth and sixth days; wives leave to spend a day at their parents' home, for example. For Buddhist prayers at home and at the graves, as described earlier, people utilize these visits from distant relatives, though these *kuyō* are viewed as an affair distinct from the New Year festivities. Though people put off their holiday garb and get back to work after the third day, the New Year is not really finished until, on the ninth or tenth, household representatives pay a group visit for prayers at Kōjin shrine and, on the fourteenth, gather together all the straw decorations for a special bonfire (*tondo*) at the crossroads in front of the housing area. The fifteenth is also a holiday, called simply "rest day."

The sharp air and clear sunlight of the New Year season contrasts with the balmy warmth that is near its end when the Fall Festival begins in October. The carefree atmosphere is equally strong, however, as the young men bring out the timbers of the large arch that is to be raised across the main road and set up the two white banners, twenty-five feet high, that proclaim the holiday. These banners stand for three days, echoed visually by identical banners in each of the six buraku that worship at Kōjin shrine and the four additional buraku that worship at its parent shrine, Upper Kamo. Household representatives go in a group from Niiike to Kōjin shrine, choosing a time that does not interfere with worship by similar groups from any of the other five buraku. Hardly anyone can prevent himself from sneaking in a little bit of work in the fields or at home— above all if he has to feed and milk dairy cows—but feasting, visiting around the neighborhood, and talking with relatives who get home for a day take up most of the holiday.

HOUSEHOLD SPIRITS AND RITUAL OBJECTS

By comparison with many villages in Japan, Niiike's homes are guarded by relatively few spirits, and the housewife who sees to the offerings tends to be considerably more punctilious about the daily prayer and offering to the ancestral tablets in the *butsudan* than about other ritual, simply because the other ritual is Shinto and so is of less concern to her. In each house, the *kamidana*, or spirit shelf, set over a doorway—generally over the doorway from the earth-floor entrance to the raised-floor anteroom— holds several small vases for floral offerings to the spirit of the little wooden shrine on the back of the shelf. This *kami* offers general protection to the house and all that belongs to the household. Fugen, the Buddhist-deity-turned-Shinto who is enshrined in the woman's part of the house, usually near the stove, has the more limited function of protecting the household welfare and health through food. The help expected from Suijin, *kami* of water, is similarly limited to keeping the well-water clean and potable. Suijin is denoted by a shingle inscribed with the name and tacked to the well post. Any other spiritual guardians of the household are entirely a matter of individual choice; for example, Iwasa Sōichi, who was not raised in Niiike but came as an adoptive husband, set up a row of four small black pottery votive boxes (*chinju*, which resemble small birdhouses) behind his house, presumably to protect the yard, though he has neglected them for too many years to recall their function and calls them simply *iwai-gami sama* ("prayer spirits"). Persons concerned about the family ox buy a cheap pottery image of an ox, set it perhaps on the *kamidana*, and make occasional offerings. Though no mark distinguishes it, one of the four main posts of the house is slightly larger than the others. It is the *Daikoku-bashira* ("wealth-god post"). From it, as the symbolic center, the wheel of zodiacal arcs is plotted that determines fortunate and unfavorable directions (see chap. 5). Special care should be taken not to deface it; nor should a person disrespectfully lean against it.

The priest from the temple, visiting the Niiike house on New Year's, brings along a *fuda* to protect the home from fire or from sickness or to prevent disease among the household animals. The *fuda* is a foot-long slip of bamboo or of stiff white paper; on it is printed the name of the temple, sometimes with a taslismanic Sanskrit character, a brief sutra, or a hardly indentifiable picture of an ox or a sheep. Should it be wanted, a small price of ¥20 or so is sufficient to get a similar *fuda* at any time, more often from a shrine than from a temple, since *fuda* are Shinto unless Sanskrit characters are used. Most *fuda* are inserted under the eave just above the regular entrance, where they pile up year after year until a vigorous housecleaning winnows them out; but some may be placed under the eave of the barn or on the well post or at any spot that seems to need protection.

Apart from the ancestral tablets and ritual equipment kept in the *butsudan* cupboard against the rear wall of the back room, no Buddhist symbols or images are regularly on view in most homes. An occasional housewife will set out a small image of Bodhidharma, a well-loved saint, or another Buddhist saint in the *tokonoma* just as a decoration to be alternated with a glass-cased doll and other secular items. Among the scrolls of almost every household, however, is a *mandara* (from Sanskrit: *mandala*), a cabalistic figure composed of esoteric Chinese and Sanskrit characters arranged to express the cosmic order of things. This scroll is hung in the *tokonoma* on all important Buddhist occasions.

COMMUNITY AND OTHER SPIRITS WITH SPECIAL FUNCTIONS

Two groups of memorial stones are set up for community use. Three stones grouped near the assembly hall have been mentioned in connection with Buddhist worship, though one of the three is for Jijin, the Shinto spirit of the earth. Jijin is honored on two days each year; the day, called *shanichi*, is set with relation to the equinox. The fall equinox, a few days later (*shōnichi*), is the center of the week of Buddhist activity called *higan;* some people use the Buddhist term, some the Shinto term, to cover the entire occasion. As mentioned earlier, Buddhist prayers and Shinto offerings and communion-meal customs intermingle in the ceremonies for this whole group of three stones; but additionally, on *shōnichi*, people are supposed to respect the earth spirit by not wounding the earth with plow or hoe. Jijin, also, as a Shinto spirit, enjoys offerings of sake, whereas no such offerings are given at the Buddhist monuments at the same spot, of course.

The second group of stones, on a terrace beside the path leading uphill from the houses; consists of two roughhewn upright stones and two stone lanterns. One stone has the characters for Yakujin ("disease spirit") carved on its face; the other is unlettered, but represents Ushi-no-kami ("ox-spirit"). Household representatives gather before each for a nearly identical ceremony, though on different days: the lunar sixth month, sixth day, for Yakujin; the lunar fifth month, fifth day, for Ushi-no-kami. Ceremonies consist in burning candles, repeating prayers, pouring a bit of sake, and offering cakes—watched by an appreciative audience of children, who know they will get the cakes after the ritual is finished. Like many *kami* of Japan that have dread and evil names but are beneficent spirits with special potency against the evil signified by their name, Yakujin, the "disease spirit," is venerated as a protector of mankind against disease, not as the deification of disease itself. The ox-*kami*, not surprisingly, protects the family ox from harm. The villagers moved the two stones together some twenty years ago apparently because their protective functions are related and their worship dates are not too far apart. On the same day as the ox-spirit ceremony and at the same spot there occurs one bit of ceremony connected with *shōbu-no-sekku* (Iris Festival), which signalizes the iris as a plant of prophylactic value; someone generally drapes a garland of twisted iris leaves over one or both of these stones. Very little time is spent in ritual gestures on any of these three days, for wheat harvest and rice transplanting keep everyone busy. For example, though each household, according to Iris Festival tradition, should lay on the eave over the house entrance a bouquet made up of iris, *miscanthus*, mugwort, and a moss called *senda*, such bouquets rarely are seen. In 1950, only one could be found in the community.

Whereas the groups of stones described above have considerable meaning to every person in the village, many villagers are actually unconscious of a small shrine they pass each day on the path running behind the housing area, though it catches the outsiders' attention immediately. This shrine appears to have been set up by a household, now extinct, in the hope of curing the young bride of a critical illness. It was dedicated to the fox (*kitsune*) spirit. Fox and badger in Japan are animals with a variety of supernal powers, and this fox-spirit power may work against illness. Grandmothers of several houses continued offerings there for some time, and a sprig of flowers and a few grains of rice still appear as offerings from time to time. But no systematic veneration continues.

Several activities or holidays that Niiike people observe purely for recreation or relaxation today, which have no conscious link with any spirit or cult, must have once been worshipful occasions as they still are in certain parts of Japan. Noting this, one is tempted to predict a similar course of evolution for other ceremonies in which the secular begins to outweigh the sacred. One example is the "mountain climb" (*yama-agari*) of the lunar third month, fourth day. On this day, girls in their brightest garments take a lunch, while the youths take bottles of sake, and all go together to climb the high hill facing Niiike, the girls for a picnic and the young men for a lighthearted binge. For Japan as a whole, the previous day is simultaneously Girls' Day, when dolls representing the ancient imperial court are arranged on shelves in the home, and Flower-viewing Day, when people go out for a picnic in the spring sun, get happily drunk on sake—and, incidentally, enjoy the brief glory of the blossoming cherry trees. Girls' Day seems wholly secular, and so, at first glance, does the Flower-viewing; to Niiike people, the mountain-climbing also is no more than a lark. Comparative evidence which need not be reviewed here, however, leaves little doubt that this spring festival period was once for fertility rituals, aimed to bring a "mountain spirit" from his winter home down to the paddy fields for the growing season. Similar evidence points to earlier religious implications for Boys' Day, *tanabata*, and several lesser festivals which now are entirely secular in Niiike and in most parts of Japan.

GREAT SHRINES AND TEMPLES

Where temples and Buddhist monuments are concerned, Niiike people have an almost total lack of interest in any apart from their own Nichiren sect temples. Throughout the countryside, for example, are small wayside shrines holding one or more stone statues of Jizō (Ksitigarbha), a Bodhisattva important to Shin sects as a guardian and patron of children. Occasional offerings to them are almost a matter of course—except to a follower of Nichiren.

A pilgrimage made to a famous temple becomes a long-cherished memory, especially for women, who have few other suitable reasons for getting out of sight of Niiike. The excitement of the journey itself, added to sectarianism, helps to explain why none of the pilgrims ever seems to aim at nearby famous temples, which are neither Nichiren nor far enough away to be exciting. Elderly men and women make most of the pilgrimages, and Kuonji temple on Mount Minobu in distant Yamanashi Prefecture is a great attraction, for it is there that Nichiren himself is buried. The ancient temple is beautifully situated in spacious groves of great trees on the side of Mount Minobu. Four or five from Niiike join a larger group from the parish of Sōrenji or Enkyūji and set off, carrying Nichiren drums, which have a distinctive fan shape, and wearing identifying sashes across their chests. A nine-hour train ride, a five-mile bus ride, and a wearying climb of more than 2,000 feet brings them to their goal, the inner sanctuary at the peak of the mountain. Under their feet is soil made sacred by the founder of their sect; rising against the sky across the valley is the magnificent cone of Mount Fuji. Long after their return home, the memory of this vision brings light to their faces.

Notable shrines not too close to home are similarly alluring. A shrine pilgrimage such as is made most often by groups of three or four young and middle-aged men is frankly about nine parts recreational and one part concern for the recovery, say, of a sick ox; but men and women may also take quite serious troubles to a shrine in the hope of getting help. The nearest great shrine is the handsome shrine of the ancient province at Kibitsu, less than four miles away. Most persons during their childhood have visited it at Fall Festival time and tend to dismiss it as being merely the *ujigami* of buraku in the eastern half of Kamo and the vicinity. A similar view is taken of the Inari shrine of Takamatsu, about three miles away, though its New Year festival (by solar calendar), which draws tremendous numbers of people from the resort service trades from all over the Inland Sea area, is an occasion so lively that some Niiike people walk over to watch the crowds. When Niiike people arrange to travel on a shrine pilgrimage, they usually go to Kompira shrine, in Shikoku across the Inland Sea; the round trip by train and boat takes at least two days to complete. If Kompira is too far away for the time available, there is the ox-spirit shrine at Jūnihonge, ten miles away in the upstream hills behind the Ashimori Valley. And not infrequent pilgrimages have been made to distant Ise to visit the national shrine there; but this was a once-in-a-lifetime venture saved for by contributions to an *Ise-kō* (see chap. 10) and has not been undertaken by anyone since the war. The prewar attraction of the Great Shrine at Ise was due to the existence of State Shinto, which is discussed below.

BUDDHIST SECTS AND ORGANIZED SHINTO

The Nichiren sect is one of the five large Buddhist sects in Japan. The census count of declared religious affiliation places the Shin sect easily in top place, followed by the Jōdō sect, the Zen sect, the Nichiren sect, and the Shingon sect. Each sect is quite independent of the others and each is further divided into branches on doctrinal grounds. Temples of each sect are in the vicinity of Niiike, though none other than Nichiren are in territory once controlled by the Hanafusa family. Thus Niiike people are more or less familiar with the doctrinal and ritual characteristics of each sect. All live in full amity; for example, Buddhist sect affiliation is never a stumbling block to marriage arrangements; nor is there any clear difference in the social class level of followers of one sect or another, except in the case of Zen, in which the proportion of families of officials and former officials is large. Nichiren is grouped sometimes with Shinshū as a democratic sect; it also has a rather special history as a militant and nationalistic sect, but this latter coloration hardly distinguishes it today. Its membership is concentrated in Core Japan.

Shrines have had no clear organization since the end of the second World War but were rigidly organized under the central government between 1868 and 1945. Though this hierarchical organization was unprecedented in earlier Japanese history, in one sense it was merely an intensification of the hoary tradition that religion is a tool of the state. State Shinto, as the organization is known, was instituted as a religious prop for the emperor as supreme ruler following the overthrow of shogun rule in 1868 and became an instrument to promote nationalist sentiment, especially after 1930. To create State Shinto the government forcibly cut the ties which, over the centuries, had grown between temples and shrines. A dual establishment was arbitrarily classified, sometimes as a temple, sometimes as a shrine. Besides breaking shrines loose from any connection with Buddhism, the government officially recognized a long list of shrines in various ranks: village shrines (*sonsha*), township shrines (*gosha*), and prefectural shrines (*kensha*). Above these were certain national shrines. Guardians were appointed to all official shrines as state employees. Unrecognized shrines, whether small or large, received no public funds, and various other moves discouraged their existence. The government went on, despite temporary open unrest, to build a cult of state worship in the person of the emperor, resurrecting myths and inventing dogma to demonstrate divine descent of the imperial line. New shrines were built for deceased emperors as *kami*. Some elements of this cult became compulsory: children bowed daily to the emperor's sacred picture, and official shrine guardians were ordered to pray for the nation and the imperial line at every ceremony, as well as to institute ceremonies for every nationally designated holiday (imperial birthdays and death days were prominent among these). Other elements of the cult were merely encouraged: low train fares were offered for pilgrims to national shrines, especially the Naiku shrine at Ise, of which an imperial family member for centuries was head priest and in which was the mirror, one of the three sacred objects —mirror, sword, and jewel—that validated the imperial family as rightful religious leaders of the nation.

Niiike's reaction to these innovations and their abolition in 1945 probably was representative of most country villages. Positive changes were accepted for the most part. People made contributions and worshiped at the Upper Kamo shrine along with the Onzaki shrine, renamed Hachiman shrine by government order (for the people of Sōzume ōaza) and the Kamo shrine (for people of Kamo ōaza and the buraku of Tsudera, Suenaga, and Hatakeda). All three, and only these three, were official shrines. Children accepted the doctrine of the divinity of the emperor and bowed at school to the imperial picture. A good many women and not a few men made the journey to the Naiku shrine at Ise. They added prayers for the emperor to their customary prayers at the shrines. But they gave up almost none of their own traditional but unofficial observances. They continued to use Kōjin shrine as their *ujigami*, even though it was not officially recognized and had no guardian. They continued to use Nichiren Buddhist prayers at the shrine and to mix shrine customs with their Buddhist services. They paid as little attention to nationally designated holidays as they now do to the set that has replaced the prewar holidays. In short, their quiet power to absorb and resist change was at least as great as their docile acceptance of new doctrines. Very little trace of Shinto as an organized cult seems to survive a decade after the end of the war; the superstructure has vanished, though nothing in the village attitude would hinder its re-establishment.

Among the evangelistic sects classed as "Shinto sects," which have risen to number more than 160 since 1945, not more than half a dozen antedate 1900. The Okayama Plain has more than its share of the earlier sects, which first appeared in the nineteenth century: the Kurozumi sect, the Konkō sect, and the Ōmoto sect all have headquarters and centers of origin within thirty miles. The Tenri sect, with headquarters in Nara Prefecture, has far the largest membership, numbering well over a million. Underneath their differences, these sects share a sense of discontent with the evils of the world, coupled with the conception that human beings aided by divine instruction and divine power can modify these evils. They stand unique among Japanese religions, especially traditional Shinto and Buddhism, in their concept of personal conversion on the part of the individual person as an acceptable and, indeed, normal way to acquire religious affiliation. Voluntary adherence is characteristic of believers in these sects. Small groups of adherents are to be found in Kamo and neighboring villages, as in other parts of Japan. A survey (1950) of six buraku in Kamo, comprising 1,283 persons, showed about two dozen Kurozumi members, and adherents in smaller numbers of Tenri and of a newer sect, called P. L. Kyōdan.

CHRISTIANITY

Iwasa Tamaichi and his household became tentative Christians while living in Okayama City, before evacuating to Niiike. To go to church, they must make the trip to Okayama; his daughters go intermittently or regularly, Tamaichi and his wife almost never. Tamaichi describes his conversion as follows: In his teens, while not yet past school age, he was drifting in Okayama City and Kobe, trying to discover a suitable job or calling and at the same time searching for grounds for faith. He happened across Christian literature, heard some talk and a few sermons, but for some time did not think of this religion seriously. As time passed, however, and he began to learn barbering, he recalled his experiences and began regular attendance at the church, which led to his conversion. Since returning to Niiike he has vacillated, reluctantly recognizing that he cannot ignore the non-Christian ceremonials and yet expect to fit into community life. Still, he hardly expects to be fully accepted. He feels that the more conservative of his neighbors, at least, carry the old attitude that barbering is a mean profession, hardly above the butchering and care of corpses and graves that are the monopoly of the *Eta*, despised outcasts. Tamaichi and his wife fret: they are discouraged under their problems, habituated to not fitting in with associates, and wish heartily to improve their status. They believe Christian faith will aid them in this.

QUALITIES OF RELIGIOUS BELIEF

State Shinto, linking the shrines to national welfare, put faith in the *kami* to a wrenching test when the nation went to war. The *kami*, and the spirit of the Japanese people, were frankly expected to substitute for wealth of war matériel in order to bring victory. Utter defeat was not only a blow to self-esteem; it was defeat of the *kami*. Or so it seemed at first. There are some who still feel disillusioned; the *kami* had no influence one way or another in wartime or in its depressing sequel, they feel, so there is no reason to expect more now. Others distinguish the *kami* of the official shrines, which could not measure up to national demands, from their own *kami*, such as at Kōjin shrine, which look after village needs and no more. Still others, without working out reasons, have felt the disillusionment of defeat healed by the passing of time. The objective consequences of these reactions have been: (1) a recrudescence of small local cults and observances that were formerly denied official sanction; (2) general slackening of shrine activities during the years of economic hardship right after the defeat; (3) general revival of shrine activities as prosperity has increased.

Many of the younger or mature men have not been to the Kōjin shrine since they were children and went up to get their share of the offerings. This absenteeism might indicate a thinning-out of belief if this were a religion which made personal choice and individual participation a religious requirement. But Shinto requires only that household representation be maintained. It seems unlikely that many of these men have come to grips with their belief or disbelief in the shrine and its powers. They do not need to stand up and be counted among the faithful. When their turn comes to represent the household, their respect for the social ties to the community is likely to prevail over questions of personal conviction. They will support the shrine overtly as their fathers did, without any battle of conscience.

Temple worship has not met a problem comparable to that of the shrine. Its reliance on ritual and formalistic prayer makes few demands on the conscience, and its reinforcement of a strongly positive veneration of parents and ancestors leads to no impasse. As in the case of the shrine, however, religious taboos seem to be of diminishing concern today, for no one really fears retribution from spirits or ghosts for plowing on the earth-spirit day or eating salt and fish on the occasion of an ascetic (shōjin) meal. Purity and personal merit are to be judged more on practical grounds than ritual grounds.

Purity and merit since long in the past have had little or no connection with morality and conscience as these are conceived in the Western world. Sin may very well weigh on a person's conscience but for reasons associated more with personal social responsibilities than with a personal religion. Accordingly, if any fading of religious convictions is observed, this can have little bearing on the nature and strength of moral convictions. Indirectly, of course, a sense of propriety and honorable conduct goes with the desire to discharge religious obligations, but the one does not cause the other. The people of Niiike are sober, responsible, and religious; their religion does not bring about their sobriety, but it comforts and reassures them of order in the world.

15. Conclusions AND EPILOGUE

Hiramatsu Hiroshi had never heard how paradoxical the people of his nation seemed to observers from abroad. Yet, when a chat with the visiting anthropologist one warm spring afternoon raised the question of marriage practices under the new constitution and civil code, he was goaded to a few remarks which might stand as his retort to those who find the Japanese mysterious, contrary, or paradoxical. His protest, in effect, was:

All these questions of yours, Sensei, get me to wondering whether you people think of us as ordinary human beings. What we do—getting married and such —isn't so hard to figure out. True, it's not just like America. But you in America try to leave everyone happy, too, I suppose, even if you do go about it differently. With us, parents have a lot to say about getting married. They have to live with the bride and be content, as well as the groom. But the youngsters have their say, too, before anything final happens. In your country, they say, only the boy and girl decide—but let that go now. Here, everyone concerned is in on the planning. To me, anyhow, our way looks like a reasonable way of fitting human nature to the circumstances. So why change things all around just because there's a new constitution? We're not living by constitutions, most of us, but by human nature and circumstances. And our way of doing it makes pretty good sense, if only your people would stop to think about it!

Without debating modes of marriage or the influence of law on customs here, we may observe that there is much in favor of Hiroshi's view. The view taken in this book has been that Niiike's practices make up a reasonable, consistent, and more or less satisfying way of life under the conditions that prevail there. A multitude of other small Japanese communities facing similar circumstances have a very similar way of life. This way is different from life in America or many other places. It is not perfectly self-consistent in every way, but it is not paradoxical unless the observer chooses to think it so. One need merely be aware of the circumstances that affect it to understand that it has logic and coherence. By presenting these circumstances we have attempted to dispel the sense of paradox that often recurs to the mind of the outsider in Japan. No doubt our presentation has not fully achieved its objective, and certain paradoxes may still linger. Yet, as our study is succeeded by others, we believe the apparent paradoxes will be reduced, not multiplied.

Let us consider a few aspects of Niiike life which may at first be thought contradictory, by comparison with life elsewhere in the world, to test whether our information is full enough to resolve the contradiction adequately. Here are three examples: First, one might well expect the most forward-looking farm villages of Japan to be not in such places as the Okayama Plain but rather in the countryside next to the modernized major cities. Niiike is overnight by express train away from Tokyo, to which almost all Japanese look for their models of progress and up-to-dateness. Yet Niiike and neighboring Inland Sea villages have outstripped the rural areas right on the fringe of Tokyo and are pace-setters in agriculture and general farm living. Second, one might expect a relatively high rural standard of living to go with relatively extensive landholdings; on the contrary, these Niiike farmers maintain a high standard, while their holdings are among the smallest per capita in the entire nation. How does it happen that, holding the least land, they make the best living? To set a third conundrum, we observe throughout Japan that the very abundance of population creates a continual problem of finding productive work for all those capable of working. The dense population around Niiike should create a particularly large labor surplus; yet, contrary to general expectation, these farmers are tending to adopt labor-saving farm machinery to offset a labor shortage. Thus, when we briefly scan the material and economic life of our community, we discover a set of apparent paradoxes. Has the information provided in this study established a perspective which can explain these paradoxes?

Analysis of Niiike's farming has shown that the advancement of farming depends greatly on the development of basic facilities, especially the systems of water control. An account has been given of the long period over which exceptional ditch and dike systems took shape on the Okayama Plain. They could not be created overnight. During these centuries, also, the plain's position as a heartland of stable, intensive farming led to the accumulation and perfection of cultivating techniques—composting, interplanting, a year-round succession of crops—so that in technology this area surpasses most other parts of Japan. The deep historical heritage we have traced in Bitchū and the rest of the Okayama Plain counts for more than a few decades of proximity to a modern city in stimulating agricultural productiveness. To the farmers of the Kanto Plain around Tokyo, proximity to a now thriving industrial city by no means compensates for their lack of comparable water-control facilities and cultivating techniques. The smaller individual landholdings on the Okayama Plain can be more efficiently used, thanks to preparation of land, control of water, and skilful techniques. These produce higher living standards in spite of greater pressure of the population on the land. Thus the first two paradoxes tend to vanish upon closer examination of the farm scene in Okayama.

The proximity of a city to Niiike, however, does help in resolving the paradoxes stated above. The city affects Niiike, not just by its modern ways, but, more specifically, by offering markets and the other economic opportunities to modern villagers. Niiike's farming is geared to supply demands of wider scope than those within each farm home. Niiike people maximize cash income by applying their traditional skill to the raising of crops that have good cash value, by being ready and able to attempt new sorts of market production, such as raising dairy cows, by processing their own rush into finished mat covers at home, and by sending their sons and daughters to take jobs in the city while living on the farm. Mat rush is outstandingly important for its distinctive virtues as a cash crop: despite price fluctuations, the market for rush as a raw material is large and perennially active, and any part of the crop can be reserved for the home looms, thus occupying spare labor while adding to its value. These features make mat rush as constant a feature of Niiike farming as the rice crop, which itself provides dependable cash income as well as subsistence.

The salaried commuters, who bring in a third of the household income, owe much to the school system that qualifies them to hold many of their jobs, much also to the bus and train network that makes daily commuting possible, and much to their proximity to the city for economical commuting. Dense population is becoming an economic asset, not a liability, as the people of Niiike exploit the opportunities offered by the city. In this fact is the key to the third apparent paradox stated above—the interest shown by Niiike farmers in saving labor in spite of their having very little land to occupy many persons. Their adoption of tractors and other labor-saving machinery makes sense because machinery frees part of the household to work outside and frees those at home for more hours at mat-cover weaving or specialty-crop cultivation. Most of all, by easing the labor pinch in harvesting and preparing fields for the next crop, machinery lets the land be filled up with marketable crops such as wheat, rice, and mat rush regardless of their overlapping work-peak periods.

It happens that the problems just examined have led to a review of features that make Niiike and its neighbors notable and distinctive among Japanese villages. Villages throughout Japan use irrigation, but not many have such highly developed water-control systems. Not many have a market crop comparable to mat rush, convenient alike for immediate sale or for household processing. Still fewer are in a situation so encouraging to mechanization of the cultivation process. To emphasize Niiike's distinctive features, however, is not the principal aim of this summary. The point has now been reached at which Niiike may be set against the background of rural life in Japan as a whole, so that its more general and typical features may be seen in perspective.

Broadly speaking, two contrasting sets of forces can be observed in most modern Japanese farm villages. Each set tends to mold the village in its distinctive way. The newer forces, originating in conditions for the most part outside the village, have been gaining momentum for some time but especially since defeat and the reconstruction that followed World War II. The other forces are rooted in conditions of population, land resources, and land use inherited from the past. These are still very important. In tolerating both sets of forces without the painful conflict and disorganization that often occurs in other parts of the world, Japanese communities such as Niiike are performing a feat well worth examination. Our survey should commence with the village as molded by traditional forces.

The thousands of small farmhouses scattered throughout Japan, whether grouped in distinct clusters or not, as a rule form definite and unambiguous communities marked by features comparable to those of Niiike. Few such communities are administrative units with salaried officials. In the postal guide, their member houses may be listed as no more than a group of consecutive addresses within a larger series, as Niiike's houses are merely a segment of the Upper Shinjō series within Kamo. Yet the inhabitants act together as a unit through community associations similar to Niiike's kōjū. Moreover, they are treated as a unit by persons and agencies on the outside, as when the government assigns a rice-requisition quota not to each individual farmer but to a buraku as a collectivity. This collectivity is a corporate entity; it has structure and regulations, owns property, and acts through a roster of members, whose arrival or departure leaves the corporate body intact. Community property—in Niiike this includes a meeting hall, fire-fighting equipment, the cemetery, and ponds but no other land—can be acquired or disposed of by action of the full membership. Thus, the community maintains a clearly defined though often unofficial corporate existence.[1]

[1] Our debt here is acknowledged to the work of Eric J. Wolf. See, for example, "Closed Corporate Peasant Communities in Mesoamerica and Central Java," *Southwestern Journal of Anthropology*, XIII (1957), 1–18.

Membership in this corporate community generally comes by birth, marriage, or adoption and is qualified by residence. It is virtually impossible for an unrelated outsider to join the community, because to build a house nearby and to rent or buy one of the community's fields does not admit him to the *kōjū* or its equivalent as a social participant in community affairs. Kinship among the members is a strong bond, but the community is a territorial entity, not a kinship group. Niiike has five separate lineages. Even more varied kinship composition characterizes most communities but does not weaken their unity. They are unified by common residence, which is an essential qualification for belonging. Persons who move away suspend their membership during their absence even though they do not renounce kinship and even though they have some right to return. Not without inconvenience and strain, Niiike reabsorbed four households during and after the war. They have dwellings of sorts, some land, and membership in the *kōjū*, whereas relatives who still live elsewhere simply have no part in the community. The combination of kinship and residential restrictions of membership gives the community a closed quality, which it reinforces by the united front it tends to present to the outer world.

The principles of collectivity and closure may be developed to various degrees. Japanese rural communities in general today do not carry collectivity to an extreme. They do not have communal ownership and cooperative utilization of all land or the sharing of its produce among all members. The member households, it is true, are subject to certain social restrictions in selling land to outsiders, but each household does hold separate title to its land, registering it in the names of individual persons. Each household takes care of its own fields and has full right to its own harvest; joint transplanting and harvesting are scarcely more than memories in the great majority of communities. Co-operation is not in disfavor; it may be the means used to acquire expensive equipment such as large pumps or insecticide sprayers. But in many communities the cooperating group is something less than the entire membership, as with the eight households that share ownership of a rice-huller in Niiike. Closure of the community also is seldom complete. Some localities do still label with the term "newcomer" households that have been in their midst for forty or fifty years, and outsiders in any community find some difficulty in winning the right to unstinted support and protection, but the boundaries of membership usually have a certain amount of flexibility.

Most communities are like Niiike in having essential relations with larger groups that date far back in time. Niiike's monthly community prayer meeting is for Niiike members alone, but, in shrine worship, its people participate collectively with those of five or nine other buraku. Collective operation of a main irrigation ditch underlies these shrine-worship groups, and Niiike participates also in still larger co-operative irrigation associations. These traditional commitments to collectivities outside of the buraku, however, involve all the people of Niiike as a unit. Such commitments actually reinforce the corporate quality of the buraku. When strains arise from conflict of interests among members of the larger co-operative organizations, the response is a polarization of buraku against buraku rather than one of individual members against other members in changing combinations. Buraku solidarity is reinforced rather than weakened by this form of participation outside of the co-resident community. The same process has been described at a still lower level, where passions and prejudices tend to create tension among the households living close together within the buraku itself. When the stresses become too intense for the community to pretend any longer that it is "one harmonious family," the community does not dissolve in unpatterned chaotic strife but tends to polarize into partisan lineage groups—Hiramatsu against Iwasa in Niiike. The lineages, of course, are also collectivities; so it may be said of this and higher levels that conflict strengthens one collective group even while it tears another apart.

We need not search far to find some of the main forces that move rural communities toward this mode of organization as closed, corporate collectivities. One is land shortage in an economy that offers little other than agriculture as a dependable livelihood. Where there is no more land to be had and people press close against the upper limit of production to make a bare living, newcomers cannot be freely admitted. The average cultivator-member cannot pile up bank accounts, insurance policies, or retirement funds against emergencies or old age. For elemental security, each person depends on his household, his household depends on the lineage, and the lineage in some degree relies on the community to alleviate crisis and to support non-productive members. Stark economic pressure lies behind the serious view taken of the symbolic monthly prayer meeting or the deliberations of the assembled householders in the assembly hall. Decreed only by custom, not by law, these gatherings are nonetheless compulsory for all members. Solidarity is evinced by harmony, and harmony implies unanimity: hence formal techniques for expressing minority dissent to any action are absent or undeveloped.

Many actions of outside government in the past have encouraged the closed, corporate quality of these communities. Officials have only gradually relinquished the view that the buraku is jointly responsible for payment of taxes. "Voluntary" contributions are still collected on a "buraku quota" basis, and the buraku members are collectively expected to maintain the small ditches, paths, and roads, all more or less at local expense. As long as government was imposed on the people from the outside and they did not participate in it, their natural response was a defensive closing of ranks, confronting officials with the same solid front that was opposed against outsiders who were after land or rents.

These various forces, and the values that rise to support them, instil characteristic attitudes and qualities of temperament in the villagers. A strong sense of attachment to one's native place may well grow out of the economic and social commitment to one particular village. Rugged individualism is out of place; instead, circumstances encourage docility in the face of group sentiment and reward with satisfaction those who conform to group traditions. Brotherly love is the attitude appropriate to kinsmen and fellow villagers, who are lifetime associates; shyness or suspicion toward outsiders is the other face of this coin. A person happily adjusted to corporate community life tends to gain warm satisfaction from the company of his fellows more than from his own achievements and is attacked by sharp loneliness when by himself or among those who have no commitment to mutual sharing with him. This is not to say that every villager possesses these qualities or is happily adjusted or that rewards come only to those whose temperament fits the communal pattern. Far from it. But strong passions, deep self-sufficiency, the search for novelty, and a host of other temperamental bents must find their rewards somehow in circumstances outside the normal village life.

These external conditions and personal attitudes may be deeply shaken and modified under the impact of the new set of forces about to be described. Before these forces are considered, however, passing note should be made of communities which, though also traditional, differ considerably from the general type of closed, corporate community, often for special local reasons. The intensely hierarchical village of Ishigami in northeastern, or Frontier, Japan will be recalled as one example. The residents of this village, living on land originally controlled by one single household, which gave small parcels of land to younger sons, servants, and protégés over a period of several generations, never were in a position to operate on a principle of mutuality. Unending subservience to the great house prevented this. Similarly, wherever landlords have been able to rise from within a community or to wedge into it from the outside, somehow defying or evading the obligation to share labor and products, or wherever special crops or alternative occupations such as mining or handicrafts provided unique, non-agricultural income to the entrepreneur, different sorts of communities were likely to develop. The growth of the egalitarian, corporate community was almost certain to be warped or thwarted under such conditions.

With the traditional Japanese community in mind we may consider the forces of change coming to rural Japan from the outside. Postwar prosperity, reduction of taxes, revision of local government, liberalization of education, and other phenomena of the period since World War II have added much momentum to these urban-industrial forces. Many Japanese villages, in consequence, are experiencing a controlled revolution more than equal to the transformations of earlier decades. In part, however, the current changes rest on ground laid long before, beginning at least as early as the late nineteenth century. The magnitude of current changes should not be permitted to obscure the ferment of "modernization" in Japan during the years of the Meiji reign, some of which led to intensified hierarchy, strengthening of family control over individual members, and to other conditions now regarded as traditional and old-fashioned by the villagers themselves as well as by some observers of Japanese customs,[2] others of which led more directly to features described here. Historical documentation of Niiike's past has been too scant to permit systematic examination of the age of these trends; yet some are certainly at least three or four generations old.

However much it is tied to the community socially, each household has been basically an independent economic unit for some time. Ways of creating income other than through rice growing are vital to the full realization of independence, provided that they do not depend on irrigation or similar communal activities. In Niiike, these activities include growing mat rush for sale on a highly competitive and fluctuating market, growing market vegetables and fruit, producing eggs and other minor market products, weaving *tatami* covers for sale, and working at salaried jobs. It is quite clear that this cluster of activities interferes with subordination of households to the interest of the community as a whole. People hesitate to use co-operative help particularly in the heavy work connected with mat rush. They pay wages instead, lest the consequent moral commitments hamper their freedom to sell the crop on an entrepreneurial basis, seeking the best time and place to market it. Mat rush, above all, is cultivated in the context of an economy of profit and loss rather than an economy of communality and sharing.

[2] Kunio Yanagida, *Customs and Manners of the Meiji Era* (Tokyo: Ōbunsha, 1957), convincingly and captivatingly shatters illusions about the antiquity of many "time-honored" customs, ranging from strict parental choice of the bride, residence after marriage with the groom's parents, and "mother-in-law trouble" to the popularity of rice in the peasant diet. He shows that some customs barely antedate the twentieth century; in the case of rice, for example, he points out that some farmers began to eat it for the first time in their lives when rice was rationed to them during World War II.

Perhaps the income tax was one of the most clear-cut steps toward individualizing the villager's relations with the agencies of government. A great many significant alterations introduced in governmental structure and processes as part of the local autonomy program of the Occupation also strike hard at habits of conceiving government to be a phenomenon outside the corporate community. These changes have been examined closely with respect to Niiike; in essentials, they are, of course, national in scope. Villagers now have a measure of opportunity to shape some local policies, thereby witnessing and participating at a lower level in the process which, at the national level, brings returns in the form of improved roads and water control, more extensive education, and public health. Evidence is appearing that rural countrymen as individuals rather than as members of some collectivity are beginning to utilize some of these opportunities to participate in the affairs of the larger community. A voting rate of 90 per cent or more in national elections, of course, does not prove that voters are interested in the political issues. Attitudinal changes in this realm are difficult to measure, to say the least. In subtle and limited ways, however, making formal means of participation available seems to encourage actual participation. To augment individualization, moreover, there now exist farm agencies and other government-supported organs for advice and aid to countrymen who bring individual and diverse problems to them.

Newspapers and the radio, almost universally available throughout the countryside even before World War II, certainly help to broaden the horizons of the local community, and the eventful years of war and its aftermath have developed habits of attention to these media. The national school system, moreover, brought systematic education to each community even before newspapers had wide circulation. As a spur to individualization, it is true, the influence of schools was limited for some time both by external circumstances and by the nature of the curriculum. Persons from Niiike of Hiramatsu Isamu's generation who chose advanced education went to the farm school, which did little to remove or estrange them from farming, the dominant concern of their agricultural community. Today's youngsters, however, have the choice of liberal or professional college education in Okayama City as an alternative to farm school; just one boy from Niiike has accepted this choice, but the total of students from farm homes is impressive. Fewer financial obstacles bar the way to participating in organizations ranging from Four-H clubs to pen pal clubs, which diversify the interests and attachments of the youth of a community. Again, Niiike's youngsters are cautious; none is a member of such a club yet. The young people participate only in the Youth Association, to which they belong as a community unit. The more diversifying associations, however, are popular in other rural communities.

The industrial-urban conditions just outlined, like those rooted in traditional agrarian conditions, tend to encourage certain attitudes and favor certain temperaments. Individualism, competitiveness, and a taste for variety, for example, fit well with the circumstances of a market economy. In these characteristics are the seeds of unrest, revolt, and unhappiness, which some persons of the older generation fear because these traits clash with many of the requirements of community life. In Niiike, as we have pointed out, few signs of such a clash have yet appeared. One suspects that a secret of the harmonious blending of these outward-oriented forces with the community-centered forces lies in the structuring of attitudes such as ambition. Ambitiousness is valued highly. Regardless of age or sex, Niiike people approve of self-betterment. The drive to accomplish things, to work hard for distant goals, is deeply implanted and strong. But ambition is harmonized with collectivity by being identified with the household. The boy or girl works hard at school to accomplish great things, not for himself alone, but in the name of the household; the househead and his wife set an example by laboring industriously for the household. This gives an outlet for competitiveness and aggression by which Niiike comes to terms with new socioeconomic forces without having to discard its precious communalism and mutuality. Change is absorbed and channeled to profitable ends, while equilibrium is maintained.

Niiike up to the end of our period of study in 1954 typified the majority of Japanese rural villages. If one were to select a single outstanding feature by which to characterize Japanese rural communities after eight decades of massive, rapid revolution in the nation as a whole, this feature would be their capacity to maintain equilibrium, while absorbing fundamental change. Whoever comes to know these villages intimately perceives through all of his senses the serene self-respect and regard for tradition maintained by its people even at the precise moment they are committing the village and themselves to fundamental innovation.

In June, 1956, after the study embodied in this book was complete, Niiike committed itself to a major transformation, ending once and for all its quality as a typical Japanese community. It accepted a project of mechanization and modernization planned by the Asia Foundation, an American non-profit philanthropic organization. The foundation was interested in demonstrating by actual example that advanced mechanization is feasible in Japan and in testing the benefits to be gained from self-directed capital improvement. The people of Niiike consented to this venture in planned change, after having been the uncomplaining and co-operative subjects of our long study, not merely because of the possible benefit to themselves, but because their consent would make possible a detailed before-and-after comparison which could not be duplicated in any other community in Japan.

The changes to be initiated required a supply of capital, which was made available over a two-year period through the Okayama prefectural government. Loans from this fund were to be repaid without interest or at low interest over a long period. A prefectural administrative committee was formed to supervise contracts, examine expenditures, and maintain public relations; the people of Niiike elected household heads to an Agri-cultural Improvement Union to plan and execute changes; and teams of Japanese social scientists were formed within the prefecture and at a national level to study the effect of changes as they would appear in the community, as well as to undertake comparisons, for control purposes, with the nearby buraku of Mukaiba, whose inhabitants also consented to be subjected to study though not participating directly in the planned changes.

A primary change was the increased mechanization of fieldwork and crop processing. An unprecedented quantity of machinery was purchased, so that the buraku as a whole was equipped with medium and light power cultivators, power threshers, power hullers, rice-polishers, power sprays, irrigation pumps, power mat rush looms, and motorcycles. Arrangements were made to supply the village with higher voltage power lines to operate the new looms. Numerous pieces of equipment are owned by the Agri-cultural Improvement Union. They are stored in a newly built machine shop and are used in rotation on the fields of the several households. Mechanization reduced the total time spent at certain jobs. For instance, completing the wheat harvest and plowing fields to transplant rice, which previously took six days, could be done in three days. The reduction in time, furthermore, facilitated making the best use of weather for impor-tant outdoor tasks.

From a new well, located high on the hill behind the buraku, pipes were laid to provide running water in every house. Many households undertook to improve their kitchen areas in other ways, such as by buying or build-ing new stoves.

According to the plan evolved, the time saved through the basic im-provements listed above was invested in other activities, for which capi-tal was provided through loans. Thus, some of the most immediate and observable consequences were important shifts in land use, varying with the households. Some households commenced clearing trees off the terraced hillside in back of the houses, where cotton once was grown, in order to plant fruit trees. Others invested in glass for a greenhouse set in dry fields or poorly drained paddy and bought root stock to raise grapes. Many increased the numbers of their chickens, building raised coops out over a plot of paddy field when other space was lacking. Some were now able to exchange their plow ox for a dairy cow. The laying of tile drains beneath ten acres of poorly drained paddy land, the improvement of paths and roads, and the exchange of fields to consolidate holdings, now that present soil and drainage characteristics were of less immediate moment, were planned and begun.

To encourage the people of Niiike in farsighted and enlightened planning for their own future, a small library was provided, containing works on poultry and pig raising, dairying, commercial fruit and vegetable raising, diet, sanitation, and child care. Additional arrangements were made for a bookmobile to visit Niiike. The village people took to an increase in the amount of time and effort available for indulging in various cultural interests as well as in outright economic improvement.

In a bare few months or even years after such large-scale changes have begun to work into the lives of a group of people, no one can be sure which of the early repercussions are transitory evidences of shock and adjustment and which are of more lasting importance. Many realignments can be anticipated only after an indeterminate period of experiment and preparation. According to an early report based on the situation a year after the program began, three changes are observed.[3] Younger people, because they have greater familiarity with machinery, are taking a relatively heavy responsibility for efficient use of the new equipment and seem to be acquiring through this a greater voice in buraku deliberations and decisions on general matters. Pressure from this group, for example, brought about an out-of-season transfer of buraku headship. Second, the report sees a tendency for fewer tasks to be undertaken by combinations of households (not overlooking the fact, however, that ownership of various pieces of new equipment is a joint matter). The third change concerns the men whose salaried jobs outside the buraku had made them junior members in much community activity. Having machinery, they can now do all their own cultivating and harrowing on Sundays alone, and so, assuming a full role as farmer, they have recovered full voice in the buraku meetings.

[3] Yuzuru Okada, "A Preliminary Report on the Social Effects of Mechanization of Agriculture in a Japanese Village," paper read before the Eighth Pacific Science Congress, Bangkok, November, 1957.

We can foresee certain effects, whatever the outcome of mechanization. The capitalization that permitted increased mechanization merely intensified certain changes that were under way when Niiike first was made a target of community study. Other changes will become evident only after the passage of time. Meanwhile, Niiike is the cynosure of eyes throughout the district merely for having accepted the new experience, whether the attitude be one of marvel or of envy. One thing is certain. Niiike, representative basic community of the Okayama Plain in 1950, will never be quite the same again.

Guide TO PRONUNCIATION

Correct pronunciation of Japanese as written in characters is a feat of memory. As transcribed in this book, however, Japanese offers few problems of pronunciation.

For precision, each syllable should have equal stress, with no appreciable accents within words.

Each vowel has only one sound, prolonged slightly when accompanied by a long mark (*ō, ū, ā*). The words for village, rice, and field—*mura, ine,* and *no*—rhyme with the words "hoorah," "we may," and "toe." The two vowels *i* and *u* may be reduced to a whisper after *s, sh, ch,* and *ts* (*shichigosan* becomes "sh¹ch¹gosan").

Each consonant is pronounced as in English. Note that *y* is always as in "yet" (never as in "my"), *g* is always as in "get" (never as in "gem").

Glossary

aki no matsuri—The Fall Festival, usually one of the three primary festivals of the year.

aza—Tract of land; also, in some areas, a small settlement. See also *buraku*.

be—Local group, often with solidarity based on occupation, and frequently subordinate to an *uji* (q.v.) (pre-Nara period).

bekke—A junior household dependent on a kindred main house. A term peculiar to certain local hierarchies.

Bon—Midsummer Buddhist festival honoring the ancestors.

bunke—A branch or cadet house of a lineage.

buraku—A primary rural community, consisting usually of fewer than one hundred houses; also, as a contraction of the euphemism *tokushū buraku* ("special community"), a settlement of *Eta* outcasts.

bushi—A person of the rank which was permitted to bear arms; a samurai (Tokugawa period).

butsudan—Shelf or cupboard for Buddhist worship of ancestors.

chigyōsho—A fief of less than ten thousand *koku* (Tokugawa period).

chō—(1) A land measure, 2.45 acres; (2) a town, or a section of a city. The character "chō" is pronounced "machi" when not in compound words.

daidokoro—Platform on which family sits at meals; in much of Japan, the entire cooking area or kitchen.

daikan—Regional deputy of the *shogun* (Tokugawa period).

daimyo—A feudal lord (Tokugawa period).

dekasegi—A person working and living away from home but contributing to its support.

dō—Administrative unit approximately equivalent to a prefecture (unique to Hokkaido).

doma—Dirt-floor area of a house.

dōzoku—Lit., "common kin"; a lineage group; a group of related households characterized by joint functions and solidarity.

Eta—Group name for the traditional class of social outcasts in Japan.

fu—Administrative unit approximately equivalent to a prefecture, but containing a metropolis.

fuda—Small, inscribed slips of paper or bamboo obtained from shrine for purification or protection.

Fujinkai—Women's Association.

furoshiki—Cloth square used as the regular means of wrapping miscellaneous packages for carrying them.

485

fusuma—Paper-covered interior sliding doors.

geisha—Trained female entertainer and hostess at men's suppers.

geta—Wooden clogs, consisting of toe straps, a wooden sole, and two wooden cross-pieces to raise the sole off the ground.

gō—A village (Nara period).

gokitō—Prayers; communal Shinto ceremony held three times annually.

gonin gumi—Group of households, usually five to twenty, held jointly responsible by government of the Tokugawa period.

goza—Inexpensive everyday matting used to cover *tatami*.

gun—Former administrative unit about equivalent in function to a county.

haiden—Roofed platform on Shinto shrine premises where offerings are made and dances are performed.

hakamairi—Visit to a grave to pay respects to the ancestors.

hara-kiri—Suicide by disembowlment. See also *seppuku*.

haregi—Festival or fine clothes.

hatamoto—A lesser vassal of the shogun (Tokugawa period).

hibachi—Heating device; a heavy pottery jar filled with ashes on which glowing charcoal is laid.

higan—The equinox; the Buddhist equinoctial ceremony of paying respect to the ancestors.

hōgaku—System of rules giving astrology-based significance to directions of the compass.

hōji—Buddhist memorial service for a particular ancestor. See also *tsuizen kuyō*.

honden—The key structure of a shrine, in which the sacred objects (*shintai*) are kept.

honke—The central or parent house of a lineage.

honke-bunke—Main and branch houses; the system of relationships linking households. See also *honke, bunke.*

hotoke—The Buddha; an ancestor.

hyō—A measure of grain; a straw sack of about six bushels quantity.

ie—House: domicile or family line.

igusa—Mat rush; the material used to cover *tatami*.

Ise-kō—A mutual help group sponsoring pilgrimages to the great shrines in Ise Province (Mie Prefecture).

jiban—Bailiwick; the area in which a politician has his main influence.

Jijin—Guardian spirit of cultivated land; originally regarded as existing half of the year as the spirit of the mountain or woodland.

jinja—Shinto shrine. See also *miya*.

jiyū kekkon—Free or romantic marriage. See also *ren'ai kekkon*.

jizō—The Ksitigarbha Bodhisattva; Buddhist guardian and patron of children.

jōri—A systematic division of irrigated farmland into numbered rectangles (Nara period).

kabuuchi—A lineage; member of a lineage.

kami—A guardian spirit or force; a "god."

kamidana—Lit., "spirit shelf"; the household shelf holding Shinto articles of ceremony and protection.

kan—A measure of weight, 8.27 pounds.

kaneoya—Lit., "metal parent"; an adult who holds a godparent type of relation with a child, usually established at a coming-of-age ceremony.

kanki—Lit., "prayer time"; a monthly assembly of households.

kazoedoshi—Japanese age-count, making a child one year old at birth and adding a year at each lunar New Year.

kazoku—Family: members of a household or, broadly, relatives within two or three degrees on the father's side.

ken—(1) Prefecture; (2) a measure of length, 1 fathom (different character).

kō—Confraternity; a traditionally organized mutual help group; originally, a religious congregation.

koaza—Parcel of agricultural or forest land represented on a single sheet of the official land map kept in a village office.

kobun—Lit., "child-role"; a person or house in a ceremonially established dependent relation to another person or house.

kōjū—Association of the households of a community (local term).

kōkaidō—Meeting hall.

koku—A measure of volume, 5.2 bushels; traditionally, a standard allowance of rice for one person for one year.

kokubunji—Official temple built at a *kokufu* (q.v.).

kokufu—Headquarters of an administrative province (Nara period).

kōri—A district (Nara period).

koseki—Family register.

kumi—A small teamwork group, consisting of persons or households.

kumiai—A joint or mutual association.

kuni—Province. Replaced by prefectures in late nineteenth century.

kura—Storeroom or storehouse with thick clay walls.

machi—Town. See also *chō*, alternative reading of same character.

mannen—Official or Euro-American age-count of total elapsed years.

miai—First meeting between prospec-

tive marriage partners, usually including the near kin of each.

miya—Shinto shrine. See also *jinja*.

mizu shōbai—Lit., "water business"; occupations concerned with recreation, entertainment, or services to travelers.

mochi—Cakes made of boiled glutinous rice, often toasted.

mompei—A woman's baggy trousers worn over kimono.

montsuki—Formal garment, black, with the family crest embroidered in white at five designated spots.

muko-yōshi—An adopted bridegroom, wedded to the daughter of the adopting parents.

mura—Village, now used officially for the smallest unit of local government.

mura hachibu—Lit., "village eight-parts"; procedure of formal ostracism from the community.

nago—A dependent, serf-like person or household, usually a tenant-farmer holding fictitious kinship to the owner.

ōaza—Subdivision of a modern *mura*, often an area which was a *mura* before 1880; also, in some localities, the principal settlement in a *mura*.

obi—Broad, stiff woman's sash.

on—A favor continuously enjoyed and continuously imposing obligation; originally, fief or land grant made to a subordinate.

oyabun—Lit., "parent-role"; person in parent-like position over others (*kobun*), protecting and directing them.

ren'ai kekkon—Marriage based on free or romantic attachment.

ri—Measure of distance, 2.44 miles.

rusuban—A person left to watch the house; a "house-sitter," rather than a baby-sitter.

sansankudo—Lit., "three and three, nine times"; the ceremony of sake drinking that binds a marriage.

Seinendan—Youth Association.

sensei—Teacher; master; doctor.

seppuku—Suicide by disembowelment. See also *hara-kiri*.

shi—City.

shikimi—A leafy shrub; star anise (*Illicium religiosum*), used for Buddhist decoration of graves.

shinden—Lit., "new field"; referring to irrigated fields created since medieval times.

shintai—Lit., "divine embodiment"; the sacred objects within a Shinto shrine through which its spirit is made manifest.

shō—A measure of volume, 1.588 quarts.

Shōbōdan—Fire-fighting Organization.

shōen—A private estate (feudal period).

shōgatsu—New Year; the New Year celebration.

shōji—Paper-covered exterior sliding doors.

sōja—A central administrative shrine (Nara period).

son—Village. See also *mura*, alternative reading of same character.

suisen—Lit., "recommendation"; in government, group acceptance of a leader's recommendation in lieu of voting.

tabi—Sock with separate division for great toe.

tan—A land measure, one-tenth of a *chō*, 0.245 acres.

tanomoshi-kō—A traditional mutual-help group formed to raise money for its members.

tatami—Rectangular, padded floor mats with rush mat as the top surface, six feet long and three feet wide.

tera—Buddhist temple.

to—Metropolitan administrative unit. Unique to Tokyo.

tō—Measure of volume; about 4 gallons.

tokonoma—The alcove; a recessed section of the end wall of the main room in a house, used for decorations.

tonarigumi—A neighborhood co-operative group.

torii—Arch or gateway to a Shinto shrine, distinguished by its double beam across the top.

tsuizen kuyō—Buddhist memorial service for all ancestors. See also *kōji*.

uji—A lineage or extended family group (pre-Nara period).

ujigami—Guardian spirit, either of a locality or (originally) of a lineage. See also *uji*.

ujiko—Lit., "children of the *uji*"; persons jointly under the protection of the *ujigami* of a shrine.

uji no kami—Chief of a lineage (pre-Nara period). See also *uji*.

wakashū gumi—Lit., "young fellows' group"; traditional name for the association of men between age about fifteen and thirty.

yome—Bride; the youngwife.

yōshi—An adopted person, male unless otherwise specified.

yuinō—Bridal gift of money from the groom's family to the bride's family.

zashiki—Main or guest room of a house; called *honza* in Niiike.

zōri—Sandals consisting of toe straps and a straw or shaped wooden base or sole.